W9-CJD-805

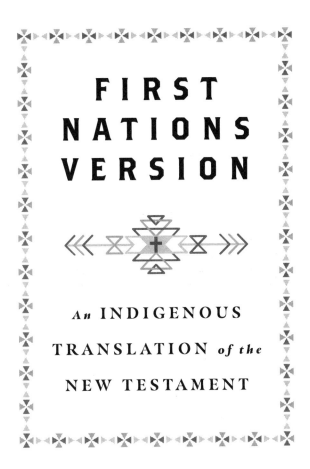

FIRST
NATIONS
VERSION

An INDIGENOUS
TRANSLATION of the
NEW TESTAMENT

An imprint of InterVarsity Press
Downers Grove, Illinois

InterVarsity Press
P.O. Box 1400, Downers Grove, IL 60515-1426
ivpress.com
email@ivpress.com
©2021 by Rain Ministries, Inc.

InterVarsity Press® is the book-publishing division of InterVarsity Christian Fellowship/USA®, a movement of students and faculty active on campus at hundreds of universities, colleges, and schools of nursing in the United States of America, and a member movement of the International Fellowship of Evangelical Students. For information about local and regional activities, visit intervarsity.org.

The publisher cannot verify the accuracy or functionality of website URLs used in this book beyond the date of publication.

Cover design and image composite: David Fassett
Interior design: Daniel van Loon
Images: old speckled paper: © pablohart / E+ / Getty Images
  old paper © Jay's photo / Moment Collection / Getty Images
  brown leather texture © Yaorusheng / Moment Collection / Getty Images
  diamond pattern © Ericbvd / iStock / Getty Images

ISBN 978-0-8308-1359-9 (casebound)
ISBN 978-0-8308-1350-6 (paperback)
ISBN 978-0-8308-2486-1 (digital)

Printed in the United States of America ∞

Library of Congress Cataloging-in-Publication Data
Title: First Nations Version : an indigenous translation of the New Testament.
Other titles: Bible. New Testament. English. First Nations Version.
Description: Downers Grove, IL : InterVarsity Press, [2021] | Includes bibliographical references.
Identifiers: LCCN 2021010363 (print) | LCCN 2021010364 (ebook) | ISBN 9780830813599 (casebound) |
  ISBN 9780830813506 (paperback) | ISBN 9780830824861 (digital)
Classification: LCC BS2095 .F57 2021 (print) | LCC BS2095 (ebook) | DDC 225.5/208—dc23
LC record available at https://lccn.loc.gov/2021010363
LC ebook record available at https://lccn.loc.gov/2021010364

P	21	20	19	18	17	16	15	14	13	12	11	10	9	8	7	6	
Y	37	37	37	36	35	34	33	32	31	30	29	28	27	26	25	24	23	22

This translation of the good story is dedicated to the Indigenous Peoples of Turtle Island (North America)—the Tribal Nations that call this land home. We pray the First Nations Version will bring healing to those who have suffered under the dominance of colonial governments who, with the help of churches and missionary organizations, often took our land, our languages, our cultures, and even our children. As our Tribal Nations work hard to reclaim what has been stolen, it is our hope that the colonial language that was forced upon us can now serve our people in a good way, by presenting Creator Sets Free (Jesus) in a more culturally relevant context.

CONTENTS

INTRODUCTION TO THE FIRST NATIONS VERSION

AN INDIGENOUS TRANSLATION OF THE NEW TESTAMENT

THE FIRST NATIONS VERSION TRANSLATION COUNCIL humbly submits this new translation of the Sacred Scriptures as our gift to all English-speaking First Nations people and to the entire sacred family, which is the body of the Chosen One.

The First Nations Version New Testament was birthed out of a desire to provide an English Bible that connects, in a culturally relevant way, to the traditional heart languages of the over six million English-speaking First Nations people of North America.

The FNV is a retelling of Creator's Story from the Scriptures, attempting to follow the tradition of the storytellers of our oral cultures. Many of our Native tribes still resonate with the cultural and linguistic thought patterns found in their original tongues. This way of speaking, with its simple yet profound beauty and rich cultural idioms, still resonates in the hearts of Native people.

The FNV takes into consideration contextual word choices, idiomatic expressions, and modifications in paragraph and sentence structure that clarify and facilitate understanding of the Scriptures. Our priority has been to maintain the accuracy of the translation and its faithfulness to the intended meaning of the biblical writers within a First Nations context. It is not a word-for-word translation, but rather it is a thought-for-thought translation, sometimes referred to as dynamic equivalence.

This translation was first envisioned by Terry M. Wildman. A while later the First Nations Version Translation Council was formed. Then with the help of OneBook and Wycliffe Associates, it expanded into a collaborative effort that included Native North Americans from over twenty-five tribes.

A small circle of interested Native pastors, church leaders, and church members gathered together under the leadership of Terry M. Wildman, OneBook, and Wycliffe Associates. They had input on the method of translation and the first biblical terms that would be used, and participated in the wording, reviewing, and editing of the Gospel of Luke.

WHY THE NAME FIRST NATIONS VERSION?

The term *First Nations*, while mostly used in Canada for the original inhabitants of the land, is increasingly being accepted and used by many Native Americans in the United States and by indigenous peoples worldwide. Following this trend, the name First Nations Version was chosen for this translation.

WHY ENGLISH?

It is conservatively estimated that over 90 percent of First Nations people do not speak their tribal language, and even fewer can read it. This is the result of several generations of governmental assimilation policies that attempted to eradicate over 250 languages spoken in North America.

This translation is not intended to be tribally specific but to present the Scriptures in a general way, attempting to represent some of the simple yet profoundly beautiful ways our languages can be expressed in English.

We aimed for a style that is easy to read, with an attempt to present, in writing, the cadence and feel of an oral storyteller. A contextual approach was adhered to, using English word choices and idiomatic phrases that are culturally relevant, with an effort to refrain from a stereotypical or culturally degrading simplicity.

PARTNERING ORGANIZATIONS

OneBook, a Canadian organization dedicated to helping indigenous peoples all over the world translate the Bible for themselves, provided financial support along with the tools and training needed for a high-quality translation. They partnered with Rain Ministries, located in the United States, to facilitate this translation. Wycliffe Associates of Orlando served this project in the beginning by providing technical support and funding for gathering the council together.

CHURCH ENGAGEMENT

The First Nations Version of the New Testament was produced in response to the consistently positive feedback given to the initial translation efforts. As samples were shared in churches and other venues, those who heard these samples began asking for more. Pastors, evangelists, missionaries, Native elders, and others began to ask whether a complete New Testament would be translated using this contextual approach. The FNV is for all the churches, and it is especially for those involved in contextual ministry with Native North Americans.

THE TRANSLATION COUNCIL

A translation council was selected from a cross-section of Native North Americans. Elders, pastors, young adults, and men and women from different tribes and diverse geographic locations were chosen to sit on the council. This council also represents a diversity of church and denominational traditions to minimize bias.

Our council consisted of twelve (one remains anonymous) First Nations individuals with tribal heritages from diverse geographical regions. This council had input into the style and method of translation to be used. From this group, a smaller council was chosen to determine how the most important biblical terms would be translated.

The members of our council are listed below with their North American tribal heritages:

- Barry D. Belindo—Kiowa/Navajo/Pawnee/Choctaw
- Garland Brunoe—Wascoe/Ojibwe
- Gordon Campbell—Kalispel/Spokane/Nez Perce
- Shándíín Church—Diné/Pokagon Band Potawatomi
- Alvin Deer—Kiowa/Creek
- John GrosVenor—Cherokee
- Antonia Belindo—Kiowa/Navajo/Pawnee/Choctaw
- Bryan Jon Maciewski—Anishinabe/Ojibwe
- Dale and Charlotte Tsosie—Diné (Navajo)
- Terry M. Wildman—Ojibwe/Yaqui

The following ministries gave of their time to participate in this project: Rain Ministries, OneBook of Canada, Wycliffe Associates, Native InterVarsity, and Mending Wings.

OTHER NATIVE PEOPLE INVOLVED

Besides the members of our council, many other First Nations people have had input into this translation as reviewers, cultural consultants, and community-feedback participants. All in all, the tribal heritages represented include but are not limited to Apache, Assiniboine, Blackfeet, Cherokee, Choctaw, Creek, Desert Cahuilla, Cayuga, Diné (Navajo), Hopi, Kalispel, Kiowa, Klickitat, Lakota, Mohawk, Métis, Miami, Muscogee, Nez Perce, Northern Cree, Odawa, Ojibwe, Pawnee, Plains Cree, Potawatomi, Tlingit, Tohono O'odham, Western Cree, Yankton Sioux, Spokane, Wascoe, Yakama, and Yaqui.

CONSULTANTS AND SUPPORT

Alongside our translation council were a number of support people on this project. Our translation consultant was the former head of Wycliffe Canada and the founder of OneBook Canada, with over fifty years of biblical translation experience with indigenous cultures. State-of-the-art translation software called Paratext was provided by OneBook along with expertise and guidance. We also had volunteer help from a retired teacher in Canada for the initial punctuation on the entire project. These friends and support partners were committed to having the First Nations people do the actual work of translation, while they provided experience, expertise, help, and feedback.

COMMUNITY CHECKING AND FEEDBACK

Our hope is that this translation will be used widely by the Native churches in North America. To facilitate this, about thirteen hundred draft versions of Luke were printed and distributed to Native churches, leaders, and many others both in Canada and the United States, asking for review and feedback. A number of pastors, church leaders, and members, along with some Bible scholars, participated in reviewing the draft version of Luke. Their input was valuable in improving this translation. Our translation council was instrumental in ensuring widespread community testing in Native communities. The feedback was overwhelmingly positive, and many great suggestions were incorporated.

For more information, visit firstnationsversion.com.

READER AIDS

Use of italics. In an attempt to present the Scriptures as a living and moving narrative, at times reasonably implied statements were added within, above, and below the text. For this, we used our imagination as we tried to picture what may have been the reaction in the voices and faces of the participants. These added statements are not intended to change the meaning of the text but rather to bring clarity. *For further clarity, these additions are in italics to distinguish them from the text of Scripture.*

History, culture, and geography. At times we also inserted comments about the history, culture, and geography within the story to add depth and understanding. This is for those without an historical understanding of the Jewish culture that is found in the New and Old Testaments. *All these additions are also in italics to distinguish them from the text of Scripture.*

Names of persons and places. We decided to follow our Native naming traditions and use the meaning of names for persons and places in this Great Story. In our community feedback, this practice was affirmed and appreciated. Most reviewers liked the standard English versions of the names in parentheses, while a few did not. We experimented with many options and finally decided to reduce the size of the font for the standard English names. Leaving the names in the text this way, instead of in footnotes, keeps the eye on the text and helps the reader's eye to more easily skip over it, if so desired.

Gender and the Great Spirit. We are of the understanding that the Great Spirit is neither male nor female. However, the original writers of the New Testament present the Great Spirit as Father, a male term. We see these terms as cultural metaphors when used of Creator. However, it is clear in the Scriptures that Creator Sets Free (Jesus) was literally born into this world as a male human. In this translation, we follow in the footsteps of the writers of the New Testament and use male pronouns for the Great Spirit. This was also the practice of many of our Native peoples as they spoke of the Supreme Being.

Names of God. Great Spirit, Creator, Great Mystery, Maker of Life, Giver of Breath, One Above Us All, and Most Holy One are a few of the names you will find in this translation. Names like these have been chosen in the retelling of this story to honor the simplicity and beauty of our Native understanding of our Great Creator.

The First Nations people of Turtle Island (North America) have many names and terms referring to the Supreme Being that created the universe. One of the names or terms that has been used predominantly is Great Spirit or Great Mystery. Among the Anishinaabe peoples Kitchi Manitou or as in many biblical translations Gizhe Manitou would be used. This would be understood generally as Great Spirit or Great Mystery. The term Creator is also used frequently among many of our peoples. While these terms are not tribally specific, the usage of Great Spirit and Creator is generally accepted by our First Nations people as a reference to the Supreme Being.

Some have asked us why we are not using the English word "God." While this term is almost exclusively used in English translations of the Bible, it is not an inspired usage. The word *god* is a translation of the Greek word *theos* in the New Testament and in the Septuagint (Greek) version of the Hebrew Scriptures. *Theos* is a general term for the divine and can be used of Yahweh (the Hebrew name for God) or for lesser divine beings. The English term *god* most likely came from a Germanic language root which was originally used for a lesser Germanic deity. In the Hebrew Scriptures, there is also a generic word for deity, the word *El*, used of both foreign gods and Yahweh. There are many names, designations, and titles used in the Bible that refer to God.

For the First Nations Version we preferred to use names, designations, and titles for God that are more relevant to our First Nations people. Even though all Christians believe in one God, they certainly have different doctrinal statements and ideas of what to correctly believe about God. Our hope is that our Native people will make the connection, through this translation, with the one who reveals perfectly who the Great Spirit is—that is Creator Sets Free (Jesus) the Chosen One.

PROLOGUE

LONG AGO, IN THE TIME BEFORE ALL DAYS, before the beginning of all things, the Great Spirit created the spirit-world above and the earth below. At that time our mother earth was an empty wasteland with no form or beauty, and great darkness was over the face of the ancient deep waters. The Breath of the Great Spirit moved over the surface of the waters like an eagle brooding over her nest. Creator sounded his voice. "Let light be!" he said. And light was! The Great Spirit could see that light was good, so he separated the light from the darkness. Creator gifted the light with the name *day*, and to the darkness he gave the name *night*. Then night faded and morning came. The first day.

In six days the Great Spirit made all things seen and unseen. He made the spirit-world above and the earth below. He created spirits to be his messengers and helpers. He also made the sun, moon, and stars, and all plants and animals. He made the great waters and all who swim in them. The winged ones who fly in the sky, the four-legged ones who walk on the ground, every creeping thing that crawls—all were shaped and molded by his hands.

On the sixth day Creator made the first man and woman and placed them in the Garden of Beauty and Harmony to be caretakers of the earth.

On the seventh day the Great Spirit rested from his work of creation, not because he was tired but because he was finished. The Great Spirit blessed the seventh day and made it a holy day. So humankind was created to enter into his day of rest and remain in harmony with Creator and care for all of creation.

But the evil snake, sometimes called Accuser (Satan), a spirit being who opposes the Great Spirit, twisted the words of Creator. He planted a seed of doubt into the minds of the first humans, so they ate the fruit of the only tree that Creator had told them not to eat from, the tree of the knowledge of good and evil. By listening to the evil snake and disobeying the Maker of Life, they brought death with all its bloodshed, violence, and destruction to all the generations of humankind that would follow.

The life of beauty and harmony was lost and the circle of life was broken. A powerful curse came upon the ground that affected all living things. Spiritual and physical death came to all. The hearts of human beings became broken, twisted together with good and evil. They could no longer live in harmony on the land and began to follow evil ways and hurt and kill one another.

Creator revealed what would come from the curse brought about by the ancient snake, then he made a promise to all humankind. He promised to one day send another human being, born of a woman, who would crush the head of the ancient snake and restore human beings and all of creation back to the life of beauty and harmony again.

After many generations, Creator found a man he would choose to make a peace treaty with, named Father of Many Nations (Abraham). Through this man and his descendants, Creator would bring to pass his promise.

When Father of Many Nations (Abraham) and his wife were too old to have children, the Great Spirit gave them a son. They named him He Made Us Laugh (Isaac) because they laughed when Creator told them they would have a child. He Made Us Laugh (Isaac) had a son whom he named Heel Grabber (Jacob), because he grabbed his twin brother's heel when he was being born. The Great Spirit later gave him a new name, Wrestles with Creator (Israel), because he wrestled with a spirit-messenger from Creator.

Wrestles with Creator (Israel) had twelve sons, who became twelve tribes. After four hundred years of mistreatment and slavery in the foreign nation of Black Land (Egypt), the Great Spirit set them free through Drawn from the Water (Moses), who became the great lawgiver.

The Great Spirit made a peace treaty with the tribes and gave them their own Land of Promise, ceremonies to purify them, and feasts to teach them to celebrate his goodness. He also gave them their tribal law, which was carved into tablets of stone, and a sacred tent lodge, where they would perform their ceremonies.

Creator wanted to be their only Chief, but the tribes wanted a human chief so they could be like the nations around them. This grieved Creator, but he gave them what they wanted. Most of these chiefs became arrogant and misrepresented the Great Spirit, but there were a few good ones. One of these chiefs was Much Loved One (David). He had a good heart toward Creator and the people, even though he, at times, also strayed from the path.

Creator chose the tribes to be a light to other nations, but they failed to keep his peace treaty, broke his laws, and misrepresented him to others. He sent many prophets to turn the hearts of the tribes back to the right ways of the Great Spirit, but they did not listen, and their hearts became like stone. The tribes went to war with each other and divided into two tribal nations. One nation kept the name Wrestles with Creator (Israel). The other nation took the name Give Him Honor (Judah).

After warning them many times, the Great Spirit finally removed his protection from them and allowed them to be conquered by the people of the Village of Confusion (Babylon). The tribes were taken captive and removed from their homeland. Their sacred lodge was destroyed, and their Village of Peace (Jerusalem) was left in ruins.

Creator's heart was full of sorrow, but he did not forget his ancient promise, so he sent more holy men to tell about his plan.

The Great Spirit spoke through the prophet Lifted by Creator (Jeremiah), saying,

Behold! The time will come when I will make a new peace treaty with the northern tribes of Wrestles with Creator (Israel) and the southern tribes of Give Him Honor (Judah). This peace treaty will be different from the one I made with their ancestors when I took them by the hand and walked them out of Black Land (Egypt). They did not honor that peace treaty, so I had to turn away from them. But here is the new peace treaty I will make with them. I will plant my laws in their minds and carve them into their hearts. I will be their Great Spirit, and they will be my people, my sacred family. (Jeremiah 31:31-33)

He also spoke through Creator Will Help Us (Isaiah), saying,

Here is the one I have chosen, who does all I ask and makes my heart glad. I have made my stand with him and love him as a father loves a son. My Sacred Spirit will rest on him and give him a message that will right the wrongs done to all people. He will not make loud arguments on the village pathways but will speak with humble dignity. He will not break a bruised reed. He will not snuff out a smoldering fire. He will never give up until all wrongs have been made right again! All Nations will hear of his reputation and put their trust and hope in him. (Isaiah 42:1-4)

The prophet Creator Will Decide (Daniel) said,

As I lay awake during the night, I was given many sacred visions. In one vision I looked and saw what appeared to be a True Human Being. He was riding on the clouds of the world above and was brought into the council house of the Ancient of Days. He stood before the Ancient of Days and was gifted with great authority over all the earth, with honor that outshines the sun, and with power that reaches beyond all the directions. All clans, tribes, nations, and languages will honor and serve this Chosen One above all others. His chiefly rule will last beyond the end of all days. For it will be a good road that can never fade away or come to a bad end. (Daniel 7:13-14)

After about seventy years in captivity, a small remnant returned to their homeland and rebuilt the sacred lodge. But the elders wept because it was pitiful in comparison to the original sacred lodge built by the great chief Stands in Peace (Solomon).

Many generations passed. Sacred ceremonies and feasts became empty rituals that were used to try to manipulate the Great Spirit to do what the spiritual leaders wanted. The ceremonies and laws were used to control people and make them afraid instead of helping them. Many spiritual leaders became even more corrupt, and they complicated and twisted the true meaning of Creator's words.

So the Great Spirit became silent and sent no more holy men to speak his words for four hundred years. But he did not forget his ancient promises.

Through the generations that followed, many powerful nations ruled over the tribes. The most recent was the People of Iron (Romans). This government took control of the tribes and dominated them for nearly two generations.

The People of Iron (Romans) forced their treaties on the tribes but did allow some freedoms. They could practice their own spiritual ways, build gathering houses called synagogues, and maintain a sacred lodge to perform their ceremonies and make their prayers.

This government also allowed them to have their own tribal chiefs. But over many years those chiefs became corrupt and were controlled more by the ways of the People of Iron (Romans) than by their ancient Sacred Ways. The People of Iron (Romans) had taken charge of appointing their holy men and their tribal chief.

The people were oppressed and feared this powerful government of the Village of Iron (Rome) with its many soldiers and weapons of war. They kept praying that the Great Spirit would fulfill the age-old prophecies and send the Chosen One, whom they hoped would be a great warrior chief to destroy the People of Iron (Romans) and set them free.

The right time had finally come for Creator to fulfill his ancient prophecies and send his Chosen One.

But he would not come in the way the tribes expected . . .

GIFT FROM CREATOR TELLS THE GOOD STORY

THE GOSPEL OF MATTHEW

1 ⪧⪦⪧⪦⪧⪦⪧⪦⪧⪦⪧⪦⪧⪦

HIS TRIBAL ANCESTRY

¹Here is the record of the ancestry of Creator Sets Free (Jesus) the Chosen One, a descendant of Much Loved One (David) and of Father of Many Nations (Abraham).

From Father of Many Nations (Abraham) to Much Loved One (David), his ancestors were:

²Father of Many Nations (Abraham), He Made Us Laugh (Isaac), Heel Grabber (Jacob), Give Him Praise (Judah) and his brothers, ³He Breaks Through (Perez) and his brother First Light (Zerah), whose mother was Fruit of Palm Tree (Tamar), Circle of Tipis (Hezron), Lifted Up (Ram), ⁴Noble Relative (Amminadab), Talks with Snakes (Nahshon), He Makes Peace (Salmon), ⁵Moves with Strength (Boaz), whose mother was Boastful Woman (Rahab), He Works Hard (Obed), whose mother was Beautiful Friend (Ruth), Original Man (Jesse), ⁶who was the father of the great chief Much Loved One (David).

From Much Loved One (David) to the removal to Village of Confusion (Babylon), the ancestors of Creator Sets Free (Jesus) were:

Much Loved One (David), Stands in Peace (Solomon), whose mother, Daughter of Seven (Bathsheba), was the wife of Fire from Creator (Uriah), ⁷Big People Maker (Rehoboam), He Is My Father (Abijah), Gathers the People (Asa), ⁸He Makes Wrongs Right Again (Jehoshaphat), Creator Is Above (Jehoram), My Great Power (Uzziah), ⁹Creator Has No Equal (Jotham), Held by Creator (Ahaz), He Will Be Strong (Hezekiah), ¹⁰He Made Them Forget (Manasseh), Burden Bearer (Amon), Good Medicine (Josiah), ¹¹and Chosen by Creator (Jeconiah) and his brothers at the time of the removal to Village of Confusion (Babylon).

¹²From the removal to Village of Confusion (Babylon) to the birth of Creator Sets Free (Jesus), his ancestors were:

Chosen by Creator (Jeconiah), Ask Creator (Shealtiel), Born in Village of Confusion (Zerubbabel), ¹³Father Boasts in Him (Abihud), He Builds Up (Eliakim), He Helps (Azor), ¹⁴Stands with a Good Heart (Zadok), Stands Firm (Achim), Power of Creator (Eliud), ¹⁵Creator Helps Him (Eleazar), Gifted by Creator (Matthan), Heel Grabber (Jacob), ¹⁶and He Gives Sons (Joseph), who was the husband of Bitter Tears (Mary), who gave birth to Creator Sets Free (Jesus), who is the Chosen One.

¹⁷And so there were fourteen generations from Father of Many Nations (Abraham) to Much Loved One (David), fourteen more generations from Much Loved One (David) until the removal to Village of Confusion (Babylon), and then

fourteen more from the removal to Creator Sets Free (Jesus), the Chosen One.

BIRTH OF THE CHOSEN ONE

¹⁸Here is the story of how the Chosen One was born:

His mother, Bitter Tears (Mary), had been promised in marriage to He Gives Sons (Joseph). But before they came together in marriage, while still a virgin, she found out that she was carrying a baby in her womb from the Holy Spirit. ¹⁹He Gives Sons (Joseph) was a man of honor. He did not want to bring her trouble and open shame, so he thought about secretly releasing her from the marriage promise.

²⁰As he wondered about these things, a messenger from the Great Spirit appeared to him in a dream and said, "He Gives Sons (Joseph), descendant of Much Loved One (David), do not be afraid to take Bitter Tears (Mary) to be your wife, because the Holy Spirit has given her this child. ²¹She will give birth to a son. You will name him Creator Sets Free (Jesus), because he will set his people free from their bad hearts and broken ways."

²²This gave full meaning to the words of Creator spoken long ago by the prophet, ²³"A young virgin will be with child and give birth to a son. They will call his name Immanuel,ᵃ which in our tribal language means Creator Is with Us."

²⁴When He Gives Sons (Joseph) woke up, he followed the guidance given him in the dream and took Bitter Tears (Mary) to be his wife. ²⁵But he did not have sexual relations with her until after the child was born, and he named the child Creator Sets Free (Jesus).

2

SEEKERS OF WISDOM

¹It was during the days of the *bad-hearted* Chief Looks Brave (Herod) that the Chosen One was born in the village of House of Bread (Bethlehem) in the Land of Promise (Judea). After his birth, Seekers of Wisdom (Magi) traveling *on a long journey* from the East came to Village of Peace (Jerusalem).

²They began to ask around, "Where is the one who has been born to be chief of the tribes of Wrestles with Creator (Israel)? We saw his star where the sun rises and have come to humble ourselves before him and honor him."

³When Chief Looks Brave heard this, he and all who lived in Village of Peace (Jerusalem) were troubled. ⁴He called a council of all the head holy men and scroll keepers and asked them where the Chosen One was to be born.

⁵"In House of Bread (Bethlehem), the village of the great chief Much Loved One (David)," they answered. "This is what the ancient prophet said: ⁶'But you, O House of Bread (Bethlehem), in the Land of Promise (Judea), even though you are small, you have a good reputation with the chiefs who watch over the land. From you will come a Great Chief who will guide my chosen people—the tribes of Wrestles with Creator (Israel).'ᵇ"

⁷Then Looks Brave (Herod) called a secret council with the Seekers of Wisdom (Magi) to find out when the star first appeared. ⁸He then sent them to House of Bread (Bethlehem) and told them, "Look everywhere for the child. Find him and tell me where he is, so that I may also come and honor him."

⁹After listening to Looks Brave (Herod),

ᵃ**1:23** Isaiah 7:14

ᵇ**2:6** Micah 5:2

the Seekers of Wisdom (Magi) went their way. ¹⁰When they saw the star rising in the East, they jumped with joy, and with glad hearts they followed until the star stopped and rested over the place where the child was. ¹¹They went into the house and saw the child and his mother, Bitter Tears (Mary). As soon as they saw the child, they bowed down to honor him. Then they opened their bundles and gifted him with gold, sweet-smelling incense, and bitter ointment of myrrh.

ESCAPE TO BLACK LAND

¹²The Seekers of Wisdom (Magi) were warned in a dream not to go back to Looks Brave (Herod), so they returned to their homeland by a different road.

¹³After the Seekers of Wisdom (Magi) had gone, a spirit-messenger from Creator warned He Gives Sons (Joseph) in a dream. "Rise up!" he said *urgently.* "Take the child and his mother and go quickly to Black Land (Egypt) and remain there until I tell you to leave. Looks Brave (Herod) is searching for the child to kill him!"

¹⁴That night He Gives Sons (Joseph) took the child and his mother, and they fled for their lives to Black Land (Egypt). ¹⁵They remained there until the death of Looks Brave (Herod). This gave full meaning to Creator's ancient prophecy: "I will call my son out from Black Land (Egypt)."ᵃ

¹⁶When Looks Brave (Herod) realized he had been outsmarted by the Seekers of Wisdom (Magi), he was full of rage. Using the knowledge he had gained from them, he gave orders for all male children in House of Bread (Bethlehem) under two winters of age to be put to death. ¹⁷This gave full meaning to another ancient prophecy spoken by Lifted by Creator

(Jeremiah): ¹⁸"A sound of weeping and wailing is heard in Highland (Ramah). Sheep Woman (Rachel) is shedding tears for her children. No one can bring her peace, because her children have been taken from the land of the living."ᵇ

DREAM GUIDANCE

¹⁹After Looks Brave (Herod) died, a spirit-messenger from Creator appeared again to He Gives Sons (Joseph) in a dream while he was still in Black Land (Egypt). ²⁰The spirit-messenger said to him, "Get up and take the child and his mother back to the land of the tribes of Wrestles with Creator (Israel), for the ones who were trying to take the child's life are dead."

²¹He Gives Sons (Joseph) got up, took the child and his mother, and began to go where he was told. ²²On the way, when he heard that Rules the People (Archelaus), the son of Chief Looks Brave (Herod), had become the new chief, he became afraid.

After being warned in another dream, he took a different path to their home through Circle of Nations (Galilee), ²³to *an out-of-the-way village most people looked down on, called* Seed Planter Village (Nazareth). This gave full meaning to the words of the prophets, "He will be called a Seed Planter (Nazarene)."

Many long winters had come and gone. Creator Sets Free (Jesus) was now thirty winters old—a mature man. The People of Iron (Romans) had many new rulers and governors, and the tribes of Wrestles with Creator (Israel) had a new chief holy man for the sacred lodge.

ᵃ**2:15** Hosea 11:1   ᵇ**2:18** Jeremiah 31:15

GIFT OF GOODWILL

¹In those days a man named Gift of Goodwill (John) appeared in the desert places of the Land of Promise (Judea). He began to speak out a message *that was loud and clear,* ²"It is time to return to the right ways of thinking. Creator's good road from above is close. *It is time to begin walking it.*"

³The prophet Creator Will Help Us (Isaiah) told about him long ago when he said, "A voice is howling in the desert, 'Clear the pathways! Make the path straight for the coming of the Great Chief!'ᵃ"

⁴Gift of Goodwill (John) came wearing a buffalo robe, with a deer-hideᵇ sash around his waist. The food he ate was grasshoppers and wild honey.

⁵The people were coming from Village of Peace (Jerusalem), from all over the Land of Promise (Judea) and the territory surrounding the river Flowing Down (Jordan). ⁶They came admitting to their bad hearts and broken ways and participated in the purification ceremony.ᶜ

SPIRITUAL LEADERS WARNED

⁷When he saw the Separated Ones (Pharisees) and Upright Ones (Sadducees) in the crowd watching, he cried out to them, "You nest of poisonous snakes! Who warned you to run and hide from the coming storm? ⁸You are like trees without fruit. Prove to others, by the way you live, that you have returned to the good road. ⁹Do you think you can say, 'Father of Many Nations (Abraham) is our ancestor'? Do you not know the Great Spirit can make these stones into his children? ¹⁰The tomahawk is already at the root of the trees, and the ones that have no good fruit will be cut down and tossed into the fire.

PURIFICATION CEREMONY WITH FIRE

¹¹"I perform the purification ceremonyᶜ with water, for the ones who have returned to the right way of thinking. But there is one you do not know, who is right here with you, and even though he comes after me, he is much greater. I am not even worthy to bend down and untie his moccasins. He is the one who will perform the purification ceremony with the fire of the Holy Spirit! ¹²His harvest basket is in his hands, to separate the grain from the husks. He will store the good grain in his barn, but the husks he will burn up with a fire no one can put out."

THIS IS MY MUCH-LOVED SON

¹³Gift of Goodwill (John) then looked up and saw Creator Sets Free (Jesus) wading out into the water of the river Flowing Down (Jordan). He had come from Circle of Nations (Galilee), *a journey of many days,* for the purification ceremony,ᶜ ¹⁴but Gift of Goodwill (John) tried to stop him.

"Why are you coming to me?" he asked *humbly.* "I am the one who should come to you."

¹⁵"This is the way it should be, for now," Creator Sets Free (Jesus) answered. "It is the right thing to do, *to bring honor to the ways of Great Spirit.*"

Gift of Goodwill (John) agreed to perform the ceremony. ¹⁶As soon as Creator Sets Free (Jesus) came up from the water, he saw the sky open. The Spirit of Creator came down like a dove and rested on him. ¹⁷A voice from the sky spoke *like distant thunder,* "This is my much-loved Son, who makes my heart glad!"

ᵃ**3:3** Isaiah 40:3
ᵇ**3:4** Lit. *garments of camel's hair and a leather belt*
ᶜ**3:6, 11, 13** Baptism

4

TESTED BY THE EVIL TRICKSTER

¹Creator Sets Free (Jesus) followed the guidance of the Spirit, who took him into the desert wilderness to be tested by Accuser (Satan), the evil trickster snake.

In the story of creation, the first man and woman lived in a Garden of Beauty and Harmony. A sly and crafty snake came to them and twisted the words of the Great Spirit to deceive them. They listened to the snake, lost the life of beauty and harmony, and fell under the curse of death. This snake, who opposes Creator's good road, is the evil spirit who rules over all evil spirits.

²For forty days and nights Creator Sets Free (Jesus) ate nothing. *His body became weak,* and his hunger grew strong.

³*When* the evil snake *saw that Creator Sets Free (Jesus) was weak and hungry, he came to him and whispered in his ear.*

"Are you the Son of the Great Spirit?" he hissed. "Prove it by turning these stones into frybread."

⁴"The Sacred Teachings are clear," Creator Sets Free (Jesus) said. "Human beings cannot live only on frybread, but on all the words that come from the mouth of the Great Spirit."[a]

⁵The evil trickster then took him to the Great Spirit's sacred lodge in Village of Peace (Jerusalem). He set him at the very top, *high above the village.*

⁶"Prove you are the Son of the Great Spirit and jump down from here!" the evil snake taunted him. "Do not the Sacred Teachings also say, 'His spirit-messengers will watch over you to keep you from harm. They will even keep your foot from hitting a stone'[b]?"

⁷"Yes," Creator Sets Free (Jesus) said back to him, "but they also say, 'Do not test the Great Spirit.'[c]"

⁸Once more the evil trickster took him to a high mountain and showed him all the great nations of the world with their power and beauty.

⁹"All of these I will give you," the snake said *smoothly,* "if you will highly honor me and walk in my ways!"

¹⁰"Get away from me, Accuser (Satan)!" he responded. "For it is written in the Sacred Teachings, 'The Great Spirit is the only one to honor and serve.'[d]"

¹¹The evil trickster could think of nothing more to test him with, so he slithered away to wait for another time.

Then spirit-messengers came to give comfort and strength to Creator Sets Free (Jesus).

GIFT OF GOODWILL JAILED

¹²After that, Creator Sets Free (Jesus) heard that Gift of Goodwill (John) was put in jail, so he left that place to return to Circle of Nations (Galilee). ¹³He left his home in Seed Planter Village (Nazareth) and went to live in Village of Comfort (Capernaum) by the sea. This was in the territory of the tribes of Honored Dwelling (Zebulun) and He Will Wrestle (Naphtali).

¹⁴The ancient prophecy of Creator Will Help Us (Isaiah) had finally found its full meaning. ¹⁵"In the territory of the tribes of Honored Dwelling (Zebulun) and He Will Wrestle (Naphtali), toward the great waters to Circle of Nations (Galilee) where many Nations dwell—¹⁶the ones

a4:4 Deuteronomy 8:3
b4:6 Psalm 91:11-12
c4:7 Deuteronomy 6:16
d4:10 Deuteronomy 6:13

who sit in darkness, where death casts a great shadow, have seen the light of a new sunrise."[a]

THE GOOD ROAD IS CLOSE

[17]From that time forward Creator Sets Free (Jesus) began to speak out, "Creator's good road from above is close. It is time to change your thinking and begin your great journey."

HIS FIRST FOLLOWERS

[18]Creator Sets Free (Jesus) was walking by the shoreline of Lake of Circle of Nations (Sea of Galilee) when he saw two fishermen throwing out their nets. They were One Who Hears (Simon), also named Stands on the Rock (Peter), and his brother Stands with Courage (Andrew).

[19]He said to them, "Come, walk the road with me, and I will show you how to fish in a new way—for two-leggeds."

[20]They dropped their nets right then and became his followers.

[21]As Creator Sets Free (Jesus) was leaving, he saw two other brothers, He Takes Over (James) and He Shows Goodwill (John), the sons of Gift of Creator (Zebedee). They were sitting with their father in a canoe getting their nets ready for fishing. [22]Creator Sets Free (Jesus) called out to them, and they dropped their nets, left their father, and also became his followers.

WALKING THE GOOD ROAD

[23]Creator Sets Free (Jesus) traveled throughout Circle of Nations (Galilee). He was teaching in their gathering houses and telling everyone the good story of Creator's good road. He was healing the people of every kind of sickness and disease. [24]His reputation as a healer spread as far as Bright Sun (Syria). Then they brought to him the ones tormented with evil spirits, along with people who suffered from seizures, and he healed them. He even healed the crippled and paralyzed among them.

[25]Large crowds from all directions began to seek after him—too many to number! They came from Circle of Nations (Galilee) and Ten Villages (Decapolis), and from Village of Peace (Jerusalem), and the Land of Promise (Judea), and from beyond the river Flowing Down (Jordan).

5

[1]When Creator Sets Free (Jesus) saw this great crowd, he went back up into the mountainside and sat down to teach the people. His followers came to him there, [2]so he *took a deep breath*, opened his mouth, and began to share his wisdom with them *and teach them how to see Creator's good road.*

BLESSINGS OF THE GOOD ROAD

[3]"Creator's blessing rests on the poor, the ones with broken spirits. The good road from above is theirs to walk.

[4]"Creator's blessing rests on the ones who walk a trail of tears, for he will wipe the tears from their eyes and comfort them.

[5]"Creator's blessing rests on the ones who walk softly and in a humble manner. The earth, land, and sky will welcome them and always be their home.

[6]"Creator's blessing rests on the ones who hunger and thirst for wrongs to be made right again. They will eat and drink until they are full.

[7]"Creator's blessing rests on the ones who are merciful and kind to others. Their kindness will find its way back to them—full circle.

---

[a]**4:16** Isaiah 9:1-2

[8] "Creator's blessing rests on the pure of heart. They are the ones who will see the Great Spirit.

[9] "Creator's blessing rests on the ones who make peace. It will be said of them, 'They are the children of the Great Spirit!'

[10] "Creator's blessing rests on the ones who are hunted down and mistreated for doing what is right, for they are walking the good road from above.

[11] "Others will lie about you, speak against you, and look down on you with scorn and contempt, all because you walk the road with me. This is a sign that Creator's blessing is resting on you. [12] So let your hearts be glad and jump for joy, for you will be honored in the spirit-world above. You are like the prophets of old, who were treated in the same way by your ancestors.

SALT AND LIGHT

[13] "As you walk the good road with me, you are the salt of the earth, bringing cleansing and healing[a] to all. Salt is a good thing, but if it loses its saltiness, how will it get its flavor back? That kind of salt has no worth and is thrown out.

[14] "As you walk the road with me, you are a light shining in this dark world. A village built on a hill cannot be hidden. [15] No one hides a torch under a basket. Instead it is lifted up high on a pole, so all who are in the house can see it. [16] In the same way, let your light shine by doing what is good and right. When others see, they will give honor to your Father—the One Above Us All.

FULFILLING THE SACRED TEACHINGS

[17] "When you hear my words, you may think I have come to undo the Law given by Drawn from the Water (Moses) and the words of the prophets. But I have come to honor them and show everyone their true meaning. [18] I speak from my heart, as long as there is a sky above and an earth below, not even the smallest thing they have said will fade away, until everything they have said has found its full meaning and purpose.

[19] "Anyone who turns away from these instructions and tells others to do the same will be looked down on, as a small one, on Creator's good road from the spirit-world above. But the ones who do them and teach others to do the same, they will be looked up to as great ones.

[20] "I will say this to you, unless you have a better reputation than the scroll keepers and the Separated Ones (Pharisees), you will not find the path that leads to the Land of Creator's good road from above."

Creator Sets Free (Jesus) then began to help the people see how the full meaning and purpose of the Law and the Prophets applied to them.

RESPECT TOWARD ALL

[21] "You have heard that our ancestors were told long ago, 'Do not take another person's life,'[b] and 'whoever does will have to answer to the tribal council.'[c] [22] But I tell you, everyone who is angry toward a fellow human being will have to give an answer to the tribal council. If they speak with disrespect to someone, saying, 'You hollow head!' they will also face the tribal council. If they curse someone by saying 'You damn fool!' they may end up in the Valley of Smoldering Fire. [23] So if you are offering a gift *at*

---

[a] **5:13** 2 Kings 2:19-22
[b] **5:21** Exodus 20:13
[c] **5:21** Deuteronomy 16:18

Creator's ceremonial lodge, and there remember that a Tribal Member has something against you, **24**leave your gift and go make things right. Then you can come back and finish the ceremony.

RESOLVING CONFLICT WITH DIGNITY

25"If someone has a complaint against you and takes you before the village council, work out an agreement before you get there. *You know how to decide things for yourselves.* The council might decide against you and turn you over to the ones who have the power to put you in prison. **26**The truth is, there is no way out of there until honor has been restored."[a]

HONORING OUR WOMEN

Most women in the time of Creator Sets Free (Jesus) were dominated by men and were often treated as property and looked down on with disrespect.

27So he said to the men, "You have heard the saying, 'You must not have sexual relations with another man's wife.'[b] **28**But I tell you this, any man who looks at a woman and wants his way with her has already done so in his heart.

"This is not how the Great Spirit wants us to see our sisters. **29**If your right eye sees in this way[c]—gouge it out and throw it away! **30**If your right hand does harm to her[c]—cut it off and throw it away! It is better to lose a part of your body than for your whole body to be thrown into the Valley of Smoldering Fire.

31"Drawn from the Water (Moses) said, 'If you put away your wife you must give her divorce papers.'[d] **32**Let me tell you why. Anyone who puts away his wife *without giving her divorce papers* makes her unfaithful when she remarries, unless she was unfaithful already. Then anyone who marries her is having sexual relations with another man's wife."

In those days men would "put away" their wives without divorcing them, leaving them destitute and unable to properly remarry.

NO SOLEMN PROMISES

33"You have heard the ancestors were told, 'When you make a solemn promise, you must keep it to honor the Great Spirit.'[e] **34**But I say this to you, do not make any solemn promises. Do not say, 'I promise by the spirit-world above,' for it is Creator's seat of honor, **35**or 'I promise by the earth below,' which is the resting place for his feet. Or 'I promise by Village of Peace (Jerusalem),' for it belongs to the Great Spirit Chief. **36**Do not even say, 'I promise by my own head.' Can you make even one hair on your head become white or black? **37**Your simple 'yes' or 'no' is enough. To say more is to speak with a forked tongue like the evil trickster snake.

EYE FOR AN EYE?

38"You have also been told, 'Take an eye for an eye and a tooth for a tooth.'[f] **39**But I tell you, do not fight back. *Violence will not be defeated by more of the same.* If someone strikes the right side of your face, turn to him the other side also. **40**If someone takes you to the tribal council for your shirt, give him your vest also. **41**If anyone, *even a soldier of the People of*

---

[a]**5:26** Lit. *until the debt is paid in full*
[b]**5:27** Exodus 20:14
[c]**5:29, 30** Lit. *offends you*
[d]**5:31** Deuteronomy 24:1
[e]**5:33** Leviticus 19:12
[f]**5:38** Exodus 21:24; Leviticus 24:20

Iron (Romans), forces you to carry his bundle one mile, *show the strength of your heart and* carry it two. **42**Give to the one who asks for help, and do not turn away from the one who wants to borrow from you.

LOVE YOUR ENEMIES

43"You have been told to love only your own people and to despise others as your enemy.[a] **44-45**But I tell you, treat your enemies with love and respect, and send up good prayers for the ones who make trouble for you and bring you pain. This will show that you are mature children of your Father from above, who sends his blessing of rain on the ones who do right and the ones who do wrong.

46"If you love and show respect only to the ones who do the same, how does that bring honor to you? Even tribal tax collectors do these things. **47**If you welcome only friends, how are you different from others? Even outsiders from other nations do these things.

48"By loving and blessing all people, you will be walking in the footsteps of your Father from the spirit-world above, who is perfect in all his ways.

THE WAY TO DO GOOD

1"Beware of doing good just so people can see you, for then you will receive no honor from your Father from above, *who is the Creator.* **2**When you give gifts to the poor and do good things for others, do not brag about it on the village pathways or in the gathering houses, like those who put on a false face,

pretending to be something they are not. The truth is, they honor only themselves and they will get nothing more.

3-4"But when you help others who are in need, do it in secret. Do not even tell your left hand what your right hand is doing. Then your Father who sees all things will honor you.

THE WAY TO PRAY

5"When you send your voice to the Great Spirit, do not be like the ones who love to stand up and pray with a loud voice in the gathering houses and along the village pathways, hoping to be seen and heard by others. The truth is, they have their honor already. They will get no more. **6**Instead, find a quiet hiding place where no one can see or hear you and send your prayers to your Father in secret. He will see what you have done and honor you.

7-8"When you pray, do not be like the people from the Outside Nations, who use empty words over and over again, thinking their many words will help them be heard. Your Father, the Creator, already knows what you need even before you ask.

9"Instead, when you send your voice to the Great Spirit, here is how you should pray:

"O Great Spirit, our Father from above, we honor your name as sacred and holy. **10**"Bring your good road to us, where the beauty of your ways in the spirit-world above is reflected in the earth below.

11"Provide for us day by day—the elk, the buffalo, and the salmon. The corn, the squash, and the wild rice. All the things we need for each day.

12"Release us from the things we have done wrong, in the same way we release others for the things done wrong to us.

---

a5:43 Leviticus 19:18

¹³"Guide us away from the things that tempt us to stray from your good road, and set us free from the evil one and his worthless ways. Aho! May it be so!

¹⁴"Remember, our Father from the spirit-world above will release you from your wrongdoings in the same manner you release others from theirs. ¹⁵But if you fail to release others, this keeps your Father, the Creator, from releasing you.

THE WAY TO FAST

¹⁶"When you go without food to seek spiritual things, do not be like the ones who put on a false face. They hang their heads down and darken their faces to look as if they are going without food. They only want people to notice them and think they are spiritual. I speak from my heart, they already have all the honor they deserve—they will get no more. ¹⁷But when you go without eating, put on your headdress and wash your face, ¹⁸so others will not notice. But know that your Father from above, who sees in secret, will honor you.

THE WAY TO SEE POSSESSIONS

¹⁹"Take care not to store up possessions on earth that can be spoiled by worms, eaten by moths, or stolen by thieves. ²⁰Instead, *give away your possessions to the ones in need*, and then you will be storing up great possessions in the spirit-world above, where nothing can be lost or stolen. ²¹For where you store your valued possessions is where your heart will be."

GOOD EYE OR BAD EYE

Among the tribes of Wrestles with Creator (Israel) a greedy person was said to have a bad eye and unable to see the good road. A generous person was said to have a *good eye, full of light and able to clearly see the good road.*

²²*So he said to them,* "Light shines into the body through the eye. If your eye is clear, your whole being is full of light. ²³But if your eye is bad, then your whole being is full of darkness. If the only light you have is darkness, then the darkness is very great!

²⁴"No one can be loyal to two rival chiefs. You will have to choose between them. You will either hate one chief and love the other, or honor one and resent the other. You cannot be loyal to the Great Provider and to possessions at the same time.

WORRY IS THE WRONG PATH

²⁵"This is why I am telling you not to be troubled about getting enough to eat or drink, or what to wear. Is eating, drinking and clothing yourself all there is? Does your life not have more meaning than this?

²⁶"Look to the winged ones who soar on the wind. Do they plant seeds and gather the harvest into a storehouse? No! But your Father from above gives them plenty to eat. Do you not know he cares even more for you? ²⁷Can worry add even one more step to the length of your life's journey?

²⁸"Why do you trouble yourself with what to wear? Have you seen how the wildflowers grow in the plains and meadows? Do you think they work hard and long to clothe themselves? ²⁹No! I tell you not even the great chieftain Stands in Peace (Solomon), wearing his finest regalia, was dressed as well as even one of these.

³⁰"If Creator covers the wild grass in the plains with such beauty, which is here today and gathered for tomorrow's fire, will he not take even better care of you?

Why is your faith so small? **31**There is no need to say, 'What will we eat? What will we drink? What will we wear?' **32**This is what the Nations *who have lost their way* have given their hearts to, but your Father from above knows you need these things. **33**"If you will make Creator's good road your first aim, representing his right ways, he will make sure you have all you need for each day. **34**So do not worry about tomorrow's troubles. It is enough to trust Creator to give you the strength you need to face today.

SEEING OTHERS CLEARLY

1"If you do not want to be judged, then do not judge others. **2**For the way you judge others will come back to you—full circle. **3***Think of it this way.* How can you see the speck of wood in the eye of another[a] when you cannot see the log in your own eye? **4**How can you say, 'Here, let me help you,' when you cannot see that you need even more help? **5**Stop pretending to be something you are not! If you will be honest about yourself, you will then see clearly enough to help others.[a]

WISDOM FOR SACRED THINGS

6"Take care not to give what is sacred to the ones who will turn on you and treat you with disrespect. For who would toss an eagle feather into the dirt to be trampled on?

KEEP DANCING YOUR PRAYERS

7"Let your prayers rise like smoke to the Great Spirit, for he will see and answer you. Every step is a prayer, and as you

---

[a]7:3, 5 Lit. *your brother*

dance upon the earth for the things you seek, the way will open before you. In the same way, as you search for the true ancient pathways, you will find them. **8**Answers will come to the ones who ask, good things will be found by the ones who search for them, and the way will open before the ones who keep dancing their prayers."

Creator Sets Free (Jesus) took a piece of fry- bread and a fish from a basket. He lifted the frybread up high for all to see.

9"What father, if his son wanted fry- bread, would give him a stone to eat?"

Then he lifted the fish up high.

10"If he asked for a fish, would he give him a snake?

11"If fathers with bad hearts know how to give good gifts to their children, then how much more will the Great Spirit, who is your loving Father from above, give good gifts to the ones who ask?

THE MEANING OF MY TEACHINGS

12"Here is the meaning of what I have been saying: whatever good you want others to do for you is what you should do for them. This is the whole purpose of the instructions given by Drawn from the Water (Moses) and the words spoken by the prophets.

SMALL GATE AND NARROW WAY

13-14"To walk Creator's good road you *must* enter this small gate and walk a narrow path that leads to the good life. Only a few find and walk this road. But the gate is large and the path is wide that leads to a bad end. Many walk this road. **15**"Some *who walk this wide road* rep- resent themselves as sheep, but inside they are hungry wolves. Watch out for these false prophets. **16**You will know them by their fruit. Do grapes come from a thorn bush or pears from thistles? **17-18**Will a sick tree give good fruit or a healthy tree bad fruit? No! Healthy trees give good fruit and sick trees give bad fruit. **19**It is the trees with bad fruit that are cut down and used to make a fire. **20**When you see the fruit of their ways, you will know them.

21"Not everyone who calls me their Great Chief is walking the good road from the spirit-world above. The ones who do what my Father from the spirit-world above wants are the ones walking this road.

22"On that day, *the time when Creator reveals all hearts,* many will say to me, 'O Great Chief, did we not speak for you, force out evil spirits, and do great things all in your name—representing you?' **23**But this is what I will have to say to them, 'Who are you? Go away from me, you who do what you know is wrong, for you never truly knew me.'**ᵃ**

WISE AND FOOLISH

24"The ones who listen to me and walk in my ways are like a wise man who built a grand lodge on solid ground. **25**The rain poured down, the streams flowed, and the strong winds came. They all beat against the lodge, but it stood strong against the storm. Nothing could shake it, for it was built on solid ground.

26"The ones who hear my words but do not walk in these ways are like another man, a foolish one, who built his lodge on top of the sand. **27**When the storm came against it, the lodge crashed to the ground, and all that was in it was lost."

28-29 Creator Sets Free (Jesus) was finished for the day with his teachings and wise stories. All the people were amazed and had great respect for him, for he was not like the other spiritual leaders—the scroll keepers. He spoke with true wisdom and dignity, showing he had the right to represent the Great Spirit.

8 ◄▷◄▷◄▷◄▷◄▷◄▷◄▷◄▷

POWER TO CLEANSE AND HEAL

1A great crowd of people followed Creator Sets Free (Jesus) as he walked down from the mountainside. **2**A man with a skin disease all over his body came up to Creator Sets Free (Jesus). He humbled himself, bowed down, and pleaded with him, "Honored One! If you want to, you can heal and cleanse me."

3"I want to!" Creator Sets Free (Jesus) said as he reached out and touched the man.

> *Tribal law says that anyone who touches anything unclean would also be unclean and in need of cleansing.***ᵇ** *But Creator Sets Free (Jesus), instead of becoming unclean himself, cleansed the man with his touch.*

"Be clean!" he said, and right away the disease left the man and he was healed.

4Creator Sets Free (Jesus) instructed the man, "Tell no one! Take the traditional ceremonial gift and show yourself to a holy man. Then have him perform the cleansing ceremony given by the lawgiver Drawn from the Water (Moses). This will show others that you have been healed and made ceremonially clean again."

ᵃ7:23 Lit. *I never knew you*   **ᵇ8:3** Leviticus 22:6

FAITH FROM A HEAD SOLDIER

[5]As Creator Sets Free (Jesus) walked into Village of Comfort (Capernaum), a head soldier from the People of Iron (Romans) came up to him. [6]"Honored One," the head soldier begged, "my household servant that I care deeply about is lying in bed, unable to move and in great pain."

[7]"I will come to your house and heal him," Creator Sets Free (Jesus) told the man.

[8]But the head soldier, *knowing the tribal traditions*, said to him, "Honored One, I am not worth the trouble that coming to my house would bring to you. If you will only speak the word, I know my servant will be healed, [9]for I am also a man under orders with many soldiers under me. I say to this one, 'Go,' and he goes, and to another, 'Come,' and he comes. My servants do what I say."

[10]Creator Sets Free (Jesus) was amazed at this answer. He turned to the ones who were following him and said to them, "I speak from my heart, I have never seen such great faith, not even among the tribes of Wrestles with Creator (Israel)."

He let his words sink deep into the hearts of the people listening.

[11]Then he said, "Listen closely, for I tell you that this man is only one of many who will come from the four directions[a] to sit in a great lodge and feast with our ancestors. They will sit down with Father of Many Nations (Abraham), He Made Us Laugh (Isaac), and Heel Grabber (Jacob) in the Land of Creator's good road from above. [12]But the ones who were first born to walk the good road will be forced out into the night. Outside in the darkness, they will howl with tears and grind their teeth together in anger and frustration."

[13]Creator Sets Free (Jesus) then turned to face the head soldier.

"Go home," he said to him, "Your faith in me has healed your servant."

And right then the head soldier's servant was healed!

IN THE HOME OF STANDS ON THE ROCK

[14]Creator Sets Free (Jesus) came to the home of Stands on the Rock (Peter). The mother-in-law of Stands on the Rock (Peter) was sick in bed with a fever. [15]When Creator Sets Free (Jesus) saw her, he reached out and touched her hand. Right then the fever left her. She *felt so good she* got up and made a meal for them.

[16]Later that day, when the sun was going down, many who were tormented by evil spirits were brought to him. He spoke to the spirits, forced them out with a word, and healed the ones who were sick. [17]All this was done to bring full meaning to the ancient prophecy spoken by Creator Will Help Us (Isaiah), "He took upon himself our sickness and carried the weight of our diseases."[b]

COST OF FOLLOWING

[18]Creator Sets Free (Jesus) saw the great number of people around him and gave his followers instructions *to prepare a canoe* to cross over to the other side of the lake.

[19]On the way to the lake, a scroll keeper walked up to him, "Wisdomkeeper," he said, "I will follow you wherever you want to go."

[20]He answered the man, "The foxes live in their holes, the winged ones who

---

[a]**8:11** Lit. *East and West*

[b]**8:17** Isaiah 53:4

fly above us live in their nests, but the True Human Being has no place to lay his head."

²¹Another follower said to Creator Sets Free (Jesus), "Honored One, let me first go home to my father *until it is time to bury him.*"

²²"Let the ones who are *spiritually* dead bury their dead," he said to the man. "You come and walk the road with me."

POWER OVER STORMS

²³*They came to the lake, and* Creator Sets Free (Jesus) and his close followers climbed into a canoe and began to paddle across the lake.

> *A dark and menacing storm began to move in quickly, and the sound of distant thunder rolled over the waters. They paddled harder, trying to get to the other shore before the storm hit.*

²⁴Suddenly the violent storm overtook them and threatened to sink the large canoe, but Creator Sets Free (Jesus) had fallen into a deep sleep. ²⁵*In desperation* they woke him up.

"Wisdomkeeper!" they cried out. "We are fighting for our lives! Save us!"

²⁶"Why are you full of fear?" he asked them, "Is your faith so small?"

He stood up and spoke sharply to the wind and the raging water. At his words a great peace fell upon the surface of the waters.

²⁷His followers were greatly amazed. They shook their heads and said to one another, "What kind of man is this? Even the wind and the waves do what he says."

POWER OVER EVIL SPIRITS

²⁸When they finished crossing the lake, they came to the territory of the people of Honored in the End (Gadarenes). As soon as Creator Sets Free (Jesus) stepped from the canoe, two men coming from the burial caves who were tormented by evil spirits came up to him. These men were so violent that no one dared to pass through that area.

²⁹"Son of the Great Spirit!" they shrieked. "What do you want from us? Are you here to torment us before Creator's chosen time?"

³⁰In the distance a large herd of pigs was feeding *on a hillside.* ³¹The evil spirits spoke through the men. "If you must force us out," they begged, "then send us into that herd of pigs."

³²"Be gone!" he said, giving them permission.

The evil spirits left and entered into the herd of pigs. Then the whole herd stampeded down the steep hill headlong into Lake of Circle of Nations (Sea of Galilee) and drowned in the deep water.

³³The ones who were watching over the pigs rushed away, *shaken and afraid.* They went to the village and told everyone all that happened.

³⁴When they heard this, the whole village went out to find Creator Sets Free (Jesus). When they found him, they begged him to leave their land.

9

WHO CAN FORGIVE BROKEN WAYS?

¹So Creator Sets Free (Jesus) *and his close followers* climbed back into the canoe and crossed over to the other side of the lake and went to the village where he was staying.

²Some people there came carrying a crippled man lying on a sleeping mat and brought him to Creator Sets Free

(Jesus). When he saw their faith in him, he said to the crippled man, "Be brave, my son, you are released from your broken ways."

3When they heard this, some of the scroll keepers began to grumble among themselves. "This man is speaking against the Great Spirit and his ways!"

4In his spirit, Creator Sets Free (Jesus) knew what they were thinking.

"Why are your hearts so full of dark thoughts?" he said to them. 5"Is it easier to tell a crippled man, 'Get up and walk,' or to say to him, 'You are released from your broken ways'?"

The crowd grew quiet as all eyes turned to Creator Sets Free (Jesus), waiting to see what he would do.

6"This is how you will know that the True Human Being has the right to forgive bad hearts and broken ways on this earth." He turned to the crippled man and said, "Get up, roll up your sleeping bundle and walk home."

7So the man stood up and began to walk home. 8Then great respect and awe filled the hearts of all who were there. They gave honor to the Great Spirit for giving such authority to human beings.

A TRIBAL TAX COLLECTOR FOLLOWS HIM

9Creator Sets Free (Jesus) left there, and as he walked on, he saw a tribal tax collector named Gift from Creator (Matthew) sitting at his tax booth.

Tribal tax collectors were often Tribal Members who were given the right to collect taxes for the People of Iron (Romans). They could force their own people, under the threat of violence, to pay them. To make a living, they would take more than the People of Iron (Romans) required. But

many of them became greedy and took even more than they were permitted. They were hated and looked down on by the people.

Creator Sets Free (Jesus), *to the surprise of all, walked up to the tribal tax collector and* said to him, "Gift from Creator (Matthew), come and walk the road with me."

So he got up from his tax booth, left it all behind, and began to walk the road with Creator Sets Free (Jesus). 10In the house of Gift from Creator (Matthew), Creator Sets Free (Jesus) and his followers were sitting down at the table eating with the guests. Among the guests were many tax collectors and outcasts.

The Separated Ones (Pharisees) called certain people outcasts. They used their strict interpretation of tribal law as a way to point them out. These outcasts were not permitted to enter the gathering houses. They were looked down on and despised by the Separated Ones (Pharisees). Outcasts included tribal tax collectors, prostitutes, people who ate and drank too much, the ones with diseases that made them ceremonially unclean, and anyone who was not a member of the tribes of Wrestles with Creator (Israel).

11When the Separated Ones (Pharisees) saw Creator Sets Free (Jesus) eating with outcasts, they complained to his followers, saying, "Why does your wisdomkeeper eat with tribal tax collectors and outcasts?"

12Creator Sets Free (Jesus) overheard them and said, "People who are well do not need medicine. It is for the ones who are sick. 13Go and learn this wise saying, 'What I want is kindness and mercy, not animal sacrifices.'[a] I have not come for the ones with good hearts. I have come to help the outcasts find the path back home again."

NEW WINESKINS FOR NEW WINE

[14]Some of the followers of Gift of Goodwill (John) came to Creator Sets Free (Jesus) and asked him, "Why do your followers feast instead of going without food and praying often, like we and the Separated Ones (Pharisees) do?"

[15]"Do you expect wedding guests to be sad and go without eating when the groom is hosting a feast?" he asked. "The time will come when he is gone. Then they will be sad and go without eating.

[16]"No one uses a new piece of cloth to patch an old garment. It would shrink and make the tear worse. [17]No one puts new wine into an old wineskin, for the new wine would burst the old skins. Then the wine would be lost and the skins ruined. New wineskins are what is needed. Then both wine and skins are preserved."

He said this to show that the old ways of the spiritual leaders did not reflect the beauty of the new way he was bringing.

COME AND HEAL MY DAUGHTER!

[18]As Creator Sets Free (Jesus) was speaking, a tribal leader came and humbled himself before him.

"My little girl has just crossed over to death! But I know that if you will come and lay your hands on her, she will live again."

[19]So Creator Sets Free (Jesus) and his followers went with him. [20]There was a woman following with the crowd who had been bleeding in an unusual way for more than twelve winters.

This would have made her ceremonially unclean and untouchable according to tribal law.

She came up close behind Creator Sets Free (Jesus), reached out her hand, and touched the fringe of his outer garment. [21]For she had said to herself, "If I can only touch his clothes, I know I will be healed."

[22]Creator Sets Free (Jesus) turned around and looked at her *with kindness in his eyes* and said, "Take courage, daughter, your faith has made you well."

Right then the blood stopped flowing, and she was healed!

POWER OVER DEATH

[23]When they arrived at the tribal leader's home, Creator Sets Free (Jesus) saw the noisy crowd of mourners and flute players.

[24]"Go from here!" he said. "This little girl is not dead. She only sleeps."

But they scorned and laughed at him, *for they knew she was dead.*

[25]After they had gone, Creator Sets Free (Jesus) went inside the house and took the little girl by the hand, and she stood up. [26]The story of this began to spread far and wide.

TWO BLIND MEN

[27]As Creator Sets Free (Jesus) left from there, two blind men followed after him. They were calling out to him, "Be kind to us, descendant of Much Loved One (David)."

[28]The blind men, *with the help of others*, followed him into a house. Creator Sets Free (Jesus) asked them, "Do you believe I can make your eyes see?"

"Yes, Wisdomkeeper," was their answer.

29He reached out, touched their eyes, and said to them, "Your trust in me will make it so."

They staggered back and rubbed their eyes.

30He had healed them! They could see! Creator Sets Free (Jesus) gave them a stern warning and said, "Tell no one about this."

31But *in their excitement, they did not listen, and* they told the news far and wide about what Creator Sets Free (Jesus) had done for them.

POWERFUL MEDICINE

32As they went from there, someone brought a man to Creator Sets Free (Jesus) who could not speak because of an evil spirit. **33**When the spirit was forced out of him, the man began to speak. All the people were amazed and said, "In all the history of the tribes of Wrestles with Creator (Israel) no one has ever seen this kind of powerful medicine."

34But the *spiritual leaders from the* Separated Ones (Pharisees) said, "It is the ruler of evil spirits who gives him the power to force out spirits."

CHIEF OF THE HARVEST

35Creator Sets Free (Jesus) continued to walk about and visit the villages. He taught in their gathering houses, helped people to understand about Creator's good road, and healed people from every kind of sickness and disease.

36When he saw the great number of people needing help, he was moved in his spirit with great compassion for them. He knew they were pushed down with no one to help and scattered about like sheep without a shepherd to watch over them.

37So he said to the ones who walked the road with him, "There is a great harvest in front of us, but only a few to gather it in. **38**Pray to the Great Spirit Chief of the harvest, so he will send out more helpers into the fields."

10

TWELVE MESSAGE BEARERS

1Creator Sets Free (Jesus) then gathered his twelve message bearers together *to prepare them for this great harvest.* He gave them authority over evil and unclean spirits, to force them out of people, and to heal all kinds of sickness and disease.

There were originally twelve tribes of Wrestles with Creator (Israel). This may be why he chose twelve message bearers.

2Here are the names of the twelve that he chose to be his special message bearers:

First there was One Who Hears (Simon), who was also called Stands on the Rock (Peter), and his brother Stands with Courage (Andrew). Then he chose He Takes Over (James) and his brother He Shows Goodwill (John), who are the sons of Gift of Creator (Zebedee).

3He also chose Friend of Horses (Philip) and Son of Ground Digger (Bartholomew) and Looks Like His Brother (Thomas) along with Gift from Creator (Matthew), the tribal tax collector.

Then he chose He Takes Charge (James), the son of First to Change (Alphaeus), along with Strong of Heart (Thaddaeus) and **4**One Who Listens (Simon) the Firebrand (Zealot). And last of all, Speaks Well Of (Judas), *also known as* Village Man (Iscariot), who later betrayed him.

INSTRUCTING HIS MESSAGE BEARERS

5Before Creator Sets Free (Jesus) sent out his twelve message bearers *to represent him,* he gave them these instructions:

"It is not the time to go to the Outside Nations or to the villages of the people of High Place (Samaria). **6**Instead, go to *your own people*—the lost sheep of the tribes of Wrestles with Creator (Israel).

7"This is what I want you to say to them: 'Creator's good road from above is close. Reach out and take hold of it!' **8**Heal all who are sick, cleanse the ones with skin diseases, raise the dead, and force evil spirits out of people. Give away the things I have given to you and ask no price for your service.

9"Take no trading goods with you or coins for your money pouches. **10**Take no traveling bundle, moccasins, or extra clothes to wear, not even a walking stick, because the ones who work hard in the harvest fields deserve to be fed and cared for.

11"Whenever you enter a camp or village, find an honorable person who will give you lodging. **12**When you come to their dwelling, greet the family with respect. **13**If they are people of honor, your greeting of peace will rest on them. **14**But if no one in that village welcomes you or listens to your message, then go from there and shake the dust from your moccasins. **15**The truth is, on the day when the fate of that village is decided, it will be worse for them than it was for Village of Bad Spirits (Sodom) and Village of Deep Fear (Gomorrah).

SHEEP AMONG WOLVES

16"Look and listen! I am sending you out like sheep into a pack of wolves, so be as crafty as snakes but as harmless and gentle as doves. **17**Look out for men with bad hearts, for they will bring you before their councils and whip you with leather straps in their gathering houses. **18**You will also be dragged before government rulers and leaders—all because you are representing me—and in this way through you both the tribes of Wrestles with Creator (Israel) and the People of Iron (Romans)[a] will hear my message.

19"When this happens, do not be afraid or worry about what you will say or how you will say it. **20**When that time comes, you will be given the words to say. For it is not you who will speak, but the Spirit of your Father will speak through you.

BETRAYAL AND HATRED

21"Brother will betray brother and parents will betray their children, even putting them to death. Children will turn against their parents and have them killed. **22**The time will come when all will hate you because you represent me and carry my name. But remember, it is the ones who never give up and make it to the end of the road who will be rescued and made whole.

23"If they hunt you down in one village, leave there and go to the next one. I speak from my heart, the True Human Being will come before you finish going through all the villages in the land of the tribes of Wrestles with Creator (Israel).

24"Followers are not greater than the one they follow. You who are my followers will be treated in the same bad ways they treat me. **25**So consider it an honor that you will be treated the same as your Wisdomkeeper. If they have called the chief of the council house

---

[a]**10:18** Lit. *Gentiles*

Worthless Ruler (Beelzebul),[a] how much worse will they speak of the members of his council?

26"Do not fear their threats. For their evil ways will be found out. Even what they say and do in secret will be made clear for all to see.

27"The things I have told you in secret at night, make them known when the sun rises! What I have whispered in your ears, stand on the rooftops and shout out loud for all to hear!

DO NOT FEAR YOUR OPPONENTS

28"Have no fear of your opponents, for they can only kill the body, but not your inner being. Instead, fear the one who can bring an end to your entire being[b] in the Valley of Smoldering Fire.

29"Two small winged ones could be traded for two poorly beaded earrings, but not one can fall to the ground unless your Father, the Creator, knows it. **30-31**Are you not worth more to him than many small winged ones? He knows the number of hairs on your head, so do not fear the ones who stand against you.

32"All who represent me before others I will represent before my Father from above. **33**But the ones who disown me will be disowned before my Father above.

FAMILY CONFLICT

34"Do you look for me to bring peace to this troubled land? **35**The message I bring will pierce like the blade of a long knife. It will turn a son against his father, a daughter against her mother, and a daughter-in-law against her mother-in-law. **36**In their own homes they will fight like enemies—all because of me.

---

[a]**10:25** Another name for Satan
[b]**10:28** Lit. *both body and soul*

37"The ones who choose their father or mother, son or daughter, over me dishonor me. **38**The ones who fail to pick up their cross and walk the road with me do not know my worth. **39**The ones who care only for their own life will fail to find life, but the ones who will lay down their life for me will find true life.

40"The ones who welcome you welcome me, and the ones who welcome me welcome the one who sent me. **41**If you welcome a prophet for who he is, you will receive the honor he brings. If you welcome a goodhearted person, you will receive the good that he brings. **42**I speak from my heart, even a drink of water given to a small one who follows me will bring great honor to the one who has given it."

11 ❈▷◁❈▷◁❈▷◁❈▷◁❈▷◁❈

1After instructing his twelve followers, Creator Sets Free (Jesus) left there to teach and announce his message in the surrounding villages.

ARE YOU THE ONE?

2From prison Gift of Goodwill (John) heard about the things the Chosen One was doing. So he sent two of his followers to ask Creator Sets Free (Jesus), **3**"Are you the one we are waiting for, or should we look for someone else?"

4Creator Sets Free (Jesus) told them, "Go back to Gift of Goodwill (John) and tell him about the things you have seen with your own eyes and heard with your own ears. **5**The blind can see again, the lame can walk, the ones with skin disease have been cleansed! Ears that cannot hear have been opened, the dead have come back to life again, and the poor are being told the good story! **6**Creator's blessing and goodwill rest on the one who does not stumble and leave the path because of me."

HONORING GIFT OF GOODWILL

7When the messengers left, Creator Sets Free (Jesus) spoke to the people about Gift of Goodwill (John):

"What were you looking for in the desert wilderness? A frail reed blowing in the wind? 8Did you see a man in soft clothes? Behold, the ones who wear soft clothes live soft lives. 9Were you looking for a true prophet? Yes! He is a true prophet but also much more! 10He is the one spoken of in the Sacred Teachings, 'Look! I am sending my messenger ahead of you. He will clear the path before you.'a

11"I speak from my heart, Gift of Goodwill (John) who performed the purification ceremonyb is a true human being. No one born of a woman has ever been greater, but now the smallest one who walks Creator's good road from above is greater than he.

12"From the time of Gift of Goodwill (John) until now, Creator's good road from above has been under attack, and the violent ones are trying to force their way upon it. 13The Law and the Prophets spoke until he came. 14If you can accept it, he is Great Spirit Is Creator (Elijah), the one the prophets said would come.c 15If you have ears to hear, you will understand.

16"This generation, what can I compare them to? They are like children at a trading post, teasing each other, saying, 17'You did not dance when we played the drum! You did not cry when we played a sad flute song.'

18"Gift of Goodwill (John) did not feast or drink wine, but they say, 'He has an evil spirit.' 19The True Human Being comes feasting and drinking and they say, 'He eats too much and is a drunk, a friend of tribal tax collectors and outcasts!' But wisdom is like a mother who knows what her children are doing and can see right through them."

VILLAGE WARNINGS

20Then Creator Sets Free (Jesus) began to warn about what would happen to the villages that saw his greatest signs and wonders but did not receive his message.

21"Sorrow and trouble will come to you, Village of Secrets (Chorazin), and the same for you, House of Fishing (Bethsaida). If the ancient villages of Rock Land (Tyre) and Hunting Grounds (Sidon) had seen the powerful signs you have seen, they would have humbled themselves long ago and with great sorrow turned their hearts back to Creator's ways. 22So then, it will be worse for you in the day when you face your end.

23"As for you, Village of Comfort (Capernaum), do you think you will be lifted up to the spirit-world above? No! You will be brought down low, to the Dark Underworld of Death (Hades). If Village of Bad Spirits (Sodom) had seen the powerful signs you have seen, that village would have remained to this day. 24But the day of their end will be better than yours."

FATHER AND SON

Creator Sets Free (Jesus) turned his eyes to the sky and sent his voice to the Great Spirit.

25"I honor you, O Great Father, Maker of earth and sky," he prayed, "for you have hidden these things from the ones who

---

a**11:10** Malachi 3:1
b**11:11** Baptism
c**11:14** Malachi 4:5

are wise in their own eyes but have shown them to the humble of heart. [26]Yes, my Father, it has made your heart glad to see this day come."

Then he turned to the ones who walked the road with him.

[27]"My Father has put everything into my hands," he said with a solemn voice. "Only the Father knows the Son and only the Son knows the Father. No one can know the Father in his fullness unless the Son makes him known."

Then he lifted his eyes to the horizon as if he were speaking to all the world.

[28]"Come close to my side, you whose hearts are on the ground, you who are pushed down and worn out, and I will refresh you. [29]Follow my teachings and learn from me, for I am gentle and humble of heart, and you will find rest from your troubled thoughts. [30]Walk side by side with me and I will share in your heavy load and make it light."

12

CHIEF OF THE DAY OF RESTING

[1]During that time on a Day of Resting, Creator Sets Free (Jesus) and his followers were walking through a field of grain. The men were hungry, so they plucked some grain, rubbed the husks off in their hands, and began to eat.

[2]When the Separated Ones (Pharisees) saw what they were doing, they said to him, "Why do your followers do what is not permitted on the Day of Resting?"

[3]He answered them, "Have you not heard about the time long ago when the great chief Much Loved One (David) was hungry? [4]How he and his followers went into the sacred lodge and ate the ceremonial bread? Tribal law says that only the holy men are permitted to eat this bread.

[5]"Have you not read in tribal law that the holy men who perform the ceremonies in the sacred lodge are permitted to ignore the sacredness of the Day of Resting—without blame?

[6]"Listen to me! The one standing before you is greater than the sacred lodge! [7]If you understood this saying, 'I want kindness and compassion, not ceremonial sacrifices,'[a] you would not have blamed the innocent ones. [8]For the True Human Being is Chief over the Day of Resting!"

HEALING ON THE DAY OF RESTING

[9]Creator Sets Free (Jesus) left there and went to their gathering house. [10]There he saw a man with a shriveled and useless hand.

The Separated Ones (Pharisees) had been keeping a close eye on him. Then they saw him looking at the man with the useless hand.

Trying to find a reason to accuse him, they asked, "Is it permitted to heal on the Day of Resting?"

Creator Sets Free (Jesus) knew what they were scheming.

[11]"Is there anyone here who would not help his sheep out of a ditch it fell into, even on the Day of Resting?" he challenged them. [12]"A human being has more value than a sheep! That is why it is permitted to do good on the Day of Resting!"

[13]Then he turned to the man and said, "Stretch out your hand."

---

[a]**12:7** Hosea 6:6

He stretched it out, and it was the same as his good hand!

14The Separated Ones (Pharisees) stormed out of there and began to scheme together about how to have Creator Sets Free (Jesus) killed. **15**But he knew what they were doing, so he left that place. A large number of people went with him, and he healed all who were sick, **16**but he warned them not to tell others who or where he was.

AN ANCIENT PROPHECY FULFILLED

17Another ancient prophecy of Creator Will Help Us (Isaiah) had now found its full meaning:

18"Here is the one I have chosen, who does all I ask and makes my heart glad. I have made my stand with him and love him as a father loves a son. My Sacred Spirit will rest on him and give him a message that will right the wrongs done to all people. **19**He will not make loud arguments on the village pathways but will speak with humble dignity. **20**He will not break a bruised reed. He will not snuff out a smoldering fire. He will never give up until all wrongs have been made right again! **21**All nations will hear of his reputation and put their trust and hope in him."ᵃ

THE SEPARATED ONES ACCUSE HIM

22They brought a man to Creator Sets Free (Jesus) who, tormented by an evil spirit, could not see or speak. He healed the man, who could then see and speak again. **23**The large crowd was amazed and said, "Could this be the promised descendant of chief Much Loved One (David)?"

24When the Separated Ones (Pharisees) heard what the people were saying, they said, "No! His power over evil spirits comes from the Worthless Ruler (Beelzebul), the one who rules over all evil spirits."

25Creator Sets Free (Jesus) knew what they were thinking and said to them, "A nation warring against itself comes to a bad end. Villages or clans warring against each other will not survive. **26**If Accuser (Satan) is warring against himself, how will he continue to rule?

27"If it is by his power that I force out evil spirits, by what power do your children do these things? So then, they are the ones who will decide against you. **28**But if I force out evil spirits by Creator's Spirit, then the good road of the Great Spirit has come close to you.

DEFEATING THE STRONGMAN

29"Who can enter the strongman's house and take away his goods, unless he first defeats him? He will then tie him up and take what is in his house.

30"The one who is not fighting with me fights against me. The one who does not help me gather scatters and makes things worse."

In this spiritual war there is no unclaimed territory.

31"That is why I say to you, the wrongdoings and evil speaking that humankind has done will be forgiven them. **32**Anyone who speaks against the True Human Being will be forgiven. But speaking evil of the Holy Spirit will not be forgiven in this present world or in the one that is coming.

GOOD AND BAD FRUIT

33"You must grow a good tree to get good fruit. If you grow a bad tree, you get bad fruit. For a tree is known by its fruit."

ᵃ**12:21** Isaiah 42:1-4

Then with fire in his eyes Creator Sets Free (Jesus) turned to the Separated Ones (Pharisees) and spoke with a voice like thunder.

34"You nest of poisonous snakes! How can you who are evil speak any good things? What is in your hearts will come out of your mouths. 35Good people speak from the good medicine stored in their hearts. Evil people speak from the bad medicine stored in their hearts. 36But I tell you, when the day comes for the final decision, human beings will have to give an answer for every worthless word spoken. 37The words that come out from your hearts will decide for or against you when you stand before the Great Spirit."

AN UNUSUAL SIGN

38Then some of the scroll keepers and Separated Ones (Pharisees) spoke back to him.

"Wisdomkeeper," they demanded, "show us a powerful sign to prove who you are."

But Creator Sets Free (Jesus) turned their words back on them, for they had just seen him do a powerful sign.

39"Only a bad-hearted and unfaithful generation would keep demanding signs," he answered. "The only sign that you will be given is the sign of the prophet Wings of Dove (Jonah). 40Just as he was in the belly of a great fish for three days and nights, the True Human Being will be in the womb of the earth for three days and nights.

41"When the time comes for the final decision to be made about the people living today, the people of Village of Changed Minds (Nineveh) will stand in

agreement against them. What they did will show your guilt, because they changed their hearts and minds when they heard the message of Wings of Dove (Jonah). Look! One who is greater than he stands before you now.

42"The female chief of the South will also be there as a witness against the people of this generation. Her reputation will show your guilt, for she journeyed from a land far away to listen to the wisdom of the great chief Stands in Peace (Solomon). Look! One greater than Stands in Peace (Solomon) is standing right in front of you.

43"When an evil spirit goes out of a person, it wanders through dry and desolate lands, looking for a place to rest. When it finds none, 44it says, 'I will go back to the house I left.' It returns to find the house empty, swept clean, and put in order. 45The spirit then finds seven other spirits, more evil than itself, who all go in and live there, making the person worse than before. This is how it will be for the generation of people living today."

ALL MY RELATIVES

46While Creator Sets Free (Jesus) was speaking to the people, his mother and brothers were outside wanting to talk with him. 47Someone noticed and told him, "Your relatives are here, waiting outside to see you."

48"Who are my relatives?" he asked the person who told him.

49Then he *looked around the circle of people*, lifted his hands toward his followers, and said, "Here they are! 50The ones who walk in the ways of my Father from the spirit-world above are my relatives—my mother, brothers and sisters."

13

THE STORIES BEGIN

¹Later the same day Creator Sets Free (Jesus) left that place and found a quiet spot to sit by Lake of Chief Garden (Gennesaret). ²Once again, people began to gather around him. The number of people was so great that he sat down in a canoe *and pushed out a little ways from the shore.* The people gathered at the shoreline on the water's edge and sat down to listen to him.

> The Great Storyteller began to tell his stories, teaching people about Creator's good road.

STORY OF THE SEED PLANTER

³Here is one of the many stories he told them: "Listen!" he said. "A seed planter went to plant some seeds and began to scatter them about on the ground.

⁴"Some seeds fell on the village pathway, and the winged ones pecked at the seeds and ate them all.

⁵"Some of the seeds fell on the rocks where there was only a little dirt. The plants sprouted up quickly, ⁶but when the sun came out, they dried up because they had no roots.

⁷"Other seeds fell into the weeds, and thistles sprouted around the seeds and choked the life out of them.

⁸"But some seeds fell on good ground, grew strong, and gave a harvest. Some gave one hundred times what was planted, some sixty, and others thirty. ⁹The ones who have ears, let them hear and understand!"

WHY TEACH WITH STORIES?

¹⁰The ones who walked the road with him came to him and asked, "Wisdom-keeper, tell us why you use stories to teach the people."

¹¹He answered them, "To you the honor has been given to understand about the mysterious ways of Creator's good road from above. This honor is not given to those who are not ready for it. ¹²The ones who understand will gain wisdom and be ready for more—much more. But the ones who do not understand or walk in the ways of wisdom will lose even the little they have.

¹³"This is the reason I tell the stories, 'for they have eyes that do not see, ears that do not hear,'[a] and hearts that do not understand.

¹⁴"These are the ones who give full meaning to the words of the prophet Creator Will Help Us (Isaiah) when he said, 'They will hear but not understand the meaning. They will see without knowing what it is they see. ¹⁵Their hearts of stone have made their ears dull and their eyes dim. If only they would see with their eyes and hear with their ears, they could open their hearts to the Maker of Life and he would heal them.'[b]

¹⁶"But Creator's blessing rests on you, for you have eyes to see and ears to hear. ¹⁷I speak from my heart, there were many prophets and goodhearted people who longed to see what you see and hear what you hear but never did.

THE MEANING OF THE STORY

¹⁸"So then," he said to his followers, "listen with your hearts and I will tell you the meaning of the story of the seed planter.

¹⁹"The seed in this story is the message from the Great Spirit about his good road.

---

[a]**13:13** Jeremiah 5:21
[b]**13:15** Isaiah 6:9-10

"The seed planted on the village pathway represents the ones who hear but do not understand the message. The evil trickster sneaks up and snatches it from their hearts.

20"The rocky ground represents the ones who hear and receive the message with a glad heart, 21but because they have no roots, their faith is shallow and does not last. As soon as the message brings them trouble or opposition, they stumble and fall away.

22"The seed planted among the weeds and thistles represents the ones who have heard the message, but they are too busy worrying about their earthly existence. The desire for more and more possessions leads them down a false path, and they never grow into mature human beings.

23"The good ground represents the ones who, when they hear the message, understand it and let it grow in their hearts to produce a harvest, some one hundred times as much, some sixty, and some thirty."

WEEDS IN THE GARDEN

24Creator Sets Free (Jesus) told the people another story. He said, "Creator's good road from above is like a man who scattered good seed in his garden. 25But during the night, while his family slept, an enemy sneaked in and scattered bad seeds in with the good ones. 26When the plants began to grow, the weeds also grew with them.

27"When the family's garden workers saw the weeds, they said to the man, 'Honored One, did you not plant good seeds in your garden? Where did these weeds come from?'

28"The man answered, 'An enemy has done this.'

"'Should we go and dig out the weeds?' the workers asked.

29"'No,' the man said, 'they are too hard to tell apart now. You might dig out the good plants with the bad. 30Wait and let them grow together until it is time for the harvest. At that time I will tell the workers: first go and gather the weeds into bundles for burning, then gather the grain into my storehouse.'"

MORE STORIES

31Creator Sets Free (Jesus) then told them more stories about the good road: "The good road from above is also like a man who plants a single grain of mustard seed, 32one of the smallest of seeds. But when planted in a garden, it grows larger than all the other plants and takes over the garden.[a] It becomes a great tree with many branches, large enough for the winged ones who soar in the sky to find lodging in its shade.

33"Again, think of the good road from above to be like the yeast a grandmother uses when she makes frybread dough. She mixes a little yeast into three big batches of flour. Then the yeast spreads throughout the dough, causing it to rise."

34Creator Sets Free (Jesus) would use only stories like these when he spoke to the crowds. He taught nothing to the crowds without using a story. 35This brought full meaning to the ancient prophecy, "I will tell many stories, stories of the ancient ways, things hidden since the beginning of the world."[b]

MEANING OF THE GOOD AND BAD SEEDS

36When he was finished, Creator Sets Free (Jesus) left the crowds and went into the house where they were staying. The

---

[a]**13:32** The mustard plant was used as an herbal medicine.
[b]**13:35** Psalm 78:2

ones who walked the road with him went in with him and asked, "Tell us the meaning of the story about the good and bad seeds in the garden."

37"The True Human Being is the one who plants the good seeds," he answered. 38"The garden is *all the nations of* the world. The good seeds are the children of the good road. The weeds are the children of the worthless ways of the world, 39and the enemy who plants the bad seeds is the evil one. The harvest is at the end of the age, and the helpers are spirit-messengers.

40"Then, when this age ends, the weeds will be gathered together and burned in the fire. 41The True Human Being will send his messengers to remove the stumbling stones from the good road, along with all who hold onto their bad-hearted ways. 42They will be gathered into bundles and used to feed the fire of a great oven. There they will weep many tears and grind their teeth together in anger and frustration. 43Then the ones who are in good standing will shine like the sun in the Land of the Father's good road. The ones with ears should hear and understand."

MORE GOOD ROAD STORIES

44"The good road from above is like a hidden treasure a man finds buried in a field. He buries it back into the ground and is then happy to go and trade everything he has for that field.

45"The good road from above is also like a trader in goods who is looking for the finest of beads.ᵃ 46When he finds one of great beauty and worth, he trades all his goods so he can have it.

47"Here is another way to see the good road from above: A large fishing net is let down into the great waters. Many different kinds of fish are caught in it. 48When it is filled up, the fishermen pull it to shore. Then they sit down and separate the good fish into baskets and throw away the bad fish.

49"It will be the same when this age comes to an end. The spirit-messengers from Creator will be sent to separate the ones who are in good standing from the ones who have bad hearts. 50The bad-hearted ones will then be thrown into a pit of fire, where they will weep with many tears and grind their teeth together in anger and frustration."

51Then Creator Sets Free (Jesus) asked his followers, "Now do you understand the things I am saying to you?"

"*Wisdomkeeper*," they said, "we do understand."

52He *smiled and* said to them, "Every scroll keeper who has learned to walk in the ways of Creator's good road is like the head of a family, an elder who opens the medicine pouch of his heart, sharing wisdom that is both new and old, *bringing new understanding to the old ways*."

HIS OWN VILLAGE REJECTS HIM

53When Creator Sets Free (Jesus) was through telling his stories, he traveled to his boyhood home *of Seed Planter Village (Nazareth)*. 54There he entered the local gathering house and began to teach the people, and they were amazed at his words.

"Where did this man get his wisdom from?" they asked. "Who gave him this powerful medicine? 55Is this not the son of the wood carver? Is his mother not Bitter Tears (Mary)? And his brothers He Leads the Way (James) and He Gives More (Joseph) and He Hears (Simon) and Speaks Well Of (Judas) 56and

ᵃ**13:45** Lit. *pearls*

all his sisters—are they not here living among us?"

57And so the people stumbled from the path because of him.

Creator Sets Free (Jesus) *with a sad heart* said to them, "A prophet is given honor everywhere except in his own village, among his own clan, and in his own house."

58So he did not do many works of power there because they failed to put their trust in him.

LOOKS BRAVE AND CREATOR SETS FREE

1Looks Brave (Herod), who ruled the territory of Circle of Nations (Galilee), began to hear reports about Creator Sets Free (Jesus).

2He said to his servants, "This man must be Gift of Goodwill (John) who performed the purification ceremony.ᵃ He has returned from the world of the dead. That is why he can do these powerful things."

THE DEATH OF GIFT OF GOODWILL

3-4 Looks Brave (Herod) had arrested Gift of Goodwill (John) and put him in chains because he had been speaking against him for breaking tribal law by living with Daring Woman (Herodias), the wife of Friend of Horses (Philip), who is the brother of Looks Brave (Herod).

5Looks Brave (Herod) would have put Gift of Goodwill (John) to death right then, but he was afraid of what the people would do, for they honored him as a prophet.

6When the birthday of Looks Brave (Herod) came, the daughter of Daring

---

ᵃ**14:2** Baptism

Woman (Herodias) danced before all the guests. Looks Brave (Herod) was so pleased **7**he made a solemn promise to give her whatever she wanted. **8**Her mother jumped at the chance and told her daughter what to ask for.

The daughter said to Looks Brave (Herod), "Give me, here and now, the head of Gift of Goodwill (John) in a basket!"

9The heart of Looks Brave (Herod) fell to the ground. But he had made a solemn promise before all of his guests. **10**So he sent a soldier to the prison, had him cut off the head of Gift of Goodwill (John), **11**put it in a basket, and bring it to the girl, who then gave it to her mother.

12The followers of Gift of Goodwill (John) took his body and gave him a proper burial. Then they went and told Creator Sets Free (Jesus).

CREATOR SETS FREE RETREATS

13When Creator Sets Free (Jesus) heard how Gift of Goodwill (John) had been put to death, he found a canoe and went off to a deserted place to be alone for a while. But the crowds of people, when they heard about it, went after Creator Sets Free (Jesus) from their villages. **14**And when he came to shore, they were waiting for him. He felt deeply for them, so he healed the ones who were sick.

HE FEEDS FIVE THOUSAND

15When the evening came, his followers said to him, "This is a deserted place, and the day is almost over. Let us send the people away to the villages in the countryside so they can find food to eat."

Creator Sets Free (Jesus) looked around at the great crowd of people, for there were over five thousand who had gathered there.

16"There is no need to send them away," he said to his followers. "You feed them."

His followers could not believe their ears!

[17]With one voice they said to him, "All we have is five pieces of frybread and two fish!"

[18]"Bring them to me," he told them. [19]Then he had all the people sit down on the grass. He took the five pieces of frybread and two fish *and held them to the sky.* He looked up, gave thanks to the Great Spirit, and began to break the frybread into smaller pieces, which he gave to his followers to give to the people. [20]Everyone ate until they were full! When they were done, they gathered the leftovers—twelve baskets full! [21]Not counting the women and children, there were about five thousand men who had eaten.

WATER WALKER

[22]Right away Creator Sets Free (Jesus) had his followers get into the canoe and go ahead of him to the other side of the great lake, while he sent the people back to their homes.

[23]After that he went up into the mountainside to be alone while he sent his voice to the Great Spirit. He stayed there and prayed as the sun set and the stars came out.

[24]His followers were still in the canoe, far from land. The wind blew strong against them, and the waves pounded the canoe and began to toss it about.

[25]Late into the night, just before the morning light, Creator Sets Free (Jesus) came near them, walking on the water! [26]When his followers saw him, they cried out in terror, "It is a ghost-spirit!"

[27]But he heard their cries and called out to them, "Do not fear, take heart. It is I."

[28]"Wisdomkeeper, is it you?" Stands on the Rock (Peter) shouted back to him. "If so, tell me now to come to you on the water."

[29]"Come!" he said to him *without any hesitation.*

With reckless abandon, Stands on the Rock (Peter) climbed over the side of the canoe and began to walk on the water toward him.

The wind howled and the waves splashed against him as he made his way toward Creator Sets Free (Jesus).

[30]But when he felt how strong the wind was, fear took hold of him. He began to sink and cried out, "Wisdomkeeper, save me!"

[31]Creator Sets Free (Jesus) quickly reached out and took hold of him. "Man of small faith," he said, "what made you hold back and doubt me?"

[32]The wind stopped blowing and the waves grew still as they climbed into the canoe. [33]All twelve of his message bearers gave honor to him, saying, "Truly, you are the Son of the Great Spirit."

ALL WHO TOUCH HIM ARE HEALED

[34]They came to shore at Lake of Chief Garden (Gennesaret). [35]When the people there recognized him, they sent messengers to all the surrounding villages, and the people brought to him all who were sick. [36]They begged him to let them touch the fringe on his outer garment—and all who touched it were healed.

15 ❧▸◂❧▸◂❧▸◂❧▸◂❧▸

CONFLICT OVER TRADITIONS

The teachings of Creator Sets Free (Jesus) were becoming a great concern to the spiritual leaders in Village of Peace (Jerusalem). So messengers were sent to spy on him to try to find ways to accuse him and make him look bad in the eyes of the people.

¹Some of the Separated Ones (Pharisees) and scroll keepers came to Creator Sets Free (Jesus) from Village of Peace (Jerusalem). ²"Why do your followers not keep the traditions given by the elders and wash their hands before they eat?" they accused him.

³Creator Sets Free (Jesus) asked them, "How is it that you use your traditions to ignore the instructions given by the Great Spirit? ⁴For he said, 'Give honor to your father and your mother,'[a] and, 'The ones who speak evil against them must die.'[b] ⁵But your tradition says, 'If you give to the Great Spirit the gifts that were meant for your father and mother, ⁶you no longer have to honor them.' This is only one of the many ways you use your traditions to do away with the instructions given by the Great Spirit."

> *He paused and let them think about what he had said. Then with fire in his eyes he raised his voice and spoke sharply to them.*

⁷"Your false faces do not fool me!" he said *loud enough for all to hear.* "The prophet Creator Will Help Us (Isaiah) was talking about you when he said, ⁸'These people honor me with their lips but their *hard, cold* hearts are far away from me. ⁹Their prayers are empty words and their ceremonies are for show. The things they tell others to do are only rules made up by weak human beings.'"[c]

¹⁰Creator Sets Free (Jesus) then gathered the people around him and said, "Listen with your hearts and understand what I tell you. ¹¹There is nothing you can take into your mouth that will make you impure. It is what comes out of your mouth that makes you impure."

¹²Then his followers came to him and said, "Do you know that what you said insulted the Separated Ones (Pharisees)?"

¹³"Every plant that has not been planted by my Father from above will be pulled out by the roots," he answered. ¹⁴Then he warned them, "The Separated Ones (Pharisees) are blind guides. The ones who follow them are also blind, and they will both fall into a ditch. You will do well to stay away from them."

¹⁵Then Stands on the Rock (Peter) said to him, "Tell us the meaning of the wise saying *about what is pure and impure.*"

¹⁶"Do you still not understand," he answered, ¹⁷"that when food enters the mouth it goes into the stomach, *not the heart,* and then out of the body? ¹⁸It is what comes out from the mouth, from deep inside, that makes people impure. ¹⁹It is from the heart that come things such as the taking of lives, unfaithful marriages, uncontrolled sexual desires, stealing, lying, and speaking against the Great Spirit. ²⁰It is things such as these that make you impure, not failing to wash your hands when you eat."

A LOWLAND WOMAN

²¹From there Creator Sets Free (Jesus) journeyed into the territory of Rock Land (Tyre) and Hunting Grounds (Sidon) *along the coast of the Great Middle Sea* (Mediterranean) *north of Circle of Nations* (Galilee).

²²A Lowlander (Canaanite) woman from that territory came to Creator Sets Free (Jesus).

"Honored One! Descendant of Much Loved One (David)," she cried out to him. "Have pity on me, for my daughter is tormented by an evil spirit."

²³Creator Sets Free (Jesus) gave no answer to the woman.

---

[a]**15:4** Exodus 20:12; Deuteronomy 5:16
[b]**15:4** Exodus 21:17; Leviticus 20:9
[c]**15:9** Isaiah 29:13

His followers came to him and begged him, "Send her away, for she is bothering us with her loud crying."

24He then said *to the woman,* "I was sent only to the lost sheep of the tribes of Wrestles with Creator (Israel)."

25She came close and humbled herself before him. "Honored One," she begged him, "help me."

26"The children's food should not be given to the dogs," he said to her.

27"That is true, Honored One," she answered, "but even the dogs can feed on the crumbs from the table of their Honored One."

28"*Dear* woman," he answered back, "your answer shows how great your faith is! What you have asked for will be yours." Her daughter was healed from that time forward.

THE GREAT HEALER

29Creator Sets Free (Jesus) journeyed from there past Lake of Circle of Nations (Sea of Galilee) to a mountainside, where he sat down *to rest.*

30Once again great crowds of people came, bringing to him the lame, the blind, the ones who could not walk or speak, and many more. They laid them down at the feet of Creator Sets Free (Jesus), and he healed them all. **31**When they saw the healings, the crowds were filled with wonder and amazement and gave honor and thanks to the Great Spirit of the tribes of Wrestles with Creator (Israel).

HE FEEDS FOUR THOUSAND

Creator Sets Free (Jesus) spent the next three days healing the sick and injured. People came from the Ten Villages (Decapolis) and surrounding area, where many people from *Outside Nations lived. The number of people had grown to over four thousand.*

32Creator Sets Free (Jesus) called his followers to his side and said to them, "I have pity in my heart for all these people, for they have been with us for three days with no food. *Some of them have come from a great distance, and* if I send them away hungry, they might lose their strength and faint."

33"This is a lonely and desolate place," they answered him. "Where could we find enough food to feed all these people?"

34"How much food do we have?" he asked.

"We have seven pieces of frybread and a few small fish," they answered.

35Creator Sets Free (Jesus) instructed all the people to sit down on the ground. **36**He then took the seven pieces of frybread and the two fish, gave thanks, and broke them into small pieces. He gave them to his followers, and they gave them out to the people.

37Everyone ate as much as they wanted, and when they were done eating, his followers gathered up the leftovers—seven baskets full! **38**They had fed four thousand men, besides women and children.

39After sending the crowds away to their homes, he climbed into the canoe *with his twelve followers* and went to the territory of Creator's High Lodge (Magdala).

16

SIGNS OF THE TIMES

1The Separated Ones (Pharisees) and Upright Ones (Sadducees) came again to Creator Sets Free (Jesus) to put him to the test *and find something to accuse him with.*

"Show us a powerful sign from the spirit-world above," they demanded, "*to prove to us who you are.*"

Creator Sets Free (Jesus) was growing weary of their ongoing attacks, but as always he was able to answer them with great wisdom.

2He looked to the west. "When the sun is setting you say, 'The sky is red. It will be a good day tomorrow.'" *He then turned to the east.* 3"At the sunrise you say, 'The sky is dark and red. There will be a storm today.'"

Then he turned to look into the faces of the spiritual leaders.

"You understand what the earth and sky are saying, but you are blind to the message of the season you live in. 4It is the bad-hearted and unfaithful people of today who look for signs, but the only sign they will be given is the sign of the prophet Wings of Dove (Jonah)."[a]

After saying this, he left them and went on his way.

CONFUSION ABOUT THE FRYBREAD

He and his followers took their canoe to cross again to the other side of the lake.

5When they came to shore, his followers realized that they had forgotten to bring frybread with them.

6Creator Sets Free (Jesus) said to them, "Be on the lookout for the yeast of the Separated Ones (Pharisees) and the Upright Ones (Sadducees)."

7His followers tried to understand why he said this. They said to each other, "Is it because we forgot to bring more frybread?"

8When Creator Sets Free (Jesus) heard them, he said, "Why are you talking like this? Why are you worried that you forgot to bring frybread? Is your faith so small? 9Do you have no understanding? Have you forgotten so soon how many baskets of broken pieces were left over when I fed the five thousand with five pieces of frybread? 10How about the seven basketsful left over when I fed the four thousand?"

11"How do you not understand that I was not talking about frybread? Beware of the yeast of the Separated Ones (Pharisees) and the Upright Ones (Sadducees)!"

12They finally understood he was talking about the teachings of the Separated Ones (Pharisees) and the Upright Ones (Sadducees), not about yeast in frybread.

YOU ARE THE CHOSEN ONE!

They journeyed on and came into the territory of Ruler of the Horsemen (Caesarea Philippi).

This territory was ruled by Chief Looks Brave (Herod) under the authority of the Ruler of the People of Iron (Caesar). There was a cave and a deep, bottomless pit there that was called by the local people "The Gate of the Dark Underworld of Death (Hades)." This was a place of bad medicine and lying spirits.

13When they came into this place, Creator Sets Free (Jesus) asked the ones who were walking the road with him, "Who do the people think the True Human Being is? What are they saying?"

His followers looked around at each other and then back to Creator Sets Free (Jesus).

---

a16:4 Jonah 1:17–2:10

[14]"Some say Gift of Goodwill (John) *who performed the purification ceremony,*"[a] they answered. "Others say Great Spirit Is Creator (Elijah), or even Lifted by Creator (Jeremiah), or one of the other prophets."

He then lowered his voice and spoke in a more serious tone.

[15]"So tell me," he asked them, "How do you see me? Who do you say that I am?"

Silent faces stared back at him. They began to look at each other, and some looked down to the ground. The moment of truth had come, but no one dared to speak. Then suddenly a voice pierced through the silence.

[16]"You are the Chosen One," One Who Hears, also called Stands on the Rock (Simon/Peter), answered, "the Son of the living Creator!"

[17]Creator Sets Free (Jesus) *smiled at him and* said, "One Who Hears (Simon), Son of Wings of Dove (Bar-Jonah), Creator's blessing rests on you, for flesh and blood did not help you see, but my Father from above opened your eyes. [18]*For this reason* I have given you the name Stands on the Rock (Peter),[b] and upon this great rock[c] I will make my sacred family stand strong. And the powers[d] of the Dark Underworld of Death (Hades) will not stand against them.

[19]"I am giving you the authority[e] of Creator's good road from above. The things you do not permit on earth will be what Creator has not permitted in the spirit-world above. The things that you permit on earth will be what Creator has permitted in the spirit-world above."

[20]He then instructed his followers not to tell anyone that he was the Chosen One.

ACCUSER TESTS HIM AGAIN

[21]Creator Sets Free (Jesus) then began to tell his followers that he must go to the Village of Peace (Jerusalem), where the elders, the head holy men, and the keepers of the scrolls would make him suffer many things and then kill him, and that on the third day he would return from the dead. [22]But Stands on the Rock (Peter) pulled him away from the others and spoke sharply to him, "Wisdomkeeper, do not even think this way! This must never happen to you!"

[23]"Get out of my way, Accuser (Satan), you evil trickster!" he said to Stands on the Rock (Peter). "You have become a stone to trip over and make me stumble on my path. Your thoughts are against the Great Spirit, for his ways are not the ways of human beings."

Creator Sets Free (Jesus) knew that his follower's thinking was being affected by Accuser (Satan).

WALKING THE ROAD OF THE CROSS

[24]"To walk the road with me," Creator Sets Free (Jesus) said to his followers, "you must turn away from your own path, and always be ready to carry your cross with me to the place of ultimate sacrifice. [25]The ones who hold on to their lives will not find life, but the ones who are willing to let go of their lives, for me and my message, will find *the true* life. [26]How will it help you to get everything you want but lose this life? Is there anything in this world worth trading for your life?

[27]"When the True Human Being comes, along with his spirit-messengers, after being honored by his Father, he will then give to everyone the honor

---

[a]**16:14** Baptism
[b]**16:18** Greek *petros*, meaning a small rock or stone
[c]**16:18** Greek *petra*, meaning a huge rock
[d]**16:18** Lit. *gates*
[e]**16:19** Lit. *keys*

they deserve for what they have done.
²⁸"I speak from my heart, there are some of you standing here today who, before you die, will see the True Human Being coming and bringing with him *the power of* his good road."

17

HE TALKS TO THE ANCESTORS

¹Six days later, Creator Sets Free (Jesus) took *only* Stands on the Rock (Peter), He Takes Over (James), and his brother He Shows Goodwill (John) up on a great high mountain. ²Right there before them his appearance began to change. His clothes turned bright white, and his face began to shine like the sun.

³Then before their eyes *two ancestors appeared—the lawgiver* Drawn from the Water (Moses) and *the ancient prophet* Great Spirit Is Creator (Elijah). They were talking with Creator Sets Free (Jesus).

They all stared in wide-eyed wonder, not knowing what to say. Then Stands on the Rock (Peter) found his voice.

⁴"Wisdomkeeper," he said out loud, "this is a good place to stay. If you want, I will put up three tipis—one for you, one for Drawn from the Water (Moses), and one for Great Spirit Is Creator (Elijah)."

⁵While he was still speaking, a bright cloud covered them. A voice spoke from the cloud, saying, "This is my much-loved Son, the one who makes my heart glad. Listen to him!"

⁶They all fell on their faces in fear, ⁷but Creator Sets Free (Jesus) laid his hands on them and said, "Do not fear! Stand to your feet."

⁸When they looked around, *the cloud was gone, the men were gone, and* all they could see was Creator Sets Free (Jesus) standing alone in front of them.

⁹As they walked down the mountainside, he instructed them to tell no one what they had seen until after the True Human Being had come back to life from the dead.

During the long walk down the mountain, the three followers had a lot to think about. Perhaps they were wondering about the ancient prophecies and how they related to what they had just seen.

¹⁰They asked him, "Why do the scroll keepers say that Great Spirit Is Creator (Elijah) must be first to come?"

¹¹"It is true," he answered, "Great Spirit Is Creator (Elijah) is the first to come to return all things to their original purpose, ¹²but I am telling you that he has already come, and no one recognized him. They did whatever they wanted with him, just as the Sacred Teachings foretold. It is also foretold that they will treat the True Human Being in the same way. They will look down on him and turn their faces away from him."

¹³Then his followers understood he was talking about Gift of Goodwill (John) who performed the purification ceremony.[a]

A GENERATION WITH NO FAITH

They continued down the mountain to re-join the other followers. When they arrived, there was a crowd of people there waiting for them.

¹⁴From the crowd of people a man came to Creator Sets Free (Jesus) and humbled himself before him. ¹⁵"Wisdomkeeper!" the man said *with desperation in his voice.* "Take pity on my

---

[a] **17:13** Baptism

son. An evil spirit has taken hold of him and makes him suffer greatly. He often falls into the fire or the water. ¹⁶I brought him to your followers, but they failed to heal him."

¹⁷"The people of this generation are bent and twisted with no faith! How much longer will I have to put up with you?" Creator Sets Free (Jesus) cried out. Then he said, "Bring the boy to me."

¹⁸He spoke sharply to the evil spirit, and it left the boy, and right then he was healed.

¹⁹Later, when Creator Sets Free (Jesus) was alone with his followers, they asked him, "Why could we not force the evil spirit out of him?"

²⁰"It is because of your weak faith," he answered and then said to them, "I speak from my heart, if you had faith like a mustard seed, you could tell this mountain to move from here to there and it would do what you say. Nothing would be too hard for you. ²¹But it takes praying and going without food to make you ready to force out a spirit of this kind."ᵃ

THE ROAD AHEAD

²²While they were in Circle of Nations (Galilee), Creator Sets Free (Jesus) gathered his followers together.

"The True Human Being will soon be taken and handed over to men ²³who will kill him," he told them, "but on the third day he will come back to life from the dead."

This filled his followers with sorrow and dread.

DUES FOR THE SACRED LODGE

From there he and his followers walked to Village of Comfort (Capernaum), where

---

ᵃ17:21 Verse 21 is not found in most ancient manuscripts.

Stands on the Rock (Peter) and his brother Stands with Courage (Andrew) lived.

²⁴When they came into Village of Comfort (Capernaum), some of the men who collected the money for the ceremonial lodge *that was in Village of Peace (Jerusalem)* came to Stands on the Rock (Peter).

"Does your wisdomkeeper pay his dues for the lodge?" they asked.

²⁵"Yes, he does," he answered them.

When he returned to his house, before he could say a word about what happened, Creator Sets Free (Jesus) said to him, *using his family name,* "Tell me, One Who Hears (Simon), do the rulers of the land collect taxes or dues from their own family members, or from others? How do you see it?"

²⁶"From others," Stands on the Rock (Peter) answered.

"So then," he said back to him, "the family members do not have to pay, ²⁷but, to keep from insulting them, *we will pay.* Go to the lake and open the mouth of the first fish you catch, and you will find a silver coin. Use that to pay the dues for both of us."

18 ⟨⟩⟨⟩⟨⟩⟨⟩⟨⟩

WHO IS TRULY GREAT?

¹The ones who walked the road with Creator Sets Free (Jesus) came to him. "Who is the greatest one on Creator's good road from above?" they asked.

²He had a small child come to him and stood the child in front of them.

³"I speak from my heart," he said to them, "unless you become like a little child, you will not find the pathway onto the good road. ⁴The ones who humble themselves, like this little child, will

become great ones in the Land of Creator's good road."

He then lifted up the child into his arms.

⁵"The ones representing me who welcome a little child like this one welcome me."

STUMBLING STONES

Then he spoke in a more serious manner.

⁶"But for the ones who put a stumbling stone in the path of one of these little ones who trust in me, it would be better for them to have a great stone tied to their necks and be drowned in the deep waters! ⁷This world of sorrow and pain will make many stumble, but how terrible it will be for the ones who go along with it!

⁸"So, if what your hand or foot does makes you stumble from the path, cut it off and throw it away! It is better to walk this life without a hand or foot than to be thrown into the fire that burns on and on. ⁹"If what your eye sees makes you stumble on the path, then gouge it out and throw it away! It is better for you to walk this life with only one eye than to be thrown into the Valley of Smoldering Fire.

¹⁰"So do not look down on even one of these little ones, for their spirit-messengers in the spirit-world above always look upon the face of my Father, the one who is above us all. ¹¹For the True Human Being has come to find the lost ones and set them free."ᵃ

THE WORTH OF THE LITTLE ONES

¹²"How do you see it?" he asked them. "If a man has one hundred sheep and one of them wanders away, will he not leave the ninety-nine on the mountainside to

---
ᵃ**18:11** Verse 11 does not appear in most ancient manuscripts.

go and find the lost one? ¹³If he finds that lost one, I speak from my heart, he will find more joy for that one than for the ninety-nine that were not lost. ¹⁴In the same way your Father from the spirit-world above does not want to lose even one of these little ones.

HANDLING CONFLICT

¹⁵"If a tribal family member wrongs you, go to him alone and tell him. If he listens, then you have won him back. ¹⁶If he cannot see the wrong, then go to him with one or two others who have seen the wrong, so he can hear them. ¹⁷If he still will not listen, take him before the sacred family council. If he will not hear the council, then he will be the same to you as an outsider or a tribal tax collector.

¹⁸"I speak from my heart, what has been decided in the spirit-world above is what you will decide on earth. ¹⁹⁻²⁰From my heart I will say it again this way: When two or three have gathered together on earth to represent me, I will be there *in spirit to guide you.* Then, *under my guidance,* whatever two or more of you agree upon and ask for will be done by my Father from above."

QUESTION ABOUT FORGIVENESS

²¹Stands on the Rock (Peter) came close to Creator Sets Free (Jesus). "Wisdomkeeper," he asked, "how many times must I forgive a brother or sister who does wrong to me? Is seven times enough?"

²²"Not just seven times," Creator Sets Free (Jesus) answered, "but seventy times seven."

STORY ABOUT FORGIVENESS

To help them see more clearly into the ways of forgiveness, he told them a story.

²³"So then, Creator's good road is like a ruler who wanted to collect the debt owed to him by his hired servants. ²⁴The first one brought to him owed ten thousand horses.[a] ²⁵The man could not repay him, so the ruler ordered that the man, his family, and all he owned be sold to pay for the debt.

²⁶"The servant fell to his knees before him and said, 'Ruler, give me time and I will repay all that I owe!'

²⁷"The ruler felt sorry for the servant, set him free, and released him from his debt.

²⁸"But that same servant went to one of his fellow servants who owed him only a small horse blanket.[b] He took hold of the man's throat and said, 'Pay me all that you owe!'

²⁹"The man humbled himself, bowed down, and pleaded, 'Please, give me more time and I will repay you!'

³⁰"But he would not even listen and threw the man into prison until he could pay all that he owed. ³¹When his fellow servants saw this, it made their hearts fall to the ground. They went to the ruler and told him the sad story.

³²"The ruler had the man brought to him and said, 'You worthless servant! *How could your heart be so cold?* I forgave you all your debt because you begged me to. ³³Why would you not do the same for your fellow servant?'

³⁴"The ruler was angry with him and put him in prison to be punished until his debt was paid in full."

Creator Sets Free (Jesus) looked deep into the eyes of the ones who walked the road with him.

³⁵"My Father from above is warning you that the same thing will happen to you unless, from your heart, you each forgive your fellow human beings."

19

¹After Creator Sets Free (Jesus) had finished speaking in the territory of Circle of Nations (Galilee), he left there and went to the territory of the Land of Promise (Judea) beyond the river Flowing Down (Jordan). ²Once again large crowds came to him there, and he healed them.

MARRIAGE AND DIVORCE

Like hungry wolves, the Separated Ones (Pharisees) began to come in packs and test him with questions about tribal law, hoping to trap him. They knew that among the spiritual leaders there was much disagreement about how to interpret the instructions about marriage and divorce.

³Some of the Separated Ones (Pharisees) came to him. "Does our tribal law permit a man to put away his wife for any and every reason?" they asked.

⁴"Have you not read in the Sacred Teachings," Creator Sets Free (Jesus) asked them, "that, in the beginning of creation, from one human being the Great Spirit made two—one male and one female? ⁵This is why a man will leave his father and mother and be joined to his wife. Together they become one flesh, ⁶no longer two, but one body joined together.[c] No human being should tear apart what Creator has put together."

Like sly coyotes they smiled at each other. They were sure that he could not answer their next question.

---

[a]**18:24** About sixteen years of wages
[b]**18:28** About a day's wages

[c]**19:6** Genesis 2:24

[7]"Why then," they asked him, "does Drawn from the Water (Moses), in the Law, instruct that a man give his wife divorce papers before sending her away?"

[8]"It is because of your cold hearts of stone that Drawn from the Water (Moses) permitted this," he answered, "but this was not the Great Spirit's original plan for men and women.

[9]"But here is how I will answer you," he told them. "Any man who sends his wife away and marries another is guilty of being unfaithful to her, unless she was the one who was not faithful."

[10]The ones who walked the road with him *shook their heads and* said, "If this is so, between husband and wife, then it must be better not to marry."

[11]"Not many can hold to this teaching," he answered them, "but only those to whom it has been gifted. *There are many reasons for not getting married.* [12]Some are born with no desire or ability for marriage. Some have lost their ability from what has been done to them. Others choose not to marry so they can put all their strength into walking the good road from above. The ones who have this gift are able to walk in this wisdom."

LITTLE CHILDREN AND THE GOOD ROAD

[13]The people were bringing their little children to Creator Sets Free (Jesus) so he would lay his hands on them and pray, but his followers spoke harsh words to the ones bringing them.

[14]"Let the little children come to me!" Creator Sets Free (Jesus) said to his followers. "Do not turn them away. Creator's good road from above belongs to the ones who are like these children."

[15]He then took the children into his arms, laid his hands on them, *blessed them*, and then went on his way.

POSSESSIONS OR THE GOOD ROAD

[16]As he was walking on down the road, a man came to him. "Wisdomkeeper," he asked, "what good must I do to find the life of the world to come that never fades away?"

[17]"Why do you ask me about what is good?" he asked the man. "There is only one who is good—*the Great Spirit.* If you want this life, then follow the instructions given in our tribal law."

[18]"Which instructions?" the young headman asked.

"You already know them," Creator Sets Free (Jesus) answered. "Do not take away the life of another, do not be unfaithful in marriage, and do not take what is not yours. Be honest in all you say and do, and never cheat a fellow human being. [19]Give honor and respect to your father and mother, and love your fellow human beings as much as you love yourself."

[20]"*Wisdomkeeper*," the man answered, "from my youth I have followed all of these instructions. What have I left undone?"

[21]"Only one thing remains," he answered. "Take all of your possessions and give them to the ones who have none, and then you will have great possessions in the spirit-world above."

Creator Sets Free (Jesus) then gave the man the same invitation that he gave to his message bearers.

"Come," he said to the man, "and walk the road with me."

[22]But when the young man heard this, his heart fell to the ground. He hung his head and walked away, for he had many possessions.

HELP TO WALK THE GOOD ROAD

[23]"I speak from my heart," Creator Sets Free (Jesus) then said to his followers,

"Finding the way onto the good road from above is a hard thing for the ones who have many possessions. ²⁴It would be easier for a moose[a] to squeeze through the eye of a *beading* needle."

²⁵His followers could not believe what they were hearing. "How then can anyone find and walk the good road?" they asked.

²⁶Creator Sets Free (Jesus) set his eyes firmly on them and said, "With two-leggeds this is impossible, but all things are possible with the help of the Great Spirit. Nothing is impossible for him."

²⁷Then Stands on the Rock (Peter) spoke up, "We have left all our possessions, and our relatives, to walk the road with you! What will become of us?"

²⁸"I speak to you from my heart," he answered. "When the new age has been birthed, the True Human Being will sit in his seat of honor, and you who have walked the road with me will sit in twelve places of honor, deciding what is good and right for the twelve tribes of Wrestles with Creator (Israel).

²⁹"All who have given up their homes and families because they represent me will receive back much more[b] than they have lost, and the life of the world to come that never fades away will be theirs."

For they now belong to Creator's sacred family, which will care for them.

³⁰"But *remember*, many who are first will be last, and many who are last will be first."

20

To help them to better understand what he was saying, Creator Sets Free (Jesus)

---

[a] 19:24 Lit. *camel*
[b] 19:29 Lit. *one hundred times as much*

told them another story about Creator's good road.

WORKERS IN A VINEYARD

¹"Creator's good road from above is like this tribal member who managed a large vineyard. He went out early in the morning to find people to harvest the grapes. ²After they agreed with him on the amount for a full day's pay, he sent them to work.

³"A few hours later he went to the trading post and saw people there doing nothing.

⁴"He told them, 'If you will join the workers in my field, I will pay you well.'

⁵"So they went to work. Then, about midday, and again at midafternoon, he went out and found others and did the same. ⁶Finally, when the day was nearly done, he found a few more people doing nothing.

"'Why are you not working?' he asked them.

⁷"'No one has hired us,' they answered. He agreed to pay them fairly and sent them to work.

⁸"At the end of the day, the headman said to his manager, 'Bring the workers in from the field and pay them, beginning from last to first.'

⁹"He paid the workers hired at the end of the day a full day's wage. ¹⁰When the workers who were hired at the start of the day were paid, they expected to receive more but were paid the same amount.

¹¹"'We have worked all day in the scorching heat,' they complained to the manager. ¹²'Why should we be paid the same as the ones who worked only one hour?'

¹³"'I am not being unfair with you, my friend,' he said to one of them. 'Did we not

agree on the amount of a full day's wages? [14]Take your pay and go *in peace.* If I want to pay these men the same, what is that to you? [15]Am I not permitted to be generous with what is mine? Or are you jealous because I have done a good thing?'"

> *Creator Sets Free (Jesus) let his followers think about the story for a moment.*

[16]"That is why I told you before," he reminded them, "the last will be first and the first will be last."

A SOLEMN REMINDER

[17]As they journeyed on toward the Village of Peace (Jerusalem), he stopped on the way and gathered his followers around him.

[18]"We are on our way up to the Village of Peace (Jerusalem)," he reminded them. "There the True Human Being will be handed over to the head holy men and scroll keepers, who will put him to death. [19]They will condemn him to death and hand him over to the People of Iron (Romans).[a] They will treat him shamefully, whip him with cords of braided cowhide, and kill him by nailing him to a tree-pole —the cross.

"*But remember,*" he added, "on the third day he will defeat death and live again."

THE GOOD ROAD IS ABOUT SERVING OTHERS

[20]The mother of *He Takes Over (James) and He Shows Goodwill (John),* the sons of Gift of Creator (Zebedee), came to Creator Sets Free (Jesus), along with her sons, and humbled herself before him to make a request.

[21]"What do you want from me?" he asked.

"Promise me," she said, "that my two sons will have an honored place when your good road comes—one on your right hand, the other on your left."

[22]"You do not know what you are asking," he said to her.

He turned to her sons and asked them, "Can you drink the cup of suffering that I will drink, or endure my purification ceremony?"[b]

"We are able!" they answered.

[23]"Yes, you will drink from my cup of suffering," he said to them, "but the place of honor on my right and left hand is not mine to give. My Father will give this honor to the ones he has chosen."

[24]When the other ten message bearers heard this, they began to look down on the two brothers.

[25]So Creator Sets Free (Jesus) called them together and said, "Other nations, *like the People of Iron (Romans),* have rulers. They like to show their power over people and push them around. [26]But this will not be the way of the ones who walk with me. The ones among you who would be great must humble themselves and serve all the others. [27]And the ones who want to be first must become the household slave of all. [28]In the same way, the True Human Being did not come to be served by others, but to offer his life in the place of many lives, to set them free."

TWO BLIND MEN SEE AGAIN

> *The road to Village of Peace (Jerusalem) took them through Moon Village (Jericho).*

[29]As they walked out from Moon Village (Jericho), a large crowd of people trailed after them. [30]Not far from the

---

village there were two blind men sitting on the side of the road.

When the blind men heard that Creator Sets Free (Jesus) was passing by, they cried out to him, "Honored One! Descendant of Much Loved One (David), have pity on us!"

31The people in the crowd scolded them and said, "Be quiet!"

That only made them cry out louder, "Honored One! Descendant of Much Loved One (David), have pity on us!"

32Creator Sets Free (Jesus) stopped walking and called out to them, "What do you want from me?"

33"Honored One," they said, "open our eyes, that we may see."

34He felt pity for them, so he touched their eyes, and right then their eyes were opened and they could see! So they went with him down the road.

21

> *Creator Sets Free (Jesus) and the ones who walked the road with him were coming to the end of their journey. As they neared Village of Peace (Jerusalem), he began to make preparations for what would be his final week with his followers. It was now time to complete the work the Great Spirit had sent him to do.*

GRAND ENTRY

1They came to House of Unripe Figs (Bethphage) at the foot of Olive Mountain, near Village of Peace (Jerusalem). There he sent two of his followers ahead of him.

2"Go into the village ahead of us," he instructed them. "As soon as you enter, you will find a donkey tied there with her colt. Untie them and bring them to me. **3**If anyone asks you what you are doing, say to them, 'Our Wisdomkeeper has need of them,' and the owner will release them to you."

4This took place to show the full meaning of the ancient prophecy, **5**"Speak these words to the daughter of Strong Mountain (Zion): 'Behold, your Chief is coming to you, in a humble way, riding upon a donkey—a colt still with its mother.'"[a]

6His followers did as they were told. When they arrived at the village, they found everything just as he had said. **7**They brought the donkey colt to Creator Sets Free (Jesus) and laid their outer garments on the colt, and he sat down on them.

8From the large crowd many began to cut branches from nearby trees and spread their outer garments on the road in front of him. **9**The crowd circled around him, front and back, and began to shout:

"Hosanna![b] To the descendant of Much Loved One (David)!

"Blessed is the one who comes representing the Great Spirit!

"Hosanna[b] to the highest one!"

> *This humble Chief did not fit the image of a conquering ruler. Instead of a warhorse, he rode on a donkey colt. No mighty warriors rode next to him. No dignitaries came out to meet him. It was mostly the common people who welcomed him that day.*

10When he rode through the gate entering the Village of Peace (Jerusalem), the whole village was in an uproar!

"Who is this?" they asked.

11"He is Creator Sets Free (Jesus), the prophet from Seed Planter Village (Nazareth) in Circle of Nations (Galilee)," the crowd answered.

---

[a]**21:5** Zechariah 9:9-10
[b]**21:9** *Set us free!*

SACRED LODGE KEEPER

[12]Creator Sets Free (Jesus) rode into the village and to the sacred lodge. He entered the lodge and began to force out the ones who were selling and buying *the ceremonial animals.* He then tipped over the tables of the money handlers and the seats of the ones who were selling the *ceremonial* doves.

[13]"It is written *from the words of the prophets,*" he cried out, "'My lodge will be called a house of prayer for all nations, but you have turned it into a hideout for thieves!'ª"

The ancient prophecies had now found their full meaning, for this was the area of the lodge called Gathering Place for the Nations. It was here that other nations could come to learn about the Great Spirit and his ways. The holy men were keeping the Outside Nations who wanted to learn of Creator's ways from entering into this Holy Place. They were stealing the ways of the Great Spirit from the nations.

[14]After that, people who could not see or walk came to him at the lodge, and he healed them. [15]The children came to him there, shouting for joy, "Hosannaᵇ to the descendant of Much Loved One (David)!"

The children then made a circle around him and laughed, danced, and sang songs.

But when the head holy men and the scroll keepers saw the wonderful things he did and heard the children shouting *and singing,* they burned with anger [16]and said to him, "Do you hear what these children are saying?"

"I hear them," he answered, "but have you not heard what the ancient Sacred Teachings say? 'From the mouths of little children and nursing babies you have created praise.'ᶜ"

[17]Then Creator Sets Free (Jesus) left Village of Peace (Jerusalem) and returned to House of Figs (Bethany), *where he was lodging.*

A FIG TREE WITH NO FRUIT

[18]The next morning, as he was returning to Village of Peace (Jerusalem), he became hungry. [19]He saw a fig tree on the side of the road and went to it, but when he came to the tree, he found only leaves.

He spoke to the tree, "You will never again grow fruit!" and the fig tree began to wither away right then and there.

[20]When the ones who walked the road with him saw the tree withering, they were amazed.

"How did it dry up and wither so quickly?" they asked.

[21]"I speak from my heart, if you put all your trust in the Great Spirit and do not doubt *that the Knower of Hearts hears you,*" he answered them, "not only will you do what was done with this fig tree, but even if you speak to this mountain and say, 'Be lifted up and go into the great waters,' it will happen. [22]So when you send your prayers to the Great Spirit, believe that he hears you, and whatever you ask for will be yours."

QUESTIONED BY THE SPIRITUAL LEADERS

[23]When he arrived at the lodge, the head holy men *were waiting for him. They* and the ruling elders of the people came to him.

"By what right do you do these things?" they challenged. "Who gave you this right?"

ª**21:13** Isaiah 56:7; Jeremiah 7:11
ᵇ**21:15** *Set us free!*
ᶜ**21:16** Psalm 8:2

²⁴"First you must answer one question from me," he challenged back, "and then I will tell you what gives me the right. ²⁵The purification ceremony[a] performed by Gift of Goodwill (John), was it from the spirit-world above, or did it come from human beings?"

They put their heads together and talked it over. "If we say it is from the spirit-world above, he will say to us, 'Why then did you not believe him?' ²⁶But if we say it is from human beings, we fear what this crowd would do, for they are sure Gift of Goodwill (John) was a prophet."

²⁷So they answered him, "We do not know."

"So then," Creator Sets Free (Jesus) said to them, "neither will I tell you what gives me the right to do these things."

STORY OF TWO SONS

> *Then, since they would not answer him, he told them the answer to his own question about Gift of Goodwill (John)—with a story.*

²⁸"How do you see it?" he asked them. "A man with two sons came to one of his sons and said, 'Son, will you work in my vineyard today?' ²⁹At first the son told him 'No,' but later changed his mind and went to work.

³⁰"Then the man went to his other son and asked him the same. He told his father, 'Yes, I will,' but never went."

³¹*Creator Sets Free (Jesus) looked right at the spiritual leaders and asked,* "Which of the two sons did what his father wanted?"

They said to him, "The first one."

"I speak truth from my heart," he said to them, "tribal tax collectors and those who sell sexual favors will find their way onto Creator's good road ahead of you! ³²Gift of Goodwill (John) came to show the good way, but you refused to hear him. You saw how the tribal tax collectors and those who sell sexual favors put their trust in him, but not even this changed your mind to believe him.

STORY OF THE VINEYARD

³³"Hear me," he said to them, "and I will tell you another story.

"There was a tribal member who planted a vineyard. He put a hedge around it, dug a pit to crush the grapes, and built a treehouse from which to watch over all the vines. He then rented the vineyard out to other tribal members *for a share of the grapes.* Then he traveled far away to another land.

³⁴"When harvest time came, the tribal member who owned the vineyard sent trusted messengers to gather his share of the grapes, ³⁵but the renters took hold of the messengers. They fiercely beat one, killed another, and even threw stones to kill another.

³⁶"Then the vineyard owner sent even more messengers than at first, but they did the same to them.

³⁷"Finally he sent his son to them, thinking, 'They will respect my son.'

³⁸"But when they saw that he had sent his son, they said to each other, 'This vineyard will one day belong to this son. If we kill him, we can take the vineyard for ourselves.'

³⁹"So they dragged him out of the vineyard and murdered him."

> *Creator Sets Free (Jesus) turned to face the spiritual leaders.*

⁴⁰"When he returns, what will the owner of this vineyard do?" he asked them.

---

[a]**21:25** Baptism

[41]They answered him, "He will bring those bad-hearted ones to a bad end and then rent out the vineyard to others who will be honorable and give him the share of the harvest he deserves."

STUMBLING OVER THE CHIEF POLE
[42]"Are you blind to the Sacred Teachings?" he said to them. "Have you not read this: 'The tree the lodge builders threw away has become the Chief Lodgepole. This is what the Great Spirit has done, and it will fill us with wonder'[a]?

[43]"So I say to you that Creator's good road will be torn from you and given to a people who will bring its fruit to a full harvest. For the ones who stumble over this Chief Lodgepole will be broken into pieces, [44]and when it falls on them, they will be crushed *and scattered like dust in the wind.*"

[45]When the head holy men and the Separated Ones (Pharisees) heard his stories, they realized they were about them. [46]They wanted to arrest Creator Sets Free (Jesus) but feared the people, since they considered him a prophet.

A REJECTED INVITATION
[1]Creator Sets Free (Jesus) continued to speak to them using stories such as this one:

[2]"Creator's good road from above is like a chief who prepared a wedding feast for his son. [3]When the feast was ready, he sent out trusted messengers to gather the ones who had been invited, but no one came.

[4]"So he sent out others with this message: 'I am serving my best meat fresh from the herd. So come, the wedding feast for my son has been prepared!'

[5]"But some ignored the messengers and returned to their work, [6]while others mistreated them and even killed them.

[7]"When the chief found out what they had done, he was filled with rage and sent his warriors to kill those murderers and burn their village to the ground.

[8]"Then the chief told his messengers, 'The wedding feast is ready, but the ones invited have proved they have no honor. [9]Waste no time, go out into the village pathways, and invite all you find to come to the feast.'

[10]"So they went and did as they were told and gathered as many as they could find, whether honorable or bad-hearted. So the lodge was filled with many wedding guests for his son.

[11]"When the chief came in to see the guests, he saw someone who was not wearing the proper regalia *that was provided for the guests at the wedding feast.* [12]He said to the guest, 'How did you get in here without the proper regalia? *Why have you dishonored my son by not wearing the outfit provided for you?*'

"There was nothing the man could say. [13]"The chief called his warriors and said to them, 'Bind him with leather straps from head to foot and throw him outside into the darkness, to weep and grind his teeth in anger.'

[14]"So you can see," Creator Sets Free (Jesus) said, "many are invited, but few accept his invitation."[b]

THE SEPARATED ONES ATTACK
[15]The Separated Ones (Pharisees) began to scheme against Creator Sets Free (Jesus). [16]They sent their followers along with

---

[a]21:42 Psalm 118:22-23

[b]22:14 Lit. *Few are chosen*

some of the Friends of Looks Brave (Herodians) to spy on him.

"Wisdomkeeper," they said to him, "we know you always speak the truth about the Great Spirit and represent him well. You show respect to human beings and treat them all the same. 17Tell us what is right, should our tribal members pay taxes to the Ruler of the People of Iron (Caesar)? Yes or no?"

18He could see right through them and knew what they were up to!

"Why are you putting me to the test? I can see behind your false faces!" he answered. 19"Show me one of their silver coins used to pay the tax *and let me take a close look at it.*"

They found a silver coin and handed it to him.

He took a good long look, holding it up to the sky to see it clearly. Then he turned the face of the coin toward them.

20"Whose image and words are carved into this coin?" he asked.

21"The Ruler of the People of Iron (Caesar)," they answered.

He *handed the coin back to them and* said, "Then give to this ruler the things that are his, and give to the Great Spirit the things that belong to the Great Spirit."

22When they heard his answer, they were amazed at his wisdom and *hung their heads in silence as they* walked away.

THE UPRIGHT ONES ATTACK
23Later that same day some of the Upright Ones (Sadducees), who say that the dead do not rise again, came to Creator Sets Free (Jesus) to question him also.

24"Wisdomkeeper," they said, "in our tribal law, Drawn From the Water (Moses) gave us these instructions: 'If a Tribal Member should die before having children, then his brother should marry his widow and give her children to carry on his brother's name.'

25"In a family of seven brothers," they continued, "the oldest took a wife but died without children. 26The next brother married her, but he also died with no children. A third brother married her, and like his other brothers, he died with no children. The same happened to all seven of them, 27and, last of all, the woman also crossed over to death. 28So, when they all come back to life in the new world, whose wife will she be, since all seven brothers married her?"

29"You are asking the wrong question," Creator Sets Free (Jesus) answered back. "You do not understand the Sacred Teachings or the power of the Great Spirit. 30When the dead rise to life, there will be no marriage, for they will be like the spirit-messengers from the spirit-world above."

31Then he added, "You say you do not believe the dead will rise again. But have you not read what was told by the Maker of Life: 32'I am the Great Spirit of Father of Many Nations (Abraham), of He Made Us Laugh (Isaac), and of Heel Grabber (Jacob)'a?

"He is not the Great Spirit of the dead but of the living."

33All the people who heard him were amazed by his teaching.

THE GREATEST OF THE INSTRUCTIONS
34When the Separated Ones (Pharisees) heard how he silenced the Upright Ones (Sadducees), they put their heads together and came up with a plan. 35One of them, who was an expert in tribal law, would put him to the test.

---

a22:32 Exodus 3:6

[36]The expert came to him. "Wisdom-keeper," he asked, "which instruction in our tribal law stands first?"

[37]Creator Sets Free (Jesus) answered him, "'You must love the Great Spirit from deep within, with the strength of your arms, the thoughts of your mind, and the courage of your heart.'[a] [38]This is the first and greatest instruction.

[39]"The second is like the first," he added. "'You must love your fellow human beings in the same way you love yourselves.'[b] [40]The Law and the words of the prophets all find their full meaning in these two instructions."

HE SILENCES HIS ADVERSARIES

[41]While the Separated Ones (Pharisees) were still gathered near him, he asked them this question, [42]"How do you see the Chosen One? Who is he descended from?"

"He is the son who is descended from Much Loved One (David)," they answered.

[43]"How can the scroll keepers call him the descendant of Much Loved One (David)," he asked, "when Much Loved One (David) himself, speaking by the power of the Spirit, called the Chosen One his Honored Chief? [44]For in the book of Sacred Songs he said, 'The Honored Chief said to my Honored Chief, "Sit down beside me at my right hand, my place of greatest honor, until I defeat and humble all your enemies"[c]'?"

He paused to let them think about his words.

[45]Then he said, "If Much Loved One (David) calls the Chosen One, 'My Honored Chief,' how can the Chosen One be his descendant?"

[46]None of the spiritual leaders could answer him. From that time on, no one dared to challenge him with another question.

His great wisdom had silenced the ones who were against him.

23

BAD SPIRITUAL LEADERS

Creator Sets Free (Jesus) cared deeply about the people, so he began to warn the people and his followers about the bad-hearted spiritual leaders.

[1-2]"The Separated Ones (Pharisees) and the scroll keepers *are leading you down the wrong path!*" he said to the people and his followers. "When they speak, they represent the lawgiver Drawn from the Water (Moses), [3]so listen when they speak the truth and do what they say but do not walk in their ways. They fail to do the things they demand of others [4]and tie heavy *spiritual* burdens on their backs, too much for them to carry, but will not lift even one finger to help them.

[5]"They want to look important to others, so to look spiritual they wear large and fancy medicine pouches and long fringes on their outfits. [6]They love to dress up in fine regalia, sit in the seats of honor at the gathering houses, [7]and have people call them 'wisdomkeeper' at the trading posts."

Then he turned to instruct the ones who walked the road with him.

THE GREAT WILL SERVE

[8-10]"Titles such as 'wisdomkeeper,' 'chief,' and 'spiritual guide' are not for you. There is only one true Wisdomkeeper,

---

[a]**22:37** Deuteronomy 6:5
[b]**22:39** Leviticus 19:18
[c]**22:44** Psalm 110:1

Chief, and Spiritual Guide—the Chosen One—and you all belong to his family. So call no one on earth by the title 'father,' for only the Great Spirit is truly the Father of us all. **11**The great ones among you will be servant of all. **12**The ones who put themselves above others will be brought down low. The ones who humble themselves will be lifted up."

> *He then turned again and began to boldly confront the bad spiritual leaders.*

SORROW AND TROUBLE

13"Sorrow and trouble is waiting for you scroll keepers and Separated Ones (Pharisees), for you have hidden from the people the way onto the good road from above. You have failed to walk the good road yourselves, and, even worse, you have barred the way for others who were trying to find the way.

14"Sorrow and trouble will come your way, you scroll keepers and Separated Ones (Pharisees), for with many words you make long empty prayers and trick widows into giving you their homes and possessions. You will come to a bad end when your fate is decided.[a]

15"Sorrow and trouble await you blind guides with false faces, for you journey far and wide, across the great waters, to find one person who will change to your ways. When you have won him over, he becomes twice as bad as you are, a true son of the Valley of Smoldering Fire.

16"And to the blind guides who say, 'A promise made outside the lodge can be broken, but one made inside must be kept,' **17**you are so foolish and blind! It is not the lodge that makes the promise

good, but it is the Great Spirit over the lodge who sees and hears all promises.

18"Or you say, 'A promise made before a ceremony can be broken, but one made during a ceremony must be kept.' **19**Are you so blind? Can you not see that the Great Spirit sees and hears all promises and expects you to keep them?

20-22"It matters not whether a promise is made inside or outside the lodge, or before or during a sacred ceremony. All promises on the earth below or in the spirit-world above are made before the eyes of the Great Spirit, who sees and hears everything.

23"Sorrow and trouble wait for you scroll keepers and Separated Ones (Pharisees). With false faces you are careful to do what tribal law says by giving a tenth of each little herb in your garden, but you ignore the more important instructions such as justice, kindness, and honesty. **24**You are spiritually blind guides, for you strain out a small flea *from your water pouch*, but swallow a whole moose.[b]

25"Sorrow and trouble will be your end, you scroll keepers and Separated Ones (Pharisees), for you wash the outside of your cups and bowls, but on the inside your hearts are full of greed and selfish ways. **26**You blind Separated Ones (Pharisees)! First clean the inside of your cup, and then the outside of the cup will become clean also.

27"Sorrow and trouble will be waiting at the end of the trail for you Separated Ones (Pharisees) and scroll keepers who hide behind false faces. You are like burial caves that have been painted white to look good on the outside, but on the inside you are full of dead men's

---

bones and rotting things. [28]You may look good to others, but you are full of falsehood and worthless ways.

[29]"Sorrow and trouble will be waiting at the end of the trail for you Separated Ones (Pharisees) and scroll keepers who hide behind false faces. You put great decorated stones on the burial grounds of the prophets and the ones who walked upright—the ones your ancestors killed.

AN OMINOUS WARNING

[30]"You say, 'If we had lived in the days of our ancestors, we would not have participated with them when they shed the blood of the prophets.' [31]But you are speaking against yourselves, for you are admitting that you are the descendants of the ones who killed them, [32]and you will finish what your ancestors started! [33]You nest of poisonous snakes! How will you escape the bad end of the Valley of Smoldering Fire?

[34]"That is why I am sending to you prophets, wisdomkeepers, and scroll keepers. You will whip some of them in your gathering houses. Others you will nail to a cross. You will threaten them and pursue them from village to village *until you shed their blood.* [35]Then you will be guilty of shedding the innocent blood of all who have lived on the earth from His Breath Goes Up (Abel), who was killed by his brother,[a] to Creator Will Remember (Zechariah), the son of He Will Be Blessed (Barachiah), who was put to death in the courtyard of the sacred lodge.[b]

[36]"I speak truth from my heart, all these things will happen to the people of this generation."

---

[a]**23:35** Abel was the second son of Adam and the first human to be killed by another. See Genesis 4:1-16 for the story.
[b]**23:35** Lit. *between the altar and the sanctuary*

O VILLAGE OF PEACE!

A dark cloud cast a shadow over Creator Sets Free (Jesus), and a look of pain and sorrow came upon his face.

[37]"Jerusalem, O Village of Peace!" *he cried out loud for all to hear.* "You who kill the prophets and stone to death the ones sent to you! How I have longed to gather your children together, like an eagle gathers her young under her wings, but you would not have it. [38]Look! Your house has fallen and will be left in ruins! [39]I speak from my heart, you will not see me again until you say, 'Blessed is the one who comes representing the Great Spirit!'"

THE SACRED LODGE WILL FALL

[1]As Creator Sets Free (Jesus) made his way out of the sacred lodge, his followers began to point out to him all the buildings that surrounded the sacred lodge.

As he stopped and looked around at the lodge and all its buildings, a look of great sadness came over his face.

[2]"Take a good long look, for I speak truth from my heart—all of these will fall to the ground. Not one log or stone will be left standing against another."

SIGNS OF THE END

[3]*Later that day* Creator Sets Free (Jesus) sat down to rest on the side of Olive Mountain.

From there he could look across the valley past the walls of Village of Peace (Jerusalem) and see the sacred lodge.

Some of his followers came to him privately. "Wisdomkeeper," they asked *with worried faces*, "when will these things happen? What will be the sign of your coming that will bring an end to this age we live in?"

4"Beware of those who would lead you down a false path," Creator Sets Free (Jesus) warned them, 5"for many will come falsely representing who I am and say, 'I am the Chosen One,' and many will follow them to a bad end.

6"When you hear of wars and stories of war breaking out, do not fear, for all of this must happen, but the end will not come all at once. 7There will be tribal wars, and nations will make war against other nations. Food will be scarce, and the earth will shake in many places— 8but this is only the beginning of the time of sorrow, like a woman feeling the pains of birth.

9"Because you represent me, you will be looked down on by all the nations. They will hunt you down and kill you, all because you follow me. 10When this happens, many will stumble on the path and even hate and betray each other.

11"Then many false prophets will rise up and lead many down false paths. 12Because evildoers will grow strong, the love in many hearts will grow cold—13but the ones who stand firm *in their faith* to the end will be set free and made whole.

14"The good story about Creator's good road will be told in truth for all the nations of this world to hear. Then the end will come.

A TIME OF SORROW AND TROUBLE

15"When you see the 'horrible thing that destroys,' that the prophet Creator Will Decide (Daniel) told about,a making its stand against the place that is holy—the reader will understand the meaning— 16you will then know it is time for those who live in the Land of Promise (Judea) to escape to the mountains. 17If you are on your rooftop, go, without taking time to get anything from your house. 18Workers in the fields should not even go back to get their outer garments. 19It will be a terrible time for women who are pregnant or nursing their babies. 20Pray that it will not happen in winter or on a Day of Resting.

21"It will be a time of trouble and sorrow like no other. A worse time has not been seen since the world was created—and there will never be a time like this again. 22If that terrible time were allowed to reach the end of the trail, no one would survive, but for the sake of Creator's Chosen Ones those days will be cut short.

23"In those days if anyone says to you, 'Look, the Chosen One is over here,' or 'Look, he is over there,' pay no attention to him, 24for false Chosen Ones will rise up and false prophets will appear. They will provide great signs and omens to mislead the people. Even Creator's Chosen Ones will be tempted to believe them.

25"Remember that I have warned you ahead of time! 26So if they say, 'The Chosen One is in the desert wilderness,' do not go with them there. Or if they say, 'The Chosen One is hidden in a secret place,' do not believe them. 27For when *the sign of*b the True Human Being appears, it will be like lightning when it flashes across the sky from the east to the west.

28"*In the same way that* gathering vulturesc are a sign of dead bodies, *so these things are a sign of the end.*

---

b**24:27** See verse 30.
c**24:28** The word for "vulture" can also be translated "eagle."

²⁹"Then, right after that time of trouble and sorrow, 'the sun will no longer shine, the moon will go dark, the stars will fall from the sky, and the powers in the spirit-world above will tremble.'ᵃ

³⁰"This is when the sign of the True Human Being will appear in the sky. Then all the tribes of the land will weep in anguish when they see the True Human Being riding on the clouds and coming with power and shining-greatness. ³¹Then he will send out his spirit-messengers, who will blow the eagle bone whistleᵇ to gather his Chosen Ones from the four winds, from one end of the sky to the other.

WISDOM FROM A FIG TREE

³²"Listen to this fig tree and hear what it is saying to you: when its branches get soft and leaves appear, you know that summer will soon be here. ³³In the same way, when you see all these things happening, you will know that the time is almost here. ³⁴I speak from my heart! All of this will happen to this generation, during the lifetime of the people who live today. ³⁵The earth and sky, as we know them, will fade away, but my words will never fade!

ALWAYS BE READY

³⁶"But no one knows the day or hour that these things will take place. Not the spirit-messengers from the spirit-world above, not even Creator's own Son, but only the Great Spirit, who is our Father from above, knows.

³⁷⁻³⁸"When the True Human Being comes, it will be like it was in the days before the great flood in the time of One

Who Rests (Noah). In those days the people were eating and drinking and getting married until the day that One Who Rests (Noah) entered the great wooden canoe. ³⁹No one knew what was happening until the floodwaters came, washed them away, and drowned them all. It will be the same when the True Human Being appears.

⁴⁰"During that time two men will be working in the field. One will be taken away and the other left. ⁴¹Two women will be husking corn. One will be taken away and the other left. ⁴²So be on the lookout, because you never know when your Honored Chief will arrive.

⁴³"But know this: If the elder of a family had known at what part of the night the thief was coming, he would have stayed awake and stopped the thief from breaking in. ⁴⁴Just like this elder, you must be ready, for the True Human Being will not come at the time you expect him to.

WHO WILL BE WISE?

⁴⁵"Who will be the wise one, worthy of trust? Will it be the uncle who was told to feed and care for the family while the elder is away? ⁴⁶A great blessing will come to that uncle when the elder returns and finds him doing so. ⁴⁷I speak from my heart, he will invite that uncle to live with the family and share everything.

⁴⁸"But what if the uncle says to himself, 'It will be a long time before he returns,' ⁴⁹then begins to abuse the family and invites the local drunks to eat and drink with him?"

ᵃ24:29 Isaiah 13:10; 34:4
ᵇ24:31 Lit. *loud trumpet*, or in Hebrew *shofar*, meaning "ram's horn"

Creator Sets Free (Jesus) paused to let his followers think about the answer and then continued.

50"The elder will return at a time the uncle does not expect. 51He will then put him out of the family to share the fate of the ones who wear false faces. There the uncle will weep with them as they grind their teeth together in anger and frustration.

25 ⟨✕⟩⟨✕⟩⟨✕⟩⟨✕⟩⟨✕⟩⟨✕⟩⟨✕⟩

WISE AND FOOLISH YOUNG WOMEN

1"When that time comes, the ones who are walking Creator's good road from above will be like ten young, unmarried women who took their ceremonial torches and went out to welcome the groom. 2Five of them were foolish and five were wise. 3-4The wise women took an extra clay pot of oil along for their torches, but the foolish ones did not bother to bring any.

5"The groom did not come when expected, and they all fell asleep as they waited. 6Then suddenly, in the dark of the night, someone cried out, 'Look! The groom is coming, let us go welcome him!'

7"All the women woke up to prepare their torches, *but the oil in the torches had run out.*

8"The foolish ones said to the wise, 'Give us some of your oil so our torches will not go out.'

9"The wise ones answered back, 'There is not enough for all of us. *Hurry,* go to the village and trade for some more.'

10"They hurried away to get more oil. But while they were gone, the groom came and all the guests went into the lodge for the wedding feast, and the gate was closed.

11"A while later the other women came to the gate and said to the gatekeeper, 'Honored one, O honored one, open the door and let us come in.'

12"But he said to them, 'I truly do not even know who you are—*why should I let you in?'"*

> *Creator Sets Free (Jesus) finished the story with these words of wisdom.*

13"Here is what I am saying to you: *be prepared like the wise women in this story and* always be ready, for you do not know the time of day or night that the True Human Being will appear."

STORY OF THE TRUSTED TRIBAL MEMBERS

14"Here is another way to see how the Creator's good road from above will come: It is like a tribal headman preparing for a long journey. He gathered three trusted tribal members together to give them charge of his goods during his journey.

15"He gave five herds of horses[a] to one, two herds to another, and one herd to the third man, giving each one according to his ability to make a good trade. After that he left on his journey.

16"The man with five herds of horses went to work right away, traded well, and earned five more herds. 17In the same way the one with two herds used them to gain two more. 18But the one who had only one kept the herd well hidden and safe from thieves.

19"Many moons passed before the headman returned from his journey. He gathered the trusted tribal members together to see how well they had traded.

20"The one given five herds came forward and said, 'Look, I have gained five more!'

21"'You have served me well, my good and trusted friend,' the headman said,

---

[a]25:15 Lit. *five talents.* A talent was worth at least fifteen years of wages.

'You have done well with a small amount, now I will give you much more. Come and live with my family and enjoy all I have.'

²²"Then the man to whom he gave two herds came forward and said, 'You gave me two herds, but I have four to give back to you.' ²³The headman honored him and did the same for him as the one with ten.

²⁴"Then the man to whom he had given one herd came to him and said, 'Headman, I know you have a reputation of being a harsh man, taking what you did not plant and gathering what is not yours. ²⁵I was afraid, so I hid the herd away to keep them safe for you. Here they are!'

²⁶"The headman said to him, 'You *have broken the trust I gave you and* have proven you are lazy and no good. If you knew I was a harsh man, ²⁷why did you not ask the trading post to trade for them so there would be something to show for them when I returned?'

²⁸"So he told them to take the herd from him and give it to the one who had ten ²⁹and said, 'The ones who do well with what they are given will be given more, but the ones who do nothing with it will lose even what they have been given.' ³⁰Then he had the man thrown out of his house into the darkness outside, the place where they weep and grind their teeth together in anger and frustration.

FATE OF THE NATIONS

³¹"When the True Human Being comes in all of his power and shining-greatness, along with all of his spirit-messengers, he will sit down in his seat of honor. ³²All nations will be gathered and come before him. He will choose between them like a shepherd separates the sheep from the goats. ³³He will put the sheep on his right side and the goats to his left.

³⁴"Then the Chief will say to the sheep on his right, 'The blessing of my Father rests upon you. Come into the Land of Creator's good road that has been prepared for you from the beginning of the world. ³⁵For I was thirsty and you gave me drink. I was hungry and you fed me. I was a stranger and you gave me lodging. ³⁶When I needed clothes, you gave me something to wear. When I was sick, you took care of me, and when I was in prison, you visited me.'

³⁷⁻³⁹"'When did we do all these things for you?' the good-hearted ones asked.

⁴⁰"'I speak from my heart,' he answered them, 'whatever you did for the least important of my fellow human beingsª who needed help, you did for me.'

⁴¹"Then the Chief will say to the goats on his left, 'Go away from me, you who have bad hearts,ᵇ into the fire that burns everything up, made for the evil trickster snake and his messengers. ⁴²For when I was hungry, you gave me nothing to eat. When I was thirsty, you gave me no drink, ⁴³and when I was a stranger, you turned me away. When I needed clothes, you gave me nothing to wear, and when I was sick and in prison, you failed to visit me.'

⁴⁴"'Honored One,' they questioned, 'when was it that we saw you like this and did nothing?'

⁴⁵"'I speak from my heart,' he answered back, 'when you did not help the ones who needed it most, you failed to help me.'

⁴⁶"Then the goats will go away to the punishment of the world to come that never fades away, and the sheep will enter

---

ª **25:40** Lit. *my brothers*
ᵇ **25:41** Lit. *cursed ones*

the life of the world to come that never fades away, full of beauty and harmony."

26

THE COUNCIL DECIDES HIS FATE

[1]After he had finished speaking about these things, Creator Sets Free (Jesus) said to the ones who walked the road with him, [2]"As you know, the Passover festival will begin after two days. It is during this time that the True Human Being will be taken captive and then killed on a tree-pole—the cross."

[3]At that time the head holy men and the elders of the people gathered in the lodge of Hollow in the Rock (Caiaphas), the chief holy man. [4]They schemed together to take Creator Sets Free (Jesus) captive on the sly and then kill him.

[5]"We should not do this during the festival," they said, "or there could be an uprising among the people."

PREPARED FOR BURIAL

[6]Creator Sets Free (Jesus) went to House of Figs (Bethany) to the home of Hearing Man (Simon), who had suffered from a skin disease. [7]While there, a woman with a pottery jar full of costly, sweet-smelling ointment came to Creator Sets Free (Jesus) and poured it over his head as he sat on the floor near the table.

[8]His followers, when they saw this, became angry and said to each other, "Why waste this costly ointment? [9]It could have been traded for food and goods to give to the ones who have none."

[10]Creator Sets Free (Jesus) heard them and said, "Why are you troubling this woman? She has done a good thing for me. [11]You can help the poor any time, for they will always be with you, but I will not.

[12]By pouring this sweet-smelling ointment on my body, she has performed a preparation ceremony for my burial. [13]I speak from my heart, when the good story is told all over the world, her story will also be told to remember what she has done."

[14]It was then that Speaks Well Of (Judas) son of Village Man (Iscariot), one of the twelve, left and went to the head holy men. [15]"How much is he worth to you," he asked them. "What price will you pay if I turn him over to you?"

They agreed on thirty pieces of silver and paid him. [16]So from then on he looked for a good time to betray Creator Sets Free (Jesus).

PREPARING FOR THE CEREMONIAL MEAL

[17]It was now the first day of the Festival of Bread Without Yeast. His followers came to Creator Sets Free (Jesus) and asked, "Where do you want us to go to prepare for the eating of the ceremonial Passover meal?"

[18]"Go into the village," he instructed them, "and there you will meet a certain man and say to him, 'Our Wisdomkeeper says, "My time has now come. I will eat the Passover meal with my followers here in your home."'"

[19]They did as he said and made everything ready for the ceremonial meal.

THE CEREMONIAL MEAL BEGINS

[20]As the sun was setting, Creator Sets Free (Jesus) sat down around the table with his twelve followers. [21]During the meal he spoke out, "I speak from my heart, one of you will turn against me."

[22]They were all worried and troubled by this and began to ask him one by one, "Wisdomkeeper, am I the one?"

[23]"It is the one who dipped his hand into the dish with me who will turn against me," he said with a look of sorrow.

24"The True Human Being must walk the path chosen for him, as the Sacred Teachings have said, but it will not go well for the one who betrays him. It would be better if that one had never been born."

25Speaks Well Of (Judas), the betrayer, looked at Creator Sets Free (Jesus) and asked, "Wisdomkeeper, you do not think I am the one, do you?"

"You have said it with your own words," he answered back.

A NEW PEACE TREATY

26Then, during the meal, Creator Sets Free (Jesus) took some of the frybread, *lifted it up*, and gave thanks. He broke it into pieces, gave some to each of his followers, and said, "This is my body. Take it and eat it."

27Then he took a cup of wine, *lifted it up*, and gave thanks. He gave it to his followers and said, "Drink from this cup, all of you, 28for this is my lifeblood of the new peace treaty, poured out to release many people from their broken ways.

29"I tell you now, I will not drink from the fruit of this vine again until I drink it with you in a fresh and new way when we walk together on my Father's good road."

30Then, after they sang a ceremonial song together, they walked to Olive Mountain.

THE SHEEP WILL SCATTER

As they walked to Olive Mountain, Creator Sets Free (Jesus) began to warn his followers about what they would face in the night ahead.

31"This very night all of you will stumble on the path and turn away because of what will happen to me. The Sacred Teachings have made it clear, 'Attack the shepherd and the sheep will scatter.'a 32But after I have risen from the dead, I will go ahead of you to Circle of Nations (Galilee)."

33Stands on the Rock (Peter) answered him, "Even if all others stumble and turn away, I will not!"

34"I speak from my heart," Creator Sets Free (Jesus) said back to him, "before the rooster crows, you will deny three times that you know me."

35"*Not so, my Wisdomkeeper!*" Stands on the Rock (Peter) replied. "Even if I must die with you, I will never turn away!"

Then all of his followers said the same thing.

PRAYING IN THE GARDEN

36Creator Sets Free (Jesus) and his followers came to the place called Where the Olives Are Crushed (Gethsemane), *a garden with many olive trees.*

"Sit here," he told his followers, "while I go over there and pray."

37He then took with him Stands on the Rock (Peter) and *He Takes Over (James) and He Shows Goodwill (John)*, the two sons of Gift of Creator (Zebedee), to a place not far from the others.

As Creator Sets Free (Jesus) began to send his voice to the Great Spirit, he became deeply troubled and full of sorrow.

38"My heart is full of sorrow to the point of death," he said to his three followers who were with him. "Stay here and watch over me."

39He went a little ways from them, dropped his face to the ground, and prayed. "O Great Father," he cried out, "is there a way to take this cup of bitter suffering away from me? But I want only your way, not mine."

40He then got up and found his followers sleeping.

---

a**26:31** Zechariah 13:7

"Could you not stay awake with me for even one hour?" he said to Stands on the Rock (Peter). **41**"Stay awake and pray so that you will be able to face the rough trail ahead of you. Your human body is weak, but your spirit is strong."

42Once again he went from them and prayed, "My Father, if this is the only way, then, as you desire, I will drink *deeply* of this bitter cup."

The night was silent and cold as Creator Sets Free (Jesus) trembled and prayed. The powers of darkness were pressing in hard. After a while he returned to the three followers, who were supposed to be praying.

43He found them and saw that their eyes were heavy with sleep, **44**so he went away from them a third time and prayed the same words.

45He then returned to his followers and said to them, "Why are you still sleeping? The time is upon us! The True Human Being has been betrayed into the hands of the ones with bad hearts. **46**Rise up! We must go! Look! The one who has turned against me is here!"

BETRAYED!

47Right then, while Creator Sets Free (Jesus) was speaking, a crowd of people stormed into the garden. Speaks Well Of (Judas), one of the twelve, was leading the way. Along with the betrayer came the large crowd, sent from the head holy men and elders of the tribal council, carrying clubs and long knives.

The air was filled with the smell of burning torches as the crowd pushed their way forward.

48The betrayer had given them a sign. "Take hold of the one I greet with a kiss, and arrest him."

49Speaks Well Of (Judas) walked right up to Creator Sets Free (Jesus).

"Greetings, Wisdomkeeper," he said and then kissed him.

50"My friend," Creator Sets Free (Jesus) said *to his face*, "Do what you came to do."

The crowd moved in and took hold of Creator Sets Free (Jesus) to arrest him. **51**But then one of his followers drew his long knife from its sheath and cut off the ear of the servant of the chief holy man.

52"Put away your long knife," he said to his follower, "for all who take up weapons will also die by them! **53**Do you not know that if I called out to my Father, he would send to me many thousands[a] of spirit-messengers? **54**But if I did, how would the ancient prophecies that foretold this find their full meaning?"

55Creator Sets Free (Jesus) then turned to the ones who had come to take him and said, "Why do you come at me with clubs and long knives as if I were a thief? Did I not sit with you every day in the sacred lodge? Why did you not take me then? **56**But now the words of the prophets have come true and found their full meaning."

After *hearing him say* this, all his followers turned and ran away.

HIS TRIAL BEFORE THE COUNCIL

57The ones who had arrested him dragged him away and brought him to Hollow in the Rock (Caiaphas), the chief holy man. The scroll keepers and elders *of the Grand Council* had gathered there *to question him.*

58Stands on the Rock (Peter) followed from a safe distance until they came to the courtyard of the chief holy man. He

---

[a]**26:53** Lit. *twelve legions*, about sixty thousand

then went inside through the gate, sat down next to the lodge guards, and waited to see what would happen. **59**The head holy men and the Grand Council kept trying to find someone who would speak against Creator Sets Free (Jesus) falsely so they could put him to death, **60**but found none *who could agree*, even though many came forward and spoke lies against him.

Finally two men came forward **61**and said, "We heard him say, 'I can tear down Creator's sacred lodge and build it again in three days.'"

62The chief holy man stood up before all. He said to Creator Sets Free (Jesus), "Have you no answer to these accusations?" **63**Creator Sets Free (Jesus) remained silent before all *and said nothing to defend himself.*

Hollow in the Rock (Caiaphas) was frustrated! His face became red with anger, and his voice thundered.

"On your honor before the living Creator I call on you to speak the truth!" he demanded. "Tell us whether you are the Chosen One, the Son of the Great Spirit!"

The room became silent. Time seemed to stand still. The air was filled with tension as they waited for his answer. When he spoke, every ear and eye in the room were fixed on him, for he must now answer.

64"What you have said is right!" he answered them. "But listen to this: from now on you will see the True Human Being sitting at the right hand of the Great Power when he comes riding the clouds of the spirit-world above!"[a]

65*They could not believe their ears!* The chief holy man tore his outer garments

and cried out, "He is guilty! His words have insulted the Great Spirit!"

He turned to the council of elders and said, "You have heard it with your own ears! Why do we even need witnesses? **66**What does the council have to say?"

With one voice the council answered, "Death is what he deserves!"

67Then they spit in his face and struck him with their fists, and others slapped him *with the back of their hands.* **68**"Prophesy to us, Chosen One," they taunted him. "Tell us who struck you!"

STANDS ON THE ROCK DENIES THE CHOSEN ONE

69Stands on the Rock (Peter) was still outside sitting in the courtyard.

A servant girl looked at him and said, "I saw you when you were with Creator Sets Free (Jesus) in Circle of Nations (Galilee)."

70"What!" he denied before them all. "I do not know what you are talking about."

71Then he went toward the gate, and another servant woman saw him and said out loud to all, "This man was with Creator Sets Free (Jesus) from Seed Planter Village (Nazareth)."

72"I swear to you," he denied with a sacred oath, "I do not know this man!"

73A short time later some of the men came up to him. "You must be one of his followers," they said. "The way you speak gives you away."

74Stands on the Rock (Peter) cursed and swore out loud, "What are you all saying? I do not know this man you are talking about."

Right then a rooster began to crow, **75**and then he remembered what Creator Sets Free (Jesus) had told him, "Before the rooster crows, you will deny three times that you know me."

---

[a]26:64 Daniel 7:13-14

Stands on the Rock (Peter) ran out of the gate and wept bitter tears *as he stumbled down the road.*

27

[1]As the sun began to rise, the head holy men and council elders laid out their plans to kill Creator Sets Free (Jesus). [2]They tied him up again and dragged him away to turn him over to Spear of the Great Waters (Pilate), the governor from the People of Iron (Romans).

THE BETRAYER TAKES HIS OWN LIFE

[3]When Speaks Well Of (Judas), the one who betrayed Creator Sets Free (Jesus), saw they had decided to have him killed, he was overcome with sorrow. He changed his mind and took the thirty pieces of silver back to the head holy men and the elders.

[4]"I have done wrong!" he told them. "I have betrayed the blood of an innocent man."

"What do we care?" they said back to him. "You did this to yourself."

[5]He threw the thirty pieces of silver on the floor of the sacred lodge and ran away in sorrow. He then left them and hanged himself.

> As the light of the sunrise grew brighter on the horizon, his lifeless body could be seen hanging from the branch of a tree. He could not live with what he had done.
>
> The head holy men did not know what to do with the pieces of silver.

[6]They picked the silver pieces up from the floor and said, "It is not permitted to put them in the storehouse of the sacred lodge, for it is blood money."

[7]So they counseled together and used the silver to purchase a clay field that had been used for making pottery to use as a burial ground for outsiders. [8]From that time on it has been called the Field of Blood.

[9]This gave full meaning to the words of the prophet Lifted by Creator (Jeremiah), "He was sold out for thirty pieces of silver by the tribes of Wrestles with Creator (Israel). This is how much they thought his life was worth. [10]With the silver they bought a field of clay, as instructed by the Great Spirit."[a]

ON TRIAL BY THE PEOPLE OF IRON

[11]Creator Sets Free (Jesus) now stood before the governor of the People of Iron (Romans) for questioning.

"Are you the chief of the tribes of Wrestles with Creator (Israel)?" the governor asked him.

"It is as you say," he answered.

[12]Then the head holy men began to accuse him, but he gave them no answer.

[13]*"Why are you silent?"* Spear of the Great Waters (Pilate) asked him, "Do you not hear their accusations?"

[14]But Creator Sets Free (Jesus) answered not one word, which amazed the governor.

WHO SHALL BE RELEASED?

[15]It was a tradition during the Passover festival to release to the crowd one criminal, whomever they wanted. [16]At that time they were holding a prisoner with a deadly reputation whose name was Son of His Father (Barabbas).

[17]"Which one shall I release?" the governor raised his voice to the crowd. "Son of His Father (Barabbas) or Creator Sets Free (Jesus), who is called the Chosen One?"

---

[a]**27:10** Jeremiah 32:6-9

18Spear of the Great Waters (Pilate) said this because he knew the head holy men and elders had handed over Creator Sets Free (Jesus) because they were jealous of his reputation with the people.

When the governor of the People of Iron (Romans) would make his final decision about the guilt and fate of a person, he would sit on a great rock carved into a seat. This seat was called the Stone of Deciding.

19While he was sitting there, a messenger came from his wife with these words: "Do no harm to this innocent man, for today I had a dream about him that troubles me greatly."

20But the head holy men and the elders talked the crowd into asking for Son of His Father (Barabbas) to be released and to have Creator Sets Free (Jesus) put to death.

21Once more the governor asked the crowd, "Whom do you want me to release?"

"Son of His Father (Barabbas)!" the crowd roared back.

22"Then what would you have me do with Creator Sets Free (Jesus), who is called the Chosen One?" he asked them.

With one voice they shouted, "Nail him to the cross!"

23"But what wrong has he done to deserve this?" he asked them again.

But their voices grew louder and louder, "Nail him to the cross!"

24Spear of the Great Waters (Pilate) could see that their minds would not be changed. He was worried that the crowd might turn violent, *so he decided to give them what they wanted.* He washed his hands in a vessel of water in front of all the people and said, "This man's blood is not on my hands. It is on yours!"

25"Let his blood be on us and on our descendants!" they answered him back.

CONDEMNED TO A VIOLENT DEATH

26So the governor released Son of His Father (Barabbas) to them. He then turned over Creator Sets Free (Jesus) to the soldiers to be whipped with cowhide strips and then nailed to a tree-pole—the cross.

The People of Iron (Romans) used a whip with many strips of leather, each braided together with bone and metal. The victim would be tied to a large rock, exposing his bare back, and then lashed. The pieces of bone and metal would rip and tear the skin from the body, leaving the victim almost lifeless.

BEATEN AND MOCKED BY THE SOLDIERS

27The governor's soldiers dragged Creator Sets Free (Jesus) into the great hall of the governor's lodge, and all the soldiers there gathered around him. 28They stripped off his clothes, wrapped a fancy purple-and-red chief blanket around him, 29and twisted together a headdress from a thorn bush and pressed it onto his head. Then they put a chief's staff in his right hand and began to bow down before him.

"Honor to the chief of the tribes of Wrestles with Creator (Israel)!" they mocked him, *making a big show of it, insulting him with cruel words and twisted faces.*

30They spat on him and took his chief's staff and clubbed him with it. Then they took turns beating him on his head, over and over again. 31When they were done, they stripped him of the chief blanket, put his own garment back on him, and took him away to nail him to a tree-pole—the cross.

The People of Iron (Romans) used a wooden pole, with a crossbeam attached, to punish criminals and anyone who dared to rise up against their empire. The cross was used as an instrument of terror and torture to keep the people in fear of the People of Iron (Romans). It was one of the most painful and cruel ways to die ever created by human beings. The crucified person's feet were fastened with iron nails to the tree-pole and their hands to a crossbeam attached to the pole—where they remained until dead.

HIS TRAIL OF TEARS

The soldiers then put a heavy crossbeam on the back of Creator Sets Free (Jesus). But he stumbled under the weight, because he was weak from the beating he had endured, too weak to bear the burden.

³²On the way they came across Listening Man (Simon), from Land of Power (Cyrene) *in northern Africa.* The soldiers forced him to carry the cross for Creator Sets Free (Jesus).

NAILED TO THE CROSS

³³They came to Place of the Skull (Golgotha) ³⁴and gave him wine mixed with bitter herbs to drink, but after tasting it, he would not drink it. ³⁵*They stripped him of his garments and,* after they nailed his hands and feet to the cross, they gambled for his clothes. ³⁶The soldiers then sat down and kept watch over him.

³⁷Above his head on the crossbeam, *carved into a piece of wood,* was the accusation against him:

THIS IS CREATOR SETS FREE
CHIEF OF THE TRIBES
OF WRESTLES WITH CREATOR

³⁸Then they also nailed two outlaws to their crosses, one on his right side, the other on his left.

MOCKED BY HIS OWN PEOPLE

³⁹As people walked by and saw him, they spoke arrogantly to him, wagged their heads, ⁴⁰and said, "You who thought you could tear down the sacred lodge and rebuild it in three days—can you even save yourself? If you are the Son of the Great Spirit, then come down off that cross!"

⁴¹The head holy men, the scroll keepers, and the elders all joined in.

⁴²"He set others free," they said, "but he cannot even free himself. So he is the chief of the tribes of Wrestles with Creator (Israel), is he? Let him come down from the cross now, and then we will believe in him! ⁴³He said, 'I am the Son of the Great Spirit,' so let the one he has put his trust in come and rescue him now—if he wants him."

⁴⁴Even the thieves who were dying next to him joined in with the others and threw insults at him.

A TIME OF DARKNESS

⁴⁵At the sixth hour of the day clouds moved in and covered the land with darkness until the ninth hour.ᵃ

⁴⁶That is when Creator Sets Free (Jesus), speaking in his native language, cried out loud, "Eli, Eli, lama sabachthani"—which means, "O Great Spirit, my Creator, why have you left me alone?"ᵇ

⁴⁷Some of the people standing there heard him and said, "He is calling on the prophet Great Spirit Is Creator (Elijah) to help him."

ᵃ**27:45** From noon until midafternoon
ᵇ**27:46** Psalm 22:1

48One of them ran and soaked a cloth with the bitter wine, put it on a staff, and put it to his mouth. **49**But the others said, "Wait, let us see whether Great Spirit Is Creator (Elijah) will come and save him."

HE BREATHES HIS LAST

50But right then Creator Sets Free (Jesus), *with his dying breath*, lifted his voice *one last time* and with a loud cry gave up his spirit.

51Suddenly the earth began to quake. Large rocks cracked and shattered. Then in the sacred lodge the great heavy blanket that hung over the entry to the Most Holy Place was torn from top to bottom.

> For the first time the inner chamber, where only the chief holy man could go, was open to all.

52-53 The burial caves opened *as the stones that covered them broke into pieces*. After Creator Sets Free (Jesus) returned to life from the dead, many of the bodies of the holy ancestors were raised to life from their sleep of death. They came out from their burial caves and appeared to many in the Sacred Village of Peace (Jerusalem).

54When the head soldier of the People of Iron (Romans) and his soldiers who were guarding Creator Sets Free (Jesus) felt the earth shake and saw what was happening all around them, they trembled with fear and said, "This man must truly be the Son of the Great Spirit!"

WOMEN WHO SERVED HIM

55Many of the honored women who had walked the road with him from the time he was in Circle of Nations (Galilee) were there, watching from a distance. These were some of the women who had served him during his journeys. **56**Strong Tears (Mary) of the village of Creator's High Lodge (Magdala) and Brooding Tears (Mary), the mother of He Takes Charge (James) and He Increases (Joses), were among them, and also the mother of the two sons of Gift of Creator (Zebedee).

BURIED IN A NEW BURIAL CAVE

57A while before sunset, He Gets More (Joseph), a man of many possessions from the tribal village of High Mountain (Arimathea), who was also one who followed Creator Sets Free (Jesus), **58**went to Spear of the Great Waters (Pilate). He asked for the body of Creator Sets Free (Jesus) *so he could prepare it properly for burial.* The governor then gave him permission to take the body.

59He took the body and ceremonially wrapped it in a traditional way using a clean, soft blanket. **60**He then laid the body of Creator Sets Free (Jesus) in his own burial cave freshly cut from the rock hillside. He rolled a large stone in front of the cave and left.

SOLDIERS GUARD HIM

61Strong Tears (Mary) of the village of Creator's High Lodge (Magdala) and Brooding Tears (Mary) were also there sitting across the garden from the tomb.

62The next day, which was after the Day of Preparing, the head holy men and the Separated Ones (Pharisees) came to Spear of the Great Waters (Pilate).

63"Honored One," they said to him, "When he was still alive, that trickster Creator Sets Free (Jesus) said, 'On the third day I will come back from the dead.' **64**We must put an end to his lies or his followers could take his body away and tell the people he has come back from the dead, making things worse for all of us. So we are asking that you order your soldiers to guard the burial cave."

⁶⁵He said to them, "Take with you a good number of my soldiers and set them to guard the burial cave securely."

⁶⁶So they went and placed a seal over the great stone and set the guards to watch.

28

A NEW SUNRISE FOR A NEW WORLD

¹Then, on the first day of the week following the Day of Resting, as the sun began to rise, Strong Tears (Mary) of the village of Creator's High Lodge (Magdala) and Brooding Tears (Mary) went to see the burial cave.

²Suddenly the earth began to shake, and a spirit-messenger from the spirit-world above came down from the sky, walked to the burial cave, rolled the stone away—and sat down on it! ³He was shining as bright as a flash of lightning, and his regalia was pure white like *freshly fallen* snow.

⁴The soldiers staggered back, trembling with fear, and fell to the ground like dead men.

⁵⁻⁶"Do not fear!" the spirit-messenger said to the women. "The one you are looking for is not here. Creator Sets Free (Jesus), who was killed on the cross, has come back to life again—just as he said. Look! Here is where they laid him. ⁷Now hurry and go tell his followers that he has risen from the dead. Tell them he is going ahead of them to Circle of Nations (Galilee), and they will see him there. Now remember what I have told you!"

HE APPEARS TO THE WOMEN

⁸The women ran from the burial cave to bring the good news to his followers. Their hearts were trembling with fear and great joy. ⁹Suddenly, Creator Sets Free (Jesus) was standing in front of them.

"It is a good morning!" he *smiled and* said to them.

They came close, held tightly to his feet, and gave great honor to him.

¹⁰"Do not fear!" he told them. "Go and tell my brothers to go to Circle of Nations (Galilee), and there they will see me."

THE SOLDIERS ARE PAID TO KEEP QUIET

¹¹After the women had left the burial cave, some of the soldiers who were guarding the place went to Village of Peace (Jerusalem) and reported everything to the head holy men. ¹²So they gathered a council together to make a plan.

They decided to pay the soldiers well to make up a story. ¹³"Tell the people that his followers came and stole his body while you were sleeping," they said. ¹⁴"Do not worry about the governor hearing of this. We will pay him whatever it takes to keep you from trouble."

Normally the People of Iron (Romans) would have put to death any soldiers who would have let someone steal a body they had been ordered to guard.

¹⁵So the soldiers took the money and did as they were told, and even to this day their story has been told far and wide among all the tribes.

FINAL INSTRUCTIONS

It was now time for Creator Sets Free (Jesus) to return to the spirit-world above. It had now been forty days since he had come back to life again. So he gathered his followers, one last time, to give them their final instructions.

¹⁶The remaining eleven of his followers journeyed to Circle of Nations

(Galilee). There, at the mountain where Creator Sets Free (Jesus) had told them to go, they met with him. **17**When they saw him, they gave to him the honor he deserved—but there were some who still doubted.

18"All the authority of the spirit-world above and the earth below has been given to me," he told them. **19**"So now I am sending you into all nations to teach them how to walk the road with me. You will represent me as you perform the purification ceremony[a] with them, *initiating them into the life of beauty and harmony represented in* the name of the Father, Son, and Holy Spirit. **20**You will then teach them all the ways that I have instructed you to walk in."

Creator Sets Free (Jesus) then looked into their faces with love and great affection. He lifted his hands toward them and spoke these final blessing words over them.

"Never forget," he said *as he began to rise up into the spirit-world above.* "I will always be with you, *your invisible guide,* walking beside you, until the new age has fully come."

Aho! May it be so!

---

[a] **28:19** Baptism

WAR CLUB TELLS THE GOOD STORY

THE GOSPEL OF MARK

1 ◊▷◁◊▷◁◊▷◁◊▷◁◊▷◁◊▷◁◊▷

THE GOOD STORY BEGINS

¹This is the good story about the Chosen One, Creator Sets Free (Jesus), who is the Son of the Great Spirit. This story began long ago and was foretold in the Sacred Teachings by the ancient prophet Creator Will Help Us (Isaiah).

²"Behold!" Creator Will Help Us (Isaiah) said, *as he spoke the words of the Great Spirit.* "I am sending my messenger ahead of you to prepare the way. ³He will be a voice howling in the desert wilderness, 'Clear away the stones and make a straight path for the coming of the Honored One!'"[a]

PURIFICATION CEREMONY

⁴The prophesied messenger appeared in the desert wilderness. He came to tell everyone to turn from their wrong ways of thinking and return to the ways of the Great Spirit. The messenger's name was Gift of Goodwill (John). He came to perform the purification ceremony[b] to show people that they had been released from their broken ways.

⁵From the surrounding territory of the Land of Promise (Judea) and from Village of Peace (Jerusalem), all the people came to him to participate in his purification ceremony[b] performed in the river

Flowing Down (Jordan). As they came, they were admitting to their bad hearts and broken ways.

PREPARING THE WAY

⁶Gift of Goodwill (John) came wearing buffalo-skin[c] garments, with a cowhide sash around his waist. The food he ate was grasshoppers and wild honey.

⁷"I am preparing the way for the one who is greater and more powerful than I," he announced to all. "I am not even worthy to bend down and untie his moccasins. ⁸I perform the purification ceremony[c] with water, but he will perform the purification ceremony[b] with the Holy Spirit!"

CREATOR SETS FREE COMES FORWARD

⁹It was in those days that Creator Sets Free (Jesus) came from his home in Seed Planter Village (Nazareth) in the territory of Circle of Nations (Galilee), to have Gift of Goodwill (John) perform for him the purification ceremony.[b]

Creator Sets Free (Jesus) was a mature man of about thirty winters. The time had come for him to show himself to all the people and begin his great work. He waded out into the river to have Gift of Goodwill (John) perform the ceremony.

¹⁰As soon as Creator Sets Free (Jesus) came up from the water, he saw the sky open. The Spirit of Creator came down

---

[a]**1:3** Isaiah 40:3
[b]**1:4, 5, 8, 9** Baptism

[c]**1:6** Lit. *camel's hair*

like a dove and rested on him. **¹¹**Then a voice from the sky spoke *like distant thunder*, "This is my much-loved Son who makes my heart glad!"

HIS VISION QUEST

¹²Right then and there the Spirit drove Creator Sets Free (Jesus) into the desert wilderness. **¹³**For forty days and nights he remained there, surrounded by wild animals and being tested by Accuser (Satan)—the ancient trickster snake. Spirit-messengers also came to give him strength and comfort.

THE MESSAGE OF THE GOOD ROAD

¹⁴Then later, after Gift of Goodwill (John) was arrested, Creator Sets Free (Jesus) traveled to the territory of Circle of Nations (Galilee) to tell the good story.

¹⁵"The time has now come!" he said to the people. "Creator's good road is right in front of you. It is time to return to the right ways of thinking and doing! Put your trust in this good story I am bringing to you."

HIS FIRST FOLLOWERS

¹⁶As he walked along the shore of the Lake of Circle of Nations (Sea of Galilee), he saw two men, One Who Hears (Simon) and Stands with Courage (Andrew), throwing their nets into the lake, for they were fishermen.

¹⁷"Come! Walk the road with me," he called out to them, "and I will teach you how to net two-leggeds instead of fish!"

¹⁸Right then and there they dropped their nets and began to walk the road with him.

¹⁹He walked a little farther down the shore and saw two more men, the brothers He Takes Over (James) and He Shows Goodwill (John), the two sons of

Gift of Creator (Zebedee). They were sitting in their canoe and mending their nets. **²⁰**Right away he called out for them to walk the road with him. They dropped their nets, left their father behind with the hired help, and also became followers of Creator Sets Free (Jesus).

NEW TEACHING FOR NEW MEDICINE

Once a week on the Day of Resting the people would come together at the local village gathering house to learn the ways of the Great Spirit.

²¹Creator Sets Free (Jesus) took his new followers and went to Village of Comfort (Capernaum). When the next Day of Resting came, he went to the gathering house and began to teach the people. **²²**They were amazed at his manner of speaking, for, unlike the scroll keepers, he spoke *clearly and boldly* as one with authority.

²³Suddenly, a man controlled by an unclean spirit cried out loud, **²⁴**"Creator Sets Free (Jesus) from the Seed Planter Village (Nazareth), what are you doing here? Have you come to put an end to us? I know who you are! You are the Holy One from the Great Spirit!"

²⁵Creator Sets Free (Jesus) spoke sharply to the spirit. "Be silent!" he said. "Come out of him!"

²⁶The unclean spirit shook the man, threw him to the ground, and, howling with a loud voice, came out of him.

²⁷The people were dumbfounded and began to ask each other, "What is this teaching? What new medicine is this? He even tells the unclean spirits what to do—and they do it!"

²⁸His reputation spread like wildfire into the territory of Circle of Nations (Galilee) and to all the surrounding territories.

POWER OVER SICKNESS

[29]As soon as they left the gathering house, they went to the home of One Who Hears (Simon) and his brother Stands with Courage (Andrew). He Takes Over (James) and He Shows Goodwill (John) were with them.

[30]The wife of One Who Hears (Simon) was there. Her mother was sick in bed with a bad fever, so they asked Creator Sets Free (Jesus) to help her. [31]He went and stood by her, took her by the hand, and lifted her up. The fever left her *and she was healed.* Then *with a glad heart* she went to prepare a meal for them.

[32]Later that day, when the sun was going down, many sick people were brought to him, along with those who were tormented by evil spirits. [33]The whole village had gathered outside the door.

[34]He healed many with different illnesses and set others free from evil spirits, but he did not permit the spirits to speak, for they knew who he was.

[35]Early the next morning, before the sunrise, he left and found a quiet, out-of-the-way place to be alone and pray. [36]One Who Hears (Simon) and the others [37]found him and said, "Everyone is looking for you!"

[38]"It's time to go to the other villages and tell them the good story," Creator Sets Free (Jesus) said to them, "for that is what I came to do."

[39]So he traveled about all the territory of Circle of Nations (Galilee). He taught in their gathering houses and forced out many evil spirits.

HE HEALS A MAN WITH SKIN DISEASE

[40]*While in one of the villages,* a man with a skin disease all over his body came to Creator Sets Free (Jesus). He humbled himself, bowed down, and pleaded with him, "Honored One! If you want to, you can heal and cleanse me."

Under tribal law anyone with a skin disease was considered ceremonially unclean and could not participate in ceremonies or attend meetings at the gathering houses. If someone touched or was touched by an unclean person, they would be considered unclean until the sun set that day. So to help people avoid this, the diseased person was required to shout, "Unclean! Unclean!"

[41]Creator Sets Free (Jesus), stirred with compassion, reached out and touched the man. "I want to!" he said. "Be cleansed!"

[42]Right away the disease left him, and he was made clean.

[43]Creator Sets Free (Jesus) sent him away at once with a warning. [44]"Tell no one!" he instructed. "Go and show yourself to a holy man, so he can see with his own eyes. Have him perform the cleansing ceremony given to us by the lawgiver Drawn from the Water (Moses)."

But the man chose not to follow his instructions.

[45]Instead, he spread the news about his healing far and wide. Soon Creator Sets Free (Jesus) was unable to show his face in the local villages, so he stayed away from them. But the people continued to come to him from all directions.

2 ◀▶◀▶◀▶◀▶◀▶

HEALING AT VILLAGE OF COMFORT

[1]After many days Creator Sets Free (Jesus) went back to Village of Comfort (Capernaum), but word got out that he had returned home. [2]So many people had gathered in the house that there was no

more room. Even the entrance was blocked. Creator Sets Free (Jesus) began to teach the people there [3]when four men came carrying a paralyzed man on a sleeping mat, [4]but they could not get past the crowd. In their desperation, they climbed up to the rooftop and broke through the roof right above Creator Sets Free (Jesus). They lowered the paralyzed man down, sleeping bundle and all.

[5]When he saw their faith in him, he said to the paralyzed man, "Young man, you are released from your broken ways *and the things in your heart that are not true to Creator's good road.*"

WHO CAN FORGIVE BROKEN WAYS?

[6]There were some scroll keepers there who began to wonder in their hearts, [7]"Who is this man to speak against the Great Spirit with such disrespect? Who but the Maker of Life can release a man from his wrongdoings?"

Under tribal law the only way to be forgiven for broken ways or wrongdoings was to go to the sacred lodge and have a ceremony performed by a holy man. By releasing this man from his broken ways, Creator Sets Free (Jesus) was claiming to have the right to do this himself, which, to the spiritual leaders, was wrong.

[8]In his spirit, Creator Sets Free (Jesus) knew right away what they were thinking and said to them, "Why are your hearts full of these thoughts? [9]Is it easier to tell a paralyzed man, 'Get up and walk,' or to say to him, 'You are released from your wrongdoings'?"

The room became quiet as he waited for an answer from them.

[10]"This is how you will know that the True Human Being has the right to forgive bad hearts and broken ways on this earth."

[11]He turned to the paralyzed man and said, "Get up, roll up your sleeping bundle, and walk home."

[12]Right away the man stood up, and, in front of them all, he rolled up his sleeping bundle and walked out.

Great amazement filled the hearts of all who were in the house as they gave praise to Creator.

"Who has ever seen this kind of mysterious and powerful medicine?" they asked.

EATING WITH OUTCASTS

[13]After this, Creator Sets Free (Jesus) went once again to walk by the lake shore. A large crowd followed him there, so he was teaching them. [14]As he walked the shore, he saw a tribal tax collector named He Brings Together (Levi), the son of First to Change (Alphaeus) sitting at his tax booth.

"Come," Creator Sets Free (Jesus) said to him, "and walk the road with me."

He Brings Together (Levi) got up from his tax booth, left that life behind him, and became a follower of Creator Sets Free (Jesus).

Tribal tax collectors were often Tribal Members who were given the right to collect taxes for the People of Iron (Romans). They could force their own people, under the threat of violence, to pay them. To make a living, they would take more than the People of Iron (Romans) required. But many of them became greedy and took even more than they were permitted. They were hated and looked down on by the people.

[15]Creator Sets Free (Jesus) went to a feast at the home of He Brings Together

(Levi) and sat down to eat with the guests. There were many other tribal tax collectors and other outcasts also sitting with Creator Sets Free (Jesus) and his close followers, for many outcasts had become his followers.

16When the Separated Ones (Pharisees) and the scroll keepers saw Creator Sets Free (Jesus) eating with outcasts, they complained to his close followers, saying, "Why does your wisdomkeeper keep company with tribal tax collectors and other outcasts?"

17Creator Sets Free (Jesus) overheard them and said, "People who are well do not need medicine. I have not come to the ones who are already walking the good road, but to help the bad-hearted and broken ones find the way back home."

NEW WAYS FOR OLD

It was a common practice among the tribal people to go without food to help their prayers and for other spiritual reasons. Sometimes it was done out of sadness and sorrow for a friend or a family member's troubles.

18Some of the followers of Gift of Goodwill (John) and the Separated Ones (Pharisees) were ceremonially going without food, so they came to Creator Sets Free (Jesus).

"Why do your followers feast," they questioned him, "instead of going without food and praying often like we do?"

19"Do you expect wedding guests to be sad and go without eating when the groom is hosting a feast?" he answered. "No! As long as the groom is there with them, they will feast! 20But the time will come when he is taken from them. Then they will be sad and go without eating."

They still did not understand, so he gave them a wise saying.

21"No one uses a new piece of cloth to patch an old garment, for it would shrink and make the tear worse. 22No one puts new wine into old wineskins, for the new wine would burst the skins. New and fresh wineskins are what is needed."

CHIEF OVER THE DAY OF RESTING

23On a Day of Resting, Creator Sets Free (Jesus) and his followers were walking through a field of grain. The men were hungry, so as they walked, they plucked some grain to eat.

24When the Separated Ones (Pharisees) saw what they were doing, they said to him, "Why do your followers do what is not permitted on the Day of Resting?"

25He answered them, "Have you not heard about the time long ago when *the great chief* Much Loved One (David) was hungry? 26How he and his followers went into Creator's ceremonial lodge, when Father of Plenty (Abiathar) was the chief holy man, and ate the ceremonial bread? Only the holy men are permitted to eat this bread.

27"Human beings were not made for the Day of Resting. Instead, the Day of Resting was made for human beings. 28So then, the True Human Being is Chief over the Day of Resting!"

3

DOING GOOD ON THE DAY OF RESTING

1Creator Sets Free (Jesus) then went to their gathering house to teach. A man was there with a shriveled and useless hand. 2The Separated Ones (Pharisees) kept a close eye on Creator Sets Free (Jesus) to see whether he would heal the man on the Day of Resting, so they could accuse him.

³Creator Sets Free (Jesus) said to the man with the useless hand, "Stand up and come forward."

⁴Then he turned to the Separated Ones (Pharisees) and asked, "On the Day of Resting, is it permitted to help or to harm, to rescue life or destroy it?"

They just glared at him and said nothing.

⁵There was fire in his eyes as he looked around the room. His anger turned to sorrow when he saw their hearts of stone. He turned to the man and said, "Stretch out your hand."

He stretched it out, and it was the same as his good hand!

⁶The Separated Ones (Pharisees) stormed out right away and went straight to the Friends of Looks Brave (Herodians) to conspire with them about how to do away with Creator Sets Free (Jesus).

CREATOR'S CHOSEN SERVANT

⁷Creator Sets Free (Jesus) and the ones who walked the road with him left that place and went to the lake. ⁸Word about him drew large crowds from Circle of Nations (Galilee), Land of Promise (Judea), and Village of Peace (Jerusalem). They also came from Red Land (Idumea), from the territory beyond the river Flowing Down (Jordan), from Rock Land (Tyre) and Hunting Grounds (Sidon).

⁹He asked his followers to keep a canoe close by, in case the crowd pressed in too close and crushed him. ¹⁰His reputation as a healer had made the sick desperate to reach out and touch him.

¹¹When the ones with evil spirits saw him, they would fall down at his feet and wail, "You are the Son of the Great Spirit!" ¹²But he warned them over and over again not to tell anyone who he was.

TWELVE MESSAGE BEARERS

¹³Creator Sets Free (Jesus) went up the mountain and gathered to himself some of his followers. ¹⁴⁻¹⁵He chose twelve of them to learn his ways by being with him, so he could send them out to tell the good story and to have the power to force out evil spirits. He called them his message bearers.

¹⁶Here are the names of the twelve he chose:

Stands on the Rock (Peter), the name he gave to One Who Hears (Simon); ¹⁷He Takes Over (James) the son of Gift of Creator (Zebedee) and his brother He Shows Goodwill (John), whom he also called Sons of Thunder; ¹⁸Stands with Courage (Andrew); Friend of Horses (Philip); Son of Ground Digger (Bartholomew); Gift from Creator (Matthew); Looks Like His Brother (Thomas); He Takes Charge (James) the son of First to Change (Alphaeus); Strong of Heart (Thaddaeus); One Who Listens (Simon) the Firebrand (Zealot); ¹⁹and Speaks Well Of (Judas), the one who would betray him.

HE HAS LOST HIS MIND

²⁰Creator Sets Free (Jesus) then returned to his house in Village of Comfort (Capernaum). Just like before, a large crowd gathered there—so many that he and his followers were not even able to eat. ²¹When his relatives heard about this, they tried to take him away from there, because the people were saying, "He has lost his mind!"

ACCUSED BY THE SPIRITUAL LEADERS

²²The scroll keepers from Village of Peace (Jerusalem) were there also.

"He stands with Worthless Ruler (Beelzebul)," they accused him, "for his power to force out evil spirits comes from the one who rules over them."

²³So Creator Sets Free (Jesus) gathered them around himself and spoke to them with wise sayings such as these:

"How can Accuser (Satan), that evil trickster, force out evil spirits? Can he defeat himself? ²⁴If a nation wars against itself, that nation cannot stand. ²⁵A family that fights against itself will fall. ²⁶In the same way, if Accuser (Satan) rises up against himself, then how will he continue to rule?

²⁷"No one can enter the house of a strongman and take away his goods, unless he first defeats him. Then he can take away his goods.

²⁸"I speak from my heart, humankind will be released from all their wrong-doing and evil speaking, ²⁹but whoever speaks evil of the Holy Spirit will not be released. This wrongdoing will follow them into the world to come and to the end of all days."

³⁰He said this because they were saying of Creator Sets Free (Jesus), "He has an evil spirit."

ALL MY RELATIVES

³¹Then his mother and brothers came to him outside the house and sent word to him to come out to them. ³²The crowd that was sitting *in a circle* around him said, "Look, your relatives are outside looking for you."

³³"Who are my relatives?" he asked them ³⁴as he looked around at the circle of people. "Here they are! ³⁵The ones who walk in the ways of the Great Spirit are all my relatives—my mother, my brothers and my sisters."

4

SEED PLANTER STORY

¹Creator Sets Free (Jesus) returned to the lakeshore and once again a very large crowd gathered around him. They pressed in so close that he got into a canoe and pushed out a little way from shore, while the people stayed at the shoreline. ²He then began to tell them stories to teach them about the ways of Creator's good road.

³"Listen!" he said. "A seed planter went to plant some seeds and began to scatter them about on the ground.

⁴"Some seeds fell on the village pathway, *but people walked on them*, and the winged ones pecked at the seeds and ate them all.

⁵"Some of the seeds fell on the rocks where there was only a little dirt. The plants sprouted up quickly, ⁶but when the sun came out, they dried up because the roots were not deep enough.

⁷"Other seeds fell into the weeds, and thistles sprouted around the seeds and choked the life out of them. None of these plants grew for a harvest.

⁸"But some seeds fell on good ground, grew strong, and gave a harvest of thirty, sixty, and even one hundred times as much."

⁹Then he said, "Let the one who has ears hear the meaning of this story."

THE REASON FOR STORIES

¹⁰Later, when the twelve message bearers and other followers were alone with him, they asked why he taught with stories.

¹¹He answered them, "To my close followers the honor has been given to understand about the mysterious ways of Creator's good road. This honor is not given to those who are not my close followers. The stories are to help them, ¹²because, 'When they look, they cannot see clearly what is in front of them. When they hear, they do not understand

the meaning. If they did, then they would return to Creator and be released from their broken ways.'ᵃ

MEANING OF THE SEED PLANTER STORY

¹³"If you do not understand this story, then how will you understand any of my stories?" he answered.

¹⁴"The seed in this story is the message about Creator's good road.

¹⁵"The village pathway represents the ones who hear but do not understand the message. Accuser (Satan), the evil trickster snake, sneaks up and snatches it away from them.

¹⁶"The rocky ground represents the ones who hear and receive the message with a glad heart, ¹⁷but because they have no roots, their faith is shallow and does not last. As soon as the message brings them trouble or opposition, they stumble and lose their way.

¹⁸"The weeds and thistles represent the ones who have heard the message, ¹⁹but they are too busy worrying about their earthly existence. This makes them stray away from the good road, wanting more and more possessions, thinking this will make them happy. The message is choked, and their faith stops growing.

²⁰"The good ground represents the ones with good and pure hearts. When they hear and understand the message, they hold on tightly to it until it grows into a harvest—thirty, sixty, and even one hundred times as great!

LIGHT SHINES IN THE DARKNESS

²¹"No one hides a torch behind a blanket or under a sleeping bundle. No! A torch belongs up high on a pole, where it can give light to everyone. ²²Nothing that has been hidden can stay a secret, and what has been covered up in darkness will be exposed by the light. ²³The ones who have ears—hear this!"

²⁴Then he added, "You must listen with an open heart. ²⁵The ones who do so will gain wisdom and be ready for more—much more. But the ones who close their hearts *to my teaching*, even what little they have will be taken away.

MORE STORIES ABOUT THE GOOD ROAD

²⁶"Here is another way to see Creator's good road," he said. "It is like a man who plants seed into the earth. ²⁷Day or night, awake or asleep, the seed grows without the man knowing how or doing anything. ²⁸The earth makes the seed grow without any help. First the stem, then the head, and finally the grain appears. ²⁹Once it is ripe, the time has come, and right away it is harvested.

³⁰"What is Creator's good road like?" he asked. "What can I compare it to? What story will help us see its meaning?

MUSTARD SEED WISDOM

³¹⁻³²"It is like a single grain of mustard seed,ᵇ one of the smallest of seeds. But when planted in a garden, it grows larger than all the other plants and takes over the garden. It becomes a great tree with many branches, large enough for the winged ones who soar in the sky to find lodging in its shade."

³³So Creator Sets Free (Jesus) taught the people with many stories like these. He would tell them as much as they were able to hear. ³⁴He would only use stories to teach the crowds, but then in private he would tell the full meaning to the ones who walked the road with him.

ᵃ**4:12** Jeremiah 5:21; Isaiah 6:9-10

ᵇ**4:31-32** The mustard plant was used as an herbal medicine.

POWER OVER STORMS

35On that same day, as the sun began to set, Creator Sets Free (Jesus) said to his followers, "Let us cross over to the other side of the lake."

36So they left the crowd and climbed into the canoe with him and pushed off from shore along with some other canoes. **37**A storm was moving in, and a fierce wind drove the waves into the canoe and threatened to swamp it.

They paddled harder, trying desperately to keep the canoe from sinking, but the wind and waves were too much for them. They were filled with fear and about to sink and needed help from their Wisdomkeeper.

38But Creator Sets Free (Jesus), *weary from a long, hard day*, was in the back of the canoe—sleeping on a soft blanket! They shook him awake and cried out loud, "Wisdomkeeper! Do you not care that we are fighting for our lives?"

39He stood up and spoke sharply to the wind and said to the raging waters, "Calm down and be still!"

Right then and there the wind died down, and a great peace fell upon the surface of the water.

40He then *turned to his followers and said to them*, "Why have you given yourselves over to fear? Where is your faith?"

41They all began to tremble with fear. They shook their heads with wonder and whispered to each other, "Who is this man? Even the wind and the waves do what he says!"

5

TERRITORY OF MANY SPIRITS

1When they finished crossing the lake, they came to the territory of Many Spirits (Gerasenes). **2**As soon as Creator Sets Free (Jesus) stepped from the canoe, a man who was tormented by an unclean spirit came up to him. **3**This man had been living at the local burial grounds, and no one could bind him, not even with iron chains.

4The people of the village had tried to capture the man and tie him down, but he would tear their ropes and break their chains. No one was strong enough to overpower him. **5**Day and night he wandered about the burial grounds and into the mountains. He would never stop wailing and cutting himself with sharp stones. **6**When the man saw Creator Sets Free (Jesus) from a distance, he ran up to him and fell down before him.

7"Creator Sets Free (Jesus), Son of the One Above Us All, what are you going to do with us?" the unclean spirits cried out through the man. "Promise me by the Great Spirit that you will not torment us."

8The unclean spirits said this because Creator Sets Free (Jesus) had said to the man, "Come out of him, you unclean spirit!"

9Then Creator Sets Free (Jesus) asked, "What is the name of the spirit you represent?"

"Our name is Many Soldiers,"[a] the evil spirits answered, "for our numbers are great."

The spirits feared Creator Sets Free (Jesus) and knew he could force them out of the man.

A HERD OF PIGS

10They kept begging him not to send them out of the territory. **11**There was a large herd of about two thousand pigs

---

[a] **5:9** Lit. *Legion*, a segment of the occupying Roman army of about five thousand soldiers

feeding nearby on the side of a mountain. ¹²"Send us to those pigs over there," they begged, "so we can enter into them." ¹³So he gave them permission. The unclean spirits then came out of the man and entered into the herd of about two thousand pigs. Then the whole herd stampeded down the mountainside headlong into the lake and drowned *in the deep water, making a frightful scene.* ¹⁴The local ones who were watching over the pigs rushed away, shaken and afraid. They went to the nearby village and told everyone all that happened. As word spread, people came from the villages and the countryside to see for themselves.

SET FREE AND MADE WHOLE

¹⁵There they found the man who had been tormented by the unclean spirits, sitting quietly at the feet of Creator Sets Free (Jesus). He was clothed and in his right mind. The people trembled with fear ¹⁶as they listened to the story of how the man was set free and to the story about the pigs. ¹⁷So they begged Creator Sets Free (Jesus) to go away from their land.

¹⁸As Creator Sets Free (Jesus) was climbing into his canoe to leave, the man who had been set free from the evil spirits begged him to take him along. ¹⁹But Creator Sets Free (Jesus) would not permit it and said to the man, "Return home to your family and friends. Tell them all the good and kind things the Great Spirit has done for you." ²⁰The man went his way and told the story far and wide in all the territory of the Ten Villages (Decapolis) of what Creator Sets Free (Jesus) had done for him—and all who heard were amazed.

A DESPERATE REQUEST

²¹Creator Sets Free (Jesus) *and his followers* canoed back to the other side of the lake. As soon as he arrived, a great crowd began to gather around him at the lakeshore.

²²A man named He Gives Light (Jairus), a headman of the local gathering house, *pushed his way through the crowd and* fell down on his knees in front of Creator Sets Free (Jesus).

²³"My little girl is almost dead!" he begged him urgently. "She is my only daughter. Please come and lay your hands on her that she may be healed and live!"

²⁴So Creator Sets Free (Jesus) went with him. The crowd also trailed along, pressing in around him from all sides.

WHO TOUCHED ME?

²⁵There was a woman in the crowd who had been bleeding for more than twelve winters. ²⁶She had spent all she had, putting up with medicine men who were not able to heal her, and she was getting worse.

Under tribal law this woman would be considered unclean and even the things she touched would be unclean also, isolating her from friends and family. She would not be able to marry or participate in the gathering house for prayer.

²⁷When she heard about Creator Sets Free (Jesus), she pressed through the crowd and came up close behind him. She reached out her hand and touched his outer garment, ²⁸for she had said to herself, "If I can only touch his clothes, I know I will be healed."

²⁹She touched him, and right away the blood stopped flowing and she felt in her body that she was healed.

³⁰Creator Sets Free (Jesus) stopped suddenly, turned, looked around the crowd, and said, "Who touched my clothes?" For he was aware that power had gone out from him.

Fear gripped the heart of this woman, for she had not announced herself as unclean, and even worse, she had touched a spiritual leader. The crowd might turn against her or even have her stoned to death. So she remained silent and said nothing.

³¹His followers *looked around, shrugged their shoulders, and* said to him, "You can see that the crowds are pushing and shoving you. How can you say, 'Who touched me?'"

³²Creator Sets Free (Jesus) continued to look around to see who had touched him. ³³The woman knew she could hide no longer, so she came forward trembling with fear, fell to the ground in front of him, and told the whole truth.

³⁴"Daughter," he said to her *with great loving kindness in his eyes,* "your trust in me has made you well. Now go in peace, for you have been healed of your disease."

POWER OVER DEATH

³⁵While Creator Sets Free (Jesus) was still speaking, some messengers came from the home of the headman of the gathering house.

"Your little girl has crossed over to death," they said *with sad faces.* "Why trouble the Wisdomkeeper any longer?"

The man's heart fell to the ground, and grief began to creep over him.

³⁶But Creator Sets Free (Jesus) paid no attention to what was said.

"Do not fear!" he said to the headman. "Trust in me alone, *and all will be well.*"

³⁷He would not permit any to go with him except Stands on the Rock (Peter) and He Takes Over (James) along with his brother He Shows Goodwill (John)—*his most trusted message bearers.*

³⁸As they came near the house of the headman, they saw and heard an uproar! People were weeping and wailing loudly.

³⁹When he entered into the house, Creator Sets Free (Jesus) said to them, "Why are you making such a noise? Do not weep. The child is not dead. She only sleeps."

⁴⁰But they only scorned and laughed at him, *for they knew she was dead.*

WAKE UP!

So he put them all out of the house except his most trusted message bearers and the father and mother. He went with them into where the girl lay, ⁴¹took hold of her hand, and said in his native language, "Talitha cumi," meaning, "Little girl, wake up!"

⁴²She stood up right away and began to walk, for she was twelve winters old. Her father and mother stood there, amazed beyond words, *weeping for joy, for their little girl was alive!*

⁴³Creator Sets Free (Jesus) had them give her some food to eat and then firmly told them not to tell anyone what had happened.

6

HIS OWN VILLAGE REJECTS HIM

¹Creator Sets Free (Jesus) and his followers left there and went to Seed Planter Village (Nazareth), where he grew up as a boy. ²On the following Day of Resting at the local gathering house, he

began to teach the people. When they heard him, they were amazed and wondered at his words.

"Where did he learn about these things?" they asked *with contempt in their voices.* "Who gave him this wisdom and ability to perform such powerful medicine? ³Is he not the wood carver, son of Bitter Tears (Mary) and brother to He Leads the Way (James), He Gives More (Joseph), Strong of Heart (Jude), and He Hears (Simon)? Look, his sisters are also here with us!"

And so they were offended and turned their faces away from him.

⁴"A prophet is given much honor," he said to them, "except in his own village, among his own clan and relatives, and even in his own family."

⁵Because of this he could do no great miracles among them, except to touch and heal a few sick people. ⁶He was troubled by their lack of trust in him. So he left his boyhood village and went about teaching in other villages.

HE SENDS HIS MESSAGE BEARERS

⁷He then gathered his twelve message bearers together, gave them power over unclean evil spirits, and began to send them out two by two. ⁸He told them to take nothing with them except a walking stick—no traveling bundle, food, or money pouches. ⁹They were to wear only one outer garment and have one pair of moccasins for their feet.

¹⁰"When you come to a village, stay in one home until you leave. ¹¹If no one in that village welcomes you or will listen to your message, then go from there and shake the dust from your moccasins as a sign against them."

¹²So the twelve went out traveling two by two, and everywhere they went, they told people to return to Creator's right ways. ¹³They forced out evil spirits and poured herbal oils on many who were sick and healed them.

LOOKS BRAVE WONDERS ABOUT HIM

¹⁴The reputation of Creator Sets Free (Jesus) reached the ears of Chief Looks Brave (Herod). Some told him, "Gift of Goodwill (John) has come back from the world of the dead. That is why he can work so much power!"

¹⁵At the same time others said, "He must be Great Spirit Is Creator (Elijah)," and still others said, "He is a prophet! Just like one of the ancient prophets."

¹⁶But Looks Brave (Herod), after hearing all this, said, "Gift of Goodwill (John), the one whose head I cut off, has come back from the dead *to haunt me.*"

¹⁷⁻¹⁸He said this because he was the one who had Gift of Goodwill (John) arrested and put in prison. Gift of Goodwill (John) had spoken out against Looks Brave (Herod) for marrying the wife of his brother Friend of Horses (Philip).

"It is not permitted in the Sacred Teachings for you to be with your brother's wife!" he told Looks Brave (Herod).

¹⁹So Daring Woman (Herodias) held this against Gift of Goodwill (John) and wanted to kill him. ²⁰But Looks Brave (Herod) knew he was a man who walked in an upright and holy manner, so he was afraid and protected him. From time to time Looks Brave (Herod) liked to sit and listen to Gift of Goodwill (John), even though his words troubled him.

A DAY OF SORROW

²¹Daring Woman (Herodias) was waiting for a chance to have him killed. This chance came on the birthday of Looks

Brave (Herod). He had a great feast prepared to celebrate his birthday and invited government officials, head soldiers, and important dignitaries from Circle of Nations (Galilee).

22-23The daughter of Daring Woman (Herodias) came in and danced before them, pleasing Looks Brave (Herod) and all the guests.

"Ask anything from me and I will give it to you," he said to her, making a solemn promise, "up to half of all that I rule over."

24So she went out to her mother and said, "What shall I ask for?"

"Ask for the head of Gift of Goodwill (John), the one who performs the purification ceremony,"[a] she replied *with a sly grin on her face.*

25Right away she hurried back to the feast, went right up to the chief, and said, "Give to me, here and now, the head of Gift of Goodwill (John) in a basket!"

26The heart of Chief Looks Brave (Herod) fell to the ground, but because he had made a solemn promise in front of his guests, he could not refuse her request. 27So right then he ordered a soldier to bring him the head of Gift of Goodwill (John). So the soldier went to where he was in prison and cut off his head. 28He brought his head to the young girl in a basket, and she gave it to her mother.

29Now, when the followers of Gift of Goodwill (John) heard about his *tragic* death, they came for his body and buried it properly.

THE MESSAGE BEARERS RETURN

30The message bearers returned from their journeys and *with full hearts* told Creator Sets Free (Jesus) about all that they had done and taught. 31There were so many people coming and going all around them that they did not even have time to eat.

So Creator Sets Free (Jesus) said to them, "Come with me, and we will find a quiet place in the wilderness to rest for a while."

32Then they left in a canoe to go to an out-of-the-way place to be alone and rest. 33But the people saw where they were going and ran ahead of them. They came from all the surrounding villages and were waiting for them when they arrived.

34As Creator Sets Free (Jesus) climbed out of the canoe, he saw the great crowd of people, and his heart went out to them again. He saw that they were like sheep with no shepherd to watch over them. He stayed there with them and began to teach and tell them stories *about Creator's good road.*

A MEAL FOR FIVE THOUSAND

35It was late in the day, so his followers said to him, "This is a deserted place, and the day is almost over. 36We should send the people away to the villages in the countryside so they can find food to eat."

Creator Sets Free (Jesus) looked around at the great crowd of people—over five thousand men and also women and children. Then he turned and looked right at his followers.

37"You feed them!" he said to them.

They could not believe their ears! How could they feed so many people?

"It would take over eight moons' worth of gathered food to feed all these," they answered him. "Do you want us to go and trade for that much?"

---

[a] 6:24 Baptism

³⁸Then he said to them, "Go and see how many pieces of frybread we have." After looking around they said, "We have five pieces of frybread and two fish."

³⁹Then Creator Sets Free (Jesus) instructed the people to sit down in groups on the green grass. ⁴⁰So the people *gathered up their traveling bundles and their children and* sat down, some in groups of one hundred and some in groups of fifty.

⁴¹Then he took the five pieces of frybread and two fish *and held them up to the sky.* He looked up into the spirit-world above and spoke words of blessing over them. He broke the frybread into smaller pieces and gave them to his followers to give to the people. Then he did the same with the fish.

⁴²Everyone ate until they could eat no more. ⁴³When they gathered up the leftovers, there were twelve baskets full. ⁴⁴The number of men fed in this great gathering of people was about five thousand!

⁴⁵Right away Creator Sets Free (Jesus) urged his followers to get into their canoe and sent them ahead to the other side of the lake toward House of Fishing (Bethsaida), while he sent the crowd on their way. ⁴⁶He then left them and went up by himself into the mountainside to send his voice to the Great Spirit.

HE WALKS ON WATER

⁴⁷As the sun was setting, his followers were still in the canoe out in the middle of the lake, while Creator Sets Free (Jesus) was alone on the land. ⁴⁸He could see them paddling hard against the wind. Then, early in the morning, just before sunrise, he walked out on the lake and was going to pass right past them.

⁴⁹His followers looked out *in the dim light* and saw him walking on the lake. Thinking he was a ghost, ⁵⁰they wailed and cried out loud as fear took hold of them.

Right away Creator Sets Free (Jesus) called out to them, "Do not fear. Take heart. It is I!"

⁵¹He then came to them and climbed into the canoe as the wind calmed down. His followers were amazed beyond words, for their hearts were still too hard. ⁵²Even the miracle of the frybread and fishes did not open their eyes *to see who Creator Sets Free (Jesus) truly was.*

⁵³They came to shore at the village of Chief Garden (Gennesaret) and tied their canoe to a rock. ⁵⁴As soon as they got out of their canoe, the people recognized Creator Sets Free (Jesus). ⁵⁵So they ran to all the nearby villages, gathered up the sick on their sleeping bundles, and brought them to Creator Sets Free (Jesus). ⁵⁶Wherever he would go—into villages, camps, or in the countryside—they would take the sick, lay them in front of the trading posts, and beg him to let them touch the fringes of his clothes. And all who touched him were healed.

7 ◆▸◀◆▸◀◆▸◀◆▸◀◆▸◀◆▸◀◆

TRADITIONS MADE BY MEN

¹The Separated Ones (Pharisees) and some of the scroll keepers had come from Village of Peace (Jerusalem). *Like hungry wolves* they gathered around Creator Sets Free (Jesus).

They were looking for ways to accuse him and make him look bad in the eyes of the people, for they were jealous of his reputation.

[2]They noticed that some of his followers had not ceremonially washed their hands before eating the food.

[3]The Separated Ones (Pharisees) and many of the tribal people will not eat until they ceremonially wash their hands, following the traditions of the elders. [4]They will not eat the food offered at the trading posts unless it is first purified by washing. They also follow many other traditions, such as the washing of drinking cups, bowls, and even the benches they sit on.

[5]So the Separated Ones (Pharisees) and the scroll keepers asked him, "Why do your followers not walk in the traditions of the elders and ceremonially wash their hands before eating?"

[6]"Your false faces do not fool me," he answered back, "The prophet Creator Will Help Us (Isaiah) was talking about you when he said in the Sacred Teachings: 'These people honor me with their lips, but their hearts are far away from me. [7]Their prayers are empty words and their ceremonies are for show. Their teachings are nothing but rules made up by weak human beings.'[a]"

He paused to let these words sink into their ears.

[8]Then he said to them, "You ignore the instructions given by the Great Spirit and use your traditions to make yourselves look good to others. [9]You are as sly as a coyote in the way you set aside Creator's instructions and replace them with your traditions.

[10]"The lawgiver Drawn from the Water (Moses) said, 'Give honor to your father and mother,'[b] and, 'The ones who dishonor them should be put to death.'[c] [11]But your tradition says, 'If someone says to their father or mother, "I have given to the Great Spirit the things that were meant to honor and take care of you," [12]then they no longer have to honor and care for their parents.' [13]This is only one of the many ways you use your traditions to do away with the words of the Great Spirit."

WHAT MAKES ONE IMPURE?

[14]Creator Sets Free (Jesus) then gathered the people around him and said, "Listen with your hearts and understand what I tell you. [15]There is nothing you can take into your mouth that will make you impure. It is what comes out of your mouth that makes you impure."[d]

[17]Later when they entered a house away from the crowds, the ones who walked the road with him asked the meaning of his wise saying.

[18-19]"Why do you also not understand?" he answered. "When food enters the mouth, it goes into the stomach, not the heart, and then out of the body."

In saying this, Creator Sets Free (Jesus) declared that nothing you eat can make you impure.

[20]"It is what comes out of a person, from within, that makes one impure. [21]From people's bad hearts and broken ways come worthless plans, sexual impurity, stealing, killing, [22]unfaithfulness in marriage, greed, evil doings, forked tongues, uncontrolled desires, selfish ways, speaking evil of others, boastful talk, and foolish ways. [23]It is things like this that make a person impure, *not failing to wash one's hands.*"

---

[a]7:7 Isaiah 29:13
[b]7:10 Exodus 20:12; Deuteronomy 5:16
[c]7:10 Exodus 21:17; Leviticus 20:9
[d]7:15 Some ancient manuscripts add verse 16: *The ones with ears to hear should listen and understand.*

HE HEALS THE DAUGHTER OF AN OUTSIDER

²⁴From there Creator Sets Free (Jesus) journeyed into the territory of Rock Land (Tyre) and Hunting Grounds (Sidon). He wanted to keep away from the crowds, so he found a house to stay out of sight but was unable to stay hidden.

²⁵⁻²⁶A woman came to him who had a daughter with an unclean spirit in her. As soon as she heard about Creator Sets Free (Jesus), she came and humbled herself before him. She was an Outsider[a] from the territory along the coastline of the Great Middle Sea (Mediterranean).[b] She begged Creator Sets Free (Jesus) to force the evil spirit out of her daughter.

²⁷"The children should be fed first," he said. "It is not right to take the children's portion and throw it to the dogs."

²⁸"But Wisdomkeeper," she answered back, "even the dogs under the table can eat the children's crumbs."

²⁹"Because your words are well chosen," he replied, "you may return home. You will find that the evil spirit has left your daughter."

³⁰The woman went home and found her daughter resting on her sleeping mat—the evil spirit had left her.

A POWERFUL HEALING

³¹From the territory of Rock Land (Tyre) Creator Sets Free (Jesus) went through Hunting Grounds (Sidon) to the Lake of Circle of Nations (Sea of Galilee) in the territory of the Ten Villages (Decapolis). ³²The people who lived there brought a man who could not hear or speak right. They begged Creator Sets Free (Jesus) to lay his hands on him. ³³So he took the man away from the crowd. When he was alone with him, he put his fingers into the man's ears, and then spit and touched the man's tongue.

³⁴He then looked up into the spirit-world above, let out a deep breath, and said in his native language, "Ephphatha!" which means, "Be opened."

³⁵Right then the man's ears were opened and his tongue was released. He could now hear and speak clearly! ³⁶Creator Sets Free (Jesus) then instructed the people to tell no one. But the more he told them not to, the more they told the story to others. ³⁷The people were amazed beyond belief and full of wonder. "He does all things well!" they told everyone. "He even heals the ones who cannot hear or speak!"

8

FOUR THOUSAND HUNGRY PEOPLE

¹On another one of those days a great crowd had gathered, and, like the time before, they were hungry with nothing to eat.

Creator Sets Free (Jesus) called his followers to his side and said to them, ²"I am concerned for all these people, for they have been with us for three days with no food. ³Some of them have come from a great distance, and if I send them away hungry, they might lose their strength and faint."

⁴"This is a desolate and out-of-the-way place," they answered him. "Where could we find enough food to feed all these people?"

⁵"How much frybread do we have?" he asked.

"We have seven pieces of frybread," they answered.

⁶Creator Sets Free (Jesus) instructed all the people to sit down on the ground. He

---

ª**7:25-26** Lit. *a Greek*
ᵇ**7:25-26** Lit. *a Syrophoenician by birth*

then took the seven pieces of frybread, gave thanks, and broke them into smaller pieces. He gave them to his followers, and they gave them out to the people.

7They also had a few small fish, so he prayed a blessing over them and told them to give them out as well.

8Everyone ate as much as they wanted, and when they were done eating, his followers gathered up the leftovers—seven baskets full! **9**They had fed about four thousand men *and also women and children.* He then sent the crowd on their way.

10Right away he climbed into the canoe with his twelve followers and went to the territory of Slow Burning Coals (Dalmanutha).

NO SIGN WILL BE GIVEN

11While they were there, the Separated Ones (Pharisees) came to argue with him. They asked from him a sign from the spirit-world above to prove who he was. **12**"Why do the people of this generation need a sign?" he asked as he breathed out a sigh from his spirit. "I tell you from my heart, this generation will not be given a sign—*not today!*"

13He then climbed back into his canoe and launched out toward the other side of the lake.

THE YEAST OF THE SEPARATED ONES

14They had only one piece of frybread with them because his followers had forgotten to bring more. **15**"Be on the lookout for the yeast of the Separated Ones (Pharisees)," he told them firmly, "and also of the Friends of Looks Brave (Herodians)."

16His followers tried to figure out why he said this. They said to each other, "Is it because we forgot to bring more frybread?"

17Creator Sets Free (Jesus) could hear what they were saying.

"Why are you thinking like this?" he said. "Why are you worried that you forgot to bring frybread? How is it that you do not understand? Are your hearts still hard? **18**Have you no eyes to see with and no ears to hear with?"

His words were sharp, and frustration showed on his face as he tried to make things clear.

"Have you forgotten so soon?" he asked. **19**"When I broke the five pieces of frybread to feed five thousand, how many baskets of broken pieces were left over?"

"Twelve," they answered.

20"When I broke the seven pieces of frybread to feed four thousand, how many baskets of broken pieces did you gather?"

"Seven," they said.

21"So, do you still not understand?" he said.

HE HEALS A MAN BORN BLIND

22They walked on to the village of House of Fishing (Bethsaida). The people there brought a blind man to Creator Sets Free (Jesus) and begged him to touch him. **23**He took the blind man by the hand and led him outside the village. He rubbed some of his spit into the man's eyes and then laid his hands on him.

"What do you see?" Creator Sets Free (Jesus) asked the man.

24He looked around and said, "I can see people, but they look like trees walking around."

25Creator Sets Free (Jesus) put his hands over the man's eyes again. His sight returned, and he could see everything clearly.

[26]He then sent the man to his home and said to him, "Do not go back into the village."

YOU ARE THE CHOSEN ONE

[27]They journeyed on and came into the villages of the territory of Ruler of the Horsemen (Caesarea Philippi).

"What are the people saying about me?" Creator Sets Free (Jesus) asked his followers as they walked along the road. "Who do they think I am?"

[28]"Some say you are Gift of Goodwill (John) who performed the purification ceremony,"[a] they answered. "Others say you are Great Spirit Is Creator (Elijah) or one of the other prophets."

[29]"But who do you say I am?" he asked.

"You are the Chosen One!" Stands on the Rock (Peter) answered.

[30]Creator Sets Free (Jesus) then sternly warned them not to tell this to anyone.

THE ROAD OF SUFFERING LIES AHEAD

[31]Creator Sets Free (Jesus) then began to instruct his followers that the True Human Being must suffer many things. The council of elders, the head holy men, and the scroll keepers would turn their faces from him. He would then be killed, and after three days he would return from the world of the dead. He said this openly to all his followers.

[32]Stands on the Rock (Peter) pulled him aside from the others and spoke sharply to him.

[33]Creator Sets Free (Jesus) turned and looked to his followers and then spoke sharply to Stands on the Rock (Peter), "Out of my way, Accuser (Satan)! These are

---

[a]8:28 Baptism

not the thoughts of the Great Spirit, but of a weak human being."

CARRYING THE CROSS

[34]He then gathered his followers and the crowd around him and said, "Any who want to walk the road with me must turn away from their own path and carry their own cross as they follow me *to the place of ultimate sacrifice.*

[35]"The ones who hold on to their lives will not find life, but the ones who are willing to let go of their lives, for me and for the good story I bring, will find the true life. [36]How will it help you to get everything you want in this world but lose the true life? [37]Is there anything in this world worth trading for it?

[38]"There are bad-hearted and unfaithful people living today, in this generation, who are ashamed of me and my message. So, when the True Human Being comes to show the power and shining-greatness of his Father along with his holy spirit-messengers, he will also be ashamed of these people."

9

[1]"I speak to you from my heart," he said to his followers and the crowd who had gathered around him. "There are some of you standing here today who, before you cross over to death, will see the coming of Creator's good road and all its power!"

THE ANCESTORS SPEAK WITH HIM

[2-3]Six days later Creator Sets Free (Jesus) took his three closest followers—Stands on the Rock (Peter), He Takes Over (James), and He Shows Goodwill (John)—and led them up a high mountain to be alone *and pray.*

Right before their eyes his appearance began to change. His clothes became shining white, whiter than anyone on earth could make them. **4**Two ancestors appeared before them also, the prophet Great Spirit Is Creator (Elijah) and the ancient lawgiver Drawn from the Water (Moses). They were both talking with Creator Sets Free (Jesus).

His three followers rubbed their eyes and looked again. They were filled with wonder and trembled with fear and excitement!

5Stands on the Rock (Peter) spoke out, "Wisdomkeeper, this is a good place to be! We should set up three tipis—one for you, one for Drawn from the Water (Moses), and one for Great Spirit Is Creator (Elijah)."

6He said this without thinking because they were all afraid and did not know what to say.

7Then, from above, a bright cloud came down around them and a voice spoke out from the cloud, "This is my Son, my Much Loved One. *He is the one who speaks for me now.* Listen to him!"

8Right then the cloud lifted. They looked around to see their ancestors, but they were gone, and standing alone before them was Creator Sets Free (Jesus).

GREAT SPIRIT IS CREATOR

9As they walked down the mountainside, he instructed them to tell no one what they had seen until after the True Human Being had come back to life from the dead. **10**So they told no one, but wondered what this "coming back to life from the dead" meant.

11*During the long walk down the mountain,* they asked him, "Why do the scroll keepers say that Great Spirit Is Creator (Elijah) must be the first to come?"

12-13"It is true," he answered, "Great Spirit Is Creator (Elijah) comes first to prepare the way for all things to be restored. And I tell you that he has already come—but none recognized him—and they did whatever they wanted to him, just as the Sacred Teachings foretold. But do you know that it has also been foretold that the True Human Being will suffer many things and be treated with scorn and disrespect?"

HIS FOLLOWERS FAIL TO FORCE OUT A SPIRIT

14When they had finished coming down the mountain to join with the other followers, they found a large crowd around them. The scroll keepers were there arguing with them *about something.* **15**As soon as the crowd saw Creator Sets Free (Jesus), they were filled with awe and ran to greet him.

Creator Sets Free (Jesus) made his way through the crowd and came to the scroll keepers, who were arguing with his followers.

16"What are you arguing with my followers about?" he asked them.

17*Before they could answer,* someone stepped out from the crowd and said to him, "Wisdomkeeper, I came and brought my son to you. He has a spirit that keeps him from speaking. **18**The evil spirit will take hold of him and throw him to the ground. He then becomes stiff and grinds his teeth together, and foam comes from his mouth. I asked your followers to force out this spirit, and they tried but failed."

19"This is a generation with no faith!" Creator Sets Free (Jesus) said to them all. "How much longer will I have to put up with you? Bring the boy to me."

20So they brought the boy to him, and right when the spirit saw Creator Sets Free (Jesus), it took hold of the boy, who then fell to the ground. He began to roll around on the ground, and foam came from his mouth.

21"How long has he been this way?" Creator Sets Free (Jesus) asked the father.

"From the time he was a child," the father answered. 22"The evil spirit has many times thrown him into a fire to burn him or into water to drown him. If you are able to do anything, have pity and help us!"

23"What do you mean 'If I am able'?" Creator Sets Free (Jesus) answered him. "Nothing is too hard for the one with faith!"

24"I do believe!" the father cried out right away. "Help my weak faith!"

25Creator Sets Free (Jesus) saw that the crowd was now pushing in closer to see, so he spoke sharply to the unclean spirit.

"Spirit that makes one unable to speak or hear," he said firmly, "I order you now to leave this boy and never enter him again!"

26The spirit cried out, and the boy began to twist and turn upon the ground. The spirit then came out, and the boy became so still it looked as if he were dead.

"He must be dead!" the people said out loud.

27Then Creator Sets Free (Jesus) took hold of the boy's hand and stood him on his feet.

28Later, when they were alone with him in the house, his followers asked him, "Why were we unable to force out the evil spirit?"

29"This kind of spirit can only be forced out by prayer,a" was his answer to them.

---

a9:29 Some ancient manuscripts add "and fasting."

HE AGAIN FORETELLS HIS DEATH

30From there, Creator Sets Free (Jesus) took his followers on through Circle of Nations (Galilee) but stayed away from the crowds 31so he could further instruct the ones who walked the road with him.

"The True Human Being will soon be taken and handed over to men who will kill him, but on the third day he will come back to life from the dead."

32But his followers did not understand what he meant and were afraid to ask.

WHO IS THE GREATEST?

33They returned again to Village of Comfort (Capernaum) and settled down into the house there.

"What were you talking about as we walked the road just now?" he asked them.

34None of them would answer him, because they had been arguing about who among themselves was the greatest. 35So Creator Sets Free (Jesus) sat down and gathered his twelve followers around him.

"The one who would be first must be the one who will serve all the others— and become last," he told them.

36He then stood a small child in front of them.

"When you represent me and welcome a child like this one, you welcome me."

37He then took the child into his arms and said, "When you welcome me, you do not welcome me alone, but also the one who sent me."

THE ONES NOT AGAINST US ARE FOR US

38Then He Shows Goodwill (John) said to him, "Wisdomkeeper, we saw a man forcing out evil spirits using your name. We told him to stop, because he does not walk the road with us."

39"Do not stop him," he answered. "No one who can do works of power using my name will suddenly turn against me. 40The ones who are not against us are for us. 41I speak from my heart, anyone who brings the gift of even a drink of water to the ones who represent me will never lose the honor that has been gained.

STUMBLING STONES

42"But let no one cause one of these little ones who have put their trust in me to stumble away from the path. It would be better to have a great stone tied to one's neck and to be thrown into the great waters. 43If what your hand does causes you to stumble off the path, then cut it off and throw it away! It would be better to live this life with only one hand than to go with two hands into the Valley of Smoldering Fire—a fire that cannot be put out. 45If where your foot walks causes you to stumble from the path, then cut it off and throw it away. It would be better to walk this life with only one foot than to walk with two feet right into the Valley of Smoldering Fire—a fire that cannot be put out.

VALLEY OF SMOLDERING FIRE

47"The same thing goes for your eye. If what it sees makes you stumble from the path, then pluck it out and throw it away. It would be better to walk Creator's good road with only one eye than to see with two eyes and be thrown into the Valley of Smoldering Fire. 48This Valley of Smoldering Fire is the place *spoken of in the Sacred Teachings*:[a] 'Where their worm does not die and the fire cannot be put out.'[b]

49"All will be salted with fire,[c] for all ceremonial offerings are salted before they are burned with fire.[d] 50Salt is a good thing, *for it purifies, heals, and makes things taste better*, but if it becomes unsalty, what will make it salty again? So make sure that you, like salt, keep your true flavor by walking with each other in the way of peace."

10

1Creator Sets Free (Jesus) then left that place and walked to the territory of the Land of Promise (Judea) beyond the river Flowing Down (Jordan). There, as he usually did, he began to teach the crowds that had once again gathered around him.

TESTED ABOUT DIVORCE

2*Like hungry wolves* the Separated Ones (Pharisees) came to test and accuse him.

"Does our tribal law permit a man to send his wife away?" they asked.

3"What did the lawgiver Drawn from the Water (Moses) instruct the people about this?" he replied.

4"He permitted a man to send her away by giving her divorce papers," they answered back.

5"It is because of your hard hearts that he permitted this," he said to them. 6"But this was not always so, for from the beginning of creation 'he made them to be male and female.'[e] 7This is why a man will leave his father and mother and be joined to his wife, 8and together they make one flesh'[f]—no longer two—but the two braided together as one. 9So

---

and in most other translations.
[c]**9:49** Most manuscripts omit the end of this verse.
[d]**9:49** Leviticus 2:13
[e]**10:6** Genesis 1:27
[f]**10:8** Genesis 2:24

[a]**9:48** Isaiah 66:24; Jeremiah 7:31-32
[b]**9:48** Some ancient manuscripts include this sentence in verse 44 or verse 46, which are omitted in this translation

no human being should tear apart what the Maker of Life has joined together."

[10]Later, back in the house, his followers asked him some more questions about this.

[11]He then said to them, "Whoever sends his wife away, *without properly divorcing her*, and marries another is guilty of being unfaithful to his *first* wife. [12]If she then, after being sent away, marries another man, then she is also guilty of being unfaithful."

In those days men would sometimes send their wives away for any reason without giving them divorce papers, leaving them destitute and unable to properly remarry.

LITTLE CHILDREN AND THE GOOD ROAD

[13]The people were bringing their little children to Creator Sets Free (Jesus) so he would lay his hands on them and bless them, but his followers spoke harsh words to the ones bringing them.

[14]When Creator Sets Free (Jesus) saw what his followers were doing, it made him angry, so he said to them, "Let the little children come to me! Do not turn them away. Creator's good road belongs to the ones who are like these children. [15]I speak from my heart, the only way onto Creator's good road is to become as trusting as a little child."

[16]He then took the children into his arms, laid his hands on them, and blessed them.

POSSESSIONS AND THE GREAT SPIRIT

[17]As Creator Sets Free (Jesus) set out walking from there, a man ran up to him and honored him.

"Good Wisdomkeeper," the man asked, "what path will lead me to the life of the world to come that never fades away?"

[18]"Why do you call me good?" he asked the man. "There is only one who is good—the Great Spirit. [19]You must know the instructions *from the lawgiver Drawn from the Water (Moses)*. 'You are not to take the life of another, or be unfaithful in marriage, or take what is not yours. Never lie about or cheat a fellow human being, and always give honor and respect to your father and mother.'"[a]

[20]"Wisdomkeeper," the man answered, "from my youth I have followed all of these instructions."

[21]Creator Sets Free (Jesus) looked at the man with love and said, "Only one thing remains. Take all your possessions, invite the poor of your village to come, and have a giveaway. Then in the spirit-world above you will have many possessions waiting for you. Then leave everything behind and come, walk the road with me."

[22]The man's heart fell to the ground. He hung his head and walked away, for he had many possessions.

POSSESSIONS AND THE GOOD ROAD

[23]Creator Sets Free (Jesus) then looked around at the people and said to his followers, "Finding and walking the good road is a hard thing for the ones who have many possessions."

[24]His followers could not believe what they were hearing.

They thought having many possessions was a sign of blessing from the Great Spirit.

[25]Creator Sets Free (Jesus) spoke again to them. "Little children," he said, "the ones who trust in their many possessions will have a hard time finding their way onto the good road. It would be

---

[a]**10:19** Exodus 20:12-16; Deuteronomy 5:16-20

easier for a moose[a] to go through the eye of a needle.”

26They shook their heads in wonder, looked at each other, and said, “How then can anyone walk the good road that sets all people free?”

27He looked at them and said, “It is not possible for weak human beings, but with Creator’s help all things are possible.”

28Stands on the Rock (Peter) spoke up, “We have left all our possessions, and our relatives, to walk the road with you! What will become of us?”

29“I speak from my heart,” he answered, “no one who has given up homes and families to follow me and walk my good road will go without. 30In this present world they will become part of an even greater family, with many homes and lands. Even though they have been abused and mistreated, they will receive much more than they have lost.[b] Then, in the world to come, they will have the life of beauty and harmony that never fades away.

31“But many who are first will be last, and many who are last will be first.”

HE FORETELLS HIS DEATH AND RISING

32Creator Sets Free (Jesus) led the way as they walked the road toward Village of Peace (Jerusalem). As they followed behind him, they began to worry *about what would happen when they arrived*, and fear began to cover them like a blanket.

Creator Sets Free (Jesus) took the twelve aside and told them once again what would happen to him.

33“This is what you must see and understand,” he said to them. “We will soon arrive in Village of Peace (Jerusalem), where the True Human Being will be turned over to the head holy men and the scroll keepers. They will condemn him to death and then turn him over to the People of Iron (Romans). 34They will mock him, spit on him, and whip him with cowhide strips. After that, they will kill him, but three days later he will come back to life again.”

A PLACE OF HONOR?

35After that, He Takes Over (James) and He Shows Goodwill (John), the sons of Gift of Creator (Zebedee), came up to Creator Sets Free (Jesus).

“Wisdomkeeper,” they said, “We want to ask you to do something for us.”

36“What is it you want from me?” he replied.

37“When your shining-greatness is revealed,” they said back to him, “permit us a place of honor beside you, one on your right hand the other on your left.”

38“You do not understand what you are asking,” he answered. “Are you able to drink the cup of suffering that I will drink, or endure the purification ceremony[c] that I will endure?”

39“We are able!” they answered.

“Yes,” he said to them, “you will drink from my cup of suffering and endure my purification ceremony,[c] 40but the place at my right and left hand is not mine to give. This honor belongs to the ones for whom it has already been prepared.”

41When the other ten message bearers heard this, they began to look down on He Takes Over (James) and He Shows Goodwill (John).

THE GOOD ROAD IS ABOUT SERVING OTHERS

42So Creator Sets Free (Jesus) called them together and said, “Other nations have

---

[a]**10:25** Lit. *camel*
[b]**10:30** Lit. *one hundred times as much*

[c]**10:38, 39** Baptism

rulers, *such as the People of Iron (Romans)*. They like to show their power over people and push them around. ⁴³But this will not be the way of the ones, like you, who walk with me. ⁴⁴The great ones among you will humble themselves and serve all the others. ⁴⁵In the same way, the True Human Being did not come to be served by others but to offer his life in the place of many lives, to set them free."

MOON VILLAGE HEALING

⁴⁶Creator Sets Free (Jesus) and his followers walked through Moon Village (Jericho), and a large crowd followed behind them as they left the village. As the crowd passed, a blind beggar, whose name was Son of Honored One (Bartimaeus), was sitting on the side of the road.

⁴⁷When he heard that Creator Sets Free (Jesus) from Seed Planter Village (Nazareth) was there, he cried out loudly, "Descendant of Much Loved One (David), have pity on me!"

⁴⁸Many in the crowd scolded him, telling him to be quiet, but this only made him cry out even louder, "Descendant of Much Loved One (David), have pity on me!"

⁴⁹Creator Sets Free (Jesus) stopped walking, *turned to the crowd*, and said, "Tell him to come to me."

So they called out to the blind man, "Have courage! He is calling for you!"

⁵⁰He jumped up, threw aside his outer garment, and walked *with the help of others* to Creator Sets Free (Jesus).

⁵¹"What do you want from me?" Creator Sets Free (Jesus) said to him.

"Wisdomkeeper," he answered, "make me see again!"

⁵²"Be on your way," he said to him, "Your trust in me has made you whole again."

Right then and there his eyes were opened! So he began to follow after Creator Sets Free (Jesus) as they continued on their way down the road.

PREPARATION FOR HIS GRAND ENTRY

¹Creator Sets Free (Jesus) and his followers came to the foot of Olive Mountain at House of Figs (Bethany) and House of Unripe Figs (Bethphage) near Village of Peace (Jerusalem). From there he sent out two of his followers.

²"Go on into the village just ahead of us," he instructed them. "Right when you enter the village, you will see a donkey colt that no one has ever ridden. Untie it and bring it to me. ³If anyone asks, 'What are you doing?' say to them, 'Our Wisdomkeeper is in need of this donkey and will soon return it.'"

⁴His followers went where they were told, found a colt tied by a gate near the village pathway, and untied it. ⁵Some of the people standing nearby said to them, "What are you doing untying that colt?"

⁶They answered them just as their Wisdomkeeper had instructed, so they were permitted to go. ⁷They brought the young donkey to Creator Sets Free (Jesus) and laid their *deer skins and Pendleton* blankets on the colt, and then he sat down upon it.

GRAND ENTRY

⁸A crowd gathered around, and some of them laid their *buffalo* robes on the road, while others spread out branches with large leaves they had cut from the fields.

The people were hoping he would be a mighty warrior chief, like their ancestor Much Loved One (David), to set them free from the People of Iron (Romans). But he did not ride a warhorse on that day, as one might expect. Instead, he rode a small, humble donkey colt. He came weeping over the Village of Peace (Jerusalem), but even this could not silence the hopes of the crowd.

⁹The people encircled him, front and back.

"Hosanna! Set us free!" they shouted. ¹⁰"Blessed is the one who comes representing the Great Spirit! The good road of our ancestor Much Loved One (David) has arrived! Hosanna, to the One Above Us All!"

¹¹Creator Sets Free (Jesus) rode into Village of Peace (Jerusalem) until he came to the sacred lodge. He went into the lodge and looked around at everything—then he left. It was time for the sun to set, so he returned to House of Figs (Bethany), along with his twelve followers, *to the place where they were lodging.*

THE FIG TREE WITHOUT FRUIT

¹²The next day, as Creator Sets Free (Jesus) was returning *to Village of Peace (Jerusalem)* from House of Figs (Bethany), he became hungry. ¹³He saw a fig tree with leaves on it in the distance and went to see whether he might find some figs on it. But when he came to the tree, he found only leaves, for it was not the season for figs.

¹⁴He responded by speaking to the tree, "No one will eat fruit from you ever again!" And his followers heard what he said.

SACRED LODGE KEEPER

¹⁵They went into Village of Peace (Jerusalem) *through the village gate, made their way through the crowded pathways,* and went straight to Creator's sacred lodge.

He came to the area called Gathering Place for the Nations. It was here that other nations could come to learn about the Great Spirit and his ways.

Creator Sets Free (Jesus) entered the lodge and began to force out the ones who were selling and buying the ceremonial animals. He turned over the benches and tables of those who were selling the doves ¹⁶and blocked the way of the ones who were carrying trading goods through the lodge.

¹⁷"It is written in the sacred teachings," he instructed them, "'My lodge will be called a House of Prayer for all Nations.'"[a] *Then his voice rose like the sound of thunder,* "'But you have turned it into a hideout for thieves!'"[b]

¹⁸The head holy men and the scroll keepers heard about what Creator Sets Free (Jesus) had said and done. They began to counsel together about how they could kill him, for they feared his reputation among the many people who respected his teachings.

¹⁹When the sun began to set, Creator Sets Free (Jesus) and his followers left the village *to return to where they were lodging.*

²⁰In the morning, as they were walking on their way to Village of Peace (Jerusalem), they saw the fig tree dried up from the roots. ²¹Stands on the Rock (Peter) remembered that it was the same tree Creator Sets Free (Jesus) had spoken against.

"Wisdomkeeper!" he said. "Look, the fig tree you spoke against has dried up from the roots!"

²²"You must put all your trust in the Great Spirit," Creator Sets Free (Jesus)

---

[a]**11:17** Isaiah 56:7
[b]**11:17** Jeremiah 7:11

replied. [23]"I speak from my heart. Anyone who says to this mountain, 'Lift up and go into the great waters,' with a heart that believes and does not doubt that what he says will happen, then it will be done. [24]That is why I say that when you send your voice to the Great Spirit, believe that he has heard you and the answer will come.

[25]"In the same way, when you stand and pray and there remember you have something against another, release them from the wrong they have done, so that your Father from above will also release you from the wrongs you have done."[a]

SPIRITUAL LEADERS CHALLENGE HIM

[27]Creator Sets Free (Jesus) returned to Village of Peace (Jerusalem) and was walking about in the sacred lodge. The head holy men and the scroll keepers came to him, along with some of the tribal elders.

[28]"By what right do you do these things?" they challenged. "Who gave you this right?"

[29]"I will give you one question to answer. If you answer me, then I will answer you. [30]The purification ceremony[b] performed by Gift of Goodwill (John), was it from the spirit-world above, or did it come from human beings?"

The spiritual leaders looked at each other. They could not decide on how to answer him. Creator Sets Free (Jesus) stood before them and held his ground.

"Answer me!" he challenged back.

[31]So they put their heads together and talked it over. "We cannot say, 'From the

spirit-world above,' for then he will say, 'Why did you not listen to him?' [32]But neither can we say, 'From human beings,' for the people honor Gift of Goodwill (John) as a prophet."

[33]They feared the people, so they said, "We do not know."

"So then, I will not answer your question," he said to them, "and tell you by what right I do these things."

12 ◆▸◆▸◆▸◆▸◆▸◆▸◆▸◆◆

[1]*Once again* Creator Sets Free (Jesus) began to speak to them using stories:

STORY ABOUT THE VINEYARD

[2]"A tribal member planted a *large* vineyard. He encircled it with a hedge, dug a hole for stomping the juice from the grapes, and built a tower for watching over it. He then rented it out to other tribal farmers *for a share of the grapes*. Then he traveled far away on a long journey to another land.

"When harvest time came, the tribal member who owned the vineyard sent a trusted messenger to gather his share of the grapes, [3]but the farmers beat him and sent him away empty-handed.

[4]"The vineyard owner sent another messenger; but they treated him shamefully, struck him on the head, and sent him away also.

[5]"So he sent a third messenger, and this one they killed. The same thing was done to many others he sent. They beat some and killed others.

[6]"Finally, the vineyard owner had only one more that he could send—his much-loved son. So, last of all, he sent his own son to them.

"'They will respect my son,' he said to himself.

---

[a]**11:25** Some ancient manuscripts also add verse 26: "But if you fail to release others, then your Father from above will not release you."
[b]**11:30** Baptism

[7]"But those tribal farmers said to themselves, 'This vineyard will one day belong to this son. If we kill him, the vineyard will be ours.'

[8]"So they killed him and threw his dead body out of the vineyard.

[9]"What do you think the owner of the vineyard will do?" Creator Sets Free (Jesus) asked *the people who were listening.*

He waited for an answer, but no one said a word.

Then he said, "He will return, put those *dishonorable* men to death, and give the vineyard to others. [10]Have you not read in the Sacred Teachings where it is said, 'The tree the lodge builders threw away has become the Chief Lodgepole. [11]This is what the Great Spirit will do, and when we see it, we will be filled with wonder?"[a]

[12]The spiritual leaders wanted to take him prisoner right then and there, for they knew the story was about them. But they were afraid of what the people might do, so they left him and went away.

THEY SET A TRAP FOR HIM

[13]The spiritual leaders sent some of the Separated Ones (Pharisees) and the Friends of Looks Brave (Herodians) to trap Creator Sets Free (Jesus) in his words.

[14]"Wisdomkeeper," they came and said to him, "we know you always speak the truth about the Great Spirit and represent him well, no matter what others may think or say. Tell us what is right," they asked. "Does our tribal law permit our people to pay taxes to the government of the People of Iron (Romans)? [15]Yes or no?"

Creator Sets Free (Jesus) could see right through their false faces!

"Why are you putting me to the test?" he said to them. "Bring to me one of their silver coins and I will look at it."

[16]So they brought one to him.

He took a good long look at it, holding it up to the sky to see it clearly. Then he turned the face of the coin for them to see.

"Whose image and words are carved into this coin?" he asked.

"The Ruler of the People of Iron (Caesar)," they replied.

[17]"Then give this ruler the things that are his," he told them, "but give to the Great Spirit the things that belong to the Great Spirit."

The spiritual leaders were amazed *at his words.*

They could not believe it. They had failed right in front of all the people and could not use his words against him, so they walked away in silence.

THE UPRIGHT ONES TEST HIM

[18]Then the Upright Ones (Sadducees), who say that there is no rising from the dead, also came to test him.

[19]"Wisdomkeeper," they said to him, "Drawn From the Water (Moses) instructed us in the Sacred Teachings that if a Tribal Member should die before having children, then his brother should marry his widow and give her children. This way the man will have descendants.

[20]"What if, in a family of seven brothers, the oldest took a wife, but died without children. [21]Then the second brother married her, but he also died leaving no children. Then the third brother also married her and he, like the others, died with no children. [22]The same happened to all seven of them, and last of all the woman also crossed over to death. [23]So then, when they all come

[a]**12:11** Psalm 118:22-23

back to life in the time when the dead rise, whose wife would she be, since all seven brothers married her?"

24"You are asking the wrong kind of question," Creator Sets Free (Jesus) answered back, "for you do not understand the Sacred Teachings or the power of the Great Spirit. 25When men or women rise again from the dead, they will not marry, for they will be like the spirit-messengers from the spirit-world above."

And then he said, 26"As for the dead rising again, do you not remember what was written in the Sacred Teachings about the time when the Great Spirit spoke to Drawn from the Water (Moses) from the burning bush? He said, 'I am the Great Spirit of Father of Many Nations (Abraham), of He Made Us Laugh (Isaac), and of Heel Grabber (Jacob).'a 27He is not the Great Spirit of the dead, but of the living! So in this matter you are greatly mistaken."

THE GREATEST INSTRUCTION OF ALL
28One of the scroll keepers overheard Creator Sets Free (Jesus) opposing the Upright Ones. When he heard the good answer he had given, he asked him, "Which instruction in our tribal law stands first?"

29"The first and greatest instruction is this," Creator Sets Free (Jesus) answered. "'Hear me, O tribes of Wrestles with Creator (Israel), there is only one Great Spirit and Maker of us all. 30You must love the Great Spirit with your whole being—with the strength of your arms, the thoughts of your mind, and the courage of your heart.'b

31"The second instruction is like the first," he added. "You must love your fellow human beings in the same way you love yourselves. There is no other instruction greater than these."

32"Wisdomkeeper," said the scroll keeper *with a smile,* "you have answered well and spoken the truth, for the Great Spirit is One and there is none other except him. 33To love him with your whole being—with the strength of your arms, the thoughts of your mind, and the courage of your heart, and to love your fellow human beings in the same way you love yourselves—is far greater than all ceremonies and offerings we make to the Great Spirit."

34When Creator Sets Free (Jesus) heard the scroll keeper's wise answer, he said, "You are not far from Creator's good road."

After that, no one dared to ask him any other questions.

A QUESTION NO ONE COULD ANSWER
35While Creator Sets Free (Jesus) was teaching at the sacred lodge, he asked, "How is it that the scroll keepers say the Chosen One is a descendant of Much Loved One (David), 36when Much Loved One (David) himself, speaking with the voice of the Holy Spirit, said, 'The Honored Chief said to my Honored Chief, "Sit down beside me at my right hand, the place of greatest honor, until I defeat and humble all your enemies"'?c

37"If Much Loved One (David) called the Chosen One 'My Honored Chief,' how then can the Chosen One be his descendant?"d

The large crowd of people listened with glad hearts, *because his wisdom was greater than the wisdom of the spiritual leaders.*

---

a**12:26** Exodus 3:6
b**12:30** Deuteronomy 6:4-5
c**12:36** Psalm 110:1
d**12:37** Lit. *his son*

FALSE SPIRITUAL LEADERS

38During his teachings he said, "Be on the lookout for the scroll keepers who like to show off by walking around in their fancy regalia, who want to be noticed at the trading posts, **39**who take the best seats at the gathering houses and the places of honor at the feasts. **40**With many words they make a big show of their prayers, and trick widows into giving them their homes and possessions. They will come to a worse end than others."

A SACRIFICIAL GIFT

41Creator Sets Free (Jesus) found a place to sit across from the storehouse of the sacred lodge. He watched as people came to put their gifts on the offering blanket. The ones with many possessions were putting down more than others. **42**Then he saw a poor widow come to the blanket and place two small, poorly beaded earrings[a] on it, worth almost nothing.

43He gathered his followers around him and told them about the widow's gift.

"I speak from my heart," he said, "this widow has given more than all the others. **44**What they gave was only a small part of their many possessions, but this poor widow has given all she had left to live on."

13 ✦✦✦✦✦✦✦✦✦✦✦✦

SIGNS OF THE END OF THE AGE

1As they were walking away from the sacred lodge, one of his followers said to him, "Look, Wisdomkeeper, these buildings are made from such handsomely carved logs and great stones!"

> *Creator Sets Free (Jesus) stopped walking, and as he looked around at all the buildings of the sacred ceremonial lodge, a look of sadness came over his face.*

2"Do you see all these great buildings?" he replied. "They will all fall to the ground! Not one log or stone will be left standing against another."

3*Later that day* Creator Sets Free (Jesus) was sitting on Olive Mountain across from the sacred lodge.

> *From there he could look across the valley and see Village of Peace (Jerusalem) and the sacred lodge.*

While he was there, *four of his followers*—Stands on the Rock (Peter), He Takes Over (James), He Shows Goodwill (John), and Stands with Courage (Andrew)— came to him in private.

4"Tell us when these things will happen," they said *with worried looks on their faces.* "What sign should we be looking for?"

STAY ON THE LOOKOUT!

5"Stay alert or you may be led down a false path!" he told them. **6**"Many will come representing me. 'I am the Chosen One,' they will claim, and many will listen to their lies.

THE SIGN OF WARFARE

7"When you hear of wars and stories of war breaking out, do not fear, for all of this must happen before the end will come. **8**There will be tribal wars, and nations will make war against other nations. Food will be scarce, and the earth will shake in many places—but this is only the beginning of the time of sorrow, like a woman feeling the pains of birth.

---

[a]**12:42** Lit. *two small coins*

THE SIGN OF TRIBAL BETRAYAL

⁹"You must stay ready and alert! Your own people will turn you over to the local tribal councils and beat you in their gathering houses. Because you are representing me, you will be brought before the governors and rulers *of the People of Iron (Romans)*. You will then tell them about Creator's good road, ¹⁰for before the end comes, the good story must first be told to all nations. ¹¹So when they put you on trial, do not worry ahead of time about what you will say. Speak what is given you at the time, for the Holy Spirit himself will give you the words to speak.

THE SIGN OF FAMILY BETRAYAL

¹²"Brother will betray brother to death, and a father his child. Children will rise up against their parents and have them killed. ¹³And because you represent me, all will look down on you and hate you, but the ones who stand strong to the end will be set free and made whole.

THE SIGN OF THE COMING DESTRUCTION

¹⁴"When you see the 'horrible thing that brings destruction' making its stand where it does not belong—the reader will know what this means[a]—the ones who live in the Land of Promise (Judea) should escape to the mountains. ¹⁵The ones who are on their rooftop should not even go back into the house to take anything. ¹⁶The ones working in the field should not go back to get their outer garments. ¹⁷It will be a time of pain and sorrow for the women who are with child and the ones nursing their babies, ¹⁸so pray that it will not happen in the winter. ¹⁹A worse time of suffering and sorrow has not been seen since the Great

Spirit created the world—and never will be seen again. ²⁰If those days were permitted to reach the end of the trail, then no one would survive, but, because of Creator's Chosen Ones, those days will be cut short.

FALSE CHOSEN ONES AND PROPHETS

²¹"So, if in those days anyone would say to you, 'Look, the Chosen One is over here,' or 'Look, he is over there,' pay no attention. ²²For false Chosen Ones will rise up, and false prophets will appear. They will provide great signs and omens to mislead, if possible, even Creator's Chosen Ones.

²³"I have told you all of this ahead of time, so stay on the lookout and be ready!

SIGNS IN THE WORLD ABOVE

²⁴"Then, right after that time of trouble and sorrow, 'the sun will no longer shine, the moon will go dark, ²⁵the stars will fall from the sky, and the powers in the spirit-world above will tremble.'[b]

SIGN OF THE TRUE HUMAN BEING

²⁶"This is when they will see the True Human Being, coming with power, riding the clouds, and shining like the sun! ²⁷He will then send out his messengers to gather his Chosen Ones from the winds of the four directions—from the spirit-world above to the earth below.

A WISE STORY ABOUT THE FIG TREE

²⁸"Listen to this wise story and learn the lesson of the fig tree: when its branches get soft and leaves appear, you know that summer will soon be here. ²⁹In the same way, when you see all these things

---

[a]**13:14** Matthew 24:15; Luke 21:20

[b]**13:25** Isaiah 13:10

happening, you will know that the time is near—almost upon you. ³⁰I speak from my heart! All of this will happen in this generation. ³¹You can be sure of what I am saying—for the earth and sky will fade away, but my words will not!

³²"But no one knows the day or hour when these things will take place—not the spirit-messengers from the spirit-world above, not even Creator's own Son—only the Father knows.

ALWAYS BE READY

³³"So keep both eyes open and be ready at all times, for no one knows when this time will come. ³⁴Be ready, like a chief who goes away on a long journey. He appoints the young men to watch over the village while he is gone, giving each of them responsibilities. Then he sets his warriors to guard the village gate. ³⁵They must stay awake and be ready, doing what he says, for they do not know when the chief will return. It may be when the sun is setting, or late into the night, or when the rooster crows early in the morning. ³⁶When the chief comes, he better not find them sleeping!

³⁷"I am telling all of you the same thing. So be ready and stay alert!"

14

PLOT TO KILL HIM

¹It was now only two days before the traditional yearly Passover and Bread Without Yeast festival would be celebrated. The head holy men and the scroll keepers were scheming together about ways to have him captured and killed.

²"We should not do it during the festival," they decided, "for that might create an uprising among the people."

PREPARING FOR HIS BURIAL

³Creator Sets Free (Jesus) was in the village of House of Figs (Bethany), in the home of Hearing Man (Simon), who had a skin disease. He was leaning back, sitting on the floor at the table, when a woman with a pottery jar full of costly, sweet-smelling ointment came to Creator Sets Free (Jesus), broke the pottery jar, and poured the ointment over his head.

⁴Some of his followers, who saw this, became angry and said to each other, "Why waste this costly ointment?ᵃ ⁵It could have been traded for food and goods to give to the poor."

So they spoke harshly to her.

⁶"Let her be!" Creator Sets Free (Jesus) spoke up. "Why are you troubling her? She has done a good thing for me! ⁷You can help the poor anytime, for they will always be among you, but I will not. ⁸This is her gift to me, to prepare me for my burial. ⁹I speak from my heart, when the good story is told all over the world, her story will also be told as a memorial."

THE BETRAYAL BEGINS

¹⁰It was then that Speaks Well Of (Judas), *also known as* Village Man (Iscariot), who was one of the twelve, left there and went to the head holy men to betray Creator Sets Free (Jesus) into their hands. ¹¹When they heard this, it pleased them, so they promised to pay him well. So Speaks Well Of (Judas) began to look for the right time to betray him.

PREPARATION FOR THE CEREMONIAL MEAL

¹²It was now the first day of Bread Without Yeast. This was when the ceremonial lamb would be killed and eaten.

ᵃ14:4 Worth almost a year's wages

"Where do you want us to go to prepare the ceremonial meal?" his followers asked their Wisdomkeeper.

13"Go into the village," he instructed two of his followers, "and there you will meet a man carrying a water pouch. Follow him 14into whatever lodging-house he enters, and say to the headman of the lodging-house, 'Our Wisdomkeeper asks: Where is the room where I can eat the ceremonial meal with my followers?' 15He will then show you a large upper room that will be set up and ready for you. There you can prepare *the ceremonial meal* for us."

16They did as he said and found everything just as he told them, so they prepared the room for the ceremonial meal.

THE CEREMONIAL MEAL BEGINS

17When the sun was setting, Creator Sets Free (Jesus) and his twelve followers went to the room that had been prepared, 18and they all sat down around the table.

"I speak from my heart," he said during the meal, "One of you who eats with me now will betray me."

19Their hearts fell to the ground, and one by one they said to him, "I am not the one, am I?"

20"It is one of the twelve, the one who has just dipped his bread into the bowl with me," he said to all. 21"The True Human Being must walk the path chosen for him, as written in the Sacred Teachings, but it will not go well for the one who betrays him. It would be better if he had never been born."

A NEW PEACE TREATY

22During the meal Creator Sets Free (Jesus) took some of the frybread and gave thanks to the Great Spirit. He then broke it into pieces and gave some to each of his followers.

"This is my body," he told them. "Take it *and eat it.*"

23He then took a cup *of wine,* gave thanks to the Great Spirit, and passed the cup to all, who then drank from it.

24"This is my lifeblood of the peace treaty, poured out on behalf of many people," he said to them. 25"I speak from my heart, I will not drink from the fruit of the vine again until the day when I will drink it with you in a fresh and new way, as we walk Creator's good road together."

ALL OF YOU WILL TURN AWAY

26They all sang a traditional song and then left to walk to Olive Mountain.

27"All of you will turn away from me," he told them as they walked along. "It was written in the Sacred Teachings, 'Attack the shepherd and the sheep will scatter.'a 28But when I return from the world of the dead, I will go on ahead of you to Circle of Nations (Galilee)."

29Then Stands on the Rock (Peter) spoke out, "Even if they all turn away from you, I will not!"

30"I speak from my heart," he said back to him. "This very night, before the rooster crows twice, you will deny three times that you even know me."

31"No!" Stands on the Rock (Peter) cried out *fiercely.* "Even if I must die with you, I will never turn away!"

And all the others said the same thing.

THE GARDEN WHERE HE PRAYED

32Creator Sets Free (Jesus) and his followers came to the place called Where the Olives Are Crushed (Gethsemane), *a garden with many olive trees.*

---

a**14:27** Zechariah 13:7

"Sit here," he told his followers, "while I go over there and pray."

33He then took with him Stands on the Rock (Peter), He Takes Over (James), and He Shows Goodwill (John) *to a place not far from the others.* There he became deeply troubled and full of sorrow.

34"My heart is full of sorrow to the point of death," he said to *his three followers who were with him.* "Stay here and watch over me."

35He went a little ways from them, dropped his face to the ground, and prayed that, if possible, he would be spared from this time of suffering.

36"Abba, Honored Father," he cried out, "nothing is too hard for you. Take this bitter cup of suffering away from me. But I want only your way, not mine."

37He then returned and found his followers sleeping.

"One Who Hears (Simon)," he said *to Stands on the Rock (Peter), using his family name.* "Are you asleep? Could you not stay awake with me for even one hour? **38**Stay awake and pray so that you will be able to face the fiery trial ahead of you. The human body is weak, but the spirit is strong."

39Once again he went from them and prayed the same words. **40**He returned and again found his followers sleeping, for their eyes were heavy, and they had no answer for him.

41After praying again, he returned a third time *and woke them up from their sleep.*

"Do you still sleep? Have you rested enough?" he said to them. "Wake up! The time is upon us! The True Human Being has been betrayed into the hands of the ones with bad hearts. **42**Rise up! We must go! Look! The one who has turned against me is here!"

BETRAYED WITH A KISS

43Right then, while Creator Sets Free (Jesus) was speaking, a crowd of people stormed into the garden. Speaks Well Of (Judas), one of the twelve, was leading the way. Along with the betrayer came the large crowd, sent from the head holy men and elders of the tribal council, carrying clubs and long knives.

44The betrayer had given them a sign, "Take hold of the one I greet with a kiss and arrest him, for he will be the one."

45Speaks Well Of (Judas), *also known as* Village Man (Iscariot), when he arrived, walked right up to Creator Sets Free (Jesus). "Wisdomkeeper!" he said, and then kissed him.

46They moved in and took hold of Creator Sets Free (Jesus) to arrest him. **47**But then one of his followers, who had drawn his long knife from its sheath, struck and cut off the ear of the servant of the chief holy man.

48Creator Sets Free (Jesus) then turned to the ones who had come to take him and said, "Why do you treat me as if I were a thief by coming with clubs and long knives to take me away? **49**Did I not sit with you every day in the sacred lodge? Why did you not take me then? But now the words of the prophets have come true and found their full meaning."

50Then all his followers left him and ran away. **51**A young man dressed only in an undercloth trailed from behind. The people tried to grab hold of him, **52**but his undergarments tore away, and the young man ran away naked into the night.

QUESTIONED BY THE CHIEF HOLY MAN

53The ones who had arrested Creator Sets Free (Jesus) dragged him away and brought him to the chief holy man. The scroll keepers and elders of the Grand Council had gathered there *to question him.*

⁵⁴Stands on the Rock (Peter) followed from a safe distance and went right into the courtyard of the chief holy man. He then sat down next to the lodge guards and warmed himself by the fire.

⁵⁵The head holy men and the Grand Council kept trying to find someone who would speak against Creator Sets Free (Jesus) so they could put him to death, ⁵⁶but found none who could agree, even though many came forward and spoke lies against him.

⁵⁷Then some false witnesses came forward and said, ⁵⁸"We heard him say, 'I will tear down this sacred lodge made with hands and in three days I will build another not made with hands.'"

⁵⁹But even about this they could not keep their stories straight.

⁶⁰The chief holy man stood before all in the center of the room.

"Have you nothing to say to these accusations?" he said to Creator Sets Free (Jesus).

⁶¹But he just stood there silently and gave no answer.

"Are you the Chosen One," the chief holy man asked him, "the Son of the One Who Is Blessed?"

The room became silent, and when he spoke, every eye and ear were fixed on Creator Sets Free (Jesus).

⁶²"I am," he answered, "and you will see the True Human Being sitting at the right hand of the Power when he comes riding the clouds of the spirit-world above!"

⁶³The chief holy man tore his regalia *and turned to the council.*

"Why do we even need witnesses?" he said to them. ⁶⁴"You have heard him

speak against the Great Spirit with your own ears! What does the council have to say?"

The decision was agreed on by all—death.

⁶⁵Some began to spit on him. They covered his face and struck him, saying, "Prophesy!" Then the lodge guards took him and struck him with the backs of their hands.

STANDS ON THE ROCK DENIES HIM

⁶⁶Below the house, outside in the courtyard, one of the servant women of the chief holy man ⁶⁷saw Stands on the Rock (Peter) warming himself by the fire. She looked closely at him and said, "You were also with Creator Sets Free (Jesus) from Seed Planter Village (Nazareth)!"

⁶⁸"I do not know him or what you are saying!" he said to her, and as he moved away toward the outside of the courtyard, a rooster crowed.

⁶⁹The servant woman, seeing him walk away, said to some of the men there, "He is one of them!"

⁷⁰But again he denied it.

After a while, some others who were standing by said to him, "You must be one of his followers. You talk like someone from Circle of Nations (Galilee)."

⁷¹Stands on the Rock (Peter) cursed, made a sacred oath, and said, "I do not know this man you are talking about."

⁷²Right then a rooster crowed for the second time. Stands on the Rock (Peter) remembered what Creator Sets Free (Jesus) had told him, "Before the rooster crows twice, you will deny three times that you know me."

Then Stands on the Rock (Peter) broke down and wept.

15

TAKEN TO THE PEOPLE OF IRON

¹As the sun began to rise, the head holy men counseled together with the tribal elders, the scroll keepers, and the Grand Council. Then with ropes they bound Creator Sets Free (Jesus) once again and took him to Spear of the Great Waters (Pilate).

> *Spear of the Great Waters (Pilate) was the local governor representing the People of Iron (Romans). He had the power to decide who would live and who would die.*

²"Are you the chief of the tribes of Wrestles with Creator (Israel)?" he asked Creator Sets Free (Jesus).

³"You have said it," he answered as the head holy men kept accusing him.

⁴"Why are you silent?" Spear of the Great Waters (Pilate) said to him. "Do you not hear all their accusations?"

⁵But, to the amazement of the governor, Creator Sets Free (Jesus) answered not one word.

WHO SHOULD BE RELEASED?

⁶It was a tradition during the Passover festival to release to the crowd one criminal, whomever they wanted. ⁷At that time they were holding a man in prison, a killer who had been part of an uprising *against the People of Iron (Romans)*, whose name was Son of His Father (Barabbas). ⁸So the crowd began to ask Spear of the Great Waters (Pilate) to release a prisoner.

⁹The governor *raised his voice and* asked the crowd, "Should I release to you the chief of your tribal nation?"

¹⁰He said this because he knew the head holy men and elders had handed over Creator Sets Free (Jesus) because they were jealous of his reputation with the people. ¹¹But the head holy men and the elders stirred the crowd into asking for Son of His Father (Barabbas) to be released instead.

¹²"What then would you have me do with the one you call chief of your tribal nation?" he asked them again.

¹³"Nail him to the cross!" they shouted *with one voice.*

¹⁴"Why? What wrong has he done to deserve this?" he said back to them.

But they only shouted louder and stronger, "Nail him to the cross!"

CONDEMNED TO DIE

¹⁵So Spear of the Great Waters (Pilate), to satisfy the crowd, released *the man of violence*, Son of His Father (Barabbas), to them. He then turned over *the man of peace*, Creator Sets Free (Jesus), to the soldiers to be whipped with cowhide strips and then nailed to a tree-pole—the cross.

> *The People of Iron (Romans) used a whip with many strips of leather, each braided together with bone and metal. The victim would be tied to a large rock, exposing his bare back, and then whipped. The pieces of bone and metal would rip and tear the skin from the body, leaving the victim almost lifeless.*

¹⁶The soldiers took Creator Sets Free (Jesus) away into the great hall of the governor's lodge, and all the soldiers gathered around him. ¹⁷They wrapped a purple chief blanket around him and twisted together a headdress from a thorn bush and pressed it onto his head. ¹⁸"Honor! Honor! To the chief of the tribes of Wrestles with Creator (Israel)," they said, mocking him ¹⁹as they bowed to the ground in front of him. Then they

spit on him and beat his head over and over again with a wooden staff.

HIS TRAIL OF TEARS

[20]When they were finished putting on their big show, they stripped him of the purple chief blanket and dressed him in his own clothes.

The soldiers forced Creator Sets Free (Jesus) to carry a heavy wooden crossbeam on his back. He stumbled under the weight, because he was weak from the beating he had endured, too weak to bear the burden.

But they continued to march him down the road to the place where they would nail him to the cross.

[21]On the way they came across a man who was just passing by, coming in from the countryside. The man's name was Listening Man (Simon), the father of Man Fighter (Alexander) and Red Man (Rufus). The soldiers forced him to carry the *heavy* crossbeam for Creator Sets Free (Jesus).

NAILED TO THE CROSS

The cross was an instrument of torture and terror, used by the People of Iron (Romans) to strike fear into the hearts of any who dared to rise up against their empire. The victim's hands and feet would be pierced with large iron nails, fastening them to the tree-pole. The victims would hang there, sometimes for days, until they were dead. This was one of the most cruel and painful ways to die ever devised by human beings.

[22]They brought Creator Sets Free (Jesus) to the Place of the Skull (Golgotha). [23]There they gave him wine mixed with bitter herbs, but he would not drink it. [24]Then they *stripped him of his clothes and* nailed him to a wooden tree-pole—

the cross—and gambled for his clothes by drawing straws to see who would win. [25]It was the third hour of the day when they nailed him to the cross. [26]Carved above his head *onto a piece of wood* was the accusation against him:

CHIEF OF
THE TRIBES OF
WRESTLES WITH CREATOR

[27]They also nailed two thieves to their own crosses, one to his right, the other to his left. [28]And so this gave full meaning to the Sacred Teachings that said, "He will be counted among the outlaws."[a]

MOCKED BY HIS OWN PEOPLE

[29]The people passing by wagged their heads and heaped insults on him.

"Aha!" they laughed out loud. "So you can destroy the sacred lodge and build it again in three days! Can you? [30]Why not come down from that cross and save yourself?"

[31]The head holy men along with the scroll keepers also mocked him.

"He set others free," they said, "but he cannot even set himself free! [32]Let the Chosen One, the Chief of the tribes of Wrestles with Creator (Israel), come down from the cross now. Then we will believe."

The men on crosses to his left and right also heaped insults upon him.

[33]At the sixth hour of the day, *when the sun was high,* darkness covered the whole land like a blanket for three hours.

HE CRIES OUT IN SORROW

[34]At the ninth hour Creator Sets Free (Jesus), speaking in his own language, cried out with a loud voice, "Eli, Eli, lema sabachthani?"—which means, "O Great

---

[a]**15:28** Isaiah 53:12. Some less ancient manuscripts omit verse 28.

Spirit, my Creator, why have you left me alone?"

35Some of the people standing there heard him and said, "He is calling on the prophet, Great Spirit Is Creator (Elijah), to help him."

36Someone then ran and soaked a cloth with bitter wine, put it on a staff, held it to his mouth, and said, "Wait, let us see if Great Spirit Is Creator (Elijah) will come and take him down."

HE BREATHES HIS LAST

37Then Creator Sets Free (Jesus), with his dying breath, lifted his voice and with a loud cry gave up his spirit.

38*At that very moment* in the sacred lodge, the great heavy blanket that hung over the entry to the Most Holy Place was torn from top to bottom.

> *For the first time the inner chamber, where only the chief holy man could go, was open to all.*

39When the head soldier of the People of Iron (Romans), who was standing in front of Creator Sets Free (Jesus), saw how he died, he said, "This man must truly be the Son of the Great Spirit!"

THE WOMEN WHO WALKED WITH HIM

40Watching from a distance were some of the women *who had walked the road with him*. Among them was Strong Tears (Mary) of the village of Creator's High Lodge (Magdala), Brooding Tears (Mary) the mother of He Takes Charge (James) the Small One and He Increases (Joses), and Peaceful Woman (Salome). **41**These were some of the women who had served Creator Sets Free (Jesus) during the times when he was at Circle of Nations (Galilee). There were also many others who had made the journey with him to Village of Peace (Jerusalem).

PREPARING FOR HIS BURIAL

42The sun would soon set, ending the Day of Preparation, and marking the beginning of the Day of Resting. **43**He Gets More (Joseph) from the tribal village of High Mountain (Arimathea), who was also looking for Creator's good road, was a respected member of the Grand Council. He found the courage to ask Spear of the Great Waters (Pilate) for the body of Creator Sets Free (Jesus).

44Spear of the Great Waters (Pilate) was surprised to hear that Creator Sets Free (Jesus) had already died, so he summoned the head soldier and asked how long he had been dead. **45**Once he was assured that Creator Sets Free (Jesus) was truly dead, Spear of the Great Waters (Pilate) released his body to He Gets More (Joseph).

46He took the dead body down *from the cross* and wrapped it in a soft blanket *in the traditional way*. He laid the body of Creator Sets Free (Jesus) in a burial cave freshly cut from the rock hillside and then rolled a large stone in front of the cave.

47Strong Tears (Mary) of the village of Creator's High Lodge (Magdala) and Brooding Tears (Mary) the mother of He Increases (Joses) were nearby watching closely where the body of Creator Sets Free (Jesus) had been laid.

16

THE BURIAL CAVE

1After the Day of Resting was over, Strong Tears (Mary) of the village of Creator's High Lodge (Magdala) and Brooding Tears (Mary) the mother of He Takes Charge (James), along with Peaceful Woman (Salome), brought herbal spices to rub into the body of Creator Sets Free (Jesus). [2]So, on the first day of the week, they came to the burial cave very early in the morning just as the sun was rising. [3]They were asking each other, "Who will roll the stone away from the opening of the burial cave?"

SPIRIT-MESSENGERS

[4]But when they arrived, they saw that the stone, which was very large, had already been rolled away. [5]When they went inside the burial cave, they saw a young man, dressed in a pure white garment, sitting to the right side of the cave. This filled the women with fear *that covered them like a blanket.*

[6]"Do not fear!" the young man said to them, "The one you are looking for is not here! Creator Sets Free (Jesus) from Seed Planter Village (Nazareth), who was killed on the cross, has returned to life. See for yourselves. Here is where they laid him. [7]Now go and tell his followers, and Stands on the Rock (Peter), that he is going ahead of them to Circle of Nations (Galilee). It is there that they will see him again—just as he told them."

[8]Terror and amazement came upon the women, and they ran as fast as they could from the burial cave.[a]

HE SHOWS HIMSELF

[9]When Creator Sets Free (Jesus) returned to life on the first day of the week, he showed himself first to *a woman,* Strong Tears (Mary) of the village of Creator's High Lodge (Magdala), the one he had set free from seven evil spirits. [10]She went to his followers, who were still grieving and weeping, and told them what she had seen and heard. [11]But when they heard

that she had seen Creator Sets Free (Jesus) alive, they would not believe it.

[12]On the same day Creator Sets Free (Jesus) also appeared to two of his followers as they were walking in the countryside, but in a different form, *so they did not recognize him.* [13]But when they returned and told the others, no one believed them.

[14]Later, at another time, he showed himself to the eleven message bearers while they were sitting around a table *eating a meal.* He scolded them for their hard hearts and failure to believe the others who had seen him alive.

HIS LAST INSTRUCTIONS

[15]"Go into all the world," he instructed them, "and tell the good story *about me* to all of creation. [16]The ones who trust in me will participate in the purification ceremony,[b] setting them free from their broken ways *and initiating them into my sacred family.* But the ones who will not walk this road with me[c] will come to a bad end.

[17]"Powerful signs will follow the ones who follow me. Here are some of the things they will do in my name, representing who I am: They will force out evil spirits, [18]pick up and throw out snakes, and even if they drink deadly poison it will not harm them. They will speak in new languages and heal the sick by laying hands on them."

HE GOES BACK TO THE FATHER ABOVE

[19]When he was finished speaking to them, Creator Sets Free (Jesus), our great chief *and Wisdomkeeper,* was taken up into the spirit-world above to sit down at the right hand of the Great Spirit—

---

[a]**16:8** Most ancient manuscripts end at this verse. Some others include verses 9-20, as we have in this translation.

[b]**16:16** Baptism
[c]**16:16** Lit. *believe*

the place of greatest honor, dignity, and power.

20His followers then went out from there, far and wide, telling everyone *the story of Creator's good road.* Our Honored Chief *through his Spirit* continued to walk with them, showing his approval of their message by powerful signs.

Aho! May it be so!

SHINING LIGHT TELLS THE GOOD STORY

THE GOSPEL OF LUKE

EYEWITNESSES

1-3O most honored Friend of Creator (Theophilus), many have told this story, given to them from those who saw these things with their own eyes, the ones who first walked out this message to hand it down to us.

Having searched out this story from the first, it seemed like a good thing for me to retell it from beginning to end. **4**In this way you will know for yourself the truth about the things you were taught.

CREATOR REMEMBERS HIS PROMISE

5It was in the time of *the bad-hearted* Chief Looks Brave (Herod), who ruled the territory of the Land of Promise (Judea), that Creator chose to send a powerful spirit-messenger to Sacred Village of Peace (Jerusalem), to a holy man whose name was Creator Will Remember (Zechariah).

He and his wife, Creator Is My Promise (Elizabeth), were both descended from the tribe the ceremonial holy people are chosen from. **6**They were in good standing in the eyes of the Great Spirit, and with good and pure hearts they walked a straight path, staying true to the tribal ways and traditions given them by the Great Spirit.

They lived in the hill country in the Land of Promise (Judea) of the tribes of Wrestles with Creator (Israel).

7But Creator Is My Promise (Elizabeth) was unable to have children, and both were growing old.

8Creator Will Remember (Zechariah) belonged to the clan of He Is My Father (Abijah), which shared the responsibility of prayers and ceremonies in the Great Spirit's ceremonial lodge that was in Village of Peace (Jerusalem).

9He was chosen in the traditional way to be the one to enter the sacred lodge and perform the sweet-smelling smoke ceremony for the evening prayer.

Most holy men could only hope for this honor once in a lifetime.

10A large number of people gathered outside to pray while he went inside.

11As the smoke went up with his prayers, suddenly a spirit-messenger from the Great Spirit appeared to him, standing to the right of the altar of sweet-smelling smoke. **12**Creator Will Remember (Zechariah) was troubled when he saw the spirit-messenger. He trembled with fear that covered him like a blanket.

13"Do not fear!" the messenger said to him. "Your prayers have been heard. The Maker of Life will give you and your wife a son. You will give him the name Gift of Goodwill (John). **14**He will bring great joy to you, and many people will be glad that he has been born."

The aroma of the sweet-smelling smoke filled the sacred lodge as the spirit-messenger continued.

15"He will be great and honorable in Creator's sight and will not drink wine or any strong drink, but will drink deeply of the Holy Spirit even in his mother's womb. **16**Because of him many of the children of the tribes of Wrestles with Creator (Israel) will *find the good road and return to the Great Spirit and his ways.*"

Creator Will Remember (Zechariah) stood silently. His whole being continued to tremble as the messenger finished.

17"He will prepare the way for the Chosen One, walking in the same spiritual powers of the prophet Great Spirit Is Creator (Elijah). He will turn the hearts of many fathers back toward their children, and many rebellious children will again honor the wisdom of their elders, so that people will be ready to participate in Creator's plan."[a]

When the spirit-messenger finished speaking, his words echoed through the lodge. Still trembling, Creator Will Remember (Zechariah) finally found his voice.

18Then he questioned the messenger, "We are too old to have children. How can I believe you?"

19The spirit-messenger answered, "My name is Creator's Mighty One (Gabriel), *his chief messenger.* I stand close to the Great Spirit! These good words I have spoken to you will come to pass, **20**but since you did not believe my words, you will not be able to speak until they are fulfilled."

21The people who were praying outside began to wonder why it was taking so long for Creator Will Remember (Zechariah) to come out of the lodge. **22**When he finally came out, unable to speak and making signs with his hands, they understood that he had seen a vision.

23When his traditional ceremonies were finished, he returned to his home in the hill country. **24**Soon afterward, Creator Is My Promise (Elizabeth) was with child. She stayed at home and for five moons did not show herself to anyone.

25She said in her heart, "The Giver of Breath has looked upon me with kindness and has taken away my shame. Now I will have respect in the eyes of my people."

BITTER TEARS

26When six moons had passed, the Great Spirit sent the same spirit-messenger, Creator's Mighty One (Gabriel), to another small, out-of-the-way place in the hill country called Seed Planter Village (Nazareth). **27**There he appeared to a young virgin woman named Bitter Tears (Mary), who was promised in marriage to a man named He Gives Sons (Joseph), a descendant of the great chief Much Loved One (David).

28Creator's Mighty One (Gabriel) said to her, "Greetings, highly favored one! You are close to the Great Spirit and greatly honored among women."

29Bitter Tears (Mary) was deeply troubled by this greeting and wondered what the spirit-messenger would say.

30"Do not fear," he comforted her, "for you have found goodwill in the eyes of the Great Mystery. **31**You will be with child and give birth to a son. You will name him Creator Sets Free (Jesus)."

It seemed like time stood still, and all creation stopped to listen as the messenger continued to speak.

32"He will be greatly honored, the Son of the One Above Us All. He will be a

---

[a] **1:17** Malachi 4:5-6

great chief like his ancestor Much Loved One (David) and will sit in his seat of honor. ³³He will always be chief over the tribes of Wrestles with Creator (Israel). His chiefly guidance will never end."

Bitter Tears's (Mary's) voice trembled with emotion, and her eyes grew wide as she looked into the face of the spirit-messenger.

³⁴She asked, "How will this be, since I have never been with a man?"

³⁵Creator's Mighty One (Gabriel) answered, "The Holy Spirit will spread his wings over you, and his great power from above will overshadow you. This holy child born to you will be the Son of the One Above Us All."

Then, to encourage her, ³⁶he said, "Your cousin Creator Is My Promise (Elizabeth), who was called barren one, is six moons with child. ³⁷See! There is nothing too hard for the Great Spirit."

She looked bravely into the face of the messenger.

³⁸"I am Creator's servant," she said with boldness. "Let it be for me just as you have said."

Then Creator's chief spirit-messenger left her.

COUSINS

³⁹Bitter Tears (Mary) quickly put together a traveling bundle and went to visit her cousin Creator Is My Promise (Elizabeth), who lived in a nearby village in the hill country of the Land of Promise (Judea). ⁴⁰When she entered the home of her relatives, she greeted her cousin.

⁴¹When Creator Is My Promise (Elizabeth) heard Bitter Tears's (Mary's) greeting, she felt her child jump inside her. She was filled with the Holy Spirit, ⁴²and with a loud cry she lifted her voice and spoke these blessing words to Bitter Tears (Mary).

"The Most Holy One has honored you more than any other woman," she laughed. "The child you carry inside you will bring great blessings to all people. ⁴³Why is Creator being so kind to me, sending the mother of the Great Chief to visit my home? ⁴⁴As soon as I heard your greeting, my baby jumped for joy inside me! ⁴⁵You have been chosen by the Maker of Life for a great honor, because you believed his words to you."

THE SONG OF BITTER TEARS

When Bitter Tears (Mary) heard this, she was filled with gladness, and her words flowed out like a song.

⁴⁶⁻⁴⁷"From deep in my heart I dance with joy to honor the Great Spirit. ⁴⁸Even though I am small and weak, he noticed me. Now I will be looked up to by all. ⁴⁹The Mighty One has lifted me up! His name is sacred. He is the Great and Holy One."

Her face seemed to shine as she continued.

⁵⁰"He shows kindness and pity to both children and elders who respect him. ⁵¹His strong arm has brought low the ones who think they are better than others. ⁵²He counts coup[a] with arrogant warrior chiefs but puts a headdress of honor on the ones with humble hearts."

She smiled, looked up to the sky, and shouted for joy!

---

[a] 1:52 "Counting coup" was a Native American practice among some of the Plains tribes of touching an enemy with a coup stick as an act of courage during battle, to show he could have killed him but chose to spare him instead. Each time the coup stick was used in battle, a mark would be placed on it. It counted the number of victories won.

53"He prepares a great feast for the ones who are hungry, but sends the fat ones home with empty bellies. **54-55**He has been kind to the tribes of Wrestles with Creator (Israel) who walk in his ways, for he has remembered the ancient promises he made to our ancestors—to Father of Many Nations (Abraham) and his descendants."

When she finished, they both laughed with joy. With hearts full of gladness they told each other their stories.

56For three moons Bitter Tears (Mary) stayed in the home of her cousin and then returned home to her own village.

A PROMISE FULFILLED

57When her time came, Creator Is My Promise (Elizabeth) gave birth to a son. **58**When her relatives and close friends heard the good news that the Great Spirit had been so kind to her, they were glad and rejoiced! **59**Then, eight days later at his naming ceremony, all the relatives wanted to name him after his father, Creator Will Remember (Zechariah).

According to tribal law, the cutting of the flesh ceremony was performed for all male children on the eighth day. The child's name was also given at that time.

60"No," she said to everyone's surprise. "His name will be Gift of Goodwill (John)!"

61But they said to her, "No one in your family has that name." **62**They made signs with their hands to Creator Will Remember (Zechariah) to see what he wanted to name him.

63He asked for a writing tablet and to their surprise wrote, "His name is Gift of Goodwill (John)." **64**Suddenly he could speak again, and when he opened his mouth, he began to give praise to the Great Spirit.

65All the people who heard about this trembled with wonder. Throughout the hills and valleys of the Land of Promise (Judea), they began to tell others what they had seen and heard. **66**All who listened began to wonder and say to themselves, "This child must have been born for some great thing." For it was clear that the hand of the Great Spirit was upon him in a powerful and good way.

67Then, with a glad heart, Creator Will Remember (Zechariah) spoke these words the Holy Spirit was giving him to say.

68"All blessings to the Great Spirit of the tribes of Wrestles with Creator (Israel)! For he has come to rescue his people from a great captivity. **69-70**Just as the prophets foretold long ago in the land of our ancestor Much Loved One (David), he has lifted up his coup stick[a] to show his great power to help us, **71**to rescue us from the arrows of our enemies and all who look down upon us with hate."

He lifted trembling hands to the sky and cried out.

72-73"He has given to us the same pity he has shown our ancestors and remembered the promise he made in the great peace treaty with Father of Many Nations (Abraham). **74-75**He has come to free us from the fear of our enemies, so we can walk all our days in his sacred and right ways."

Then he turned to his newborn son, and from deep in his spirit he spoke these words of blessing to him.

---

[a] **1:69-70** The coup stick was a stick with an eagle or hawk claw attached to its tip. It was used by some of the tribes of the Plains. A warrior in battle would scratch an enemy with it as an act of courage to show he could have killed him but chose to spare him instead.

76"And you, my son, will be a prophet from the One Above Us All. You will make a clear path for the coming of the Great Chief, 77to show his people that he will heal our broken ways by cleansing us from our bad hearts and releasing us from our wrongdoings. 78Because Creator is kind and gentle, he will come to us as the sunrise from above, 79to shine on the ones who sit in darkness and in the land of death's shadow, to guide our feet on the good path of peace."

80Gift of Goodwill (John) grew strong in *body and* spirit and stayed in the desert, waiting until the time was right to show himself to the tribes of Wrestles with Creator (Israel).

2 ✦◀✦▶◀✦▶◀✦▶◀✦▶◀✦▶◀✦▶

HUMBLE BIRTH

1-2When the time drew close for Bitter Tears (Mary) to have her child, the government of the People of Iron (Romans) ordered that the people be numbered and put on government rolls. This happened during the time that Powerful Protector (Quirinius) was the governor of Bright Sun (Syria). 3All the Tribal Members were required to travel to their own ancestral village to register.

4-5He Gives Sons (Joseph) and Bitter Tears (Mary) set out on a long journey from Seed Planter Village (Nazareth) in Circle of Nations (Galilee), to House of Bread (Bethlehem) in the Land of Promise (Judea), the village of their ancestor, the great chief Much Loved One (David).

The journey took several long days and cold nights as they traveled over high hills and through the dry desert. When they arrived, tired and weary, they entered the crowded village.

6The time for Bitter Tears (Mary) to have her child was upon her! 7But no place could be found in the lodging house, *so He Gives Sons (Joseph) found a sheep cave where it was warm and dry.* There she gave birth to her son. They wrapped him in a soft, warm blanket *and laid him on a baby board.* Then they placed him on a bed of straw in a feeding trough.

8That night, in the fields nearby, shepherds were keeping watch over their sheep. 9Suddenly a great light from above was shining all around them. A spirit-messenger from Creator appeared to them. They shook with fear and trembled 10as the messenger said to them, "Do not fear! I bring you the good story that will be told to all nations. 11Today in the village of Much Loved One (David) an Honored Chief has been born who will set his people free. He is the Chosen One!"

12The spirit-messenger continued, "This is how you will know him—you will find the child wrapped in a blanket and lying in a feeding trough."

13Suddenly, next to the messenger, a great number of spirit-warriors from the spirit-world above appeared giving thanks to Creator, saying, 14"All honor to the One Above Us All, and let peace and good will follow all who walk upon the earth."

15When the messengers returned to the spirit-world above, the shepherds said to each other, "Let us go and see this great thing Creator has told to us." 16So they hurried to the village of Chief Much Loved One (David) and found Bitter Tears (Mary), He Gives Sons (Joseph), and the child, who, just as they were told, was lying in a feeding trough!

17The shepherds began to tell everyone what they had seen and heard about this child, 18and all who heard their story were amazed.

¹⁹Bitter Tears (Mary) kept these things hidden in her heart and wondered what all this would mean. ²⁰The shepherds returned to their fields, giving thanks to the Great Spirit for the wonders they had seen and heard.

KEEPING THE TRADITIONS

²¹Eight days after the birth of their son, in keeping with the traditional cutting of the flesh ceremony,ᵃ they named him Creator Sets Free (Jesus), the name given them by the spirit-messenger before the child was born.

²²⁻²³Then, about one moon later, the time came for them to present their child to the Great Spirit in the Sacred Village of Peace (Jerusalem). This was for their cleansing ceremony, an ancient tradition from the lawgiver Drawn from the Water (Moses), who said, "Every male child who is first to open the womb will be holy in the Great Spirit's sight. ²⁴Bring two turtledoves or two young pigeons to be burned with fire as a sweet-smelling smoke offering."

This shows they were poor, for this was the offering a poor family was permitted to bring according to tribal law.

²⁵When they arrived at the sacred lodge in Village of Peace (Jerusalem), they were welcomed by Creator Hears (Simeon), a respected elder who did what was right in the Great Spirit's sight, and waited patiently for him to fulfill his promises to the tribes of Wrestles with Creator (Israel). ²⁶The Holy Spirit rested on him and told him he would not die until he saw Creator's Chosen One with his own eyes.

²⁷As Creator Hears (Simeon) followed the guidance of the Spirit, he arrived at the sacred lodge just in time to see He Gives Sons (Joseph) and Bitter Tears (Mary) bringing their child for the traditional ceremony given in their tribal law. ²⁸Creator Hears (Simeon) took the child into his arms and spoke words of blessing over him.

²⁹⁻³²"O Great Father," he prayed, "I now see with my own eyes the one you have prepared for all Nations, the one who will heal our broken ways and set us free. He will make a clear path for all people to see and bring honor to the tribes of Wrestles with Creator (Israel). Now, just as you have said, I can cross over in peace."

³³The child's father and mother were amazed at what was being said. ³⁴So Creator Hears (Simeon) spoke blessing words over them also.

He then turned to Bitter Tears (Mary) and spoke softly in her ear.

"This child has been chosen for the fall and rising of many in the tribes of Wrestles with Creator (Israel). He will be a sign that will be spoken against, ³⁵exposing the thoughts of many."

His voice softened as she looked sadly into his eyes.

He said to her, "Even your own spirit will be pierced through like a sharp arrow."

³⁶⁻³⁷As they pondered his words, a holy woman named Woman of Goodwill (Anna) welcomed them. She was an elder from the tribe of Walks with a Glad Heart (Asher) and the daughter of Face of Creator (Phanuel). She had married at a young age and lived with her husband for seven winters, but had now been a widow for eighty-four winters. She served the Great Spirit at his sacred lodge night and day

---

ᵃ**2:21** Circumcision

with fasting and many prayers. **38**When she saw the child, she gave thanks to Creator and began telling about the child to all who were waiting for Creator to fulfill the promises he made to the Sacred Village of Peace (Jerusalem).

39After they performed all the ceremonies that Creator's Law required, they returned to Circle of Nations (Galilee), to their home in Seed Planter Village (Nazareth). **40**In this village the child grew strong in his spirit and was filled with wisdom, for the blessing of the Great Spirit was resting on him.

COMING OF AGE

41By traditional law it was a custom for all the families of the tribes of Wrestles with Creator (Israel) to journey to Village of Peace (Jerusalem) to participate in the ancient Passover festival.

This festival celebrated the time when the lawgiver, Drawn from the Water (Moses), had set them free from captivity to the powerful nation of Black Land (Egypt). He did this by using the great power Creator gave him to perform many signs and wonders.

42When Creator Sets Free (Jesus) was twelve winters old, his family traveled together to celebrate this traditional feast.

43When the festival was over, his parents began their journey home. Without telling his parents, Creator Sets Free (Jesus) stayed behind in Village of Peace (Jerusalem). **44**They thought he was with the other relatives and friends traveling with them. After a *long* day's journey, they began to look for him but were unable to find him, **45**so they returned to Village of Peace (Jerusalem) to look for him there.

46After searching for three days, they found him at Creator's ceremonial lodge. He was sitting with the elders, listening to them and asking questions. **47**All who heard his answers were amazed at his wisdom and understanding of the spiritual ways.

48His parents were surprised and at a loss for words, but then his mother scolded him, "Son, why have you treated us this way? Your father and I were worried and our hearts were heavy as we looked everywhere for you!"

49"Why were you looking everywhere for me?" he asked. "I thought you would know to look for me here, in my Father's lodge, doing what he sent me to do."

50But they did not understand the meaning of what he was saying to them. **51**He then returned to Seed Planter Village (Nazareth) with them and continued to be a respectful son following the guidance of his parents. But his mother hid these words in her heart.

52Creator Sets Free (Jesus), as a young man, grew in wisdom and strength, and had respect in the eyes of the people and the Great Spirit.

GIFT OF GOODWILL COMES FORWARD

Eighteen long winters had now come and gone. The People of Iron (Romans) had many new rulers and governors, and the tribes of Wrestles with Creator (Israel) had a new chief holy man for the sacred lodge.

1It was now the fifteenth year of the rule of Son of the Great River (Tiberius Caesar). Under him was Spear of the Great Waters (Pontius Pilate), the governor ruling over the Land of Promise (Judea).

The bad-hearted Chief Looks Brave (Herod) had been chosen by the People of Iron (Romans) to rule over the territory of Circle of Nations (Galilee). His brother Friend of Horses (Philip) ruled over the nearby territory of Guarded Mountains (Iturea) and Place of Stones (Trachonitis), and End of Sorrow (Lysanias) ruled the territory of the Ten Villages from its chief village Many Meadows (Abilene).

²Walks Humbly (Annas) was still the chief holy man, along with Hollow in the Rock (Caiaphas), who would soon replace him.

It was during this time that Creator's message came down from above *like a burden basket*[a] and rested on Gift of Goodwill (John), the son of Creator Will Remember (Zechariah), while he was praying in the desert wilderness.

> *The time had come for him to begin his work with the tribes of Wrestles with Creator (Israel) and prepare the way for the Chosen One.*

³Gift of Goodwill (John) began to walk the territory around the river Flowing Down (Jordan). His message was for all to return to Creator's right ways of thinking and come to the river to perform the purification ceremony[b] to be released from their bad hearts and broken ways.

⁴The prophet Creator Will Help Us (Isaiah) told about him long ago, "*He will be* a voice howling in the desert, 'Clear the pathways! Make a straight path for the coming of the Honored One! ⁵The valleys will be filled in. The mountains

and hills will be brought down low. The crooked places will be made straight and the rough road smooth. ⁶Then all people will clearly see the good road that sets them free.'"[c]

PREPARING THE WAY

⁷Large crowds of people were coming out to hear his message and have him perform the purification ceremony.[d] He noticed *some of the spiritual leaders in* the crowd and warned them, "You nest of poisonous snakes! Who warned you to run and hide from the coming storm? ⁸Prove to others by the way you live that you have returned to the good road. Do not think you can say, 'Father of Many Nations (Abraham) is our ancestor.' Do you not know that the Great Spirit can make these stones into his children? ⁹The tomahawk is at the root of the trees. The ones that have no good fruit will be cut down and tossed into the fire."

¹⁰When the crowds heard his words, they *were afraid and* asked, "What should we do?"

¹¹He answered, "If you have two blankets, give one to someone who has none, and the one with food should share it."

¹²There were tribal tax collectors who came to participate in the ceremony who asked him, "Wisdomkeeper, what should we do?"

¹³"Collect no more taxes than the People of Iron (Romans) permit," he answered. "*To take more is to steal from the people and dishonor the Great Spirit.*"

¹⁴When the lodge soldiers heard this, they said, "What about us? What can we do?"

---

[a] **3:2** The Apache and a few other Southwestern tribes have burden baskets. They are often used in a coming-of-age ceremony, symbolizing the transition from the old generation to the new. We use it here to show that John carries the burden of transition from the old covenant to the new covenant (peace treaty).
[b] **3:3** Baptism
[c] **3:6** Isaiah 40:3-5
[d] **3:7** Baptism

"Do not use fear or violence to force money from people or accuse them falsely," he answered, "and be satisfied with your pay."

¹⁵When the people heard these words, they began to have hope. They were pondering in their hearts, "Could Gift of Goodwill (John) be the Chosen One?"

¹⁶He gave them this answer, "I perform the purification ceremony[a] with water, but there is one coming who is greater and more powerful than I."

He paused for a moment and softened his voice.

Then he said, "I am not even worthy to bend low and untie his moccasins."

Then he lifted his hands and cried out with a loud voice!

"He is the one who will perform the purification ceremony[a] with the fire of the Holy Spirit! ¹⁷He will separate the grain from the husks. His harvest basket is in his hands. He will store the good grain in his barn, but the husks he will burn away with a fire no one can put out."

¹⁸With many more words Gift of Goodwill (John) warned and encouraged the people with the good story *of Creator's good road.*

¹⁹Gift of Goodwill (John) warned Chief Looks Brave (Herod) about stealing his own brother's wife and his many other bad-hearted ways. ²⁰So Looks Brave (Herod) had him put in prison, adding this to his many evil deeds.

CREATOR SETS FREE COMES FORWARD

The time had now come for Creator Sets Free (Jesus) to show himself to all the people. He was now a mature man of about

thirty winters. *He came from Circle of Nations (Galilee) to the river Flowing Down (Jordan) to have Gift of Goodwill (John) perform the purification ceremony.*

²¹While the people were coming to Gift of Goodwill (John) for the ceremony, Creator Sets Free (Jesus) came also. Then the ceremony was performed for him, and while he was praying, the sky opened up ²²and the Holy Spirit came down in the form of a dove and rested on him. A voice from the spirit-world above spoke *like distant thunder,* "You are my much-loved Son who makes my heart glad!"

HIS FAMILY TREE

²³Creator Sets Free (Jesus) was about thirty winters old when he began his great work. He was the son, so it was thought, of He Gives Sons (Joseph), the son of One Above Us (Heli), ²⁴son of Gift of the Great Spirit (Matthat), son of He Brings Together (Levi), son of My Chief (Melchi), son of He Grows Strong (Jannai), son of He Gathers Much (Joseph), ²⁵son of Gift from Above (Mattathias), son of Burden Bearer (Amos), son of He Gives Comfort (Nahum), son of Protected One (Esli), son of Light Bringer (Naggai), ²⁶son of Small One (Maath), son of Gift from Above (Mattathias), son of He Listens (Semein), son of He Gathers Much (Joseph), son of Gives Honor (Judah), ²⁷son of Shows Goodwill (Joanan), son of Walks Friendly (Rhesa), son of Born in Village of Confusion (Zerubbabel), son of Ask Creator (Shealtiel), son of Burning Light (Neri), ²⁸son of My Chief (Melchi), son of Clothed in Beauty (Addi), son of Talks to Spirits (Cosam), son of Love Beyond Measure (Elmadam), son of He Looks Around (Er), ²⁹son of Creator Gives Freedom (Joshua), son of Creator Helps Him (Eliezer), son of Honored by Creator (Jorim), son of Gift of the Great Spirit (Matthat), son of He Brings

---

[a]**3:16** Baptism

Together (Levi), ³⁰son of Creator Hears (Simeon), son of Give Him Praise (Judah), son of He Gathers Much (Joseph), son of Creator Shows Goodwill (Jonam), son of He Builds Up (Eliakim), ³¹son of He Makes Full (Melea), son of He Is Ready (Menna), son of Gift Giver (Mattatha), son of He Will Give (Nathan), son of Much Loved One (David), ³²son of Original Man (Jesse), son of He Works Hard (Obed), son of Moves with Strength (Boaz), son of He Makes Peace (Salmon), son of Talks with Snakes (Nahshon), ³³son of Noble Relative (Amminadab), son of He Is Lifted Up (Admin), son of Lifted Up High (Arni), son of Circle of Tipis (Hezron), son of He Breaks Through (Perez), son of Give Him Praise (Judah), ³⁴son of Heel Grabber (Jacob), son of He Made Us Laugh (Isaac), son of Father of Many Nations (Abraham), son of He Made Them Wait (Terah), son of Snorting Buffalo (Nahor), ³⁵son of Growing Stem (Serug), son of Faithful Friend (Reu), son of Where the Water Divides (Peleg), son of Over the River (Eber), son of Shooting Arrow (Shelah), ³⁶son of Made Straight (Cainan), son of Son of His Mother (Arphaxad), son of His Name Is Known (Shem), son of One Who Rests (Noah), son of Strong Wild Man (Lamech), ³⁷son of Long Arrow (Methuselah), son of Walks with Creator (Enoch), son of He Came Down (Jared), son of Full of Praise (Mahalaleel), son of Made Straight (Cainan), ³⁸son of Weak Human Being (Enos), son of Drinks Too Much (Seth), son of Red Clay (Adam), son of the Great Spirit.

4

VISION QUEST

¹Creator Sets Free (Jesus) was now filled with the Holy Spirit. From the river Flowing Down (Jordan), the Spirit guided him into the desert wilderness, *a dry and lonely place filled with wild animals and many other dangers.* ²There, for forty days, he would be put to the test by Accuser (Satan), the evil trickster snake.

In the story of creation, the first man and woman lived in a Garden of Beauty and Harmony. The evil trickster snake came to them and twisted the words of the Great Spirit to deceive them. They listened to the snake, lost the life of beauty and harmony, and fell under the curse of death—both physical and spiritual. This snake is an evil spirit, sometimes called Accuser (Satan), who opposes the good things Creator wants for all two-leggeds.

For forty days and nights Creator Sets Free (Jesus) ate nothing. His body became weak, and his hunger grew strong.

When the evil trickster snake saw that Creator Sets Free (Jesus) was weak and hungry, he came to him and whispered in his ear.

³"Are you the Son of the Great Spirit?" he hissed. "Prove it by turning these stones into frybread."

⁴"It is written in the Sacred Teachings," Creator Sets Free (Jesus) said, "'frybread is not the only food for two-leggeds.'ᵃ"

⁵Once more Accuser (Satan) took him up *to a high mountain* and, in a moment of time, showed him all the great nations of the world. ⁶"All of their power and beauty can be yours!" the snake said smoothly. "They were given over to me, and I can give them to anyone I choose. ⁷If you will bow down to me and my ways, they will all be yours!"

⁸"Go away from me, you evil trickster!" he answered. "For it also says in the

---

ᵃ4:4 Deuteronomy 8:3

Sacred Teachings, 'The Great Spirit is the only one to bow down to and walk in his ways.'[a]"

⁹The evil snake took him to the Great Spirit's sacred lodge in Village of Peace (Jerusalem). He took him to the very top of the lodge, high above the village. "Prove you are the Son of the Great Spirit and jump down from here!" the snake taunted him. ¹⁰"Do not the Sacred Teachings also say, 'His spirit-messengers will watch over you to keep you from harm. ¹¹They will not even let your foot hit a stone'[b]?"

¹²"Yes," Creator Sets Free (Jesus) said back to him, "but they also say, 'Do not put the Great Spirit to a foolish test.'[c]"

¹³Creator Sets Free (Jesus) had passed every test. The evil snake could think of nothing more, *so he slithered away* to wait for another time.

HIS OWN VILLAGE REJECTS HIM

¹⁴The power of the Spirit was now resting on Creator Sets Free (Jesus), so he returned to the territory of Circle of Nations (Galilee). News about him began to spread like wildfire throughout the villages, ¹⁵for he was teaching in their gathering houses, and the people gave him much honor.

In the Law given by Drawn from the Water (Moses), all the tribes were instructed to keep a Day of Resting called the Sabbath. This was the seventh day of the week, to honor and remember the time when Creator rested on the seventh day after making all things. On that day no work was to be done, and how far one could walk was limited. The tribal people would meet together at their village gathering houses on this day.

¹⁶On one of these Days of Resting, Creator Sets Free (Jesus) returned to his boyhood home in Seed Planter Village (Nazareth). As was his tradition, he entered the gathering house and stood up to read from the ancient Sacred Teachings. ¹⁷The headman handed him the scroll with the words from the prophet Creator Will Help Us (Isaiah). He opened the scroll and began to read.

He spoke with deep respect in his voice as he held the scroll in a sacred manner. His words were strong and clear, and his eyes were bright and full of life as he read.

¹⁸"The Spirit of Creator has come to rest on me. He has chosen me to tell the good story to the ones who are poor. He has sent me to mend broken hearts, to tell prisoners they have been set free, to make the blind see again, and to lift up the ones who have been pushed down— ¹⁹to make it known that Creator's Year of Setting Free[d] has come at last!"[e]

²⁰He rolled up the scroll, returned it to the headman, and sat down. All eyes were fixed on him, wondering what he would say.

He looked around at them and spoke clearly, with a strong voice, ²¹"Today these words you have heard have found their full meaning."

Then he began to teach and share his wisdom with them.

²²At first they were amazed at the power and beauty of his words.

But soon the meaning of his words sank into their hearts, and the mood of the people began to change.

---

[a]**4:8** Deuteronomy 6:13
[b]**4:11** Psalm 91:11-12
[c]**4:12** Deuteronomy 6:16

[d]**4:19** Jubilee (see Leviticus 25:8-17)
[e]**4:19** Isaiah 61:1-2

"Is this not the son of *Bitter Tears (Mary) and* He Gives Sons (Joseph), the wood carver?"

23So he said to them, "I am sure you will tell me this wise saying, 'Healer, use your medicine on yourself.' And you will say, 'We want to see you do here in your own village the powerful signs you did in Village of Comfort (Capernaum).' 24But the truth is, a prophet is given much honor except in his own village, among his own clan, and in his own house."

Those who were listening continued to grumble out loud, shaking their heads and rolling their eyes.

25"I speak from my heart," he said to them. "There were many widows in the land of Wrestles with Creator (Israel) during the days of the prophet Great Spirit Is Creator (Elijah). It was a time of great hunger, and food was hard to find. It had not rained for more than three winters. 26But Great Spirit Is Creator (Elijah) was not sent to any of these widows. Instead, he was sent to Refining Fire Woman (Zarephath), a widow in the territory of Hunting Grounds (Sidon), *an Outside Nation.*[a] 27And there were many with a skin disease in the days of the prophet Creator Saves Us (Elisha), but none were healed and cleansed except for Looks Handsome (Naaman), an outsider from Bright Sun (Syria), *the head soldier of the enemy's army.*"[b]

28The people in the gathering house were insulted and furious at his words. 29Together they herded him out to the village hillside to throw him off the cliff, 30but he slipped through the crowd and went on his way.

[a]4:26 1 Kings 17:8-24
[b]4:27 2 Kings 5:1-19

VILLAGE OF COMFORT

31From there he went to Village of Comfort (Capernaum) in the territory of Circle of Nations (Galilee). On the Day of Resting 32he was teaching in their gathering house and the people were amazed at his manner of speaking, for he spoke boldly with authority, *not like the other spiritual leaders.*

33There was a man that day in this gathering house who had an unclean evil spirit. Suddenly, the man wailed out loud, 34"AAAIIIEEE! Creator Sets Free (Jesus) from Seed Planter Village (Nazareth). What are you doing here? Have you come to put an end to us? I know who you are! You are the Holy One from the Great Spirit!"

35Creator Sets Free (Jesus) spoke sharply to him, "Be silent! Leave this man now!" The evil spirit shook the man, threw him to the ground, and came out without hurting him.

36The people were in awe and began to ask each other, "What is he teaching? What new medicine is this? He even tells the unclean spirits what to do—and they do it!"

37Because of this, his reputation spread like wildfire throughout the Circle of Nations (Galilee) and to all the surrounding territories.

HOME OF ONE WHO HEARS

38After he left the gathering house, Creator Sets Free (Jesus) went to the home of One Who Hears (Simon). The wife of One Who Hears (Simon) was there. Her mother was sick in bed with a bad fever, so they asked Creator Sets Free (Jesus) to help her. 39He went and stood over her and told the fever to go, and it left! *With a glad heart* she got up and went to prepare a meal for them.

⁴⁰Later that day, when the sun was going down, many sick people were brought to him. He touched them all and healed them. ⁴¹Many were set free from evil spirits. As the spirits left them, they howled with loud voices, saying, "You are the Chosen One, Creator's own Son!" But he spoke sharply to them and did not let them speak, for they knew who he was.

⁴²The next day, before the sunrise, he found a quiet, out-of-the-way place to be alone and pray. But the crowds found him again and would not let him go. ⁴³He said to them, "I was sent to tell you the good story about Creator's good road. You must let me go to other villages, so they can also hear."

⁴⁴So he continued to teach and tell his stories in the gathering houses of the Land of Promise (Judea).

5

FISHING FOR TWO-LEGGEDS

¹As Creator Sets Free (Jesus) was teaching at Lake of Chief Garden (Gennesaret), a great number of people pressed in close to hear him speak the words of the Great Spirit. ²He was standing on the shore and saw two fishing canoes, but the fishermen had left their canoes and were washing their nets. ³He climbed into the canoe belonging to One Who Hears (Simon) and asked him to push out a little from the shore. He then sat in the canoe and taught the large gathering of people.

⁴When he had finished speaking, he said to One Who Hears (Simon), "Push out farther into the deep water and throw in your nets for a catch."

⁵"Wisdomkeeper," he answered, "we have been fishing all night and caught nothing, but because it is you who ask, I will do it."

⁶They threw the net out into the water.

Before they knew what was happening, the net became heavy. They struggled with the weight of it and began to pull it in.

But the net was so full of fish it began to tear. ⁷They called out to the other canoe for help. The men came and began to pull in the nets. *Fish of every size poured into the two canoes until they were so full they began to sink.*

⁸⁻¹⁰When One Who Hears (Simon), along with his fishing partners—He Takes Over (James) and He Shows Goodwill (John), the sons of Gift of Creator (Zebedee)—saw what happened, they were filled with wonder and awe at the great catch of fish.

One Who Hears (Simon) fell to his knees in front of Creator Sets Free (Jesus). "Wisdomkeeper!" he groaned. "Go away from me! For I am a bad-hearted and unholy man."

"Do not fear!" Creator Sets Free (Jesus) told him. "From now on your nets will catch two-leggeds."

¹¹When they returned to the shore, they left everything and began to walk the road with him.

SKIN DISEASE CLEANSED

¹²While he was in one of these villages, a man with a skin disease all over his body came to Creator Sets Free (Jesus). He humbled himself, bowed down, and pleaded with him. "Honored One!" he cried. "If you want to, you can heal and cleanse me."

¹³Creator Sets Free (Jesus), stirred with compassion, reached out and touched the man. "I want to!" he said. "Be

cleansed!" And right away the disease left him and he was healed.

[14]Creator Sets Free (Jesus) sent him away at once. "Tell no one!" he said. "Go and show yourself to a holy man and have him perform the cleansing ceremony given to us by the lawgiver Drawn from the Water (Moses), to show the holy man what the Great Spirit has done for you."[a]

Tribal law instructed that a person healed of a skin disease must be pronounced ceremonially clean by a holy man.

[15]The reputation of Creator Sets Free (Jesus) began to grow among the people as word about him spread. The crowds came from everywhere to hear him speak and be healed of their sicknesses. [16]But he often left the crowds and went out into the desert wilderness to pray.

SPIRITUAL LEADERS OFFENDED

[17]On another day he was teaching *at a house in Village of Comfort (Capernaum).* The Separated Ones (Pharisees) and the scroll keepers had come from the surrounding villages of Circle of Nations (Galilee) and from as far as the Land of Promise (Judea) and Village of Peace (Jerusalem) to hear him speak.

The healing power of the Great Spirit was there, resting on Creator Sets Free (Jesus).

[18]Several men came carrying a paralyzed man on a sleeping mat to bring him to Creator Sets Free (Jesus), [19]but they could not get past the crowd. In their desperation, they climbed up to the rooftop and broke through the roof tiles. They lowered the paralyzed man down, sleeping mat and all, right in front of Creator Sets Free (Jesus). [20]When he saw

[a]5:14 Leviticus 14:2-32

their trust in him, he said to the paralyzed man, "Young man, you are released from your broken ways and wrongdoings."

[21]The scroll keepers and the Separated Ones (Pharisees) began to grumble among themselves, "Who is this man to speak lies against the Great Spirit with such disrespect? Who but the Maker of Life can release a man from his wrongdoings?"

[22]In his spirit, Creator Sets Free (Jesus) knew what they were thinking and said to them, "Why are your hearts full of dark thoughts and questions? [23]Is it easier to tell a paralyzed man, 'Get up and walk,' or to say to him, 'You are released from your wrongdoings'?"

The room became quiet as he waited for an answer.

[24]*When no one answered, he said to them,* "This is how you will know the True Human Being has the right to forgive bad hearts and wrongdoings on this earth." He turned to the paralyzed man and said, "Get up, and when you have rolled up your sleeping bundle, walk to your home." [25]Right away the man stood up in front of them and did what he said, giving thanks to the Great Spirit for his healing.

[26]Great respect and awe filled the hearts of all who were in the house. They gave honor to Creator, saying, "Today we have seen how mysterious the ways of the Great Spirit can be."

EATING WITH OUTCASTS

[27]After this he taught again by the lakeshore. As he walked by, he saw a tribal tax collector sitting at his tax booth.

Tribal tax collectors were often Tribal Members who were given the right to collect taxes for the People of Iron (Romans). They could force their own people, under the threat of violence, to pay them. To make a living, they would take more than the People of Iron (Romans) required. But many of them became greedy and took even more than they were permitted. They were hated and looked down on by the people.

The name of this tribal tax collector was He Brings Together (Levi).[a] Creator Sets Free (Jesus) went to him and said, "Come, walk the road with me." [28]He got up from his booth, left it all behind, and began to walk the road with him.

[29]He Brings Together (Levi) hosted a great feast for Creator Sets Free (Jesus). *He invited all his friends to come.* Tribal tax collectors, along with other outcasts, were all sitting around the table with Creator Sets Free (Jesus).

The Separated Ones (Pharisees) called certain people outcasts. They used their strict interpretation of their tribal law as a way to point them out. These outcasts were not permitted to enter the gathering houses. They were looked down on and despised by the Separated Ones (Pharisees). Outcasts included tribal tax collectors, prostitutes, people who ate and drank too much, ones with diseases that made them ceremonially unclean, and anyone who was not a member of the tribes of Wrestles with Creator (Israel).

[30]When the Separated Ones (Pharisees) and the scroll keepers saw Creator Sets Free (Jesus) eating with outcasts, they complained to his followers, saying, "Why does your wisdomkeeper keep company with tribal tax collectors and outcasts?"

[31]Creator Sets Free (Jesus) overheard them and said, "People who are well do

---

[a]**5:27** Later known as Matthew

not need medicine. [32]I have not come for the ones with good hearts. No! I have come to help the outcasts find the path back home again."

FRESH SKINS FOR NEW WINE

[33]Then they asked Creator Sets Free (Jesus) another question. "The followers of Gift of Goodwill (John) often go without eating to pray, and so do the followers of the Separated Ones (Pharisees). So why do your followers feast and eat so much?"

A gentle smile came across the face of Creator Sets Free (Jesus), and with a sigh he responded.

[34]"Do you expect wedding guests to be sad and go without eating when the groom is hosting a feast?" he asked. [35]"The time will come when he is gone. Then they will be sad and go without eating."

They still did not understand, [36]so he told them this wise saying, "No one uses a new piece of cloth to patch an old garment, for it would shrink and make the tear worse. [37]No one puts new wine into an old wineskin, for the new wine would burst the skins. [38-39]New and fresh wineskins are what is needed, but the ones who have a taste for the old do not want the new."

He said this to show that the old ways of the spiritual leaders did not reflect the beauty of the new way he was bringing.

CHIEF OF THE DAY OF RESTING

[1]On another Day of Resting, Creator Sets Free (Jesus) and his followers were walking through a field of grain. The men were hungry, so they plucked some grain, rubbed the husks off in their

hands, and began to eat. ²When the Separated Ones (Pharisees) saw what they were doing, they said to him, "Why do your followers do what is not permitted on the Day of Resting?"

³⁻⁴He answered them, "Have you not heard about the time long ago when the great chief Much Loved One (David) was hungry? How he and his followers went into Creator's sacred lodge and ate the ceremonial bread? Only the holy men are permitted to eat this bread."

He paused to let them think about his words.

⁵And then he added, "The True Human Being is Chief over the Day of Resting!"

HEALING ON THE DAY OF RESTING

⁶On another Day of Resting Creator Sets Free (Jesus) went into a gathering house and began to teach the people. A man was there with a shriveled and useless hand. ⁷The scroll keepers and the Separated Ones (Pharisees) kept a close eye on Creator Sets Free (Jesus) to see whether he would heal the man, so they could accuse him of not honoring the Day of Resting.

⁸Creator Sets Free (Jesus) knew what they were scheming, so he said to the man, "Come, stand here, where everyone can see you." So the man did what he said. ⁹Then Creator Sets Free (Jesus) asked them, "On the Day of Resting, is it permitted to help or to harm, to rescue or destroy?"

They just looked at him and said nothing. At first there was fire in his eyes! But his anger turned to sorrow when he saw their hearts of stone.

¹⁰He looked around the room and then turned to the man and said, "Stretch out your hand." He stretched it out, and it was the same as his good hand!

¹¹The Separated Ones (Pharisees) stormed out in a fit of rage and began to counsel together about what could be done with Creator Sets Free (Jesus).

TWELVE MESSAGE BEARERS

The crowds were growing larger. The task of healing and helping this great number of people was too much for Creator Sets Free (Jesus) to do alone. He knew that he needed help from the ones who were walking the road with him.

¹²He went by himself to a mountain, where he prayed all night to the Great Spirit. ¹³In the morning, on the mountainside, he gathered the ones who had been walking the road with him. He chose twelve of them to be his message bearers.

Here are the names of the ones he chose:

¹⁴First there was One Who Hears (Simon), whom he named Stands on the Rock (Peter), and his brother Stands with Courage (Andrew). Then he chose two brothers whom he called Sons of Thunder—He Takes Over (James) and He Shows Goodwill (John).

Next there was Friend of Horses (Philip) and Son of Ground Digger (Bartholomew) ¹⁵along with He Brings Together (Levi)[a] and Looks Like His Brother (Thomas).

Then he chose He Takes Charge (James), son of First to Change (Alphaeus), along with One Who Listens (Simon) the Firebrand (Zealot) ¹⁶and Speaks Well Of (Judas) the son of He Takes Hold (James). And last of all he chose Speaks Well Of (Judas), who later betrayed him.

---

[a] 6:15 Later known as Matthew

¹⁷Creator Sets Free (Jesus), along with his twelve message bearers and a large number of his followers, went down from the mountain to where the ground is flat. A great number of people came to hear him speak and to be healed. They came from all over the Land of Promise (Judea), from Village of Peace (Jerusalem), and from the coast of Rock Land (Tyre) and Hunting Grounds (Sidon).

¹⁸The ones tormented by unclean spirits were being set free. ¹⁹All the people were trying to touch him, for great power was flowing out from him to heal them all!

WAYS OF BLESSING OR SORROW

²⁰Creator Sets Free (Jesus) looked out over the crowd of his followers and began to teach them about the ways of Creator's good road.

"Creator's blessing rests on you who are poor and in need. The good road is yours to walk.

²¹"Creator's blessing rests on you who hunger now, for you will be filled to the full.

"Creator's blessing rests on the ones who weep now, for your sorrow will turn into laughter.

²²"Creator's blessing rests on you when you are hated and rejected, looked down on and treated as worthless, all because you have chosen to walk the good road with the True Human Being.

²³"When this happens, let your hearts be glad and jump for joy! The spirit-world above will honor you, for this is the same way your ancestors treated the prophets of their day. *You are walking in their moccasins now!*"

Here is what he said to the privileged among the people:

²⁴"Sorrow and trouble will be the end of you who store up possessions for yourselves, for you have already had a life of ease.

²⁵"Sorrow and trouble will be the end of you who eat your fill now. You will go hungry later.

"Sorrow and trouble will be the end of you who are laughing about this now, for your own trail of tears is coming.

²⁶"Sorrow and trouble will be your end, when others say only good things about you, for that is what our ancestors said about the prophets who told lies.

THE WAY TO TREAT YOUR ENEMIES

²⁷"Hear me, you who are listening now, I am telling you to love to your enemies, do good to the ones who look down on you, ²⁸return blessing for cursing, and send up good prayers for the ones who give you trouble and pain.

²⁹"If someone slaps you on the side of your face, show the strength of your heart and offer the other side. In the same way, if a thief takes your coat, offer your shirt also.

³⁰"When someone in need asks, do not hold back. Do what you can to help. If someone takes what is yours, let them keep it."

"*Here is another way to see what I am saying:* ³¹Help others in the same way you would want them to help you.

³²⁻³⁴"Where is the honor in only showing love to the ones who do the same for you? Why should you be given respect for doing good to the ones who do you good, or for lending only to the ones who can repay you? Even tribal tax collectors and outcasts do these things.

³⁵"Instead, show love and respect to your enemies, help them when they are in need without asking them to repay you. This will show that you are children of your Father from above, for he is kind

and takes pity on the ones with bad hearts, even when they do not thank him for it. ³⁶So then, show kindness to others in the same way as your Father the Great Spirit.

BLIND GUIDES

³⁷"Do not judge others, and you will not be judged. When you release others from their wrongdoings, you will be released from yours. ³⁸The amount you measure out to others is the amount that comes back, like a basket that has been filled to the top, shaken down, and packed together, until it overflows. What you give out will come back to you—full circle."

³⁹He gave them a wise saying, "How can a blind person guide another who is blind? Will they not both stumble and fall? ⁴⁰The one guided cannot rise above his guide but will be just like him—*blind.*

"*Think of it this way,* ⁴¹how can you see the speck of wood in someone else's eye when you cannot even see the log in your own eye? ⁴²How can you say, 'Here, let me help you,' when you cannot see that you are the one who needs help? Stop pretending to be something you are not!

GOOD AND BAD TREES

⁴³"Healthy trees give good fruit and rotten trees give bad fruit. ⁴⁴Do grapes come from a thorn bush or figs from thistles?

⁴⁵"*The human heart is like a medicine pouch.* Good-hearted people speak from the good medicine stored in their hearts. Bad-hearted people speak from the bad medicine stored in their hearts. For the mouth will speak what the heart is filled with.

⁴⁶"How is it that you call me 'Great Chief' but do not walk in my ways? ⁴⁷The ones who listen to me and walk in these ways are like a man who built a lodge. ⁴⁸He dug deep to find solid ground to build on. When a flood came, the waters beat against the lodge, but it stood strong. Nothing could shake it, for it was built on solid ground.

⁴⁹"The ones who hear my words but do not walk in these ways are like another man, who built his lodge on soft ground. When the flood came against it, the lodge crashed to the ground, and all that was in it was lost."

7 ◈◈◈◈◈◈◈◈◈

A SOLDIER FROM THE PEOPLE OF IRON

¹When Creator Sets Free (Jesus) was finished speaking to the people, he went to Village of Comfort (Capernaum).

²A head soldier of the People of Iron (Romans) had a servant he cared deeply about who was sick and near death. ³When the head soldier heard about Creator Sets Free (Jesus), he asked some elders from the tribes of Wrestles with Creator (Israel) to go to him and ask him to heal the servant.

⁴⁻⁵The elders found Creator Sets Free (Jesus) and begged him to help the head soldier. "He is a man of honor who loves our nation and has built a gathering house for us. He is worth helping."

⁶So Creator Sets Free (Jesus) followed them. They were not far from the house when the head soldier sent some messengers to say to him, "Honored One, I do not want you to bring trouble on yourself by coming into my house. ⁷That's why I did not think it wise to come to you myself. If you will only speak a word, my servant will be healed. ⁸I too am a man under orders and have many soldiers under me. I say to this one 'go,' and he goes, and to another 'come,' and he comes. My servants do what I say."

⁹Creator Sets Free (Jesus) was amazed at this answer. He turned to the large crowd that was with him and said, "I have never seen such great faith, not even among the tribes of Wrestles with Creator (Israel)."

¹⁰When the elders returned to the head soldier, they found the servant well.

THE SON OF A WIDOW

¹¹Not long after this, Creator Sets Free (Jesus) and the ones who walked the road with him went to Village of Harmony (Nain). A large crowd of people trailed behind him. ¹²As he came near the village gate, a man who had crossed over was being carried, wrapped in a blanket, to a burial site. He was the only son of his mother, a widow. A crowd of people from the village were walking with her. ¹³When Creator Sets Free (Jesus) saw her, he felt pity for her and said, "Do not weep. *The Great Spirit has seen your tears.*"

¹⁴He walked up, opened the blanket, and laid his hands on the young man. The ones carrying it stopped *and waited to see what he would do.* "Young man," he said out loud, "rise up!" ¹⁵To the amazement of all, he sat up and began to talk. Creator Sets Free (Jesus) then gave him back to his mother.

Her weeping turned to joy as she threw her arms around her son and kept kissing his face.

¹⁶Great fear and trembling fell on the crowd. They gave honor to the Great Spirit and said, "A great prophet has been sent to us! The Giver of Breath has come to visit his people!" ¹⁷News about this traveled far and wide throughout the Land of Promise (Judea) and into the surrounding villages and territories.

ARE YOU THE ONE?

¹⁸Followers of Gift of Goodwill (John), who performed the purification ceremony,ᵃ told him what Creator Sets Free (Jesus) had done. ¹⁹He sent two of his followers to ask the Wisdomkeeper a question. ²⁰When they found Creator Sets Free (Jesus), they asked him the question from Gift of Goodwill (John), "Are you the one who is to come, or should we look for someone else?"

²¹The messengers watched as he healed many who were sick and tormented by evil spirits, and gave sight to the ones who were blind.

²²He told them, "Go back to Gift of Goodwill (John) and tell him about the things you have seen with your own eyes and heard with your own ears. The blind can see again, the lame can walk, the ones with skin disease have been healed and ceremonially cleansed! Ears that cannot hear have been opened and the poor have been told the good story! Even the dead have come back to life again!"

Creator Sets Free (Jesus) sent them back to him with these last words:

²³"Creator's blessing rests on the ones who do not stumble and leave the path because of me."

A TRUE PROPHET

²⁴When the messengers left, Creator Sets Free (Jesus) spoke to the people about Gift of Goodwill (John). "What were you looking for in the desert wilderness? A frail reed blowing in the wind? ²⁵Did you see a man in costly garments? No! The ones who wear costly clothes and buy whatever they want live in grand houses. ²⁶Were you looking for a true prophet?

ᵃ7:18 Baptism

Yes! He is a true prophet but also much more! 27He is the one spoken of in the Sacred Teachings, 'Look! I am sending my messenger ahead of you. He will make a clear path.'[a]

28"Listen closely, no one born of a woman has ever been greater, but now the smallest one who walks Creator's good road is greater than he is."

29When the people and tribal tax collectors heard this, they agreed that the ways of the Great Spirit were true and right, for they had received the purification ceremony[b] of Gift of Goodwill (John). 30But the scroll keepers and Separated Ones (Pharisees) turned away from the Great Spirit's plan for them, for they had refused the ceremony of Gift of Goodwill (John).

31"This generation, what can I compare them to?" Creator Sets Free (Jesus) told the crowd. 32"They are like children at a trading post, teasing each other, saying, 'You did not dance when we played the drum! You did not cry when we played a sad flute song.'

33"Gift of Goodwill (John) did not feast or drink wine, but you say, 'He has an evil spirit.' 34The True Human Being comes feasting and drinking and you say, 'He eats too much and is a drunk, a friend of tribal tax collectors and outcasts with broken ways!' 35But wisdom is proved right through the behavior of her children."

A MEAL WITH A SPIRITUAL LEADER

36A spiritual leader from the Separated Ones (Pharisees), named Man Who Listens (Simon), invited Creator Sets Free (Jesus) to a meal. So he went to his house and joined the guests at the table.

37There was a woman in the village, an outcast with broken ways, who heard that Creator Sets Free (Jesus) was eating with the spiritual leader. So she went to the house and brought with her a small pottery jar of sweet-smelling ointment. 38She came up behind Creator Sets Free (Jesus) and began to weep at his feet. Her tears fell on his feet, and she wiped them with her hair. Then she kissed his feet and rubbed the ointment on them.

39When the spiritual leader saw this, he thought to himself, "If this man were a true prophet he would know who is touching him. He would see what kind of woman this is—an outcast!"

40Creator Sets Free (Jesus) *knew what he was thinking and* said to him, "Man Who Listens (Simon), I have something to say to you."

"Wisdomkeeper," he answered, "say what you will."

41"Two men were in debt to the same person. One owed him five hundred horses, the other two buffalo hides. 42Neither of them had enough to pay him back, so he released them from their debt. Which one do you think will love him the most?"

43"I suppose it would be the one who owed him the most."

"You have answered well," Creator Sets Free (Jesus) told him.

44Then he turned to the woman and said to Man Who Listens (Simon), "Do you see this woman? When I entered your house, you did not offer me water to wash the dust from my feet, but she washed them with her tears and wiped them with her hair. 45You did not welcome me with a kiss, but this woman is still kissing my feet. 46You did not put oil on my head, but she has rubbed sweet-smelling ointment on my feet. 47I

---

[a]**7:27** Malachi 3:1
[b]**7:29** Baptism

tell you, she is forgiven and set free from her broken ways because of her great love. But small is the love of one who has been forgiven only for small things."

Creator Sets Free (Jesus) looked at her with kindness in his eyes.

48"You are forgiven!" he said to her. **49**The other guests at the table began to grumble to each other and say, "Who is this man who thinks he can forgive wrongdoings?"

50Creator Sets Free (Jesus) *ignored them and* said to the woman, "Your faith in me has healed your broken ways. Go in peace."

8

WOMEN OF HONOR

1After this, Creator Sets Free (Jesus) began to walk from one village to another telling stories about Creator's good road. The twelve he had chosen were with him **2**and also some women who had been healed and set free from evil spirits. One was Strong Tears (Mary) from the village of Creator's High Lodge (Magdala), who had been set free from seven evil spirits. **3**Another was Woman of His Goodwill (Joanna), the wife of Vision Seer (Chuza), the headman of the household of Chief Looks Brave (Herod). And then there was Water Flower (Susanna). These women and many others helped out with their own goods.

FOUR KINDS OF SOIL

4The people began to gather in crowds as they came from village after village to Creator Sets Free (Jesus). As the crowds gathered, he told them a story.

"Listen!" he said. **5**"A seed planter went to plant some seeds and began to scatter them about on the ground.

"Some seeds fell on the village pathway, but people walked on them, and the winged ones pecked at the seeds and ate them all.

6"Some of the seeds fell on the rocks, where there was only a little dirt. The plants grew, but they dried up because they had no water.

7"Other seeds fell into the weeds, and thistles sprouted around the seeds and choked the life out of them.

8"But some seeds fell on good ground, grew strong, and gave a harvest of one hundred times what was planted. If you have ears to hear, you will understand this story."

BLIND EYES AND DEAF EARS

9But his followers did not understand, so they asked him for the meaning of the story.

10He answered them, "To you the honor has been given to understand the mysterious ways of Creator's good road. *This honor is not given to those who are not ready for it.* I speak to them in stories because 'even though they have eyes to see, they do not see, and even though they have ears to hear, they fail to understand.'[a]

MEANING OF FOUR KINDS OF SOIL

11"This is what the story means," he told them. "The seed in this story is the teaching from the Great Spirit *about his good road.*

12"The village pathway represents the ones who hear, but then Accuser (Satan), the evil snake, sneaks up and steals the words out of their hearts to keep them from believing the teaching and being set free.

---

[a] **8:10** Isaiah 6:9

¹³"The rocky ground represents the ones who hear and receive the teaching with glad hearts, but because they have no roots, their faith is shallow and does not last. As soon as the teaching brings them trouble or opposition, they stumble and fall away.

¹⁴"The weeds and thistles represent the ones who have heard the teaching, but they are too busy worrying about their earthly possessions, so the teaching is choked and their faith stops growing good fruit.

¹⁵"The good ground represents the ones who hear the teaching with good and pure hearts, hold on tightly to it, and never let go until it grows good fruit in their lives.

¹⁶"No one after lighting a lamp hangs a blanket in front of it. Instead, they would put it on a table so everyone can see. ¹⁷The ones who have ears to hear will understand this teaching.

¹⁸"But they must listen carefully, for the ones who understand will gain wisdom and be ready for more—much more. But the ones who do not listen wisely will lose even the little they think they understand."

ALL MY RELATIVES

¹⁹The mother of Creator Sets Free (Jesus) and his brothers came to see him. They were unable to get to him because of the great number of people gathered there. ²⁰Someone told him, "Your relatives are here, waiting to see you."

²¹Creator Sets Free (Jesus) *smiled and* told the messenger, "The ones who listen to the teachings of the Great Spirit and walk in his ways are all my relatives—my mother, aunts and uncles, brothers and sisters."

POWER OVER VIOLENT STORMS

²²On another day Creator Sets Free (Jesus) said to his followers, "Let us cross over to the other side of the lake." They climbed into a large canoe and pushed off from the shore.

Tired from a long day, ²³Creator Sets Free (Jesus) fell into a deep sleep.

His followers let him sleep and continued to paddle across the lake. A windstorm came up suddenly and began to move over the waters. They paddled harder, trying to get to shore before the storm hit.

Soon the storm overtook them and threatened to sink the canoes. ²⁴*In desperation* they woke him from his sleep and cried out, "Wisdomkeeper! Wisdomkeeper! We are all going to drown."

He woke up from his sleep, *stood up,* and spoke sharply to the wind and the raging water. At his words the wind stopped blowing and the waves calmed down. Great peace fell upon the surface of the waters. ²⁵He turned to his followers and said to them, "Where is your faith?"

Amazed and afraid, they *shook their heads and* whispered to each other, "Who is this man? Even the wind and the waves listen to him!"

POWER OVER EVIL SPIRITS

²⁶When they finished crossing, they came to the territory of the people of Honored in the End (Gadarenes), across the Lake of Circle of Nations (Sea of Galilee). ²⁷As soon as he stepped from the canoe, a man from the village was there. This man had been tormented with evil spirits for a long time. His clothes had worn off him, and he was homeless, so he lived in the local burial grounds.

²⁸When the man saw Creator Sets Free (Jesus), he fell to the ground in front

of him. The evil spirit cried out through the man, "Creator Sets Free (Jesus), Son of the One Above Us All, what do you want with me? I beg you not to torment me!" [29]He said this because Creator Sets Free (Jesus) had ordered the evil spirit to leave the man.

In the past this evil spirit had often taken hold of the man, so the villagers had kept the man bound with chains and under close watch. But the man had broken the chains, and the evil spirit had forced him out into the desert.

[30]Creator Sets Free (Jesus) asked, "What is your name?"

"Many Soldiers,"[a] he answered, because thousands of spirits had entered into him. [31]They begged him not to send them into the deep dark pit of the world below.[b]

[32]There was a large herd of pigs feeding on a nearby mountainside, so the spirits begged him to permit them to enter the pigs. [33]When he gave them permission, the evil spirits left the man and entered into the herd of pigs. Then the whole herd stampeded down the mountainside headlong into the lake and drowned.

[34]The ones who were watching over the pigs were scared to death and ran away. They went to the nearby village and told them everything that had happened. [35]As word spread, people came from the villages and the countryside to see for themselves. There they found the man whom the evil spirits had come out of, sitting quietly at the feet of Creator Sets Free (Jesus). He was clothed and in his right mind. This filled the hearts of the people there with awe and fear.

[36]The ones who had seen what happened told the people how the man with evil spirits had been set free. [37]Then the people from the territory of Honored in the End (Gadarenes) begged Creator Sets Free (Jesus) to go away from their land.

[38]As Creator Sets Free (Jesus) entered the canoe to return to the other side, the man who had been set free from the evil spirits begged him to take him along. Creator Sets Free (Jesus) would not permit it and said to the man, [39]"Return home to your family and friends." He told the man, "Tell them all the powerful things the Great Spirit has done for you."

The man went his way and told his story in the villages, telling everyone the great things Creator Sets Free (Jesus) had done for him.

A DESPERATE REQUEST

[40]Creator Sets Free (Jesus) canoed back to the other side of the lake. A great crowd, waiting for him at the lakeshore, welcomed him with glad hearts. [41]A man named He Gives Light (Jairus), the headman of the local gathering house, pushed his way through the crowd and fell down on his knees in front of Creator Sets Free (Jesus) and begged him to come to his house. [42]He had an only daughter, about twelve winters old, who was dying.

As Creator Sets Free (Jesus) went with the man, the crowd also trailed along, pressing in around him from all sides.

WHO TOUCHED ME?

[43]There was a woman in the crowd who had been bleeding in an unusual way for more than twelve winters.

Under tribal law this woman would be considered unclean. She was also required to warn people nearby of her condition by

---

[a]8:30 Lit. *legion*, a segment of the occupying Roman army of about five thousand soldiers
[b]8:31 Abyss or underworld

saying out loud, "Unclean! Unclean!" Instead, she pushed her way through the crowd to get to the Wisdomkeeper.

She spent all she had on medicine men who were not able to heal her. **44**She came up close behind him, reached out her hand, and touched the fringe of his outfit, and right away the blood stopped flowing.

Creator Sets Free (Jesus) stopped, turned, and looked around the crowd.

45"Who touched me?" he asked.

The ones who heard him shrugged their shoulders and began to look around also.

When no one came forward, Stands on the Rock (Peter) said to him, "Wisdomkeeper, the crowds are pushing, shoving, and touching you, what do you mean?"

46"Someone touched me," he said again. "I felt power go out from my body."

Fear took hold of the heart of this woman, for she had not announced herself as unclean, and even worse, she had touched a spiritual leader. The crowd might turn against her or even have her stoned to death.

47The woman knew she could hide no longer. She came forward, trembling with fear, and fell down before him. In front of all the people she told the story of why she touched him and how she was healed right then.

48Creator Sets Free (Jesus) looked at her with kindness in his eyes and said, "Daughter, your faith has made you well. Go in peace."

POWER OVER DEATH

49As they continued on, a messenger from the home of the headman of the gathering house came. *With sadness on his face* he said to He Gives Light (Jairus), "There is no need to trouble the Wisdomkeeper any longer. Your little girl has died."

The man's heart fell to the ground, and grief began to creep over him.

50Creator Sets Free (Jesus) overheard *and quickly* said to him, "Do not fear, simply trust me and all will be well."

51When they came to the house, Creator Sets Free (Jesus) did not permit anyone to go in with him except the child's parents and his most trusted followers—Stands on the Rock (Peter), He Shows Goodwill (John), and He Takes Over (James).

52All the people there were crying for the little girl. Creator Sets Free (Jesus) said to them, "Do not cry. The child is not dead. She only sleeps."

53They mocked him and laughed, for they knew she was dead. **54**So he sent them outside, and then, taking the little girl by the hand, he said, "Little girl, stand up!" *She drew in a deep breath as* **55**her spirit returned to her body, and she stood up. Creator Sets Free (Jesus) had them give her some food.

56Her father and mother stood there, amazed beyond words, *weeping for joy. Their little girl was alive!* Then he firmly told them not to tell anyone what had happened.

MESSAGE BEARERS SENT OUT

1He then gathered his twelve message bearers together. He gave them the authority over all evil spirits and the power to heal all kinds of sickness and disease.

²He then sent them out to tell the story of Creator's good road and heal the sick.

³"Take nothing with you," he instructed them, "not even walking sticks for your journey. Take no coins for your money pouches, no food for your traveling bundle, and only one outer garment for warmth.

⁴"When people welcome you into their home, stay there until you move on. ⁵If no one in that village welcomes you, when you go from there, shake the dust from your moccasins to warn them that you have done all that you can do."

⁶The twelve went out to represent Creator Sets Free (Jesus) to all the villages, telling all who would listen about the good story and healing the sick everywhere they went.

HIS REPUTATION GROWS

⁷The reputation of Creator Sets Free (Jesus) *had spread far and wide, until it finally* reached Chief Looks Brave (Herod). He was troubled because some were saying that Gift of Goodwill (John) had come back to life from the dead. ⁸Others were saying that the ancient prophet, Great Spirit Is Creator (Elijah), had been seen again, and some said that one of the prophets of old had come back to life from the dead.

⁹Chief Looks Brave (Herod) wondered about this and said, "I cut off the head of Gift of Goodwill (John), but who is this one I am hearing about?" So he began to look for Creator Sets Free (Jesus) to see for himself who he was.

¹⁰The twelve message bearers returned from their journeys and told Creator Sets Free (Jesus) all the things they had done. He then took them to a deserted place near House of Fishing (Bethsaida) to be alone. ¹¹The crowd of people saw where they were going and followed him.

When Creator Sets Free (Jesus) saw the great crowd of people, his heart went out to them again. He welcomed them and took the time to tell stories and help them understand many things about Creator's good road. He also healed the ones among them who were sick.

HE FEEDS FIVE THOUSAND

¹²It was becoming late in the day, so his message bearers said to him, "This is a deserted place. Let us send the people away to the villages in the countryside so they can find food to eat."

¹³"You feed them!" he said *with a smile on his face.*

"We have only five pieces of frybread and two small fish—unless you want us to go and buy food for this many people." ¹⁴For there were about five thousand men there, and also women and children.

Creator Sets Free (Jesus) said to them, "Have the people gather together in groups of fifty and sit down on the grass." ¹⁵So they did what he asked.

The people began to scoop up their children and belongings and gather together. Creator Sets Free (Jesus) waited patiently for them to finish. When they were all settled down, he had his message bearers bring baskets and stand in a circle around him.

¹⁶He took the five pieces of frybread with the two fishes and held them up to the sky. He looked up, spoke words of blessing over them, broke them into smaller pieces, and gave them to his message bearers to give to the people. ¹⁷Everyone ate until they were full!

When they gathered up the leftovers, it took twelve baskets to hold them all.

WHO DO THE PEOPLE SAY I AM?

One morning, [18]after praying alone with his followers, he asked them, "Who do all the crowds say that I am?"

They *looked around at each other and* said, [19]"Some say you are Gift of Goodwill (John) who performed the purification ceremony.[a] Others say you might be Great Spirit Is Creator (Elijah), or one of the prophets of old come back to life from the dead."

Creator Sets Free (Jesus) lowered his voice and spoke with a more serious tone.

[20]"So tell me," he asked them. "Who do you say I am?"

Silent faces stared back at him. They began to look at each other, and some looked down to the ground. The moment of truth had come, but no one dared to speak. Then suddenly a voice pierced through the silence.

"You are Creator's Chosen One!" Stands on the Rock (Peter) answered.

[21]He then warned them all not to tell anyone that he was the Chosen One [22]and said to them, "The True Human Being must enter a time of much suffering. The elders, the head holy men, and the scroll keepers will turn their faces from me. They will have me killed, but I will come back to life on the third day.

[23]"If you want to walk the road with me, each day you must also be ready to give up your own life and carry your own crossbeam with me [24]*to the place of ultimate sacrifice.* The ones who hold on to their lives will lose them, but the ones who are willing to lay down their lives for me and my message will live. [25]How will you it help you to get everything

you want but lose what it means to be who Creator made you to be? Is there anything in this world worth trading for that?

[26]"If anyone is ashamed of me and my teaching, then the True Human Being will be ashamed of them when he comes in his bright-shining greatness, to be honored by the Father above and all of his Holy Spirit-messengers.

[27]"I speak from my heart, there are some of you standing here with me today who, before you cross over to death, will see Creator's good road."

THE MOUNTAIN WHERE HE SHINED

[28]About eight days later Creator Sets Free (Jesus) took Stands on the Rock (Peter), He Takes Over (James), and He Shows Goodwill (John) up on a mountain to be alone and pray. [29]As he was sending his voice to the Great Spirit, the appearance of his face began to change, and his clothes turned white as snow.

[30]Two men appeared and began to talk with him. One was the prophet of old, Great Spirit Is Creator (Elijah), and the other the ancient lawgiver Drawn from the Water (Moses). [31]They were shining like the sun and were talking to him about his crossing over from this life to the next, which would take place in Village of Peace (Jerusalem).

[32]Stands on the Rock (Peter) and the others were deep asleep, but they woke up and shook the sleep from their eyes. They saw Creator Sets Free (Jesus) with his face and clothes shining. They also saw the two men standing with him. [33]As the men with him turned to go, Stands on the Rock (Peter) spoke *without thinking.* "Wisdomkeeper!" he said. "This is a good place to stay. Let us make three tipis— one for you, one for Drawn from the

---

[a]**9:19** Baptism

Water (Moses), and one for Great Spirit Is Creator (Elijah)."

³⁴While he was saying this, a bright cloud from above began to fall on them. Their knees shook as the cloud surrounded them. ³⁵A voice spoke from the cloud, saying, "This is my Son, the one I have chosen. Listen to him!"

³⁶When the voice finished speaking, they saw Creator Sets Free (Jesus) standing there alone in front of them. After this they kept silent and told no one at that time what they had seen.

A GENERATION WITH NO FAITH

³⁷The next day, when Creator Sets Free (Jesus) finished coming down from the mountain, a large crowd was there. ³⁸A man called out from the crowd, "Wisdomkeeper!" he said *with desperation in his voice*. "I beg you, have pity on my son, my only child! ³⁹A spirit takes hold of him, making him scream out loud, then foam comes from his mouth. It seldom stops tormenting him—leaving him beaten and bruised. ⁴⁰I asked your followers to force this spirit to go from him, and they tried but failed."

⁴¹"Your generation is bent and twisted—with no faith," Creator Sets Free (Jesus) said. "How much longer will I have to be with you and put up with you? Bring your son to me."

⁴²As they were bringing the boy to him, the evil spirit took hold of him and threw the boy to the ground. But Creator Sets Free (Jesus) spoke sharply to the evil spirit, healed the boy, and gave him back to his father. ⁴³Everyone there stood in awe at Creator's great power.

While the crowd stood there in amazement, Creator Sets Free (Jesus) turned to his followers and said to them, ⁴⁴"Let these words sink deep into your ears: The True Human Being will soon be betrayed and turned over to others."

⁴⁵But still they did not understand. The meaning was hidden from them. Their hearts would not let them believe what they heard with their ears. His words filled them with sorrow and dread, and they were afraid to ask him what it all meant.

WHO IS THE GREATEST?

⁴⁶The ones who walked the road with Creator Sets Free (Jesus) began to argue with each other over which one of them was the most important. When they got back to the house, Creator Sets Free (Jesus) asked them, "What were you arguing about as we walked on the road?"

But they just looked around at each other, not wanting to answer him.

⁴⁷Creator Sets Free (Jesus) knew the thoughts of their hearts, so he had a small child come and sit next to him. ⁴⁸"The ones representing me who welcome this little child are welcoming me. When you welcome me, you are not only welcoming me but also the one who sent me. That is what I meant when I said, 'The lowest among you will become the greatest of all.'"

⁴⁹He Shows Goodwill (John) came close to him and said, "Wisdomkeeper, we saw a man forcing out evil spirits using your name. We told him to stop because he does not walk the road with us."

⁵⁰"Do not stop him," Creator Sets Free (Jesus) told them. "The ones who are not against us are for us."

THE WRONG SPIRIT TO FOLLOW

⁵¹His work on earth was coming to an end, and Creator Sets Free (Jesus) would soon be returning to the spirit-world

above. So he *drew strength from deep within and* made up his mind to go to the Sacred Village of Peace (Jerusalem) *and finish what his Father sent him to do.*

⁵²He sent some other messengers ahead to High Place (Samaria) to find lodging, ⁵³but the people of High Place (Samaria) would not welcome him, for they knew he was on his way to Village of Peace (Jerusalem), and they wanted nothing to do with the people there.

⁵⁴When He Takes Over (James) and He Shows Goodwill (John) found out he was not welcome there, they said, "Wisdom-keeper, do you want us to call down fire from the spirit-world above to burn them up, like the prophet Great Spirit Is Creator (Elijah) did?"

⁵⁵Creator Sets Free (Jesus) spoke sharply to them, "You do not know what spirit you are listening to, ⁵⁶for the True Human Being came to help people, not hurt them."

After that, they walked *silently* with him toward another village.

WALK THE ROAD WITH ME

⁵⁷As they traveled on, a man walked up to Creator Sets Free (Jesus). "*Honored One*," he said, "I will follow you wherever you go."

⁵⁸He answered the man, "The foxes live in their holes, the winged ones who fly above us live in their nests, but the True Human Being has no place to lay his head."

⁵⁹Creator Sets Free (Jesus) turned to another man and said, "Come, walk the road with me."

"Honored One," he said, "let me first go home to my father *until it is time* to bury him."

⁶⁰"Let the ones who are dead bury their own dead," he said to the man.

"*You are alive*, go and tell others about Creator's good road."

⁶¹Another said to him, "Honored One, I will walk the road with you, but first let me go home and prepare my family."

⁶²Creator Sets Free (Jesus) told him, "No one who begins a journey and then turns back is ready to walk Creator's good road."

10

THE GREAT HARVEST

¹After this, Creator Sets Free (Jesus) chose seventy men from the ones who walked the road with him. He sent them out, two by two, to prepare the way for him in the villages he was about to visit *on his way to the Sacred Village of Peace (Jerusalem).*

²He said to them, "There is a great harvest before us, but there are not enough helpers. Pray to the Harvest Chief, so he will send more helpers. Go and represent me. ³You will be like lambs walking among wolves. ⁴Take no money pouch or traveling bundle with you—not even a second pair of moccasins. Waste no time greeting others on the way.

⁵"When you lodge with someone, say to them first, 'Peace be to this house.' ⁶If people of peace live there, you will be welcomed. If not, your blessing of peace will return to you as you leave. ⁷Stay with the ones who welcome you. There is no need to move around from house to house. Share their food and drink with them, for the ones who work hard are worth feeding.

⁸"In any village that welcomes you, eat whatever they set before you. ⁹Offer healing prayers for any who are sick and say to them, 'Creator's good road has come close to you.'

¹⁰"If you enter a village and no one welcomes you, go into the village pathways and say, ¹¹'We must wipe the dust of your village from our *clothes* as a sign against you, for Creator's good road has come close to you, *but you would not welcome it.*' ¹²I speak from my heart, that village will face a worse end than Village of Bad Spirits (Sodom)."

Creator Sets Free (Jesus) began to warn about what would happen to the villages that saw his greatest signs and wonders but did not believe his message.

¹³"Sorrow and trouble will come to you, Village of Secrets (Chorazin), and the same for you, House of Fishing (Bethsaida). If the ancient villages of Rock Land (Tyre) and Hunting Grounds (Sidon) had seen the powerful signs you have seen, they would have thrown dirt and ashes on their heads and turned their hearts back to Creator's ways. ¹⁴It will be worse for you in the day when you face your end.

¹⁵"As for you, Village of Comfort (Capernaum), do you think you will be lifted up to the spirit-world above? No! You will be brought down low, to the Dark Underworld of Death (Hades)."

Then he turned to his followers and said, ¹⁶"The ones who welcome you welcome me. The ones who send you away are sending me away. The ones who send me away send away the one who sent me."

So, after he said these things, the seventy went out, two by two, to all the villages.

THE HARVESTERS REPORT BACK

¹⁷The seventy who were sent out by Creator Sets Free (Jesus) returned. Their hearts were overflowing with joy as they reported back to him. "Wisdomkeeper!"

they said. "Even the evil spirits did what we said when we spoke to them in your name, representing you."

Creator Sets Free (Jesus) looked up to the sky and back down at them.

¹⁸Then he said to them, "With my own eyes I have seen Accuser (Satan) fall down like lightning from the spirit-world above. ¹⁹Look and see! I have given you authority over snakes and spiders and over all the power of this enemy. Nothing will be able to harm you."

But then he gave them some words of wisdom.

²⁰"Yes, the spirits must listen to you, but do not be too happy about this. Instead, let your hearts be glad that your names are carved into the rock cliffs of the spirit-world above."

²¹The Holy Spirit filled the heart of Creator Sets Free (Jesus) with joy. "O Great Father, maker of the earth and sky," he prayed, "you have hidden these things from the ones who are wise in their own eyes but have shown them to the humble of heart. Yes, my Father, it has made your heart glad to see this day come."

²²He then turned to the seventy who walked the road with him and said, "My Father has put everything into my hands. Only the Father knows the Son, and only the Son knows the Father. No one can truly know the Father in his fullness unless the Son makes him known."

²³Then he turned to his twelve *message bearers and whispered to them,* "You have been given a great honor to see these things. ²⁴There were many prophets and chiefs who wanted to see and hear the things you have but did not."

A SLY SCROLL KEEPER SETS A TRAP

25A scroll keeper, *one who was skilled in his knowledge of tribal law*, came to Creator Sets Free (Jesus) to test him and trap him in his words.

"Wisdomkeeper," he said. "What path must I walk to have the life of the world to come that never fades away, full of beauty and harmony?"

26He answered him, "What is written in our tribal law about this? Tell me, how do you see it?"

27The scroll keeper spoke from the words of the law, "You must love the Great Spirit from deep within, with the strength of your arms, the thoughts of your mind, and the courage of your heart,[a] and you must love your fellow human beings in the same way you love yourselves."[b]

28"You have answered well," Creator Sets Free (Jesus) said back to him. "If you walk this path you will live."

29But the scroll keeper, wanting to look good to others, asked him, "Who are my fellow human beings?"

HE TURNS THE TRAP WITH A STORY

30Creator Sets Free (Jesus) answered him with a story.

"There was a man walking the road from Village of Peace (Jerusalem) to Moon Village (Jericho). On the way he was attacked by thieves, who beat him, stripped him of his clothes, and left him bleeding to death.

31"Now it happened that a holy man was on the same road, not far behind. When he saw the man, he went around him on the other side of the road. 32Not far behind him was another man, also from the tribe holy men are chosen from.

When he saw the wounded man, he did the same thing as the holy man.

33"Then a man from High Place (Samaria),[c] who was also walking the road, saw the wounded man. *Even though he was not a Tribal Member but a mixed blood despised by the tribal people*, he felt pity for the man. 34He helped him by pouring good medicine on his wounds and wrapping them in a cloth. He put the man on his own animal and took him to a lodging house to care for him.

35"The next day, when the man of High Place (Samaria) was leaving, he gave from his own money pouch to the keeper of the lodging house. 'Use this to care for him,' he said, 'and when I return, I will give you anything more that is needed.'"

36Creator Sets Free (Jesus) then *looked at the scroll keeper and* said, "Which one of these three acted as a fellow human being to the man who was attacked by the thieves?"

37The scroll keeper answered, "The one who had pity on him."

"Go," Creator Sets Free (Jesus) said, "and walk in the same way."

CHOOSING THE BEST PART

38As they journeyed on, they went to a village where a woman named Head Woman (Martha) gave them lodging at her house. 39Her sister Healing Tears (Mary), who lived with her, sat next to Creator Sets Free (Jesus) on the floor, listening to his teaching.

As their Wisdomkeeper, Creator Sets Free (Jesus) would teach the men who gathered around him, but this would not have been proper for a woman of that culture.

---

[a]**10:27** Deuteronomy 6:5
[b]**10:27** Leviticus 19:18

[c]**10:33** The people of Samaria were mixed bloods who had changed the traditional ceremonial ways and were despised by the Jewish people of that day.

40Head Woman (Martha) was distracted, trying to get the meal ready for the honored guests. When she saw Healing Tears (Mary) sitting down, she walked up to Creator Sets Free (Jesus) and said, "Wisdomkeeper, do you not care that my sister has left me to work alone? Tell her to help me."

41"Head Woman (Martha), O Head Woman (Martha)," he said, "I know many things worry and trouble you. **42**But you must set your heart on the one thing that matters. That is what Healing Tears (Mary) has done, and I will not take it from her."

HE GIVES HIS FOLLOWERS A PRAYER

1Another time, after Creator Sets Free (Jesus) had finished praying, one of his followers said to him, "Wisdomkeeper, teach us how to pray in the same way Gift of Goodwill (John) taught his followers."

2Creator Sets Free (Jesus) *smiled and* said to them, "*When you send your voice to the Great Spirit,* here is how you should pray:

"O Great Spirit, our Father from above, your name is sacred and holy.

"Bring your good road to us, where the beauty of your ways in the spirit-world above is reflected in the earth below.

3"Provide for us day by day—the elk, the buffalo, and the salmon. The corn, the squash, and the wild rice. All the good things we need for each day.

4"Release us from the things we have done wrong in the same way we release others for the things done wrong to us.

And guide us away from the things that tempt us to stray from your good road."

MORE WISDOM ABOUT PRAYING

5*Then he added,* "Suppose you went to a friend in the middle of the night and said, 'I need three pieces of frybread! **6**A relative of mine has come from a long way to see me, and I have nothing for him to eat.' **7**But he says to you, 'Quit bothering me! I cannot help you. My children and I are all in bed.' **8**Do not give up! If your friendship is not enough, then he will do it just because you will not give up asking.

9"So, keep dancing your prayers, and the way will open before you. Search *for the ancient pathways,* and you will find *them.* Keep sending up your prayers, and they will be heard.

10"Answers will come to the ones who ask, good things will be found by the ones who search for them, and the way will open before the ones who keep dancing their prayers.

11"What kind of father, if his son wanted a fish, would give him a rattlesnake, **12**or, if he asked for an egg, would give him a deadly spider? **13**If even fathers with bad hearts will give good gifts to their children, how much more will the Creator, who is your Father from the spirit-world above, give the Holy Spirit to all who ask!"

SPIRITUAL LEADERS ACCUSE HIM

14One day Creator Sets Free (Jesus) was setting a man free from a spirit that kept him from speaking. When the spirit left the man, he could speak again, and the crowd was amazed. **15**But some of them said, "His power over evil spirits comes from the Worthless Ruler (Beelzebul),[a] the one who rules over all evil spirits."

16And others were putting him to a test, asking him for a sign from the spirit-world above.

---

[a]**11:15** Beelzebul, another name for Satan

17Creator Sets Free (Jesus) knew what they were thinking and said, "Any nation warring against itself comes to a bad end. **18**A village or clan warring against each other will not survive. If Accuser (Satan) is against himself, how will he continue to rule? I say this because you have accused me of forcing out evil spirits by the power of the Worthless Ruler (Beelzebul).

19"If my power over evil spirits comes from the Worthless Ruler (Beelzebul), then by what power do your children do these things? They are the ones who will decide against you. **20**If I force out evil spirits by the finger of the Great Spirit, then Creator's good road has come close to you.

21"When a strong warrior, who is dressed for war, guards his own belongings, they are safe. **22**But when someone who is stronger attacks and defeats him, he will strip him of his war garments that he trusted in, take away all his goods, and give them away to others.

23"*In this spiritual battle there is no unclaimed territory.* The one who is not fighting with me fights against me. The one who does not help me gather scatters and makes things worse.

24"When an evil spirit goes out of someone, it wanders through dry wastelands, looking for a place to rest. When it finds none, it says, 'I will go back to the house I left.' **25**It returns to find the house empty, swept clean, and put in order. **26**The spirit then finds seven other spirits, more evil than itself, who all go in and live there, making the person worse than before."

27As Creator Sets Free (Jesus) was speaking, a woman from the crowd raised her voice and said to him, "Creator's blessing is on the womb that birthed you and the breasts that nursed you!"

"*That may be,*" **28**he answered her, "but a greater blessing belongs to the ones who listen to the words of the Great Spirit and walk in his ways."

THE SIGN OF WINGS OF DOVE

29More and more people came to hear Creator Sets Free (Jesus), so he said to them, "This is a generation of bad-hearted people, looking only for powerful signs. The only sign you will be given is the sign of Wings of Dove (Jonah)." **30**In the same way he was a sign to the people of Village of Changed Minds (Nineveh), the True Human Being will be to the people living today.

31"The reputation of the female chief of the south will speak against the people of today. What she did will show your guilt, for she journeyed from a land far away to listen to the wisdom of the great chief Stands in Peace (Solomon). Look! A greater one is standing right in front of you.

32"When Creator decides the fate of the people living today, the reputation of people of Village of Changed Minds (Nineveh) will speak against them. What they did will show your guilt, because they changed their minds when they heard the message of Wings of Dove (Jonah). Look! One who is greater than he stands before you now.

THE WAY TO SEE POSSESSIONS

33-34"No one, after lighting a lamp, hides it or puts it under a basket. Instead it will be lifted up high on a pole so all who enter can see it."

Among the tribes of Wrestles with Creator (Israel) a greedy person was said to have a bad eye and unable to see the good road. A generous person was said to have a good eye, full of light and able to clearly see the good road.

So he said to them, **35**"Light shines into the body through the eyes. If your eyes are clear, your whole being is full of light. **36**But, if your eyes are bad, then your whole being is full of darkness. Make sure your eyes are full of light and not darkness, and then you will clearly see the path you walk, like a torch in the night."

HE CONFRONTS THE SPIRITUAL LEADERS

37When Creator Sets Free (Jesus) finished speaking, one of the Separated Ones (Pharisees) invited him to a meal, so Creator Sets Free (Jesus) sat with him at his table. **38**The Separated One (Pharisee) was upset that he did not ceremonially wash his hands before eating.

39"You Separated Ones (Pharisees) always wash the outside of your cups and bowls, but on the inside your hearts are full of greed and worthless ways. **40**How can you be so foolish? The one who made the outside also made the inside! **41**If you will give food to the hungry from the inside of you, *from the pity in your heart,* then all things will be clean for you.

42"Sorrow and trouble await you Separated Ones (Pharisees)! For you are careful to do what tribal law says by giving a tenth of each little herb in your garden, as you should without ignoring the more important instructions, such as treating others equally and walking in the love of the Great Spirit.

43"Sorrow and trouble await you Separated Ones (Pharisees)! For you love to sit in the seats of honor at the gathering houses and to be noticed at the trading posts.

44"Sorrow and trouble will be waiting at the end of the trail for you, for you are like unmarked burial grounds that others walk over without even noticing."

45A scroll keeper, one who was an expert in tribal law, spoke up. "Wisdom-keeper," he complained, "when you say these things, you insult us also."

46Creator Sets Free (Jesus) did not hold back. "Sorrow and trouble is coming your way," he warned the scroll keeper, "for you put heavy spiritual loads on the backs of others, too much for them to carry, but will not lift even one finger to help them.

47"Sorrow and trouble are waiting for you, for you carve statues on the burial grounds of the prophets of old to honor them, but it was your ancestors who murdered them. **48**Your actions show you are walking in their moccasins, for they killed the prophets, and you decorate their burial grounds.

49"But here is what the Great Spirit in his wisdom says to you, 'I will send to you prophets and message bearers. Some you will murder, and others you will track down and torture.'

50"The people living today will have to give an answer for shedding the blood of all the prophets who have lived since the beginning of the world, **51**from the blood of His Breath Goes Up (Abel) to the blood of Creator Will Remember (Zechariah), who was murdered in the courtyard of the sacred lodge.

52"Sorrow and trouble await you experts in tribal law, for you have taken for yourselves the secrets of wisdom and understanding. You have failed to walk in them, and even worse, you have stood in the way of others who were trying to get in."

53As Creator Sets Free (Jesus) began to leave, the scroll keepers and Separated Ones (Pharisees) grew fierce in their anger toward him. [54]They began to attack him with sharp questions, trying to trap him in his words.

12

CREATOR SEES ALL

[1]Many thousands of people were now crowding around Creator Sets Free (Jesus), so many that they were trampling on each other. Before he spoke to the crowd, he first said to his followers, "Be on the lookout for the teachings[a] of the Separated Ones (Pharisees) who put on a false face. [2]*Remember*, nothing can be hidden from Creator's eyes. He will uncover all secrets. [3]What is spoken in darkness will be heard in the light, and what is whispered in secret will be shouted from the rooftops.

[4]"Hear me, my friends, do not fear the ones who can kill only the body. For there is nothing more they can do. [5]You should fear the one who, after you have been killed, has the right to throw you into the Valley of Smoldering Fire. This is what should make you tremble.

[6]"Five small winged ones could be traded for two stones, yet Creator cares for each of them. [7]He even knows the number of hairs on your head. Do not fear. Are you not worth more to him than many small winged ones?

[8]"Listen! When you represent me before others, the True Human Being will represent you before Creator's spirit-messengers. [9]But the ones who disown me will be disowned before them.

[10]"Anyone who speaks against the True Human Being can be forgiven, but speaking evil of the Holy Spirit will not be forgiven.

[11]"When they drag you into their gathering houses and before government rulers, do not worry how to defend yourselves or what to say. [12]When that time comes, the Holy Spirit will give you the words to speak."

LOOK OUT FOR GREED

[13]Someone from the crowd pushed forward and said to him, "Wisdom-keeper, tell my brother to give me my part of what our father left to us."

[14]Creator Sets Free (Jesus) said to him, "Who made me the one to decide this between you and your brother? [15]Watch your step, or greed will make you stumble. Remember, one's life is not made up of many possessions."

There were many people in the crowd who heard what he said about possessions, [16]so he told this story to help them see more clearly.

"A man with many possessions had a field that was growing a great harvest of food. [17]'What will I do with all this food?' he said to himself. 'I have no room in my storage barns for this great harvest.'

"The man *thought about it and then* said to himself again, [18]'I know what I will do, I will tear down my old storage barns and build larger ones. [19]I will have enough to last me many winters. Then I will take my rest, eat, drink, and celebrate.'

[20]"But the Great Spirit said to him, 'Why are you being so foolish? This is the day you will cross over to death and give an answer for your life. Now who will get the goods you have stored up for yourself?'"

Creator Sets Free (Jesus) let the people think about the story, and then he said, [21]"This is how it will be for the ones who make themselves rich but forget about Creator's true riches."

---

[a]12:1 Lit. *yeast*

FEAR NOT, LITTLE FLOCK

²²Then he said to the ones who walked the road with him, "This is why I am telling you not to be troubled about getting enough to eat or drink, or what to wear. Is eating, drinking, and clothing yourself all there is? ²³Does your life not have more meaning?

²⁴"Look to the ravens, the winged ones who fly above us. Do they plant seeds and gather the harvest into a storehouse? No! But the Great Spirit gives them plenty to eat. Do you not know he cares even more for you? ²⁵Will worrying about these things help you live one hour longer? ²⁶If you cannot do such a small thing, why worry about other things?

²⁷"Have you seen how the wildflowers grow in the plains and meadows? Do you think they work hard and long to clothe themselves? No! I tell you, not even the great chieftain Stands in Peace (Solomon), wearing his finest regalia, was dressed as well as even one of these.

²⁸"If the Great Spirit covers the wild grass in the plains with such beauty, which is here today and gathered for to-morrow's fire, will he not take even better care of you? Why is your faith so small? ²⁹Why worry so much about what to eat or drink? ³⁰This is what the Nations of the world, *who have lost their way*, have given their hearts to, but your Father from above knows you need these things.

³¹"If you will make Creator's good road your first aim, he will make sure you have all you need for each day. ³²Do not fear, for even though you are a small flock, it makes your Father's heart glad to give you the good road!

³³"Share your possessions with the ones in need, and you will have money pouches that never wear out, filled with possessions from the spirit-world above. ³⁴For where you store your possessions is where your heart will be.

³⁵"Be ready at all times, with your torches burning bright. ³⁶Be like the ones who, waiting for their chief to return from a distant wedding feast, are watching and ready to welcome him. ³⁷When he returns and finds them ready, he will take off his chiefly garments, dress himself in servant's clothes, sit them at his own table, and serve them a great feast. ³⁸He will do this whether he returns late in the night or early in the morning.

³⁹"Here is another way to see what I am saying. If the elder of a family had known what night the thieves were coming, he would not have let them break in. ⁴⁰In the same way you must always be ready, for the True Human Being will return at a time you do not expect."

WHO IS THIS STORY FOR?

⁴¹Hearing this, Stands on the Rock (Peter) said to him, "Wisdomkeeper, is this story for us, or for all people?"

⁴²"You tell me," Creator Sets Free (Jesus) answered, "who is the wise one, worthy of trust? The uncle who feeds and cares for the family while the elder is away? ⁴³⁻⁴⁴Yes, and when the elder returns, he will honor that uncle, take him into his home, and share everything with him.

⁴⁵"But what if the uncle says to himself, 'It will be a long time before he returns,' then begins to abuse the family, eat all the best food, and get drunk on the wine? ⁴⁶I will tell you what will happen," Creator Sets Free (Jesus) continued. "The elder will return at an unexpected time and find the uncle abusing his family. He will then put him out of the family and send him away to live with the other outcasts.

"Who is the story for?" Creator Sets Free (Jesus) asked his followers. [47]"Like the bad-hearted uncle, it is for the ones who know Creator's right ways but fail to walk in them. They will be given the greatest punishment, [48]for more is required from the ones who are given and trusted with more. As for the ones who do not know but still fail to do what is right, their punishment will not be as great."

MY MESSAGE WILL BRING DIVISION

Creator Sets Free (Jesus) knew that his followers were not prepared for the effect his message would have on their nation and what would soon happen to him in the Sacred Village of Peace (Jerusalem).

[49]"I came down from above to ignite a fire on this land, and how I long for it to burn!" he said to his followers. [50]"I have a purification ceremony[a] with fire to accomplish—and I am desperate to finish it!

[51]"Do you look for me to bring peace to this land? No! I tell you, first there will be great conflict. [52]The message I bring will pierce like the blade of a long knife. It will even separate family members. A family of five will take sides, three against two and two against three. [53]Fathers and sons, mothers and daughters, uncles and nephews, aunties and nieces. They will all fight like enemies, *all because of me and my message."*[b]

[54]Creator Sets Free (Jesus) then said to the crowd, "When a cloud rises in the west, you say, 'It will rain soon,' and so it does. [55]The wind blows from the south and you say, 'It will be a hot day,' and so it is."

Then he spoke to the spiritual leaders, [56]"You who wear false faces! You understand what the earth, wind, and sky are saying, but you are blind to the message of the season you live in.

[57-58]"If someone has a complaint against you, why not work things out on the way to tribal council? Can you not decide on your own what is right and come to an agreement? The council may decide against you and turn you over to ones who have the power to banish you [59]where there is no way back until honor is restored."

13 ▶◀▶◀▶◀▶◀▶◀▶◀▶◀▶◀▶◀

TAKE A NEW PATH

[1]Then some of the people there told Creator Sets Free (Jesus) about the people from Circle of Nations (Galilee) whom Spear of the Great Waters (Pilate) had put to death and mixed their blood with their own ceremonial offerings.

[2]He said to them, "Do you think it was because of their bad hearts and wrongdoings that they suffered? Do you think their hearts were worse than all the others in Circle of Nations (Galilee)? [3]No, I say to you! But if you, *the people of Village of Peace (Jerusalem),* do not change your ways of thinking and take a new path, you will all die in the same way.

[4]"What about the eighteen people on whom the tower in Sending Village (Siloam) fell? Do you think they were worse than all others living in Village of Peace (Jerusalem)? [5]No, I say to you! But if you, *the people of the Sacred Village of Peace (Jerusalem),* do not change your ways of thinking and take a new path, you will all die in the same way."

[6]So he told them this story, "There was a man who planted a fig tree in his garden, but when he came to find fruit,

---

[a]**12:50** Baptism
[b]**12:53** Micah 7:6

there was none. [7]He said to the keeper of the garden, 'I have been looking for fruit on this tree for three seasons and have found none. Cut the tree down! Why waste good dirt on it?'

[8]"But the garden keeper answered the man, 'Give me another season. I will dig around the tree and fertilize it. [9]If it has no fruit after that, then cut it down.'"

CONFLICT ABOUT THE DAY OF RESTING

[10]On another Day of Resting, Creator Sets Free (Jesus) was teaching at a gathering house. [11]There was a woman there who had a spirit of weakness for eighteen winters. Her back was bent and twisted, so she could not stand up straight.

[12]When Creator Sets Free (Jesus) saw her, he told her to come to him and said, "Honored woman, you are set free from your weakness." [13]He put his hands on her, and right away she stood up straight and gave thanks to the Great Spirit.

[14]The headman of the gathering house was offended because Creator Sets Free (Jesus) had healed on the Day of Resting. He stood up and told the people, "Are there not six other days to do your work? Come on one of those days to be healed, not on the Day of Resting."

Creator Sets Free (Jesus) helped the woman back to her seat. He then turned to the headman with a look of sorrow mixed with anger on his face.

[15]"You who wear false faces!" he said to the headman. "Is there anyone who would not untie his horse on the Day of Resting and take it to a watering hole? [16]This woman is a daughter of Father of Many Nations (Abraham). Accuser (Satan), that evil trickster, has kept her this way for eighteen winters. Why should she not be set free on the Day of Resting?"

[17]The enemies of Creator Sets Free (Jesus) were put to shame by his words, but the hearts of the people jumped for joy because of the wonderful things he was doing.

THE GOOD ROAD WILL FILL THE EARTH

[18]"What is Creator's good road like? What can I compare it to?" Creator Sets Free (Jesus) asked. [19]"It is like a man who planted in his garden a single grain of mustard seed,[a] where it grew into a great tree, large enough for the winged ones who soar in the sky to find lodging in its branches.

[20]"Again, think of Creator's good road [21]like the yeast a grandmother uses when she makes frybread dough. She mixes a little yeast into a large amount of flour, then the yeast spreads throughout all of the dough."

WILL ONLY A FEW FIND THE GOOD ROAD?

[22]Creator Sets Free (Jesus) continued to travel on to Village of Peace (Jerusalem). As he passed through the villages on the way, he would stop and teach the people. [23]At one of these villages a man asked him, "Wisdomkeeper, will only a few find their way onto the good road and be set free?"

[24]"Yes," Creator Sets Free (Jesus) said to the man, "so make it your aim to enter in by the narrow way *that I have taught you.* There will be many who try to enter some other way but will not be able.

[25]"Once the elder of a home has closed the door, others will come *pound on the door and* say to him, 'Elder! Elder! Open the door for us!'

"But the elder will tell them, 'I do not know who you are.'

---

[a]**13:19** The mustard plant was used as an herbal medicine.

26"'But did we not eat and drink with you?' they will argue. 'Did you not teach on our village pathways?'

27"'No!' he will say to them, 'I do not know where you are from. Go away from me, you bad-hearted trouble makers!'

28"For there will be much weeping and grinding of teeth in anger when you see Father of Many Nations (Abraham), He Made Us Laugh (Isaac), Heel Grabber (Jacob), and all the prophets of old, feasting in the Land of Creator's good road, but you are on the outside looking in! 29People will come from many Nations, from the east, south, west, and north, and sit down to join in the feast.

"So you see," Creator Sets Free (Jesus) said to the man, 30"some who are last will be first, and some who are first will be last."

> The man's face became pale as the meaning of the words of Creator Sets Free (Jesus) sank into his heart.

NO PEACE IN VILLAGE OF PEACE

31At that time some of the Separated Ones (Pharisees) came to him and said, "You should leave this place! Looks Brave (Herod) is looking for you—to put you to death."

32He answered them, "You can tell that sly coyote to look out! I am forcing out evil spirits and healing the sick today and tomorrow. On the third day I will finish the work I came to do. 33That is why I will go from this place today, tomorrow and the day after. For a prophet cannot be put to death this far from Village of Peace (Jerusalem)!

34"O Village of Peace (Jerusalem), you who kill the prophets and stone to death the ones sent to you! How I have longed to gather your children together, like the eagle gathers her young under her wings, but you would not have it. 35Look! Your house has fallen and will be left in ruins!

"I speak from my heart, you will not see me again until you say, 'Blessed is the one who comes representing the Great Spirit!'"[a]

14

HEALING AGAIN ON THE DAY OF RESTING

1On a Day of Resting, Creator Sets Free (Jesus) was invited to the house of a headman of the Separated Ones (Pharisees) for a meal. All were keeping their eyes on him.

2A man with a sickness that made parts of his body swell up came and stood in front of him. 3Creator Sets Free (Jesus) asked the Separated Ones (Pharisees) and the scroll keepers, who are experts in tribal law, "Is it permitted to heal on the Day of Resting? Yes or no?"

4The spiritual leaders glared at him in silence. 5So he took hold of the man, healed him, and sent him on his way.

He then turned to the spiritual leaders and said, "If your child, or even a horse, fell into a watering hole, would you not pull it out on the Day of Resting?"

6The spiritual leaders had no answer for him.

HUMILITY INSTEAD OF SELF-IMPORTANCE

7He noticed how the invited guests had chosen the best seats at the table, so he gave them some wise counsel.

8"If you are invited to a wedding feast, do not sit in the best seats, for someone with greater honor may be invited.

---

[a] **13:35** Psalm 118:26

⁹Then the host will come to you and say, 'Give your seat to this person.' Then, hanging your head, you will have to take the lowest seat. ¹⁰"Instead, take the lowest seat and the host may say to you, 'Friend, come and sit in the seat of honor.' You will then be honored in the eyes of all the guests."

Creator Sets Free (Jesus) looked around the table at all the guests.

¹¹He said to them, "The ones who put themselves above others will be brought down, but all who humble themselves will be lifted up."

¹²Creator Sets Free (Jesus) then turned to the headman who had invited him and said, "When you have a feast, do not invite only your friends, relatives, and the ones with many possessions, who can repay you. ¹³Instead, invite the poor, the blind, and the crippled, who cannot repay you. ¹⁴Then you will be honored when the good-hearted ones are brought back to life again."

¹⁵One of the guests at the feast said to Creator Sets Free (Jesus), "Creator's blessing rests on the ones who will feast at the table in the Land of Creator's good road!"

STORY OF THE GREAT FEAST

Creator Sets Free (Jesus) could see they still did not understand, so he told them another story.

¹⁶"There was a man who prepared a great feast and invited many people. ¹⁷When the feast was ready, he sent a messenger to tell the ones he had invited, 'Come to the table, the feast is ready!' ¹⁸But one by one they all began to make excuses.

"One said, 'I must go and tend to my new field. Please excuse me.'

¹⁹"Another said, 'Please excuse me also, for I must try out the horses[a] I just traded for.'

²⁰"And another, 'I cannot come, for I have just been married.'

²¹"When the messenger told the man their answer, he became angry and said, 'Waste no time! Go out into the village pathways and invite the ones who are poor, crippled, blind and lame.'

²²"When the messenger returned, he told the man, 'I have done what you said, but there is still room for more.'

²³"So he told the messenger, 'Go out to the mountain trails, look behind all the bushes, and urge them to come, so that my house may be filled with people. ²⁴None of the ones I first invited will even taste of this feast!'"

COUNTING THE COST

Creator Sets Free (Jesus) was coming near to Jerusalem.

²⁵Large crowds were following him, so he turned to them and said, ²⁶"*The ones who come to me must put me first, above all others.* To walk the road with me, they must love and respect me above their own fathers and mothers, wives and children, and aunties and uncles. They must love me even more than their own lives. ²⁷Only the ones who are willing to follow me and carry their own crossbeam are ready to walk the road with me and learn my ways.

²⁸"Who would build a great lodge without first making sure he had enough trees to finish it? ²⁹If he only built the floor and then ran out of trees, others would laugh at him and say, ³⁰'How will you finish what you started?'

---

[a] **14:19** Lit. *oxen*

³¹"Would a chief go to war against another chief if he only had half as many warriors? ³²No! He would send messengers ahead to make a peace treaty!

³³"You must count the cost of following me, for all who are not willing to give up all they have are not ready to walk the road with me and learn my ways."

³⁴Then he added, "Salt is a good thing, but if it loses its saltiness, how will it get its flavor back? ³⁵That kind of salt is thrown away. It is no good for the garden or the manure pile.

"Let the ones who have ears hear what I am saying!"

15

THE WORTH OF THE LOST ONES

¹Tribal tax collectors and other outcasts would often gather around Creator Sets Free (Jesus) to listen to him tell his stories. ²But the Separated Ones (Pharisees) and the scroll keepers would complain about this. They would say things like, "This man welcomes outcasts to join him at the table and eat with him."

³On one of those occasions Creator Sets Free (Jesus) answered them with a story.

⁴"Who among you, if you were caring for one hundred sheep and one of the lambs wandered away, would not leave the ninety-nine and search for that lost lamb until you found it? ⁵Would you not put that lamb on your shoulders, hurry home, ⁶and invite your friends to a celebration, saying to them, 'Rejoice with me, for I have found my lost lamb!'?

⁷"In the same way, the spirit-world above will celebrate even more over one outcast who finds the way back home than for ninety-nine who are already safely there.

⁸"Let me say it another way," he explained. "What man who has ten eagle feathersª and loses one would not light a torch, sweep the house clean, and look everywhere until he found it? ⁹Then, after he finds it, would he not gather his friends together for a celebration? ¹⁰In the same way, Creator's spirit-messengers will celebrate when even one outcast finds the way back home."

A STORY ABOUT TWO SONS

Creator Sets Free (Jesus) then told them another story to help them see even more clearly.

¹¹"There was a man with two sons. ¹²The younger son said to his father, 'Father, give me now my share of what is coming to me.'"

This was a great insult to the father, for this would not have been done until the father had crossed over to death.

"But the Father, who was good-hearted and loved his sons, divided all he had with his two sons anyway.

¹³"Not many days later, the younger son took his share and went far away to another land. He began to spend it all on wild living and soon had nothing left. ¹⁴The time came when there was not enough food in the land for everyone, and he found himself poor and hungry. ¹⁵So he went to work for a rancher, who sent him out to feed the pigs. ¹⁶He became so hungry that he wanted to eat the husks he was feeding the pigs, but no one would even give him a meal.

¹⁷"Soon the younger son came back to his right mind and said to himself, 'Look, here I am naked and starving, but the

---

ª15:8 Lit. woman who has ten silver coins

servants who work for my father are well fed! **18**I am going back to humble myself to my father. I will tell him that I have dishonored both him and the spirit-world above, **19**and I am no longer worthy to be called his son. I will ask him just to let me be a hired servant to work in his fields.'

20"He then made up his mind and began to go home. While he was still far away, his father saw him walking. The father's heart opened wide and he ran to his son, threw his arms around him, and kissed him.

21"The son said, 'Father, I have failed the spirit-world above and you. I am not worthy to be called your son.'

22"But the father ignored his son's words, turned to his servants, and said, 'Go! Find my best regalia and put it on him. Give him a headdress of feathers for his head and new moccasins for his feet! **23**Go get the fattest calf and prepare a great feast for a celebration. **24**This is my son! He was lost, but I have found him. He was dead to me, but now he is alive!' Then they all began to feast, sing, and dance.

25"Now, the older son was just returning from a hard day's work in the field. He heard the music and dancing, **26**so he asked one of the servants what was going on. **27**The servant told him, 'Your brother has come home and your father has prepared a great feast for him, because he is alive and well.'

28"Hearing this, the older brother became very angry and refused to go into the lodge. The father saw him *brooding outside*, so he went to him and urged him to come in.

29"The older son said to his father, 'Why can you not see? I have worked hard for you all my life, and done all that you have asked of me, but you have not

even given me one small goat to have a feast with my friends. **30**But when this son of yours, who wasted all you gave him on sexual favors with women, comes home, you kill the fattest calf for him.'

"The father looked kindly into his older son's face.

31"'My son,' he said to him, 'you are always close to my heart, and everything I have is yours. **32**But it is a good thing for us to celebrate with glad hearts, for your brother was dead but now is alive. He was lost, but now we have found him!'"

16

POSSESSIONS AND THE GOOD ROAD

1He then told the ones who walked the road with him another story:

"There was a man with so many possessions, he had to have someone to oversee them all. The rich man was told that his overseer was mishandling his possessions. **2**He sent for the man and said to him, 'Why am I hearing these things about you? Give me an account of all I possess, for I can no longer trust you to oversee my belongings.'

3"The man said to himself, 'What will I do? I am too old to dig ditches and too proud to beg from others.'

"Then an idea came to his mind. **4**'I know what to do so that others will help me and give me a place to live.' **5**He went to each person who was in debt to the rich man.

"He said to the first one, 'How much do you owe?' **6**'One hundred containers of oil,' the man answered. 'Make it to be fifty,' the overseer told him.

7"He then said to another, 'How much do you owe?' 'One hundred baskets of wheat,' he answered. 'Make it to be eighty,' the overseer said back to him.

8"When the rich man found out what the dishonest overseer had done, he *shook his head but* admired the man's craftiness.

"Do you see what this means?" Creator Sets Free (Jesus) asked. "The children of darkness are *sometimes* wiser in the ways of this world than the children of light are in the ways of the spirit-world above.

9"So then, use the possessions of this world to help others in need, who will become your friends. Then when possessions run out, these new friends *of Creator's good road* will always welcome you into their homes.

10-12"If Creator cannot trust you with the possessions of this world, then how will he trust you with the treasures of the spirit-world above? But if you do well with the small things *of this world*, you will do well with the great things *of the spirit-world above.*

13"No one can be loyal to two rival chiefs. He will have to choose between them, for either he will hate one chief and love the other, or he will honor one and resent the other. You cannot be loyal to the Great Provider and to possessions at the same time."

14When the Separated Ones (Pharisees) heard him, they shrugged their shoulders and rolled their eyes, for they loved their many possessions.

15Creator Sets Free (Jesus) said to them, "You always make yourselves look good to others, but the Great Spirit sees your heart. What many see as valuable he sees as worthless.

NOTHING IN TRIBAL LAW WILL FAIL

16"Tribal Law and the Prophets spoke until Gift of Goodwill (John) came. From his time until now, the good story about Creator's good road has been told, but people are trying to force their way upon it. **17**Not one thing the Law or the Prophets have said will fail to come to pass. Their words are as sure as the sky above and the earth below."

ABOUT DIVORCE

In those days men would sometimes send their wives away for no good reason without giving them divorce papers, leaving them destitute and unable to properly remarry. Drawn from the Water (Moses), in the Law, said they must give a woman divorce papers before sending her away.[a] *To protect the honor and dignity of women, Creator Sets Free (Jesus) set them straight about how to apply this law.*

18"Whoever sends his wife away, *without properly divorcing her*, and marries another is guilty of being unfaithful to his first wife. Anyone who then marries her is guilty of marrying another man's wife.

THE RICH MAN AND THE BEGGAR

19"There was once a man with many possessions who always dressed in the best clothes, had more than enough to eat, and lived a life of ease. **20**Every day a beggar named Creator Helps Him (Lazarus) was laid at the gate of his lodge. **21**Dogs would come and lick the sores that covered his body as he begged for crumbs from the rich man's table.

22"When the time came for the beggar to cross over to the world of the dead, spirit-messengers carried him into the welcoming arms of his ancestor, Father of Many Nations (Abraham).

---

[a] **16:18** Deuteronomy 24:1; Matthew 5:31

"At the same time the rich man also crossed over to death, and his body was buried. **23**In the Dark Underworld of Death (Hades) he was suffering and in pain. He looked up and saw his ancestor, Father of Many Nations (Abraham), far off in the distance. He could see Creator Helps Him (Lazarus) being comforted in his arms.

24"He cried out in his pain, 'Father of Many Nations (Abraham), my ancestor, have pity on me. Send Creator Helps Him (Lazarus) to dip the tip of his finger in water and cool my thirsty tongue. Help me, for I am suffering in this flame.'

25"Father of Many Nations (Abraham) said to him, 'My son, do you not remember? All your days were filled with good things, but the days of Creator Helps Him (Lazarus) were filled with sorrow and pain. It is now his time for comfort, but it is your time for sorrow and pain. **26**Look! There is a great canyon between us, so wide that none can make the journey from here to there.'

27"The rich man *hung his head and* said, 'Please, my ancestor, send him back to the lodge **28**of my father and my five brothers. He can warn them of this place of suffering and pain, so they will not have to come here also.'

29"Father of Many Nations (Abraham) said to him, 'They have the words of Drawn from the Water (Moses) and the words of the prophets. Let your family listen to them.'

30"'No!' the rich man cried out. 'If someone goes back to them from the world of the dead, they will turn their hearts back to Creator.'

31"Father of Many Nations (Abraham) *shook his head and* said, 'If your family will not listen to Drawn from the Water (Moses) and the prophets, then they will not listen even to one who comes back to life from the dead.'"

TROUBLE WILL COME

1Creator Sets Free (Jesus) said to the ones who walked the road with him, "This world of sorrow and pain will make many stumble, but how terrible it will be for the ones who go along with it. **2**It would be better to be thrown into the deep waters with a great stone tied to your neck than to cause even one of these little ones, who trust in me, to stumble on the path.

"When you are wronged, **3-4**look first at what is in your own heart. If one of your brothers or sisters *in the sacred family* has wronged you, then tell them face to face. If they turn around and ask forgiveness, then release them—even if they do this seven times in one day."

5"Wisdomkeeper," his message bearers said, "help our weak faith!"

6"If you had faith as small as a mustard seed," he replied, "you could also say to this mulberry tree, 'Come out by the roots and be planted in the sea,' and it would do what you say.

DOING ONLY WHAT IS EXPECTED

7"Would an elder who sent a young man out to hunt for a deer, when the young man returned, say to him, 'Sit down while I skin the deer and cook the meal for you'? **8**No, but he would say, 'Now skin the deer, then clean up and cook for me, then when I am finished, you can eat.'

9"The young man is only doing what is expected and deserves no special thanks. **10**In the same way, when you have done everything the Great Spirit expects of you, serve him as you would an elder and do not expect to be honored for doing only what you should do."

HONOR FROM AN OUTSIDER

11On his way to Village of Peace (Jerusalem), Creator Sets Free (Jesus) took the path following the border between High Place (Samaria) and Circle of Nations (Galilee). **12**He went into a small village where ten men with a skin disease came across his path. **13**They *kept a respectful distance from him and* called loudly, "Creator Sets Free (Jesus)! Honored One!" They pleaded, "Have pity on us!"

14Creator Sets Free (Jesus) looked at them and said, "Go to the holy men and show yourselves to them."ᵃ

Tribal law instructed that a person healed of a skin disease must be pronounced ceremonially clean by a holy man.

They did what he said, and as they were on the way, they were healed. **15**One of the ten men, when he saw he was healed, returned to Creator Sets Free (Jesus), giving loud praise to the Great Spirit. **16**He then bowed down to honor Creator Sets Free (Jesus) and offered him thanks. This man was from High Place (Samaria).

All the people from there were despised and looked down on by the tribes of Wrestles with Creator (Israel).

17Creator Sets Free (Jesus) said *to those who were watching*, "Were not ten men healed? Where then are the other nine? **18**Was the only one who returned to give thanks and honor to the Great Spirit an outsider from High Place (Samaria)?"

19Then he said to the man, "Stand up and be on your way. Your trust in me has healed you."

THE GOOD ROAD HAS COME

20Another time the Separated Ones (Pharisees) asked him, "When will we see the Land of Creator's good road?"

He said to them, *"Creator's good road is not what you expect.* It does not come with the outward signs you are looking for. *You will need new eyes to see it.* **21**No one will say, 'Here it is! I found it!' or 'Look! It is over there!' For Creator's good road is already here—in me, as I walk among you."

SIGNS OF TROUBLED TIMES

22He then said to his message bearers, "In the time of trouble ahead, you will long for the days when the True Human Being walked among you. Those days will be no more. **23**People will say, 'Look! He is over there or over here!' Do not listen to them, **24**for when the day of the True Human Being comes, it will be like lightning when it flashes and lights the whole sky. **25**But first he will suffer many terrible things and be turned away by the people living today.

26"The days of the True Human Being will be the same as it was in the days of One Who Rests (Noah), before the great flood. **27**The people were eating and drinking and getting married until the day that One Who Rests (Noah) entered the great wooden canoe. No one believed what was coming until the floodwaters came, washed them away, and drowned them all.

28"It will be the same as it was in the days of Covers His Head (Lot). The people were eating and drinking, trading goods, planting seeds, and building their lodges

²⁹until the day came that Covers His Head (Lot) left Village of Bad Spirits (Sodom). Then rocks burning with fire fell from the sky and destroyed them all. ³⁰This is how it will be when the True Human Being is revealed.

³¹"When that day comes, the ones on their rooftops should flee, not even taking the time to get their belongings from inside their house. The ones who are working in the field should not take time to go home. ³²Remember what happened to the wife of Covers His Head (Lot)."

In the days of Covers His Head (Lot), the ancient Village of Bad Spirits (Sodom) was destroyed by fire-rocks that fell from the sky. He and his wife had to flee, leaving all behind. But his wife held back, and the ashes from the fire covered her, turning her into a mound of salt.

³³"The ones who cling to their life's *belongings* will lose their own lives, but whoever is willing to leave everything behind will survive.

³⁴"During that night two people will be asleep in bed. One will be taken away and the other left. ³⁵Two women will be husking grain. One will be taken away and the other left."

³⁶⁻³⁷"Taken where?" his followers asked him.

"To the place where the dead bodies lie and the eagles[a] gather over them," he answered.

18

NEVER GIVE UP PRAYING

¹Creator Sets Free (Jesus) told them a story to show that they should pray at all times and never lose heart.

---

[a]**17:36-37** The same word for "eagle" can also be translated "vulture."

²"*Listen!*" he said. "There was a village that had a tribal council chief who did not fear the Great Spirit or respect his fellow human beings. ³A woman of that village, who had lost her husband, kept bothering him. She would say to him, 'Stand up for me against the one who has done me wrong!'

⁴⁻⁵"The tribal council chief ignored her at first, but the woman kept demanding that he help her. The council chief grew weary, changed his thinking, and said, 'This woman really troubles me. If I do not help her and right this wrong, she will never stop bothering me! I will see that she gets justice, not because I respect her or even fear the Great Spirit, but only because she will not give up until I help her.'"

⁶Creator Sets Free (Jesus) then said, "Can you hear the words of this bad-hearted tribal council chief? ⁷If a council chief like that will do what is right, how much more will the Great Spirit right the wrongs done to the ones who cry out to him day and night? Will he ignore their cries? No! ⁸I tell you, he will not be slow to bring justice to them. But when the True Human Being comes, will he find this kind of faith anywhere in this land?"

ARROGANCE AND HUMILITY

⁹He then told a story to warn the ones who trusted in themselves and thought they were better than others.

¹⁰"Two men, a Separated One (Pharisee) and a tribal tax collector, went to the Great Spirit's sacred lodge to send up their prayers.

¹¹"The Separated One (Pharisee) kept his distance from the tribal tax collector and prayed out loud, 'Creator, I thank you that I am not like the rest of humankind—like the ones who use force

to get from others what they want, or who are not faithful in marriage, or who have no understanding of right or wrong. I thank you also that I am not like this tribal tax collector standing here! [12]I go without food twice a week for spiritual reasons, and I give a tenth of all my gain.'

[13]"Now the tribal tax collector hung his head down and would not even lift his face to the spirit-world above. He beat his hands against his chest and cried out, 'Creator! Be kind and have pity on me. I am a pitiful man, full of bad thoughts and wrongdoings!'

[14]"Can you not see?" Creator Sets Free (Jesus) said. "The tribal tax collector returned home in good standing with Creator, but the Separated One (Pharisee) did not! The ones who think too highly of themselves will be brought down low. The ones who humble themselves will be lifted up."

LITTLE CHILDREN AND THE GOOD ROAD

[15]The people were bringing their little children to Creator Sets Free (Jesus) so he would lay his hands on them *and bless them*, but his followers spoke harsh words to the ones bringing them.

[16]So Creator Sets Free (Jesus) said to them, "Let the little children come to me! Do not turn them away. Creator's good road belongs to the ones who are like these children. [17]I speak from my heart, unless you welcome Creator's good road in the way a little child does, you will never walk it."

POSSESSIONS OR THE GREAT SPIRIT?

[18]A spiritual leader came to Creator Sets Free (Jesus). "Good Wisdomkeeper," he asked, "what must I do to have the life of the world to come that never fades away, full of beauty and harmony?"

[19]"Why do you call me good?" he asked the man. "Only the Great Spirit is good. [20]You know the sacred instructions from tribal law: Do not be unfaithful in marriage, do not take the life of another, or take anything that is not yours. Do not lie about others, and always give honor and respect to your parents."[a]

[21]"*Wisdomkeeper*," the man answered, "from my youth I have followed all of these instructions."

[22]"Then only one thing remains," Creator Sets Free (Jesus) told him, "Take all of your possessions and give them to the ones who have none. Then you will have great possessions in the spirit-world above. And then come, walk the good road with me."

[23]The young man's heart fell to the ground, and he hung his head, for he had many possessions.

[24-25]A great sadness came to the face of Creator Sets Free (Jesus) as he looked at the man. And then he said, "Walking the good road is a hard thing for the ones who have many possessions. It would be easier for a moose[b] to squeeze through the eye of a beading needle."

[26]After hearing this, they asked him, "How then can anyone walk the good road that sets all people free?"

[27]Creator Sets Free (Jesus) *looked at them and* said, "This is only possible with the help of the Great Spirit."

[28]Stands on the Rock (Peter) spoke up. "Can you see that we have left all our possessions *and our relatives* to walk the road with you?"

[29]"I speak from my heart," he said to them, "No one who has left homes and families to walk Creator's good road will

---

[a]**18:20** Deuteronomy 5:16-20
[b]**18:24-25** Lit. *camel*

go without. [30]For in this world they will gain an even greater family with many homes, and in the world to come, the life of beauty and harmony will be theirs."

THE ROAD AHEAD

[31]Creator Sets Free (Jesus) took the twelve aside and told them again about what was coming on the road ahead.

"Consider closely what I am telling you," he reminded them. "We are on our way to the Sacred Village of Peace (Jerusalem), where all the words of the prophets about the True Human Being will come to pass. [32]He will be handed over to the People of Iron (Romans).[a] They will treat him shamefully, spit on him, [33]and put him to death, but on the third day he will come back to life."

[34]But his twelve message bearers did not understand what he was saying. The meaning was hidden from their eyes.

A BLIND MAN HEALED

[35]As they walked the road toward Village of Peace (Jerusalem), they came to Moon Village (Jericho). A blind man was sitting by the road begging for food. [36]When he heard the sound of the passing crowd, he asked what was happening. [37]He was told that Creator Sets Free (Jesus), from Seed Planter Village (Nazareth), was passing by.

[38]The blind man cried out in a loud voice, "Creator Sets Free (Jesus), descendant of Much Loved One (David), have pity on me!"

[39]The people in the front of the crowd scolded him and said, "Be quiet!"

That only made him cry out louder, "Descendant of Much Loved One (David), have pity on me!"

---

[a]**18:32** Lit. *Gentiles*

[40]Creator Sets Free (Jesus) stopped walking and told them to bring the man to him. When the man was close, Creator Sets Free (Jesus) asked him, [41]"What do you want from me?"

"Wisdomkeeper," he said, "heal my eyes, so I can see again."

[42]"Open your eyes and look around," he told the man. "Your trust in me has healed you."

[43]As soon as he said this, the man could see!

> *The people laughed with joy as the man blinked his eyes and looked into their faces.*

Right then the man began to walk the road with Creator Sets Free (Jesus), giving honor to the Great Spirit. And all the people who saw this also sang songs to thank the Great Spirit.

19

RESTORING PURE OF HEART

[1]Creator Sets Free (Jesus) was walking through Moon Village (Jericho). [2]There, a man named Pure of Heart (Zacchaeus), who was a head tribal tax collector with many possessions, [3]was trying to see who was coming but was too short to see over the crowd. [4]So he ran ahead and climbed up a tall tree to get a better view.

[5]When Creator Sets Free (Jesus) came to the tree, he looked up and said, "Pure of Heart (Zacchaeus), come down from there and take me to your house, for I need a place to rest."

[6]He quickly climbed down the tree and with a glad heart welcomed him into his house. [7]But when the people saw this, *they shook their heads.* "What is he doing?" they grumbled out loud. "Why would he go into the house of an outcast?"

⁸Pure of Heart (Zacchaeus) stood up to the crowd and said to Creator Sets Free (Jesus), "Hear me, Wisdomkeeper. I will give half my possessions to the ones who have none. If I have cheated anyone, I will give them back four times as much."

⁹Creator Sets Free (Jesus) smiled and said, "This is a good day, because this man and his family have finally been set free. For he also is a descendant of Father of Many Nations (Abraham) *who had lost his way.* ¹⁰The True Human Being has come to find the ones who have lost their way and guide them back again to the good road."

REJECTING THE NEW CHIEF

¹¹Since they were now close to Village of Peace (Jerusalem), and his followers thought that Creator's good road would appear as soon as they arrived, he decided it was time to tell them another story.

¹²"There was a man who was born to be chief of a large tribal nation. The time had come for him to take his place as chief. But first he had to take a long journey to another land, *to meet with a council of many nations,* to be approved.

¹³"Before he left, he called together ten trusted tribal members who worked for him. He gave each one a woven blanket of great value. 'Go,' he told them, 'and trade well until I return.'

"He then left on his journey to meet with the council.

¹⁴"But many of his own people despised him, so they sent some messengers ahead of him to speak with the council. 'We do not want this man to be our chief,' they said.

"But the council did not listen to them.

¹⁵"*Much later,* after being appointed as chief, he returned to his own tribal nation. He called together the trusted tribal members to whom he had given the woven blankets, to see how well they had traded.

¹⁶"The first to come to him said, 'Honored chief, look, I now have ten blankets to return to you.'

¹⁷"'You have done well!' the chief replied, 'Since you did well with this small thing, you will now represent me in ten villages.'

¹⁸"The second man came to him, and said, 'Look, my chief, your one blanket is now five.'

¹⁹"'Well done. You will now represent me in five villages,' the chief told him.

²⁰"Another came to him and said, 'See, my chief, I have returned to you the blanket you gave me. I folded it and hid it safely away. ²¹I dared not trade with it, for I know you to be a harsh man and I was afraid. You take from others what is not yours and harvest food you did not plant.'

²²"'You have betrayed my trust,' he said to the man. 'Your own words will decide your fate! If you thought I was this way, ²³why did you not give your blanket to the trading post and at least have something to show for it when I returned?'

²⁴"Then the newly appointed chief turned to the ones who stood close by and said, 'Take the blanket from him and give it to the one who has ten.'

²⁵"They were confused by this. 'But, honored chief,' they said, 'he already has ten blankets!'

²⁶"The chief said to them, 'The ones who do well with what they have will be given more. But for the ones who do nothing, even what they have will be taken away.'

"Then the chief turned to the tribal members who had opposed his appointment.

27"'Now bring to me the ones who opposed me before the council,' he said with authority. 'They will now have to die, while I watch, because they have made themselves my enemies.'"

He told them this so they would see that the good road would not come in the way they expected.

HIS GRAND ENTRY

28After he told this story, Creator Sets Free (Jesus) walked on ahead of his followers to Village of Peace (Jerusalem). **29-30**When he came to House of Figs (Bethany) at the foot of Olive Mountain, he said to two of his followers, "Go to House of Unripe Figs (Bethphage) on the other side of the mountain. When you come into the village, you will see a young donkey colt tied there that no one has ever ridden. Untie it and bring it to me. **31**If anyone asks what you are doing, say this to them, 'Our Wisdomkeeper is in need of it.'"

32His followers did as they were told. When they arrived at the village, they found everything just as he had said. **33**When they started untying the colt, the owners asked them, "What are you doing?" **34**They answered the owners just as they had been instructed, so they were permitted to go.

35They brought the young donkey colt to Creator Sets Free (Jesus) and laid their *deer skins and tribal* blankets on the donkey colt. He then mounted the colt and began his ride.

Creator Sets Free (Jesus) came riding into the Sacred Village of Peace (Jerusalem) down Olive Mountain toward the eastern

entry into Village of Peace (Jerusalem) that is called Beautiful Gate. His twelve followers encircled him and led the colt forward. He did not fit the powerful image of a conquering ruler, for he was not riding a warhorse. Instead, he rode a small, humble donkey colt. No mighty warriors rode next to him. No dignitaries came out to meet him. It was mostly the common people who welcomed him that day.

36As he rode forward, some of the people began to spread their *buffalo* robes on the road in front of Creator Sets Free (Jesus). **37**When he reached the foot of Olive Mountain, the whole village was in an uproar. His followers began to sing to Creator and shout out loud, praising him for the powerful signs they had seen.

38"Blessed is the Grand Chief who comes representing the Great Spirit! Peace to the spirit-world above and honor and shining-greatness to the One Above Us All!"[a]

39Some of the Separated Ones (Pharisees) who were in the crowd spoke up. "Wisdomkeeper!" they cried out, "Warn your followers to watch what they are saying."

It was a dangerous thing to call anyone a chief or ruler in front of the soldiers of the People of Iron (Romans) who were guarding the area.

40"I will tell you this," he said to them. "If they were silenced, the very stones and rocks *we are walking on* would lift their voices and cry out!"

THE TRAIL WHERE HE CRIED

41As he rode forward, he could see the Sacred Village of Peace (Jerusalem), and tears began to run down his face.

---

[a] **19:38** Psalm 118:26

He could taste the salt from his tears as he opened his mouth in anguish.

⁴²"*Jerusalem, O Jerusalem, you are the Sacred Village of Peace,*" he wept out loud. "Of all people, you should be the ones who would know the way of peace, but on this sacred day, the way of peace is hidden from your eyes.

⁴³"In the days ahead your enemies will encircle you and close in on you from every side. You will be crushed and trampled down, along with all your children. ⁴⁴Every lodge will fall, and not even one pole, log, or stone will be left standing against another. All of this will happen because you did not know it was your time for the Great Spirit to visit you."

⁴⁵Then he rode through the Beautiful Gate, into the village and up to the sacred lodge.

He entered the lodge and came into the area called Gathering Place for the Nations. It was here that other nations could come to learn about the Great Spirit and his ways. The holy men were using this place to buy and sell the ceremonial animals. But it was so crowded that there was not enough room for the people from other nations who wanted to learn about Creator's ways. They were not honoring the purpose of this holy place.

He entered the lodge and began to force out the ones who were buying and selling the ceremonial animals. ⁴⁶"It is written in the Sacred Teachings," he cried out, "'my lodge will be a house of prayer; but you have turned it into a hideout for thieves!'ª"

⁴⁷In the days that followed, Creator Sets Free (Jesus) came each day to the sacred lodge to teach and tell his stories. The head holy men, the scroll keepers, and the spiritual leaders took counsel together to plan new ways to have him killed. ⁴⁸But they could not figure out what to do, for the people had great respect for him and held on to every word he said.

20

THE SPIRITUAL LEADERS CHALLENGE HIM

¹One day that week when Creator Sets Free (Jesus) was telling the good story at the sacred lodge, the head holy men and the scroll keepers came to him, along with the elders. ²"By what right do you do these things?" they challenged. "Who gave you this right?"

³"I will answer your question," he said to them, "but first you must answer mine.

⁴"The purification ceremonyᵇ performed by Gift of Goodwill (John), was it from the spirit-world above, or did it come from human beings?" he asked them.

The spiritual leaders looked at each other. They did not know how to answer him. All the people there kept their ears wide open to hear what the spiritual leaders would say. Creator Sets Free (Jesus) stood before them and quietly held his ground.

⁵They put their heads together and talked it over. "If we say it is from the spirit-world above, he will ask us why we did not listen to him. ⁶If we say it is from human beings, the people would stone us to death, for they think Gift of Goodwill (John) is a great prophet."

ª19:46 Isaiah 56:7; Jeremiah 7:11

ᵇ20:4 Baptism

[7]So they said to him, "We do not know." [8]Creator Sets Free (Jesus) looked straight at them and said, "Then I will not answer your question either."

STORY OF THE VINEYARD

[9]Then he turned again to the people and began to tell them this story.

"A tribal member planted a large vineyard and rented it out to other tribal members for a share of the grapes. Then he traveled far away to another land to stay for a long time.

[10]"When harvest time came, the tribal member who owned the vineyard sent a trusted messenger to gather his share of the grapes; but the farmers beat him and sent him away empty-handed. [11]The vineyard owner sent another messenger, but they treated him shamefully, beat him, and sent him away also. [12]So he sent a third messenger, but they did the same things to him.

"The tribal member who owned the vineyard was at the end of his rope.

[13]"'What can I do?' he wondered. 'I know,' he said to himself, 'I will send my much-loved son. They will have to respect him.'

[14]"When they saw that he had sent his son, they put their heads together and came up with an evil plan. 'This vineyard will one day belong to this son,' they schemed. 'If we kill him, the vineyard will be ours.'

[15]"So they dragged him out to the edge of the vineyard, murdered him, and left his dead body there."

Creator Sets Free (Jesus) turned to the spiritual leaders.

"What will the owner of the vineyard do?" he asked.

He waited for an answer, but no one said a word.

[16]Then he said, "He will return, put those dishonorable men to death and give the vineyard to others."

The spiritual leaders were insulted by this story.

"That must never happen!" they said. [17]Creator Sets Free (Jesus) looked at the spiritual leaders and said, "Then what do the Sacred Teachings mean when they say, 'The tree the lodge builders threw away has become the Chief Lodgepole'? [18]The ones who stumble over this pole will be broken into pieces, and when it falls on them, they will be crushed *and scattered like dust in the wind.*"[a]

THE SEPARATED ONES ATTACK

[19]When the head holy men and the scroll keepers realized that this story was about them, they looked for a way to arrest him, but they could not, for they were afraid of what the people might do. [20]They kept an eye on him and sent spies who pretended to be good-hearted to trap him in his words, so they would have a reason to turn him over to the power of the governor of People of Iron (Romans).

[21]"Wisdomkeeper," the spies said to him. "We know you always speak the truth about the Great Spirit and represent him well. [22]Tell us what is permitted, should our tribal members pay taxes to the Ruler of the People of Iron (Caesar)? Yes or no?"

[23]Creator Sets Free (Jesus) could see right through them. [24]"Show me one of their silver coins."

They found a silver coin and handed it to him. He took a good long look, holding it up

---

[a]**20:18** Psalm 118:22

to the sky to see it clearly. Then he turned the face of the coin toward them.

"Whose image and words are carved into this coin?" he asked.

"The Ruler of the People of Iron (Caesar)," they answered.

He handed the coin back to them.

25"Then give to this ruler the things that are his," he said, "and give to the Great Spirit the things that belong to the Great Spirit."

26The spiritual leaders had failed, right in front of the people, and could not use his words against him. They were amazed at his wisdom and hung their heads in silence.

THE UPRIGHT ONES ATTACK

27Then some of the Upright Ones (Sadducees), who say there is no rising again from death, came to Creator Sets Free (Jesus) 28to question him also.

"Wisdomkeeper," they said, "in the law Drawn from the Water (Moses) gave us these instructions: 'If a Tribal Member should die before having children, then his brother should marry his widow and give her children. This way the man will have descendants.'a

29"In a family of seven brothers, the oldest took a wife, but died without children. 30The next brother married her, but he also died with no children. 31A third brother married her, and, like his other brothers, he died with no children. The same happened to all seven of them, 32and, last of all, the woman also crossed over to death. 33When they all come back to life in the new world, whose wife would she be, since all seven men married her?"

34"Marriage belongs to this present world and to the ones who live in it," he answered. 35"The ones who are chosen to rise to life in that world will not marry, for they will be like the spirit-messengers. 36They will never die, for they are the children of the Great Spirit who raises them again to new life."

37*And then he said,* "As to the dead rising again, listen to what the Sacred Teachings tell us that Drawn from the Water (Moses) said when he saw the burning bush. He calls Creator the 'Great Spirit of Father of Many Nations (Abraham), He Made Us Laugh (Isaac), and Heel Grabber (Jacob).'b

38"He is not the Great Spirit of the dead, but of the living. To him all are alive."

39Hearing this, some of the scroll keepers said to him, "Wisdomkeeper, you have answered well."

40After that none of the Upright Ones (Sadducees) dared to ask him any more questions.

41So Creator Sets Free (Jesus) asked them a question, "How is it that you call the Chosen One the descendant of Much Loved One (David), 42when Much Loved One (David) in the Sacred Songs (Psalms) says, 'The Great Chief said to my Great Chief, 'Sit down beside me at my right hand, my place of greatest honor, 43until I defeat your enemies and humble them before you'?"c

He paused to let his words sink in.

44"If Much Loved One (David) calls the Chosen One, 'My Great Chief,'" he asked them, "then how can the Chosen One be his descendant?"

The Upright Ones (Sadducees) had no answer for him.

---

a20:28 Deuteronomy 25:5-6

b20:37 Exodus 3:6
c20:43 Psalm 110:1

⁴⁵Then Creator Sets Free (Jesus) said to his followers, loud enough for all to hear, ⁴⁶"Beware of the scroll keepers, who walk about dressed up in fancy regalia, who love to be noticed at the trading posts, who take the seats of honor at the gathering houses and the best seats at the feasts. ⁴⁷With many words they make long, empty prayers to trick widows into giving them their homes and possessions, but they will all come to a worse end than others."

21

A SACRIFICIAL GIFT

¹Creator Sets Free (Jesus) looked up and saw people with many possessions bringing their gifts to the giveaway at the sacred lodge. ²He then saw a poor widow walk up and place two poorly beaded earrings on the blanket, worth almost nothing.

³"I speak from my heart," he said to his followers, "this widow's gift is better than all the others. ⁴When they put their gifts on the blanket, they gave only a small part of their many possessions, but this poor widow has given all she had."

SIGNS AND WARNINGS

⁵Some of his followers began to point out to him the beauty of the great lodge with its handsomely carved logs, its large stones, and ceremonial gifts.

A look of sadness came over the face of Creator Sets Free (Jesus).

⁶"Take a good long look," he said, "for in the days ahead, all of this will fall to the ground. Not one log or stone will be left standing against another."

They looked at him with worried faces.

⁷"Wisdomkeeper, when will this happen?" they asked. "What will be the sign?"

⁸"Make sure no one leads you down the wrong path," he warned them, "for many will falsely represent me and say, 'I am the Chosen One, *follow me*, there is no time left!' Do not follow after them.

⁹"When you hear of wars and uprisings, do not fear, for these things will come first—but the end is not yet. ¹⁰Tribal wars will break out, and nations will war against nations. ¹¹There will be great earthquakes, food will be scarce, sickness will spread everywhere, and bad signs will appear in the sky.

¹²"Before all of this happens, you will be betrayed by your own people. They will hunt you down, drag you into their gathering houses, and put you in jail. They will hand you over to the government and officials *of the People of Iron (Romans).* All of this they will do to you because of me and my name. ¹³But remember, this will be your chance to represent me and tell them the good story. ¹⁴Do not worry about what to say ahead of time to defend yourselves, ¹⁵for I will give you the mouth of a wisdomkeeper, and no enemy will be able to answer you or prove you wrong.

¹⁶"You will be betrayed by your own family members and friends. They will even have some of you killed. ¹⁷They will all hate you because you are representing me and my teachings.

¹⁸"But none of these things can truly harm you,[a] ¹⁹so you must stand up strong and never give up trusting in me, for my life inside you will help you walk with firm steps."

---

[a] **21:18** Lit. *Not one hair on your head will perish*

THE DAY OF SORROW AND DESTRUCTION

20"When you see Village of Peace (Jerusalem) surrounded and encamped about by the armies *of the People of Iron (Romans)*, you will know that the time of her destruction has come.[a] 21The people of the Land of Promise (Judea) should run to the mountains for safety, and the ones who are inside the walls of Village of Peace (Jerusalem) must get out, and the ones outside should not go in. 22For this is the time when Creator will let justice have its way, to bring about the bad end spoken of in the Sacred Teachings.

23"It will be hard for women who are pregnant or nursing their babies, for great sorrow and trouble will come like an angry storm upon the land and against this people. 24The great Village of Peace (Jerusalem) will be cut down by the long knives. The people will be taken captive and scattered into all the nations. The Sacred Village of Peace (Jerusalem) will then be trampled down by the Outside Nations until their time has come to an end.

25"There will also be signs in the sun, moon, and stars, and on the earth the nations will tremble with fear. Panic and confusion will grow strong when they hear the sea roar and see the waves swell. 26The people will shake with fear, and hearts will fall to the ground when they see what is happening to the world around them. Even the powers of the spirit-world above will tremble and shake. 27"Then they will look up and see the True Human Being coming with power, riding on the clouds, and showing his shining-greatness![b]

28"When you see all these things begin to happen, stand strong, my followers.

Lift up your heads! For the time of your captivity will soon come to an end!"

STORY ABOUT THE FIG TREE

29Then he told them a wisdom-story: "Look at this fig tree or any tree, and see what it is saying to you. 30When the branches of a tree grow soft and buds appear, you know that it is nearly summer. 31In the same way when you see these things happening, you will know that Creator's good road is about to come into full bloom.

32"I speak from my heart! All of this will happen to this generation, during the lifetime of the people who live today. 33What I have told you is sure, for my words will last longer than the sky above and the earth below.

34"So keep your eyes straight. Do not let your hearts fall to the ground. Do not give yourselves to drinking or worrying about your life's possessions, or that day will take you by surprise. 35For it will come without warning, to all who live on the land, like a beaver that is snared in a trap. 36So stay on guard, praying that you will find a safe path through this time and stand strong before the True Human Being."

37During the day Creator Sets Free (Jesus) would teach and tell his stories at the sacred lodge. Then at night he would go to where he was lodging on Olive Mountain. 38Then, in the morning, all the people would gather again at the lodge to listen to him.

22

THE BETRAYER MAKES HIS MOVE

1It was time once again for the traditional feast of Bread Without Yeast,

---

[a] **21:20** Matthew 24:15; Mark 13:14
[b] **21:27** Daniel 7:13

called Passover. ²The head holy men and the scroll keepers were looking for a way to capture Creator Sets Free (Jesus) and have him put to death, for they feared his influence over the people.

³During that time, Accuser (Satan) wrapped himself around the heart of Speaks Well Of (Judas), *also called* Village Man (Iscariot), who was one of the twelve followers of Creator Sets Free (Jesus).

⁴He went to the head holy men and the lodge guards and told them of his plan to turn against Creator Sets Free (Jesus). ⁵With glad hearts they agreed to pay him. ⁶He agreed to the amount and began to wait for the right time to betray Creator Sets Free (Jesus) when there were no crowds around him.

PREPARING FOR THE CEREMONIAL MEAL

⁷It was now the day of Bread Without Yeast, when the ceremonial Passover lamb would be sacrificed *and eaten.*

⁸Creator Sets Free (Jesus) chose Stands on the Rock (Peter) and He Shows Goodwill (John). "Go and prepare a place for us to eat the ceremonial meal," he instructed them.

⁹"Where should we go?" they asked him.

¹⁰"Go into the village," he instructed them, "and look for a man carrying a pouch of water. He will take you to a lodge. Go in with him ¹¹and say to the headman of the house, 'Our Wisdom-keeper wants to know where the room is to eat the Passover meal with his followers.' ¹²He will then take you to a large upper room that will be ready for you. There you can prepare the meal."

¹³They did as he said and found everything was just as he told them, so they prepared the ceremonial meal.

THE CEREMONIAL MEAL BEGINS

¹⁴When it was time for the ceremonial meal to begin, Creator Sets Free (Jesus) and his twelve message bearers sat down *around a table.*

Creator Sets Free (Jesus) looked into the faces of his followers.

¹⁵"How I have longed to sit and eat this Passover meal with you before I suffer," he said.

¹⁶⁻¹⁸He then lifted up a cup of wine, gave thanks for it, and said, "Take this and share it with one another."

The cup was then passed from Creator Sets Free (Jesus) to each of them, and one by one they all drank from it.

Creator Sets Free (Jesus) said to them, "Listen to me closely, I will not drink from the fruit of this vine again until it finds its full meaning in the Land of Creator's good road."

During the meal ¹⁹Creator Sets Free (Jesus) took some of the frybread, lifted it up, and gave thanks. He broke it into pieces, gave some to each of his followers, and said, "This is my body, my gift to you. Take it and eat it. Do this to remember me."

They all passed the frybread around the table and ate it with wondering hearts, because this was something new. Creator Sets Free (Jesus) was showing his followers that this ancient ceremony was finding its full meaning in him.

²⁰In the same way, after the meal was over, he took a cup of wine, lifted it up, and gave thanks. He gave it to his followers and said, "This cup of wine is for the new peace treaty. It is my lifeblood poured out for you."

²¹"But look and see!" he said to the surprise of all. "The one who has turned

against me is sitting at this table. ²²The True Human Being will walk the path that has been chosen for him, but it will not go well for the one who betrays him."

²³His message bearers looked around at one another, asking who among them would do such a thing.

WHO IS THE GREATEST?

²⁴This led to an argument about which one of them was to be seen as the first and greatest among them.

²⁵So Creator Sets Free (Jesus) reminded them, "Rulers from the Nations show their power by forcing their way upon people and then call it 'helping them.' ²⁶This will not be the way of the ones who walk my road. The greatest among you will be least, like a child, and the rulers will be like household servants."

He let his words sink into their hearts.

²⁷"Who is the greater one?" he asked. "The one who is being served, or the one who serves?"

They all hung their heads and would not look him in the eye.

"Is it not the one being served?" he responded. "But here I am serving you."

The voice of Creator Sets Free (Jesus) became full of compassion and love. His followers lifted their heads up and looked at their Wisdomkeeper.

²⁸"You have stood with me even in my time of sorrow and testing. ²⁹My Father has made me the Chief of the good road. As Chief, I give you the right to walk this road with me ³⁰and share my table. There you will sit in twelve council seats and decide all things for the tribes of Wrestles with Creator (Israel)."

ALL OF YOU WILL TURN AWAY

The Passover meal was coming to an end. It was time to close the ceremony and face the dark night ahead. Turning to Stands on the Rock (Peter), Creator Sets Free (Jesus) spoke to him using his family name.

³¹"One Who Hears (Simon), hear me!" he said. "Accuser (Satan) has asked to put you all to the test, like one who separates the grain from the husks. ³²But I have prayed for you that your failure will not turn you from the good road. When you turn back once again, then help the others to do the same."

³³But One Who Hears (Simon) *could not hear, so he* said, "Wisdomkeeper, I am ready to go with you to both prison and death!"

³⁴Creator Sets Free (Jesus) *looked at him with sad eyes and* said, "Stands on the Rock (Peter), listen to me! Before the rooster crows, this very night, you will deny that you know who I am. *Not once, not twice, but* three times."

TROUBLE AHEAD

Creator Sets Free (Jesus) knew that trouble was coming, ³⁵so he said, "When I sent you out *to tell the good story to the villages,* you took no money pouch, no traveling bundle, not even extra moccasins. Did you need anything?"

"Nothing," they answered.

³⁶*"That is good,"* he said, "but now take your money pouch and your traveling bundle with you."

Then he spoke of what they would need to face that very night.

"Also, if you have no long knife, then trade your outer garment for one, ³⁷for there is another prophecy in the Sacred Teachings that tells what will happen to me. It says, 'He was numbered with the rebels.'[a] This also must find its full meaning and come to an end in me."

[38]"Wisdomkeeper!" they said, "Look, here are two long knives."

"That will be enough," he answered.

PRAYER OF SUFFERING

[39]Creator Sets Free (Jesus) and his followers left from there and went to the place where he often prayed at Olive Mountain. [40]When they arrived, he said to them, "Pray that you will have the strength to face this time of testing ahead of you."

[41-42]He went from them about as far as one can throw a stone. He lowered himself to the ground, fell on his face, and sent his voice to Creator, "If you want, my Father, you can take this bitter road of pain and sorrow away from me, but even so I want to walk your path, not my own."

The night was silent and cold as Creator Sets Free (Jesus) trembled and prayed. The powers of darkness were pressing in hard.

[43]While he prayed, a spirit-messenger from the spirit-world above appeared, giving him strength. [44]In great agony he prayed with renewed strength, until his sweat began to fall like great drops of blood watering the ground.

[45]When he had finished sending his voice to the Great Spirit, he got up and found his followers sleeping. [46]"Why are you sleeping?" he asked. "Wake up and pray for strength to face this time of testing!"

THE FIERY TRIAL BEGINS

[47]While Creator Sets Free (Jesus) was speaking, suddenly a crowd stormed in led by Speaks Well Of (Judas), one of the

twelve. He walked up to Creator Sets Free (Jesus) to greet him.

[48]"Will you betray the True Human Being with a kiss?" he said to him.

[49]When his followers saw what was happening, they said, "Wisdomkeeper, should we strike with our long knives?"

[50]Before he could answer them, one of them drew his long knife from its sheath and cut off the right ear of the servant of the chief holy man.

[51]"Stop! No more fighting!" Creator Sets Free (Jesus) cried out. Then he touched the man's ear and healed it. [52]He then turned to the head holy men, the lodge soldiers, and the council elders, who had come to take him.

"Why do you come at me with clubs and long knives as if I were a thief?" he asked them. [53]"Did I not sit with you every day in the sacred lodge? Why did you not take me then? This is your time, and you have given the powers of darkness their day."

[54]The lodge soldiers grabbed hold of him, dragged him away, and took him to the house of the chief holy man. Watching from a distance, Stands on the Rock (Peter) followed them.

STANDS ON THE ROCK DENIES HIM

[55]Some of the men built a fire in the courtyard and sat down to warm themselves. Stands on the Rock (Peter) sat down with them. [56]When a servant girl noticed him sitting by the fire, she looked closely into his face and said, "This man was with Creator Sets Free (Jesus)!"

[57]"Woman," he denied, "I do not know the man."

[58]A short time later someone else noticed him, and said, "You are one of his followers."

"I am not!" he argued back.

[a]**22:37** Isaiah 53:12

59About one hour later another man accused him, "He must be one of his followers, for he is also from Circle of Nations (Galilee)."

60"Man!" Stands on the Rock (Peter) defended himself, "I do not know what you are talking about."

Before he could get the words out of his mouth, a rooster crowed. 61Then Creator Sets Free (Jesus) turned and looked at him *from a distance.*

Stands on the Rock (Peter) remembered what he had been told earlier, "Before the rooster crows today, you will deny three times that you know me."

62Then Stands on the Rock (Peter) ran out of the gate, *at the first light of dawn,* and wept bitter tears *as he stumbled down the road.*

THE GRAND COUNCIL QUESTIONS HIM

63The soldiers who were guarding Creator Sets Free (Jesus) began to mock and beat him with their fists. 64They put a blindfold over his eyes. "Prophesy to us! Tell us who struck you!" 65they laughed, insulting him *with cruel words and twisted faces.*

66As the sun began to rise, the Grand Councila of elders, along with the head holy men and the scroll keepers, all came together. They brought Creator Sets Free (Jesus) into the council house.

67"If you are the Chosen One, then tell us!" they demanded.

"If I say that I am, you will not believe me, 68and if I ask for your answer, you will not tell me." 69And then he said, "But from now on the True Human Being will be seated at the right hand of the Great Power."b

70Then with one voice they asked, "Are you then the Son of the Great Spirit?"

"You have said it," he answered them. "I am."

71"Why question any more witnesses?" the council ruled. "We have heard it ourselves from his own mouth."

23 ◂▸◂▸◂▸◂▸◂▸◂▸◂▸

QUESTIONED BY THE PEOPLE OF IRON

1When they were done, they tied ropes around him again. All the ones who had gathered there got up and followed as they took Creator Sets Free (Jesus) to Spear of the Great Waters (Pilate), the governor of the People of Iron (Romans).

Spear of the Great Waters (Pilate) represented the People of Iron (Romans). His job was to keep the "peace" and make sure there were no uprisings among the tribes. He came out of his lodge to hear the charges against Creator Sets Free (Jesus).

2So they began to accuse him, "We caught this man misleading our nation and telling people not to pay taxes to the government of the People of Iron (Romans). He tells the people that he is the Chosen One, a Great Chief."

3Spear of the Great Waters (Pilate) turned to Creator Sets Free (Jesus) and asked him, "Do you say that you are chief of the tribes of Wrestles with Creator (Israel)?"

"It is you who have said it," he replied.

4Spear of the Great Waters (Pilate) turned to the head holy men and said in front of all the people, "I see no reason to find this man guilty."

5But they kept accusing him and saying, "He is making trouble with the people of the Land of Promise (Judea),

---

a**22:66** The Sanhedrin, the council of seventy that served as supreme court for Israel
b**22:69** Psalm 110:1

spreading his teachings from Circle of Nations (Galilee) to Village of Peace (Jerusalem)."

⁶After hearing this and finding out Creator Sets Free (Jesus) was from Circle of Nations (Galilee), ⁷he decided to send him to Looks Brave (Herod), who was in Village of Peace (Jerusalem) for the festival, for Looks Brave (Herod) was chief of the territory of Circle of Nations (Galilee).

QUESTIONED BY CHIEF LOOKS BRAVE

⁸Chief Looks Brave (Herod) was happy to see him. He had waited a long time for this, for he had heard much about Creator Sets Free (Jesus). He was hoping to see some powerful medicine come from him.

⁹⁻¹⁰The head holy men and scroll keepers made strong accusations against him, so Looks Brave (Herod) dug deep with many questions.

But Creator Sets Free (Jesus) stood silent and gave no answer.

¹¹Chief Looks Brave (Herod) mocked him along with his soldiers. They dressed him in a fancy robe and sent him back to the People of Iron (Romans). ¹²Looks Brave (Herod) and Spear of the Great Waters (Pilate) had been enemies, but on that day they became friends.

BACK TO THE PEOPLE OF IRON

¹³When they brought Creator Sets Free (Jesus) back to Spear of the Great Waters (Pilate), he then gathered the head holy men, the spiritual leaders, and the people together ¹⁴and said to them, "You told me this man was a troublemaker, but I questioned him and found him not guilty of your accusations. ¹⁵Looks Brave (Herod), one of your own people, also questioned him and found nothing wrong with him. Can you not see that this man has done nothing that deserves

death? ¹⁶I will have him whipped and release him."

¹⁷By tradition the People of Iron (Romans) would release one criminal during the festival. ¹⁸But they all shouted, "No! Not Creator Sets Free (Jesus)! Instead release Son of His Father (Barabbas)!" ¹⁹Now this man was a troublemaker who had caused an uprising and had been imprisoned for murder.

²⁰Spear of the Great Waters (Pilate) wanted to release Creator Sets Free (Jesus), so he asked again what they wanted to do with Creator Sets Free (Jesus). ²¹The crowd began to roar, "Death! Death on the cross!"

²²Spear of the Great Waters (Pilate) *quieted the crowd and* a third time said, "Why! What evil has he done? I have not found him guilty or worthy of death. I will have him beaten and then set him free."

²³The crowd would not back down. Louder and louder they demanded his death on the cross again and again, ²⁴until Spear of the Great Waters (Pilate) finally gave them what they wanted. He made his official decision, ²⁵released Son of His Father (Barabbas), a man of violence, guilty of uprising and murder, and he turned Creator Sets Free (Jesus), *the man of peace,* over to what the people wanted.

The cross was used by the People of Iron (Romans) as an instrument of torture to strike fear into criminals or anyone who dared to rise up against their empire. Iron nails would be used to pierce the hands and feet of the victims, fastening them to the tree-pole and its crossbeam. They would then hang there until dead. It was one of the most painful and cruel ways to die ever created by human beings. Often the victim was forced to carry the large wooden crossbeam to the place where they would be executed.

NAILED TO THE CROSS

²⁶The soldiers then marched Creator Sets Free (Jesus) away. A man named Listening Man (Simon), from Land of Power (Cyrene) *in northern Africa,* was just entering Village of Peace (Jerusalem). The soldiers forced him to walk behind Creator Sets Free (Jesus) and carry the crossbeam for him.

²⁷A large crowd of people trailed behind. Some of the women were wailing and crying out loud. ²⁸Creator Sets Free (Jesus) turned to them and said, "Daughters of Village of Peace (Jerusalem), weep not for me but for yourselves and your children.

²⁹"The time is coming soon when people will say, 'It is better for the women who have borne no children, *for they will not have to watch them die.'* ³⁰People will say to the mountains and the hills, 'Fall on us and cover us over.'ᵃ

³¹"If they do this to a green tree, what will they do to the trees that are dead and dry?"

³²Two other men, both of them criminals, were also walking the road with him to be put to death.

³³When they came to the place called "The Skull," they nailed the hands and feet of Creator Sets Free (Jesus) to a tree-pole—the cross. They did the same for the two criminals, putting one on each side of him.

³⁴"Father, forgive them!" Creator Sets Free (Jesus) cried out. "They do not know what they are doing."

The soldiers divided up his garments and gambled for them by drawing straws.ᵇ

³⁵The people watched as the spiritual leaders mocked him. "He set others free," they said, "why can he not free himself, if he is Creator's Chosen One?"

³⁶The soldiers offered Creator Sets Free (Jesus) wine mixed with bitter herbs ³⁷and mocked him. "If you are the Great Chief of the tribes," they laughed, "then set yourself free."

³⁸Above his head, carved above the crossbeam, were these words in three languages:

THIS IS THE CHIEF OF
THE TRIBES OF
WRESTLES WITH CREATOR

³⁹One of the thieves next to him spewed out angry words, "If you are the Chosen One, save yourself and us!"

⁴⁰Then the other thief spoke up and said, "Have you no fear or respect for the Great Spirit? ⁴¹We are guilty and suffering for our own wrongdoings, but this man has done nothing wrong!"

⁴²The man *turned to Creator Sets Free (Jesus) and* said to him, "Honored One, remember me when you come into the power of your good road."

⁴³Creator Sets Free (Jesus) looked at the man and said, "Listen closely, before the sun sets today, you will walk with me in the beautiful garden."ᶜ

⁴⁴It was now midday, for the sun had reached the center of the sky.ᵈ A great shadow of darkness covered the land like a blanket, and the sky remained dark until midafternoon.ᵉ ⁴⁵The light of the sun grew dim, and the great heavy blanket that hung over the entry to the Most Holy Place in the sacred lodge was torn in two down the middle.

ᵃ**23:30** Hosea 10:8
ᵇ**23:34** Psalm 22:18
ᶜ**23:43** Paradise
ᵈ**23:44** Lit. *the sixth hour*
ᵉ**23:44** Lit. *the ninth hour*

⁴⁶At the same time Creator Sets Free (Jesus) cried out with his last breath, "O Great Father, my spirit is in your hands!"ᵃ

▌ *Creator Sets Free (Jesus) was dead.*

⁴⁷One of the head soldiers of the People of Iron (Romans), who saw all these things, honored the Great Spirit by saying, "He must have been an upright man, not deserving death."

⁴⁸When the large crowd that had gathered to watch saw and heard all that was happening, they began to wail and beat their fists against their chests as they walked home.

⁴⁹Many friends of Creator Sets Free (Jesus) stood watching from a distance, along with the women who had walked the road with him from Circle of Nations (Galilee).

PREPARATION FOR HIS BURIAL

⁵⁰⁻⁵¹A man named He Gets More (Joseph) sat on the Grand Council of elders but had not agreed with the decision to put Creator Sets Free (Jesus) to death. He was a good-hearted and upright man from the tribal village of High Mountain (Arimathea), one who looked for Creator's good road.

⁵²He went to Spear of the Great Waters (Pilate) and asked for the body of Creator Sets Free (Jesus). ⁵³He then took it down from the cross and ceremonially wrapped his body with soft cloths. Then he laid the body in a newly carved burial cave that had never been used.

⁵⁴It was still the Day of Preparation for the Passover, and the Day of Resting would soon begin. ⁵⁵After the women who had walked the road with him from Circle of Nations (Galilee) saw where they

ᵃ**23:46** Psalm 31:5

put his body, ⁵⁶they left and went to prepare herbal spices and sweet-smelling ointments. Then they settled into their homes and followed the instructions for Day of Resting.

24

DEATH DEFEATED

¹It was now sunrise on the first day of the week. The women who had prepared the spices and oils were on their way to the burial cave. ²When they arrived, they saw that the large stone in front of the cave had been rolled away. ³They went inside, only to find the body of Creator Sets Free (Jesus) was gone!

⁴They were standing there in amazement and wonder when suddenly two men appeared beside them dressed in shining white outfits. ⁵The women, trembling with fear, fell down to the ground on their faces.

The men said, "Why do you look for the living in the place of the dead? ⁶He is not here. He has returned to life. Do you not remember what he told you in Circle of Nations (Galilee)? ⁷That the True Human Being would be turned over to the ones with bad hearts. They would put him to death on the cross, but he would come back to life on the third day."

⁸Then the women remembered what he had said. ⁹They hurried back to tell the eleven message bearers and the others what they had seen and heard. ¹⁰There was Strong Tears (Mary) of the village of Creator's High Lodge (Magdala), Woman of His Goodwill (Joanna), and Brooding Tears (Mary) the mother of He Takes Charge (James), and other women with them.

These women told the message bearers and the others what they saw with their own eyes. **11**But the men did not believe the women, thinking it was only empty talk.

12But Stands on the Rock (Peter) ran to the burial cave. He bent down to look inside and saw strips of cloth lying there, *but no sign of the body of Creator Sets Free (Jesus).* He then walked away wondering what had happened.

THE ROAD TO WARM SPRINGS

13On the same day, two of the followers of Creator Sets Free (Jesus) were walking to Village of Warm Springs (Emmaus), seven miles out from Village of Peace (Jerusalem). **14**As they walked along, they were talking about all that had happened. **15**Creator Sets Free (Jesus) came alongside them as they walked, **16**but their eyes were kept from seeing who he was.

17He said to them, "What are you talking about?"

They stopped walking and a look of sadness fell over their faces. **18**One of the men, Honored by His Father (Cleopas), answered him, "How can you not know about the things that have happened in Village of Peace (Jerusalem)? You must be coming from far away."

19"What things are you talking about?" he asked.

"About Creator Sets Free (Jesus) from Seed Planter Village (Nazareth). He was a prophet from the Great Spirit, with powerful medicine, who did many good things among all the people. **20**The head holy men and other leaders handed him over to the People of Iron (Romans) to be put to death on the cross. **21**We had hoped that he would free the tribes of Wrestles with Creator (Israel) *from the People of Iron (Romans).* It is now the third day since they killed him on the cross, **22-23**but today some women told us an amazing story. Early this morning they went to his burial cave and found that his body was not there. They told us about visions of spirit-messengers who told them he was alive! **24**Some of our men went to see with their own eyes and found the empty cave, but they did not see Creator Sets Free (Jesus)."

25"Why are your hearts so slow to believe the words of the prophets?" he said. **26**"It should be clear to you that the Chosen One would suffer first before he would be lifted up and honored above all."

27So Creator Sets Free (Jesus) told them his story, beginning with Drawn from the Water (Moses) and all the prophets. He showed them how all the ancient Sacred Teachings were written about the Chosen One and pointed the way to him.

> *They still did not know it was Creator Sets Free (Jesus) talking to them.*

28As they entered the village, he walked on as if to go farther. **29**They said to him, "Please, stay with us. It is late, and the sun will soon set."

So he went into the lodging house with them. **30**When they sat down to eat a meal together, Creator Sets Free (Jesus) took some frybread into his hands. He gave thanks and broke it, giving each of them a piece. **31**Suddenly, their eyes were opened and they knew who he was, but he vanished right in front of them.

32The men looked at each other in wide-eyed wonder and said, "It felt like our hearts were on fire when he was talking with us on the road, showing us the meaning of the Sacred Teachings!"

33They got up without finishing their meal and walked back to Village of Peace (Jerusalem) as fast as they could, for the sun was setting. They found where the eleven had gathered together with the others.

34They were saying, "Our Wisdom-keeper is alive! He has shown himself to One Who Hears (Simon)."

35So the two men told them what happened on the road and how their eyes were opened when Creator Sets Free (Jesus) broke the frybread into pieces.

THE MESSAGE BEARERS SEE HIM

36Before the men finished speaking, suddenly Creator Sets Free (Jesus) himself was standing there among them. "Peace be with you!" he said to them.

37Filled with fear, they all moved back from him, thinking he was a ghost. **38**"Why are you trembling?" he asked. "Why do you doubt what your eyes see? **39**Look at my hands and feet. Touch me. A spirit does not have flesh and bone, as you can see I have."

40Then he showed them his hands and feet. **41**They still could not believe their eyes, and with glad but fearful hearts they could only stare at him.

Then he said to them, "Give me something to eat." **42**They gave him some cooked fish **43**and he ate it in front of them. **44**As he ate, he said this to them, "When I was with you before, I told you that all the words of Drawn from the Water (Moses), the Prophets, and the Sacred Book of Songs (Psalms) must find their full meaning in me."

45He then opened their minds so they could see the full meaning of the Sacred Teachings **46**and said to them, "The Sacred Teachings foretold long ago that the Chosen One would walk a path of suffering. He would then die and rise to life on the third day.

47"It was also foretold that, beginning in the Sacred Village of Peace (Jerusalem), the good story would be told to all nations. This story will change hearts and minds and release people from their bad hearts and broken ways.

48"You, my message bearers, have seen these things with your own eyes so that you can go and tell others. **49**But first you must wait in Village of Peace (Jerusalem) until I send to you the Holy Spirit, just as my Father promised. He will dress you in my regalia, with power coming down from the spirit-world above."

HE RETURNS TO THE WORLD ABOVE

50Creator Sets Free (Jesus) then walked with them to House of Figs (Bethany). He lifted his hands and spoke blessing words over them, **51**and as he spoke, he was taken up into the spirit-world above.

52As he went up, his followers bowed down to honor him, and then with glad hearts they returned to the Sacred Village of Peace (Jerusalem). **53**Day by day they gathered at the sacred lodge, praying and giving thanks to the Great Spirit.

Aho! May it be so!

HE SHOWS GOODWILL TELLS THE GOOD STORY

THE GOSPEL OF JOHN

1

CREATOR'S WORD COMES DOWN

1-2 Long ago, in the time before all days, before the creation of all things, the one who is known as the Word was there face to face with the Great Spirit. This Word fully represents Creator and shows us who he is and what he is like. He has always been there from the beginning, for the Word and Creator are one and the same. **3**Through the Word all things came into being, and not one thing exists that he did not create.

4Creator's life shined out from the Word, giving light to all human beings. This is the true Light that comes to all the peoples of the world and shines on everyone. **5**The Light shines into the darkness, and the darkness cannot overcome it or put it out.

6-7 Into the wilderness of the Land of Promise (Judea) came a man named Gift of Goodwill (John). He was sent by the Great Spirit to tell what he knew about the Light so everyone could believe. **8**He was not the Light but came to speak the truth about the Light. **9**The true Light that shines on all people was coming into the darkness of this world.

10He came down into this world, and even though he made all things, the world did not recognize him. **11**Even his own tribe did not welcome or honor him. **12**But all who welcome and trust him receive their birthright as children of the Great Spirit. **13**They are born in a new way, not from a human father's plans or desires, but born from above—by the Great Spirit.

14Creator's Word became a flesh-and-blood human being and pitched his sacred tent among us, living as one of us. We looked upon his great beauty and saw how honorable he was, the kind of honor held only by this one Son who fully represents his Father—full of his great kindness and truth.

15Gift of Goodwill (John) told what he knew about him and cried out with a loud voice, "The one I have told you about is here! He comes after me, but is much greater—*my elder! He has more honor, for even though he is thought to be younger,* he existed before I was born."

16From the fullness of his being we have all had many gifts of kindness poured out on us. **17**Drawn from the Water (Moses) gave us our tribal laws, but the gift of great kindness and truth came from Creator Sets Free (Jesus), the Chosen One.

18No one has ever seen the Great Spirit, but the one Son, who is himself the Great Spirit and closest to the Father's heart, has shown us what he is like.

TRIBAL LEADERS QUESTION HIM

[19]Some of the holy men and tribal leaders from the tribes of Wrestles with Creator (Israel) were sent from Village of Peace (Jerusalem).

"Who are you?" they asked.

[20]He knew what they were asking, so he hid nothing and said plainly, "I am not the Chosen One."

[21]"Who are you, then?" they demanded. "The prophet from long ago, Great Spirit Is Creator (Elijah)?"

"No," he answered, "I am not."

"Are you the Prophet[a] *who is to come?*" they asked.

"No," was his answer again.

[22]So they said to him, "Tell us who you are, so we will have an answer for the ones who sent us. What do you have to say about yourself?"

Gift of Goodwill (John) looked at the spiritual leaders straight in the eyes and spoke with authority as he announced the full meaning of the ancient prophecy.

[23]"I am saying the same thing the prophet Creator Will Help Us (Isaiah) said. I am a voice howling in the desert, 'Make a straight pathway for our Honored Chief.'"

[24]These tribal leaders were sent by the Separated Ones (Pharisees), [25]so they asked Gift of Goodwill (John), "Why do you perform the purification ceremony[b] if you are not the Chosen One, or Great Spirit Is Creator (Elijah), or the Prophet who is to come?"

[26]"I perform the purification ceremony[b] with water," he answered, "but there is one you do not know, who is walking among you. [27]He is the one who comes after me, but with greater honor. I am not even worthy to untie his moccasins."

[28]These things took place in House of Figs (Bethany) on the far side of the river Flowing Down (Jordan).

CREATOR'S LAMB

The tribes of Wrestles with Creator (Israel) performed a ceremony every year where a lamb was killed and then ceremonially eaten. This was to remind them of the time when the Great Spirit set them free from their slavery to the ruler of Black Land (Egypt) and took them to a new land.[c]

[29]The next day Gift of Goodwill (John) saw Creator Sets Free (Jesus) walking toward him from a distance. "Behold!" he said to the ones gathered with him. "There is Creator's Lamb, the one who carries away and heals the bad hearts and broken ways of the world!"

The crowd of people looked to see the one Gift of Goodwill (John) was talking about.

[30]"He is the one I said is greater than I, for he existed before I was born. [31]The reason I perform the purification ceremony[d] with water is to make him known to the tribes of Wrestles with Creator (Israel). [32]With my own eyes I saw the Holy Spirit come down from above like a dove and rest on him. [33]I now know he is the one, because the Father above who sent me said, 'The man you see the Spirit come down and rest on will perform the purification ceremony[d] with the Holy Spirit.'"

The people could only stare in amazement at Creator Sets Free (Jesus) as they listened to the words that they had longed to hear for many generations.

---

[a]1:21 Deuteronomy 18:15
[b]1:25, 26 Baptism
[c]1:28 See Exodus 12.
[d]1:31, 33 Baptism

34Gift of Goodwill (John) finished by saying, "With my own eyes I have seen the one who has been chosen by the Great Spirit."

COME AND SEE

35The next day, Gift of Goodwill (John) was standing with two of his followers. **36**They saw Creator Sets Free (Jesus) walking nearby.

He said to them, "Look! There is Creator's Lamb!"

37So they took off after Creator Sets Free (Jesus).

38When they caught up to him, he saw them and asked, "What are you looking for?"

"Wisdomkeeper," they asked, "where are you staying?"

39"Come," he said, "and you will see."

So they went with him, saw where he was staying, and spent the rest of the day with him, for the day was almost over.

40One of the two men, Stands with Courage (Andrew), went to find his brother, One Who Hears (Simon), also named Stands on the Rock (Peter). **41**When he found him, he ran up to him and said, "My brother! We have found the Messiah" (which means "the Chosen One"[a]). **42**So he took his brother to meet Creator Sets Free (Jesus).

Creator Sets Free (Jesus) *looked deep into his eyes and* said, "You are One Who Hears (Simon), son of Gift of Kindness (John). I will give you the name Stands on the Rock (Peter)."

THE GREAT LADDER

43The next morning Creator Sets Free (Jesus) walked to the territory of Circle of Nations (Galilee). There he found a man named Friend of Horses (Philip) and said to him, "Come, and from now on walk the road with me."

44Friend of Horses (Philip) was from House of Fishing (Bethsaida), the same village where Stands with Courage (Andrew) and Stands on the Rock (Peter) also lived. **45**Friend of Horses (Philip) looked for his friend Creator Gives (Nathanael) *and found him sitting under a fig tree.*

"We have found him!" he said *as he ran up to him.* "The one the lawgiver Drawn from the Water (Moses) told us about, the one foretold by the prophets of old. He is Creator Sets Free (Jesus), son of He Gives Sons (Joseph), from Seed Planter Village (Nazareth)."

46Creator Gives (Nathanael) *crossed his arms and, shaking his head,* said to him, "How can anything good come from Seed Planter Village (Nazareth)?"

"Come," he said, "and you will see!"

47When Creator Sets Free (Jesus) saw Creator Gives (Nathanael) walking toward him, he said, "Look, a true descendant of Wrestles with Creator (Israel)! There is nothing false in him."

48Creator Gives (Nathanael) asked him, "How do you know me?"

Creator Sets Free (Jesus) *smiled and* said, "Before Friend of Horses (Philip) found you, I saw you under a fig tree."

49"Wisdomkeeper!" Creator Gives (Nathanael) answered. "You are the Son of the Great Spirit and the Chieftain of the tribes of Wrestles with Creator (Israel)!"

50"You believe me because I said I saw you under the fig tree?" he said to him. "I speak truth from my heart. You will see much more than this! **51**You will see the sky open wide and the spirit-messengers from Creator climbing up and down a

---

[a]**1:41** Lit. *Anointed One*

great ladder.ᵃ On the True Human Being they will climb from the spirit-world above to the earth below and back again."

2

HIS FIRST SIGN

¹Three days later there was a wedding in Village of Reeds (Cana), in the territory of Circle of Nations (Galilee). Bitter Tears (Mary), the mother of Creator Sets Free (Jesus), was there. ²Creator Sets Free (Jesus) and the ones who walked the road with him were invited as guests to the wedding.

³During the celebration, they ran out of wine.

This would have been a great embarrassment to the groom and his family.

So the mother of Creator Sets Free (Jesus) said to him, "Son, they have no more wine."

⁴"*Honored* woman," he said to her. "Why are you telling me? Is this our concern? It is not yet my time to show who I am."

⁵But his mother turned to the helpers and said, "Do whatever he says."

They looked to him and waited for his instructions.

⁶There were six *traditional* stone water pots, used for purification ceremonies, that could hold large amounts of water.

⁷⁻⁸"Fill them to the top," Creator Sets Free (Jesus) told them, "and take some to the headman of the feast."

They filled the pots until they could hold no more and did what he said.

⁹⁻¹⁰The water had turned into wine. The headman did not know where it had come from, but the helpers who were serving the wine knew.

The headman took a drink and called to the groom, "Everyone serves the best wine first, and after the guests have had enough to drink, they bring out the watered-down wine. But *even though you served good wine at first*, you have saved the best wine for last."

¹¹This was the first of the signs through which Creator Sets Free (Jesus) displayed his power. When his *new* followers saw this, their trust in him grew stronger. All of this happened in the territory of Circle of Nations (Galilee) at Village of Reeds (Cana). ¹²After this he went with his mother, his brothers, and his followers to Village of Comfort (Capernaum), where he stayed for a few days.

PASSOVER FESTIVAL

It was a custom for all the families of the tribes of Wrestles with Creator (Israel) to journey to Village of Peace (Jerusalem) to participate in an ancient festival called Passover. This festival celebrated the time when the lawgiver, Drawn from the Water (Moses), had set them free from captivity to the powerful nation of Black Land (Egypt). He did this by using the great power Creator gave him to perform many signs and wonders.

¹³The time of the year had come for the ancient Passover festival. Creator Sets Free (Jesus) made his way to the Great Spirit's lodge in Village of Peace (Jerusalem).

This was the custom for all the families of the tribes of Wrestles with Creator (Israel).

He came into the area in the lodge called Gathering Place for the Nations. It

---

ᵃ1:51 Genesis 28:12

was here that other nations could come to learn about the Great Spirit and his ways.

14As Creator Sets Free (Jesus) entered the lodge, he saw people sitting at money tables. There were also others who were trading, buying, and selling the cattle, sheep, and doves for the ceremonies—inside the lodge!

SACRED LODGE KEEPER

It was so crowded that there was no room for the people from other nations who had come to learn about the Great Spirit. They were not honoring the purpose of this holy place.

15So Creator Sets Free (Jesus) took some leather straps and made a whip. He cracked the whip *to startle and move the animals, and* to drive all the people from the lodge. He tipped over the tables, which scattered their money on the floor. **16**He then turned to speak to the ones who were selling the ceremonial doves.

"Go!" he roared at them. "Take these things out from here. Do not make my Father's sacred lodge into a trading post!"

17The ones who walked the road with him listened and remembered the ancient prophecy, "My desire to honor your sacred lodge burns like a fire in my belly."[a]

18"What gives you the right to do these things?" the tribal leaders said to him. "Prove yourself and show us a sign!"

19"Tear down this sacred lodge," he answered, "and in three days I will raise it up again."

20The people *shook their heads and* said to him, "It took forty-six winters to build this great lodge. How could you raise it up in three days?"

21They did not understand that he was speaking about the lodge of his own body. **22**After he was raised up from the dead, his followers remembered what he said and then believed the ancient Sacred Teachings and the words he spoke to them.

23During the Passover festival many people began to believe in him because they saw the powerful miracles he was performing. **24**But he did not trust himself to them, for he could see right through them. **25**He did not need anyone to tell him about human beings, for he knew the hearts of humankind.

3

BORN FROM ABOVE

1-2A man named Conquers the People (Nicodemus) came to Creator Sets Free (Jesus) in secret at night. He was one of the Separated Ones (Pharisees) and a headman of the tribes of Wrestles with Creator (Israel) who sat in the Great Council.

Out of the shadows he whispered, "Wisdomkeeper, we know the Great Spirit sent you to teach us. No one can perform powerful signs like these unless the Maker of Life walks with him."

3"I speak from my heart," Creator Sets Free (Jesus) answered, "Only one who has been born from above can see Creator's good road."

4Conquers the People (Nicodemus) *was surprised by this strange answer, so he* asked, "Can a man be born when he is old? Can he enter his mother's womb to be born a second time?"

5"Listen closely," Creator Sets Free (Jesus) answered. "One must be born of both water and spirit to walk Creator's good road. **6**The human body only gives

---

[a] **2:17** Psalm 69:9

birth to natural life, but it takes the Spirit of Creator to give birth to spiritual life.[a] [7]Do not be surprised that I said to you, 'You must be born from above.' [8]Everyone born in this way is like the wind that blows wherever it wants. You can hear its sound, but no one knows where it comes from or where it goes."

[9]"How can these things be?" Conquers the People (Nicodemus) asked.

Creator Sets Free (Jesus) looked gently but firmly into his eyes and continued.

[10]"How can it be that a wisdomkeeper and spiritual leader of the tribes of Wrestles with Creator (Israel) does not understand these things? [11-12]Listen closely, for you fail to hear what we are talking about. We are speaking about things we know to be true, but if you do not believe me when I talk about things on earth, how will you believe me when I talk about the things from the spirit-world above? [13]For there is only one who has gone up and come down from the world above—the True Human Being.

[14-15]"*Do you not remember when* Drawn from the Water (Moses) lifted up a pole with a snake on it in the desert wilderness?[b] This is what will happen to the True Human Being, so people will put their trust in him and have the life of the world to come that never fades away, full of beauty and harmony."

Long ago, when the tribes of Wrestles with Creator (Israel) were wandering in the desert, they did not listen to the Great Spirit. Poisonous snakes came and bit them, and many were dying. Drawn from the Water (Moses) prayed for them, so Creator told him to put a snake on a pole and lift it up so the people could see it. When they looked at it, they were healed and did not die.

Conquers the People (Nicodemus) remained silent, listening to the words of Creator Sets Free (Jesus).

[16]"The Great Spirit loves this world *of human beings* so deeply he gave us his Son—the only Son who fully represents him. All who trust in him and his way will not come to a bad end, but will have the life of the world to come that never fades away, full of beauty and harmony. [17]Creator did not send his Son to decide against the *people of this* world, but to set them free from *the worthless ways of* the world.

[18]"The ones who trust in him are released from their guilt, but, for the ones who turn away from him *to follow the ways of this world*, their guilt remains. This is because they are turning away from the life of beauty and harmony the Great Spirit offers through his Son.

[19]"This is what decides for or against them. My light has shined into this dark world, but because of their worthless ways people loved the dark path more than the light. [20]When they choose the dark path, they do not want others to see, so they hide in the darkness and hate the light. [21]But the ones who are true and do what is right are walking in the daylight so others can clearly see they are walking with Creator."

GIFT OF GOODWILL STEPS BACK

[22]Creator Sets Free (Jesus) and the ones who walked the road with him went to the nearby countryside in the Land of Promise (Judea). They stayed there and began to perform the purification ceremony[c] as the people came to the river.

---

[a]3:6 Or more literally: *Flesh gives birth to flesh, and spirit to spirit*
[b]3:14-15 Numbers 21:9

[c]3:22 Baptism

²³*About a two-day walk to the north,* Gift of Goodwill (John) was also performing the purification ceremony,ᵃ at Spring of Water (Aenon), near Peaceful Village (Salem), where there was much water. ²⁴This was before Gift of Goodwill (John) had been put in prison.

²⁵Some of the followers of Gift of Goodwill (John) began to argue with a local Tribal Member about the purification ceremony.ᵃ ²⁶They took their argument to Gift of Goodwill (John).

"Wisdomkeeper," they said to him, "the one you told us about at the river Flowing Down (Jordan) is performing the purification ceremony.ᵃ All of the people are going to him now."

²⁷"No one has anything," Gift of Goodwill (John) answered, "unless it is gifted from the spirit-world above. ²⁸You heard me say, 'I am not the Chosen One.' I was sent to clear the way for him. ²⁹The bride at a wedding belongs to the groom, and like the best man, a friend who stands with the groom, I am glad to hear his voice. ³⁰But it is time for me to step back and for him to come forward into his place of honor. My part is fading away.

³¹⁻³²"The one who is greater than all speaks from the spirit-world above. The one who is from the earth speaks only about earthly things. The one from above speaks about the things he has seen and heard, but who believes him? ³³But I am one who receives his words, and I know for sure that the Great Spirit approves of all he says and does.

³⁴"The one whom Creator sent is the one who has all the fullness of Creator's Spirit and clearly speaks his words. ³⁵The Father above loves his Son and gives him all things.

³⁶"The ones who trust in his Son have the life of the world that never fades away, but the ones who do not walk in his ways will not have this life. Instead, they will remain *under the power of death,* which reveals Creator's great anger."

4

LIVING WATER

Many people were now coming to Creator Sets Free (Jesus) at the river Flowing Down (Jordan) for the purification ceremony.

¹⁻³Creator Sets Free (Jesus) was gathering more followers for the purification ceremonyᵇ than Gift of Goodwill (John), although it was not he but his followers who were performing the ceremony. When Creator Sets Free (Jesus) found out that the Separated Ones (Pharisees) knew of this, ⁴he left the Land of Promise (Judea) to return to Circle of Nations (Galilee). On the way he had to journey through the territory of High Place (Samaria).

Many of the people from High Place (Samaria) were mixed bloods and despised by the tribes of Wrestles with Creator (Israel). They had their own sacred lodge and ceremonies, and did not respect the Tribal Members or consider Village of Peace (Jerusalem) to be a holy place. Both of them would go out of their way to keep from having contact with the other.

The sun was beating down from high above the head of Creator Sets Free (Jesus) as he journeyed through High Place (Samaria).

⁵There he came to a place called Burial Site (Sychar), which was near a piece of

---

ᵃ3:23, 25, 26 Baptism

ᵇ4:1-3 Baptism

land Heel Grabber (Jacob) had passed down to his son Creator Gives More (Joseph).

6-8 Weary from his journey, about the sixth hour of the day, Creator Sets Free (Jesus) sat down to rest at the ancient watering hole of Heel Grabber (Jacob), while the ones who walked the road with him went to the nearby village to find some food.

A WOMAN FROM HIGH PLACE

The sun had reached midpoint in the sky. It was now the time of day when no one would normally come to the watering hole.

A woman from High Place (Samaria) came to the well to draw water. Creator Sets Free (Jesus) saw the woman and said to her, "Would you give me some water to drink?"

This surprised the woman, because a traditional man would not speak to a woman in public.

9She *found her voice and* asked, "Why would you, a man from the tribes of Wrestles with Creator (Israel), ask me for a drink, seeing I am a woman from High Place (Samaria)?"

She said this because the tribes of Wrestles with Creator (Israel) have no dealings with the people from High Place (Samaria).

10"If you only knew about Creator's good gift," he answered, "and who it is who asks you for a drink, you would ask him for living water and he would give it to you."

11She said to him, "Honored One, this watering hole is deep, and you have no way to draw out the water. Where will you get this living water? **12**Are you greater than our ancestor Heel Grabber (Jacob), who gave us this well and was

first to drink from it with his children and animals?"

13"The ones who drink from this well will thirst again," Creator Sets Free (Jesus) answered. **14**"But the ones who drink the water I give will never thirst, for this water will become a river flowing from inside them, giving them the life of the world to come that never fades away, full of beauty and harmony."

15"Honored One, please give me this water," she said to him, "so I will never thirst again or need to walk this long path to get a drink."

16He said to her, "Go to your husband and bring him here."

17"I have no husband," she answered.

"Yes, that is true," Creator Sets Free (Jesus) said. **18**"You have had five husbands, and the man you are with now is not your husband."

Her eyes grew wide as she lifted a trembling hand to her mouth.

19"Oh! I see. You are a prophet!" she said back to him. **20**"Our ancestors honored and served the Great Spirit on this mountain. But your people say the only place to make our prayers and perform our ceremonies is in Village of Peace (Jerusalem)."

This was a very old argument between the people of High Place (Samaria) and the tribes of Wrestles with Creator (Israel).

21-23"Honored woman, trust my words," Creator Sets Free (Jesus) said to her. "Your people honor and serve him, but in ways they do not fully understand. We honor and serve him with understanding, for the good road that sets us free has been entrusted to the tribes of Wrestles with Creator (Israel).

SPIRIT AND TRUTH

"But the time is coming when all who honor and serve the Great Mystery will not need to do so in this mountain, nor in Village of Peace (Jerusalem). The Father is looking for the ones who will honor him in spirit and truth—and the day for this has now come. ²⁴The One Above Us All is spirit, and all who honor and serve the Great Spirit must do so in spirit and truth."

²⁵"I know the Chosen One will come," she said, "and when he comes, he will make all things clear to us."

²⁶Creator Sets Free (Jesus) said to her, "I am the Chosen One, the one who is speaking to you now."

²⁷Just then his followers returned. They wondered why he was talking to a woman, but no one said to her, "What do you want?" or to him, "Why are you talking to her?"

THE HARVEST IS NOW

²⁸The woman left her water pouch, went to the village, and told the people, ²⁹"Come and see this man who knows everything about me. Could he be the Chosen One?"

³⁰The people of the village went out to find him. ³¹Meanwhile, the ones who walked the road with him said, "Wisdom-keeper, here is some food to eat!"

³²"I have food to eat you know nothing about," he said.

³³His followers whispered to each other, "None of us brought him anything to eat."

³⁴*He knew what they were saying, so* he said to them, "What feeds me is to do the will of the one who sent me and to finish his work. ³⁵It has been said, 'Is it not four moons until the harvest?' Open your eyes! The harvest is upon you now! ³⁶The ones who reap the harvest are rewarded because they are gathering grain for the life of the world to come that never fades away. Both the ones who plant the seed and the ones who harvest will celebrate together. ³⁷This is a true saying, 'One plants and another reaps.' ³⁸I send you to reap where others have done the work of planting, and now it is you who will gather."

MANY BELIEVE

³⁹Soon many people from the woman's village in High Place (Samaria) arrived. Many believed in him because the woman had said, "He knows everything about me." ⁴⁰They asked him to stay, so he remained there for two more days. ⁴¹When they heard him speak, many more believed in him.

⁴²They said to the woman, "We believe now, not just because of your words, but because we have heard him ourselves. We now see that this is the one who will restore the world and set all people free."

HE CONTINUES HIS JOURNEY

⁴³After the two days he continued on his journey to Circle of Nations (Galilee), the territory near his boyhood home. ⁴⁴Creator Sets Free (Jesus) had said that a prophet is given much honor except in his own village, among his own clan, and in his own house. ⁴⁵But even so, the people there welcomed him, because they had seen with their own eyes the powerful things he had done at the Passover festival.

SECOND SIGN

⁴⁶He returned to Village of Reeds (Cana), where he had turned the water into wine. At Village of Comfort (Capernaum), *almost a day's walk away*, the son of a government official was sick and near death.

47When the man heard that Creator Sets Free (Jesus) had come to Circle of Nations (Galilee) from the Land of Promise (Judea), he came to him and asked him to come and heal his son.

48Creator Sets Free (Jesus) *looked around at the crowd and* said, "Why do you need to see signs and wonders before you will believe?"

49"Honored one," the man spoke, *with desperation in his voice.* "Please come before my child dies!"

50"Go home!" Creator Sets Free (Jesus) instructed him. "Your son will live."

The man believed him and left to go home. **51**On the way his servants met him and told him his son was getting stronger. **52**He asked them the hour when this occurred.

"Yesterday, at the seventh hour, the fever left him," they answered.

53The father knew it was the same time that he was told, "Your son will live," so he and his family believed.

54This was the second powerful sign Creator Sets Free (Jesus) performed in Village of Reeds (Cana), having come from the southern territory of the Land of Promise (Judea) to Circle of Nations (Galilee).

5

WORKING ON THE DAY OF RESTING

1A short time later Creator Sets Free (Jesus) went again to Village of Peace (Jerusalem) to another traditional feast for all the tribes of Wrestles with Creator (Israel).

2In Village of Peace (Jerusalem) near the Sheep Gate, there is a water hole with five covered porches called House of Kindness (Bethesda) in our tribal language. Under these porches **3**lay a great number of people who were sick, blind, or could not walk or stand. They were waiting for the swirling of the water, **4**because from time to time a spirit-messenger would go down into the water hole and make the water swirl. Then the first one to get into the water would be healed.

5A man was there who had been ill for thirty-eight winters. **6**Creator Sets Free (Jesus) saw him lying there and knew that he had been sick for a long time.

He asked him, "Do you want to be healed?"

7"Honored One," the man answered. "When the water swirls, there is no one to help me into the water, and someone else gets there first."

8"Get up!" Creator Sets Free (Jesus) said to the man. "Roll up your sleeping bundle and walk."

The man felt his body begin to change. Strength rushed into his legs and arms.

9Right then the man was healed! He got up, rolled up his bundle, and walked.

Creator Sets Free (Jesus) healed this man on the Day of Resting. **10**The strict traditional Tribal Members saw the healed man carrying his bundle.

"It is the Day of Resting," they said to him. "Tribal law forbids you to carry your sleeping bundle."

11He said to them, "The one who healed me instructed me to take up my bundle and walk."

12"Who is the man who told you this?" they asked.

13But the man who was healed did not know who he was. Creator Sets Free (Jesus) had left because too many people were there.

14Later on, Creator Sets Free (Jesus) saw the man in the sacred lodge.

"Look! You are healed," he said to him. "Now that you have been set free, do not use your freedom to walk a path that leads to broken ways, or something worse may come to you."

¹⁵The man went back to the strict traditional people and told them it was Creator Sets Free (Jesus) who had made him well again. ¹⁶Because of this, the tribal leaders were giving Creator Sets Free (Jesus) trouble and wanted to put him to death, because he was doing this on the Day of Resting.

¹⁷Creator Sets Free (Jesus) made it clear to them, "My Father has been working, so I am working also."

¹⁸This made them want to kill him all the more, for he not only showed no regard for the Day of Resting, but he also was making himself out to be equal with the Great Spirit—calling him his own Father.

EQUAL HONOR BELONGS TO THE SON

¹⁹"I speak from my heart," he said to them, "the Son only does what he sees the Father doing, for the Father and the Son do the same things. ²⁰The Father loves the Son and shows him everything he does. He will show him great and powerful medicine, things that will fill you with wonder. ²¹You will see the Son give life to whomever he wants and bring the dead back to life again—just like the Father does.

²²"The Father does not make the final decision about anyone. He has given that decision to the Son. ²³He did this so all will honor the Son in the same way they honor the Father. The ones who do not honor the Son do not honor the Father who sent him.

²⁴"I speak from my heart. The ones who listen to me and trust the one who sent me have the life of the world to come that never fades away. The final

decision about their end has been made, for they have already crossed over from death to life. ²⁵The time has now come when the ones who are *spiritually* dead will hear the voice of Creator's own Son, and all who hear it will live. ²⁶Just as all life comes from the Father, in the same way he has made all life come from the Son.

²⁷"I speak from my heart. The final decision about everyone has been given to the Son. It is his right, because he is the True Human Being.

²⁸"Do not look so surprised! For the day is dawning when the dead and buried will hear his voice and come out of their graves. ²⁹The ones who have done good will rise to a new life, but the ones who do what has no worth will rise to face the final decision about their end.

FATHER AND SON

³⁰"I do nothing on my own. I listen *to my Father* before I decide about anyone. What I decide is right because I am not seeking my own way but the way of the one who sent me. ³¹If I am the only one who speaks for myself, then my words are empty, ³²but there is another who speaks for me, and what he says is true.

³³"You sent messengers to Gift of Goodwill (John), and he told you the truth about me, ³⁴⁻³⁵but I do not need a human being to speak for me. Gift of Goodwill (John) shined like a burning torch, and for a short time you were glad to walk in his light. Now, to be set free from your broken ways, you must listen to me. ³⁶My words carry more weight than his and are proven by the things I do. I have done the things the Father sent me to do. That is all the proof that is needed.

³⁷"The Father is the one who sent me, and he is the one who speaks for me. But,

since you have never seen his form or heard his voice, 38you do not trust the one he sent, so his words have no root in you. 39"You search the Sacred Teachings, for you think they will give you the life of the world to come—but they tell my story. 40Why do you refuse to come to me for this life?"

The tribal leaders had heard enough! They just shook their heads and started to walk away.

41*Creator Sets Free (Jesus) said to them,* "I came representing my Father, yet you show me no respect. But I am not looking for honor or respect from you, 42for I know you are empty inside, and the love of the Great Spirit has no place in you. 43But you will honor the one who comes representing himself. 44If you only look for honor from each other, and not from the only Creator, how will you believe? 45"I have not come to tell the Father how wrong you are. It is Drawn from the Water (Moses), the one you have put your hope in, who will do this. 46If you trust him, then you should trust me, for he told my story. 47But if you do not believe his words, how will you ever believe mine?"

6 ⟫⟨⟫⟨⟫⟨⟫⟨⟫⟨⟫⟨⟫⟨

HE FEEDS FIVE THOUSAND

1After this Creator Sets Free (Jesus) went over to the other side of Lake of Circle of Nations (Sea of Galilee), also called Sea of Rolling Water (Sea of Tiberias). 2A great crowd of people followed him because they saw the powerful signs he performed, healing the sick. 3Creator Sets Free (Jesus) walked up to the mountainside and sat down with his followers. 4Soon it would be time again for the yearly Passover festival for the tribes of Wrestles with Creator (Israel).

5From the mountainside Creator Sets Free (Jesus) could see how large the crowd following behind him had become. *There were over five thousand men, along with women and children!*

He then looked at Friend of Horses (Philip) and said, "Where will we find enough food to feed all these people?" 6He said this to test him, for he already knew what he would do.

Friend of Horses (Philip) took a step back and looked at him with wide eyes. He was not sure whether Creator Sets Free (Jesus) was serious or not.

7Friend of Horses (Philip) answered, "'Eight moons' worth of gathered food would only give them enough for one small bite apiece!"

8Stands with Courage (Andrew), one of the twelve, the brother of Stands on the Rock (Peter), *tried to be helpful and* said, 9"Here is a boy with five pieces of frybread and two small fish, but how would that possibly be enough?"

10Creator Sets Free (Jesus) said to them, "Have the people sit down on the grass." There was much grass there, so all of the five thousand men began to sit down, *along with women and children.*

Creator Sets Free (Jesus) waited patiently for them to finish. When they were all settled down, he had the ones who walked the road with him bring baskets and stand in a circle around him.

11He took the five pieces of frybread given by the little boy and held them up to the sky. He gave thanks to the Great Spirit and began to break the frybread into smaller pieces and gave them to his followers to give to the people. In the same manner he also divided the two fish, and they were given out to the people. ¹²Everyone ate until they were full!

When they were done eating, he instructed them to gather the leftovers of fish and frybread, so nothing would go to waste. ¹³It took twelve baskets to hold it all.

HE MUST BE THE PROPHET

¹⁴The people began to realize what had happened. This was a powerful sign that Creator Sets Free (Jesus) had just performed.

> They began to wonder who this man was who could do such amazing things. Like wildfire, the hopes and dreams of many generations began to rise in their hearts and minds.

They were saying to one another, "This must be the Prophet, spoken of long ago, who would come into the world!"

¹⁵Creator Sets Free (Jesus) knew in his spirit that the people were about to take him by force to make him their chief, so he left the crowd and went to a quiet place on the mountainside to be alone and pray.

WATER WALKER

¹⁶Later, as the sun began to set, his followers climbed into a canoe to go to Village of Comfort (Capernaum) on the other side. ¹⁷Darkness was beginning to creep across the water with no sign of Creator Sets Free (Jesus), so they pushed off from shore.

> As they continued to paddle, lightning flashed in the distance, and the sound of thunder rolled across the sky.

¹⁸⁻¹⁹A strong wind blew in over the waters. The waves grew large and pounded against them, *threatening to overturn the canoe.* They were pulling hard on the paddles, trying to make headway, but had only traveled partway across[a] the great lake *and were still a long way from land.*

They looked out through the storm, *and their eyes grew wide* with fear, for they saw Creator Sets Free (Jesus) coming toward them, walking on the water!

²⁰Creator Sets Free (Jesus) *saw the fear in their faces and* called out to them, "Do not fear. *Take heart,* it is I!"

²¹When they knew it was Creator Sets Free (Jesus), they were glad to bring him into the canoe, and suddenly they were at the shoreline on the other side of the great lake.

LOOKING FOR THE WRONG FOOD

²²It was now morning, and the crowd of people on the other side of Lake of Circle of Nations (Sea of Galilee) began to look for Creator Sets Free (Jesus), for they knew there was only one canoe and that he did not go with his followers. ²³Just then some canoes arrived from Rolling Water (Tiberias) at the same place where Creator Sets Free (Jesus) had given thanks for the frybread and fed them all. ²⁴When they could not find Creator Sets Free (Jesus) or his followers, they climbed into the canoes to go to Village of Comfort (Capernaum) to find him.

²⁵When they arrived on the other side and found Creator Sets Free (Jesus), they asked, "Wisdomkeeper, when did you get here?"

²⁶Creator Sets Free (Jesus) *ignored their question and* said to them, "Listen closely to my words, you are not looking for me because of the powerful sign you saw,

---

[a]**6:18-19** About three and a half miles

but only because you filled your bellies with food. **27**Why are you working so hard for food that fades away? You should work for the food that gives you the life of the world to come that never fades away. The True Human Being will give you this food, for he has the Father's full approval."

28"What does Great Spirit require from us," they asked, "so we can do what he wants *and have his approval also?*"

29"Here is what he wants you to do," he answered, "put your trust in the one he has sent."

BREAD FROM THE WORLD ABOVE

30"What powerful sign will you show us, that we should trust in you?" they asked. "What sign will you perform? **31**When our ancestors were wandering in the desert they ate bread, just as the Sacred Teachings tell us, 'From the spirit-world above he gave them bread to eat.'ᵃ"

32"Listen closely," Creator Sets Free (Jesus) answered. "Drawn from the Water (Moses) did not give you the bread from the spirit-world above. It is my Father who gives you the true bread that comes down from the spirit-world above. **33**This bread gives the life of beauty and harmony to the world."

34"Honored One," they said, "from now on give us this bread."

35Creator Sets Free (Jesus) *smiled, held out his arms to them, and* said, "I am the bread of life that came down from the spirit-world above. The ones who come to me will hunger no more. The ones who trust me will thirst no more."

36"*He lowered his arms and with a heavy heart he continued,* "But even as I told you before, you have seen me but you still do not trust me. **37**The ones my Father has given to me will come to me. They are a gift from my Father that I will always keep.

38"I came down from the spirit-world above, from the one who sent me, to walk his path, not to walk my own. **39**He wants me to keep safe the ones he has given me and bring them back to life again at the end of all days. **40**The ones who see who the Son truly is will put their trust and hope in him and have the life of the world to come that never fades away. Yes! I will bring them back to life again at the end of all days, for this is what my Father who sent me wants."

41Upon hearing this, the Tribal Members complained, "Who is this 'Bread from the spirit-world above'? **42**Is this not the son of He Gives Sons (Joseph)? We know who his mother and father are. How can he say 'I came down from the spirit-world above'?"

43"Stop grumbling to each other," he answered. **44**"The only ones who come to me have been drawn by my Father. These are the ones I will bring back to life at the end of all days. **45**The Sacred Teachings from the prophets of old tell us, 'There will come a time when the Great Spirit will instruct everyone.'ᵇ That is why the ones who hear and listen to the Father come to me.

46"The only one who has seen the Father is the one sent from the Great Spirit. This one has clearly seen the Father. **47**I speak truth from my heart, the ones who trust in me have the life of the world to come that never fades away, full of beauty and harmony.

48"I am the bread that gives this life. **49**Your ancestors ate bread in the desert

---

ᵃ**6:31** Exodus 16:15

ᵇ**6:45** Isaiah 54:13

wilderness, and they died. ⁵⁰Here, standing before you, is the bread that comes down from above. The ones who eat this bread will not die. ⁵¹I am the living bread from above. The ones who eat this bread will live beyond the end of all days. And this is the bread that I will give as a gift to the world—my human body."

⁵²His words caused a great division among the Tribal Members, and they began to argue with one another.

"How can this be?" they asked. "Will he give us his flesh to eat?"

⁵³"I speak from my heart," he answered. "The only way to have my life in you is to eat the body of the True Human Being and drink his blood. ⁵⁴Then, the life of the world to come will be yours, and at the end of all days I will bring your body back to life. ⁵⁵My body is true food. My blood is pure drink. ⁵⁶The ones who eat and drink my body and blood live in me, and I live in them. ⁵⁷In the same way the living Father sent me and gave me his life, the ones who feed on me will have my life. ⁵⁸The bread from above is not like the bread our ancestors ate—and then died. This bread gives the life of the world to come that never fades away, full of beauty and harmony."

⁵⁹These are the words he spoke to the people at the gathering house in Village of Comfort (Capernaum).

MANY FOLLOWERS WALK AWAY

⁶⁰When the ones who walked the road with Creator Sets Free (Jesus) heard this, many of them said, "These words are too hard to hear. Who can even listen to them?"

⁶¹Creator Sets Free (Jesus) knew in his spirit what was troubling them, so he said, "Do these words make you stumble from the path? ⁶²What will you do when you see the True Human Being going back up to where he came from?

⁶³"Life comes from the spirit, not from the human body.ᵃ My words have spirit and life in them—⁶⁴but some of you have no faith in who I am."

He said this because he knew, from the beginning, the ones who did not believe and who would betray him.

⁶⁵He then finished by saying, "That is why I said no one can come to me on their own, but only as a gift from my Father."

⁶⁶When they heard this, many who followed him turned and walked away. ⁶⁷Creator Sets Free (Jesus) looked at the twelve and said, "Do you also want to walk away?"

⁶⁸"Wisdomkeeper," One Who Hears (Simon), also named Stands on the Rock (Peter), answered him, "who else would we walk the road with? You have the words that give the life of the world to come that never fades away, full of beauty and harmony. ⁶⁹We have come to know and trust in you as the Holy One from the Great Spirit."

⁷⁰Creator Sets Free (Jesus) said to them, "Even though I chose all twelve of you, one of you is an enemy."ᵇ

⁷¹He was talking about Speaks Well Of (Judas), one of the twelve, who would later turn on him and betray him.

7 ◀▶◀▶◀▶◀▶◀▶◀▶◀▶◀▶

FESTIVAL OF SHELTERS

¹Creator Sets Free (Jesus) left the Land of Promise (Judea) because the Tribal Members there wanted to put him to death. To avoid conflict with them, he had been staying in the territory of

---

ᵃ6:63 Lit. *flesh*
ᵇ6:70 Lit. *devil* or *adversary*

Circle of Nations (Galilee), going from village to village. ²But now it was almost time for the Festival of Shelters in Village of Peace (Jerusalem), which all the tribes participated in.

This festival was celebrated at the end of the harvest. The tribes were instructed to make temporary shelters from tree branches. In this way they remembered the time after they had been set free from their captivity in Black Land (Egypt), when their ancestors migrated in the desert wilderness under the care of the lawgiver, Drawn from the Water (Moses).

³The brothers from the family of Creator Sets Free (Jesus) came to him and said, "You should leave here and go back to the Land of Promise (Judea) for the festival. This way more of your followers will see the powerful signs you can do. ⁴Why not show everyone who you are? The ones who want to be well known do not hide in secret. You should show all the world who you are."

⁵Even his own brothers did not believe *that he was the Chosen One.*

⁶⁻⁷Creator Sets Free (Jesus) answered them, "You are free to go anytime you want, for the people there do not hate you. But they do hate me, because I show them their bent and crooked ways. ⁸You can go to the festival, but I am not going now—it is not my time yet."

⁹After he said this, he stayed behind in Circle of Nations (Galilee) ¹⁰until his family left. Then he went to the festival, not openly, but in secret.

LOOKING FOR HIM AT THE FESTIVAL

Tribal Members from all directions came to the festival. Village of Peace (Jerusalem) was crowded and overflowing with thou-sands of people walking, donkeys pulling carts, and merchants selling their crafts.

¹¹Many were looking for Creator Sets Free (Jesus) at the festival. The people who had gathered there were whispering and wondering about him.

"Where is he?" they asked.

¹²Some of them said, "He is a true human being with a good heart."

But others were saying, "No! He is leading the crowds down a false path."

¹³No one was saying these things out in the open, because they feared what the tribal leaders might do to them.

WHY DO YOU WANT TO KILL ME?

¹⁴Creator Sets Free (Jesus) *came secretly to the festival and stayed away from the crowds. He* waited until the midpoint of the festival, went to the sacred lodge, and began to teach.

¹⁵The tribal leaders were amazed at his teaching.

"Where did he get this wisdom and understanding?" they asked. "He has not studied *under our wisdomkeepers or attended our learning houses.*"

¹⁶Creator Sets Free (Jesus) answered them, "The wisdom I share is not my own but comes from the one who sent me. ¹⁷The ones who desire to walk in the ways of the Great Spirit will understand my wisdom comes from him. ¹⁸The one who represents himself is seeking his own honor. The one who represents the one who sent him is true and upright, and there is nothing false in him.

¹⁹"Drawn from the Water (Moses) gave you the law, but none of you keep it. Why do you want to kill me?"

²⁰"You must have an evil spirit!" they answered back. "Why else would you think we are trying to kill you?"

²¹He answered them, "I did one work. I healed a man. You were amazed to see such power, but you were offended because this was done on the Day of Resting.

²²"*Do you not see?* Drawn from the Water (Moses) gave you the cutting of the flesh ceremony, handed down to him from the ancestors. Sometimes this ceremony is performed for a baby boy on the Day of Resting. ²³If this is permitted on the Day of Resting, then why are you angry with me for healing a man's whole body on that day? ²⁴Do not decide things by their outward appearance. Instead, make your decisions in a good way, looking beyond what you see with your eyes."

HOW COULD HE BE THE CHOSEN ONE?

²⁵Some of the people who lived in Village of Peace (Jerusalem) began to say, "Is this not the one they are seeking to put to death? ²⁶Look, he speaks boldly to all, and they have nothing to say to him. Does our tribal council think he truly is the Chosen One? ²⁷But how could this be? When the Chosen One comes, no one will know where he comes from, but we know where this man is from."

²⁸⁻²⁹Creator Sets Free (Jesus) then lifted up his voice in the sacred lodge and cried out, "You may think you know me and where I am from, but I know where I am truly from—the Father. He is the one who sent me. You do not know who I am or where I am from, because you do not know him."

SOLDIERS SENT TO ARREST HIM

³⁰The tribal leaders were looking for a way to arrest him, but no one could even lay a hand on him, for it was not yet his time. ³¹Many of the people chose to trust in him.

They said, "When the Chosen One comes, will he do more powerful signs than this man has done?"

³²When the Separated Ones (Pharisees) and the head holy men heard what the crowds were saying about him, they sent the lodge soldiers to arrest him.

³³"I will be gone soon," he said to them. "I am returning to the one who sent me. ³⁴You will look for me, but you will not find me. Where I am going you cannot follow."

³⁵The Tribal Members began to grumble, "Where will he go that we cannot find him? Will he go to where the Tribal Members live among the Wisdom Seekers (Greeks)? ³⁶Will he teach them there? What does he mean by saying, 'You will look for me, but will not find me,' and, 'Where I am going you cannot follow'?"

SOURCE OF LIVING WATER

³⁷It was now the last and greatest day of the Festival of Shelters.

It has been said that on this day, by ancient tradition, a holy man would be chosen to take a golden pot to the Waters of Sending Village (Pool of Siloam) and fill it with water. He would then bring the water to the sacred lodge for a special ceremony and celebration. The holy man would take the water to the great altar, and then at the sound of the ram's horn, called the shofar, he would pour out the water on the altar. They would recite the words of the prophet Creator Will Help Us (Isaiah), "With glad hearts we will draw from the wells, water that will set us free."[a]

After the ceremony Creator Sets Free (Jesus) stood before the people and cried

a7:37 Isaiah 12:3

out with a loud voice, "The ones who thirst must come to me and drink! **38**Put your hope and trust in me. I am the one the Sacred Teachings spoke of when they said, 'Rivers of living water will flow out from inside him.'ᵃ"

39He was saying this about the Spirit, who would soon be given to the ones who believed in him. The Spirit had not yet been poured out, for Creator Sets Free (Jesus) had not yet risen to his place of honor, power, and beauty.

CONFLICT ABOUT WHO HE IS

40When they heard these words, some of the people gathered there were saying, "This must be the Prophet, the one of whom it was foretold would come."

41Others were saying, "*No!* He is the Chosen One."

Still others did not agree and said, "How can this be? Will the Chosen One come from Circle of Nations (Galilee)? **42**Do not the Sacred Teachings tell us that the Chosen One will be a descendant of Chief Much Loved One (David) and come from House of Bread (Bethlehem), the village where he was born?"

43So the people could not agree about him. **44**The lodge soldiers were amazed by his words and could not bring themselves to arrest him. **45**They returned to the head holy men and the Separated Ones (Pharisees), who asked them, "Where is he? Why did you not arrest him?"

46The soldiers answered, "No one has ever spoken like this man!"

47"Has he turned you from the path also?" they said. **48**"Does even one tribal leader or Separated One (Pharisee) believe in him? **49**These people are ignorant of the Sacred Teachings given by

Drawn from the Water (Moses). They are under a curse!"

50Conquers the People (Nicodemus), the same one who came to Creator Sets Free (Jesus) in secret at night, was one of the Separated Ones (Pharisees). **51**He *boldly* said to the other tribal leaders, "Our tribal law does not permit us to decide against a man without giving him a chance to stand before the council and give an answer for what he does."

52The other tribal leaders *scorned him and* said, "Are you also from Circle of Nations (Galilee)? Look into the Sacred Teachings for yourself. You will see that no prophet comes from Circle of Nations (Galilee)."

53*The Festival of Shelters was over, and* the people all returned to *the peace and safety of* their own homes.

8

CONFLICT BETWEEN LAW AND KINDNESS

1But Creator Sets Free (Jesus) went to Olive Mountain *to find lodging there.* **2**Early in the morning at the sunrise, he returned again to the sacred lodge. All the people began to gather around him, so he sat down and *once again* began to teach *and tell his stories.*

Across the plaza a cloud of dust was rising from a group of people who were walking toward Creator Sets Free (Jesus) as he was teaching. They were forcefully dragging a woman along with them. He could see her tears and the look of terror on her face.

3It was the scroll keepers and the Separated Ones (Pharisees). They brought the woman to Creator Sets Free (Jesus) and forced her down on the ground in front of him and all the people.

ᵃ**7:38** Jeremiah 2:13

4"Wisdomkeeper," they said, "we found this woman in the very act of being unfaithful to her husband. 5Drawn from the Water (Moses) instructed us in the law to throw stones at her until she dies. What do you have to say about this?"

6They were putting him to a test, so they could have a way to accuse him.

The crowd was silent and waited to see what he would say, but he said nothing.

He bent over and with his finger wrote something in the dirt.

When he did not answer right away, the Separated Ones (Pharisees) *became angry and* kept questioning him.

7Creator Sets Free (Jesus) looked up at them and said, "The one who has done no wrong should be the first to throw a stone at her."

8He then bent over and again began to write in the dirt with his finger.

9When they heard his words, they all stood there silently. Then, beginning with the elders, one at a time they dropped their stones and walked away. Soon all were gone except for Creator Sets Free (Jesus) and the woman. 10He stood up and looked at her.

"Honored woman," he said. "Where are the ones who were accusing you? Is there no one who finds fault with you?"

11The woman *looked up timidly into his eyes and* said, "No one, Wisdom-keeper."

"Then I also find no fault with you," he said to her. "You may go your way, but take care not to return to this broken path you have been walking."

CONFLICT BETWEEN LIGHT AND DARKNESS

After the woman left, the people began to gather around him again, waiting to hear what he would say.

12Creator Sets Free (Jesus) *lifted up his voice and* said to them, "I am the light shining on this dark world. The ones who walk with me will not stumble in the darkness but will have the light that gives them life."

13When they heard this, the Separated Ones (Pharisees) said to him, "When you say these things about yourself, you are the only one who says they are true. If no one else speaks for you, then we cannot receive your words."

14Creator Sets Free (Jesus) answered them, "If I am the only one who speaks for myself, my words are still true. I know where I came from and where I am going. You are the ones who do not know where I came from or where I am going. 15You are deciding about me with weak human minds. I am not deciding about anyone, 16but even if I did, my decisions would be true, for I do not stand alone. My Father who sent me is the one who stands with me. 17Your tribal law tells you it takes the word of two people to know the truth. 18So then, I speak for myself, and the Father speaks for me also."

WHO IS YOUR FATHER?

19"Where is your Father?" they said back to him.

"You do not know me or my Father," he told them. "If you knew me, you would know who my Father is."

20Creator Sets Free (Jesus) said these things at the sacred lodge, where he was teaching, near the storehouse where they keep the ceremonial gifts. No one laid a hand on him, for his time had not yet come.

The people began to argue among themselves about him.

21So he *lifted up his voice again and* said, "You are not able to go where I am going. When I am gone, you will *wander in the darkness* looking for the Chosen One,[a] and your bad hearts will lead you down the path of death *to a bad end.*"

22The people said to each other, "Is he going to kill himself, since he says he is going where we cannot follow?"

23So he said to them, "You are from below and belong to *the ways of* this world. I am from above, and this world and its ways have no place in me. **24**This is why I said that your bad hearts and broken ways will lead you down a path of death. Unless you put your trust in who I am *and follow my ways*, your end will be death."

WHO DO YOU THINK YOU ARE?

25When they heard this, they said to him *in anger*, "Who do you think you are?"

He answered, "From the beginning I have been telling you who I am. **26**I have many more things I could say and decide about you. The words I speak to the *people of this* world come from the one who sent me, and he is the Truth."

27But no one could see that he was talking about the Father, *who is the Great Spirit.*

28So Creator Sets Free (Jesus) said to them, "When you lift up the True Human Being *on the cross*, then you will know that I am who I say I am. For I only do and say the things taught to me by my Father. **29**The one who sent me is with me now. He has never left me alone, for I always walk in the ways that make his heart glad."

CONFLICT ABOUT FREEDOM

30Many began to trust in him as they listened to his words, **31**so Creator Sets Free

(Jesus) said to the Tribal Members who believed in him, "If you walk in my footsteps and follow my teachings, you will truly be my followers. **32**Then you will see and understand the truth that sets all people free."

33But they questioned him, "We are the descendants of Father of Many Nations (Abraham) and have never been anyone's slave. How can you say, 'You will be set free'?"

34"I speak truth from my heart," he answered them. "All who walk in the broken ways of this world become slaves to their bad hearts. **35**A slave is not a member of the family and will not always live with the family. But a son of the family always has a home. **36**The freedom the Son gives you is the way of true freedom.

CONFLICT OVER FATHERHOOD

37"I know you are the descendants of Father of Many Nations (Abraham), but you still want to kill me **38**because my message has no home in you. I am telling you the things my Father has shown me, but you are doing the things you have heard from your father."

39"Father of Many Nations (Abraham) is our father," they said back to him *in anger.*

Creator Sets Free (Jesus) said to them, "If you were truly the children of Father of Many Nations (Abraham), you would do the same things he did. **40**Instead, you want to put to death the one who has told you truth from the Great Spirit. This is not what Father of Many Nations (Abraham) did. **41**You are doing the same things your father does."

"We were not born from an unmarried woman," they said. "We have but one Father—the Great Spirit."

THE BATTLE LINES ARE DRAWN

42Creator Sets Free (Jesus) told them, "If the Great Spirit were truly your Father, you would love me *and show respect*, for I came from him. I did not send myself. He is the one who sent me.

43"Why can you not hear what I am saying to you? Are my words not clear? *Then I will speak more clearly.* **44**Your father is Accuser (Satan), the evil trickster. You are doing what he wants, for he was the first to take the life of another. He stands outside of the truth, because truth has no home in him. He speaks with a forked tongue and twists his words. His lies show who he truly is. He is a liar and the father of all that is false.

45-46"Even though I am telling you the truth, you do not believe me. Which one of you can show that I have done anything wrong? **47**The ones who come from the Great Spirit can hear his words. The reason you do not hear me is that you are not from him."

ACCUSED OF HAVING AN EVIL SPIRIT

48"Now we have the right to call you a *mixed blood* from High Place (Samaria) and one who has an evil spirit," they said to him *in anger.*

49He answered them back, "I have no evil spirit. I honor my Father, but you dishonor me. **50**I am not trying to honor myself, but there is one who honors me, and he has the final decision. **51**I speak from my heart, death will not have the final word for the ones who walk in my message."

52"Now we are sure you have an evil spirit," they said. "Father of Many Nations (Abraham) and all the prophets crossed over to death. How can you say that the ones who walk in your word will not taste of death? **53**Do you think you are greater than Father of Many Nations (Abraham) and the prophets? Who are you making yourself out to be?"

MY FATHER HONORS ME

54Creator Sets Free (Jesus) answered them, "If I honor myself, then I have no honor. The one who honors me is my Father, the one of whom you say, 'He is our Great Spirit.' **55**You do not truly know him, but I do. If I were to say, 'I do not know him,' I would be a liar, like you! But I know him deeply and walk in all his ways. **56**Father of Many Nations (Abraham) looked ahead to my day. He saw it, and it made his heart glad!"

57"How could you have seen Father of Many Nations (Abraham)?" they asked, shaking their heads. "You have not even seen fifty winters."

58"I speak from my heart," he answered. "I was there before Father of Many Nations (Abraham) was born—for I AM."[a]

The tribal leaders had heard enough! **59**They picked up stones to throw at him, but he hid himself *in the crowd*, passed them by, and walked out of the sacred lodge.

WHO IS BLIND AND WHY?

1After walking *safely away from the lodge*, Creator Sets Free (Jesus) saw a man blind from birth *sitting by the pathway. They stopped near the man and* **2**the ones who walked the road with him asked, "Wisdomkeeper, why was this man born blind? Was it his wrongdoings or his parents' that caused this?"

---

[a]**8:58** A possible reference to the name of the Great Spirit. See Exodus 3:14.

3"The wrongdoings of neither he nor his parents caused this," he told them, "but that the healing power of the Great Spirit would be seen in him, **4**for while the sun still shines, we must be doing what he wants. A time of darkness is coming when no one will do what he wants. **5**But as long as I am in the world, I will be its light."

HE HEALS A MAN BORN BLIND

6-7 After saying this, he spit on the ground. Then he made mud from his spit and rubbed it on the man's eyes and instructed him to go and wash in the Waters of Sending Village (Pool of Siloam). *With the help of others*, the man went and washed *the mud out of his eyes* and returned with his sight restored.

8The people who lived near him, and others who knew he was a blind beggar, saw him and said *in amazement*, "Could this be the blind man who sat and asked for handouts?"

9Some were saying it was he, others said he only looked like him, but he kept saying, "I am the one!"

10So they asked him, "How did your sight return to you?"

11He said, "A man named Creator Sets Free (Jesus) made some mud and rubbed it on my eyes. He told me to go to the Waters of Sending Village (Pool of Siloam) and wash. So I did what he said, and now I can see."

12"Where is he?" they asked.

"I do not know where he is," the man answered.

HOW WERE YOU HEALED?

13-14 Since it was on the Day of Resting that Creator Sets Free (Jesus) had healed the man, they decided to take him to the Separated Ones (Pharisees) *to see what they*

would say. **15**The Separated Ones (Pharisees) asked the man how he was healed.

He said to them, "He rubbed mud on my eyes. I washed off the mud, and now I can see."

16Then some of the Separated Ones (Pharisees) said, "This man, who does not honor the Day of Resting, cannot be from the Great Spirit."

But others were saying, "How can someone with a bad heart perform powerful signs such as these?"

17The tribal leaders could not agree, so they said to the blind man, "You are the one he healed. What do you have to say about him?"

The man answered them, "He must be a prophet from the Great Spirit."

18The tribal leaders could not believe the man had been blind. So they found his parents **19**and asked them, "Is this your son, whom you say was born blind? How does he now see?"

20-22 His parents were afraid of the tribal leaders who had said that anyone who says Creator Sets Free (Jesus) is the Chosen One would be put out of the gathering house.

23"Yes, this is our son, and he was born blind," they answered, "but we do not know how he sees, or who opened his eyes. He is a full-grown man. Ask him. He will tell you for himself."

I WAS BLIND BUT NOW I SEE

24They went back to the man who was blind and said to him, "Give honor to the Great Spirit for healing you, not to Creator Sets Free (Jesus), for we know he is an outcast with a bad heart."

25"I do not know whether this man has a bad heart," he answered them. "But this I do know—I was blind but now I see."

²⁶They asked the man again, "What did he do to open your eyes?"

²⁷He said to them, "You did not listen the first time I told you. Why do you want to hear it again? Do you also want to become one of his followers?"

This made the leaders angry, so they tried to insult the man.

²⁸"You are his follower!" they said with disrespect in their voices. "We follow Drawn from the Water (Moses), ²⁹for we know the Great Spirit has spoken to him, but we do not know where this man is from."

³⁰The man answered them, "This is a strange thing! You, who are tribal leaders, do not know where this man comes from, yet he is the one who opened my eyes. ³¹The Great Spirit does not listen to people with bad hearts. He listens to the ones who humbly serve him and do what is right. ³²From the creation of the world no one has ever seen a man healed who was born blind. ³³If he were not from the Great Spirit, he could not have done this."

BANNED FROM THE GATHERING HOUSE

The Separated Ones (Pharisees) were furious! How could this outcast talk back to them like this?

³⁴They *puffed up their chests and* said, "You were born an outcast, and you think you can teach us?"

Then they threw him out *and banned him from his gathering house.*

³⁵When Creator Sets Free (Jesus) heard that they had put the man out of the gathering house, he went to him and said, "Will you put your trust in the True Human Being?"

³⁶"Honored One, tell me who he is," the man answered, "and I will put my trust in him."

³⁷"Look at me and see the True Human Being," Creator Sets Free (Jesus) said. "He is talking with you now."

³⁸The man bowed down to him and said, "Honored One, I believe!"

³⁹Creator Sets Free (Jesus) said, "I came to show what is right and wrong about the ways of this world, so that the blind will see—and that the ones who see may become blind."

BLIND GUIDES

⁴⁰Some of the Separated Ones (Pharisees) overheard what he said to the man. "Are you saying that we are blind?" they asked.

⁴¹"If you were truly blind, you would have no guilt," he answered them. "But since you claim to see, your guilt remains."

10 ◆◆◆◆◆◆◆◆◆◆◆

THE GOOD SHEPHERD

Creator Sets Free (Jesus) told this story to the Separated Ones (Pharisees), for they were blind guides, leading the tribes of Wrestles with Creator (Israel) down a false path to a bad end.

¹"I speak from my heart," Creator Sets Free (Jesus) said *to the blind tribal leaders.* "Thieves and outlaws do not use the gate to the sheep pen but sneak in some other way. ²But the shepherd uses the gate to enter, ³⁻⁴and the gatekeeper opens the way. The sheep know their shepherd's voice, for he calls each one of them by name, and they follow him as he leads them *in and out of the sheep pen.*

⁵"The sheep will not follow the voice of a stranger. They will run away, for they do not recognize a stranger's voice."

⁶Because he was using a story to teach them, Creator Sets Free (Jesus) could see that they did not understand, ⁷so he told them the meaning of the story.

THE GATE FOR THE SHEEP

"I speak again from my heart," he said. "I am the gate for the sheep. ⁸All who put themselves before me are thieves and outlaws—*false shepherds*. My sheep do not listen to them.

⁹"I am the gate for the sheep. The ones who enter by me will be safe *and well cared for.* Following the Shepherd, they will go in and out and find good food to eat.

¹⁰"Thieves enter only to take away life, to steal what is not theirs, and to bring to ruin all they cannot have. I have come to give the good life, a life that overflows with beauty and harmony.

GOOD SHEPHERD

¹¹"I am the Good Shepherd, *the one who watches over the sheep.* I will lay down my life for them. ¹²The ones who watch the sheep only for pay will run away when a wolf comes, because the sheep are not theirs. Then the wolf preys upon the sheep and scatters the flock. ¹³The ones who do it only for pay are not true shepherds, for they do not care for the sheep *but only for themselves.*

¹⁴⁻¹⁵"I am the Good Shepherd, the one who lays down his life for the sheep. The Father knows me, and I know him. In the same way, I also know each one of my sheep, and they know me. ¹⁶I have other sheep who are not from this flock. I will go and find them, and they will also hear my voice. Then there will be only one flock, with one Shepherd.

¹⁷"My Father has a great love for me, for I lay my life down to take it back

again. ¹⁸No one takes my life from me, for I lay it down on my own. I have the right to lay my life down and the right to take it back. It is my Father who gives me this right."

DISAGREEMENT

¹⁹This story brought much disagreement among the Tribal Members, and they began to argue about him.

²⁰Many were saying, "He has lost his mind and has an evil spirit. Why do we even listen to him?"

²¹At the same time others were saying, "These are not the words of someone with an evil spirit. Can an evil spirit open blind eyes?"

FEAST OF DEDICATION

Two moons had passed since the Festival of Shelters, and ²²it was now time for the people to celebrate the Feast of Dedication[a] in Village of Peace (Jerusalem).

> *This festival was to remember the time when the Great Spirit's lodge was cleansed after it had been made ceremonially unclean by an evil ruler.*

²³It was winter, and Creator Sets Free (Jesus) was walking near the sacred lodge under the entryway named after the great chief Stands in Peace (Solomon). ²⁴The tribal leaders came to him and said, "How long will you make us wait? If you are the Chosen One, then tell us!"

²⁵"I already told you who I am," he said to them, "but you did not believe me. The things I do, representing my Father, speak the truth about me. ²⁶*As I told you before*, you do not trust me because you are not my sheep. ²⁷I know who my sheep are, for they know my voice and go

---

10:22 Also called Hanukkah and Festival of Lights

where I lead them. ²⁸My gift to them is the life of the world to come, full of beauty and harmony, and they will never fade away or come to a bad end. ²⁹My Father gave them to me, and no one can take them from me, because no one is greater than my Father. My sheep are safe in his hands, ³⁰for I and my Father are one."

TRIBAL LEADERS REJECT HIM

³¹The tribal leaders *became furious and* picked up stones to kill him.

³²Creator Sets Free (Jesus) *stood his ground and* said to them, "I have done many good things, representing my Father. For which of these do you mean to stone me?"

³³They answered, "Not for any good thing you have done, but for speaking lies against the Great Spirit. How can you, a weak human being, represent yourself as the Great Spirit?"

³⁴Creator Sets Free (Jesus) answered them, "In your tribal law it says, 'You are powerful spiritual beings.'ᵃ ³⁵If Creator's word, which came to you, says you are 'powerful spiritual beings,' and the Sacred Teachings are clear and cannot be changed, ³⁶then how can you say that the one the Father has set apart and sent into the world is speaking against the Great Spirit when he says, 'I am the Son of the Great Spirit'?

³⁷"If I am not doing what my Father does, then do not believe me. ³⁸But even if you do not believe me, then at least believe in the powerful things I do. Then you will see clearly that I am in the Father and he is in me."

³⁹The tribal leaders moved toward him to take him by force, but he slipped through their hands and walked away.

CREATOR SETS FREE RETREATS

Creator Sets Free (Jesus) decided it was time to leave Village of Peace (Jerusalem) again.

⁴⁰He went to the place on the east side of the river Flowing Down (Jordan) where Gift of Goodwill (John) first performed the purification ceremony.ᵇ He *and his followers* remained there *for a time.*

⁴¹Many people from the area came *to hear him* and, *after seeing Creator Sets Free (Jesus) teach, tell his stories, heal the sick, and force out evil spirits*, the people were saying, "Gift of Goodwill (John) never performed a miracle or did any powerful signs, but what he told us about this man is true."

⁴²And so many of the people there believed in him *that he was the Chosen One.*

11

A FRIEND CROSSES OVER

¹⁻²In House of Figs (Bethany), *near Village of Peace (Jerusalem)*, a man named Creator Helps Him (Lazarus) was very sick. He was the brother of Healing Tears (Mary) and Head Woman (Martha). Healing Tears (Mary) is the one who poured ointment over *the head and feet of* Creator Sets Free (Jesus) and wiped his feet with her hair.ᶜ

³The sisters sent a messenger to Creator Sets Free (Jesus), who said to him, *"Our brother, Creator Helps Him (Lazarus), the one you care deeply about, is sick."*

⁴When Creator Sets Free (Jesus) heard the message, he said, "This sickness will not end in death. Instead, this will bring honor to the Great Spirit and shine a light on his Son."

ᵃ**10:34** Lit. *You are gods.* See Psalm 82:6.
ᵇ**10:40** Baptism
ᶜ**11:1-2** See Mark 14:3; John 12:1-8.

HIS LIGHT SHINES BRIGHTER

5Even though Creator Sets Free (Jesus) loved this family dearly, **6**he stayed where he was for two more days. **7**Then he said to his followers, "Let us go back to the Land of Promise (Judea)."

8But his followers said to him, "Wisdomkeeper, the Tribal Members there tried to throw stones at you to kill you! Why would you want to go back there?"

9He answered them, "Does not the sun give us a full day of light? The ones who walk during the day never stumble, because they see the light that shines on this world. **10**But the ones who walk at night stumble in the darkness, because there is no light for them to see."

He was telling them that he was the light shining in this dark world and that it was time to let his light shine even brighter.

11Creator Sets Free (Jesus) explained to them, "Our good friend, Creator Helps Him (Lazarus), has fallen asleep and I am going to wake him."

12They said to him, "Wisdomkeeper, if he is only sleeping, he will get well."

13They did not understand that Creator Sets Free (Jesus) meant that Creator Helps Him (Lazarus) had died. **14**They thought he was sleeping naturally. He then told them plainly, "Creator Helps Him (Lazarus) has crossed over to death. **15**It is a good thing that I was not there, so you will believe. But we must go to him now."

16Looks Like His Brother (Thomas) said to the others, "Yes, we should go and die with him."

FOUR DAYS DEAD

17When Creator Sets Free (Jesus) came to House of Figs (Bethany), he found out that Creator Helps Him (Lazarus) had died four days earlier and was laid in a burial cave. **18**House of Figs (Bethany) was a close walk[a] from Village of Peace (Jerusalem). **19**Many of the local Tribal Members had gathered, along with the women, to give comfort to Head Woman (Martha) and Healing Tears (Mary) for the loss of their brother.

I AM THE RISING FROM THE DEAD

20When Head Woman (Martha) heard that Creator Sets Free (Jesus) was coming, she went out to greet him, but Healing Tears (Mary) stayed home.

21When she found Creator Sets Free (Jesus), she said to him, "Wisdomkeeper, if you had been here, my brother would still be with us. **22**Even so, I know if you ask anything of the Great Spirit, he will give it to you."

23"Your brother will live again," he answered.

24"I know he will live again," she said, "when the dead rise up at the end of all days."

25-26"I am the rising from the dead and the life that follows," he told her. "The ones who trust me will live again, even after death. Death will never be the end of the ones who are alive and trust in me. Do you believe what I am saying to you?"

27"Yes, Wisdomkeeper!" she *smiled and* said. "I believe you are the Chosen One, the Son of the Great Spirit—the one who came *down* into this world *from above.*"

HE WEEPS WITH THOSE WHO WEEP

28After she said this, she left him and went in private to her sister Healing Tears (Mary) and said to her, "The Wisdomkeeper is nearby and wants you to come to him."

---

[a]**11:18** About two miles

29-30 Creator Sets Free (Jesus) was still waiting outside the village where Head Woman (Martha) had met him. When Healing Tears (Mary) heard this, she got up right away and went to see him. **31**The Tribal Members who were comforting Healing Tears (Mary) saw her get up and leave quickly, so they went with her, thinking she was going to the burial cave to weep.

32When Healing Tears (Mary) found Creator Sets Free (Jesus), she crumpled at his feet and wept.

"Wisdomkeeper!" she said *as tears ran down her face*. "If only you had been here, my brother would still be alive."

33Creator Sets Free (Jesus) stood there watching Healing Tears (Mary) weeping at his feet. He looked around and saw all the Tribal Members who came with her also weeping. A deep anguish began to well up inside him, and he was troubled in his spirit.

He cried out, **34**"Where did they bury him?"

"Wisdomkeeper, come with us," they said to him. "We will show you."

35Creator Sets Free (Jesus) wept.

36When the Tribal Members saw his tears, some said, "See how deeply he cared for him!"

37But others said, "If this man could open the eyes of a blind man, why could he not have kept this man from dying?"

POWER OVER DEATH

38Creator Sets Free (Jesus), still deep in anguish, found his way to the family burial place. It was a cave, and a large stone blocked the entrance.

39Creator Sets Free (Jesus) cried out, "Take away the stone!"

Head Woman (Martha) whispered to him, "Wisdomkeeper, he has been dead four days. There will be a terrible smell."

40He *looked at her and* said, "Do you not remember what I told you? If you believed, you would see the shining-greatness of the Great Spirit."

Head Woman (Martha) could say nothing. She watched as **41**they rolled the stone away from the burial cave.

Creator Sets Free (Jesus) turned his eyes upward toward the sky and said, "I thank you, Father, that you have already heard my prayers and always listen to me. **42**The reason I say this out loud is so that all who are standing around me can hear and believe that you sent me."

The men and women gathered there stood silently, listening to his prayer.

43*Then the voice of* Creator Sets Free (Jesus) *pierced the silence as he* cried out with a loud voice, "Creator Helps Him (Lazarus), come out of there!"

The sound of his voice echoed from out of the burial cave and then faded into the distance. The people looked at Creator Sets Free (Jesus) and then back to the cave. No one dared say anything, so they all waited. Then suddenly, gasps could be heard from the crowd. There was movement in the cave!

44Creator Helps Him (Lazarus) came *stumbling* out of the burial cave with his ceremonial wrappings still clinging to his head, hands, and feet.

He was alive!

Creator Sets Free (Jesus) told the people, "Take off his wrappings and set him free."

Head Woman (Martha) and Healing Tears (Mary) wept for joy as they tore the ceremonial wrappings from their brother.

They could not stop hugging and kissing him! All the people were full of joy and began to celebrate.

⁴⁵When many of the local Tribal Members saw what Creator Sets Free (Jesus) had done, they put their trust in him. ⁴⁶But some of them went to find the Separated Ones (Pharisees) to tell them what had happened.

A WAR COUNCIL IS CALLED

⁴⁷When the Separated Ones (Pharisees) and the head holy men heard about this great miracle, they called the Grand Council together.

"What are we going to do?" they asked each other. "This man has powerful medicine and performs many signs and wonders. ⁴⁸If we do not stop him, all the people will believe in him. Then the People of Iron (Romans) will come and take away our sacred lodge and, with it, our *power to rule this* nation."

⁴⁹Hollow in the Rock (Caiaphas), the chief holy man for that year, said to the council, "Is it too hard for you to see? ⁵⁰It would be better for us if one man were to die for the people than for our whole nation to be destroyed."

⁵¹Hollow in the Rock (Caiaphas) was not aware that, as the chief holy man for that year, he prophesied that Creator Sets Free (Jesus) would die for their nation. *Little did he know that* ⁵²he would not only die for their nation but also to gather together all of Creator's scattered children *from every nation* and make them into one people.

⁵³From that day forward the Grand Council set in motion a plan to have him killed.

⁵⁴Knowing this, Creator Sets Free (Jesus) no longer walked openly among the people. He went into the countryside near the desert wilderness to the Village of Fruitful Place (Ephraim). There he stayed *for a time* with his close followers.

ON THE LOOKOUT FOR CREATOR SETS FREE

⁵⁵It was time again for the traditional Festival of Bread Without Yeast, called Passover. Tribal Members would travel from their homelands to Village of Peace (Jerusalem). Many would arrive early to perform a purification ceremony *to prepare for the festival.*

⁵⁶The tribal leaders were all looking for Creator Sets Free (Jesus). As they stood in *the courtyard of* the sacred lodge, they asked each other, "What do you think? Surely he will not come here to the festival?"

⁵⁷For the head holy men and the Separated Ones (Pharisees) had given instruction that anyone who saw Creator Sets Free (Jesus) should report back to them so they could arrest him.

12 ✖◀✖▶◀✖▶◀✖▶◀✖▶◀✖▶◀✖▶◀✖▶

PREPARATION FOR HIS BURIAL

¹It was now six days before the Passover festival. Creator Sets Free (Jesus) returned to House of Figs (Bethany) to lodge at the home of Creator Helps Him (Lazarus), whom he had brought back to life from the dead. ²That night, they had a meal to honor Creator Sets Free (Jesus). Head Woman (Martha) was preparing the meal, and her brother, Creator Helps Him (Lazarus), was sitting with Wisdomkeeper and the other guests.

³Healing Tears (Mary), *the sister of Head Woman (Martha),* took a small pottery jar that held some costly

ointment, broke it, and poured the sweet-smelling ointment on the feet of Creator Sets Free (Jesus). She then wiped his feet with her hair, and the scent of the sweet-smelling ointment filled the whole house.

⁴When Speaks Well Of (Judas), *also known as* Village Man (Iscariot), the one who would soon betray Creator Sets Free (Jesus), saw this, he said, ⁵"This could have been traded for a year's wages and given to the poor."

⁶He said this not because he cared for the poor, but because he was a thief, and, as the keeper of the money pouch, he would take what he wanted.

⁷"Let her be!" Creator Sets Free (Jesus) said to all. "She has done a good thing, saving this for the day of my burial. ⁸You can help the poor anytime, for they will always be with you, but I will not."

⁹Word got out that Creator Sets Free (Jesus) was there. Many people came from all around to see him, and not only him but also Creator Helps Him (Lazarus), the one he had brought back from the dead. ¹⁰The head holy men were also making a plan to kill Creator Helps Him (Lazarus), ¹¹for because of him many of the Tribal Members believed in Creator Sets Free (Jesus), *that he was the Chosen One.*

HIS GRAND ENTRY

¹²The following day, the people who had come to the Passover festival heard that Creator Sets Free (Jesus) was entering Village of Peace (Jerusalem). ¹³A great crowd of them took branches from palm trees and went out to greet him.

Waving palm branches in their hands, they began to shout, "Hosanna!" meaning "Help us!" They cried out with glad hearts. "We honor you as the one who is to come representing the Great Spirit. You are the Great Chief of the tribes of Wrestles with Creator (Israel)!"

¹⁴Creator Sets Free (Jesus) was riding on the colt of a donkey to give full meaning to the ancient prophecy, ¹⁵"Do not fear, O daughter of Strong Mountain (Zion). Your Great Chief is coming to you, in a humble way, riding on a young donkey."[a]

¹⁶At the time his followers did not understand these things. It was not until some time later, when he had entered his place of honor and bright shining-greatness, that they remembered how the things done to him had first been written down by the ancient prophets long ago.

¹⁷⁻¹⁸Among this crowd were the ones who had seen Creator Sets Free (Jesus) bring Creator Helps Him (Lazarus) back from the dead. They were telling everyone about this great miracle. That is why the crowd was so large that day.

Creator Sets Free (Jesus) came riding down Olive Mountain and went into Village of Peace (Jerusalem). His twelve followers encircled him and led the donkey forward.

He did not fit the powerful image of a conquering ruler, for he was not riding a warhorse. Instead, he rode a small, humble colt of a donkey. No mighty warriors rode next to him. No dignitaries from Village of Peace (Jerusalem) came out to meet him. It was mostly the common people who welcomed him that day.

¹⁹The Separated Ones (Pharisees) *huddled together near the crowd.*

"Nothing we have done to stop him has worked," they complained. "Look! The whole world is now following him."

---

[a]**12:15** Zechariah 9:9-10

WISDOM SEEKERS SEEK HIM

Along with the Tribal Members of Wrestles with Creator (Israel) who came to participate in the Passover festival, there were also many outsiders from other nations who would come.

20There were people from these nations who came to celebrate the festival from Land of Wisdom Seekers (Greece).

These were people who often prided themselves in their study of wisdom and knowledge.

21They went up to Friend of Horses (Philip), who was from House of Fishing (Bethsaida) in Circle of Nations (Galilee). *Knowing him to be one who walked with Creator Sets Free (Jesus),* they said to him, "Honored friend, we would like to see Creator Sets Free (Jesus), your Wisdomkeeper."

22Friend of Horses (Philip) *did not know what to do, so he* found Stands with Courage (Andrew) and asked him what he thought. Then together they both went to see Creator Sets Free (Jesus) and told him that the Wisdom Seekers (Greeks) wished to see him.

23He answered them, "It is time for the True Human Being to be lifted up to his place of honor. 24I speak from my heart. If a seed is unplanted, it remains only one seed, but if it dies, falls to the earth, and enters the ground, it will then grow and become many seeds.

25"The ones who love the kind of life this world gives will lose the life they seek, but the ones who let go of their life *in this world and follow my ways* will find the life of the world to come that never fades away, full of beauty and harmony.

"Tell these Wisdom Seekers (Greeks) to walk the road with me. 26Anyone who wants to serve me will walk in my footsteps, and I will take them to the same place I am going. If they give up their lives to serve me in this way, my Father will honor them."

THE TIME OF HONOR HAS COME

A look of sorrow came over the face of Creator Sets Free (Jesus).

27"But now I am deeply troubled and in anguish!" he said. "Should I ask my Father to rescue me from this hour that has now come? No! I came into the world for this time and for this purpose."

He then lifted his face, looked up to the sky, and sent his words to the Great Spirit.

28"Father," he prayed, "honor your name and show the world the beauty of it."

Suddenly, a voice from above spoke out of the sky, "I have honored my name, *for it represents who I am,* and I will once again honor and show the beauty of it."

29Some of the people standing nearby heard the voice and said, "Was that thunder?"

Others said, "No, a spirit-messenger has spoken to him."

30Creator Sets Free (Jesus) said to them, "This voice you heard was not for my sake, but for yours. 31It is a sign to you that it is now time for the Great Spirit to make his final decision about this world. The evil one who now rules this world will be defeated and thrown down. 32But I, *the True Human Being,* will be lifted up from the ground *and nailed to a cross.* This is the way I will bring all things, *in the spirit-world above and the earth below,*[a] to myself."

---

[a]**12:32** Colossians 1:19-20

33Creator Sets Free (Jesus) said this to show the kind of death he would die *and what his death would accomplish.*

34The people who heard him said, "How can this be? We have been told from our Sacred Teachings that the Chosen One, when he comes, will remain beyond the end of all days. How can you say the True Human Being will be lifted up like this? Who are you talking about?"

35Creator Sets Free (Jesus) spoke to them *with sadness in his voice.* "My light will shine on you for only a little while longer, so walk in my light before the darkness comes, for the ones who walk in darkness cannot see the path. **36**Put your trust in the one who gives you light, and then you will become children of light."

He looked around at the people, knowing that these were nearly the last public words he would speak.

He then went away to hide himself from the crowds.

BLIND EYES AND HARD HEARTS

37Even though Creator Sets Free (Jesus) had *healed the sick, brought the dead back to life, and* shown the people powerful medicine from the Great Spirit, his own tribal nation still did not believe in him or trust him.

38-39 This showed the full meaning of the ancient prophecy, "Who will believe such a thing? Who will see that Creator's great power *would be shown in weakness?*"[a] **40**and, "His great light has blinded their eyes and his great love has hardened their hearts. If only they would open their hearts to him, then they would see clearly and he would make them whole."[b]

41The prophet Creator Will Help Us (Isaiah) saw the true beauty of Creator Sets Free (Jesus) long ago and prophesied the reasons the people could not believe. **42**But even so, many tribal leaders did believe in him but would not tell anyone because they feared the Separated Ones (Pharisees). They knew if they openly confessed their faith in him they would be put out of the gathering houses. **43**In the end, their reputation with the people was more important to them than bringing honor to the Maker of Life.

MY MESSAGE WILL DECIDE

As he was leaving, **44**Creator Sets Free (Jesus) *turned around, lifted his voice, and cried out to the people one last time,* "If you trust me, you are not only trusting me, but the one who sent me. **45**When you see me, you see the one who sent me. **46**I came into this dark world as a shining light, so the ones who trust me will no longer have to stumble in the darkness.

47"I have not come to decide against the ones who have heard my words but fail to walk in them. Instead, I have come to rescue them from the *worthless ways of this* world and set them free. **48**But a day is coming when the ones who have turned away from me and my words will be decided against. In the end, it will be the message I have spoken that will decide for or against them.

49"The message I have spoken is not from myself. It is from the one who sent me. I have spoken only what my Father gave me to speak, nothing more. **50**The instructions my Father gave me lead to the life of the world to come that never fades away, full of beauty and harmony."

[a]**12:38-39** Isaiah 53:1
[b]**12:40** Isaiah 6:10

13

THE CEREMONIAL MEAL BEGINS

¹The Passover festival was drawing near. Creator Sets Free (Jesus) knew it was time to leave this world and go back to his Father. His love for the ones who walked the road with him had always been great, and now, at the end, his love for them remained strong.

²The evil trickster snake had already twisted the heart of Speaks Well Of (Judas), *also known as* Village Man (Iscariot), son of Man Who Hears (Simon), to betray Creator Sets Free (Jesus).

³Creator Sets Free (Jesus) knew that his Father had put all things in his hands and that he had come from the Great Spirit and was returning to him.

FOOT-WASHING CEREMONY

⁴Knowing all of this, during the meal Creator Sets Free (Jesus) got up from the table, took off his outer garments, and wrapped a cloth around himself like a sash. ⁵He poured water into a vessel and, one by one, he began to wash the feet of his followers and dry them with the cloth.

This was a task reserved for only the lowest servant of the household.

⁶He came to Stands on the Rock (Peter), who said to him, "Wisdomkeeper, are you going to wash my feet?"

⁷"You do not understand now what I am doing, but later you will," he answered.

⁸"No!" Stands on the Rock (Peter) lifted his voice, "This can never be!"

Creator Sets Free (Jesus) *looked deep into his eyes and* said, "If you refuse this, then you have no part in who I am."

⁹"Wisdomkeeper," he answered back, "*if this is so*, then wash my hands and head also!"

¹⁰Creator Sets Free (Jesus) replied, "If you have already had a bath, only your feet need washing, and then you will be clean all over. Now, you are all clean. Except for one."

¹¹He said this because he knew who would betray him.

After he had finished washing all their feet, ¹²he put his outer garment back on and sat down again at the table.

"Do you see what I have done?" he said to them. ¹³"You are right to call me Wisdomkeeper and Chief—because I am. ¹⁴If I, your Wisdomkeeper and Chief, have washed your feet, then you should wash each other's feet. ¹⁵So follow my footsteps and do for each other what I have done for you.

¹⁶"I speak from my heart. The one who serves is not greater than the one who is served. A message bearer is not greater than the one who sent him. ¹⁷If you walk in this way of blessing, you will do well, and it will return to you—full circle.

ONE OF YOU WILL BETRAY ME

¹⁸"I am not talking about all of you, for I know *the hearts of* the ones I have chosen. Now you will see the full meaning of the Sacred Teachings that said, 'The one who ate with me has turned against me.'ᵃ ¹⁹I am telling you this ahead of time, so when it happens you will believe that I am *the Chosen One.*

²⁰"I speak from my heart. The one who welcomes the one I send welcomes me. The one who welcomes me welcomes the one who sent me."

²¹When he finished saying this, Creator Sets Free (Jesus) became deeply troubled in his spirit. *As sorrow moved*

ᵃ**13:18** Psalm 41:9

over his face, he said to all, "From my heart I tell you, one of you will turn against me."

²²His followers' *hearts fell to the ground. They* looked around at each other, wondering who would do such a thing. ²³*He Shows Goodwill (John),* the much-loved follower of Creator Sets Free (Jesus), was sitting next to him. ²⁴Stands on the Rock (Peter) motioned him to ask Creator Sets Free (Jesus) who it was. So he leaned back on his chest and whispered into his ear, "Wisdomkeeper, who is it?"

²⁵"When I dip my frybread into the dish," he whispered back, "I will give it to the one who will turn against me."

He did as he said and handed the frybread to Speaks Well Of (Judas), *also known as Village Man (Iscariot),* the son of Man Who Hears (Simon). ²⁶When Speaks Well Of (Judas) took the frybread, the evil snake took hold of his heart.

²⁷"Go now," Creator Sets Free (Jesus) said to him, "and do what you have planned."

²⁸None of the others understood what Creator Sets Free (Jesus) was saying to him. ²⁹Since he was the keeper of the money pouch, they thought he was going to pay for the ceremonial meal or give something to the poor. ³⁰As soon as he had taken the frybread, Speaks Well Of (Judas) got up from the table and went out into the night.

A NEW ROAD

³¹After he left, Creator Sets Free (Jesus) said to them all, "The time has now come for the True Human Being to honor the Great Spirit and to be honored by him. ³²As soon as the Son gives him honor, it will come back again—full circle."

The Passover meal was coming to an end. It was time to close the ceremony and face the dark night ahead. The heart of Creator Sets Free (Jesus) was full of compassion and love for the ones who had walked the road with him for over three winters.

³³"My little children," he said to them, "my time with you is almost gone. You will look for me, but where I am going you cannot follow. This is the same thing I said to the other Tribal Members and I now say to you."

His followers lifted their heads up and looked into the face of their Wisdomkeeper.

³⁴"I am giving you a new road to walk," he said. "In the same way I have loved you, you are to love each other. ³⁵This kind of love will be the sign for all people that you are walking the road with me."

WHERE ARE YOU GOING?

³⁶Stands on the Rock (Peter) spoke up and asked, "Wisdomkeeper, where are you going?"

"The path I walk tonight you cannot walk with me," he answered, "but you will walk it later."

³⁷"Wisdomkeeper!" he replied. "Why can I not walk with you now? I am ready to give my life for you!"

³⁸"Will you truly lay down your life for me?" Creator Sets Free (Jesus) asked. Then he said, "Before the rooster crows in the morning, you will deny three times that you know who I am!"

14

NO OTHER GUIDE

His followers hung their heads as his words sank deep into their hearts. Creator Sets Free (Jesus) gathered them together and had them sit down in a circle, like an eagle gathering her young under her wings. He spoke softly but clearly to them.

¹"Do not let your hearts fall to the ground," he encouraged them. "Trust in the Great Spirit, and trust in me. ²My Father's lodge has room for everyone. If this were not so, then why would I tell you that I am going to prepare a place for you? ³When I am finished, I will come back to you, so that you will always be with me. ⁴You already know the path to where I am going."

⁵Looks Like His Brother (Thomas) interrupted and said, "Wisdomkeeper, if we do not know where you are going, how can we know the path?"

⁶"I am the *Great Spirit's* pathway, the truth *about who he really is,* and the life *of beauty and harmony he offers to all.* There is no other guide who can take you to the Father. ⁷To know me is to know my Father, so from now on you know him and have seen him."

SHOW US THE FATHER

⁸Friend of Horses (Philip) said to him, "Wisdomkeeper, show us the Father, and that will be enough."

⁹"Friend of Horses (Philip)," Creator Sets Free (Jesus) said, "how long have you walked with me, and still you do not know me? How can you say, 'Show us the Father'? The ones who have seen me have seen the Father. ¹⁰Do you not believe that the Father is in me and I am in the Father?

"The words I speak to you are not my own. It is the Father speaking in me. ¹¹Trust in me, for I am in the Father and he is in me. Or at least trust in the works my Father does through me.

¹²"I speak from my heart. The ones who trust in me will do the same things

I do, and even greater things, for I am going away to my Father. ¹³⁻¹⁴When you ask the Father for anything, ask it in my name, representing who I am. When you ask for anything in this way, I will do it to bring honor to my Father.

PROMISE OF THE HOLY SPIRIT

¹⁵"If you love me, you will walk in my ways. ¹⁶I will ask the Father to send one who will always walk beside you and guide you *on the good road.* ¹⁷He is the Spirit of Truth, the one this world is not able to accept because it does not see or know him. But you know him, for he is with you now and will soon be in you.

¹⁸"I will not leave you like a child with no parents. I will come back to you. ¹⁹Soon this world will no longer see me, but you will see me. Because I will live again, you will also live. ²⁰When that day comes, you will know that I am in the Father, that you are in me, and that I am in you. ²¹The ones who walk in my ways and stay true to my message love me. They will be loved by my Father, and I will love them and show them my true self."

²²Speaks Well Of (Judas), not the one who betrayed him, asked, "Wisdomkeeper, how will you show yourself to us and not to the rest of the world?"

²³"I will show myself to the ones who love me and are staying true to my teachings. They will be loved by my Father, and we will come and make our home in and among them. ²⁴The ones who do not *return my* love will not walk in my message. This message is not only mine. It is from my Father, the one who sent me.

²⁵"I have told you these things while I am still with you, ²⁶but there is one whom the Father is sending to represent me. He will walk beside you and be your spirit guide. He is the Holy Spirit, who will be

your Wisdomkeeper and will help you to remember all that I have told you.

GREAT PEACE

27"I leave you now with my great peace. It is my gift to you. It is not the kind of peace the world gives. Do not let the troubles of this world fill you with fear and make your hearts fall to the ground, and do not let fear hold you back. 28I told you I am going away and that I will come back. This should make your hearts glad if you truly love me, for I am going to the one who is greater than I am—to my Father, *the One Above Us All.*

29"I have told you all these things beforehand, so when you see them happen you will believe. 30There is only a little time left for me to talk with you. The dark ruler of this world is coming. His power over me is nothing, 31but I must walk the path the Father has for me, so the world will know the great love I have for him.

"Get up!" he said to them. "It is time for us to go from here."

15

THE TRUE VINE

1"I am the true grapevine. My Father is the Vine Keeper. 2He cuts off the branches in me that have no fruit. He carefully trims back the branches with fruit, so they will grow more fruit.

3"My teachings have purified you, 4but you must stay joined to me in the same way a branch is joined to the vine. A branch cannot grow fruit unless it is joined to the vine. It is the same with you and me.

5"I am the vine and you are the branches. The ones who stay joined to me will grow much fruit, for without me nothing grows. 6The ones who do not stay joined to me are broken off and dry up, and then they are gathered up and used to make a fire.

7"If you are joined to me and my words remain in you, you can ask me for anything and it will be done. 8When you grow a harvest of fruit, this will show that you are walking my road. You will then bring great honor to my Father.

THE ROAD OF LOVE

9"In the same way the Father loves me, I have loved you. Never stop walking this road of love. 10By doing what the Father has told me, I have remained in his love. 11As you walk in my ways, my love will remain in you. I am saying this so your hearts will be filled with the same joy I have.

12"To walk the road with me, you must love each other in the same way I have loved you. 13There is no greater way to show love to friends than to die in their place. 14You are my friends if you walk in my ways and do what I say. 15I no longer see you as my servants but as friends. Masters do not share their hearts and plans with their servants, but I have shown you everything I have heard from my Father.

16"You may think you chose me, but I am the one who chose you. You are my new garden where I will grow a great harvest of my love—the fruit that remains. When you bear this fruit, you represent who I am—my name. Then the Father will give you whatever you ask for. 17I am telling you this so you will walk the road of love with each other.

THE WORLD WILL HATE YOU

18"If you are hated by the world, remember, it hated me first. 19The ones who walk in the ways of this world love the ones who do the same but look down on and hate the ones who do not. I have chosen you to walk away from the ways of this world, on a different path, and that is why the world will hate you. [20]Remember, I told you a servant is not greater than the one he serves. If I was hunted down, it will be the same for you. If they walk in my message, they will walk in yours.

[21]"The *people who walk in the ways of this* world will do this to you because you walk in my ways, representing me. This shows they do not know the one who sent me.

[22]"If I had not come to them and represented the truth, they would not be guilty of this, but now their guilt remains. [23-24]If I had not done the things no one else has done, they would have no guilt. But now they have seen with their own eyes and hated me and my Father. [25]The full meaning of their own Sacred Teachings have become clear, 'They hated me for no reason.'[a]

SPIRIT OF TRUTH

[26]"I am sending you the Spirit of Truth, the one who is coming from the Father. He will walk close by your side, representing me, and telling the truth about me. [27]You will also represent me as truth tellers, for you have walked with me from the first and have seen these things with your own eyes.

16

IT IS BETTER IF I GO AWAY

[1]"I am telling you these things to keep you from stumbling away from the path.

[2]The tribal leaders will force you out of their gathering houses. The time will come when they will put you to death, thinking they are doing what the Great Spirit wants, [3]all because they do not know me or my Father. [4]I am telling you this so when the time comes you will remember I told you ahead of time. I did not tell these things from the first because I was with you— [5]but now I am going away.

"I am returning to the one who sent me, but none of you are asking, 'Where are you going?' *You are thinking only of yourselves* [6]because my words have made your hearts fall to the ground. [7]I speak from my heart, it is better for you that I go away. If I remain, the one who will guide you will not come. If I go, I will send him to you.

THE HOLY SPIRIT'S WORK

[8]"When the Holy Spirit comes, he will clearly show the wrong ways of this world, the right ways of the spirit-world above, and the answer that will be required of them in the end. [9]He will show them that the answer to their broken ways is to trust in me. [10]The right ways of the spirit-world above will come when I return to the Father and they no longer see me. [11]The final decision *about this world* will come because *Accuser (Satan)*—the ruler of this world—has been found guilty.

[12]"There are many more things I want to say to you, but your hearts are not strong enough to hear them now. [13]When the Spirit of Truth comes, he will be the one to tell you. He will be your *one true* spirit guide and will lead you down the path of truth. He will fully represent me and will tell you only what I have told him. The Spirit

will show you what is coming on the road ahead. ¹⁴He will honor me by making known to you everything I have shown him. ¹⁵All that I am and all that I have comes from the Father. He has not held back one thing from me, and the Spirit will not hold back anything from you.

A LITTLE WHILE

¹⁶"Soon I will be gone and you will not be able to see me, and then after a little while you will see me again."

¹⁷⁻¹⁸His followers began to whisper to each other, "What is he saying? We do not know what he means by 'a little while' and not seeing him and then seeing him again. What does he mean by 'I go to the Father'?"

¹⁹Creator Sets Free (Jesus) knew what they wanted to ask him, so he said, "You want to know what I meant when I said 'soon you will not see me, but then you will see me again.'

²⁰"I speak from my heart. Your tears will be many, and your hearts will fall to the ground, because of what will happen to me, but the world around you will have glad hearts. ²¹All of you will be filled with sorrow, but your sorrow will turn into dancing!

"When a woman is giving birth, she has sorrow, for her time of pain has come. But when she gives birth to her child, she forgets her pain, for a new human being has been born into the world. ²²It will be the same for you. You will have sorrow for now, but when I see you again, you will dance for joy. And no one will be able to take your joy from you.

A NEW WAY OF ASKING

²³⁻²⁴"When that time comes, your questions will be answered, not by asking me but by asking the Father himself. You will then ask the Father in my name, fully representing me. I know you have never asked in this way before, but it is now time. I speak from my heart. When you ask in this new way, the Father will answer, and your hearts will know the full meaning of joy.

THE END OF STORIES

²⁵"I have told you truths from the spirit-world above, using earthly stories. The time is coming when I will not have to use stories but will tell you plainly about the Father. When that time comes, you will not need me to ask the Father for you, because you will ask him yourself. ²⁶When you ask in my name, you are representing me. ²⁷Your love and trust in me will bring the Father's love to you—full circle. ²⁸You now believe that I came from the Great Spirit. Yes, I came into this world from the Father, and now I am leaving this world and returning to the Father."

²⁹His followers said to him, "Now you are speaking plainly to us instead of using stories! ³⁰We now see that you know all things and can answer a question before it is asked. This helps us to believe that you came from the Great Spirit."

I HAVE DEFEATED THE WORLD

³¹"You say you believe now," Creator Sets Free (Jesus) said to them, ³²"but soon you will all be scattered and return to your families. You will leave me alone, but I will not be alone, for my Father is with me.

³³"I have told you all these things so you will have my peace. This world is full of sorrow, pain and trouble, but have strong hearts, for I have defeated the world."

HE PRAYS FOR HIS FOLLOWERS

1When Creator Sets Free (Jesus) was finished speaking to his followers, he lifted his eyes to the spirit-world above and sent his voice to the Great Spirit.

"O Great Father," he prayed, "it is time for you to bring honor to your Son, so he may bring honor to you. **2**You have put all human beings under the care of your Son, so he can give them the life of the world to come that never fades away, full of beauty and harmony. **3**This life comes from knowing you, the only true and Great Spirit, and from knowing the Chosen One, Creator Sets Free (Jesus), the one you have sent into this world.

4"I have brought you honor on earth by finishing the work you sent me to do. **5**It is now time, my Father, for you to honor me with the beauty I shared at your side before you created all things.

6"I have shown who you truly are to the ones you gave me from this world. They were always yours and you trusted me with them, and they have walked in your ways. **7**They now know that everything I have comes from you. **8**The message you gave to me I have given to them. They have welcomed the truth about who I am and trust that you sent me. **9**These are the ones I now pray for. I am not praying for the ones who walk in the ways of the world, but for the ones you gave to me, for they belong to you. **10**My followers bring honor to me. They are a gift from you, a gift we share together.

11"*Since I am returning to you,* I will no longer be in the world, but my followers will still be here. O Father of all that is holy, watch over them with the loving care that we share with one another. In this way, they will also share the love that makes us one.

12"During my time on earth representing you, I kept them safe in your loving care. Not one of them has been lost, except for the one foretold in the Sacred Teachings, the one doomed to a bad end.

13"I am returning to you now. But while I am still here, I pray for my followers, so they may share in my joy. **14**Your message, which I gave them, has taken root in their hearts. Like me, they have chosen not to walk in the ways of this world, and so the world hates them. **15**I am not asking you to remove them from the world but that you keep them safe from the evil one and his ways. **16**They no longer belong to *the ways of* this world, any more than I do. **17**Make them holy through the beautiful message of your truth.

18"You sent me into the world, and now, in the same way, I send them into the world. **19**I set my life apart for them in a sacred manner, so they may also set their lives apart to walk in the beauty of your truth.

20"My prayers are not only for them, but for all who will trust in me through their message. **21**I pray that all who walk with me will be joined together as one, in the same way that you, Father, are in me and I am in you—that they may be one in us. This is how the world will believe that you have sent me.

22"The beauty you gave to me I have given to them. This will join them together with us. **23**In the same way you are in me, I will be in them, beautifully joined together as one. This is the reason you sent me into this world, to show that you love them just as you love me.

²⁴"O Great Father, I want the ones you have given to me to share this place of beauty that I have with you, so they can see the power of your love for me, a love that we shared before you created all things.

²⁵"O Father of all that is good and right, the world does not know you, but I know you, and my followers know you sent me. ²⁶I have represented and will always represent who you truly are so that the love you have for me will be in them and I will live in them also."

18

BETRAYAL

¹When he finished sending up his prayers, he and the ones who walked the road with him walked across the Valley of Darkness (Kidron) and entered a garden with many olive trees.

²Speaks Well Of (Judas), the betrayer, knew about this place because Creator Sets Free (Jesus) would often go there with his followers. ³The betrayer came into the garden, and with him came a band of lodge soldiers sent from the scroll keepers, head holy men, and Separated Ones (Pharisees), *representing the elders of the Grand Council*. The air was filled with the smell of burning torches as they entered the garden carrying clubs and long knives.

⁴Creator Sets Free (Jesus) knew all this would happen, yet he turned to the soldiers and asked, "Who have you come for?"

⁵*With one voice* they answered back, "Creator Sets Free (Jesus) from Seed Planter Village (Nazareth)!"

The betrayer, Speaks Well Of (Judas), was standing there with the lodge soldiers when Creator Sets Free (Jesus) answered, "I am he!"

⁶At the sound of his voice they all moved back and fell to the ground.

⁷He asked them again, "Who have you come for?"

They answered, "Creator Sets Free (Jesus) from Seed Planter Village (Nazareth)."

⁸"I told you already, I am the one you are looking for," he said. "Let these other men go."

⁹He said this to fulfill his promise, "None of the ones you gave to me have been lost."[a]

¹⁰Right then, Stands on the Rock (Peter) drew his long knife from its sheath and cut off the right ear of the servant of the chief holy man. The servant's name was Chieftain (Malchus).

¹¹Creator Sets Free (Jesus) turned to Stands on the Rock (Peter) and cried out, "*Enough of this!* Put your long knife back into its sheath. Shall I not drink the cup of suffering my Father has asked of me?"

CREATOR SETS FREE IS ARRESTED

¹²The lodge soldiers, along with their head soldier and the Grand Council representatives, took hold of Creator Sets Free (Jesus), tied him securely with cowhide strips, ¹³and took him first to Walks Humbly (Annas), one of the high holy men. He was the father of the wife of Hollow in the Rock (Caiaphas), the chief holy man ¹⁴who had advised the Grand Council by saying, "It will be better if one man dies for all the people."[b]

FIRST DENIAL

¹⁵Stands on the Rock (Peter) and one other follower[c] had been watching from a distance. Since this follower was known by the chief holy man, he entered the courtyard of the house. ¹⁶But Stands on

---

[a]**18:9** John 6:39
[b]**18:14** John 11:49-50
[c]**18:15** John, the author, is speaking of himself.

the Rock (Peter) stood outside the gate. This follower spoke to the gatekeeper, a young woman, who then let Stands on the Rock (Peter) in. **17**She said to him, "Are you not one of his followers?"

"No!" he told her, "I am not."

18The night was growing cold, so some of the men, along with the soldier guards from the lodge, built a fire in the courtyard to keep warm. Stands on the Rock (Peter) stood there with them, trying to stay warm.

CREATOR SETS FREE QUESTIONED

19Back inside, the chief holy man began to question Creator Sets Free (Jesus) about his followers and his teachings. **20**Creator Sets Free (Jesus) said to him, "I have spoken openly to all, in the gathering houses and the sacred lodge. I said nothing in secret. **21**Why ask me? Ask the ones who heard me. They will know."

22One of the head soldiers struck him in the face and said, "Is that how you answer a chief holy man?"

23Creator Sets Free (Jesus) answered him back, "If I have spoken wrongly, tell me what I said wrong. If I spoke what is true, then by what right do you strike me?"

24Walks Humbly (Annas) decided to send Creator Sets Free (Jesus) to Hollow in the Rock (Caiaphas), the chief holy man. So they took him, still bound by ropes, to Hollow in the Rock (Caiaphas).

THE ROOSTER CROWS

25Outside in the courtyard Stands on the Rock (Peter) was still warming himself by the fire. The others asked him, "You are not one of his followers, are you?"

"No!" Stands on the Rock (Peter) denied. "I am not!"

26One of the servants of the chief holy man, a relative of the man whose ear had been cut off, looked at him, and said, "Yes, you are! I saw you in the garden with him!"

27Stands on the Rock (Peter) shook his head in denial—and right then a rooster began to crow.

TO THE PEOPLE OF IRON

28Creator Sets Free (Jesus) was taken from the house of Hollow in the Rock (Caiaphas) to the lodge of the governor of the People of Iron (Romans). The tribal leaders stayed outside, for they did not want to become ceremonially unclean by going inside. It was early in the morning, and many of them had not yet eaten the ceremonial meal of Passover.

29Spear of the Great Waters (Pilate) came outside to meet them.

They took Creator Sets Free (Jesus) and stood him before Spear of the Great Waters (Pilate). He took a good long look at him, then turned back to the crowd.

"What has this man done wrong?" he asked them.

30"If he were not a criminal, would we have brought him to you?" they answered.

"Take him away!" **31**Spear of the Great Waters (Pilate) said to them. "Use your own law to decide what to do."

"Our tribal law will not permit us to put him to death," they answered.

32This proved that Creator Sets Free (Jesus) was right when he told them how he would die—*by being nailed to a tree-pole—the cross.*

ARE YOU THEIR CHIEF?

33Spear of the Great Waters (Pilate) went back into his lodge and had Creator Sets Free (Jesus) brought to him, *so he could question him in private.*

Once inside, he said to him, "Are you the chief of the tribes of Wrestles with Creator (Israel)?"

³⁴"Is this your question," Creator Sets Free (Jesus) asked, "or are you listening to others?"

³⁵"I am not from your tribes," Spear of the Great Waters (Pilate) answered. "It is your own people and their head holy men who have turned you over to me. What have you done?"

³⁶"My way of ruling is a good road. It is not in the ways of this world. If it were, my followers would have fought to keep me from being captured."

³⁷"So then, you are a chief," he said back to him.

"It is you who have said it," Creator Sets Free (Jesus) answered. "I was born for this and have come into the world for this purpose—to tell about the truth. The ones who belong to the truth will listen to my voice."

³⁸Spear of the Great Waters (Pilate) *shook his head and* said, "What is truth?"

I FIND NO GUILT IN HIM

³⁹Then Spear of the Great Waters (Pilate) went outside to the tribal leaders and said to them, "I find no guilt in this man. By your own tradition we set free one criminal during your Passover Festival. Do you want me to release Creator Sets Free (Jesus), your chief?"

⁴⁰"No! Not him," the crowd roared back. "Release Son of His Father (Barabbas)!"

Son of His Father (Barabbas) was a troublemaker who had caused an uprising.

19

CROWN OF THORNS

¹Spear of the Great Waters (Pilate) turned Creator Sets Free (Jesus) over to his soldiers to have him beaten. ²The soldiers twisted together a headdress from a thorn bush, pressed the thorns into his head, and wrapped a purple chief blanket around him. ³They bowed down before him, making a big show of it, and kept mocking him, saying, "Honor! Honor to the Great Chief of the tribes of Wrestles with Creator (Israel)."

They took turns hitting him on his face *until he was bruised and bloodied.*

⁴Spear of the Great Waters (Pilate) stood before the crowd again and said, "I bring to you the one in whom I have found no guilt."

Creator Sets Free (Jesus) was brought forward, *blood flowing down his bruised face.* ⁵He was wearing the headdress of thorns and the purple chief blanket that was wrapped around him.

"Behold the man!" Spear of the Great Waters (Pilate) said to them. ⁶"Take a good long look at him!"

The crowd stared at him in stunned silence.

But then the head holy men and the lodge guards began to shout, "Death! Death on the cross!"

"Then take him and kill him yourselves," Spear of the Great Waters (Pilate) said to them. "I find no guilt in him!"

⁷They answered him back, "Our law tells us he must die, for he has represented himself as the Son of the Great Spirit."

POWER OF LIFE AND DEATH

⁸When Spear of the Great Waters (Pilate) heard this, his fear grew stronger, ⁹so he took Creator Sets Free (Jesus) back inside his lodge.

"*Who are you, and* where are you from?" he questioned him.

Creator Sets Free (Jesus) *stood there and* remained silent.

¹⁰"Speak to me! Do you not know I have the power of life and death over you? I can have you killed or set you free," he warned him. "Have you nothing to say?"

¹¹"The only power you have is what has been given you from above," he answered. "The ones who turned you over to me carry the greater guilt."

¹²Spear of the Great Waters (Pilate) tried harder to have Creator Sets Free (Jesus) released, but the people would not have it.

They stood their ground, saying, "If you release a man who says he is a chief, you are not honoring the ruler of your people, for anyone who claims to be a chief challenges his power."

STONE OF DECIDING

¹³When Spear of the Great Waters (Pilate) heard this, he took Creator Sets Free (Jesus) and went to the Stone of Deciding, called Gabbatha in the tribal language, and sat down. ¹⁴It was now midday on the Day of Preparation for the Passover Festival.

He brought Creator Sets Free (Jesus) before the people and said, "Here is your chief."

¹⁵"Take him away! Take him away!" the crowd shouted with one voice. "Nail him to the cross!"

"Would you have me nail your chief to the cross?" he asked them.

This time the head holy men answered back, "We have no other chief than the Ruler of the People of Iron (Caesar)."

¹⁶Spear of the Great Waters (Pilate) then turned Creator Sets Free (Jesus) over to the soldiers to have him put to death on a tree-pole—the cross—so they took him away.

The cross was an instrument of torture and terror used by the People of Iron (Romans) to strike fear into the hearts of any who dared to rise up against their empire. The victim's hands and feet would be pierced with large iron nails, fastening them to the cross. The victims would hang there, sometimes for days, until they were dead. This was one of the most cruel and painful ways to die ever devised by human beings.

ULTIMATE SACRIFICE

The soldiers placed a wooden crossbeam on his back and forced him to carry it to the place where he would be executed.

¹⁷Creator Sets Free (Jesus) carried the crossbeam to the Place of the Skull, which is called Golgotha in the tribal language. ¹⁸There they nailed his hands and feet to the cross, along with the two others, and placed his cross between the two of them.

¹⁹Spear of the Great Waters (Pilate) fastened a sign to the top of the cross where they attached the crossbeam with these words written on it:

CREATOR SETS FREE
FROM SEED PLANTERS VILLAGE
CHIEF OF THE TRIBES
OF WRESTLES WITH CREATOR

²⁰This was near Village of Peace (Jerusalem). *So that many of the Tribal Members could read it*, the sign was written in Aramaic, their tribal language, but also in Latin and Greek, *the languages of the People of Iron (Romans).*

²¹The chief head holy men and the tribal leaders said to Spear of the Great Waters (Pilate), "Do not write 'chief of the tribes.' Instead write, 'He said he is chief.'"

²²But he answered, "What I have written will stand."

²³The soldiers stripped his clothes from him when they nailed his hands and feet to the cross. They tore one of his garments into four pieces, one for each guard. His long outer garment was woven together into one piece, ²⁴so they said, "Let us not tear this, we can draw straws for it."

This gave full meaning to the Sacred Teachings that said, "They divided my clothes between them and gambled for my garment."ᵃ This is what the soldiers did *as they kept watch over Creator Sets Free (Jesus).*

²⁵⁻²⁶Standing near the cross was Bitter Tears (Mary), the mother of Creator Sets Free (Jesus), who had come to see him, along with her sister. Two other women also came with her, Brooding Tears (Mary) the wife of Trader (Clopas), and Strong Tears (Mary) from Creator's High Lodge (Magdala). *He Shows Goodwill (John),* the much-loved follower of Creator Sets Free (Jesus), was also there with them.

When Creator Sets Free (Jesus) looked down and saw them, he said to his mother, *"Honored* woman, look to your son." ²⁷Then he said to his follower, "Look to your mother."

From that time the follower took Bitter Tears (Mary) into his family and cared for her.

²⁸Creator Sets Free (Jesus), knowing he had done all the ancient Sacred Teachings had foretold, said, "I thirst."

²⁹There was a vessel of sour and bitter wine standing nearby. One of the soldiers dipped a cloth in it to soak up some wine. He wrapped the cloth around the tip of a hyssop branch and held it up to the mouth of Creator Sets Free (Jesus).

³⁰He then tasted the bitter wine, *turned his head to the sky* and cried out loud, "It is done!"

He then lowered his head to his chest and, *with his last breath,* gave up his spirit.

Creator Sets Free (Jesus) was dead.

NOT ONE BONE BROKEN

³¹Soon the sun would set and a special Day of Resting would begin, *when no work could be done.* It was time to prepare for this day, so the Tribal Members asked Spear of the **Great Waters** (Pilate) to have the legs of the men on the crosses broken, *which would make them die sooner.* Then they could take the bodies down and prepare them for burial.

³²The soldiers came and broke the legs of the two men on each side of Creator Sets Free (Jesus). ³³When they came to him, they saw he was already dead. Instead of breaking his legs, ³⁴one of the soldiers took a spear and pierced his side. Blood and water flowed out from the wound.

³⁵The one who saw these things with his own eyes is telling the truth about this—so that all will believe. ³⁶This was foretold in the ancient Sacred Teachings that say, "Not one of his bones was broken,"ᵇ ³⁷and, "They will look upon the one they have pierced."ᶜ

TRADITIONAL BURIAL

³⁸He Gets More (Joseph) from High Mountain (Arimathea), *a man with many possessions,* was a follower of Creator Sets Free (Jesus), but in secret, because he

---

ᵃ**19:24** Psalm 22:18

ᵇ**19:36** Psalm 34:20
ᶜ**19:37** Zechariah 12:10

feared the tribal leaders. *Since it would soon be sunset, when the Day of Resting would begin,* he went to Spear of the Great Waters (Pilate) and asked permission to remove the body of Creator Sets Free (Jesus) from the cross.

Spear of the Great Waters (Pilate) released the body to him. So he and another man, ³⁹Conquers the People (Nicodemus), who had come to Creator Sets Free (Jesus) in secret at night, took his body away *to prepare it ceremonially for burial.* Conquers the People (Nicodemus) had brought a mixture of myrrh and oils weighing about seventy-five pounds. ⁴⁰Together they ceremonially wrapped his body for burial in the traditional way, using strips of cloth and herbal spices and oils.

⁴¹⁻⁴²So because it was the Day of Preparation for the Passover Festival, *and the day of resting was about to begin,* they laid the body of Creator Sets Free (Jesus) in a nearby burial cave that had never been used *and then returned to their homes.*

20

HIS BODY IS GONE

¹Early on the first day of the week, Strong Tears (Mary) from Tower of Creator's High Lodge (Magdala) came to the burial cave early in the morning while it was still dark. When she saw the stone had been removed from the burial cave, ²she ran to find Stands on the Rock (Peter) and *He Shows Goodwill (John),* the much-loved follower of Creator Sets Free (Jesus).

She found them and, *catching her breath, she* said to them, "They have taken the body of our Wisdomkeeper away, and we do not know where he is!"

³⁻⁴Stands on the Rock (Peter) raced to the burial cave, but the other follower outran him and came there first. ⁵⁻⁷He stooped low to look inside but did not go in all the way. He saw strips of cloth lying there, but the cloth that had been wrapped around the head of Creator Sets Free (Jesus) was rolled into a bundle, lying by itself. Stands on the Rock (Peter) arrived behind him and came to the cave. When he went inside, he saw the same things.

⁸The other follower, who arrived first, now found the courage to go inside all the way. He saw the burial cave was empty—and believed. ⁹But they still did not understand from the Sacred Teachings that he would return from death. ¹⁰Then they went back to the place where they were staying.

A WOMAN SEES HIM FIRST

After the men left, Strong Tears (Mary) from Creator's High Lodge (Magdala) went back to the garden.

¹¹Her heart was on the ground as she stood outside the cave, weeping. As the tears ran down her face, she looked inside. ¹²There she saw two spirit-messengers dressed in white. They were sitting, one at the head, the other at the feet, of where the body of Creator Sets Free (Jesus) had once lain.

¹³They looked at her and said, *"Honored woman,* why do you weep?"

"My Wisdomkeeper is gone," she answered, "and I do not know where they have taken him."

¹⁴She turned around to see a man standing behind her. It was Creator Sets Free (Jesus), but she did not recognize him.

¹⁵*"Honored* woman, why the tears?" he said to her. "Who are you looking for?"

She thought he was the keeper of the garden, so she said, "If you have carried him away, tell me where, and I will find him."

¹⁶"Strong Tears (Mary)," he said to her *in a soft and kind voice.*

She looked closer at him and her eyes grew wide. Then she hugged him close and whispered in his ear in her native language.

"Rabboni!" she said, meaning Wisdomkeeper.

¹⁷"You must let me go," he said back to her. "I have not yet gone up to the Father. Go to my brothers who walked the road with me and say to them, 'I am going up to my Father and your Father, to the one who is the Great Spirit and Father of us all.'"

Creator Sets Free (Jesus) had chosen to show himself first to a woman, Strong Tears (Mary) from Creator's High Lodge (Magdala), the one he had set free from seven evil spirits.

¹⁸Strong Tears (Mary) then went and found the followers of Creator Sets Free (Jesus) and said, "I have seen our Wisdomkeeper!"

She then told them everything she had heard from him.

HIS FOLLOWERS SEE HIM

¹⁹It was now late in the same day, the first day of the week. His followers were all hiding behind locked doors in fear of being captured by the tribal leaders.

Suddenly, Creator Sets Free (Jesus) himself was standing in front of them and said, "Peace be with you!"

²⁰He then showed them where the iron nails had pierced his hands and where the spear had cut into his side.

When they saw their Wisdomkeeper, the hearts of his followers were filled with joy, ²¹so he said to them again, "Peace be with you! In the same way the Father above has sent me, I am now sending you."

²²He blew his breath on them and said, "*You will breathe in and receive the Holy Spirit. With his wisdom and guidance,* ²³if you release others from their bad hearts and broken ways, they are released. If you do not release them, they are not released."

PUT AWAY YOUR DOUBTS

²⁴Looks Like His Brother (Thomas), one of the original twelve followers, was not there when Creator Sets Free (Jesus) showed himself to the others. ²⁵They told him, "We have seen the Wisdomkeeper with our own eyes."

But he said to them, "Unless I see the nail marks in his hands, and put my finger into them, and put my hand into the hole in his side, I will not believe."

²⁶Eight days later his followers were gathered together again, and Looks Like His Brother (Thomas) was with them. The doors were all locked, but Creator Sets Free (Jesus) came in and stood before them all.

"Peace be with you," he said. ²⁷Then he turned to Looks Like His Brother (Thomas) and said, "Look closely at my hands and touch my scars with your finger. Put your hand into the wound in my side. Then put away your doubts and trust in me."

²⁸"You are my Honored Chief and my Creator," he said.

²⁹"Now you believe, because you have seen me?" he said to him. "A greater blessing will rest on the ones who have not seen but still believe."

³⁰Creator Sets Free (Jesus) did many more powerful signs before the eyes of his followers that have not been written down in this book. ³¹But I have told this

much so you will believe that Creator Sets Free (Jesus) is the Chosen One, the Son of the Great Spirit. When you put your trust in all that his name represents, the life of beauty and harmony he has promised to all will be yours.

21

BACK TO FISHING

1A while later, Creator Sets Free (Jesus) showed himself again to his followers by Lake of Circle of Nations (Sea of Galilee), *also called Sea of Rolling Water (Sea of Tiberias).*

2Stands on the Rock (Peter) along with other followers of Creator Sets Free (Jesus) had gathered there. With him were Looks Like His Brother (Thomas), Creator Gives (Nathanael) from Village of Reeds (Cana) in Circle of Nations (Galilee), the two sons of Gift of Creator (Zebedee), and two other followers.

3Stands on the Rock (Peter) said to them, "I am going fishing."

They all agreed and said, "Take us with you."

So they took a canoe out onto the lake. *Under the light of the moon and stars* they worked hard all night. Again and again they threw out their nets and drew them back in—empty.

4Just as the first light of day was dawning, Creator Sets Free (Jesus) came and stood on the shore. But they did not know it was he.

5"Friends," he called out to them, "have you netted any fish?"

"No!" they answered.

6"Throw out your nets to the right of your canoe," he shouted to them. "You will find some fish there."

They did as he said, and the net was filled with so many fish they could not pull it into the canoe. **7***He Shows Goodwill (John),* the much-loved follower of Creator Sets Free (Jesus), said to Stands on the Rock (Peter), "It is our Wisdomkeeper!"

Stands on the Rock (Peter) had taken off his outer garment to fish. He put it back on and jumped into the water. **8**The shore was not far, so the others made their way in, dragging the net full of fish behind the canoe.

They came to the shore and stepped out of the canoe. **9**They saw a warm fire with fish cooking over the coals and some frybread to eat.

HE FEEDS HIS FOLLOWERS

10Creator Sets Free (Jesus) *looked up from cooking and* said, "Bring me some of the fish you caught."

11Stands on the Rock (Peter) climbed into the canoe and pulled the net to shore. The fish were large, and they counted them—one hundred and fifty-three in all! But even with so many fish the net did not tear.

12Creator Sets Free (Jesus) said, "Let us eat."

They all sat down to eat, but no one dared ask, "Who are you?" They knew it must be their Wisdomkeeper.

13He took the frybread and gave some to each of them, along with a piece of fish. **14**This was the third time he had shown himself to them after coming back to life from the dead.

STANDS ON THE ROCK RESTORED

15When they had finished eating, Creator Sets Free (Jesus) took Stands on the Rock (Peter) *and sat down with him by the lake.*

He spoke to him, *using the name his family gave him,* "One Who Hears (Simon), son of Gift of Kindness (John), do you love me more than the others love me?"

"Yes, Wisdomkeeper," he answered, "you know I am your friend."

"Then feed my lambs," he said.

They sat looking out over the water and listening to the sound of the waves coming in to the shore.

16Then a second time Creator Sets Free (Jesus) asked, "One Who Hears (Simon), son of Gift of Kindness (John), do you love me?"

"Yes, Wisdomkeeper," he answered him again, "you know how deeply I care for you."

"Then watch over my sheep," he said.

The sound of the water birds could be heard in the distance, and the sun felt warm as it rose higher in the sky.

17Creator Sets Free (Jesus) asked him a third time, "One Who Hears (Simon), Son of Gift of Kindness (John), do you love me as a friend?"

Stands on the Rock (Peter) felt his heart sink because he asked the third time, "Do you love me as a friend?"

"Wisdomkeeper!" he said, "you know all things, you must know how deeply I care for you. I am your friend!"

Creator Sets Free (Jesus) said to him again, "Feed my sheep."

18Creator Sets Free (Jesus) then said to him, "I tell you from my heart, when you were a young man, you dressed yourself and walked wherever you wanted. But when you grow old, you will stretch out your hands and someone else will dress you and take you to a place you do not want to go."

19He was telling him the kind of death he would die, to bring honor to Creator. Then he said to Stands on the Rock (Peter), "Come, walk the road with me."

This was the same invitation he had given years earlier to Stands on the Rock (Peter) in Circle of Nations (Galilee) after the canoes had been filled with fish.

WALK THE ROAD I HAVE CHOSEN

20Stands on the Rock (Peter) looked over at *He Shows Goodwill (John)*, the much-loved follower of Creator Sets Free (Jesus). He was the same one who, during the ceremonial meal, had leaned back and asked, "Wisdomkeeper, who will betray you?"

21When Stands on the Rock (Peter) saw him, he said to Creator Sets Free (Jesus), "Wisdomkeeper, what about this man, *how will he die?*"

22Creator Sets Free (Jesus) answered him, "If I want him to remain alive until I return, why would it matter? You must walk the road I have chosen for you."

23When the others heard what Creator Sets Free (Jesus) had said about He Shows Goodwill (John), talk began to go around that he would never die. But Creator Sets Free (Jesus) did not say he would not die. He said, "If I want him to remain alive until I return, why would it matter to you?"

THE PURPOSE OF THIS STORY

24The one telling you this story has seen and heard these things with his own eyes, and all can agree he is telling the truth. 25Many more things could be told about Creator Sets Free (Jesus), the message of his good road, and the people his life touched. This story has been written down in a book, but not everything. For he did so many things, if they were all written down in books, the whole world would not have room for them.

Aho! May it be so!

THE GOOD STORY CONTINUES

ACTS

THE STORY CONTINUES

1 O most honored Friend of Creator (Theophilus), I have already told you the story of Creator Sets Free (Jesus), about the many things he did and taught among the people ²*from his birth* until the day he returned to the spirit-world above. ³After he had suffered by being put to death on the cross, he returned to life and then appeared to his message bearers, giving them many proofs that he was truly alive again.

FORTY DAYS OF INSTRUCTION

For forty days he continued to appear to them, and through the Holy Spirit he instructed them further about Creator's good road. ⁴Once, during a meal with his followers, he said to them, "Wait here in the Sacred Village of Peace (Jerusalem), for the gift from my Father that I already told you about—the Holy Spirit. ⁵He Shows Goodwill (John) performed the purification ceremony[a] with water, but not many days from now, you will participate in the purification ceremony[a] with the Holy Spirit."

They were all full of wonder about what was taking place. Was this the beginning of the new world the prophets of old had promised to the tribes of Wrestles with Creator (Israel)?

---

[a]**1:5** Baptism

⁶They crowded around Creator Sets Free (Jesus). "Wisdomkeeper," they asked him, "will you now give the good road back to the tribes of Wrestles with Creator (Israel)?

⁷"Times and seasons are in the Father's hands," he answered. "These things are not for you to know. ⁸Instead, set your hearts and minds on the Holy Spirit, who will give you strong medicine when he comes. You will then tell my story in Village of Peace (Jerusalem), in all the Land of Promise (Judea) and High Place (Samaria), and then to the farthest parts of the earth—*to all languages, tribes, and nations.*"

⁹As he spoke these words, he was taken up and went into a cloud where they could no longer see him.

His followers bowed down to honor him, and then, full of wonder and awe, they stood there looking up into the sky.

¹⁰As they watched him go up into the spirit-world above, two men appeared before them in pure white garments.

¹¹"Men of Circle of Nations (Galilee)!" they said. "Why are you looking up into the sky? This same Creator Sets Free (Jesus), whom you saw going up into the spirit-world above, will return in the same manner you have seen him go."

THE UPPER ROOM

¹²Village of Peace (Jerusalem) was nearby, about as far as one is permitted to walk on

a Day of Resting. [13]So the followers of Creator Sets Free (Jesus) walked down Olive Mountain and returned to the village and to the place where they were staying, at a lodging house in an upstairs room.

Here are the names of some of the follow-ers of Creator Sets Free (Jesus) who were gathering together to pray:

Stands on the Rock (Peter), He Shows Goodwill (John), He Takes Over (James), Stands with Courage (Andrew), Friend of Horses (Philip), Looks Like His Brother (Thomas), Son of Ground Digger (Bar-tholomew), Gift from Creator (Matthew), He Takes Charge (James) son of First to Change (Alphaeus), One Who Listens (Simon) the Firebrand (Zealot), and Speaks Well Of (Judas),[a] the son of He Takes Hold (James).

[14]Bitter Tears (Mary), the mother of Creator Sets Free (Jesus), was there along with some of his brothers. Also many of the honored women were welcomed among them. They were all gathering together, night and day, to send their voices to the Great Spirit.

[15]This group had grown into *one big family*, about a hundred and twenty of them, who all trusted in Creator Sets Free (Jesus), that he was the Chosen One.

A NEW MESSAGE BEARER CHOSEN

There were now only eleven message bear-ers. Speaks Well Of (Judas), the one who betrayed Creator Sets Free (Jesus), was no longer among them. Since Creator Sets Free (Jesus) chose twelve message bearers to represent the twelve tribes of Wrestles with Creator (Israel),[b] someone had to be chosen to replace him.

So during this time Stands on the Rock (Peter) stood up to speak.

[16]"Friends and family," he said to all, "Much Loved One (David), guided by the Holy Spirit, foretold in the Sacred Teachings the things that found their full meaning in Speaks Well Of (Judas), who betrayed Creator Sets Free (Jesus) into the hands of the ones who arrested him.

[17]"From the first, Speaks Well Of (Judas) was one *of the twelve* chosen to walk with us as one of his followers.

[18]"*After he betrayed Creator Sets Free (Jesus)*, he used the blood money he was paid to buy a field. *There he hung himself on a tree.*[c] His body fell to the ground and broke open, spilling out his insides. [19]News about this spread throughout Village of Peace (Jerusalem), and so that place became known *in our native language* as Akeldama, meaning Field of Blood."

[20]*Stands on the Rock (Peter) continued,* "This gives full meaning to the words of the Sacred Book of Songs (Psalms), 'Let his land become deserted, a place where no one will live.'[d] It also says, 'Let another take his place in the council.'[e]

[21]"*We must now choose another to re-place Speaks Well Of (Judas).* He must be one who was with us the whole time while we were walking the road with our Wisdomkeeper, [22]from the time he participated in the purification cer-emony[f] with He Shows Goodwill (John) until the day Creator Sets Free (Jesus) was taken up from us to the spirit-world above. Then, along with us, he will be able to tell what his own eyes have seen, about the rising from the dead of Creator Sets Free (Jesus)."

---

[a]**1:13** John 14:22
[b]**1:15** Matthew 12:28

[c]**1:18** Matthew 27:5
[d]**1:20** Psalm 69:25
[e]**1:20** Psalm 109:8
[f]**1:22** Baptism

THE COUNCIL OF TWELVE IS RESTORED

²³Two men were selected who met the requirements: He Adds More (Joseph), who was called Son of Resting (Barsabbas), also known as Stands Upright (Justus), and Gifted From Creator (Matthias). ²⁴They *stood the men before the council and* prayed over them, "O Great Chief, Knower of Hearts, show to us the one you have chosen ²⁵to be your message bearer in the place of Speaks Well Of (Judas), who left the path given him and chose his own path." ²⁶They decided to choose by drawing straws. The straw was in favor of Gifted From Creator (Matthias), and so he was added to the eleven message bearers *to form a council of twelve—representing the twelve tribes of Wrestles with Creator (Israel).*

2 🟫▪️🔷▪️🔷▪️🔷▪️🔷▪️🔷▪️🔷

FESTIVAL OF WEEKS

The tribes of Wrestles with Creator (Israel) celebrated another great feast called the Festival of Weeks or Pentecost, meaning "fifty," because it was celebrated seven weeks after the Passover festival, on the fiftieth day. This was a harvest festival when the people would bring the firstfruits of the harvest to Creator's lodge in the Sacred Village of Peace (Jerusalem) and give thanks for his provision. Creator was about to send the Holy Spirit, promised by Creator Sets Free (Jesus), to begin the time of the great harvest and gather people from all nations who would represent the Great Spirit.

¹The time for *the full meaning of* the ancient festival had now arrived.

The followers of Creator Sets Free (Jesus), numbering about one hundred and twenty, *were waiting and praying in the upstairs room where they were lodging. It had now been fifty days since the Passover festival.*

WIND AND FLAMES OF FIRE

They had all gathered together in one place, ²when suddenly the sound of a great windstorm came from the spirit-world above and could be heard throughout the house where they were sitting. ³They saw flames of fire coming down from above, separating and resting on each of their heads. ⁴The Holy Spirit had come down upon them and began to fill them *with his life and power.* New languages began to flow out from their mouths, languages they had never learned, given from the Holy Spirit.

⁵The Sacred Village of Peace (Jerusalem) was filled with devoted members of the tribes of Wrestles with Creator (Israel), *who had come for the festival* from every nation under the sun. ⁶A crowd began to gather when they heard the loud noise.

⁷In wonder and amazement the crowd began to ask, "How is it that these people from Circle of Nations (Galilee) are speaking in our many languages? ⁸For we all can understand them in the languages of the places we have come from! ⁹⁻¹¹There are people here for the festival from nations and places close by and far away who are members of the tribes of Wrestles with Creator (Israel), and those from Outside Nations who have been taken into the tribes.

"They come from Land of Victory (Parthia), Land in the Middle (Media), and Land of the Ancient Ones (Elam). Many come from Land Between Rivers (Mesopotamia), Land of Promise (Judea), Land of Handsome Horses (Cappadocia), Land of Black Waters (Pontus), and Land of the

Rising Sun (Asia). Some come from Dry Wood (Phrygia) and Many Tribes (Pamphylia), and the territory of Land of Tears (Lybia) near the village of Strong Wall (Cyrene). There are travelers from Village of Iron (Rome), both Tribal Members and Outsiders who have become Tribal Members, along with those who come from Flesh Eater Island (Crete) and Land of Wanderers (Arabia).

"We can hear them, in the languages of these nations, telling about the great and powerful things done by the Great Spirit!" 12Many were amazed and confused and began to ask each other, "What can this mean?" 13But others in the crowd just laughed and said, "They are drunk on new wine!"

STANDS ON THE ROCK SPEAKS OUT

14Stands on the Rock (Peter), along with the other eleven message bearers, stood up to the crowd, and with a loud voice said, "Tribal members from far away and all who live in Village of Peace (Jerusalem), listen closely to me. I will tell you what this means!"

The crowd became quiet and turned to hear Stands on the Rock (Peter).

15"No one among us is drunk on wine, for it is still the middle of the morning. This is not what you think it is. 16This is what the prophet Creator Is the Great Spirit (Joel) spoke of long ago when he said, 17"'In the last days,' says Creator, "I will rain down my Spirit upon all human beings from every nation. Your sons and daughters will prophesy. Young warriors will see visions and elders will have dreams. 18When that time comes, my Spirit will rain down on all who serve me, both men and women, and they will boldly speak my words. 19There will be

powerful signs and omens in the spirit-world above and on the earth below— blood and fire with clouds of smoke. 20The sun will grow dark and the moon will be red like blood, as the great and dreadful day of Creator shines like the sun. 21Then the ones who cry out to the Great Spirit will be made whole and set free.""a

22Stands on the Rock (Peter) cried out, "Listen to me, you men of the tribes of Wrestles with Creator (Israel)! You already know about Creator Sets Free (Jesus) from Seed Planter Village (Nazareth) and about the powerful signs and the wonders he performed among the people that proved Creator was with him. 23-24Creator knew, before it happened, that the tribes would use the power of the People of Iron (Romans)b to have him violently killed by nailing him to a tree-pole—the cross. But the Maker of Life let you have your way with him, because he had made a plan, long ago, to bring him back to life. Creator Sets Free (Jesus) was released from the painful grip of death, for even death itself could not hold him captive.

ANCIENT PROPHECIES FULFILLED

25"When the great chief Much Loved One (David) spoke these words long ago, he was telling us about Creator Sets Free (Jesus). Listen to what he said, 'The Great Spirit will never leave me. I will not tremble with fear, for he is close by my side, and guides me on the pathways of life. 26My heart is glad and my mouth sings! I have hope that 27even after my body is dead, I will not be left alone in the ground to return to dust. You will not leave your Holy One in the Dark Underworld of Death (Hades). 28For you have

---

a2:21 Joel 2:28-32
b2:23-24 Lit. those outside the law

given me a clear path to your life of beauty and harmony. When I stand before you face to face, my heart will leap for joy!'"[a]

> *Stands on the Rock (Peter) waited while the crowd thought about his words.*

[29]*Then he said,* "My fellow Tribal Members, there is no doubt that our ancestor, Much Loved One (David), died and was buried long ago. His burial cave is with us to this very day. [30-31]The Great Spirit gave him a sacred promise that one of his descendants would be a Great Chief to rule over all the tribes. Much Loved One (David) was a prophet and saw, ahead of time, that the Chosen One would rise from the dead and that he would not be left alone in the Dark Underworld of Death (Hades), nor would his body return to the dust of the earth.

[32]"Creator Sets Free (Jesus) is this Chosen One who has been raised to life from death! We have seen him with our own eyes. [33]He has now returned to his seat of honor at the right hand of the Great Spirit. The Father above has gifted him with the Holy Spirit whom he promised to send. This Spirit has now been poured out upon us like the rain. This is the meaning of what you now see and hear.

[34]"Much Loved One (David) did not go up into the spirit-world above, so when he says, 'The Great Chief said to my Great Chief, "Sit down beside me at my right hand, my place of greatest honor, [35]until I defeat and humble all your enemies,"'[b] *he was not talking about himself. He was talking about the Chosen One.*

[36]"So let all the tribes of Wrestles with Creator (Israel) have no doubt about what the Great Spirit has done. He has made

Creator Sets Free (Jesus), the one you put to death on a tree-pole—the cross—to be both Chief *of all the tribes* and the Chosen One, *the one he promised to send long ago.*"

THE CROWD RESPONDS

[37]When they heard this, the words pierced their hearts *like a long knife.* With troubled hearts they lifted their voices to Stands on the Rock (Peter) and all the message bearers.

"Fellow Tribal Members," they said, "tell us what we must do."

[38]"Change your thinking," Stands on the Rock (Peter) instructed them, "and participate in the purification ceremony[c] that is done in the name of Creator Sets Free (Jesus), the Chosen One, representing him *and initiating you into his right ways.* You will then be healed from your bad hearts, released from your broken ways, and gifted with the Holy Spirit, *who will give you the strength to walk the good road with him.* [39]He has promised this to all generations of the tribes of Wrestles with Creator (Israel), and to all *the Nations* who live far away. For the Great Spirit, our Creator, is calling out to all who will, to share in this life of beauty and harmony."

[40]Stands on the Rock (Peter) said many more things to the ones who were listening. With strong words he kept telling them, "This is how you will be set free and rescued from the bent and twisted ways of this generation."

[41]The ones who believed the words of Stands on the Rock (Peter) became a part of Creator's new sacred family and participated in the purification ceremony.[c] About three thousand people were added to the family on that day!

---

[a]**2:28** Psalm 16:8-11
[b]**2:35** Psalm 110:1

[c]**2:38, 41** Baptism

A NEW FAMILY IS FORMED

⁴²This newly formed family continued daily to learn from the twelve message bearers. They lived together in harmony, ate ceremonial meals, and prayed with one another. ⁴³Great respect and awe came down upon all, and the message bearers performed many powerful signs. ⁴⁴As these new followers lived together in peace, their harmony grew stronger, and they shared all things. ⁴⁵Many of them had a giveaway to provide for all who were in need.

⁴⁶Each day they gathered at the sacred lodge. With good and pure hearts they feasted together in their homes and shared the ceremonial meal of frybread and wine given to them by Creator Sets Free (Jesus). ⁴⁷They gave honor and thanks to the Great Spirit and were respected by the people. Each day Creator sent more people who were being set free to join with them.

3

RISE UP AND WALK

¹In the middle of the afternoon the people would gather at the sacred lodge for a time of prayer. Stands on the Rock (Peter) and He Shows Goodwill (John) were walking together on their way to the lodge. ²Some people were carrying a man who had been unable to walk from his birth. Each day they would lay him down by the entrance to the lodge called the Beautiful Gate, so he could ask for handouts from the ones who were going into the lodge.

³When the man saw Stands on the Rock (Peter) and He Shows Goodwill (John) passing by, he asked them for a handout. ⁴They stopped right in front of the man, looked straight at him, and said, "Look at us!"

⁵The man did as they said, hoping they would give him something.

⁶⁻⁷Stands on the Rock (Peter) said to him, "I have no silver or gold to give to you, but I have a gift for you *that is worth much more.*"

He reached his hand out to the man and said, "I represent the Chosen One, Creator Sets Free (Jesus) from Seed Planter Village (Nazareth). In his name I tell you now—stand up and walk!"

Stands on the Rock (Peter) took hold of his hand and began to pull him up. ⁸The man felt strength returning to his legs and feet and pushed himself up on his own feet and began to walk! He danced through the Beautiful Gate and went into the lodge, walking and leaping and giving praise to the Great Spirit.

⁹All the people looked at the man ¹⁰and saw that he was the same one who sat and asked for handouts at the gate. Wonder and amazement swept through the crowd *like a wildfire* when they saw him healed and strong.

¹¹The man threw his arms around Stands on the Rock (Peter) and He Shows Goodwill (John) and would not let go of them. A great crowd of people ran up and began to circle around them under the covered walkway named after the great chief Stands in Peace (Solomon). They looked at Stands on the Rock (Peter) and He Shows Goodwill (John) with wonder and amazement on their faces.

STANDS ON THE ROCK
SPEAKS OUT AGAIN

¹²When Stands on the Rock (Peter) saw all the people, he lifted up his voice to give the people an answer for the healing of the crippled man.

"Fellow Tribal Members," he said to them, "you should not be amazed at us, or think that we are holy enough to make a crippled man walk. [13]It was the one who walked with Father of Many Nations (Abraham), He Made Us Laugh (Isaac), and Heel Grabber (Jacob)—the Great Spirit of our ancestors, who has done this.

"The Giver of Life has honored Creator Sets Free (Jesus), the one who served him and did all he asked. The same one you turned over to Spear of the Great Waters (Pilate), the governor from the People of Iron (Romans), to be put on trial for his life. The same one you turned your back on, in front of Spear of the Great Waters (Pilate), when he wanted to release him.

[14]"But you turned your back on the Holy and Upright One and then asked for a violent murderer to be set free. [15]In doing so you killed the Maker of Life! But the Giver of Breath brought him back to life from the dead! This we have seen with our own eyes.

[16]"It is only because of Creator Sets Free (Jesus), and all that his name represents, that this man stands before you healed and strong now. You can see for yourselves what trusting in Creator Sets Free (Jesus) has done for him."

THIS IS WHAT THE PROPHETS FORETOLD

Stands on the Rock (Peter) continued to speak boldly.

[17]"Fellow Tribal Members," he said, "I understand that neither you nor your leaders knew what they were doing *when they had Creator Sets Free (Jesus) killed.* [18]But this is how the Great Spirit fulfilled all that the prophets foretold when they spoke of the suffering of the Chosen One.

[19]"You must think in a new way and return to the Great Spirit to walk this new path he has chosen for us all. Then you will be healed of your broken ways,

[20]and Creator will shine his face on you and give you cool, fresh water to drink from his river of life. He will then give to you the one he selected to be his Chosen One—Creator Sets Free (Jesus). [21]He has gone up into the spirit-world above to remain there until the time comes when Creator will restore all things.

"Creator spoke of these things long ago through his holy prophets. [22]Listen to the words of Drawn from the Water (Moses), when he said, 'The Great Spirit Chief will raise up a prophet from among the tribes, in the same manner he raised me up. You must listen to this prophet and do all he says, [23]for any among the tribes who fail to follow his ways will come to a bad end.'[a]

[24]"All the prophets, from Creator Hears Him (Samuel) and all who spoke in the generations that followed, told about these very days we are living in. [25]Every Tribal Member is a descendant of those prophets and of the peace treaty Creator made with our ancestors. Did not the Great Spirit promise our ancestor Father of Many Nations (Abraham) that through his descendants he would bless all the families who dwell on earth?

[26]*"That day has come!* The Great Spirit has raised up his servant, Creator Sets Free (Jesus), and sent him first to the tribes of Wrestles with Creator (Israel) to bless you and turn you back from your worthless, evil ways."

ARRESTED AND IMPRISONED

[1]While Stands on the Rock (Peter) and He Shows Goodwill (John) were speaking to the people, the head lodge soldier, along

---

[a]**3:23** Deuteronomy 18:15, 18-19

with the Upright Ones (Sadducees) and some holy men, came up to them. ²They were offended because the message bearers were telling the people that the rising from the dead had begun with Creator Sets Free (Jesus). ³They took hold of Stands on the Rock (Peter) and He Shows Goodwill (John) *to bring them to the council,* but because it was late in the day, they held them in prison until the next day. ⁴But a large number of over five thousand men who heard Stands on the Rock (Peter) speak believed the message!

FACING THE GRAND COUNCIL

⁵On the following day the headmen, elders, and scroll keepers held a council in Village of Peace (Jerusalem). ⁶Both Walks Humbly (Annas) the chief holy man and Hollow in the Rock (Caiaphas) sat in the council along with He Shows Goodwill (John), Man Fighter (Alexander), and other members of the family of the chief holy man. ⁷They brought Stands on the Rock (Peter) and He Shows Goodwill (John) to sit before them and give an answer to the council.

"Where did the power to heal this man come from? What is the name of the one you represent? Tell us!" they demanded.

⁸The Holy Spirit rose up inside Stands on the Rock (Peter).

"Headmen and elders among the people," he said with boldness, ⁹"if we are being questioned today before this council about the kindness we showed to a man who could not walk, by healing him, ¹⁰then let all the tribes of Wrestles with Creator (Israel) know the truth. It is because of the name of Creator Sets Free (Jesus) the Chosen One, and all he represents, that this man stands before you healed and whole! Yes! The same Creator Sets Free (Jesus) from Seed Planter Village (Nazareth) whom you killed on a tree-pole—the cross. The Maker of Life has brought him back to life from the world of the dead. ¹¹He is 'the log you builders threw away, which has become the Chief Lodgepole.'ᵃ ¹²No one else can restore us. No other human being can represent the Great Spirit and carry in his name the kind of power needed to rescue us and set us free."

THE COUNCIL DECIDES

¹³When the council saw the courage of Stands on the Rock (Peter) and He Shows Goodwill (John), they were amazed to find that they were common and unschooled men. They also took notice that they had walked the road with Creator Sets Free (Jesus). ¹⁴But what could they say? The man who had been healed was standing right there with them! ¹⁵They ordered them to wait outside of the council house while they decided what to do with them.

As the men were taken outside, the council lowered their voices and looked around at each other with troubled faces.

¹⁶"What should we do with these men?" they asked. "Anyone living in Village of Peace (Jerusalem) can see that a powerful sign has been done by them. We cannot deny this. ¹⁷But to keep this from spreading to more people, we must warn them to no longer represent Creator Sets Free (Jesus) or to speak to anyone in his name."

¹⁸The council agreed and summoned the message bearers to face their decision. They warned them, "You must never again say anything representing Creator Sets Free (Jesus) or instruct others in his teachings."

ᵃ**4:11** Psalm 118:22

[19]Stands on the Rock (Peter) and He Shows Goodwill (John) disagreed with the council's decision.

"We will let you decide for yourselves whether we should follow the Great Spirit or weak human beings like yourselves," they said with boldness. [20]"But we cannot stop speaking about what we have seen with our own eyes and heard with our own ears!"

The council could not believe their ears! How could these backward people from Circle of Nations (Galilee) stand up to them?

[21]So the council warned and threatened them again, but released them and let them go on their way. The council dared not do anything to punish them, because the people were giving thanks to Creator for this powerful sign. [22]For the man who had been healed was over forty winters old.

THE MESSAGE BEARERS RETURN

[23]Stands on the Rock (Peter) and He Shows Goodwill (John) went back to their newly formed family and told them what had happened to them and what the council had decided. [24]When the sacred family members heard this, they formed a circle around the message bearers, joined their hearts together, and sent their voices to the Great Spirit.

PRAYER FOR HELP

"O Great Father of the sky above and the earth below, of the great waters and all that is in them," they prayed. "Hear our cry! [25]Long ago your Holy Spirit spoke these words through our ancestor Much Loved One (David), who served you.

"The Spirit said, 'Why did the Nations, in their great anger, make empty threats? Why did the people waste their time

forming useless plans? [26]The war chiefs of the land took their stand, and the war councils schemed together. But who were they planning to fight? It was against the Great Spirit Chief and his Chosen One!'[a]

[27]"The truth of this is plain to see, for right here in the Village of Peace (Jerusalem) they gathered together and took their stand against your Holy Servant, Creator Sets Free (Jesus). Chief Looks Brave (Herod) and Spear of the Great Waters (Pontius Pilate) together with the People of Iron (Romans) and the tribes of Wrestles with Creator (Israel) [28]did what you, in your great wisdom, had decided long ago would be done.

[29]"So we ask, O Great One, look down and see their threats against us. Help us to be brave and tell your story well [30]by performing many powerful signs as we represent your Holy Servant, Creator Sets Free (Jesus)."

[31]When they finished praying, the place where they had gathered began to rumble and shake. The Holy Spirit filled them *with his power*, and with brave and strong hearts they began to tell Creator's Story!

THEY SHARE THEIR POSSESSIONS

[32]With one heart and mind all who trusted in Creator Sets Free (Jesus) shared their possessions with each other. No one claimed their belongings to be only for themselves. [33]With great power the message bearers told the story of how their Honored Chief Creator Sets Free (Jesus) had defeated death and returned to life. Creator's gift of great kindness was covering all of them *like a warm blanket,* [34]and no one among them was in

[a]4:26 Psalm 2:1-2

need. Those who owned houses or land sold them and brought what they had gained [35]and gave it to the message bearers to share with everyone.

[36]There was a man among them named Creator Adds More (Joseph), who was also given the name Son of Comfort (Barnabas) by the message bearers. He was from the tribe of Holy Men (Levites), who was born in Island of Flowers (Cyprus). [37]He sold a piece of land that was his and brought the money and gave it to the message bearers.

5

LYING TO THE HOLY SPIRIT

[1-2]A man named Creator Shows Kindness (Ananias), along with his wife, Stone of Beauty (Sapphira), sold some of their land. He, with his wife knowing about it, gave the money to the message bearers. *They let them think they had given all,* but they *secretly* held back some for themselves.

[3]But Stands on the Rock (Peter) said to Creator Shows Kindness (Ananias), "Why did you let Accuser (Satan), that evil trickster snake, fill your heart to lie to the Holy Spirit? You have kept back some of the money from the sale of your land for yourself! [4]You did not have to sell your land, and even after selling it you still could do whatever you wanted. So why did you try to deceive us? You have lied not *only* to human beings but to the Great Spirit himself!"

[5]When Creator Shows Kindness (Ananias) heard this, he fell to the ground and breathed out his last breath. Great fear and awe fell on all who heard what had happened. [6]Some of the young men wrapped his body in a blanket, carried him out, and buried him.

[7]About three hours later the wife of Creator Shows Kindness (Ananias) came in, but she did not know what had happened.

[8]Stands on the Rock (Peter) asked her, "Was this how much you sold the land for?"

"Yes," she said, "That is the right amount."

[9]Stands on the Rock (Peter) then said to her, "How could both of you agree to put Creator's Spirit to the test? Look! The ones who buried your husband are coming to do the same for you."

[10]Right then she fell down in front of him and breathed her last. The young men came in, and when they saw she had crossed over to death, they carried her away and buried her next to her husband. [11]Once again great fear and awe took hold of all in the sacred family and also of all who heard what had happened.

SIGNS AND WONDERS CONTINUE

[12]The message bearers were performing many powerful signs among the people. The people were all gathering together under the entryway *at the sacred lodge* named after the great chief Stands in Peace (Solomon). [13]The people respected them greatly, but many did not dare to join in with them. [14]Even so, the crowds grew, and more and more people put their trust in Creator and his Son.

[15]The people carried the sick into the village pathways and laid them on their sleeping bundles and mats so that when Stands on the Rock (Peter) walked by, his shadow might fall on them. [16]The crowds came from the villages near Village of Peace (Jerusalem). They brought the sick and the ones tormented by evil spirits— and all of them were healed!

OPPOSITION FROM THE SPIRITUAL LEADERS

17When the chief holy man and other spiritual leaders of the Upright Ones (Sadducees) heard what was happening, the fire of jealousy burned in their bellies. **18**They took hold of the message bearers and put them in the local jail. **19**But a spirit-messenger from Creator came in the night and set them free.

20"Go and stand in the sacred lodge," the spirit-messenger instructed them, "and speak all the words of this new life to the people."

21They did what they were told and went to the sacred lodge, and just as the sun was rising, they began to teach the people.

When the chief holy man arrived, along with the spiritual leaders, they called together the Grand Council and the elders of the tribes of Wrestles with Creator (Israel). They sent some lodge soldiers to the local jail to have the message bearers brought before the council. **22**When the lodge soldiers arrived at the jail, they could not find the prisoners, so they returned to report to the Grand Council.

23"When we arrived at the jail," they said to the council, "we found the jail doors locked and guarded. But when we opened the doors, there was no one to be found!"

24The head lodge soldier and the head holy men could not believe their ears! While they were wondering about this, **25**a messenger came up to them.

"Look!" the messenger said, "the ones you put in jail are standing in the sacred lodge and teaching the people!"

26The head lodge soldier, along with his soldiers, went to arrest the message bearers again, but not by force, for they were afraid the people might throw stones at them.

THEY STAND BEFORE THE GRAND COUNCIL

27So they took the message bearers to stand before the Grand Council to be questioned by the chief holy man.

28"We clearly instructed you not to speak representing this man's name or his teaching. Now Village of Peace (Jerusalem) has been filled with your teaching. Do you mean to bring this man's blood upon our heads *by blaming us for his death?*"

STANDING STRONG

29Stands on the Rock (Peter) and the other message bearers answered back, "We must obey the Great Spirit instead of weak human beings. **30**The Great Spirit of our ancestors has raised up Creator Sets Free (Jesus), the one you killed by hanging him on a tree. **31**Creator has honored him to the highest place, at his own right hand to be our Chief, the one who will set us free and give us a new path to walk. This is how we, the people of the tribes of Wrestles with Creator (Israel), will be set free from our bad hearts and broken ways. **32**We have seen these things with our own eyes! The Holy Spirit also agrees with these things, the one Creator will give to those who walk in his ways."

WISE WORDS FROM A COUNCIL MEMBER

33When the Grand Council heard this, the anger in them burned like a fire—they wanted to kill them. **34**But then, Creator Has Honored (Gamaliel) stood up to speak. He was a highly respected council member, a Separated One (Pharisee) and a teacher of tribal law. He instructed them to remove the message bearers outside for a while.

35Then he said to the council, "You men of the tribes of Wrestles with Creator (Israel), think carefully about what you plan to do with these men. 36Remember when Flows with Water (Theudas) made himself out to be a great one, with a following of four hundred men? He was killed, and all his followers were scattered and came to nothing. 37After him, Speaks Well Of (Judas) from Circle of Nations (Galilee) rose up during the days of the census. He also had many follow him, but he was also killed and his followers scattered.

38"My counsel to you is to let these men go and trouble them no longer. If what they do is a weak human idea, then it will come to nothing. 39But if Creator is with them, you will not be able to stand against them, and you may find yourselves fighting the Great Spirit!"

THE MESSAGE BEARERS ARE RELEASED

The Grand Council listened to his wisdom. 40They brought the message bearers back in, beat them with a whip, and instructed them to speak no longer in the name of Creator Sets Free (Jesus) *or represent his teachings.*

41So the message bearers left the Grand Council. Their hearts were glad that they had been considered worthy to suffer dishonor for the reputation of Creator Sets Free (Jesus). 42Day by day, in the sacred lodge and from house to house, they kept telling the good story about Creator Sets Free (Jesus) and showing the truth that he is the Chosen One.

6 ◀▸◀▸◀▸ ◀▸◀▸ ◀▸◀▸ ◀▸◀▸

THE SACRED FAMILY GROWS

1In those days, when the sacred family was growing in number, the Tribal Members who spoke the language of the Wisdom Seekers (Greeks) grumbled against the Tribal Members who spoke their own language. They complained *to the twelve* that their widows were being overlooked during the daily meals. 2So the twelve message bearers invited everyone to a council meeting.

They said to all, "It is not a good thing for us to give so much of our time to seeing over these meals. This gives us little or no time to teach about Creator's message. 3We want you to choose seven men of good reputation, who are filled with Creator's Spirit and wisdom, who will serve in our place. 4Then we can give ourselves to prayer and to the *teaching of Creator's* message."

5This seemed like a good thing to all the people, so they chose Many Feathers (Stephen), a man strong in his faith and full of the Holy Spirit. They also chose Lover of Horses (Philip), Head Singer (Prochorus), Man of Victory (Nicanor), Man of Honor (Timon), Stands Close By (Parmenas), and He Overcomes (Nicolas), an outsider from Stands Against (Antioch) who had been taken into the tribes of Wrestles with Creator (Israel). 6They stood these men before the message bearers, who then placed their hands on them and sent their voices to the Great Spirit.

7Creator's message was told far and wide. In Village of Peace (Jerusalem) the number of followers continued to grow, and many holy men believed and began to walk in this new way.

MANY FEATHERS TAKEN CAPTIVE

8Many Feathers (Stephen), who was filled with Creator's good medicine, was performing powerful signs among the people. 9But some men, from what is called the gathering house of Men Set

Free, opposed him. They were Tribal Members from Land of Power (Cyrene), Village of Defense (Alexandria), Turns Over (Cilicia), and from Land of the Rising Sun (Asia). **10**Even though they stood against Many Feathers (Stephen) with strong words, they were not strong enough to defeat the wisdom given to him by the Spirit.

11So they talked some men into telling lies about him.

"We have heard him speak against Drawn from the Water (Moses) and against the Great Spirit!" they said to the people, elders, and scroll keepers.

12This turned them against Many Feathers (Stephen), so they took hold of him and brought him before the Grand Council. **13**Then they brought in the ones who were falsely accusing him to speak to the council.

"This man keeps speaking against the sacred lodge and against our tribal law," they said to the Grand Council. **14**"We heard him say that Creator Sets Free (Jesus) from Seed Planter Village (Nazareth) will bring an end to this Holy Place and change the tribal traditions given to us by Drawn from the Water (Moses)."

15But all who were sitting in the council were staring at the face of Many Feathers (Stephen) because his face was *shining* like the face of a spirit-messenger.

MANY FEATHERS ANSWERS THE COUNCIL

1"Are these things spoken against you true?" the chief holy man asked him.

2He said to them, "Fellow Tribal Members, my brothers and fathers, hear what I have to say! The Great Mystery, the one who shines like the sun,

appeared to our ancestor Father of Many Nations (Abraham) while he was still living in Land Between Rivers (Mesopotamia), before he pitched his tipi at Mountain Where the Roads Cross (Haran).

3"'Leave your people and the land of your ancestors,' Creator instructed him, 'and go to the land that I will show to you.'[a]

4"So he went out from the people of the land of Field of Spirits (Chaldeans) and pitched his tipi at Mountain Where the Roads Cross (Haran) until his father crossed over to death. Creator then moved him to the land where you now live, **5**but he found no place to live there, not even a piece of ground to set his foot on. It was there that Creator promised him and his descendants a lasting home—even though he had no children.

6"The Great Spirit told him that his descendants would be wanderers in a land of strangers, who would force them to work hard for them and mistreat them for four hundred winters. **7**'But I will decide against this nation that forced them to be slaves,' Creator promised, 'and when they are set free, they will honor and serve me in this land.'[b]

8"Creator gave to Father of Many Nations (Abraham) the peace treaty that was sealed with the cutting of the flesh ceremony. Then Father of Many Nations (Abraham) became the father of He Made Us Laugh (Isaac) and, eight days after he was born, performed the cutting of the flesh ceremony on him. He Made Us Laugh (Isaac) became the father of Heel Grabber (Jacob), and he became the father of the twelve ancestors of our nation.

9"Our ancestors became jealous of Creator Gives More (Joseph) and sold him as a slave into Black Land (Egypt), but the

---

[a]**7:3** Genesis 12:1
[b]**7:7** Genesis 15:13-14

Great Spirit stood with him and [10]set him free from all his troubles. Creator then honored him in the eyes of Great House (Pharaoh), the ruler of Black Land (Egypt), who made him a ruler over Black Land (Egypt) and over his own family.

[11]"A time of hunger came upon Black Land (Egypt) and Lowland (Canaan). It was a time of great suffering for our ancestors, for they could not find enough food. [12]When Heel Grabber (Jacob) heard that there was grain in Black Land (Egypt), he sent his sons—our ancestors—there to trade for some. [13]When Heel Grabber (Jacob) sent them a second time, their brother, Creator Gives More (Joseph), *whom they had sold as a slave*, made himself known to them. That is how Great House (Pharaoh) learned about his family. [14]Then Creator Gives More (Joseph) sent a message to his father Heel Grabber (Jacob) and welcomed him and all his family—seventy-five in all—to come to Black Land (Egypt) *under his protection*.

[15]"So Heel Grabber (Jacob) pitched his tipi in Black Land (Egypt). It was there that he and our ancestors all crossed over to death. [16]Their bones were later moved to Burden Carrier (Shechem) and placed in a burial cave that Father of Many Nations (Abraham) had traded for from the sons of Red Donkey (Hamor).

[17]"*Many generations later*, when the time had come for the Great Spirit to keep his promise to Father of Many Nations (Abraham), the number of our people in Black Land (Egypt) had grown from small clans to a great tribe. [18]But a new ruler arose in Black Land (Egypt) who did not know about Creator Gives More (Joseph). [19]This new ruler oppressed our people and forced them to leave their newborn children outside to die, *to make our numbers smaller*.

[20]"It was during this time that Drawn from the Water (Moses) was born—a beautiful baby. Creator's eye was on this one! For three moons his family fed and cared for him. [21]When the time came that they had to leave him outside to die, the daughter of Great House (Pharaoh) rescued him and raised him as her own son. [22]So that is how Drawn from the Water (Moses) was taught all the wisdom of the people of Black Land (Egypt) and became powerful in his words and in all that he did.

[23]"When he was a full-grown man of forty winters, he decided to visit his tribal family—the descendants of Wrestles with Creator (Israel). [24]When he saw one of them being mistreated, he came to his defense and, on fire for justice, he struck down the man of Black Land (Egypt). [25]He thought his tribal family would understand that the Great Spirit had sent him to set them free—but they did not.

[26]"The following day Drawn from the Water (Moses) saw two Tribal Members fighting and tried to make peace between them.

"'Men!' he said to them. 'You are brothers. Why do you want to hurt each other?'

[27]"But the one who had attacked his fellow Tribal Member pushed Drawn from the Water (Moses) away from him.

"'Who made you our ruler and judge?' the man said *in anger*. [28]'Do you want to kill me the way you killed that man of Black Land (Egypt) yesterday?'

[29]"When he heard the man's words, Drawn from the Water (Moses) ran from there as fast as he could and went to live as an outsider among the people in Land of Conflict (Midian). It was there that he had two sons.

[30]"Forty winters later, in the desert wilderness near Mountain of Small Trees (Sinai), a spirit-messenger appeared to him in the flames of a burning thorn bush. [31]When Drawn from the Water (Moses) saw it, he wondered what it was. As he came close to see it better, he heard the voice of Creator.

[32]"'I am the Great Spirit of your ancestors. The Great Spirit of Father of Many Nations (Abraham), and of He Made Us Laugh (Isaac), and of Heel Grabber (Jacob).'[a]

"Drawn from the Water (Moses) began to tremble with fear, and he dared not to even look at the bush.

[33]"'Take your moccasins off and let your feet touch the earth,' Creator said to him, 'for the ground you are standing on is sacred.'"

With trembling hands Drawn from the Water (Moses) took off his moccasins. His knees grew weak as he stood before the fire of the Great Spirit and listened as Creator continued to speak.

[34]"'With my own eyes I have seen the way my people have suffered in Black Land (Egypt). I have heard their deep sighs and groanings, and I have come down to set them free. Come now, it is time to go, for I am sending you back to Black Land (Egypt).'[b]

[35]"So Creator sent back the same man who had been rejected by his own people when they said, 'Who made you our ruler and judge?' Through the spirit-messenger, who appeared to him in the burning thorn bush, the Great Spirit sent Drawn from the Water (Moses) to be both their ruler and the one who would pay the price to set them free. [36]With the

powerful signs and omens he performed in Black Land (Egypt), at the Red Sea, and in the desert wilderness, he set them free and guided them through the desert wilderness for forty winters.

[37]"Drawn from the Water (Moses) was the same one who said to the descendants of Wrestles with Creator (Israel), 'The Great Spirit will raise up a prophet like me from among your own people.'

[38]When our ancestors were gathered together in the desert wilderness, Drawn from the Water (Moses) was there with them. On the Mountain of Small Trees (Sinai) a spirit-messenger from Creator spoke to him. It was there that he and our ancestors were given the words of life, which have been handed down to us.

[39]"But our ancestors were not willing to follow his guidance. They turned away from him and turned their hearts back to the ways of Black Land (Egypt). [40]They said to Light Bearer (Aaron), *the brother of Drawn from the Water (Moses)*, 'We do not know what has become of Drawn from the Water (Moses), so carve for us an image of spirit-beings who can guide us.'

[41]"So they formed an image shaped like a calf, offered ceremonial sacrifices to it, and celebrated what their own hands had formed. [42]But the Maker of Life turned his face away from them and then handed them over to serve the evil warrior-spirits who rule in the dark spirit-world above and around us.

"In the book of the prophets, it says, 'Was it to me that you offered ceremonial sacrifices for forty winters in the desert?' Creator asked the family descendants of Wrestles with Creator (Israel). 'No! [43]Instead you carried an altar for Child-Burning Spirit (Moloch) and one for Wandering Star Spirit (Rephan). These were images you formed with your own

---

[a]7:32 Exodus 3:6
[b]7:34 Exodus 3:5,7,8,10

hands that you chose to serve. So, because you have chosen this path, I will make you walk it to and beyond Village of Confusion (Babylon).'[a]

44"Our ancestors carried the sacred tent of Creator's peace treaty with them during their desert wanderings. The Great Spirit gave Drawn from the Water (Moses) a vision for this sacred tent and the full instructions on how to make it. **45**When the time came to enter the Land of Promise, our ancestors carried this sacred tent with them as Creator Gives Freedom (Joshua) led the way. The Great Spirit removed the Outside Nations from the land, and our ancestors took possession of it. The sacred tent remained there until the days of Much Loved One (David). **46**Creator's great kindness rested on Much Loved One (David), so he asked whether he could build a lodge for the Great Spirit of Heel Grabber (Jacob). **47**But it was his son Stands in Peace (Solomon) who built a lodge for him.

48"But the One Above Us All does not live in lodges built by human hands, for the prophet *Creator Will Help Us (Isaiah)* has said, **49**'The spirit-world above is my seat of honor, and the earth below is a resting place for my feet. Could you build me a lodge like this?' says the Great Spirit. 'One that I could rest in? **50**Have I not formed all of these things with my own hands?'"[b]

A great boldness rose up in Many Feathers (Stephen) as he made his stand before the Grand Council. A look of fire came from his eyes as he raised his voice and spoke from his heart.

51"You are a bullheaded people! Your hearts of stone and deaf ears have made you no different from the nations around you. Just like your ancestors, you continue to oppose the Holy Spirit. **52**Did not your ancestors hunt down, torture, and kill the prophets who foretold the coming of the Upright One? You have now become his betrayers and murderers! **53**You, the ones to whom our tribal law was given by spirit-messengers, a law that you have not followed!"

THE GRAND COUNCIL HAS HIM KILLED

54When the council heard these words, they were filled with rage and ground their teeth in anger and frustration at him. **55**But then the Holy Spirit filled Many Feathers (Stephen) with a great vision. He looked up into the spirit-world above and saw a bright light shining from the Great Spirit, and standing next to him at his right hand was Creator Sets Free (Jesus)!

56"Look!" he said, "I can see into the spirit-world above! The sky has opened, and there at the right hand of the Great Spirit is the True Human Being!"

57But they put their hands over their ears and screamed out loud as they all rushed together to take hold of him. **58**They dragged him outside of the village and began to throw stones at him to kill him. Those who spoke against him laid their outer garments at the feet of a young man whose name was Man Who Questions (Saul).

59As they threw the stones at Many Feathers (Stephen), he was sending his voice to the Great Spirit.

"Creator Sets Free (Jesus) my Honored Chief," he called out to Creator. "Welcome my spirit *as I come to you!*"

60He then fell to his knees and cried out with a loud voice, "Honored One, do not hold this wrong against them!"

[a]**7:43** Amos 5:25-27
[b]**7:50** Isaiah 66:1, 2

Then, with a final breath, he fell asleep and crossed over to death.

A GREAT PERSECUTION BEGINS

¹Man Who Questions (Saul) stood in agreement with the death of Many Feathers (Stephen), and on that same day a great persecution of the sacred family in Village of Peace (Jerusalem) began. All except for the message bearers were scattered about in the territories of the Land of Promise (Judea) and High Place (Samaria). ²With loud cries and many tears, some good-hearted men buried Many Feathers (Stephen). ³But Man Who Questions (Saul) was bringing great harm to the sacred family. Going from house to house, he dragged both men and women away to put them in prison.

LOVER OF HORSES GOES TO HIGH PLACE

⁴Everywhere the ones who had been scattered went, they told others the story *about Creator Sets Free (Jesus)*. ⁵Lover of Horses (Philip) went to a village in High Place (Samaria) and began to tell them about the Chosen One. ⁶When the people heard him and saw the powerful signs that he did, they all agreed to listen to what Lover of Horses (Philip) had to say. ⁷The evil spirits shrieked out loud as he forced them out, and many who could not walk or move about were healed. ⁸This filled the hearts of the people of that village with great joy!

A BAD MEDICINE MAN BELIEVES

⁹In that same village there was a man named Man Who Hears (Simon), who had practiced bad medicineᵃ and had made

himself out to be someone great. ¹⁰He had a reputation among the people, both small and great, that he was the power of the Great Spirit. ¹¹His reputation came from the bad medicine he amazed them with.

¹²But when Lover of Horses (Philip) told them about Creator's good road and the name and reputation of Creator Sets Free (Jesus) the Chosen One, both men and women put their trust in him and participated in the purification ceremony.ᵇ ¹³Even Man Who Hears (Simon) believed and participated in the ceremony. After the ceremony he stayed close to Lover of Horses (Philip), for he was amazed at the powerful signs and miracles he saw.

SOME MESSAGE BEARERS COME TO PRAY

¹⁴The message bearers in Village of Peace (Jerusalem) heard that the people in High Place (Samaria) had welcomed Creator's message. So they sent Stands on the Rock (Peter) and He Shows Goodwill (John) to them. ¹⁵The two went there and prayed for them to receive the Holy Spirit, ¹⁶for they had only participated in the purification ceremonyᵇ in the name our Honored Chief, Creator Sets Free (Jesus), and the Spirit had not yet come down on them.

MAN WHO HEARS LEARNS A LESSON

¹⁷When Stands on the Rock (Peter) and He Shows Goodwill (John) placed their hands on them *and prayed*, they received the Holy Spirit. ¹⁸But Man Who Hears (Simon), when he saw that the Holy Spirit was given through the hands of the message bearers, offered them money to get this power.

¹⁹"Give me also this power," he said to them, "so that anyone I place my hands on will receive the Holy Spirit."

ᵃ8:9 Lit. *magic or sorcery*

ᵇ8:12, 16 Baptism

²⁰"Both you and your money are on a path to a bad end," Stands on the Rock (Peter) warned him, "because you thought Creator's gift could be bought with money! ²¹This message has found no home in you, for your heart is not straight before the Great Spirit. ²²Turn away from these evil thoughts and pray that, if possible, Creator will forgive you for this wrong way of thinking. ²³For I see that a bitter root has poisoned you and an evil power has captured your thinking."

²⁴"Pray to Creator for me!" Man Who Hears (Simon) said *with a trembling voice*, "so that nothing you have said will happen to me."

²⁵So Stands on the Rock (Peter) and He Shows Goodwill (John) continued to speak Creator's words of truth and then returned to Village of Peace (Jerusalem). On the way they told the good story about Creator Sets Free (Jesus) to many more people in the villages of High Place (Samaria).

A SPIRIT-MESSENGER SPEAKS

²⁶A spirit-messenger from Creator came and spoke to Lover of Horses (Philip).

"Rise up," the spirit-messenger told him, "and go south on the road that will take you from Village of Peace (Jerusalem) to Strong Place (Gaza)."

This road goes through the desert wilderness. ²⁷⁻²⁸*So Lover of Horses (Philip) followed the guidance of the spirit-messenger.* He got up and began to go toward the south.

MAN FROM EYES OF FIRE

While on the road, he came across a man from Eyes of Fire (Ethiopia). He had great authority because he was a trusted official[a] of the female chief of Eyes of Fire (Ethiopia) and managed all her wealth and possessions. This man had traveled to Village of Peace (Jerusalem) to participate in the lodge ceremonies and was returning home.

As this man was traveling, he was sitting in a fancy horse-drawn covered wagon[b] and reading from the Sacred Teachings of the prophet Creator Will Help Us (Isaiah).

²⁹The Spirit *of Creator* said to Lover of Horses (Philip), "Go and walk next to this covered wagon."

³⁰So Lover of Horses (Philip) ran to where the man was and overheard him reading from the prophecies of Creator Will Help Us (Isaiah).

"Do you understand what you are reading?" Lover of Horses (Philip) asked him.

³¹"How can I," the man answered, "unless someone guides me?"

So he welcomed Lover of Horses (Philip) to sit with him. ³²The man was reading these words from the Sacred Teachings: "Like a sheep led to the slaughter or like a lamb being sheared, he was silent and did not open his mouth. ³³He was shamed and denied a fair trial. No one even imagined he had a future, for he was cut down in the prime of his life."[c]

³⁴"I ask you," the man said to Lover of Horses (Philip), "is the prophet speaking about himself or someone else?"

³⁵Then Lover of Horses (Philip) *took a deep breath*, opened his mouth, and began from that prophecy[d] to tell him the good story about Creator Sets Free (Jesus). ³⁶As they traveled the road, they came to a watering hole.

---

given positions of trust by ancient rulers.
[b]**8:27-28** Lit. *chariot*
[c]**8:33** Isaiah 53:7-8
[d]**8:35** Lit. *Scripture*

[a]**8:27-28** These trusted officials, called eunuchs, were men who could not physically father children. They were often

PURIFICATION CEREMONY

"Look!" the man said, "There is much water here. Why should I not participate in the purification ceremony?"[a]

37"If from your heart you truly believe," Lover of Horses (Philip) answered, "you may."

"I believe that Creator Sets Free (Jesus) is the Son of the Great Spirit," the man replied.[b]

38He instructed them to stop the carriage, and they both waded out into the water, and Lover of Horses (Philip) performed the purification ceremony[a] for him. **39**When they came up from the water, Creator's Spirit snatched Lover of Horses (Philip) away from the man's sight. So he continued on his journey with a glad heart.

But what happened to Lover of Horses (Philip)?

40He found himself in Strong Fort (Azotus), and as he walked throughout the territory, he told everyone the good story until he arrived at Chief Village (Caesarea).

A RAMPAGE OF THREATS AND MURDER

1Man Who Questions (Saul) was on a rampage, breathing threats and murder against the followers of our Honored Chief, Creator Sets Free (Jesus). He went to the chief holy man **2**and asked for written documents to give to the tribal gathering houses in the village of Silent Weaver (Damascus). This would permit him to take any followers of the Way, men or women, bind them in chains, and take them to Village of Peace (Jerusalem).

---

[a]**8:36, 38** Baptism
[b]**8:37** Most ancient manuscripts leave out verse 37.

A VOICE FROM THE WORLD ABOVE

3So on his way to Silent Weaver (Damascus), just as he came near the village, without warning a light from the spirit-world above shone down all around him. **4**He fell to the ground and then heard a voice speaking.

"Man Who Questions (Saul), Man Who Questions (Saul)," the voice called out his name twice, "why are you pursuing and mistreating me?"

Man Who Questions (Saul) trembled with fear at the sound of the voice that was coming from the blinding light.

5"Honored One," he asked, "who are you?"

"I am Creator Sets Free (Jesus)," the voice answered, "the one you are pursuing and mistreating. **6**Now stand to your feet and go into the village. There you will be told what you must do."

7The men who were traveling with him stood silent, saying nothing, for they heard the voice but saw no one. **8**Man Who Questions (Saul) stood to his feet and opened his eyes, but he could not see. The ones who were with him took him by the hand and guided him into the village of Silent Weaver (Damascus). **9**He stayed there without eating or drinking, and after three days he still could not see.

GUIDANCE FROM A SACRED VISION

10Now in that village there was a man named Creator Shows Kindness (Ananias), a follower of Creator Sets Free (Jesus). He was given a sacred vision from the Great Spirit.

"Creator Shows Kindness (Ananias)!" the voice called out to him in the vision.

"I am here, Honored One!" he answered back.

11"Get up and go to the house of Speaks Well Of (Judas), on the village pathway called Straight. There you must ask for a man from Tree Village (Tarsus) named Man Who Questions (Saul). He is praying right now. [12]In a vision he has seen a man with your name come to him and lay his hands on him so that he might see again."

[13]"Honored One," Creator Shows Kindness (Ananias) answered him back, "I have heard of this man and how much harm he has done to your holy people in Village of Peace (Jerusalem). [14]The head holy men have given him the authority to put in prison all who call upon your name."

[15]"Go to him," Creator Sets Free (Jesus) answered him, "for I have chosen this man to represent me to the Outside Nations, to their rulers and to the tribes of Wrestles with Creator (Israel). [16]I will show him how much he must suffer in order to represent who I am."

HE FOLLOWS THE VISION

[17]Creator Shows Kindness (Ananias) followed the guidance given to him in the vision and went to the house, and there he placed his hands on Man Who Questions (Saul).

"Man Who Questions (Saul), my brother," he said to him, "Creator Sets Free (Jesus), our Honored Chief, the one who appeared to you on the road, has sent me to you so you may see again and be filled with his Holy Spirit."

[18]Right then something like fish scales fell from his eyes and he could see again! Then he stood up and went to participate in the purification ceremony.[a] [19]After that he ate some food and his strength returned. He stayed in the village of Silent Weaver (Damascus) for a few days with some followers of Creator Sets Free (Jesus).

---

[a]9:18 Baptism

HE BEGINS TO TELL THE STORY

[20]Right away he went to the local gathering houses and began to tell them that Creator Sets Free (Jesus) is the Son of the Great Spirit, [21]and all who heard him could not believe their ears!

"Is this not the man who in Village of Peace (Jerusalem) was waging war against the ones who called upon this name?" they asked. "Did he not come here to take them bound to the head holy men?"

[22]But Man Who Questions (Saul) became more powerful in his speech, proving that Creator Sets Free (Jesus) was the Chosen One, leaving the local tribal leaders confused and unable to argue against him.

THE PLOT TO KILL MAN WHO QUESTIONS

[23]A few days later the tribal leaders formed a council to put him to death, [24]but he found out what they were planning. They kept watch day and night at the village gates so they could take and kill him. [25]But some of his followers snuck him out at night by lowering him down in a basket from an opening in the village walls.

[26]He went to Village of Peace (Jerusalem) and tried to join together with the followers of Creator Sets Free (Jesus), but they were afraid and did not trust that he was a true follower. [27]But Son of Comfort (Barnabas) came alongside him and took him to the message bearers.

Man Who Questions (Saul) then told them the story of what happened on the road, how he had seen and heard the voice of our Honored Chief. He also told them that he had been representing Creator Sets Free (Jesus) and speaking out boldly to the Tribal Members in the village of Silent Weaver (Damascus).

SPEAKING BOLDLY

²⁸So Man Who Questions (Saul) stayed with them. He walked the roads all around Village of Peace (Jerusalem) representing Creator Sets Free (Jesus) by speaking out boldly about him.

²⁹He spoke to the Greek-speaking tribal leaders arguing with them, but it just made them look for a way to kill him. ³⁰When the members of the sacred family heard about this, they took him away to Chief Village (Caesarea) and from there sent him to Tree Village (Tarsus).

³¹Finally, the sacred family in the territory of the Land of Promise (Judea), Circle of Nations (Galilee), and High Place (Samaria) were at peace and growing strong. As they walked in a sacred manner with great respect for Creator, the Holy Spirit comforted them and made their numbers grow.

A POWERFUL HEALING

³²Stands on the Rock (Peter) was walking the road from place to place. On his journey he came upon some of Creator's holy ones who lived in the village of Almond Tree (Lydda). ³³There he found a man named Man of Honor (Aeneas), who could not move his body and had been unable to leave his bed for eight winters.

³⁴"Man of Honor (Aeneas)," Stands on the Rock (Peter) said to him, "Creator Sets Free (Jesus) the Chosen One heals you! Stand up and fold up your bed blankets."

The man stood right up, ³⁵and all who lived in Almond Tree (Lydda) and those who lived in Flatland (Sharon) saw him and turned their hearts to Creator's Honored One.

A RESPECTED WOMAN CROSSES OVER

³⁶Now in the nearby Village of Beauty (Joppa) there lived a follower of Creator Sets Free (Jesus) whose name was Deer Woman (Tabitha), which is translated into our tribal language as Deer Eyes (Dorcas). She was a doer of many good deeds and always gave to the ones who had little. ³⁷During the time that Stands on the Rock (Peter) was in Almond Tree (Lydda), she became ill and crossed over to death. So they ceremonially washed her body and laid her in an upstairs room.

³⁸Since Almond Tree (Lydda) is near to Village of Beauty (Joppa), the followers there sent two men to Stands on the Rock (Peter), begging him to come right away.

³⁹Stands on the Rock (Peter) got right up and went with the men. When they arrived, they took him to where her body lay in the upstairs room. The widows came and stood next to him. The tears rolled down their faces as they showed him the beautiful garments Deer Eyes (Dorcas) had made when she was with them.

POWER OVER DEATH

⁴⁰Stands on the Rock (Peter) sent them all outside. He then fell to his knees and sent his voice to the Great Spirit. After he prayed, he turned toward the dead body of the woman.

"Deer Woman (Tabitha)," he said to her, "get up!"

She opened her eyes, and when she saw Stands on the Rock (Peter), she sat up. ⁴¹He reached out his hand to her and helped her up. He then called all the holy ones and the widows and stood her before them. She was alive! ⁴²Word of this spread throughout all of Village of Beauty (Joppa), and many put their trust in our Honored Chief, *Creator Sets Free (Jesus)*.

⁴³Then Stands on the Rock (Peter) stayed a good number of days in Village

of Beauty (Joppa) in the home of Hearing Man (Simon), a tanner of leather.

10

A POWERFUL VISION

1Now there lived a man in Chief Village (Caesarea) whose name was Little Horn (Cornelius). He was a head soldier in the Young Bulls (Italian) band of the People of Iron (Romans). **2**He was a spiritual man who had deep respect for the Great Spirit. He, along with all his family, gave with a big heart to the poor and prayed to Creator at all times.

3One day, in the middle of the afternoon, he had a sacred vision. He could clearly see a spirit-messenger from Creator coming toward him.

"Little Horn (Cornelius)!" the messenger said to him.

4Little Horn (Cornelius) could only stare at the spirit-messenger and tremble with fear.

"What is it you want, Honored One?" he asked the messenger.

"Your prayers and gifts of kindness have been remembered. They have risen like sweet-smelling smoke to the Great Spirit. **5**Now you must send messengers to Village of Beauty (Joppa) to find One Who Hears (Simon), who is also named Stands on the Rock (Peter) and ask him to come to your home. **6**He is lodging at a house near the great waters at the home of Hearing Man (Simon), the tanner of hides."

7After the spirit-messenger who spoke to him had left, Little Horn (Cornelius) called two servants and a trusted soldier from the ones who were under his command. **8**After he told them everything they needed to know, he sent them to Village of Beauty (Joppa).

ANOTHER SACRED VISION

9On the next day, as the messengers were traveling and coming close to the village, Stands on the Rock (Peter) climbed up onto the *flat* roof of the house to send his voice to Creator. It was about midday. **10**He became hungry and wanted something to eat. As they were cooking the food, he fell into a trance and had a sacred vision.

11He saw an opening in the sky and something like a large, soft blanket that was being lowered to the ground by its four corners. **12**On the blanket were all kinds of four-legged animals, creeping things from the ground, and winged ones who soar in the sky.

13"Stands on the Rock (Peter), rise up!" a voice said to him. "Kill and eat."

> *This would have been a hard thing for Stands on the Rock (Peter) to hear, because their tribal law forbade them to ceremonially offer or eat any unclean animal, and many of these animals were unclean or impure.*

14"I cannot, O Honored One!" he answered. "I have never eaten anything impure or unclean."

15Then the Voice spoke to him a second time, "What the Great Spirit has made clean, you must not consider impure."

16This was repeated three times, and then the blanket was taken right back up into the spirit-world above.

THE MESSENGERS FROM LITTLE HORN ARRIVE

17Stands on the Rock (Peter) was troubled, trying to understand the meaning of the vision. At the same time the men who were sent by Little Horn (Cornelius) stood at the gate **18**and called out to see whether Stands on the Rock (Peter) was lodging there.

[19]While Stands on the Rock (Peter) was meditating on the vision, the Spirit said to him, "Look, three men are searching for you. [20]Now rise up, go down into the house, and do not hesitate to go with these men, because I have sent them."

[21]So Stands on the Rock (Peter) went down from the rooftop to where the men were and said to them, "I am the one you are looking for. What is it you want from me?"

[22]"Little Horn (Cornelius), who is a head soldier of the People of Iron (Romans), sent us. He is a man with a good heart who has deep respect for the Great Spirit and is well spoken of by all in your tribal nation. He was instructed by a sacred spirit-messenger to send messengers to you, to ask you to come to his house so he can hear your words."

HE GOES WITH THE MESSENGERS

[23]Stands on the Rock (Peter) then welcomed them into the house and gave them lodging for the night. The next day he awoke and set out with them, and some of his *spiritual* brothers from Village of Beauty (Joppa) also went along.

[24]On the following day they came to Chief Village (Caesarea). Little Horn (Cornelius), who was waiting for them to come, had gathered together many relatives and close friends.

IN THE HOUSE OF OUTSIDERS

[25]As soon as Stands on the Rock (Peter) came into the house, Little Horn (Cornelius) dropped to his knees and began to pray to him.[a] [26]But Stands on the Rock (Peter) made him stand to his feet.

"Stand up!" he said to him, "I am only a weak human being, just as you are."

---

[a]10:25 Lit. *worship him*

[27]Stands on the Rock (Peter) kept talking to him as they went inside the house. There he saw all the people who had gathered to hear him.

This was the first time Stands on the Rock (Peter) had ever been in the home of someone from another nation. These people were considered to be outsiders and unholy. This was new territory that he was walking into, so he took a deep breath and began to speak to them.

[28]"As all of you must know," he said to them, "it is against our law for a Tribal Member like myself to have anything to do with someone from an Outside Nation. But Creator has helped me to see that I should not consider anyone to be impure or unclean. [29]So when I was asked to come here, I did not hesitate to come. So tell me, why have you sent for me?"

LITTLE HORN TELLS HIS STORY

[30]Little Horn (Cornelius) spoke up and said to him, "It has now been four days to this very hour. In the middle of the afternoon, while I was praying, I looked up and saw a man standing before me, and his garments were shining bright.

[31]"'Little Horn (Cornelius),' he said to me, 'your prayer has been heard, and your gifts to the poor have risen like sweet-smelling smoke before the Great Spirit. He has remembered what you have done. [32]Send messengers to Village of Beauty (Joppa) to One Who Hears (Simon), who is also named Stands on the Rock (Peter), and ask him to come. He is lodging at the house of Hearing Man (Simon), a tanner of hides, who lives near the great waters.'

[33]"I sent for you right away, and I thank you for coming. So we have all gathered here, in the sight of the Great

Spirit, to hear what Creator has instructed you to tell us."

STANDS ON THE ROCK SPEAKS TO ALL

34Stands on the Rock (Peter) *took another deep breath, opened his mouth, and began.*

"I speak from my heart," he said to them. "I now see that Creator does not favor one human being over another. **35**He accepts people of all nations who have a deep respect for him and do what is right.

36"This is the message he has given to the tribes of Wrestles with Creator (Israel), a message of peace that comes through Creator Sets Free (Jesus) the Chosen One. He is the one who has been honored above all others!

37"You must have heard about it. It all began with the purification ceremony[a] announced by He Shows Goodwill (John) in Circle of Nations (Galilee). From there his message has spread *like wildfire* throughout the Land of Promise (Judea).

38"It is the story of how the Great Spirit chose Creator Sets Free (Jesus) from Seed Planter Village (Nazareth), and how the power of Holy Spirit came to rest upon him. How he walked the land, with Creator at his side, doing good and healing all who were pushed down and crushed by the evil trickster.

39"We are his message bearers, telling the truth about all that he did in the territory of our Tribal Members and in Village of Peace (Jerusalem), where they had him killed by hanging him on a tree. **40**He is the one whom Creator, on the third day, brought back to life from the world of the dead. He then appeared, **41**not to everyone, but to us, the ones he chose ahead of time to tell the truth about what

---

[a]**10:37, 47, 48** Baptism

we saw, we who ate and drank with him after he returned to life from the dead.

42"He has instructed us to tell this story in a sacred manner, so that all people will know that Creator Sets Free (Jesus) has been chosen by the Great Spirit to decide the fate of the living and the dead. **43**All the prophets *from long ago* have spoken of him, that all who put their trust in him will be released from their bad hearts and broken ways through his name."

THE HOLY SPIRIT COMES DOWN

44While Stands on the Rock (Peter) was still speaking, the Holy Spirit came down upon all who were listening to his words. **45-46**They began to speak in *new* languages and give praise and honor to the Great Spirit. This amazed the Tribal Members who came with Stands on the Rock (Peter), for they could hear *and see with their own eyes* that even on people from Outside Nations, the gift of the Holy Spirit had been poured out.

Then Stands on the Rock (Peter) said to all, **47**"Who can now refuse water for these people to participate in the purification ceremony?[a] For they have received the Holy Spirit in the same manner that we did."

48So he instructed them to participate in the purification ceremony[a] in the name of the Chosen One Creator Sets Free (Jesus) *and all he represents, welcoming them into the sacred family.*

After that they asked Stands on the Rock (Peter) to remain with them for a number of days.

11

STANDS ON THE ROCK IS QUESTIONED

1Back in the Land of Promise (Judea), the message bearers and other followers of

Creator Sets Free (Jesus) heard that people from the Outside Nations had welcomed Creator's message. ²So when Stands on the Rock (Peter) returned to Village of Peace (Jerusalem), the *strict* Tribal Members there began to question him.

³"How is it that you went into the house of Outsiders and ate with them?" they asked.

STANDS ON THE ROCK RETELLS HIS STORY
⁴So he told them, step by step, the journey he had been on.

⁵"In the Village of Beauty (Joppa), where I was lodging, I was sending my voice to the Great Spirit. I went into a trance and was given a sacred vision. I saw something that looked like a large, soft blanket coming down from the sky, being lowered by its four corners. As it came near to me, ⁶I looked into it wondering what it was. I saw four-legged animals of the land, wild animals, snakes, creeping things, and winged ones who soar in the sky.

⁷"Then I heard a Voice say, 'Stands on the Rock (Peter), kill and eat.'

⁸"'I cannot! O Honored One,' I answered, 'I have never eaten anything impure or unclean.'

⁹"Then the Voice from the spirit-world above spoke to me a second time, 'If Creator has made it clean, then you must not consider it impure.'

¹⁰"This happened three times. Then the blanket was taken back up into the spirit-world above. ¹¹Right then three men who had been sent to me from Chief Village (Caesarea) arrived at the house where we were lodging. ¹²The Spirit told me to have no doubts about going with them. So I and six *spiritual* brothers went to the man's house and were welcomed inside.

¹³"The man of the house told us how he had seen a spirit-messenger standing in his house. The messenger told him to send a message to Village of Beauty (Joppa) to One Who Hears (Simon), who is also named Stands on the Rock (Peter), ¹⁴who will tell you and all your family and friends how to be set free and made whole.

¹⁵"Just as I was beginning to speak to them, the Holy Spirit came down upon them in the same manner he did for us at first. ¹⁶Then I remembered what our Wisdomkeeper had said to us: 'He Shows Goodwill (John) performed the purification ceremony[a] with water, but you will participate in the purification ceremony[a] with the Holy Spirit.'

¹⁷"If Creator gave them the same gift he gave to us when we put our trust in our Honored Chief Creator Sets Free (Jesus), the Chosen One, who was I to stand in the way of the Great Spirit?"

¹⁸When they heard these words, they sat there in silence with nothing to say. Then they gave honor to Creator.

"So then," they said *with wondering voices*, "the Great Spirit has also given the Outside Nations the way to return to the path of life."

TELLING THE GOOD STORY
¹⁹The ones who had been scattered because of the persecution that began when Many Feathers (Stephen) was killed had made their way as far as Land of Palm Trees (Phoenicia), Island of Flowers (Cyprus), and Stands Against (Antioch). They were telling the good story, but only to the Tribal Members, not to anyone from the Outside Nations.

²⁰But there were others, men from Island of Flowers (Cyprus) and Land of

---

[a]11:16 Baptism

Power (Cyrene), who came to Stands Against (Antioch) and began to tell the Wisdom Seekers (Greeks) from Outside Nations about Creator Sets Free (Jesus), our Honored Chief. 21The strong hand of the Great Spirit was with them, and a large number of them trusted in our Honored Chief.

22Word of this came to the ears of the sacred family in Village of Peace (Jerusalem). 23-24So they sent to them Son of Comfort (Barnabas), a good-hearted man who was full of the Holy Spirit and faith. When he saw Creator's great kindness at work in them, it made his heart glad. He then spoke wise counsel to them, telling them to have brave hearts and to stand strong, looking to our Honored Chief.

> There were so many new followers there that Son of Comfort (Barnabas) knew he needed more help.

25So he went to Tree Village (Tarsus) to look for Man Who Questions (Saul). 26When he found him, he took him back to Stands Against (Antioch). For a whole year they gathered there, together with the sacred family. There they taught a large number of people. It was in the village of Stands Against (Antioch) that the followers of Creator Sets Free (Jesus) were first called Followers of the Chosen One.

27It was in those days that some prophets came down from Village of Peace (Jerusalem) to the village of Stands Against (Antioch). 28One of them, named Grasshopper (Agabus), foretold by the Spirit that soon there would be a shortage of food all over the territory of the People of Iron (Romans). This happened during the rule of Walks with a Limp (Claudius).

29So the followers who lived in Stands Against (Antioch) decided to send help to

the sacred family in the Land of Promise (Judea)—as much as they could spare. 30Son of Comfort (Barnabas) and Man Who Questions (Saul) hand-carried the gifts to the elders.

12 ▷▶◁▷◀▷◀▷◀▷◀▷◀◁▷◀◁

MORE PERSECUTION

1During those days, Looks Brave (Herod)[a] used his power as chief to bring harm to the sacred family. 2He had He Takes Over (James) the brother of He Shows Goodwill (John) killed with the long knife. 3When he found out that this pleased the corrupt tribal leaders, he decided to take Stands on the Rock (Peter) captive also—during the Festival of Bread Without Yeast. 4After capturing him, he put him in prison and assigned sixteen soldiers to guard him—four at a time. Looks Brave (Herod) planned to bring him before the people during the Passover festival.

RESCUED BY A SPIRIT-MESSENGER

5But while Stands on the Rock (Peter) was in prison, the sacred family prayed for him with strong hearts as they sent their voices to the Great Spirit.

6On the night before Looks Brave (Herod) was planning to bring him before the people, Stands on the Rock (Peter) was sound asleep between two soldiers who were guarding him. He was bound with two chains, and more guards were guarding the prison gate.

7Out of nowhere a spirit-messenger from Creator appeared, and a light shone all around them. The spirit-messenger nudged Stands on the Rock (Peter) in his side to wake him up.

---

[a]12:1 This is the great-grandson of Herod the Great, who tried to kill Jesus when he was a baby.

"Get up quickly!" the messenger instructed him, and right then the chains fell from his hands. **8**"Tighten your sash and put on your moccasins," he added. He did so, and the messenger said, "Now put on your outer garment and follow me."

9Stands on the Rock (Peter) went out with the spirit-messenger, but he thought he was having a vision and did not know it was really happening. **10**They had passed by the first guard, then the second, when they came to the iron gate that leads into the village. The gate opened by itself, they walked down a village path, and right then the messenger left him.

He rubbed his eyes and looked around and finally realized that he was not in a vision. This was really happening!

11After his thoughts cleared up, he said to himself, "Now I know for sure that Creator has sent his spirit-messenger to rescue me from the hand of Looks Brave (Herod) and from all that the Tribal Members thought would happen to me."

AT THE HOUSE OF SOBER TEARS

12So Stands on the Rock (Peter) went to the home of Sober Tears (Mary), the mother of Walks in Kindness (John), who is also named War Club (Mark). Many of the sacred family had gathered there praying *for him.*

13He knocked at the gate outside the door, and a servant girl named Rose Bush (Rhoda) went to answer. **14**When she recognized the voice of Stands on the Rock (Peter), she ran back inside without opening the gate and told everyone it was Stands on the Rock (Peter) who was at the gate.

15"You have lost your mind!" they said to her, but she assured them that it was he.

"It must be his spirit-messenger," they kept saying to each other.

16Meanwhile Stands on the Rock (Peter) was still knocking at the gate. When they opened the door and saw him at the gate, they could not believe their eyes. **17**Stands on the Rock (Peter) motioned to them with his hand to be silent. He then told them how Creator had rescued him from the prison.

"Tell He Leads the Way (James) and the others what has happened," he said to them. He then left to go to another place.

18The next morning the soldiers who were guarding Stands on the Rock (Peter) were in a big uproar, for he was gone! **19**Looks Brave (Herod) came and searched for him also. When he could not find him, he questioned the guards and then ordered them to be put to death. He then traveled down from the Land of Promise (Judea) to Chief Village (Caesarea) and stayed there.

EATEN BY WORMS

20Looks Brave (Herod) was angry with the people of Rock Land (Tyre) and Hunting Grounds (Sidon), so they sent some messengers to him to make peace, for their people depended on the food that came from the land Looks Brave (Herod) ruled over. The messengers won the favor of Budding Branch (Blastus), the most trusted servant of Looks Brave (Herod).

21After that Looks Brave (Herod) chose a day to make his decision about this matter. He put on his chiefly regalia and sat down on the Seat of Deciding to speak to the people using many words.

22The crowd began to shout, "This is not the voice of a man, but of a great spirit!"

²³Because Looks Brave (Herod) did not give the honor over to the Great Spirit, a spirit-messenger from Creator struck him down. He was then eaten by worms and crossed over to death.

²⁴Meanwhile, Creator's message continued to grow strong among the people and to spread far and wide. ²⁵*Their task was now complete*, so Son of Comfort (Barnabas) and Man Who Questions (Saul) returned from Village of Peace (Jerusalem) to Stands Against (Antioch), taking with them Walks in Kindness (John) who was also named War Club (Mark).

13

PROPHETS AND TEACHERS

¹There were prophets and teachers among the sacred family that gathered in Stands Against (Antioch). There was Son of Comfort (Barnabas), Creator Hears (Simeon) who was also called Black Man (Niger), also Bright Light (Lucius) from Land of Power (Cyrene), Man of Comfort (Manaen) who was taken into the family of Chief Looks Brave (Herod),ᵃ and Man Who Questions (Saul).

²They were performing their ceremonies to Creator and going without food when the Holy Spirit spoke to them, "Set apart Son of Comfort (Barnabas) and Man Who Questions (Saul), so they can do what I have chosen them to do."

NEW MESSAGE BEARERS SENT OUT

³So after they continued to go without food and pray, they laid their hands on them and sent them on their way. ⁴Then Son of Comfort (Barnabas) and Man Who Questions (Saul) followed the guidance of

---

ᵃ**13:1** Lit. *Herod the tetrarch*, meaning ruler of one of four parts of a territory

the Holy Spirit and journeyed to Crashing Waves (Seleucia). From there they canoed to Island of Flowers (Cyprus).

⁵When they came to Village of Salt (Salamis), they went to the local tribal gathering house. There, with the help of Walks in Kindness (John), they began to share Creator's message with them.

CONFLICT WITH A FALSE PROPHET

⁶They traveled the whole island as far as Foaming Water (Paphos). There they met a man named Son of He Sets Free (Bar-Jesus), a Tribal Member and false prophet who practiced bad medicine. ⁷He was with the local official of the People of Iron (Romans), whose name was Small One Who Serves (Sergius Paulus), a man of understanding, who had sent for Son of Comfort (Barnabas) and Man Who Questions (Saul) because he wanted to hear Creator's message.

⁸But the bad medicine man, who was also called Wise One (Elymas) in the local language, opposed them and tried to turn the official from believing their message. ⁹Then Man Who Questions (Saul), with the power of the Holy Spirit, looked straight into his eyes.

¹⁰"You son of the evil trickster!" he spoke sharply to Wise One (Elymas). "You who speak with a forked tongue! You are the enemy of all that is good and right. When will you ever stop making Creator's straight paths crooked? ¹¹Keep your eyes open while you can. Creator's hand is against you, and for a while your eyes will not see, even the light of the sun."

As soon as Man Who Questions (Saul) finished speaking, a mist of darkness came upon the man, and he stumbled about looking for someone to take him by the hand. ¹²When the official saw what happened, he believed and was struck with wonder at the lesson Creator had given.

THEY CONTINUE THEIR JOURNEY
[13]At Foaming Water (Paphos) Small Man (Paul)[a] and the ones who were with him set out in their canoes and journeyed to Earth Village (Perga) in the territory of Many Tribes (Pamphylia). From there Walks in Kindness (John) left them and returned to Village of Peace (Jerusalem).

SMALL MAN TELLS THE GOOD STORY
[14]But Small Man (Paul) and the others continued on and went to another village, named Stands Against (Antioch) in the territory of Tree Sap (Pisidia). On the next Day of Resting they went into the local tribal gathering house and sat down. [15]After the people read out loud from the Law and the Prophets, the headmen of the gathering house sent a message to them.

"Fellow Tribal Members," the message said, "If there is anything you want to say to encourage the people, please speak up."

[16]So Small Man (Paul) stood up, motioned with his hands, and said, "Men from the tribes of Wrestles with Creator (Israel) and all who have deep respect for the Great Spirit, listen to me now! [17]The Great Spirit of our people chose to make our ancestors into a great nation when they were still slaves in Black Land (Egypt). He then lifted them up with his strong arm and led them out into the desert wilderness. [18]There he put up with their ways for forty winters. [19]He then defeated seven nations in the territory of Lowland (Canaan) and gave their land to the tribes of Wrestles with Creator (Israel) for the generations that would follow. [20]All this took about four hundred and fifty winters in all.

"After that he gave them spiritual leaders[b] until the days of the prophet Creator Hears Him (Samuel). [21]When they asked for an earthly chief, Creator gave them Man Who Questions (Saul) the son of Sets His Trap (Kish) from the tribe of Son of My Right Hand (Benjamin), who was their chief for forty winters.

[22]"After removing him as chief, Creator chose Much Loved One (David) to be the chief of our ancestors. This is what he said about him: 'I have found one who makes my heart glad, who will do all that I ask of him. He is Much Loved One (David) son of Original Man (Jesse).'

[23]"Creator has kept his promise to the tribes of Wrestles with Creator (Israel) and has raised up a descendant of Much Loved One (David) to be the one to set his people free *from their bad hearts and wrongdoings*. This descendant is Creator Sets Free (Jesus).

[24]"Before Creator Sets Free (Jesus) came to us, the Great Spirit first sent He Shows Goodwill (John), who announced a purification ceremony[c] to return our tribes to the right way of thinking and walking. [25]When the work of He Shows Goodwill (John) was coming to an end, he said many times, 'Do you think I am the Chosen One? I am not. I am not worthy to untie the moccasins of the one who is coming after I am done.'

[26]"My fellow members of the sacred family, descendants of Father of Many Nations (Abraham), and all who have deep respect for the Great Spirit, it is to *all of us* that this message has been given. This

---

[a]**13:13** This is where Saul takes on the name Paul. Paul is the Greek form of Saul.

[b]**13:20** Lit. *judges*
[c]**13:24** Baptism

is a message that will set us free and make us whole.

27-28"It was the people who live in Village of Peace (Jerusalem), and their leaders, who had him put to death because they did not recognize him. Even though they failed to understand the words of the prophets, which are read out loud on every Day of Resting, they fulfilled these words when they had Spear of the Great Waters (Pilate) put him to death—even though he had done nothing wrong.

29"Then, when they did all that was foretold about him, they lowered him from the tree and laid him in a burial cave. 30But the Great Spirit brought him back to life, 31and for many days he was seen by the ones who had walked the road with him from Circle of Nations (Galilee) to Village of Peace (Jerusalem). They are now his truth tellers to the tribes of Wrestles with Creator (Israel).

THE PROMISE HAS COME TRUE

32"Today, we are here to tell you this good story that completes the promise that was made to our ancestors. 33The Giver of Life has made his promise come true for us, their descendants, by raising up Creator Sets Free (Jesus), just as it says in the second Sacred Song (psalm), 'You are my Son. Today I have become your Father.'ª

34"To show that he would raise up Creator Sets Free (Jesus) from the dead, to never die again, he said, 'I will gift you with the sacred promises spoken to Much Loved One (David).'ᵇ

35"And, here is another verse from the book of Sacred Songs (Psalms), where it

says, 'You will not let the body of your Holy One return to the ground.'ᶜ

36"It is clear that Much Loved One (David), after he served Creator's purpose for the people of his own day, crossed over into the death-sleep, was buried with his ancestors, and his body returned to the ground. 37But the body of the one that Creator raised up did not return to the ground.

FINAL WORDS

38-39"My fellow Tribal Members, I want you to know that it is through Creator Sets Free (Jesus) that we are released from our bad hearts and broken ways. Whoever trusts in him is set free and put into good standing with Creator. This is something the law given by Drawn from the Water (Moses) could never do.

40"So then," *Small Man (Paul) said as he finished his talk,* "make sure that another thing the prophets foretold does not happen to you, for they said, 41'Watch out, you who laugh and scorn! You will die in your amazement, for I am doing something you will not believe even when you are told that it has happened!'ᵈ"

THE PEOPLE WANT TO HEAR MORE

42As they were leaving, the people begged them to stay and talk with them again on the next Day of Resting. 43After the meeting at the gathering house ended, many of the Tribal Members and others who had been ceremonially taken into the tribe followed after Small Man (Paul) and Son of Comfort (Barnabas), who urged them to keep walking in Creator's gift of great kindness.

ª**13:33** Psalm 2:7
ᵇ**13:34** Isaiah 55:3

ᶜ**13:35** Psalm 16:10
ᵈ**13:41** Habakkuk 1:5

A LIGHT TO THE OUTSIDE NATIONS

44Seven days later, on the following Day of Resting, almost the whole village gathered together to hear Creator's word. **45**But the local Tribal Members became jealous when they saw how large the crowd was. They spoke lies against Small Man (Paul) and argued against everything he said. But both Small Man (Paul) and Son of Comfort (Barnabas) stood up to them.

46"It was of great importance," they said with strong hearts, "that we would bring Creator's message first to you who are our Tribal Members. But now that you have shown no respect for this message and decided that you are not worthy of the life of the world to come, we will turn to the people from the Outside Nations.

47"For this is what the Great Spirit instructed us to do when he said, 'I have chosen you to be a light to all nations, so that all who live upon the earth may know Creator's power to rescue and make them whole.'"[a]

48When the ones who were from other nations heard this, it made their hearts glad, and they honored Creator's message. And all who had been chosen from long ago for the life of the world to come that never fades away, put their trust in the message.

49So Creator's message spread throughout the whole territory. **50**But the Tribal Members stirred up the spiritual leaders, both the women and men, against Small Man (Paul) and Son of Comfort (Barnabas) and forced them out of that area. **51**So they shook the dust from their moccasins, as a sign against them, and went from there to Spirit Village (Iconium).

---

[a] **13:47** Isaiah 49:6

52The followers of Creator Sets Free (Jesus) were filled with joy and with the Holy Spirit.

CONFLICT IN SPIRIT VILLAGE

1The same thing happened at Spirit Village (Iconium). Small Man (Paul) and Son of Comfort (Barnabas) went to the local tribal gathering house and spoke with such powerful words that many Tribal Members and Wisdom Seekers (Greeks) put their trust in Creator Sets Free (Jesus).

2But the Tribal Members who did not believe poisoned the minds of the people from Outside Nations and turned them against their new family members. **3**So the message bearers, Small Man (Paul) and Son of Comfort (Barnabas), remained there a long time and spoke with boldness about our Honored Chief. Through their hands Creator did many wonderful and powerful signs, confirming the message of the gift of his great kindness.

4But the people of Spirit Village (Iconium) were split apart. Some stood with the Tribal Members and some with the message bearers. **5-6**But when the message bearers heard that some of the Tribal Members and Outsiders, along with their rulers, were planning to harm them and even stone them to death, they fled for safety. They went to the villages of She Wolf (Lycaonia), Set Free (Lystra), Hide Tanner (Derbe), and their surrounding territories. **7**And everywhere they went they told the good story.

A POWERFUL HEALING

8Now in the village of Set Free (Lystra) sat a man who was born with bad feet and unable to walk. **9**He sat listening as Small

Man (Paul) was speaking. Small Man (Paul) looked closely at the man and saw that he had faith to be healed.

¹⁰"Stand up on your feet!" he said with a loud voice.

The man jumped to his feet and began walking.

¹¹When the crowd of people saw what Small Man (Paul) had done, they all began to shout in their local language, "Powerful spirits[a] have come down to us in the form of human beings!"

¹²Son of Comfort (Barnabas) they called Skyfather (Zeus), and Small Man (Paul) they called High Messenger (Hermes) because he was the chief speaker. ¹³The sacred lodge of Skyfather (Zeus) was at the village gate, and the holy man of the lodge, along with the people, brought out cattle wearing ceremonial wreaths to make an offering to Small Man (Paul) and Son of Comfort (Barnabas).

¹⁴When the two message bearers heard what was happening, *in humble desperation* they tore their clothes and rushed out to the center of the crowd.

¹⁵"Friends!" they shouted. "Why are you doing this? We are only weak two-leggeds like yourselves. We came to tell you the good story so you would turn away from these empty ways *and turn* to the Great Spirit, who is the maker of the sky, the earth, the great waters, and everything in them. ¹⁶In past generations he permitted all nations to walk in their own ways, ¹⁷yet in his goodness he gave each of us signs of his existence. He gave us rain from the sky above and seasons of harvest to feed us and make our hearts glad."

¹⁸Even these words barely kept the people from sacrificing an offering to them. ¹⁹But some Tribal Members from

Stands Against (Antioch) and Spirit Village (Iconium) came and caused people to listen to their lies and turned them against Small Man (Paul). They threw stones at him and dragged him outside the village, thinking he was dead. ²⁰But when some followers gathered around him, he got up and returned to the village. The next day he and Son of Comfort (Barnabas) left to go to the village of Hide Tanner (Derbe).

THEY FINISH THEIR JOURNEY

²¹After telling the good story in that village and making many new followers, they made their way back through the village of Set Free (Lystra), then on to Spirit Village (Iconium), and back to Stands Against (Antioch), *where they began their journeys.*

²²*On the way* they strengthened the hearts of the new followers, telling them to stand tall as they walked this path of trusting.

"Following Creator's good road to the end," they counseled them, "is a difficult path with many hardships."

²³They chose elders *to watch over* every sacred family gathering. After praying and going without food, they dedicated them to our Honored Chief in whom they had put their trust.

²⁴On their journey they walked *back* through the territory of Tree Sap (Pisidia) and Many Tribes (Pamphylia). ²⁵There in Earth Village (Perga) they told the good story to the people before traveling on to the village of Grows More (Attalia). ²⁶From there they traveled by water to Stands Against (Antioch), where, by Creator's great kindness, they had been sent out on this journey that was now complete.

²⁷After arriving, they gathered the sacred family together and told the story

---

^a**14:11** Lit. *gods*

of all that Creator had done among them, about how he had opened a pathway of faith for all Nations. **28**And they remained there with the sacred family for a long time.

THE COUNCIL AT VILLAGE OF PEACE

1*While Small Man (Paul) and Son of Comfort (Barnabas) were in Stands Against (Antioch),* some men came down from the Land of Promise (Judea) and began to teach the followers there.

They said, "Unless you have participated in the traditional cutting of the flesh ceremony, given by Drawn from the Water (Moses), you cannot be set free and made whole."

2But Small Man (Paul) and Son of Comfort (Barnabas) did not agree with them and had a strong argument with them. It was decided that Small Man (Paul) and Son of Comfort (Barnabas), along with a few others, would go to the message bearers and elders at Village of Peace (Jerusalem) to settle this among them.

3So, having been sent on their way by the sacred family, they traveled through Land of Palm Trees (Phoenicia) and High Place (Samaria). As they traveled, they told how the Outside Nations had come to faith. This made the hearts of all the followers glad.

4When they came to Village of Peace (Jerusalem), the message bearers, elders, and the sacred family welcomed them. They told them the stories of all that the Great Spirit had done through them. **5**But some of the sacred family members who belonged to the band of the Separated Ones (Pharisees) stood up among them *to make their voice heard.*

"The Outside Nations," said the Separated Ones (Pharisees), "must participate in the cutting of the flesh ceremony and be required to follow our tribal law given by Drawn from the Water (Moses)."

6The message bearers and elders sat in council together to discuss this matter. **7**After much talk and debate, Stands on the Rock (Peter) stood up among them.

"My fellow members of the sacred family," he said to all, "you know that a good while ago Creator chose me to be the one to help the Outside Nations come to faith by telling them the good story. **8**The Knower of Hearts made this clear when he gave them the Holy Spirit in the same manner as he did for us. **9**The Great Spirit made no difference between us and them, purifying their hearts when they trusted in him. **10**So why put Creator to the test by putting a burden on their shoulders that neither our ancestors nor we have been able to carry?

11"So then," *Stands on the Rock (Peter) finished,* "we believe it is because of the gift of great kindness from Creator Sets Free (Jesus), the Chosen One, that we will be set free and made whole. It is the same for us and them!"

12Silence fell upon all who had gathered there as they listened to Son of Comfort (Barnabas) and Small Man (Paul) tell about the wondrous and powerful signs the Great Spirit had done through them when they were with the Outside Nations.

MORE DISCUSSION

13When they were finished speaking, He Leads the Way (James) stood up and spoke to the gathering.

"My fellow Tribal Members," he said. "Hear what I have to say. **14**One Who Hears (Simon) has spoken well to remind us of how the Great Spirit first showed *to us* his concern for the Outside Nations, by choosing from among them those who would represent him. [15]This agrees with the words of the prophets *from long ago.*

"It is written in the Sacred Teachings, [16]'At that time I will return and repair the sacred tent of Much Loved One (David) that has fallen to the ground. I will raise it up from its tattered ruins and mend its tears, [17]so that the rest of humankind may search for the Great Spirit—all the Outside Nations who have *also* been chosen to represent me. This is what Creator is saying, [18]for he made these things known long ago.'[a]

[19]"So, as I see it, we should not put stumbling stones in the path of the ones in these Outside Nations who are turning to the Great Spirit. [20]The message we should send to them is that they should stay away from things offered to evil spirits,[b] from sexual impurity, from the meat of a strangled animal, and from *drinking* blood. [21]For from ancient times the ways of Drawn from the Water (Moses) have been taught in every village, and his words are read out loud in the tribal gathering houses on every Day of Resting."

THE COUNCIL DECIDES

[22]Then the message bearers, the elders, and all of the sacred family agreed that it was a good thing to choose some men, along with Small Man (Paul) and Son of Comfort (Barnabas), to take a message to Stands Against (Antioch). They chose Speaks Well Of (Judas) who is also called Son of Resting (Barsabbas) and Woods Man (Silas), spiritual leaders among the sacred family.

---

[a]**15:18** Some ancient manuscripts read *For the Great Spirit knew long ago what he would do.*
[b]**15:20** Lit. *idols*

THE COUNCIL WRITES A MESSAGE

[23]Here is the message they sent in a letter: "Greetings, from the message bearers and elders of the sacred family, to our brothers *and sisters* who are from the Outside Nations in the villages of Stands Against (Antioch), Bright Sun (Syria), and Turns Over (Cilicia).

[24]"We heard that some of our people came to you, even though we did not send them, and that they said things that troubled and confused you. [25]We all agreed it would be good to send some men to represent us—along with our much-loved Son of Comfort (Barnabas) and Small Man (Paul). [26]These are men who have risked their lives representing our Honored Chief Creator Sets Free (Jesus), the Chosen One. [27]So we sent Speaks Well Of (Judas) and Woods Man (Silas) to tell you the same things we have written.

[28]"So then, it seemed good to the Holy Spirit and to us to place on you no burden other than these necessary things: [29]that you stay away from things offered to evil spirits, from *drinking* blood, from the meat of strangled animals, and from sexual impurity. If you stay away from these things you will be walking in a good way. Safe journeys to you."

THE MESSAGE IS SENT

[30]So they sent the messengers to Stands Against (Antioch). [31]When they gathered everyone together and read the message, their hearts were encouraged and made glad. [32]Speaks Well Of (Judas) and Woods Man (Silas), who were also prophets, lifted their spirits and made their hearts strong with many words.

RETURN TO VILLAGE OF PEACE

[33]After some time there, they sent the messengers back with a blessing of

peace on those who had sent them. **34**Woods Man (Silas) thought it good to remain there.ᵃ **35**Small Man (Paul) and Son of Comfort (Barnabas) *also* remained in Stands Against (Antioch). There, along with many others, they taught the message of the good story about our Honored Chief.

SEPARATE WAYS

36After they had stayed there for a while, Small Man (Paul) said to Son of Comfort (Barnabas), "Come with me and we will visit the sacred family in every village where we taught Creator's message, to see how well they are doing."

37Now Son of Comfort (Barnabas) wanted Walks in Kindness (John), who is also named War Club (Mark), to go with them. **38**But Small Man (Paul) did not think it wise, for he had deserted them in the territory of Many Tribes (Pamphylia) and did not complete his task.

39Their argument became so strong that they split apart and went their separate ways. Son of Comfort (Barnabas) took War Club (Mark) and set out by water for Island of Flowers (Cyprus), **40**but Small Man (Paul) chose Woods Man (Silas). So they were given Creator's blessing by the sacred family and set out, **41**traveling through Bright Sun (Syria) and Turns Over (Cilicia). There they gave strength to the sacred family gatherings *in that territory.*

16 ◁▷◁▷◁▷◁▷◁▷◁▷◁▷

HE GIVES HONOR JOINS THE JOURNEY

1Small Man (Paul) also went to the village of Hide Tanner (Derbe) and then to Set Free (Lystra). In that village was a follower named He Gives Honor (Timothy). His mother was a Tribal Woman who trusted *in Creator Sets Free (Jesus),* and his father was from an Outside Nation.ᵇ **2**He Gives Honor (Timothy) was well spoken of by the sacred family at Set Free (Lystra) and Spirit Village (Iconium).

3Small Man (Paul) wanted to take He Gives Honor (Timothy) with him, so he performed the cutting of the flesh ceremony for him, because of the Tribal People in the area who knew his father was from an Outside Nation.ᵇ

4As they journeyed through the villages, they instructed the sacred family gatherings to follow the decisions made by the message bearers and elders who were in Village of Peace (Jerusalem). **5**So the members of the sacred family were made strong in the faith, and their numbers grew larger each day.

GUIDANCE FROM THE HOLY SPIRIT

6Small Man (Paul) and He Gives Honor (Timothy) continued their journey through the territory of Dry Wood (Phrygia) and Land of Pale Skinned People (Galatia), for the Holy Spirit had held them back from telling the good story in Land of the Rising Sun (Asia). **7**When they came to Land of Beech Trees (Mysia), they tried to go to Rushing Storm (Bithynia), but the Spirit of Creator Sets Free (Jesus) would not permit them. **8**So they went around Land of Beech Trees (Mysia) and traveled on to the village of Cut Through (Troas).

9During the night Small Man (Paul) had a vision in which he saw a man from Land of Tall People (Macedonia) standing in front of him. The man was begging him and saying, "Come over to our land and help us!"

ᵃ**15:34** Most manuscripts do not include verse 34.   ᵇ**16:1, 3** Greek

[10]When the vision was done, right away we tried to go into the Land of Tall People (Macedonia), trusting that Creator had chosen us to tell them the good story.

[11]So we set off by water straight from Cut Through (Troas) to Sign of Rags (Samothrace). The next day we came to New Village (Neapolis), [12]and from there we went on to Village of Horses (Philippi), the chief village of Land of Tall People (Macedonia) under the rule of the People of Iron (Romans). There we remained for a number of days.

WELCOMED BY A WOMAN OF FAITH

[13]Then on the Day of Resting we went outside of the village gate to a nearby river to find a place to send our voices to the Great Spirit. We sat down on the riverbank and spoke to some women who had gathered there. [14]One of the women there, named Bitter Fruit (Lydia), from High Rock House (Thyatira), was a trader in purple cloths and had great respect for Creator. As Small Man (Paul) spoke, she listened closely to the message, and Creator opened her heart. [15]She and her family then participated in the purification ceremony.[a]

"If you consider me to be one who trusts in our Honored Chief," she said to us firmly, "then you must come and stay at my house." And she would not take no for an answer.

THEY FORCE OUT AN EVIL SPIRIT

[16]As we were on our way to where we gathered for prayer, a slave-girl who had an evil snake spirit met us.[b] She brought her owners much gain by fortune-telling.

[17]She began to follow after Small Man (Paul) and shout out loud, "These men, who serve the One Above Us All, are showing us the way to be set free and made whole."

[18]She did this for many days. *By so doing,* she greatly troubled Small Man (Paul), who finally turned and spoke to the *evil* spirit, "As one who represents Creator Sets Free (Jesus), the Chosen One, I tell you now to come out of this woman!"

[19]Right away the spirit left her. When her owners saw that the hope of their gain was gone, they took hold of Small Man (Paul) and Woods Man (Silas) and dragged them to the village rulers at the trading post.

ARRESTED AND IMPRISONED

[20]They brought them before the village council and said, "These men are from the tribes of Wrestles with Creator (Israel). They are bringing trouble to our village [21]by trying to force their tribal customs on us. Since we are of the People of Iron (Romans), we are not permitted to accept or follow these customs."

[22]The people who had gathered there also began to speak against them, so the village council stripped their clothes off them and gave orders for them to be beaten with sticks. [23]When they finished beating them, they threw them into prison and told the headman of the prison to lock them up. [24]So he followed his instructions, put them deep into the prison, and locked their feet in iron bindings.

AN EARTHQUAKE OPENS PRISON DOORS

[25]In the middle of the night Small Man (Paul) and Woods Man (Silas) were sending up prayers and singing sacred songs to the Great Spirit. The other prisoners were listening, [26]when suddenly the earth began to shake violently, and the stones holding the prison up began to tremble. Right then the prison doors

---

[a]**16:15** Baptism
[b]**16:16** Lit. *spirit of python*

were opened, and everyone's iron bindings fell off.

THE HEADMAN BECOMES A FOLLOWER

²⁷When the headman of the prison woke up and saw all the prison doors standing open, he took his long knife and was going to kill himself, for he thought all the prisoners had escaped.

²⁸But Small Man (Paul) shouted out to him, "Do not harm yourself, we are all here!"

²⁹The headman of the prison asked for a torch, and, trembling with fear, he rushed inside and fell down before Small Man (Paul) and Woods Man (Silas).

³⁰He then took them outside and said, "What must I do to be set free and made whole?"

³¹"Put your trust in Creator Sets Free (Jesus), our Honored Chief," they said to him. "He will make you whole and set you and all your family free *to follow him.*"

³²Then they told Creator's good story to him and all his family. ³³It was still late in the night, but the headman took Small Man (Paul) and Woods Man (Silas) and washed their wounds. Then right away the headman and his family all participated in the purification ceremony.ᵃ ³⁴He then invited them into his home and fed them. His heart was glad because he and all his family had put their trust in the Great Spirit.

THE COUNCIL RELEASES THEM

³⁵In the morning the village council sent messengers, saying, "Release these men."

³⁶So the headman of the prison told Small Man (Paul), "The council has instructed me to release you. You may go in peace."

³⁷But Small Man (Paul) said, "We are citizens of the People of Iron (Romans)! They have beaten us before the village without a trial and thrown us in prison, and now they would send us away in secret? No! Let them come here and take us out themselves!"

³⁸The messengers went back and reported what they said to the village council. When they heard that they were citizens of the People of Iron (Romans), they were afraid. ³⁹So they came and apologized to them, released them, and asked them to leave the village. ⁴⁰So after they left the prison, they went to the home of Bitter Fruit (Lydia). There they encouraged the sacred family, *and then left to continue their journey.*

17

THE MESSAGE BRINGS COMFORT AND CONFLICT

¹After traveling through Circle Village (Amphipolis) and Village of Destroyer (Apollonia), they came to a tribal gathering house at the village of False Victory (Thessalonica). ²As was his custom, Small Man (Paul) went to the gathering house on the next three Days of Resting. He tried to convince them from the Sacred Teachings, ³explaining and proving to them that the Chosen One had to suffer and then rise again from the dead.

Then he said to them, "Creator Sets Free (Jesus), the one I have been telling you about, is the Chosen One!"

⁴Some of them were won over and joined with Small Man (Paul) and Woods Man (Silas), including a large number of Wisdom Seekers (Greeks) who had deep respect for Creator and also many of the local headwomen.

ᵃ**16:33** Baptism

⁵But the Tribal Members became jealous. Banding together with some troublemakers from the trading post, they gathered a crowd and caused an uprising in the village. They broke into the house of a man named Healer (Jason), looking for Small Man (Paul) and Woods Man (Silas) so they could bring them before the people. ⁶Not finding them there, they took hold of Healer (Jason) and some of the other sacred family members and dragged them before the village council.

"The ones who have turned the world upside down," they shouted, "have also come here! ⁷And Healer (Jason) has welcomed them into his house. They are going against the laws of the Ruler of the People of Iron (Caesar), by saying there is another ruler—Creator Sets Free (Jesus)."

⁸This troubled the people and the village council, ⁹so after taking payment as a promise from Healer (Jason) and the others *that there would be no more trouble*, they let them go.

SMALL MAN IS SENT AWAY

¹⁰Right away, under the cover of night, members of the sacred family sent Small Man (Paul) and Woods Man (Silas) to Much Water (Berea). When they arrived, they went to the local tribal gathering house. ¹¹The Tribal Members there were more honorable than the ones in False Victory (Thessalonica), for they welcomed the message with glad hearts, and each day they searched the Sacred Teachings to see whether their message agreed. ¹²In this way many Tribal Members came to the faith, including honored women and men from the Wisdom Seekers (Greeks).

¹³When the Tribal Members from False Victory (Thessalonica) found out that Small Man (Paul) was telling the Sacred Story in Much Water (Berea), they also came there to stir up the crowds and make trouble for them. ¹⁴So right away the sacred family sent Small Man (Paul) away to the great sea, but Woods Man (Silas) and He Gives Honor (Timothy) remained behind.

¹⁵The ones who went with Small Man (Paul) took him to Wondering Place (Athens). Small Man (Paul) told them to send Woods Man (Silas) and He Gives Honor (Timothy) to him right away, and so they went back to Much Water (Berea).

SMALL MAN AT WONDERING PLACE

¹⁶While Small Man (Paul) was waiting for them at Wondering Place (Athens), he saw that this large village was filled with images of powerful spirit-beings. ¹⁷So every day at the tribal gathering house he would argue with the Tribal Members, and at the trading posts he would talk with any spiritual people who happened to be there. ¹⁸Some traditional wisdom seekers[a] also argued with him.

Others wondered, "What is this talking head saying?" while others said, "He seems to be talking about strange and powerful spirits."

SMALL MAN SPEAKS AT MARS HILL

They said this because he was telling them the good story about Creator Sets Free (Jesus) and his rising from the dead. ¹⁹So they took him to the council at Mars Hill (Areopagus).

"Explain this new teaching to us," they asked him, ²⁰"for your message is strange to us, and we want to know its meaning." ²¹The people who lived in Wondering Place (Athens) would spend all their time telling or hearing about some new thing.

---

[a]17:18 Epicureans and Stoics

[22]So Small Man (Paul) stood up in the center of Mars Hill (Areopagus) and said, "People of Wondering Place (Athens), I can see that in all things you are a very spiritual people. [23]As I walked around, I saw some of your sacred objects. One altar had this message carved into it:

DEDICATED TO AN UNKNOWN
POWERFUL SPIRIT

"So then, the one you sacredly honor without knowing is the one I will make known to you. [24]The Great Spirit is the one who created the universe and all things in it. Since he is the rightful ruler of the spirit-world above and the earth below, he does not live in lodges built by human hands. [25]Creator does not really need human beings to do things for him, since he is the one who gives all people life and breath and everything we need.

[26]"Beginning with the first human being, he made all tribes and nations. He wanted people to live all over the face of the earth. He decided ahead of time when and where each tribe would live. [27]He did this so that all people could look for him and find the trail that leads to him. Creator is not far away from any one of us. [28]It is through him that we live, walk, and have our being.

"As some of your song makers have said, 'We are children of the Great Spirit.' [29]Since we are his children, we should not think that he is made of gold or silver or wood or stones. He is not like the carvings that people have thought up in their minds and made with their hands.

[30]"In times past Creator overlooked this empty way of thinking. But now he wants all people everywhere to return to the right way of thinking, [31]because he has chosen a day when he will decide, for all people, who has done right and

who has done wrong. He has chosen a man who will do this and has shown all people who he is by bringing him back to life again from the dead."

[32]When they heard about the rising from the dead, some mocked him, but others said, "We will hear you again about this."

[33]So Small Man (Paul) went on his way. [34]Some of the people believed and joined with him, including one of the council members of Mars Hill (Areopagus) named Shining Tree (Dionysius) and a woman named Good Wife (Damaris), along with a few others.

18

SMALL MAN AT VILLAGE OF PLEASURE

[1]Small Man (Paul) left from Wondering Place (Athens) and went to Village of Pleasure (Corinth). [2]There he found a Tribal Member named Strong Eagle (Aquila) who lived in Land of Black Waters (Pontus). He and his wife, Lives Long (Priscilla), had recently moved from Land of Young Bulls (Italy) because Walks with a Limp (Claudius), the Ruler of the People of Iron (Caesar), had ordered the removal of all Tribal Members from that territory.

[3]Small Man (Paul) found out they were both tentmakers, as he was, so he lodged with them and joined them in their work. [4]Then on every Day of Resting in the gathering houses he debated with his local Tribal Members and the Wisdom Seekers (Greeks), trying to convince them *about Creator Sets Free (Jesus).*

[5]After Woods Man (Silas) and He Gives Honor (Timothy) came from Land of Tall People (Macedonia), Small Man (Paul) became like a man on fire—trying to convince his Tribal Members that

Creator Sets Free (Jesus) was the Chosen One. **6**But when they stood against him and spoke evil of him, he shook the dust from his clothes.

"You have decided your own fate!" he told them. "I have done all I can do. From now on I will go to the Outside Nations."

THE HEADMAN BELIEVES

7So he left them and went to the house of Stands Upright with Fire (Titius Justus), a man with deep respect for Creator and whose house was next door to the tribal gathering house. **8**A man named Curly Hair (Crispus), who was headman of the gathering house, put his trust in our Honored Chief, and both he and his family participated in the purification ceremony.[a] When others who lived in Village of Pleasure (Corinth) heard about this, they also believed and participated in the purification ceremony.[a]

9During the night Creator spoke to Small Man (Paul) in a sacred vision.

"Do not fear!" he said to him. "Keep speaking and do not be silent, **10**for I am standing with you. No one will harm you, for I have many people in this village."

11So Small Man (Paul) stayed there for one year and six moons, teaching Creator's message to the people.

AN UPRISING AGAINST SMALL MAN

12During the days when Rooster (Gallio) was the governor of Land of Sorrow (Achaia), the Tribal Members joined together in an attack on Small Man (Paul) and took him before the governor to accuse him of wrongdoing.

13"This man is convincing people to serve the Great Spirit in ways that go against our tribal law," they accused.

14But before Small Man (Paul) could open his mouth to defend himself, the governor spoke to the Tribal Members.

"If a wrong had been done or some kind of evil had been committed, then I would hear your accusations," he said to them, **15**"but if this is simply a question about words and names and how to interpret your own laws, then you must decide for yourselves. I want nothing to do with deciding these things."

16So he sent them away from his council house. **17**The Tribal Members then took Strong Protector (Sosthenes), the headman of the gathering house, and began to beat him right in front of the governor. But he turned his head the other way.

SMALL MAN'S JOURNEY

18After staying there for a number of days, Small Man (Paul) said farewell to the sacred family. Then he, along with Lives Long (Priscilla) and Strong Eagle (Aquila), set off by water to Bright Sun (Syria). At Small Seed Village (Cenchreae) Small Man (Paul) ceremonially shaved his head because he had made a solemn promise.

19From there they traveled to Village of Desire (Ephesus). Small Man (Paul) left his traveling friends in the village, but he went to the local tribal gathering house to speak with the Tribal Members there. **20**They asked him to stay, but he turned them down and said his farewells.

21"If Creator permits it," he told them, "I will return."

He then set out from the village by water. **22**He came to land at Chief Village (Caesarea), greeted the sacred family there, and then made his way to Stands Against (Antioch).

23He stayed there a number of days, then left and walked here and there,

---

[a]**18:8** Baptism

strengthening the hearts of the sacred family members throughout the territory of Land of Pale Skinned People (Galatia) and Dry Wood (Phrygia).

BACK IN THE VILLAGE OF DESIRE

²⁴There was a Tribal Member named He Tears Down (Apollos) from Village of Defense (Alexandria) who came to Village of Desire (Ephesus). He was a powerful wisdom speaker who had a deep understanding of the Sacred Teachings. ²⁵Even though he had only participated in the purification ceremonyᵃ of Gift of Goodwill (John), he was well instructed in the Way of our Honored Chief, and a fire burned in his spirit as he spoke clearly about Creator Sets Free (Jesus).

²⁶At the local tribal gathering house he began to speak openly. But when Lives Long (Priscilla) and Strong Eagle (Aquila) heard him speak, they took him with them and helped him see Creator's Way more clearly. ²⁷Then, when he desired to go to Land of Sorrow (Achaia), the sacred family sent along a message to instruct the followers there to welcome him. When he arrived, he was a great help to the ones who had trusted in the gift of Creator's great kindness, ²⁸for he spoke powerfully to his Tribal Members, proving to them from the Sacred Teachings that Creator Sets Free (Jesus) was the Chosen One.

19

VILLAGE OF DESIRE

¹While He Tears Down (Apollos) was at Village of Pleasure (Corinth), Small Man (Paul) journeyed through the inland ter-

ritories and arrived at Village of Desire (Ephesus), where he found some followers. ²"When you put your trust in Creator Sets Free (Jesus)," Small Man (Paul) asked them, "did you receive the Holy Spirit?"

"What do you mean?" they replied. "We have not even heard about this 'Holy Spirit.'"

³"What kind of purification ceremonyᵃ did you participate in?" he asked.

"It was the purification ceremonyᵃ performed by Gift of Goodwill (John)," they answered.

⁴"Gift of Goodwill (John) performed a purification ceremonyᵃ for the ones who turned to Creator's right ways of thinking and doing," Small Man (Paul) said to them. "In this way they would be ready to put their trust in Creator Sets Free (Jesus), the one he was preparing the way for."

⁵When they heard this, they participated in the purification ceremonyᵃ done in the name of our Honored Chief Creator Sets Free (Jesus). ⁶⁻⁷Small Man (Paul) then laid his hands on the men, about twelve in all, and they spoke in languages they had not learned and prophesied when the Holy Spirit came down upon them.

SMALL MAN TELLS THE GOOD STORY

⁸Then for three moons Small Man (Paul) went to their tribal gathering house and spoke out boldly to convince the people living there about Creator's good road. ⁹But some, who were stubborn, with hearts like stone, refused to believe and spoke evil of the Way to all who gathered there.

So Small Man (Paul) left there, taking with him the new followers. He went to the teaching lodge of Harsh Ruler (Tyrannus) to teach there. ¹⁰He continued this for two winters, until all the Tribal

Members and Wisdom Seekers (Greeks) who lived in Land of the Rising Sun (Asia) had heard the message about our Honored One.

POWERFUL SIGNS AND WONDERS

[11]Through the hands of Small Man (Paul), Creator was doing some unusually powerful signs. [12]Face cloths and sashes that had touched his body were taken to heal the sick and force out evil spirits.

[13]Then some Tribal Members who traveled about forcing out evil spirits tried to use the name of Creator Sets Free (Jesus) over those with evil spirits, saying, "I force you out by the sacred power of Creator Sets Free (Jesus), the one whom Small Man (Paul) proclaims."

[14]These men were the seven sons of Weak Hand (Sceva), a Tribal Member who was *representing himself as* a chief holy man.

[15]But the evil spirit spoke back to them, "I know of Creator Sets Free (Jesus) and I have heard of Small Man (Paul), but who are you?"

[16]Then the man with the evil spirit jumped on them and so overpowered them that they ran from the house naked, bruised, and bleeding.

[17]Word spread to all the Tribal Members and the Wisdom Seekers (Greeks) who lived in Village of Desire (Ephesus). Great awe and respect came upon all, and the name of Creator Sets Free (Jesus) was spoken of with respect.

[18]Many who had chosen to follow Creator Sets Free (Jesus) came forward and admitted to their evil practices. [19]A number of them who had practiced bad medicine gathered their mystic writings and burned them in the sight of all. These books were found to be worth about fifty thousand silver coins.[a] [20]In this way Creator's message grew strong and spread like wildfire.

[21]After this, Small Man (Paul) decided in his spirit that he should travel through Land of Tall People (Macedonia) and Land of Sorrow (Achaia) and then on to Village of Peace (Jerusalem). "After that," he said, "I must also go to Village of Iron (Rome)." [22]So he sent his two helpers, He Gives Honor (Timothy) and Much Desired (Erastus), ahead of him to Land of Tall People (Macedonia), while he remained for a time in Land of the Rising Sun (Asia).

AN UPRISING IN THE VILLAGE

[23]Now during that time there was a great uprising at Village of Desire (Ephesus) about the Way. [24]There was a man there named Corn Spirit (Demetrius), who worked with silver and made little silver lodges for the spirit-image of Hunting Woman (Artemis). His work helped support many of the artists who traded there. [25]He gathered them together, along with the others who also worked with silver.

"Fellow workers," he said to them, "you all know that this work we do provides for us. [26]You have all seen and heard what this Small Man (Paul) has done, not only in our village but also in most of Land of the Rising Sun (Asia). He has convinced many people to turn away from our spirit-images, saying that spirit-images made by hands are not powerful spirits."

The crowd began to grumble and grow restless as he continued to speak.

[27]"We are in danger that the work we do will be looked down on, and that the

---

[a]19:19 Each coin was worth a day's wages.

sacred lodge of the spirit-image of Hunting Woman (Artemis), the one whom all in Land of the Rising Sun (Asia) and the world bows down to, will be seen as worthless, and her great beauty and power will fall to the ground."

28When the crowd heard this, a great anger filled their hearts, and they shouted, "Great is Hunting Woman (Artemis) of Village of Desire (Ephesus)!"

29The whole village was thrown into confusion. With one purpose they ran into the teaching lodge, dragging with them Glad Heart (Gaius) and Good Chief (Aristarchus) from Land of Tall People (Macedonia), who were traveling with Small Man (Paul).

30Small Man (Paul) wanted to go into the crowd, but the other followers would not let him. **31**Also, some of the village leaders who were friendly toward him sent word for him not to come into the teaching lodge.

32The gathering became one of turmoil and confusion. Some were shouting one thing, some another. Most did not even know why they had gathered!

33Some of the Tribal Members in the crowd pushed Man Fighter (Alexander) to the front, instructing him *what to say*. He motioned with his hand that he wanted to speak, **34**but when they saw that he was a man of the tribes of Wrestles with Creator (Israel), they cried out with one voice, "Great is Hunting Woman (Artemis) of Village of Desire (Ephesus)!"

Over and over again they kept shouting as the day wore on,[a] **35**until the village scroll keeper finally quieted them down.

"People of Village of Desire (Ephesus)," he said to all, "who among us does not

know that the people of Village of Desire (Ephesus) are the sacred lodge keepers of the great Hunting Woman (Artemis) and of her spirit-image that fell from the spirit-world above? **36**Since these things cannot be denied, you should lower your voices and do nothing without thinking clearly first.

37"The men you have brought here did not come to steal from your sacred lodge and they do not speak against Hunting Woman (Artemis). **38**If Corn Spirit (Demetrius) and the other artists with him want to accuse anyone, let them bring these accusations to the village council or the local officials. **39**Anything else should also be brought to the village council meeting. **40**For we are in danger today of being charged with causing an uprising, with no good reason for it."

41After saying this, he sent the crowd away.

20

SMALL MAN CONTINUES HIS TRAVELS

1After the uprising had calmed down, Small Man (Paul) gathered the local sacred family members together to strengthen their hearts and say his farewell to them. He then left for Land of Tall People (Macedonia).

2As he traveled through that territory, with many words he lifted the hearts of the members of the sacred family who lived there. He then came to Land of Wisdom Seekers (Greece) **3**and stayed there for three moons. Just as he was about to set out by water to Bright Sun (Syria), the Tribal Members there hatched a plot against him, so he decided to return through Land of Tall People (Macedonia).

---

[a] **19:34** Lit. *for about two hours*

SMALL MAN'S TRAVELING FRIENDS

[4]The men who went with him are Defends His Father (Sopater) the son of Red Fire (Pyrrhus) from Much Water (Berea), Good Chief (Aristarchus) and Second Blessing (Secundus) from False Victory (Thessalonica), also Glad Heart (Gaius) from Hide Tanner (Derbe), He Gives Honor (Timothy), and He Is at Ease (Tychicus) and He Eats Well (Trophimus) from Land of the Rising Sun (Asia).

[5]These men traveled ahead of us and were waiting for us at Cut Through (Troas). [6]They had to wait five days because we stayed for the Festival of Bread Without Yeast. Then we set out by water from Village of Horses (Philippi) and joined with them at Cut Through (Troas) and stayed there for seven days.

POWER OVER DEATH

[7]It was the first day of the week, when we gather to eat our sacred meal together.[a] Small Man (Paul) was doing the talking because he planned to leave the next day. He was long-winded and kept talking until the middle of the night. [8]There were many torches burning in the upper room of the house where we had all gathered.

> The number of people and the torches in this room, using up the air, may have made some people sleepy or lightheaded.

[9]As Small Man (Paul) spoke on and on, a young man named Greatly Blessed (Eutychus), who was sitting on the window ledge, began to sink into a deep sleep. When the sleep overcame him, he fell from the third-floor window and was found dead. [10]Small Man (Paul) went down, bent over the young man, and put his arms around him.

"Do not fear!" he said to all. "His life has returned to him."

[11]Small Man (Paul) went back to the upper room, ate the ceremonial meal with them, and continued speaking until sunrise. He then went on his way, [12]and with glad hearts they took the young man home alive!

MORE TRAVELS

[13]We all climbed into our canoes and headed to Move Toward (Assos), where we would take Small Man (Paul) aboard, for he had decided to travel there on land. [14]So he met us there and joined us as we went on to Bent Horn (Mitylene). [15]We set off from there, and on the following day we came to shore across from Snow Island (Chios). The next day we touched shore at Sand Cliff (Samos), and the day after that we came to White Sheep Wool (Miletus).

[16]We did not stop at Village of Desire (Ephesus), because Small Man (Paul) was in a hurry to get to Village of Peace (Jerusalem), if possible, for the Festival of Weeks,[b] and did not want to take the time to go to Land of the Rising Sun (Asia).

[17]From White Sheep Wool (Miletus), Small Man (Paul) sent a messenger to Village of Desire (Ephesus) to ask the elders of the sacred family to come to him.

[18]He said to them, "You all know how I lived among you the whole time I was with you, from the first day that I set foot in Land of the Rising Sun (Asia). [19]I did all Creator asked of me with a humble heart, as I walked a trail of tears when the Tribal Members schemed against me. [20]You also know that I held back nothing that would help you, as I taught openly

---

[a]20:7 Lit. *break bread*

[b]20:16 See the glossary of biblical terms.

and from house to house. ²¹I spoke truth in a sacred manner to both the Tribal Members and the Wisdom Seekers (Greeks), as I told them about turning their thoughts and hearts to the Great Spirit by trusting their lives to Creator Sets Free (Jesus), our Honored Chief.

²²"And now, a captive of the Spirit, I am on my way to Village of Peace (Jerusalem). I do not know what will happen to me there. ²³I only know the Holy Spirit has made it clear to me that in every village I will be hunted down and taken captive. ²⁴But my life means nothing to me. I only want to finish walking the road the Maker of Life has set before me, telling the good story of the gift of his great kindness as I follow Creator Sets Free (Jesus), my Honored Chief.

²⁵"I now know that none of you will see my face again. You are the ones I have taught clearly about the good road. ²⁶Hear me this day! I speak from my heart, I am no longer responsible for the fate of any of you, ²⁷for I held back nothing from you. All that Creator has made known to me, I have given to you.

²⁸"Stay alert and care for one another. The Holy Spirit has given you elders the task of watching over his people. Like shepherds that guard the sheep, you will watch over his sacred family, the ones he paid the highest price for with his own lifeblood.

²⁹"I know that after I am gone savage wolves will sneak in who care nothing for the sheep. ³⁰Even some of your own elders will rise up and lead people down a false path, just to have their own followers. ³¹So I tell you again, stay alert! Do not forget that night and day, for three winters, I kept giving you wise counsel and warning each of you with many tears.

³²"I now give you over to the Great Spirit's care and to the message of the gift of his great kindness. A message that will make you stand strong and give you his promised blessings, together with all the ones he has made holy.

³³"I never asked anyone for their silver, gold, or fine clothes. ³⁴You all have seen that I worked hard with my own hands to provide for myself and for the ones who traveled with me. ³⁵In this way, I have walked a path for you to follow, working hard to give help to the weak. We must never forget the words of Creator Sets Free (Jesus) when he said, 'Giving to others is a greater blessing than getting from others.'"

³⁶When Small Man (Paul) had finished speaking, he knelt down beside the elders of the sacred family and sent his voice to the Great Spirit. ³⁷With many tears they put their arms around his neck and kissed him. ³⁸Their greatest sorrow was from his words, "You will not see my face again."

Then they walked with him to our canoe *to see us on our way.*

21

JOURNEY TO VILLAGE OF PEACE

¹After we had torn ourselves away from them we set out in our canoe and followed the shortest distance to the island of High Point (Kos). On the next day we went to Rose Island (Rhodes), and then to Walked Over (Patara). ²From there we found a large canoe that was headed for Land of Palm Trees (Phoenicia) and traveled with them. ³We could see Island of Flowers (Cyprus) to our left as we traveled on toward Bright Sun (Syria), and then went to shore at Rock Land (Tyre) to unload trading goods from the canoe.

⁴We looked for members of the sacred family *who lived there* and, after finding them, we stayed with them for seven days. Guided by the Spirit, they kept telling Small Man (Paul) not to go to Village of Peace (Jerusalem). ⁵At the end of our time with them, as we were on our way to leave, the men of the sacred family, along with their wives and children, followed us outside the village. We all knelt down at the shoreline, sent our voice to the Great Spirit, ⁶and said our farewells. We then climbed into the canoe as they went back to their homes.

⁷From Rock Land (Tyre) we continued on to Village of War (Ptolemais). We were welcomed by the sacred family and stayed the rest of the day with them. ⁸The next day we left and went to Chief Village (Caesarea) and lodged there at the home of Lover of Horses (Philip), a teller of the good story and one of the seven. ⁹Lover of Horses (Philip) had four unmarried daughters who spoke words of prophecy from the Holy Spirit.

> Lover of Horses (Philip) *was one of the seven who had been chosen by the message bearers in Village of Peace (Jerusalem) to be in charge of serving the meals. He also went about telling the good story in High Place (Samaria).*[a]

¹⁰We stayed there a number of days. During our stay a prophet named Grasshopper (Agabus) came to us from Land of Promise (Judea). ¹¹He took the sash from Small Man's (Paul's) waist and tied it around his own feet and hands.

"This is what the Holy Spirit is saying," he prophesied. "'The tribal leaders in Village of Peace (Jerusalem) will do the same to the owner of this sash. They will tie him up and turn him over to the People of Iron (Romans).'"[b]

¹²When we, along with the sacred family there, heard this, we all urged Small Man (Paul) not to go to Village of Peace (Jerusalem).

¹³"Why are you weeping and breaking my heart?" he said to them. "I am representing our Honored Chief, Creator Sets Free (Jesus). I am ready not only to be bound but even to die for him in Village of Peace (Jerusalem)."

¹⁴Nothing we could say would change his mind. "Let Creator's will be done," we said and then remained silent.

ARRIVAL AT VILLAGE OF PEACE

¹⁵We then prepared to leave on our journey to Village of Peace (Jerusalem). ¹⁶Some of the sacred family members from Chief Village (Caesarea) traveled with us, along with a longtime follower named He Will Remember (Mnason), from Island of Flowers (Cyprus), in whose house we would stay. ¹⁷When we arrived at Village of Peace (Jerusalem), the sacred family welcomed us with glad hearts.

MEETING WITH THE COUNCIL

¹⁸The next day Small Man (Paul) went with us to meet with He Leads the Way (James) and the elders who were with him. ¹⁹After giving them a respectful greeting, he told them about all the things Creator had done as he had worked among the Outside Nations. ²⁰When they heard this, they gave praise to the Great Spirit.

"Our brother," they said to him, "you can see how many thousands of our Tribal Members have become followers of Creator Sets Free (Jesus), and how our tribal law *given by Drawn from the Water (Moses)* burns like a fire in them!"

---

[a]**21:9** See Acts chapters 6 and 8.

[b]**21:11** Lit. *Gentiles*

But then their manner changed, and their voices lowered as they looked around and then back to Small Man (Paul).

21"They have heard that you are teaching our Tribal Members who live among the Outside Nations to turn away from Drawn from the Water (Moses). They have also heard that they should not perform the cutting of the flesh ceremony for their children or follow our tribal traditions. 22What will happen when they find out you are here? What can be done?"

But it seemed that they already had made plans about what to do.

23"Listen, and do what we say," they said to him. "We have four men who have taken a solemn vow of dedication. 24Go and join with them in this vow and provide for the shaving of their heads. In this way you will show everyone that these rumors are false and that you still walk in our traditional tribal law.a"

This was the Law of Dedication (Nazarite). The men and women who make this solemn vow to the Great Spirit must drink no wine, vinegar, or strong drink, and eat no grapes or the juice of grapes. Among other things, they also must not touch a dead person, or cut their hair or beard during all the days of this vow. The vow must be kept for at least thirty days. After the days of the vow are complete, they must shave their heads in a holy ceremony at the sacred lodge in Village of Peace (Jerusalem).

He Leads the Way (James) continued giving instructions to Small Man (Paul).

25"As for the ones from the Outside Nations who have trusted in Creator Sets Free (Jesus), we sent them a message with our decision that they should stay away from things offered to evil spirits,b from *drinking* blood, from the meat of a strangled animal, and from sexual impurity."

26So the next day Small Man (Paul) went with the men to the sacred lodge. He purified himself with them and told them the number of days before the vow would be complete and the sacrifice that would be offered for them.

SMALL MAN TAKEN CAPTIVE

27Seven days later, when the time was complete, *Small Man (Paul) returned to the sacred lodge.* Some Tribal Members were there from Land of the Rising Sun (Asia). When they saw him in the sacred lodge, they took hold of him and began to stir up the crowd against him.

28"Fellow Tribal Members!" they shouted out to the crowd. "Help us! This is the man who teaches everywhere against our people, our tribal law, and this *holy* place! Even worse, he has brought Wisdom Seekers (Greeks) into the lodge and has defiled this holy place."

29They said this because they had seen He Eats Well (Trophimus) from Village of Desire (Ephesus) with Small Man (Paul) in Village of Peace (Jerusalem), and thought he had brought him into the sacred lodge.

30The village was in an uproar! A group of people came together, took hold of Small Man (Paul), dragged him outside the lodge, closed the gates behind him, and tried to kill him.

31A messenger went from them and told the local head soldier of the People of Iron (Romans) that there was an uprising in the Village of Peace (Jerusalem). 32At once

---

a**21:24** Numbers 6:1-21

b**21:25** Lit. *idols*

he took some soldiers and their officers with him and ran to where they were attacking Small Man (Paul). When the crowd saw the head soldier and his men, they stopped beating Small Man (Paul).

33The head soldier arrested him and had him bound with two chains of iron. He then asked the crowd who this man was and what he had done. **34**Some in the crowd shouted one thing and some another. Since the head soldier could not figure out what happened, he decided to take Small Man (Paul) back to the soldiers' lodge. **35**The crowd became so violent that Small Man (Paul) had to be carried up the stairs.

36"Take him away!" they shouted over and over again as they pressed close, following behind the soldiers.

37Just before they got to the soldiers' lodge, Small Man (Paul) turned to the head soldier.

"Is it permitted for me to speak to you?" he asked in the soldier's language.

38"You speak the language of the Wisdom Seekers (Greeks)," he replied. "Then you are not the man from Black Land (Egypt) who some time ago caused an uprising and took four thousand assassins out into the desert wilderness."

39"I am a Tribal Man of the tribes of Wrestles with Creator (Israel)," Small Man (Paul) answered, "from Tree Village (Tarsus) in the territory of Turns Over (Cilicia), a citizen of a well-known village."

He now had the full attention of the head soldier, so he made a request.

"I beg you," he said to the head soldier, "let me speak to my people!"

40The head soldier gave him permission, so Small Man (Paul) stood on the steps overlooking the crowd and motioned his hand to the people. A great hush settled over them, so Small Man (Paul), speaking in the language of his own people, *took a deep breath and with respect* began to speak to them.

22

SMALL MAN SPEAKS TO THE CROWD

1"My fellow Tribal Members, my fathers," he said, "hear me now as I explain myself to you."

2When the people heard him speak in their native language, they quieted down even more.

3"I am a fellow Tribal Man, born in Tree Village (Tarsus) in the territory of Turns Over (Cilicia), but I was raised in Village of Peace (Jerusalem) and was taught at the feet of Creator Has Honored (Gamaliel). I learned to closely follow all of our traditional tribal laws, and a fire for the Great Spirit burned in my belly, just as it does in yours today.

4"I hunted down and even killed the followers of this Way. I put both men and women in iron chains and took them to prison. **5**Our chief holy man and the whole council of elders are witnesses to the truth of what I say. I asked for and received written authority to give to the local Tribal Council in Silent Weaver (Damascus), with instructions to capture any followers of the Way and take them to Village of Peace (Jerusalem) to be punished.

6"It was midday on the journey to Silent Weaver (Damascus). As I came near the village, suddenly a bright light from the spirit-world above was shining all around me. **7**I fell to the ground and heard a voice speaking to me *and twice calling out my name.*

"'Man Who Questions (Saul), Man Who Questions (Saul),' the voice said, 'why are you pursuing and mistreating me?'

[8]"'Honored One,' I asked, 'who are you?'

"'I am Creator Sets Free (Jesus) from Seed Planter Village (Nazareth),' the voice answered, 'the one you are pursuing and mistreating.'

[9]"The men who were traveling with me saw the light but did not hear the voice of the one speaking to me.

[10]"'Honored One,' I asked, 'what is it you want me to do?'

"'Stand to your feet and go into the village,' he said to me, 'and there you will be told all that I want you to do.'

[11]"Since I was still unable to see because of the bright light, the men with me led me by the hand to Silent Weaver (Damascus).

SMALL MAN AND CREATOR SHOWS KINDNESS

[12]"A man named Creator Shows Kindness (Ananias), who had deep respect for our tribal law and had a good reputation among our Tribal Members who lived there, [13]came and stood beside me.

"'Man Who Questions (Saul), my brother,' he said to me, 'look up and see again!'

"I looked up, and right then sight returned to my eyes!

[14]"Then he said to me, 'The Great Spirit of our ancestors has chosen you to know his will, to see the Upright One and hear his voice, spoken from his own mouth. [15]You will tell all people the truth of what you have seen and heard. [16]What are you waiting for? Rise up and participate in the purification ceremony,[a] washing you clean from your broken ways, as you call out to him, trusting in all that his name represents.'

[a]**22:16** Baptism

[17]"*Sometime later*, after I had returned to Village of Peace (Jerusalem), I was in the sacred lodge sending my voice to the Great Spirit. I fell into a sacred vision [18]and saw Creator Sets Free (Jesus).

"'You must hurry and leave Village of Peace (Jerusalem) right away,' he said to me, 'for they will not believe what you tell them about me.'

[19]"'Honored One,' I said to him, 'they know that I used to go from one gathering house to another, capturing and whipping the ones who trusted in you. [20]When the blood of Many Feathers (Stephen) your truth teller was being shed, they saw that I was standing in agreement and guarding their garments while they killed him.'

[21]"'Go!' he said to me. 'I am sending you far away to the Outside Nations.'"

THE CROWD TURNS AGAINST HIM

[22]The Tribal Members listened to him, up until this last word.

"Away with this one!" they shouted, "He has no right to even live on this earth!"

[23]The crowd was wailing out loud! They tore off their outer garments and threw dust into the air. [24]The head soldier ordered his men to take Small Man (Paul) back to their lodge with instructions to beat him with whips until he told them the reason the crowd was so angry with him.

[25]But as they stretched him out and prepared to whip him, Small Man (Paul) turned to the head soldier standing there.

"Does your law permit you to whip a citizen of Village of Iron (Rome)," he asked, "without a fair trial?"

[26]Hearing this, the head soldier reported to his head officer.

"What are you doing?" he asked. "This man is a citizen of the People of Iron (Romans)."

27The head officer went to Small Man (Paul).

"Tell me," he asked, "Are you a citizen of Village of Iron (Romans)?"

"Yes, I am," Small Man (Paul) replied.

28"I paid a high price to become a citizen," the officer said to him.

"But I was born a citizen of Village of Iron (Rome)," Small Man (Paul) replied.

29Right away the soldiers who were about to question him backed away. Fear came upon the head officer as he realized that he had bound a citizen of Village of Iron (Rome) in chains.

BEFORE THE GRAND COUNCIL

30But the head officer wanted to know what Small Man (Paul) was being accused of by the Tribal Members, so, before releasing him, he instructed the head holy men and the Grand Council to meet. He then brought in Small Man (Paul) and stood him before them.

23

HE SPEAKS TO THE GRAND COUNCIL

1Small Man (Paul) looked deeply into the eyes of the members of the Grand Council.

"My fellow Tribal Members," he said to the council, "All my life I have walked in a good way, with a pure heart before the Great Spirit."

2*Hearing this*, Creator Shows Kindness (Ananias) the chief holy man ordered the ones standing near Small Man (Paul) to strike his mouth.

3"Creator will strike you, you false-faced pretender!" Small Man (Paul) said

back to him. "Do you sit there using our own tribal law to decide my fate, and then break the same law by ordering me struck?"

4The ones standing near him said, "How dare you speak in a disrespectful manner to Creator's chief holy man?"

5"Fellow Tribal Members," he replied, "I did not recognize that he was the chief holy man, for it is written in the Sacred Teachings, 'You must not speak against a leader of your people.'[a]"

6Small Man (Paul), knowing that both the Upright Ones (Sadducees) and the Separated Ones (Pharisees) sat on the Grand Council, said to them, "My fellow Tribal Members, I am a Separated One (Pharisee). It is because of my hope that the dead will rise to life again that I am on trial here today."

THE COUNCIL IS DIVIDED

7When he said this, an argument broke out between the Separated Ones (Pharisees) and the Upright Ones (Sadducees). This created a division in the council, **8**for the Upright Ones (Sadducees) say the dead will not rise and that there are no spirits or spirit-messengers, but the Separated Ones (Pharisees) believe in them all.

9The arguments grew louder and louder. Then some scroll keepers who were among the Separated Ones (Pharisees) stood up and voiced their argument forcefully.

"We find no reason to condemn this man," they cried out. "It could be that a spirit or spirit-messenger has spoken to him!"

10The division broke out into violence. The head officer, afraid that Small Man (Paul) would be torn apart by them,

---

[a] **23:5** Exodus 22:28

ordered his soldiers to take him by force and bring him back to their lodge.

[11]That night Creator Sets Free (Jesus) came and stood near him *in a sacred vision.*

"Be strong of heart," he said to him, "for in the same manner you have represented me in Village of Peace (Jerusalem), you must also represent me in Village of Iron (Rome)."

THE PLOT TO KILL SMALL MAN

[12]Early the next day, some of the Tribal Members schemed together against Small Man (Paul). They bound themselves in a solemn promise that they would not eat or drink until they had killed him. [13]There were more than forty men who bound themselves to each other in this twisted plan.

[14]They went to the head holy men and elders and said to them, "We have bound ourselves with a solemn promise to neither eat nor drink until we have killed Small Man (Paul). [15]So we want you and the council to ask the head officer to bring him to you. Tell him that you plan to ask Small Man (Paul) some more questions. We will then be ready to ambush him on the way and kill him."

WARNING FROM A NEPHEW

[16]But when Small Man's (Paul's) nephew heard about the ambush, he snuck into the place where Small Man (Paul) was being held and warned him.

[17]Small Man (Paul) then called out to one of the head soldiers, "This young man has something important to report, so take him to your head officer."

[18]Hearing this, the head soldier took him to the head officer, and said, "The prisoner Small Man (Paul) asked me to bring this young man to you. He has something important to tell you."

[19]So the head officer took the young man aside, and asked, "What is it you want to report to me?"

[20]"Some Tribal Members from the council have agreed to ask you to bring Small Man (Paul) before them, as if they want to question him some more," he told the head officer. [21]"But do not let them fool you, for there are more than forty men waiting to ambush him on the way. They have bound themselves by a solemn promise to neither eat nor drink until they have killed him. They are ready now and waiting for you to agree to bring him."

[22]The head officer told the young man to say nothing, sent him away, [23]and then called two head soldiers to himself.

SMALL MAN SENT TO THE GOVERNOR

"I want you to be ready by the third hour of the night," he instructed them. "Gather seventy horsemen and two hundred spearmen and take them as far as Chief Village (Caesarea)."

[24]The head officer also provided a horse and horsemen for Small Man (Paul), to bring him safely to Happy Man (Felix), the governor for the People of Iron (Romans).

[25]Then he wrote a letter *for them* to give to the governor:

[26]"Greetings from Limping Man Who Sets Free (Claudius Lysias) to the most noble Happy Man (Felix), governor representing the People of Iron (Romans).

[27]"This man, *who has been brought before you,* was taken captive by the Tribal People, who were about to kill him. But when I learned that he was *also* a citizen of the People of Iron (Romans), I had my soldiers rescue him. [28]To find out what he was accused of, I took him before their Grand Council. [29]I learned

that he was being accused of matters relating to their own tribal laws, but nothing deserving death or imprisonment. ³⁰When I was told of a plot against this man, I had him sent to you at once, and told his accusers to bring their accusations to you."

³¹So the soldiers, following their instructions, took Small Man (Paul) by night to First Ancestor Village (Antipatris). ³²The next day the soldiers let the horsemen take him further, while they returned to their lodge. ³³When the horsemen came to Chief Village (Caesarea), they gave the letter to the governor and turned Small Man (Paul) over to him. ³⁴After reading the letter, the governor asked which territory he was from. Learning that Small Man (Paul) was from Turns Over (Cilicia), he agreed to hear his case.

³⁵"I will make my decision," he said to Small Man (Paul), "after your accusers arrive."

He then ordered that Small Man (Paul) should be kept under guard in their lodge, which used to be the lodge of Looks Brave (Herod), *the bad-hearted chief of the tribes of Wrestles with Creator (Israel).*

24

SMALL MAN ACCUSED

¹Five days later Creator Shows Kindness (Ananias) the chief holy man, along with some of the elders and a legal expert named Third (Tertullus), came before Happy Man (Felix), and with many words they brought to him their accusations against Small Man (Paul). ²When they brought Small Man (Paul) before them, the legal expert began to accuse him.

"O Most Honored Happy Man (Felix)," he began his speech, "our hearts are glad

that under your guidance we have had many winters of peace. Because of your wisdom, many good changes have come to the people, ³changes that we fully welcome with glad and open hearts. ⁴So we beg you, in your kindness, to hear our short complaint.

⁵"We have found this man to be a troublemaker who, all over the world, stirs up our Tribal People in a bad way. He is a headman of the wayward band called Seed Planters (Nazarenes). ⁶When he tried to defile our sacred lodge, we arrested him ªand would have judged him by our own tribal law. ⁷But the head officer Limping Man Who Sets Free (Claudius Lysias) came and forcefully took him out of our hands. He then ordered his accusers to come to you. ⁸When you question him for yourself, you will learn from him that we speak the truth."

⁹The Tribal Members who were there also joined in the accusations, saying it was all true.

¹⁰The governor then motioned for Small Man (Paul) to speak.

"I know that for many winters you have been a judge over this nation," Small Man (Paul) said. "My heart is glad that I can clear the air regarding these things. ¹¹As you will find out from others, it has not been more than twelve days since I went to Village of Peace (Jerusalem) to offer my prayers and participate in traditional ceremonies at the sacred lodge.

¹²"No one there found me making trouble or stirring up a crowd. Not at the sacred lodge, the gathering house, or in the village. ¹³No one here can prove the accusations they now bring against me.

¹⁴"I speak from my heart. I am only guilty of following the Way, which they

---

ª**24:6** The remainder of verse 6 along with verse 7 are not included in many ancient manuscripts.

say is false. But this is the way I follow the Great Spirit of my ancestors. This Way is in agreement with the law of my people and what has been foretold by our prophets. **15**This gives me the same hope in Creator that my accusers have. That all who have died, both those who do good and those who do bad, will rise to life again. **16**Knowing this, my aim is to walk with a clear heart toward the Great Spirit and my fellow human beings.

17"After being away for a number of winters, I returned to Village of Peace (Jerusalem). I brought gifts for the poor of my nation, as well as ceremonial offerings. **18**When they found me, I was in the sacred lodge participating in a ceremony. There was no crowd or disturbance. **19**Some Tribal Members from Land of the Rising Sun (Asia) were there at that time. If they have any accusation against me, they are the ones who should make it.

20"Let these men who are here tell you what I did wrong when I stood before the council. **21**The only thing they can say against me is what I said to them: 'I am on trial today because I believe in the rising of the dead!'"

22But Happy Man (Felix), who knew more about the Way, delayed his decision.

"I will make my decision," he said, "when Limping Man Who Sets Free (Claudius Lysias) arrives."

23He then ordered the head soldier to keep Small Man (Paul) under guard but to give him some freedom and permit his friends to care for his needs.

24A number of days later Happy Man (Felix) returned with Tender Woman (Drusilla), his wife, who was a member of the tribes of Wrestles with Creator (Israel). He had Small Man (Paul) brought to him,

and he *and his wife* listened to him tell about his trust in Creator Sets Free (Jesus), the Chosen One. **25**They talked back and forth about Creator's right ways, about self-control, and about the judgment that was to come. But Happy Man (Felix) became afraid.

"Leave me for now," he said. "I will send for you when I have more time to talk."

26He was hoping that Small Man (Paul) would offer him a bribe, so from time to time he would send for him and talk with him, *but Small Man (Paul) remained under guard.* **27**Two winters later Happy Man (Felix) was replaced as governor by Pig Festival (Porcius Festus). Then to gain favor with the Tribal Members, he left Small Man (Paul) in prison.

25

SMALL MAN PUT ON TRIAL

1Three days after Festival (Festus) arrived, he went from Chief Village (Caesarea) to Village of Peace (Jerusalem). **2**So the head holy men and other tribal leaders *wasted no time and* brought to him their accusations against Small Man (Paul). They begged him, **3**as a favor to their nation, to have Small Man (Paul) returned to Village of Peace (Jerusalem). They were hatching a plot to have him killed along the way.

4"Small Man (Paul) is being guarded in Chief Village (Caesarea)," Festival (Festus) said to them, "and I am returning there soon. **5**Have your tribal leaders travel with me. If this man has done wrong, I will hear your accusations against him there."

6So after eight or ten more days he left for Chief Village (Caesarea). The next day he sat down in his council chair, where he would decide this case, and ordered Small Man (Paul) to be brought before him. **⁷**As soon as he arrived, the Tribal Members who had come from Village of Peace (Jerusalem) circled around him and began to make accusations against him that they could not prove.

⁸Small Man (Paul) stood up and said, "I have not spoken against our tribal law, our sacred lodge, or against the Ruler of the People of Iron (Caesar)."

⁹But then Festival (Festus), wishing to gain the favor of the tribal leaders, responded to Small Man (Paul) and asked, "Do you wish to stand trial before me in Village of Peace (Jerusalem)?"

Small Man (Paul) could see right through him.

¹⁰"I am making my stand here, before you, at the council chair of the People of Iron (Romans). This is where the decision about me should be made. By now, it should be clear to you that I have done nothing wrong against my own people."

Small Man (Paul) paused to draw strength from deep within. He made up his mind to do what was right and follow the path Creator had set before him.

¹¹"If I have done anything to deserve death," he continued, "I will not try to escape. But if their accusations are false, you have no power to turn me over to them. I appeal to the Ruler of the People of Iron (Caesar)."

¹²Festival (Festus), after speaking to his council, said to him, "You have made your appeal to the Ruler of the People of Iron (Caesar), and to him you will go."

SMALL MAN AND CHIEF WILD HORSE

Chief Wild Horse (Agrippa) was a Tribal Member who ruled over some of the territory near Circle of Nations (Galilee) under the power of the People of Iron (Romans). He was the son of Looks Brave (Herod) also named Wild Horse (Agrippa) and the great grandson of Looks Brave (Herod) called the Great.

¹³A number of days later Chief Wild Horse (Agrippa), along with his sister Bringer of Victory (Bernice), came to pay their respects to *the new governor* Festival (Festus). **¹⁴**Since they were lodging with him for a number of days, he explained to the chief about the accusations made against Small Man (Paul) by the tribal leaders.

"There is a man here who was left by Happy Man (Felix) as a prisoner. **¹⁵**When I went to Village of Peace (Jerusalem), the head holy men and the tribal elders told me about him. They wanted me to find him guilty. **¹⁶**I informed them that the laws of the People of Iron (Romans) would not permit me to hand over anyone until they could stand face to face with their accusers and make a defense for themselves.

¹⁷"So when they came here, I wasted no time. The next day I sat as head of the council and sent for him to stand trial. **¹⁸**I expected to hear from his accusers about some great evil, **¹⁹**but instead their accusations were about their own spiritual ways and about a man named Creator Sets Free (Jesus), who was dead but who Small Man (Paul) said was alive.

²⁰"Since I knew nothing about these things, I asked if he wished to go to Village of Peace (Jerusalem) and face his accusers there. **²¹**But he appealed his case to the Ruler of the People of Iron (Caesar) and to be kept under guard until I could send him to our Ruler for his decision."

²²Wild Horse (Agrippa) then said to Festival (Festus), "I would like to hear from this man for myself."

"You will hear him tomorrow," Festival (Festus) replied.

SMALL MAN BEFORE CHIEF WILD HORSE

²³The next day Wild Horse (Agrippa) and Bringer of Victory (Bernice), making a big show of it, came into the council room along with the head officers and leaders of the village. Festival (Festus) gave the order, and Small Man (Paul) was brought in.

²⁴"Chief Wild Horse (Agrippa) and all who are here," the governor said, "standing before you is the man whom the whole tribal nation has asked me to condemn to death. ²⁵But I have not found him guilty of anything deserving death. Since he has appealed to the Ruler of the People of Iron (Caesar), I will send him to Village of Iron (Rome).

²⁶"But, since I am not sure what message to send to my Ruler about him, I have decided to bring him to you all, and above all to you, Chief Wild Horse (Agrippa), so you can give me counsel in this matter. ²⁷For it seems unwise to me to send a prisoner there without a clear report of the accusations made against him."

26

SMALL MAN TELLS HIS STORY

¹Then Wild Horse (Agrippa) said to Small Man (Paul), "You are permitted to speak and tell your side of this story."

So Small Man (Paul) stretched out his hand and began to tell his side of the story.

²"Chief Wild Horse (Agrippa)," he began, "Since my accusers are all Tribal Members, *like yourself*, it seems good to me that I can defend myself before you today, ³mainly because you know so well how we disagree about many of our tribal traditions. So I humbly ask that you listen to me with patience.

⁴"All of our Tribal People know the manner I have walked, even from the days of my youth, when I lived among our people in Village of Peace (Jerusalem). ⁵They have known from the first, if they will admit to it, that I walked in the way of a Separated One (Pharisee), the most demanding of all our spiritual paths.

⁶"The reason I stand here on trial before you today is my hope in the promise made by the Great Spirit to our ancestors. ⁷It is a promise our twelve tribes solemnly strive for as they serve him night and day with prayers and ceremonies. It is for this hope, O honored chief, that I stand here accused by our tribal leaders! ⁸Why would any of our people find it impossible to believe that the Great Spirit raises the dead?

⁹"*At first,* I myself was convinced that I should do as much harm as I could to destroy the reputation of Creator Sets Free (Jesus) of Seed Planter Village (Nazareth). ¹⁰In Village of Peace (Jerusalem), I obtained permission from the head holy men to capture and put many of Creator's holy ones into prison. Not only that, but I voted against them when they were being killed. ¹¹In all our gathering houses I violently punished them, trying to force them to speak against Creator Sets Free (Jesus). Like a threatening storm I took out my anger on them, even pursuing them to faraway places.

SMALL MAN TELLS HIS SACRED VISION

¹²"On one of these journeys I was on my way to Silent Weaver (Damascus) with the full approval and authority of the head

holy men. **¹³**Then at midday, O honored chief, I saw a light from the spirit-world above shining down on me and my fellow travelers. **¹⁴**We all had fallen to the ground when I heard a voice speaking to me in our tribal language.

"'Man Who Questions (Saul), Man Who Questions (Saul),' the voice *called my name twice, and* asked, 'why are you pursuing and mistreating me? It is a hard and painful thing to fight against me, like a horse pushing back against the spurs.'

¹⁵"'Honored One,' I said back to the voice, 'who are you?'

"'I am Creator Sets Free (Jesus),' the voice answered, 'the one you are pursuing and mistreating. **¹⁶**Now rise up! Stand to your feet! I have chosen you to be my servant, a witness who will tell others what you have seen with your own eyes and what I will reveal to you.

¹⁷"'I will rescue you from your own people and from the Outside Nations, the ones to whom I am sending you. **¹⁸**My message will open their eyes so they may turn from the path of darkness to walk the road of life, and turn away from the power of the Accuser (Satan) to the power of the Great Spirit, so they may be released and set free from their bad hearts and wrongdoings. In this way, they will find their place among all who are made holy by trusting in me.'

SMALL MAN FINISHES HIS STORY

¹⁹"So then, Chief Wild Horse (Agrippa), I was true to this sacred vision. **²⁰**First I told those in Silent Weaver (Damascus). Then I told the people in Village of Peace (Jerusalem) and all in the territory of the Land of Promise (Judea), and to the Outside Nations. I told them all that they should change their thinking, return to

Creator's ways, and walk in a manner worthy of this change of heart.

²¹"This was the reason that these Tribal Members took hold of me at the sacred lodge and tried to kill me. **²²**Up to this day, with the help of the Great Spirit, I have told the truth to both small and great. I have said only what was foretold by the ancient prophets and by Drawn from the Water (Moses). **²³**I said that the Chosen One must suffer, and then, being the first to rise from the dead, he would be the light bearer, shining both on our people and on the Outside Nations."

²⁴Right then, as Small Man (Paul) was still speaking, Festival (Festus) interrupted. "Small Man (Paul)," he shouted, "you are sick in the head! Your much learning is twisting your mind!"

²⁵"O most noble Festival (Festus)," Small Man (Paul) replied, "what I am saying is clear and understandable. **²⁶**Chief Wild Horse (Agrippa) understands these things, so I am speaking boldly to him and holding nothing back. I am convinced that he is aware of all that I speak of, for none of these things happened in a cave."

Small Man (Paul) then turned and faced Chief Wild Horse (Agrippa).

²⁷"Chief Wild Horse (Agrippa)," he boldly asked, "do you believe in what the prophets have spoken? I know that you do!"

²⁸"Do you think that in such a short time I could be talked into becoming a follower of the Chosen One?" he replied.

²⁹"I pray to the Great Spirit that, whether in a short time or long, all who hear me today would become as I am—except for these chains."

³⁰*After hearing these words* Chief Wild Horse (Agrippa) stood to his feet. The governor and Bringer of Victory (Bernice) and all the others stood up with him. **31**They left the room, and after talking together they said, "This man has done nothing that deserves prison or death." **32**Then Chief Wild Horse (Agrippa) said to the governor, "This man could have been set free if he had not appealed to the Ruler of the People of Iron (Caesar)."

27

VOYAGE OF TROUBLE

1They decided to send Small Man (Paul) by a great canoe to Land of Young Bulls (Italy).

Village of Iron (Rome) was the head village of the Ruler of the People of Iron (Caesar) in the territory of Land of Young Bulls (Italy).

So Small Man (Paul), along with some other prisoners, was turned over to a head soldier of the Royal Guard, named Soft Haired Man (Julius). **2**At Harbor of Death (Adramyttium) we climbed aboard a canoe that was going our way, making stops at harbors along the shoreline of Land of the Rising Sun (Asia). So we launched out into the great waters. A man named Good Chief (Aristarchus) from False Victory (Thessalonica), in the territory of the Land of Tall People (Macedonia), also journeyed with us. **3**On the following day we came ashore at Hunting Grounds (Sidon). There Soft Haired Man (Julius) was kind to Small Man (Paul) and permitted him to go to his friends so they could care for him. **4**From there we launched out again into the great waters but remained close to the shoreline of the Island of Flowers (Cyprus), for the winds were strong against us. **5**From there we crossed the open waters near Turns Over (Cilicia) and Many Tribes (Pamphylia), and then came to land at Weeping Waters (Myra) in the territory of Land of Wolves (Lycia). **6**At Weeping Waters (Myra) the head soldier found a great wooden sea canoe on its way from Man Fighter (Alexandria) to Land of Young Bulls (Italy) that would give us passage, so we climbed aboard. **7**For a number of days we traveled along slowly until with difficulty we came near Old Village (Cnidus). The wind was against us and began to force us off course, so we remained close to the shoreline of Flesh Eater Island (Crete) near Village of Garments (Salmone). **8**From there we struggled along the shoreline until we came to a place called Good Harbor, near Shaggy Village (Lasea).

9The journey was no longer safe. Too much time had passed, for the Festival of Release from Wrongdoings[a] had already passed. So Small Man (Paul) gave them his advice.

10"Fellow travelers," he said to them, "I can see that this journey ahead of us will end in injury and loss, not only of the canoe and its goods, but also of our lives." **11**But the head soldier was more convinced by the headman of the canoe than by the words of Small Man (Paul). **12**And because the harbor was not a good place to stay the winter, a greater number of people decided it was best to launch out into the great waters and try to reach Palm Tree (Phoenix). This was a harbor on the shore of Flesh Eater Island (Crete), facing both to the southwest and to the northwest.

13But then, when a gentle south wind began to blow, they thought they could reach their journey's end. So they

---

a27:9 Day of Atonement, a festival of the Jews

prepared their canoe and launched out into the great waters again. They stayed close to the shoreline of Flesh Eater Island (Crete) for safety, **14**but it was not long before a violent wind roared down from the island—a wind they call the Northeaster.

15The canoe was caught in the wind, and when we could make no headway against it, we gave up trying and let it force us along. **16**Then, when we came under some cliffs, we were finally able to get the canoe under control. **17**We roped the life raft we were towing behind us to the side of the canoe, and then tied the ropes around the canoe to hold it together. Then, fearing we would be caught in the shallow sandbars, we lowered our anchor rock and let the canoe be dragged along by the fierce winds.

18But the next day, after being pounded by the storm, they began to throw the goods overboard. **19**Then, on the third day, with their bare hands they threw the benches and whatever else they could find into the water. **20**For many days the storm continued to rage, the sun did not shine, nor could the stars be seen at night. All hope of being rescued was gone.

VISITED BY A SPIRIT-MESSENGER

21After they had gone for many days without food, Small Man (Paul) stood up among them.

"Fellow travelers," he said to them, "if you would have listened to me and not set out from Flesh Eater Island (Crete), you would not have suffered this injury and loss. **22**But I say to you now, do not lose your courage. For even though our canoe will be lost, not one of us will lose our lives. **23**Last night a spirit-messenger

from the Great Spirit, the one I belong to and serve, stood by my side. **24**"'Do not fear,' he said to me, 'for you must stand before the Ruler of the People of Iron (Caesar). Behold! The Giver of Life has gifted you with the lives of all who journey with you!'"

> The men just stared at Small Man (Paul) with wondering eyes and said nothing. So he once again spoke courage into their hearts.

25"Be strong of heart," Small Man (Paul) said to them, "for I have faith that the Great Spirit will do everything he told me. **26**But we will have to find an island to land on."

THEY COME NEAR LAND

27It had now been fourteen nights that we had been driven about by the wind and waves of the Sea with No Wood (Adriatic Sea). In the middle of the night, the men who guided the canoe could feel that we were near land. **28**They began to test the depth of the water and found it was as deep as a tall tree.[a] Then a short distance later they tested it again and found that it was not as deep.[b]

29Since they knew the shoreline was rocky, they were afraid we might run into a large rock under the water, so they dropped four anchor rocks from the back of the canoe and prayed for the sun to rise.

SOME OF THE MEN TRY TO ESCAPE

30But then, some of the men, trying to escape, untied the life raft and lowered it into the water, pretending they were putting out more anchor rocks.

---

a 27:28 About 120 feet
b 27:28 About 90 feet

Small Man *(Paul)* saw what they were doing and went to the head soldier.

³¹"If these men leave the canoe," he said to him and the other soldiers, "you will not be saved *and all will be lost.*"

³²So the soldiers cut the leather straps from the life raft and let it drift away.

HE ENCOURAGES THE MEN

³³Just before the sun began to rise, Small Man *(Paul)* urged everyone to eat something.

"For fourteen days now you have been constantly worrying and have not eaten any food," he said to them. ³⁴"Please eat something now. You will need it to survive. *Do not fear! No one will die or be harmed.* Not even one hair from your heads will be lost."

³⁵After he said this, he took a piece of frybread and, giving thanks to the Great Spirit in front of them all, he broke it and began to eat. ³⁶This gave the men courage, so they also began to eat.

³⁷All in all there were two hundred seventy-six persons in this great wooden canoe. ³⁸When they finished eating, they tossed the rest of the grain over the side to lighten the canoe.

SUNRISE AND A ROUGH LANDING

³⁹When daylight came, they did not recognize the shoreline, but they could see a bay with a beach. They decided to try to run the canoe up into the sandy beach, if possible. ⁴⁰So they cut the ropes to the anchor rocks and left them in the water. At the same time they untied the ropes holding the rudders in place. Then they set the men to the paddles, and they paddled with all their mightᵃ heading toward the beach.

ᵃ**27:40** Lit. *They put up the sails into the wind*

⁴¹But on the way the canoe struck a sandbar and stayed there, stuck in the sand. The front of the canoe began to break from the force of the waves. ⁴²The soldiers made a plan to kill the prisoners so none could escape by swimming away. ⁴³But the head soldier, wanting to spare the life of Small Man *(Paul)*, stopped them. He ordered the ones who could swim to jump overboard and swim to land. ⁴⁴The rest he sent floating on wooden poles and pieces of the canoe. In this way all who were aboard made it safely to the land.

28

A WARM WELCOME

¹After everyone was safe on the shore, we found out that this land was called Island of Honey *(Malta)*. ²The indigenous people there showed great kindness to us. It was raining and cold, so they built us a warm fire and welcomed us all.

SNAKE BITE

³Small Man *(Paul)* gathered a bundle of sticks and threw them on the fire, but the heat forced out a poisonous snake that bit into his hand and would not let go.

⁴When the local natives saw the snake hanging from his hand, they said, "This man must be a murderer. Even though he escaped from the great waters, the spirit who rights wrongs will not let him live."

⁵Then Small Man *(Paul)* shook the snake from his hand into the fire, and nothing bad happened to him. ⁶The local people were sure that he would swell up or fall down dead. They waited a long time, but when they saw that nothing bad had come to him, they changed their minds and said he must be a powerful spirit.

SMALL MAN HEALS THE SICK

⁷There was a piece of land belonging to From the People (Publius), the chief of the island. He welcomed us into his home for three days and took care of all our needs. ⁸At that time the father of From the People (Publius) was sick in bed with a high fever and a bloody stool. Small Man (Paul) went to see him and, after praying, laid his hands on the man and healed him.

⁹After that, the rest of the island natives who were sick came to Small Man (Paul), and they were also healed. ¹⁰The people honored us with many gifts, and when we were leaving, they loaded our canoe with all that we needed.

ARRIVAL AT VILLAGE OF IRON

¹¹Three months later we again launched out into the great waters in another very large wooden canoe. This canoe was made by the people from Man Fighter (Alexandria). The front of the canoe was carved into the images of two powerful lookalike spirits, Bright Star (Castor) and Much Sweet (Pollux).

¹²We came to land at Smelly Swamp (Syracuse) and lodged there for three days. ¹³From there we launched out and came to Royal Place (Rhegium). The next day, with the help of a south wind, we arrived at Deep Water Hole (Puteoli). ¹⁴It was there that we found some sacred family members, who welcomed us to stay with them for seven days.

After that we left again toward Village of Iron (Rome). ¹⁵The sacred family members who lived there, when they heard we were coming, came to greet us from as far away as the Great Trading Post (Appius Market) and the Three Lodging Houses *along the Great Trail (Appian Way)*. When Small Man (Paul) saw them, he gave thanks to the Great Spirit, and his heart was strengthened. ¹⁶Then, upon our arrival to Village of Iron (Rome), Small Man (Paul) was permitted to live by himself with a soldier to guard him.

HE MEETS THE LOCAL COUNCIL

¹⁷Three days later Small Man (Paul) asked to meet with the local tribal leaders. When they had gathered together, he told them the story of what had happened to him.

He stood there in chains under the guard of a soldier of the People of Iron (Romans). Yet he spoke with dignity as he faced the leaders of his own people.

"Fellow Tribal Members," he said to them, "I have done nothing against our people or the traditions of our ancestors, but even so I was arrested in Village of Peace (Jerusalem) and handed over to the People of Iron (Romans). ¹⁸They questioned me and were about to release me, since I had done nothing deserving death. ¹⁹But when our tribal leaders refused to agree, I had no choice but to appeal to the Ruler of the People of Iron (Caesar), not that I have any accusation to bring against my own people.

²⁰"It is for this very reason that I have asked to see and speak with you, for I wear these chains because I have the same hope held by all the tribes of Wrestles with Creator (Israel)."

Small Man (Paul) then stopped speaking, looked calmly into their faces, and waited for them to reply.

²¹"No one from the Land of Promise (Judea) has come with a bad report," they said to him, "nor have we received any written message about you from them. ²²But we want to hear how you see this

new Way that some are following. We know that people everywhere speak against this Way."

SENT TO THE OUTSIDE NATIONS

[23]They made plans to meet again with Small Man (Paul) on another day. When that day came, they arrived in large numbers at the place where he was lodging. From sunrise to sunset, using the law of Drawn from the Water (Moses) and the teachings of the prophets, he spoke many words to clearly show them the truth about Creator's good road and about Creator Sets Free (Jesus).

[24]Some were convinced by his words, but others refused to believe. [25]So they disagreed with each other and began to leave after Small Man (Paul) said these last words to them, "The Holy Spirit was right when he spoke these words through the prophet Creator Will Help Us (Isaiah):

[26]"'Go and tell this people, "You will hear but not understand, you will see but not know what you are seeing, [27]because the heart of this people has become like stone. Their ears have grown dull and they have closed their eyes. If only they would open their ears and eyes, then their hearts would understand, and they would return to me and be healed.[a]"'"

FINAL WORDS

A look of sorrow came over the face of Small Man (Paul) as he watched his own people turn and walk away.

[28]"So let it be known to you," he said to them, "that this message about the Great Spirit's plan to rescue and make whole has been sent to the Outside Nations. And they will listen!"

[29]Hearing this, the Tribal Members argued fiercely with one another as they walked away.[b]

[30]Small Man (Paul) continued to live in his own rented house and welcomed all who came to him. [31]With great boldness he spoke openly about Creator's good road and kept teaching others about our Honored Chief Creator Sets Free (Jesus), the Chosen One.

Aho! May it be so!

---

[a]**28:27** Isaiah 6:9-10
[b]**28:29** Some ancient manuscripts do not include verse 29.

SMALL MAN TO THE SACRED FAMILY IN VILLAGE OF IRON

ROMANS

1

GREETINGS AND BLESSINGS

¹From Small Man (Paul), a servant of the Chosen One, Creator Sets Free (Jesus).

The Great Spirit has called me to be a message bearer, one who has been set apart to tell his good story. ²The Sacred Teachings tell us about this good story that was promised by the prophets *from long ago, who spoke from the Great Spirit.*

³This is the good story about Creator's own Son. In his human body he was descended from *Chief* Much Loved One (David), ⁴and in a powerful way he was shown to be the Son of the Great Spirit when his human body was raised from the dead by the Spirit of all that is sacred.

⁵It is because of the gift of his great kindness that we have been chosen to be his message bearers. We are telling his good story to all Nations so they can put their trust in Creator, follow him in all his ways, and bring honor to his name. ⁶This sacred task is also yours, because you have been called to belong to Creator Sets Free (Jesus) the Chosen One.

⁷I write this message to the ones who live in Village of Iron (Rome). You are all deeply loved by the Great Spirit and are called to be his holy ones. I send to you great kindness and peace from our Father the Creator and from our Honored Chief, Creator Sets Free (Jesus) the Chosen One.

⁸First of all, I thank the Great Spirit, along with Creator Sets Free (Jesus) the Chosen One, for all of you, because all over the world people are hearing about your trust in his good story.

PRAYERS AND DESIRES

⁹⁻¹⁰The Great Spirit, whom I serve from my spirit by telling others the good story about his Son, knows how much I pray for you. I never stop bringing your name before Creator when I send my voice to him, asking whether this is the time that he will finally open the way for me to come and be with you.

¹¹I am longing to see you face to face, so I can pass on to you some spiritual gift that will give you strength, ¹²so that we can strengthen our trust in him and together become firmly rooted *in the good story.*

¹³I want you to know, my sacred family members, how often I have tried to come to you, but many things have held me back. I have desired to share in some of the spiritual fruit Creator has grown from you, in the same way I have from others who are of the Outside Nations.

¹⁴Because of the great debt *of love* that I owe, I must tell the good story to both the civilized and uncivilized—to all who walk in the ways of wisdom and to all

who do not. [15]And now I am able and ready to tell the good story to you who live in Village of Iron (Rome).

NOT ASHAMED

[16]I am not ashamed of this good story, for to all who trust in its message it has Creator's power to set free and make whole. This is true, first for our Tribal People, and then to all the Outside Nations![a] [17]For this good story tells about Creator's great faithfulness to do what is good and right. It is the story of faithfulness and trust from beginning to end. It is written in our Sacred Teachings, "The ones in good standing will find life by trusting[b] *in what the Great Spirit has done for them.*"

NO EXCUSE FOR HIDING THE TRUTH

[18]From the spirit-world above, Creator's great anger is being shown to the ones who hide the truth by following their bad hearts and wrongful ways. [19]*The Great Spirit has a reason to be angry,* because he has clearly made himself known to all human beings. [20]Ever since the world was made, his invisible, never-fading power and Sacred Spirit[c] have been understood and clearly shown through the things that he has made.

So they have no good reason *not to trust in what Creator has done for them.* [21]For even though they knew him as Creator, they did not thank him or give him the honor he deserved. This empty way of thinking took hold of their foolish hearts and led them into darkness.

FOOLISH WAYS

[22]Even though they thought they were wise, they became only foolish two-

leggeds. [23]They traded the beauty and honor of the Great Spirit, who has always existed, for carved images of short-lived human beings, winged ones, four-leggeds, and snakes that crawl on the ground.

[24]For this reason the Great Spirit permitted them to go their own way and follow the dark desires found in their own hearts, desires with one another that failed to honor the sacred purpose their bodies had been created for. [25]In doing so, they traded Creator's truth for something false, and honored and served created things more than the Great Spirit. He is the one who is to be given honor and blessing to the time beyond the end of all days. Aho! May it be so!

[26]So then, the Great Spirit permitted them to go their own way to dishonor themselves by following these dishonorable desires. Their women traded what was their natural sexual desire for what was not natural. [27]Their men did the same things, giving up their natural desire for women and fanning into flame a hunger for one another, men with men, dishonoring their own bodies. In doing so, they had to face for themselves the end result of this wrong thinking. [28]Since they did not want to know the Great Spirit, he turned them over to their worthless ways of thinking, to do things that should not be done.

FROM BAD TO WORSE

[29-30]Filled with these wrong ways, they followed their bad hearts and made evil their aim. Keeping all things for themselves and not sharing, they became filled with greed, hatred, and violence. This took them down a dark path of fighting and killing, of lies and telling bad stories about others. They became puffed up, disrespectful and arrogant,

---

[a]**1:16** Lit. *Greeks*
[b]**1:17** Habakkuk 2:4
[c]**1:20** Lit. *divinity or divine nature*

finders of new ways to do evil things, disobedient to parents, and they even began to hate the Great Spirit. **³¹**This turned them into foolish, ruthless treaty breakers, with hearts like stone!

³²Even though they know that Creator is right when he says these worthless ways deserve death and will lead others there, they continue to walk in these ways, and *even worse*, they give their approval to other people who also walk this path.

2

WHO ARE YOU TO JUDGE?

¹But you who judge and decide the guilt of those who walk in these broken ways have no excuse for doing so. When you decide the guilt of others, you are only proving your own guilt, because you are doing the same kinds of things. **²**For we know that when the Great Spirit decides the guilt of the ones who do this, his judgment is always honorable and true.

³Tell me, when you do the same kinds of things that you judge others for, do you think what you have done will be hidden from the eyes of the Great Spirit? **⁴**Or do you hold bitter thoughts about Creator's kindness, patience, and willingness to bear with others? Do you not know that it is the kindness of the Great Spirit that draws you back to the path of his right ways?

⁵Because your hearts are unwilling to bend to the ways of the Great Spirit, your lives are becoming filled with the things that make the Great Spirit angry. A day is coming when Creator's great anger against these things and his decision to do what is right will be made clear.

CREATOR WILL BE THE ONE TO DECIDE

⁶Creator will honor each of us for what we have done. **⁷**He will honor the ones who have walked with firm steps on a path of doing good, and those who seek to live in the ways of beauty, honor, and spiritual purity.[a] The life of the world to come that never fades away, full of beauty and harmony, will be waiting for them.

⁸But the ones who live only for themselves, who refuse to walk the path of truth and stand against the right ways of the Great Spirit, will face a coming storm of great anger.

CREATOR TREATS ALL THE SAME WAY

⁹Trouble and sorrow await all human beings who walk an evil path. This is true, first of all for the members of the tribes of Wrestles with Creator (Israel) but also for the Outside Nations.[b] **¹⁰**But beauty, honor, and peace await all who walk in a good way. To the Tribal Members first, and also for the Outside Nations. **¹¹**For the Great Spirit does not favor one over the other.

¹²For all *the Outside Nations* who have followed their bad hearts and broken ways, even though they had no *written* law to follow, will come to a bad end. And all who were given the tribal law but also followed their bad heart and broken ways, their own tribal law will decide against them. **¹³**For it is not the ones who hear the law who have good standing with Creator but the ones who do what it says.

CREATION'S LAW WRITTEN ON HEARTS

¹⁴If the Outside Nations, who never heard the law, naturally do what they

---

[a] **2:7** *Spiritual purity* is our translation for a word that could mean immortality, incorruptibility, or integrity.
[b] **2:9** Greeks

know is right, the things instructed by the law, this natural law is all they need. [15]They show that creation's law is already at work within them, carved into their hearts. There is a voice deep within their inner being that speaks to them about what is right and what is wrong. [16]The good story that I tell says there will come a day when the Knower of Hearts, through Creator Sets Free (Jesus) the Chosen One, will bring to light what is good and bad about the secrets hidden in every human heart.

A WORD OF WARNING

[17]To those among you who call yourselves Tribal Members, who take your stand on tribal law and boast about your knowledge of the Great Spirit, [18]because you have been instructed by this law, you are sure you know what Creator wants and what is honorable to him. [19]You see yourselves as guides to the blind, lights to those in dark places, [20]wisdomkeepers to the unwise, and instructors of children. You, because you have the law, claim be the holders of all truth.

[21]So then, you who teach others, do you not teach yourself? You who tell others not to steal, do you take what is not yours? [22]You who instruct others to be faithful in marriage, do you sleep around from lodge to lodge? You who despise those who pray to spirit-images, do you steal from their sacred lodges?

[23]When you fail to follow the same tribal law you brag about, you bring insult to the Great Spirit. [24]This is in agreement with the Sacred Teachings that say, "It is because of you that the Outside Nations are speaking against the Great Spirit."[a]

---

[a]**2:24** Ezekiel 36:21

[25]The cutting of the flesh ceremony has honor if you follow the instructions of our tribal law. But if you fail to follow the law, your cutting of the flesh ceremony is worthless. [26]If someone who has never participated in the ceremony walks by nature in the right ways that the law teaches, then it will be as if he had participated in that ceremony.

[27]So then, if someone from an Outside Nation, who never participated in the cutting of the flesh ceremony, does by nature what the law instructs, that Outsider's ways will expose the guilt of the one who participated in the ceremony. For if he does not walk true to the whole written law, he remains guilty of breaking the law.

A MATTER OF THE HEART

[28-29]Being a true Tribal Member is a matter of the heart, not of blood or ceremonial law. It is the same with the cutting of the flesh ceremony. It is a spiritual matter, not a physical one. One might perform the ceremony perfectly according to tribal law for all to see, but it is not what happens on the outside that counts. It is what happens spiritually, on the inside, that has true meaning. Such a person seeks honor from the Great Spirit and not from human beings.

**THE BLESSINGS OF BEING
A TRIBAL MEMBER**

[1]So, *you might ask,* "What advantage do Tribal Members have that others do not have? What good does the cutting of the flesh ceremony do for them?"

[2]Being a Tribal Member is a blessing in many ways. The greatest blessing is

that they were entrusted with the Sacred Teachings of the Great Spirit!

WILL CREATOR BE TRUE TO HIS PROMISE?

³But, *you might also ask,* "What if some of them failed to honor this trust? Will their failure stop the Great Spirit from keeping his promises?"

⁴Never! Creator will be true to his promise, even if every human being fails to be true to him. This is what the Sacred Teachings say *about Creator,* "You will be true to your word and always decide what is best."

⁵As human beings we might think that our wrongdoing only proves that the Great Spirit was right about us all along. Would we then be able to say that it is wrong for him to show his anger toward us?

⁶This is a weak way of thinking, for if this were true, then how could Creator ever make things right again for the whole world?

⁷"But if the Great Spirit is proved to be right by my failure to stand true, why am I found to be in the wrong?"

⁸If this were true, then we might as well say what some have accused us of saying, "We should do evil that good may come of it." But their own words are proving them to be in the wrong and will take them to a bad end.

TRIBAL MEMBERS AND THE OUTSIDE NATIONS

⁹So what are we to say? Are we Tribal Members in a better place than the Outside Nations? I tell you without a doubt that we are not! For I have already made my argument that all human beings have followed their bad hearts and broken ways.

¹⁰It is written in our Sacred Teachings of our tribal law, "There is no one who stands upright. Not even one! ¹¹No one walks in wisdom. No one is seeking to walk with the Great Spirit. ¹²All have turned away from the good path to walk in worthless ways. No one is good and kind. Not even one!"ᵃ

¹³The Sacred Teachings also say, "Their throats are like open graves. They speak with forked tongues."ᵇ "From their lips come words full of snake venom."ᶜ ¹⁴"Their mouths are filled with bitter curses."ᵈ ¹⁵"Their feet are swift to shed blood. ¹⁶They leave behind a trail of misery and trouble wherever they go. ¹⁷The path of peace is beyond their way of thinking."ᵉ ¹⁸"They turn their eyes from the path of giving honor and respect to the Great Spirit."ᶠ

ALL HAVE FAILED

¹⁹From these Sacred Teachings we can see that we Tribal Members have not followed our own tribal laws. Our Sacred Teachings have spoken against us, giving us nothing to say in our own defense, and proving that we, along with all the people of the world, stand guilty. And we must give an answer to the Great Spirit for what we have done.

²⁰So then, it should be clear to all that no one can be in good standing in the eyes of the Great Spirit by doing what our tribal law says. What is clear is that the law shows us how bad our hearts have become and how broken our lives truly are.

GOOD STANDING IS A GIFT

²¹But there is a way to be in good standing with the Great Spirit that does not

---

ᵃ**3:12** Psalms 14:1-3; 53:1-3; Ecclesiastes 7:20
ᵇ**3:13** Psalm 5:9
ᶜ**3:13** Psalm 140:3
ᵈ**3:14** Psalm 10:7
ᵉ**3:17** Isaiah 59:7-8
ᶠ**3:18** Psalm 36:1

depend on us keeping tribal law! Even our Law and the Prophets have spoken the truth about this. [22]We can stand in a good way before the Great Spirit by trusting in Creator Sets Free (Jesus) the Chosen One and what he has done for us. This good standing is a gift to all who believe. It does not matter whether you are a Tribal Member[a] or from any other nation. [23]We are all the same because all of us have followed our bad hearts and broken ways, [24]but because of the gift of his great kindness all of us are put in good standing with the Great Spirit through what Creator Sets Free (Jesus) has done to set us free and make us whole.

[25]The Great Spirit sent Creator Sets Free (Jesus) to show through him the full meaning and purpose of the ancient mercy-seat ceremony, where our broken ways are washed clean when we trust in what the shedding of his lifeblood has accomplished.

The tribes of Wrestles with Creator (Israel) were given this ceremony to show that the Great Spirit had washed them clean from their bad hearts and broken ways. Once a year the chief holy man would take the blood of a ceremonial animal into the Most Holy Place in Creator's sacred lodge and sprinkle the blood onto the lid of a wooden box covered with gold. This lid of this wooden box was called the mercy seat.

The Great Spirit did this to prove that he was in the right when he released people from their bad hearts and broken ways in the ages past. [26]He also did this to show people in this present age that he has the right to put people in good standing with himself because they trust in what Creator Sets Free (Jesus) has done.

NO ROOM FOR BOASTING

[27]There is now no room for anyone to brag or boast. Why not? Because the Great Spirit has given us a new kind of law, not one that depends on what human strength or desire can do, but one that depends on trusting in what Creator Sets Free (Jesus) has done.

[28]Here is another way to see it. Good standing with the Great Spirit does not come by following our tribal law but by putting all our trust in what Creator has done for us. [29]For is not the Great Spirit the maker of all people, not just our Tribal People? Yes! He is the Great Spirit of all Nations!

[30]Since there is only one Great Spirit and Creator, he will treat us all the same. We have good standing with him by trusting in what he has done. It does not matter whether we are Tribal Members who have the cutting of the flesh ceremony or whether we are people from the Outside Nations who do not have this ceremony. [31]Does this new way of trusting in Creator Sets Free (Jesus) undo our tribal law? Not at all! Instead, it shows us the law's true meaning and purpose.[b]

FATHER OF MANY NATIONS

[1]How does our tribal ancestor, Father of Many Nations (Abraham), fit into this way of trusting? What can we learn from what he found? [2]If Father of Many Nations (Abraham) found good standing with Creator because he earned it by hard work, then he would be able to boast. But not in the eyes of the Great Spirit.

[3]But what do the Sacred Teachings tell us? "Father of Many Nations (Abraham)

---

put his trust in Creator. This is what gave him good standing in the eyes of the Great Spirit."[a]

[4]We know that what people gain from hard work is not a gift, but something earned. [5]But when people do no work but simply trust in Creator to release them from their spiritual darkness, this kind of trusting gives them good standing in the eyes of the Great Spirit.

[6]Chief Much Loved One (David) also speaks of the goodwill that is poured out on the ones who did no work to be in good standing in the eyes of Creator. [7]He says, "Creator's blessing rests on the ones who are released from their broken ways and those who have been set free from their wrongdoings. [8]His blessing rests on the ones whose bad hearts and broken ways are not held against them by the Great Spirit."[b]

[9]Is this blessing only for our Tribal Members who have the cutting of the flesh ceremony? Or is it also for the Outside Nations who do not have this ceremony?

> The "cutting of the flesh ceremony" was an initiation ceremony given to the men of the tribes of Wrestles with Creator (Israel) that made one a Tribal Member in good standing and a participant in the peace treaty the Great Spirit made with the tribes.

Now we have already said that it was by trusting that Father of Many Nations (Abraham) had good standing in the eyes of the Great Spirit. [10]So when was it that he trusted Creator and was counted to be in good standing? Was it before or after he performed the cutting of the flesh ceremony? We all know it was before. [11]He was given the cutting of the flesh ceremony to mark him as Creator's own, as a sign that he had already put his trust in the Great Spirit and that he was in good standing even before he performed the ceremony.

This means Father of Many Nations (Abraham), *just as his name says*, is the ancestor of all the Outside Nations who believe and trust in the Great Spirit. Even though they have never performed the ceremony, they are now in good standing with Creator. [12]He is also the ancestor of all of our Tribal Members who not only have performed the cutting of the flesh ceremony but who also follow the trust-filled path that Father of Many Nations (Abraham) walked before he performed the ceremony.

[13]The promise to Father of Many Nations (Abraham) that all the *nations of the world* would belong to him and his descendants did not come to him because he kept our tribal law, but because of the good standing that comes from trusting in the Great Spirit's promise. [14]But if the promise depends on walking the path of the law, then trusting means nothing and the promise falls to the ground.

[15]The law produces only anger *for those who fail to walk in it.* Where there is no law, *only a promise*, then no one would be failing to keep a law. [16]That is why the promise comes from trusting in the gift of Creator's great kindness, so that all the descendants of Father of Many Nations (Abraham) can be sure to receive it. This promise is not only for the ones who are under our tribal law, but for all who walk the same path of trust and faith that Father of Many Nations (Abraham) walked. For he is the father of us all!

[17]The Sacred Teachings tell us, "I have made you the father of many nations."[c] And in the eyes of the Great Spirit he is

---

[a]**4:3** Genesis 15:6
[b]**4:8** Psalm 32:1-2

[c]**4:17** Genesis 17:5

our father, for he put his trust in the Great Spirit, the one who gives life to the dead and speaks into being things that are not yet as if they already were.

[18]When all hope seemed to be gone, he trusted in the promise that he would become the father of many nations. The Great Spirit had said to him, "Your descendants will be *like the stars, too many to count.*"[a]

[19]When Father of Many Nations (Abraham) was about one hundred winters old, he could see that his body was as good as dead and that the womb of Noble Woman (Sarah) was barren. Even so, his faith did not become weak, [20]and he did not stumble from the path as he kept walking toward Creator's promise. His trust grew even stronger as he gave honor to the Great Spirit. [21]He knew deep down in his bones that whatever Creator had promised, he had the power to do. [22]This is why he was counted as one in good standing with the Great Spirit.

[23]These words, "he was counted as one in good standing," were not written down for him only, [24]but also for us, whom the Great Spirit will count among those who are in good standing with him, the ones who trust in him who raised our Honored Chief Creator Sets Free (Jesus) from the dead. [25]We are the ones who through our wrongdoings betrayed and killed him, but his rising from the dead proves we have good standing with the Great Spirit.

5 ⟨X⟩◀⟨X⟩▶◀⟨X⟩▶◀⟨X⟩▶◀⟨X⟩▶◀⟨X⟩▶

PEACE WITH THE GREAT SPIRIT

[1]This good standing we have brings peace with the Great Spirit. This peace comes from trusting in Creator Sets Free (Jesus)

---

[a]**4:18** Genesis 15:5

---

the Chosen One and what he has done for us. [2]Our trust in him opens the way into Creator's great kindness and is now the solid ground on which we stand. Now our boasting is in him, as we look forward to being the kind of people the Great Spirit created us to be, a people filled with his beauty and shining-greatness.

[3-4]But we must also find joy in our sufferings on his behalf. For we know that when the trail gets rough, we must walk with firm steps to reach the end. As we walk firmly in his footsteps, we gain the strength of spirit that we need to stay true to the path. [5]This gives us the hope we need to reach the end of the trail with honor. All of this is because of Creator's great love that has been poured into our hearts by the Holy Spirit, who is his gift to us from above.

SET FREE FROM BROKEN WAYS

[6]When the time was right, while we were still weak human beings following our bad hearts and broken ways, the Chosen One died for us. [7]It is not easy to find someone who is willing to die for a good person, even though we might find someone with the courage to die for a very good person. [8]But here is the way the Maker of Life proves how deep his love is for us: even when we were still following our bad hearts and broken ways, the Chosen One gave his life for us. [9]The lifeblood that he poured out puts our lives back into harmony and promises us good standing with the Great Spirit. What he has done sets us free from the storm of great anger caused by our bad hearts and broken ways.

[10]So, if the lifeblood poured out by the Chosen One has put us in good standing with the Great Spirit, then how much more will his life of beauty and harmony,

which has defeated death, now set us free to walk in his ways!

11But taking this a step further, we can now boast with glad hearts about what the Great Spirit has done through our Honored Chief Creator Sets Free (Jesus) the Chosen One! He is the one who has restored us back into friendship with the Great Spirit!

FROM RED CLAY TO CREATOR SETS FREE

12Here is another way to see what I am saying. Red Clay (Adam) was the first human being to fail to live the life he was created for. His broken ways brought death to all who followed in his footsteps, for death comes from following bad hearts and broken ways. **13**These broken ways were already at work in the world, even before our tribal law was given. But where there is no law, no one can be guilty of breaking it.

14Even so, death still came to all who lived from Red Clay (Adam) to Drawn from the Water (Moses), who gave us the law. Yes, death ruled over all who walked in broken ways, even over the ones who did not fail in the same way Red Clay (Adam) failed. But, as we will see, Red Clay (Adam) was in many ways like the one who would come later, the Chosen One.

15But not in all ways, for the false step of Red Clay (Adam) cannot be compared with the gift of Creator's great kindness shown to us in the Chosen One. If one man's failure brought death to human beings, then how much more will Creator's great kindness, gifted to us through the goodwill of one man— Creator Sets Free (Jesus) the Chosen One— overflow to all with new life!

16Here is another way to see it. Red Clay's (Adam's) one failure was repeated over and over again, bringing guilt and shame to all who followed in his footsteps.

But the gift of Creator's great kindness overcame those many failures and gave human beings a path to good standing with him once again.

17If death overcame all human beings because of the wrongdoing of one man, then how much greater will it be for the ones who receive this gift of good standing and overflowing kindness? I will tell you! Through Creator Sets Free (Jesus) the Chosen One, they will guide others with the wisdom and honor of a chief as they walk this road of life!

18And if the false steps of one man led to guilt and shame for all human beings, then another man's true and firm steps will bring life and good standing to all human beings. **19**Again, if one man who followed his bad heart passed it on to many others, then one man who walks with a good and upright heart will pass on that good heart to many others.

THE LIFE OF THE WORLD TO COME

20Our tribal law stepped in to show us how bad our broken ways had become, and this only made our broken ways grow worse. But the worse our broken ways grew, even stronger grew the gift of Creator's great kindness. **21**Our broken ways ruled over us leading to death. But the gift of Creator's great kindness that gives us good standing with him now rules over us. This leads to the life of the world to come that never fades away, full of beauty and harmony. This is his gift to us because of what our Honored Chief Creator Sets Free (Jesus) the Chosen One has done.

PURIFICATION CEREMONY

1What can we say about this? Should we continue to walk in our broken ways so that Creator will show us even more kindness? [2]This kind of thinking takes us nowhere! How can we who have died to our bad hearts and broken ways continue to walk that path? [3]Or have you forgotten that we who have participated in the purification ceremony[a] of Creator Sets Free (Jesus) the Chosen One have ceremonially died with him?

[4]This ceremony shows that we have been buried with him in death, so that in the same way the Chosen One was raised from the dead by the power of our Father the Great Spirit, we should walk this new road of life to bring honor to him. [5]If we have joined with him in his death, then, like him, we will also rise again to a new life. [6]For we know that our old self was nailed to the cross with him, killing the evil desires in our bodies, so that our broken ways will not rule over us. [7]For dead people can no longer follow their bad hearts and broken ways.

DYING TO BROKEN WAYS

[8]*I will say it another way.* If we have died with the Chosen One, we believe we will also live with him. [9]For we know that once the Chosen One was raised to life from the dead, he would never die again. Death no longer has the power to rule over him. [10]He died, once for all, to bring an end to humanity's broken ways. The life he now lives is a life that brings honor to the Great Spirit.

[11]So think about yourselves in the same way, dead to broken ways and alive to the Great Spirit in harmony with the Chosen One Creator Sets Free (Jesus). [12]You must no longer give in to the desires of your weak human bodies, letting your broken ways turn you away from the good path.

[13]So then, you should no longer permit broken ways to use your bodies for wrongdoing. Instead, as people whom the Great Spirit has raised from death to life, offer your bodies to him for doing what is right. [14]Your bad hearts and broken ways have no power to rule over you now, for you are not under the restrictions of our tribal law, but under the freedom that the gift of Creator's great kindness brings.

FOLLOWING THE RIGHT PATH

[15]What then does this mean? Should we continue to walk in broken ways since we are not under our tribal law, but under the gift of Creator's great kindness? Let that kind of thinking fall to the ground! [16]You must know that if you follow a path, you will end up where it takes you. Which path will you follow? Will you follow the path of broken ways that leads to death, or the path that leads to good standing in the eyes of the Great Spirit?

[17]I am giving thanks to the Great Spirit! For even though you once followed your bad hearts and broken ways, you turned from that path, and now from the heart you follow the sacred ways that you have been taught. [18]You have now been set free from your broken ways to walk a path of doing what is right.

WALKING IN A SACRED MANNER

[19]I am using weak human words to speak to weak human beings! You used to walk in impure ways and became the slaves of doing wrong, leading to even worse things. So now, in the same way, begin to walk as slaves of doing what is good and right, living life in a sacred manner.

[20]When you followed your old ways, you did not even think about walking in a sacred manner. [21]But what good came

---

[a]**6:3** Baptism

from the things you are now ashamed of? For those things are a sure path to death.

²²But now you have been set free from broken ways to follow the ways of the Great Spirit. Good fruit grows along this path as you walk in a sacred manner on the road that leads to the life of the world to come that never fades away, full of beauty and harmony.

²³Following the path of broken ways only earns us death, but Creator's free gift to us is the life of the world to come that never fades away, full of beauty and harmony. This free gift is ours in the Chosen One, who is our Honored Chief Creator Sets Free (Jesus).

7

GUIDANCE FOR TRIBAL MEMBERS

¹Now I, *Small Man (Paul)*, will speak to the members of the sacred family who understand our tribal law. You must know that our law applies only to someone who is alive. ²For example, under our law of marriage a woman is bound to her husband as long as he lives, but if her husband dies, she is released from that law.

³So if she gives herself to another man while her husband lives, she will be guilty of unfaithfulness to her husband. But if her husband is no longer alive, she would not be guilty of unfaithfulness. His death has released her from the law of marriage.

⁴So my sacred family members, when the Chosen One died in his human body, you died with him. This death released you from our tribal law, so you could join with the one who has been raised from the dead. So now our lives can bear much fruit for the Great Spirit.

⁵For when we walked in our broken human ways,ª the law stirred up our evil desires, so that we bore fruit for death. ⁶But now that we have died, we have been released from the law that kept us bound. We now walk in the new way of the Spirit, and not in the old way of a law carved in stone and written with ink on paper.ᵇ

THE LAW IS HOLY, UPRIGHT, AND GOOD

⁷But if you think I am saying our tribal law is at fault or that it is the reason we walk in our broken ways, you are not thinking straight. What I am saying is that the law shows us how bad our broken ways have become. I would not have known that some desires are wrong if the law had not said, "Do not desire what belongs to another."

⁸But my broken ways of thinking turned the law's instruction into a temptation that created in me all kinds of wrong desires. For if there were no law, then the temptation to walk in broken ways would not be awakened. ⁹I once lived my life not knowing the law, but when I heard the law's instructions, my broken ways came to life and I died.

¹⁰So the law's instructions, which were supposed to give me life, instead brought death to me. ¹¹But it was my broken ways of thinking that tricked me and turned the law's instructions into a temptation that ended up bringing death to me.

¹²So then, our tribal law is sacred, and its instructions are holy, upright, and good. ¹³Does that mean this good law brought death to me? No! It was my broken ways that did it, by using the law to stir up temptation in me, so I could see how bad my broken ways truly were.

ª**7:5** Lit. *the flesh*
ᵇ**7:6** See 2 Corinthians 3:3, 7.

THE INNER STRUGGLE TO DO GOOD

14For we know that our tribal law is spiritual, but I am a weak human being. My broken ways rule over me as if I were their slave. **15**I do not understand why I do the things I do. I want to walk in a good way, but I end up doing the things I hate.

16And if I hate doing wrong, then it is a good thing for me to agree with the law that these things are wrong. **17**So the part of me that hates doing wrong is not to blame. It is the broken ways that have taken root in my heart that hold me to this wrong path.

18I can now see that there is nothing good in this weak part of me[a] that gives in to wrong desires, for it keeps me from doing what I know to be right. **19-20**But since I want to do what is right but keep doing what is wrong, then it is not I but the broken ways within me that keep me doing wrong.

A LAW OF BROKEN WAYS

21I can now see that no matter how much I want to do good, evil is right there with me—a law of broken ways—taking charge and ruling over me. **22**In my inner being I dance for joy in Creator's law, **23**but there is another law, rooted in my humanity, that fights against Creator's law in my thoughts and makes me a prisoner of the law of broken ways that has taken root in my weak and broken humanity.[b]

24_Someone_ have pity on me, for I am a man trapped in sorrow! Who will set me free from my broken humanity? **25**I give thanks to the Great Spirit, for he is the one who set me free through Creator Sets Free (Jesus) the Chosen One!

So then, when I set my mind on what Creator Sets Free (Jesus) has done I serve Creator's law, even though in my broken humanity I remain a slave to broken ways.

8

1So now, no one can use our tribal law to decide the guilt of the ones who have trusted in Creator Sets Free (Jesus) the Chosen One! **2**For the Chosen One, Creator Sets Free (Jesus), has brought the new law of the Spirit's life to release us from the death sentence of our tribal law, given because of our bad hearts and broken ways. **3**That law did not have the power to set us free, because of our broken humanity.[c] But Creator found a way by sending his Son, in the likeness of broken and weak human beings, to bear the weight of our broken ways in his own human body and set us free from our guilt and shame.

4Now our tribal law can never have the say over the ones who walk in the new ways of the Spirit, and not in the old ways of our broken humanity. **5**The ones who walk in these broken ways are still thinking like weak human beings, but the ones who walk in step with the Spirit are thinking like true human beings.

6If we set our minds on the broken desires of our bodies, we will see only death. But if we look to the power of the Spirit, we will have life and walk the road of peace. **7**For the thoughts of our weak human minds are against the ways of the Great Spirit. These thoughts will not and cannot surrender to Creator's law. **8**The ones who follow only their broken desires are not able to please the Great Spirit.

9But if Creator's Spirit lives in you, then the desires of your broken human

---

[a]**7:18** Lit. _my flesh_
[b]**7:23** Lit. _flesh_

[c]**8:3** Lit. _flesh_

ways cannot overpower you. Remember, the ones who belong to the Chosen One have his Spirit. [10]So then, if the Chosen One lives in you, even though your broken human desires doom your bodies to death, the Spirit gives you life because of Creator's power to restore you back to his right ways. [11]If the same Spirit that brought Creator Sets Free (Jesus) the Chosen One back from the dead lives in you, then that same Spirit will also bring your death-doomed bodies back to life again.

[12-13]Can you not see, my relatives? We must no longer let our weak and broken human ways guide us, for that path led us only to death. But if we let the Spirit put to death these broken ways, we will share in his life, [14]for it is the ones who follow the guidance of Creator's Spirit who are truly his children. [15]We must no longer surrender like slaves to the spirit of fear. The Great Spirit has taken us into Creator's family now, and we lift our voices and cry out to him, "Abba! My Father!"

[16]His Spirit talks to our spirit and tells us we are his children. [17]If we are his children, then we share with the Chosen One in all his blessings. But to be honored with him in the world to come, we must also be willing to suffer with him in this world.

[18]For it is clear to me that the suffering we now share with him is a small price to pay compared to the beauty and honor that is coming to us. [19]The creation all around us is waiting on tiptoe for Creator's sons and daughters to be revealed in the full beauty of who he has created them to be.

[20-21]Creation itself became weak and powerless, unable to fulfill its destiny, not by its own choice but because of the one who had the power over it. But there is hope, for Creator has a plan to restore human beings. Then all of creation will share in the freedom of the life of beauty and harmony given to all of Creator's children.

[22]It is plain to see that all creation is still groaning in pain like a mother giving birth. [23]And even we who have first tasted of his Spirit are groaning on the inside, as we wait for Creator to finish the purpose for which he took us into his family, by giving us our new bodies that will never die. [24]This is what Creator was planning when he set us free by his Spirit. It is the hope of all creation. We cannot fully see this hope yet, for who hopes for what has already happened? [25]So we must be patient and wait for Creator to bring everything to completion.

[26]In the same way, his Spirit helps us in our weakness, for our prayers are often empty words, but Creator's own Spirit groans deep within us, without words, making our weak prayers strong. [27]The one who sees into our hearts knows the Spirit's thoughts and prays with us in our weakness, so we can become who he created us to be.

[28]In all these things, Creator is working to bring good to the ones who love him, the ones he chose according to his ancient purpose. [29]For he knew long ago what kind of people he would choose. He decided ahead of time to make them to be like his firstborn Son who is the Elder of the sacred family. [30]The Great Spirit chose them, invited them, set them right with him, and gave them a life that shines with beauty and honor.

[31]What more can be said? If Creator stands with us, who can stand against us? [32]If the Great Spirit did not hold back his own Son, but instead gave him up for us all, will he then hold back on anything

else? Along with his Son, he will give us all there is to give. [33]No one can accuse Creator's chosen ones of being guilty, for the Great Spirit himself has decided in their favor. [34]Who could speak against them when it is Creator Sets Free (Jesus) the Chosen One who speaks for them? Yes, the one who died and was raised now sits at Creator's right hand and represents them in his prayers.

[35]What could come between us and the power of this kind of love? Could times of sorrow and suffering do it? How about not having enough food to eat or clothes to wear? What about danger from weapons and warfare? [36]It is written in our Sacred Teachings, "Because of you we face death every day. We are counted only as sheep to be violently killed." [37]But as we walk the path of the one who loved us, then, like him, we are greater and more powerful than all who come against us.

[38]One thing I know for sure. Nothing can separate us from Creator's love. Not death or life. Not spirit-messengers or dark spirit-rulers. [39]Nothing from the spirit-world above or on the earth below. Nothing today or in the days to come. Not one thing in all creation can separate us from his great love, a love that is ours in the Chosen One, Creator Sets Free (Jesus), our Honored Chief!

9

SMALL MAN LAMENTS OVER HIS PEOPLE

[1]From my heart I speak truth in the Chosen One. I am not speaking with a forked tongue. My spirit is in harmony with the Holy Spirit when [2]I tell you of the great sorrow that burns like a never-ending fire in my heart. [3]If it would help my Tribal Family members to find the truth *that would set them free and make them whole*, I would be willing to be cursed, cut off from the Chosen One!

[4]They are members of the tribes of Wrestles with Creator (Israel) and my flesh-and-blood relatives. They were chosen by the Great Spirit and taken into his family. They were given honor, sacred treaties and promises, laws to live by, and a sacred lodge in which to perform ceremonies.

[5]They are related to our honored ancestors *Father of Many Nations (Abraham)*, *He Made Us Laugh (Isaac), and Heel Grabber (Jacob)*, who are the human ancestors of Creator Sets Free (Jesus)—the Chosen One. He is the Great Spirit who is above all, over all, and blessed to the time beyond the end of all days. Aho! May it be so!

CREATOR'S PROMISE HAS NOT FAILED

[6]Even if my human relatives have turned away, this does not mean the promise[a] of the Great Spirit has fallen to the ground. For not all who are from the tribes of Wrestles with Creator (Israel) are the true Tribal Members. [7]Just because they are descendants of Father of Many Nations (Abraham) does not make them the children of promise. For the Sacred Teachings say, "It is the descendants of He Made Us Laugh (Isaac) who will carry on your name."[b]

[8]This means it is not the children physically descended from Father of Many Nations (Abraham) who are counted as children of the Great Spirit, but only the ones who are born because of Creator's promise.

He Made Us Laugh (Isaac) was born because of a promise the Great Spirit

---

[a]**9:6** Lit. *word*
[b]**9:7** Genesis 21:12

made to Father of Many Nations (Abraham). [9]For the promise said, "Next year at this time I will return and your wife Noble Woman (Sarah) will have a son."[a]

[10-12]There is more to this story. She Holds Together (Rebecca), the wife of our ancestor He Made Us Laugh (Isaac), gave birth to twins. But before they were born, the Great Spirit said to her, "The elder son will serve the younger."[b] The reason Creator chose one son over the other had nothing to do with what they had done, good or bad, but only to show that the Knower of Hearts chooses according to his own purpose. [13]That is why the Sacred Teachings say, "My love caused me to choose Heel Grabber (Jacob) over Hairy Man (Esau)."

CREATOR WILL DO WHAT IS RIGHT

[14]Do not get the wrong idea. We are not saying that the Great Spirit chooses unfairly. [15]We are saying the same thing that Creator said to Drawn from the Water (Moses), "If I want to show kindness to someone, that is what I will do. I will have pity on anyone I choose."[c]

[16]The choice does not depend on the desire of one's heart or the strength of ones legs, but on the pity and kindness of the Great Spirit.

[17]The Sacred Teachings make this clear when the Great Spirit said to Great House (Pharaoh), "I raised you up, so that when I defeated you, my power and reputation would be known to all the earth."[d]

[18]So the Great Spirit does whatever he desires. He gives hard hearts to some and takes pity on others. [19]But, some might ask, "If Creator is the one who decides these things, then what choice do we have, for who can stand against what he wants?"

SMALL MAN ANSWERS

[20]How can anyone talk back to the Great Spirit? We are weak human beings with small minds who do not understand his ways. Does a clay pot say to its maker, "Why did you give me this shape?" [21]Does not the one who forms the clay give it its purpose? From one lump of clay he can make one pot for ceremonial use and the other for everyday use.

[22]So then, what if Creator, who has the right to show his great anger and power against pots of clay he is angry with, which are ready to be broken into pieces, has instead shown them great patience? [23]Does not the Great Spirit also have the right, from the treasures of his beauty, to pour out his kindness and mercy on pots of clay he has already chosen from the Outside Nations? [24]He did this so everyone can see how honorable he is. He still chose us, whether we are Tribal Members or from the Outside Nations.

THE SACRED FAMILY IS FROM MANY NATIONS

[25]For the prophet He Helps Us (Hosea) has said, "To Nations who are not mine I will give the name 'You Are My People.' To Nations who have not known my love I will give the name 'You Are Loved!'"[e]

[26]He Helps Us (Hosea) also said, "In the same place where they were told, 'You are not my people,' they will be called 'The family[f] of the living Creator.'"[g]

[a]9:9 Genesis 18:10
[b]9:10-12 Genesis 25:23
[c]9:15 Exodus 33:19
[d]9:17 Exodus 9:16

[e]9:25 Hosea 2:23
[f]9:26 Lit. *sons*
[g]9:26 Hosea 1:10

[27]But the prophet Creator Will Help Us (Isaiah) cries out to the tribes of Wrestles with Creator (Israel), "Even though the number of the children of the tribes of Wrestles with Creator (Israel) are as many as the grains of sand on the seashore, only a small number will return to be made whole and set free. [28]For very soon the word of Creator will be fully carried out on the land."[a]

[29]And just as Creator Will Help Us (Isaiah) has foretold, "If the Chief of Spirit Warriors had not left some of our descendants alive, we would have become like the people of Village of Bad Spirits (Sodom) and Village of Deep Fear (Gomorrah)."

Long ago, in the time of Father of Many Nations (Abraham), Village of Bad Spirits (Sodom) and Village of Deep Fear (Gomorrah) were destroyed, and none of the people survived.

THE PATH TO GOOD STANDING

[30]What can we say about this? We are saying that the Outside Nations found good standing in the eyes of the Great Spirit even though they did not follow our tribal law. Instead, they trusted in what Creator has done. [31]We are also saying that our own Tribal People, who worked so hard to earn this good standing by following the law, have failed.

[32]Why did they fail? It was because they were depending on what they could do, by keeping the law, instead of trusting in what the Great Spirit would do for them. They tripped over the great stumbling stone,[b] [33]just as it is written in our Sacred Teachings, "Be aware! For in Strong Mountain (Zion) I have set a lodgepole that many will trip over, a large chief pole that will make them stumble—and the hearts of all who trust in him will never fall to the ground."[c]

10

SMALL MAN'S LONGING FOR HIS PEOPLE

[1]Hear me, my sacred family! I want you to know that when I send my voice to the Great Spirit my heart beats with a great longing to see my own Tribal People set free and made whole. [2]I speak the truth when I say that their dedication to the Great Spirit burns like a wildfire! But this fire has been set ablaze with no understanding. [3]Since they did not understand Creator's path to good standing, they tried to make their own way. But in doing so, they did not walk Creator's path and never found good standing in his eyes. [4]The law finds its true meaning and purpose in the Chosen One, for good standing with the Great Spirit comes from trusting in what he has done.

THE PATH TO GOOD STANDING

[5]Here is what the lawgiver Drawn from the Water (Moses) has written down about finding good standing by following the law: "The man who seeks good standing through the law must find it by keeping the law all the days of his life."[d]

[6]But here is what is written down for the ones who trust in Creator for their good standing: "Do not say in your heart, 'Who will go up into the spirit-world above?'[e]"—to bring the Chosen One down—[7]"or 'Who will go down into the

---

[a]**9:28** Isaiah 10:22-23
[b]**9:32** Isaiah 8:14
[c]**9:33** Isaiah 8:14 and 28:16
[d]**10:5** Leviticus 18:5
[e]**10:6** Deuteronomy 30:12

deep dark pit of the world below?"ᵃ"—to raise the Chosen One up from the dead.

⁸But *if it does not say that,* what does it say to us? It says, "The word is not far away from you. It is in your mouth and in your heart."ᵇ It is not far away in the spirit-world above or buried in the earth below.

So then, this is the message of trusting that we speak: ⁹if you will lift up your voice and make it known that Creator Sets Free (Jesus) is the Honored Chief over all the earth, and trust in your heart that the Great Spirit has raised him from the dead, you will be set free and made whole. ¹⁰For trusting comes from the heart and leads to good standing. Then the mouth says what the heart believes, which takes us down the path of being set free and made whole.

¹¹The Sacred Teachings tell us, "All who trust in him will never be dishonored or put to shame."ᶜ ¹²So it matters not whether one is a Tribal Memberᵈ or from an Outside Nation,ᵉ for the same one we call Chief is the Great Spirit of all people. He pours out his treasures on all who call out to him. ¹³For "anyone who calls out to our Great Spirit Chief *Creator Sets Free (Jesus)* will be set free and made whole."ᶠ

GOOD STORY BRINGERS

¹⁴But how can anyone trust in or call out to one they have never heard of? And how can they hear if no one has told them? And how will his message reach their ears if no one is sent? ¹⁵Just as it is written down in the Sacred Teachings,

"How beautiful are the feet of the good story bringers, who tell about the good things Creator has done for us *through the Chosen One!*"ᵍ

THE GOOD STORY AND
THE TRIBAL PEOPLE

¹⁶But not everyone who heard this good story has trusted in its message. For the prophet Creator Will Help Us (Isaiah) has said, "Great Spirit, who has trusted in our message?"ʰ ¹⁷So you can see that hearing and trusting must walk together and follow the path given to us by Creator's Chosen One.

¹⁸But our Tribal People have not heard this message, have they? Yes, they have! *The book of Sacred Songs tells us,* "The voice *of the stars in the night sky* has spoken to all the land. Their message has traveled the four directions to the furthest places on earth."ⁱ

¹⁹But the tribes of Wrestles with Creator (Israel) did not know that this message was also for the Outside Nations, did they? Yes, they did! For Drawn from the Water (Moses) was the first to say to them, "I will make you jealous by a nation that has no standing in my eyes," says the Great Spirit. "I will make you angry by a nation that does not understand my ways."ʲ ²⁰And Creator Will Help Us (Isaiah), speaking with bold words, also said, "A people who were not looking for me found me. I made myself known to a people who never asked for me."ᵏ

²¹But here is what he has to say about the tribes of Wrestles with Creator (Israel), "From the rising of the sun to its setting,"

ᵃ**10:7** Deuteronomy 30:13
ᵇ**10:8** Deuteronomy 30:14
ᶜ**10:11** Isaiah 28:16 (Septuagint)
ᵈ**10:12** Jew
ᵉ**10:12** Greek
ᶠ**10:13** Joel 2:32

ᵍ**10:15** Isaiah 52:7
ʰ**10:16** Isaiah 53:1
ⁱ**10:18** Psalm 19:4
ʲ**10:19** Deuteronomy 32:21
ᵏ**10:20** Isaiah 65:1

says the Great Spirit, "I have reached my hands out *with love* to people who are stubborn and fail to represent me in a good way."[a]

11

CHOSEN AND BLESSED

[1]If you think that I am saying the Great Spirit has turned away from his own people in the tribes of Wrestles with Creator (Israel), you are mistaken. I am proof that he did not. I myself am a Tribal Member, a descendant of Father of Many Nations (Abraham), from the tribe of Son of My Right Hand (Benjamin). [2]Creator has not turned away from ones he knew ahead of time would be his people. Do you remember the story of Great Spirit Is Creator (Elijah) as it is told in the Sacred Teachings, when he was complaining to the Great Spirit about the tribes of Wrestles with Creator (Israel)?

[3]He said, "O Great Spirit, your people have put to death your prophets and have torn down your sacred altars. I am the only one left, and they are trying to kill me!"[b]

[4]How does Creator answer him? "I have seven thousand men who have not bowed down to serve Dark Ruler (Baal)."[c]

[5]It is the same for the time we live in. There are some from among our Tribal People who have been chosen not by working to keep our tribal law, but through the gift of his great kindness. [6]Now if they are chosen by the gift of Creator's great kindness, then this choosing cannot come from working hard to keep the law, but only by his great kindness. Otherwise it would not truly be a gift.

ONLY A FEW HAVE FOUND THE PATH

[7]This means that only a chosen few have found what all the tribes of Wrestles with Creator (Israel) were looking for. The rest have hearts that have become as hard as stone.

[8]It is written in the Sacred Scrolls, "Creator has given them over to a spirit that makes them slow to understand. To this very day, they have eyes but fail to see and ears but fail to hear."[d]

[9]Chief Much Loved One (David), *speaking of our tribes*, also says, "Let their traditional food laws[e] become a trap to catch them by surprise, so they will stumble and have their own ways fall back on their heads. [10]Let the darkness blind their eyes, and let their backs be always bent *under the weight of their broken ways*."[f]

THE WAY BACK

[11]Have our Tribal People then stumbled with no way to get back up again? I tell you they have not! Creator knew ahead of time that they would fail, and he knew their failure would open the way for the people of all Nations to be set free and made whole. One reason the Great Spirit did this was to make the tribes of Wrestles with Creator (Israel) jealous by giving the people from the Outside Nations equal standing in his eyes. [12]But if the failure and loss of our Tribal Members brings such great blessings to the nations of this world, how much greater these blessings will be when they fully become the people he created them to be!

[a]**10:21** Isaiah 65:2
[b]**11:3** 1 Kings 19:10, 14
[c]**11:4** 1 Kings 19:18
[d]**11:8** Deuteronomy 29:4; Isaiah 29:10
[e]**11:9** Lit. *table*
[f]**11:10** Psalm 69:22-23

A MESSAGE TO THE OUTSIDE NATIONS

¹³I am now speaking to you who are the people from the Outside Nations. I consider it an honor that I have been sent to you as a message bearer. ¹⁴I make sure that my flesh-and-blood Tribal Members know how much I honor you, in the hope that it will make some of them jealous, so that they can also trust in Creator Sets Free (Jesus) to be set free and made whole.

¹⁵So think about it this way. If the turning away of our Tribal Members from the Great Spirit means that he then turned toward the rest of the world, to bring them back to himself, then what will it mean when our Tribal Members turn back to welcome him? It can only mean that they have come back to life from the dead!

¹⁶If the piece of ceremonial bread that is offered first to the Great Spirit is sacred, then the whole loaf is also sacred. If the root of a tree is holy, then its branches are also holy.

DO NOT THINK YOU ARE BETTER

¹⁷Some of the branches of this olive tree were broken off, and you Outside Nations have been grafted in from a wild olive tree. This means you now share in the health-giving sap that comes from the roots. ¹⁸So do not think that you are better than those broken-off branches. For you are also a branch supported by what the root supplies.

¹⁹But someone might say, "Those branches were broken off so I could be grafted in."

²⁰What you say is true. But they were broken off because they did not believe, and you stand only by your faith. So do not get big-headed, but show deep respect. ²¹For if Creator did not have pity on the original branches, why should he have pity on you?

CREATOR IS KIND BUT MUST BE STRICT

²²So you can see how kind and how strict the Great Spirit can be. He was strict toward the ones who walked away but is kind toward you, as long as you keep walking in his kindness. If not, you also will be cut off. ²³And if the ones who walked away turn around and begin trusting again, then Creator has the power to graft them back in because of his great kindness. ²⁴It is not a natural thing for wild branches to be grafted into an olive tree that is grown in a garden. It is much easier for the natural branches to be grafted back into the same olive tree they were cut from.

ANOTHER MYSTERY REVEALED

²⁵My sacred family members, to keep you from being wise in your own eyes, I want you to know about a great mystery Creator has shown to me. A hardening of hearts has come upon a part of the tribes of Wrestles with Creator (Israel) until the Outside Nations have fully entered in. ²⁶And this is the way all of the tribes of Wrestles with Creator (Israel) will be set free and made whole.

As the Sacred Teachings tell us, "The one who Sets Us Free will come from Strong Mountain (Zion). He is the one who will turn Heel Grabber (Jacob) from his worthless ways, back to the ways of the Great Spirit. ²⁷This is the peace treaty[a] I will make with them when I take away their bad hearts and broken ways."[b]

ENEMIES OF THE GOOD STORY AND ALSO LOVED

²⁸Looking through the eyes of the good story, the tribes of Wrestles with Creator (Israel) have become its enemy. But looking

[a]**11:27** Covenant
[b]**11:27** Isaiah 59:20-21

through the eyes of the ancestors, they are greatly loved because Creator chose them for his good purposes. [29]For the Great Spirit will never take back his calling and gifts once he has given them.

[30]Here is another way to see what I am saying: In the past you Outside Nations said no to these ways of the Great Spirit. But now, because the tribes of Wrestles with Creator (Israel) have said no to Creator's good story, you have said yes to it, and received the mercy they turned away from. [31]Since they have also failed the Great Spirit, they can now receive mercy from him in the same way you have. [32]Creator has rounded up into one corral all who have failed to do what he wants, so that he can show his great kindness and mercy to everyone.

GIVING HONOR TO THE GREAT MYSTERY

[33]O how deep are the treasures of both the wisdom and knowledge held by the Great Mystery![a] His decisions go far beyond our weak ways of thinking! [34]"For who has understood the thoughts of the Great Spirit? Who has given him counsel?"[b] [35]"Who could give him a gift that would require a gift in return?"[c]

[36]For from him all things come, by him all things exist, and in him all things find their true meaning and purpose. All honor belongs to him, both now and in the world to come, to the time beyond the end of all days. Aho! May it be so!

12 ◇▷◇▷◇▷◇▷◇▷◇▷◇▷◇▷◇▷

BECOMING A TRUE HUMAN BEING

[1]So then, my sacred family members, because Creator has shown us such mercy

and kindness, I now call on you to offer your whole beings, heart, mind, and strength, to the Great Spirit as a living sacrifice. Do this in a sacred and spiritual manner that will make his heart glad.

[2]Do not permit the ways of this world to mold and shape you. Instead, let Creator change you from the inside out, *in the way a caterpillar becomes a butterfly*. He will do this by giving you a new way of thinking, seeing, and walking. Then you will know for sure what the Great Spirit wants for you, things that are good, that make the heart glad, and that help you to walk the path of becoming a mature and true human being.

WISDOM FROM SMALL MAN

[3]Because Creator, in his great kindness, has made me a message bearer,[d] I give this message to each of you. Do not think too highly of yourself. Instead, understand that the Great Spirit calls us to different purposes in answer to our trust in him. [4]For just as our bodies have many members and each member has a different purpose, [5]it is the same way with the body of the Chosen One. We are members of his body, and each member belongs to all the others.

USE YOUR GIFTS IN A GOOD WAY

[6]Creator's gift of great kindness has been poured out on us in many ways, giving us different kinds of gifts. If your gift is to speak the heart and mind of the Great Spirit in a prophecy, then let trust guide your words. [7]If your gift is helping others, then give yourself to help others. If teaching is your gift, teach well. [8]If your gift is to speak courage and strengthen the hearts of others, then speak bravely.

---

[a]**11:33** Job 11:7
[b]**11:34** Isaiah 40:13
[c]**11:35** Job 41:11

[d]**12:3** Romans 1:5

The one whose gift is giving should not hold back. If your gift is leading, lead with honor. And the one whose gift is showing mercy and kindness to others should do so freely, with a glad heart!

MORE WISDOM FROM A WISDOMKEEPER

[9]Love with a true heart. Hate what is evil and hold on tight to what is good. [10]Love like family and honor others by putting them first.

[11]Be a good fire keeper, and never let your spiritual fire go out as you serve our Honored Chief. [12]Let hope make your heart glad. Keep sending your voice to the Great Spirit, even when the road gets hard to walk.

[13]Give what you can to help the sacred family members[a] who are in need. Open your homes and hearts to others.

[14]Bless the ones who seek to harm you. Bless and do not curse! [15]Dance with the ones who dance for joy, and shed tears with the ones whose hearts have fallen to the ground.

[16]Seek to live in harmony with all. Do not think you are better than others. Walk the road of life with the humble of heart, and do not be wise in your own eyes.

[17]No one should pay back evil with evil. Do what you know to be honorable in the eyes of another. [18]If it is within your power, walk the road of peace with everyone.

[19]My much-loved family members, do not take the punishment of others into your own hands. Instead, turn all anger and wrath over to the Great Spirit. For the Sacred Teachings tell us, "Punishment for wrongs belongs to me," says the Great Spirit Chief. "I will make sure that wrongs are made right again."[b]

[20]You should do the opposite. "If your enemy is hungry, feed him. If your enemy thirsts, give him a drink. Your kindness will be like burning coals poured on his head, *as his shame for the way he has treated you bursts into flame.*"[c] [21]Do not let evil take over in your heart, but overcome evil with good.

13

GOVERNMENTS, RULERS, AND THE GREAT SPIRIT

[1]The Great Spirit is over all powers and authorities that rule the lands. Since he is the one who created them to serve his purposes by providing protection and order for all, then each person should follow the laws that have been set in place. [2]Do not rise up against these authorities, for you will be going against what Creator has put in place. This will only bring their laws down on your head.

[3]Rulers need only be feared by evildoers, not by those who walk in a good way. So do what is good, and the rulers should honor you, [4]for they are Creator's servants to bring good to you. But if you follow evil ways, you will have something to fear, for this will be a reason for them to use their power to punish you. When they punish evil, they are serving Creator's purpose, for his anger is against all who walk a path of evil. [5]So you should follow their laws, not just because of Creator's anger against evil, but because you know deep inside it is the right thing to do.

[6]This is also the reason you pay taxes, so that government officials can serve the purpose given to them by the Great

---

[a]**12:13** Lit. *holy ones*
[b]**12:19** Deuteronomy 32:35
[c]**12:20** Proverbs 25:21

Spirit. [7]So pay all the different kinds of taxes you owe, and show respect and honor to all. [8]Owe no one anything but love. If you follow the trail of the law to its end, you will find love. For the one who loves others has found the law's true meaning and purpose.

THE LAW AND THE ROAD OF LOVE

[9]There are many instructions in the law, such as, "Do not be unfaithful in marriage," "Do not kill a fellow human being," "Do not take what is not yours," and "Do not long for what belongs to another."[a] All of these, and any other instructions there might be, all come together in this one saying, "Love your fellow human beings in the same way you love yourself."[b] [10]Love does no harm to another, so loving others fulfills the purpose of the law.

[11-12]So keep walking the road of love. This is what is needed for the times we live in. The night is almost over. The first rays of the new day are already shining! For the day when Creator will finish setting us free and making us whole is now closer than when we first began walking this road. We must turn away from the path of darkness and put on the war garments of light.

[13]Let the light of this new day guide you onto a path of honor. We must walk away from wild drinking parties, from sexual impurity and improper desires, and from arguing and jealousy. [14]Instead, wrap our Honored Chief Creator Sets Free (Jesus) the Chosen One around you like a blanket, and do not let your broken human desires control you.

---

[a]13:9 Exodus 20:13-17
[b]13:9 Leviticus 19:18

14

FOOD, DRINK, AND SACRED DAYS

[1]Welcome *into our sacred gatherings* those who are weak in their understanding of our spiritual ways. Do not try to prove them wrong about the things they have decided for themselves.

[2]One person trusts that all foods are good to eat, while another whose understanding is weak might only eat herbs and plants. [3]The one who eats all foods must not look down on the one who eats only herbs and plants. In the same way, the one who eats only herbs and plants should not decide the other is wrong, for the Great Spirit has accepted both of them.

[4]What gives anyone the right to judge the servant of another? It is before the one they serve that they will stand or fall. And they will stand, for the Great Spirit has the power to make them stand.

[5]One person may decide that one day is more sacred than another, while another may decide that all days are the same. Each of you should be sure in your own mind that you have made the right decision. [6]The one who keeps a day as sacred does so to honor the Great Spirit. It is the same for the one who eats all foods and for the one who does not. For they are both doing so to honor and give thanks to the Great Spirit.

LIFE, DEATH, AND HONORING THE GREAT SPIRIT

[7]For we who follow Creator Sets Free (Jesus) do not live or die to bring honor to ourselves. [8]If we live, it is to honor the Great Chief with our lives. If we die, it is to bring honor to him with our deaths. So in life or in death we belong to him. [9]The reason the Chosen One chose to die

and rise to life again was to be Chief of both the dead and the living.

[10]Since this is true, why then do you look down on and decide the guilt of a sacred family member? For the time will come when we all will stand before the Great Spirit, and he will be the one to decide who has done right and who has done wrong.

[11]For it is written in the Sacred Teachings, "As surely as I live," says the Great Spirit, "Every knee will bow down to honor me, and every tongue will speak truth to Creator."[a]

[12]So then, each of us must give an answer to the Great Spirit for how we have walked on this earth. [13]Since this is true, we should no longer point the finger at each other. Instead, we should decide to never do anything that would make a sacred family member stumble and fall as they walk this good road.

THE GOOD ROAD IS A ROAD OF LOVE

[14]Creator Sets Free (Jesus) the Chosen One has shown me that no food by nature is ceremonially impure, but if someone considers it to be impure, for that person it is impure. [15]If you cause pain and sorrow by looking down on how a sacred family member sees food, then you are no longer walking the road of love. Do not let your strong feelings about food become the ruin of one for whom the Chosen One died.

[16]Give no one a reason to speak evil of what you see as good. [17]For Creator's good road is not about eating or drinking. Instead, it is about doing what is right in Creator's eyes, about walking his path of peace, and finding the joy that comes from the Holy Spirit. [18]For all who serve the Chosen One in this manner find goodwill in the eyes of the Great Spirit and will be honored by their fellow human beings.

WALKING IN THE WAY OF PEACE

[19]So then, let us walk the path of peace in a manner that lifts up and strengthens the heart of each person. We must not tear down the good things Creator has done because of how we see food. [20]While it is true that all foods are ceremonially pure, it is not good to force the way you eat on others and make them stumble. [21]It would be better not to eat, drink wine, or do anything that would make a sacred family member stumble on the path.

[22]So in these situations keep what you believe about these things between you and the Great Spirit. The ones who are doing what they know to be right have no reason to feel any guilt, for Creator's blessing rests on them. [23]But the ones who are not sure they are doing right will feel their guilt, for whatever does not come from trusting in Creator comes from our broken ways.

15

THE STRONG AND THE WEAK

[1]So we who are strong in our spiritual ways should be willing to lend a shoulder to the ones who are weak and unable to walk this road with firm steps. For this road is not only for our own good, [2]but also for the good of all who walk with us. [3]When the Chosen One walked this earth, he came not only to please himself but to help others.

The Sacred Teachings say, "The insults they spoke against you have landed on me."[b]

---

[a]**14:11** Isaiah 45:23

[b]**15:3** Psalm 69:9

[4]These words were written down long ago so we would learn from them. It is from the Sacred Teachings that we find the hope and strength we need to walk this road of life. [5]I pray that the Great Spirit who walks beside you, keeping your steps firm, will help you walk together in step with Creator Sets Free (Jesus) the Chosen One. [6]In this way you will speak with one voice, giving honor to the Great Spirit, the Father of Creator Sets Free (Jesus) our Honored Chief, who is the Chosen One.

THE OUTSIDE NATIONS
ARE SACRED FAMILY

[7]So welcome each other with open arms in the same way the Chosen One has honored the Great Spirit by welcoming you. [8]This is what I am saying: the Chosen One came as a servant to our Tribal People, to show that the Great Spirit has kept the promises he made to our ancestors. [9]He also came to show his kindness and mercy to the Outside Nations so they would also give honor to the Great Spirit.

For the Sacred Teachings say, "I will tell the truth about you to all the Nations, I will sing songs to them to honor your name."[a]

[10]They also say, "Dance for joy, all you Nations, along with his people."[b]

[11]And again, "Give praise to the Great Spirit, all you Outside Nations. Let all people honor him!"[c]

[12]And again the prophet Creator Helps Us (Isaiah) says, "The one who is the root of Original Man (Jesse) will rise up to rule over the Outside Nations, and they will put their hope and trust in him."[d]

---

[a]**15:9** Psalm 18:49
[b]**15:10** Deuteronomy 32:43
[c]**15:11** Psalm 117:1
[d]**15:12** Isaiah 11:10

A PRAYER FOR THE OUTSIDE NATIONS

[13]My prayer for the Outside Nations is that the Great Spirit, who gives you this hope, will fill you with the joy and peace that comes from trusting him, so that this hope will flow like a river through your lives by the power of his Holy Spirit.

[14]My sacred family members, I can see that goodness and wisdom have already found a home in you. You have become wise teachers able to instruct each other in the ways of the Great Spirit.

[15-16]Even though this is true, I have used strong words to remind you about these things. I have spoken boldly because, in his great kindness, the Great Spirit has chosen me to be a holy man in the way of Creator Sets Free (Jesus) the Chosen One. He has called me to perform the sacred task of telling Creator's good story. In this way I can present the Outside Nations as a sweet-smelling smoke offering, pleasing to him and set apart in a sacred manner by the Holy Spirit.

SMALL MAN'S SERVICE TO
THE OUTSIDE NATIONS

[17]The Chosen One Creator Sets Free (Jesus) has given me reason to brag about my work among you Outside Nations, but only to bring honor to Great Spirit. [18]For I can only speak about what the Chosen One has done through me. He used my words and what I have done to bring the Outside Nations into step with Creator's plan for them. [19]It was through signs and wonders, done by the power of Creator's Spirit, that I was able to finish the work of telling them the good story about the Chosen One. I traveled from Village of Peace (Jerusalem) all the way around to Land of Outside Nations (Illyricum).

[20]It has been my aim to tell this good story to people who have never heard

about the Chosen One. In this way I am not trying to build on the work that someone else has already started. [21]For the Sacred Teachings say, "The Ones who have not been told about him will see, and the ones who have never heard will understand."[a]

SMALL MAN'S DESIRE TO VISIT VILLAGE OF IRON

[22]This is the reason it has taken me so long to come to Village of Iron (Rome) to see you face to face. [23]It has been my desire for many winters to do so, and now that I have finished my work here, it is my plan to see you [24]on my journey to Setting Sun (Spain). I hope to stay with you for a while, for some good food and talk, and then have you sing a traveling song over me and send me on my way.

[25]But for now I am on my way to the sacred family members[b] who live in Village of Peace (Jerusalem) to bring some much-needed help to the ones who live there. [26]For the sacred family members from Land of Tall People (Macedonia) and Land of Sorrow (Achaia) are happy to give of their goods to help the poor among our sacred family members in Village of Peace (Jerusalem). [27]For since the Outside Nations have shared in the spiritual blessings of our Tribal People, they are bound by honor to also share their material blessings with them—which they do with glad hearts!

[28]Once I have brought to them this offering and delivered it safely to them, then I will visit you who live in Village of Iron (Rome) on my way to Setting Sun (Spain). [29]And I know that when I come to you, I will bring with me a heart-basket full of the blessings of the Chosen One!

WRESTLE WITH ME IN YOUR PRAYERS

[30]My sacred family members, I now call on you by the power of our Honored Chief Creator Sets Free (Jesus) the Chosen One, and by the love of the Spirit, to wrestle with me in prayer when you send your voice to the Great Spirit. [31]Pray that he will be a shield to protect me from the ones in the Land of Promise (Judea) who have refused to believe our message. Also pray for the sacred family members in Village of Peace (Jerusalem), that they will have open hearts to receive what I bring to them.

[32]Then, with the help of your prayers, and by the will of the Great Spirit, I will come to Village of Iron (Rome). Then with a glad heart I will be refreshed as we sit together with good food and much talk!

[33]I pray that the Great Spirit of Peace will be close to all of you. Aho! May it be so!

16

LOVE AND GREETINGS TO ALL

[1]I am sending to you Morning Light (Phoebe). She is of the sacred family that gathers at Small Seed Village (Cenchreae). She is a sacred servant[c] and a woman of honor. [2]Welcome her, as one who trusts in our Honored Chief, in a manner that brings honor to our sacred family. Help her with anything she needs, for she has helped not only me but many others as well.

[3]Give my greeting to Lives Long (Priscilla)[d] and her husband Strong Eagle (Aquila), who have worked side by side with me as sacred servants of the Chosen One, Creator Sets Free (Jesus). [4]They have risked their own lives for my sake, for

---

[a]**15:21** Isaiah 52:15
[b]**15:25** Lit. *holy ones*

[c]**16:1** Lit. *a deaconess*, meaning servant
[d]**16:3** Lit. *Prisca*, which was probably a nickname for Priscilla. See Acts 18:1-3.

which they have not only my thanks, but also the thanks of the sacred family members of the Outside Nations. **5**Also greet the sacred family members who gather for ceremony at their house.

I also send greetings to Worthy of Praise (Epaenetus), our much-loved one, who was the firstfruits of Land of the Rising Sun (Asia), the first to walk the road with the Chosen One in that territory.

6Give my greeting to Tears of Sorrow (Mariam), who has worked tirelessly for you.

7I send greetings also to Victory Man (Andronicus) and Younger One (Junia), my fellow Tribal Members and fellow prisoners, who have a good reputation as message bearers. They walked with the Chosen One before I did.

8Greet Large Man (Ampliatus), who is a much-loved one in our Honored Chief.

9Greet Village Dweller (Urbanus), who has worked side by side with us for the Chosen One, and Ear of Corn (Stachys), who is also a much-loved one.

10Greet Stands Alone (Apelles), who by walking a rough road has proven himself to be a faithful follower of the Chosen One. Also greet Gives Wise Guidance (Aristobulus) and his family.

11Greet Walks Brave (Herodion), a member of my Tribal Family. Greet the family of Sleepy Head (Narcissus) who are also in our Honored Chief.

12Greet Soft Garden (Tryphaena) and Sweet Garden (Tryphosa), who work hard for our Honored Chief. Also greet my much-loved friend Woman Rides Horses (Persis), another who has worked hard for our Honored Chief.

13Greet Red Man (Rufus), one who stands tall for our Honored Chief, and his mother, who has also been a mother to me.

14Greet No One Like Him (Asyncritus), Fire Starter (Phlegon), High Messenger (Hermes), Follows His Father (Patrobas), Keeps Things Steady (Hermas), and the sacred family members who are with them.

15Give my greeting to Likes to Talk (Philologus), Soft Haired Woman (Julia), Shining River (Nereus) and his sister, Bright Mountain (Olympas), and all the sacred family members who gather with them.

16When you greet each other, do so with a holy kiss. All the Chosen One's sacred family gatherings under my care also send their greetings to you.

A WISE WARNING

17And now, my sacred family members, I warn you to be on the lookout and stay away from the ones who cause trouble and place stumbling stones in your path by teaching things that are against what you have learned. **18**For the ones who do this are not walking in the ways of our Honored Chief and Chosen One. Instead, they are feeding their own selfish desires, and like tricksters they use smooth words and big talk to fool the hearts of the ones who lack wisdom.

19Even though you have a good reputation for following Creator's ways, which makes my heart glad, I still felt the need to give you this counsel. But I want you to walk in wisdom toward what is good and to keep your path free from evil ways. **20**For it will not be long before the Great Spirit of Peace flattens the head of Accuser (Satan), *that evil snake*, under your feet.[a] May the great kindness of our Honored Chief Creator Sets Free (Jesus) be your guide on the road of life.

21He Gives Honor (Timothy), who works side by side with me, greets you, along

---

16:20 Genesis 3:15

with Bright Light (Lucius), Healer (Jason), and Sets His Father Free (Sosipater), my tribal relatives.

²²I, Third Born (Tertius), the one who is writing this message from Small Man (Paul), send my greetings to you as one who also trusts in our Honored Chief.

²³Glad Heart (Gaius), who has opened his home not only to me but to all the sacred family, greets you. Much Desired (Erastus), who keeps track of the money pouch for the village, and Fourth Born (Quartus), a member of the sacred family, also greet you.

²⁴May the great kindness of our Honored Chief Creator Sets Free (Jesus) rest on all of you.ᵃ

²⁵*I pray that* the Great Spirit *will* make you stand strong and firm by my telling of the good story about Creator Sets Free (Jesus) the Chosen One. From the time before all days this message has been kept secret, ²⁶but it has now been made clear. The Great Eternal One told his prophets to write this down in our Sacred Teachings, so that all nations would hear, put their trust in his good story, and follow all his ways.

²⁷May the Great Mystery, from whom all wisdom comes, be honored through Creator Sets Free (Jesus) the Chosen One, to the time beyond the end of all days.

▌ *Aho! May it be so!*

ᵃ**16:24** Some manuscripts do not have verse 24.

FIRST LETTER FROM SMALL MAN TO THE SACRED FAMILY IN VILLAGE OF PLEASURE

1 CORINTHIANS

GREETINGS

1From Small Man (Paul), called to be a message bearer for Creator Sets Free (Jesus) the Chosen One, and from Safe and Strong (Sosthenes), our *spiritual* brother.

2To the members of Creator's sacred family who gather in Village of Pleasure (Corinth).

I write to you, the ones who have been made holy in harmony with the Chosen One, Creator Sets Free (Jesus), who have been chosen to walk the road of life with him in a sacred manner. I also write this to all people everywhere who call out to and put their trust in Creator Sets Free (Jesus) our Honored Chief and all that his name represents. He is their Honored Chief and ours.

WORDS OF ENCOURAGEMENT

3Great kindness and peace to you from our Father the Great Spirit and from our Honored Chief Creator Sets Free (Jesus), the Chosen One. **4**I am always giving thanks to Creator for you, for the gift of his great kindness given to you in Creator Sets Free (Jesus), the Chosen One. **5**He has blessed you with the right words to speak and a deep understanding of all things. **6**So we can now be sure that your lives are telling the true story of the Chosen One. **7**This shows that you have all the spiritual gifts you need as you wait with pounding hearts for the great revealing of our Honored Chief Creator Sets Free (Jesus), the Chosen One.

8He will keep your feet on solid ground and guide you to the end of the trail so that you will have a good reputation when the day comes for our Honored Chief Creator Sets Free (Jesus) the Chosen One to be revealed. **9**Creator can be fully trusted for these things, for he is the one who chose you to walk side by side with Creator Sets Free (Jesus), who is the Chosen One and our Honored Chief.

FIRM WORDS OF CORRECTION

10My sacred family members, I come to you representing our Honored Chief Creator Sets Free (Jesus), the Chosen One. I am speaking to you from my heart with firm words. To keep the family from splitting into opposing groups, you must seek harmony with each other and speak with one voice. In this way, you will be joined together with one mind and purpose.

11My sacred family members, some who gather at the house of Tender Grass (Chloe) have made it clear to me that there is much conflict among you. **12**It was told to me that one says, "I follow Small Man (Paul)." Another says, "I follow He Tears Down (Apollos)." Another says, "I follow Stands on the Rock (Cephas)."[a] And someone else says, "I follow the Chosen One."

13Has the Chosen One been broken into pieces? Was Small Man (Paul) killed on a cross for you? Did you participate in the purification ceremony[b] under the name of Small Man (Paul)? **14**I thank the Great Spirit that I performed the purification ceremony[b] for only Curly Hair (Crispus), Glad Heart (Gaius), and no one else, **15**so no one can say their purification ceremony[b] was done in my name.

16I also remember that I performed the purification ceremony[b] for Headdress of Many Feathers (Stephanas) and his family, but I do not remember performing the ceremony for anyone else. **17**For the Chosen One did not send me to perform the purification ceremony.[b] He sent me to tell the good story, not with the wisdom found in high-sounding words, because that kind of wisdom empties the cross of the Chosen One of its power.

THE WISDOM OF THE GREAT SPIRIT

18The message of the cross seems foolish to the ones who are walking a path to a bad end. But for us who are being set free and made whole, the message itself is the power of the Great Spirit.

19For it has been written in the Sacred Teachings, "I will tear down the wisdom of the *ones who see themselves as* wise and undo the understanding of those who think they know all things."[c]

20So then, where are the *ones who think they are* wise? Where is the scroll keeper who explains the meaning of our tribal law? Where is the trained speaker of this present world? Has not the Great Spirit made *the ones who are trusting in* the wisdom of this world look foolish? **21**In his great wisdom Creator knew that the world through its wisdom would not come to know him. So his heart was glad to rescue and set free the ones who trust in the "foolishness" of the good story we tell.

22The people of the tribes of Wrestles with Creator (Israel) require powerful signs. The Wisdom Seekers (Greeks) search for wisdom. **23**But we tell the good story about the Chosen One, who died on a tree-pole—the cross. This message puts a stumbling stone in the path of our Tribal People and is nothing but foolishness to the Outside Nations. **24**But to the ones who have been called out from among our Tribal People and the Wisdom Seekers (Greeks), the Chosen One is the power and wisdom of the Great Spirit. **25**Creator's foolishness is wiser than the wisest of human beings, and his weakness is more powerful than the strongest of all.

WHO CREATOR CHOOSES

26My sacred family members, take a look at your own calling. In the eyes of the world, there are not many wise or powerful or of noble birth among you. **27**For the Great Spirit has chosen the foolish to shame the wise and the weak to shame the strong. **28**He has chosen the ones the world looks down on, those who seem to have nothing to offer, to bring to nothing the ones the world looks up to. **29**In this way, no one will be able to boast when they stand before the Great Spirit.

30It is the Great Spirit himself who has brought you into harmony with the Chosen One, Creator Sets Free (Jesus). The Chosen One has become Creator's wisdom for us. He put us in good standing and

---

[a] **1:12** Cephas is Aramaic for Peter.
[b] **1:13, 14, 15, 16, 17** Baptism
[c] **1:19** Isaiah 29:14

made us holy, by paying the highest price to set us free.

³¹This brings full meaning to the Sacred Teachings that say, "Let the one who boasts boast in what the Great Spirit has done."ᵃ

WISDOM FOR THE SPIRITUAL

¹My sacred family members, when I came among you to tell you about Creator's mysterious ways, I did not use big words or high-sounding wisdom. ²For I decided not to know anything while I was with you except about Creator Sets Free (Jesus), the Chosen One—and his death on the cross. ³I came to you as a weak human being in fear and trembling. ⁴I did not come with strong words or great wisdom, but with the Spirit showing his power *in my weakness*. ⁵In this way your trust would not rest on the wisdom of human beings, but in the Great Spirit's power.

⁶On the other hand, there is a wisdom that we speak among those who are mature in the Chosen One. It is not the wisdom of this present world or of its rulers, who are fading away. ⁷Instead, with a strong voice we make known the wisdom of the Great Spirit. A wisdom that is mysterious and hidden away *in Creator's heart*. He decided long ago, before the world began, that this wisdom would be for our honor.

SPIRIT WISDOM

⁸None of the rulers of this present world have understood this wisdom. If they had, they never would have killed our great and shining Honored Chief. ⁹The

Sacred Teachings tell us that no human being has ever seen or heard or imagined all the good things the Great Spirit has planned for the ones who love him.ᵇ ¹⁰But Creator has revealed these things to us by his Spirit.

The Spirit searches everything, even the deep things found in the mind and heart of the Great Spirit. ¹¹No one can know the thoughts of another except for that person's own spirit. In the same way no one can know Creator's thoughts except his own Spirit. ¹²We have not received the spirit of the world, but we have received Creator's Spirit. This is how we can know the things that have been gifted to us by the Great Spirit.

¹³So when we speak, we do not use words taught by human wisdom. Instead we use words taught by the Spirit—speaking in a spiritual manner about spiritual things. ¹⁴Humans without the Spirit are not able to see the things revealed by Creator's Spirit. These things sound foolish and are beyond their understanding, for they must be interpreted in a spiritual manner. ¹⁵*On the other hand*, the spiritual are able to see into the meaning of all things in ways the unspiritual do not understand.

¹⁶"For who understands the mind and heart of the Great Spirit and can sit in council with him?"ᶜ But we *who share his Spirit* do understand the mind *and heart* of the Chosen One!

MILK FOR SPIRITUAL INFANTS

¹My sacred family members, *the first time I came to you* I could not speak to

---

ᵃ**1:31** Jeremiah 9:24

ᵇ**2:9** Isaiah 64:4
ᶜ**2:16** Isaiah 40:13

you as I would to the spiritually mature. Instead, I had to speak to you as I would to the unspiritual, as infants in the Chosen One. ²I had to feed you with milk, since you were not ready for solid food. Even now you are not ready. ³As long as there is jealousy and fighting among you, are you not unspiritual and walking like weak and broken human beings?

⁴When one of you says, "I follow Small Man (Paul)," and another says, "I follow He Tears Down (Apollos)," does this not prove you are walking like weak and broken human beings? ⁵Who is He Tears Down (Apollos)? Who is Small Man (Paul)? Only servants who with the help of our Honored Chief led you down the path of trusting. ⁶I planted the seed, and He Tears Down (Apollos) watered it, but it was the Great Spirit who made it grow.

⁷So it does not matter who plants or who waters. What matters is the one who makes the plants grow. ⁸The one who plants and the one who waters both share the same purpose, and each will be honored according to how well they have served. ⁹For we are working side by side with the help of the Great Spirit. You are Creator's garden where he grows good fruit, and you are the sacred lodge where he has chosen to live.

BUILDING THE SACRED LODGE

¹⁰In his great kindness Creator gave me the wisdom of a skilled lodge builder. I set the stone in place for the lodge to rest on, and others are building on what I laid down. But each person must take care to see how the lodge is to be built. ¹¹For this lodge cannot be built on just any stone, but only on the stone that has already been set in place. That stone is Creator Sets Free (Jesus), the Chosen One.

¹²⁻¹³Each builder must use the right building materials, for a day is coming when the quality of each one's work will be tested by fire. Then it will be clearly shown whether the builder has used gold, silver, and costly stones, or wood, dried grass, and corn stalks. ¹⁴If what has been built survives *the fire*, then the builder will be honored. ¹⁵If what has been built is burned up, then the builder *will have no honor and* will lose all that was done. The builder's life will be spared, but as one who has escaped through the fire.

TRUE AND FALSE WISDOM

¹⁶Do you not know that Creator's Spirit lives in all of you, making you his sacred lodge? ¹⁷Creator will bring ruin to anyone who ruins his lodge, for Creator's lodge is holy, and you are his sacred lodge. ¹⁸Do not trick yourself. All who think they are wise in the ways of this present world need to become foolish, so that they may become wise *in Creator's ways.* ¹⁹For the wisdom of this world is foolishness in the eyes of the Great Spirit.

Our Sacred Teachings tell us, "He is many steps ahead of the wise who think they can trick him."[a] ²⁰They also say, "Human beings may think they are wise, but Creator can see how weak and empty their thoughts truly are."[b]

²¹So you can stop bragging about human teachers! ²²Men such as Small Man (Paul) or He Tears Down (Apollos) or Stands on the Rock (Cephas) are all yours *in the Chosen One.* All things are already yours—whether it is this world, or life, or death, or today and all the days that will

---

[a] **3:19** Job 5:13
[b] **3:20** Psalm 94:11

follow. ²³For you are of the Chosen One, and the Chosen One is of the Great Spirit.

SERVING IN A SACRED MANNER

¹So you should think of us message bearers as servants of the Chosen One who have been entrusted with the sacred task of making known the mysteries of the Great Spirit. ²The ones who have been chosen for this sacred task must walk it out in a sacred manner, to prove they are worthy of it.

³I am not at all troubled about how worthy you think I am, because deciding how well I have performed this sacred task is not up to you or any human council. It is not up to me to decide how well I have done. ⁴I know of nothing in which I have failed, but this does not prove me to be in the right. That decision belongs to our Honored Chief.

⁵So do not keep deciding these kinds of things ahead of time. Instead, wait until the coming of our Honored Chief. *On that day* he will shine his light on the things hidden in darkness and make known the plans of all human hearts. The Knower of Hearts will then give to each person whatever honor is due.

WISDOM LEADS TO HUMILITY

⁶Now, my sacred family members, I have made an example of myself and He Tears Down (Apollos) so you will not get big heads bragging about how one teacher is better than another. You should not think of human beings beyond what is written *in our Sacred Teachings.*

⁷Who made you better than others? Do you have anything that was not gifted to you? If it was a gift, then why do you behave as if you gained it by yourselves? ⁸You think you need nothing more. You think you are well-to-do. You think you have become grand chiefs with no help from any of us! How I wish you really were. Then we could serve together as chiefs.

MESSAGE BEARERS ARE IN THE WORST PLACE

⁹I am thinking that the Great Spirit has put us message bearers in the worst place. We are like captured warriors being dragged through the village pathways to their death—for all to see. He is making a big show of us to all the world, to both humans and spirit-messengers. ¹⁰We look like sacred clowns for the Chosen One, but you are seen as his wisdom keepers! You seem powerful, while we are seen as weak.

¹¹Even now we are hungry and thirsty. We are dressed in rags. We are often badly beaten and wander about with no regular place to lay our heads. ¹²We have had to work hard with our own hands *to have enough to eat.* We have blessed those who cursed us and have been patient with the ones who bring harm to us. ¹³To those who speak against us, we wage peace. To those *who walk in the ways* of this world, we are the mud they scrape from their moccasins and the buffalo chips they wipe from between their toes. Yes, to this very day we message bearers have suffered all these things.

WISDOM FROM A SPIRITUAL FATHER

¹⁴I tell you these things not to shame you, but to give you wise counsel as my much-loved children. ¹⁵Even though you may have countless spiritual teachers to instruct you in the ways of the Chosen One, you do not have many *spiritual* fathers.

It is Creator Sets Free (Jesus) the Chosen One who has made me a *spiritual* father to you through the good story. [16]So I urge you to follow in my steps as I show you the way.

[17]This is why I sent He Gives Honor (Timothy) to you. He is my trustworthy and much-loved son in our Honored Chief. He will remind you of how I walk the road of life with Creator Sets Free (Jesus) the Chosen One. He will guide you with the same message I teach everywhere at every sacred family gathering.

A WORD OF WARNING

[18]There are some of you who have become puffed up, thinking I will not come face to face with you. [19]But I will come to you soon if that is what our Honored Chief wants. Then I will see whether these puffed-up ones speak only hollow words, or whether *Creator's* power is behind their words. [20]For Creator's good road does not depend on talk alone but also on power. [21]Which is better? Should I come to you with a big stick, or with love and a gentle spirit?

5 ◀◆◀◀◆◀▶◀◆◀▶◀◆◀▶◀◆◀▶

IMPURITY AMONG THE SACRED FAMILY

[1]I have heard from many that there is an impurity among your sacred family members, the kind of impurity not found even among the Outside Nations. A man is having relations with his stepmother, the wife of his father. [2]Why does this make you proud? You should be weeping tears of sadness for this man. For his own good and yours, he should be removed from among you.

[3]Even though I am absent in body, my spirit is there with you. In this manner, I

have already decided what must be done on behalf of this man. [4]So when you gather together representing our Honored Chief, my spirit will be there with you. Then, with the power of our Honored Chief Creator Sets Free (Jesus), [5]hand this man over to Accuser (Satan) so that his broken human ways may die and his spirit may be set free and made whole in the day of our Honored Chief.[a]

FALSE PRIDE SPREADS LIKE YEAST

[6]You have become prideful. This is not good. Do you not know that just a little yeast will spread through the whole lump of bread dough? [7]You must cleanse yourselves from this yeast *of false pride.*[b] Then you will be a new, clean lump of dough, which is what you really are *in the Chosen One and what you have been created to be.* For the Chosen One is our Passover Lamb who has given his life in sacrifice.[c]

The people of the tribes of Wrestles with Creator (Israel) participated in the ceremonial Passover meal that was eaten the evening before the seven-day Bread Without Yeast festival started. The bread used in the Passover meal was made without yeast. The day after the Passover meal, the sacrificial lamb would be ceremonially killed before sundown, when the Bread Without Yeast festival began. Creator Sets Free (Jesus) ate this meal with his close followers the night before he was killed on the cross.

[8]So then, we should not eat this ceremonial meal with the old bread dough filled with the yeast of wrongdoings and evil ways. Instead we should feast with a

---

[a]**5:5** Romans 8:12-13
[b]**5:7** Yeast puffs up bread dough. Pride, in this case, means to be puffed up.
[c]**5:7** Mark 14:12

new piece of bread made without yeast, filled with honesty and truth.

THE SACRED FAMILY MUST BE KEPT PURE

⁹When I wrote to you before, I told you to stay away from those who walk a path of sexual impurity. ¹⁰But I did not mean with the people of this world who walk in this way or with those who behave like tricksters to steal from others. I did not even mean with the ones who pray to spirit-images. To stay away from people like these, you would need to leave the whole world. ¹¹What I meant was for you to stay away from any who call themselves sacred family members who walk in these ways. This includes those who walk in sexual impurity, those filled with greed, and those who pray to spirit-images. *It also includes* big-mouth troublemakers, drunks, and thieves. You should not even eat a meal with any sacred family members who walk in these ways.

¹²Our task is not to make guiding decisions for those outside the sacred family. Our task is to make these kinds of decisions within our sacred family. ¹³It is up to the Great Spirit to judge the ones on the outside. So then, you must remove the one who has done this evil from among you.

KEEPING DISAGREEMENTS WITHIN THE SACRED FAMILY

¹How can any of you, when you have something against another, be so bold as to take your dispute before those outside our sacred family? The outsiders who decide these matters have no understanding of our ways. Why not call a council within the sacred family to decide these things?

²⁻³Do you not know that Creator's holy ones will decide for the whole world who has done right and who has done wrong, both for human beings and spirit-messengers? If you will take part in such a great matter as this, are you not able to call together a sacred family council to decide on small matters for your daily lives?

⁴If you have your own councils to decide on these matters, why would you let outsiders who have no standing in the eyes our sacred family decide these things? ⁵Have you no shame? Is there no one among you wise enough to restore harmony between sacred family members? ⁶Instead, one sacred family member takes another to be judged by those who know nothing of our spiritual ways. ⁷When this happens, you have already lost *everything*! Why not let yourselves be wronged or cheated? ⁸Instead, you wrong and cheat the members of your own sacred family.

WALKING THE WRONG PATH

⁹Do you not know that the ones who wrong and cheat each other will not share in the blessings of Creator's good road? Do not let anyone mislead you. Anyone who walks an impure path of uncontrolled desires,[a] or anyone who prays to spirit-images, or any who are unfaithful in marriage, or weak men who let other men use them for sex, or any who abuse *the sacred gift of* sex with each other. ¹⁰Nor those filled with greed, or drunks, or big-mouth troublemakers, or those who behave like tricksters— none of these will share in the blessings of Creator's good road.

¹¹Some of you used to walk in these ways, but no more. You have been washed

---

[a] **6:9** Ephesians 5:3-5

clean. You have been made holy. You have been given good standing *in the eyes of the Great Spirit*. All this was done through the name of our Honored Chief Creator Sets Free (Jesus) the Chosen One, and by the Spirit of our Creator.

FREEDOM MEANS DOING GOOD

[12]*Someone has said, "I am free to do whatever I desire." This may be true,* but not all things one can do will lead to harmony with each other. So then, even if I am free to do whatever I desire, I will not let my desires tell me what to do.

[13]*It has been said, "Our stomachs want food, so why not give our stomachs what they want?"* But we must remember that Creator will do away with both the need for food and for stomachs. We should use our bodies for the purpose they were created for, not for uncontrolled desires, but to bring honor to our Great Chief.

[14]Creator has raised up our Honored Chief from death to life. The same power that raised him will also raise up our bodies in the same way. Do you not know that this means that we are part of the body of the Chosen One? [15]Should I take a part of the body of the Chosen One and join it to someone who trades the use of their body for possessions? May it never be so!

[16]Can you not see that a man who joins together with such a woman becomes one body with her? For it says in our Sacred Teachings, "The two will be joined together and become one body."[a] [17]But the one who is joined together with our Honored Chief is one spirit with him.[b]

[18]Run away from these kinds of impure desires. No other broken human ways affect the body in this way. The ones who treat sex in this manner are

going against Creator's purpose for their own bodies. [19]Or have you forgotten that the Holy Spirit lives in you as Creator's gift to you, and that your body is not your own *but is his sacred lodge?* [20]A great price was paid to make you his own, so use your body to bring honor to the Great Spirit and not dishonor.

7 ▶◀▶◀▶◀▶◀▶◀▶◀▶◀▶◀

GUIDANCE FOR MARRIAGE AND SEXUAL RELATIONS

[1]Now I will give an answer to the things you wrote to me about *the sacred gift of marriage and sexual relations.* I think it would be a good thing not to marry or have sexual relations. [2]But because of the strong temptation to misuse these desires, each man should have his own wife and each woman her own husband. [3]Both husband and wife should honor each other in marriage and fulfill each other's sexual needs. [4]In this matter neither wife nor husband have the right over their own bodies. Their bodies belong to each other.

[5]So do not deny each other unless you both agree for *spiritual reasons such as* prayer. Only deny yourselves for an agreed-upon time, then renew your relations with each other. In this way, if you lack self-control, then Accuser (Satan) cannot tempt you.

[6]I am not telling you what you must do. I am only guiding you by what I have learned *as a weak human being.* [7]I wish that everyone could be unmarried just as I am, but the Great Spirit has gifted each of us in different ways.

[8]Now I will counsel those who are not married or widowed: Follow in my footsteps and remain as you are. [9]But if any

---

[a]**6:16** Genesis 2:24
[b]**6:17** John 17:21

of you lack self-control, you should get married, for that is better than letting your desires burn like a wildfire.

GUIDANCE FOR MARRIAGE
IN THE SACRED FAMILY

[10]To those who are married I give this instruction, not from me but from our Honored Chief: A wife should not leave her husband, [11]but if she does, she is to remain *as one who is* unmarried, or go back and work things out with her husband. And *in the same manner*, a husband should not leave or send away his wife.

[12]I know nothing more about this from our Honored Chief, but here is my counsel to all the others: If a sacred family member has a wife who does not trust in our spiritual ways, but she is willing to live with him, he should not send her away. [13]It is the same for a wife who has a husband who does not believe. [14]For both husband and wife, even if they do not believe, are made holy by being joined in marriage. If this were not so, your children would be ceremonially impure, but now they are holy.

[15]But if the one who does not believe wants to end the marriage, let it be so. In a situation like this a sacred family member is not bound, for the Great Spirit has called us to live in harmony with each other. [16]So I give this counsel to both wives and husbands who find themselves in this situation: How can you be sure that you will guide your marriage partners away from their broken ways to be set free and made whole?

[17]In every situation you find yourself, walk in a manner pleasing to the Great Spirit. This is the guidance I give to all the sacred families *Creator has called me to serve.*

WISE COUNSEL FOR NEW FOLLOWERS

[18]Any man who has participated in the cutting of the flesh ceremony before he was called should not remove the marks of that ceremony. In the same way, any who have not participated in the ceremony have no further need to participate. [19]Whether or not you participated in that ceremony no longer means anything. What has meaning is walking the road in the ways of the Great Spirit.[a]

[20]All should walk in a good way in whatever condition they were in when called *to follow* Creator Sets Free (Jesus).

[21]Were you a slave when you answered the call? Think nothing of it. But if you are able to gain your freedom, do so. [22]Remember, the one who was a slave when called by our Honored Chief is his freedman. In the same way, the one who was free when he was called is now a slave of the Chosen One. [23]A great price was paid to set you free, so do not become slaves to human beings.

[24]My sacred family members, all should walk in a good way in whatever condition they were in when they were called to follow Creator Sets Free (Jesus).

COUNSEL FOR THOSE WHO
ARE NOT MARRIED

[25]Now about those who have not yet married. I have no instructions from our Honored Chief in this matter, but I will give you my counsel as one whom our Honored Chief in his kindness has proven to be worthy of trust. [26]In the light of the troubled times we face, it would be a good thing for a man who is not married to remain so. [27]So then, if you have a wife, do not look for a way out of marriage. Have you been freed

---

[a]**7:19** Galatians 5:6

from a wife? Then do not look for another. [28]But if you do marry, you have not done wrong. If a young maiden marries, she has done nothing wrong. But those who marry will find it hard to face troubled times in this world, and I want to keep you from those things.[a]

[29]Here is what I am saying to you who are members of the sacred family: There is not much time left *before these troubled times come.* So those who are married should now prepare themselves to live as if they were not. [30]It is not the time to wallow in tears and self-pity, or for glad hearts and festivals, and it is not the time to gather many possessions. [31]Those who depend on the world as it is must be ready to let go of it, for the world as we know it will soon pass away.

[32]I want you to walk free from worry about these things. A man who is not married can give all his time to please our Honored Chief. [33-34]But a man who is married will have to give more of his time to the things of this world in order to please his wife. It is the same for a woman who is not married, or for a young maiden. They are able to give all their time to our Honored Chief, to keep their body and spirit holy and pleasing to him. But a married woman will have to give more of her time to the things of this world in order to please her husband. [35]I am saying these things for your own good, not to put a rope around your necks, but so that you will be able to keep both eyes on our Honored Chief as you walk his good road.

COUNSEL FOR NEW MARRIAGES

[36]Now in the case of a man who has been promised in marriage to a young maiden,

and his desire for her is becoming strong: if he wants to marry her and is no longer able to wait, and she is of age, then it is not wrong for them to marry.[b]

[37]On the other hand, if a man has a strong heart, if he is able to bridle his desires, and has decided for himself not to marry the promised young maiden, then for him it is the right thing to do.

[38]So the one who marries has done a good thing, and the one who does not marry is doing even better.

[39]A wife is bound by the law of marriage to her husband as long as he lives.[c] If her husband dies, she is then free to marry whomever she desires, but only to one who belongs to our Honored Chief. [40]I think she would be much happier to remain unmarried. That is how I see it, and I think Creator's Spirit also agrees with me.

8

OFFERINGS TO SPIRIT-IMAGES

[1]Now I will give my answer to you about offering food to spirit-images. We *may think we* know all the answers about these things. Knowledge puffs up *the individual,* but love strengthens and builds up *the sacred family. Knowledge makes big heads, but love makes big hearts.* [2]Those who think they have all the answers still have much to learn, [3]but the Great Spirit knows the ones who love him.

[4]So as to eating food offered to spirit-images: we know that none of this world's spirit-images can take the place of the one Great Spirit, *for he stands alone and is above all created things.*

---

⁵There are spirits in this world and in the spirit-world above that are called powerful spirit-beings or spirit-rulers. Even if there are many of these, ⁶for us there is only one Great Spirit. He is the Father from whom all things exist, and we were made for him. Creator Sets Free (Jesus) the Chosen One is the only Honored Chief. Through him all things were made, and we were created for him.

⁷But not all human beings have this knowledge. There are some who are familiar with spirit-images. So when they eat food they know has been offered to a spirit-image, they feel bad about it deep inside. Their understanding is weak, and so they feel they have done something wrong. ⁸*Now, the truth is* our good standing with the Great Spirit has nothing to do with what we eat. Eating food will not make us any worse or better in the eyes of our Creator.

⁹But you must take care not to use this freedom you have in a way that could make a weaker family member stumble along the path. ¹⁰If these *weak* family members were to see you eating in a lodge dedicated to a spirit-image, they might find strength in the moment to go along with you and eat this food, even though they feel deep inside that it is wrong to do so. ¹¹Your knowledge would cause them to lose their way, and you would end up bringing harm to a sacred family member that the Chosen One died for.

¹²When you wrong family members in this way, you have wounded them in their weakness, and you have done the same to the Chosen One. ¹³So then, if what I eat causes any of my family members to stumble along the path, then I will never again eat meat in a way that will make them stumble.

SMALL MAN DEFENDS HIS CALLING

¹Am I not free? Am I not a message bearer? Did I not come face to face with Creator Sets Free (Jesus) the Chosen One? Are you not the fruit of the work given to me by our Honored Chief? ²Others may not see me as a message bearer, but I must be in your eyes. You are the proof that our Honored Chief has chosen me.

³Here is how I will answer the ones who have decided to put me on trial: ⁴Do we message bearers not have the right to expect food and drink from you? ⁵Do we not have the right to travel with a wife, as do the other message bearers, such as the brothers of our Honored Chief and Stands on the Rock (Cephas)? ⁶Or is it only Son of Comfort (Barnabas) and I who have no right to these things and are forced to work to provide for ourselves?

⁷What nation would not care for the warriors who fight to keep them safe? Who plants a vineyard and is not permitted to eat fruit from it? Who watches over a flock of sheep and does not drink from its milk?

⁸I am not just looking through human eyes, for our Sacred Teachings tell us the same things. ⁹The law given to us by Drawn from the Water (Moses) says, "When an ox is used to harvest corn, do not cover its mouth and keep it from eating."ᵃ

Do you think the Great Spirit was only speaking of oxen, ¹⁰or was he also speaking about human beings? Yes, he meant it for human beings also, because the one who plows the ground does so in the hope of a good harvest, and the one

---

ᵃ**9:9** Deuteronomy 25:4

who gathers the corn expects to share in the harvest.

[11]If we have planted spiritual seeds into your lives, is it too much to ask for you to meet our physical needs? [12]If you have given others this right, should we not expect the same? But we have not asked for this right. Instead we have taken this burden on our own shoulders. In this way, nothing will stand in the way of us telling the good story of the Chosen One.

[13]Do you not know that the ones who perform the sacred ceremonies eat food from the sacred lodge? And that the holy men who tend to the altar receive their share of the ceremonial meat offered there? [14]In the same way, our Honored Chief instructed *his followers* that the ones who are tellers of the good story should receive their living from the good story.[a]

SMALL MAN LAYS DOWN HIS RIGHTS

[15]But as for me, I have not asked for this right, and I am not saying this so you will give it to me. I would rather die than have anyone take away my dignity in this matter. [16]I should not be given special honor for telling the good story, for it is a burden that has been laid on my shoulders. Trouble waits for me if I have failed in this sacred task! [17]If I chose this for myself, then I would expect to be honored for it. But if this was chosen for me, then I am only a keeper of this sacred task, requiring no special honor.

[18]So what honor do I take to myself? It is my honor to tell the good story without expecting anything in return. In this way, I lay down any rights that I could ask for as I tell the good story. [19]For even though I am free and a slave to no man, I have made myself a slave to all, in order to win many more.

FINDING COMMON GROUND

[20]When I am among my own Tribal Members, like them I honor our traditions that I might win them over to the good story. To the ones who are under the law, I come under the law when among them, even though I am no longer under our tribal law. I do this to gain their respect and win them over to the good story.

[21]When I am among the ones who are outside of our tribal law, I consider myself as also outside of our tribal law. Even so, I am not truly outside Creator's law, but under the law of the Chosen One. I do this to gain their respect and win them over to the good story.

[22]When I am among those who are poor and weak, I join with them in their struggle. I look for common ground with everyone, so that I can tell them the good story that will make them whole and set them free. [23]I do all of this so I can tell everyone the good story, so that together we may share in its blessings.

RUN THE RACE TO WIN

[24]Do you not know that in a race there are many who run, but only one is honored for winning the race? So run with the honor of winning in mind. [25]All who make it their aim to run in races work hard and practice self-control in all things. They do this for a headdress *of flowers* that only grows old and fades away, but we who *follow Creator Sets Free (Jesus)* do this for a *spiritual* headdress that will never grow old or fade away.

[26]So when I run, I do not run in circles but toward a goal. When I fight, I do not swing my arms like a wild man. I aim my

---

[a]**9:14** Matthew 10:10; Luke 10:7

punches. 27I am rough on my body and bring it under my power, so that after I have instructed others, I myself will not grow weary and drop out of the race.

10

LESSONS FROM THE SACRED STORIES

1My sacred family members, never forget that our tribal ancestors, *who are our spiritual fathers, when they left Black Land (Egypt)* were all guided to safety under a cloud. They all walked through the Red Sea *on dry land when the waters opened before them.* 2The cloud and the water became for them a purification ceremonya that was performed by Drawn from the Water (Moses). 3They all ate the same spiritual food 4and they all drank the same spiritual drink. They drank from the spiritual rock that traveled with them, and that rock was the Chosen One.

5But the Great Spirit was not pleased with most of them, so their dead bodies were left scattered over the desert wasteland.

6We should see in this story a spiritual warning for us today. It means we must not desire wrong things like they did. 7We must not honor spirit-images, as some of our ancestors did, for our Sacred Teachings tell us, "The people sat down to eat and drink, and then got up to dance and sing *in honor of the golden calf.*"b

8We must not give in to wrong sexual desires, as some of our ancestors did, and twenty-three thousand fell in one day.c 9We should not put our Honored Chief to the test, as some of our ancestors did, and were killed by poisonous snakes.d 10And

we must not grumble, as some of our ancestors did, who were then destroyed by the spirit-messenger of death.e

11These things happened to them as a warning to us. These stories were written down so we would learn not to walk in their footsteps. We are the people who live in the time when Creator's plan has reached its full meaning and purpose.f 12So the ones who think they stand strong should watch out that they do not fall.

13*You are not so different from your ancestors who all faced temptation.* All human beings are tempted in similar ways. So remember, the Great Spirit is faithful. He will not permit you to be tempted beyond your ability to resist. For when temptation comes, he will show you how to break free from it and stand firm.

14So then, my much-loved family, break free and run away from following after spirit-images *and what they represent.* 15I speak to you as wisdomkeepers. You are well able to decide for yourselves if what I say is true.

16*Think about it in this way*: When we give thanks and drink from the cup Creator has blessed, are we not participating ceremonially in the blood of the Chosen One? When we ceremonially break and eat the frybread, are we not participating in the body of the Chosen One? 17For we who are many all eat from one piece of frybread. This shows that we are all one body.

18Think about those who by human ancestry are of the tribes of Wrestles with Creator (Israel). When they eat from the sacred offerings, are they not participating in the sacred altar?

19So am I saying that a spirit-image or the food offered to a spirit-image is

---

a**10:2** Baptism
b**10:7** Exodus 32:19
c**10:8** Numbers 25:9
d**10:9** Numbers 21:5

e**10:10** Numbers 11
f**10:11** Lit. *those upon whom the ends of the ages has come*

anything at all? [20]No, but *I am saying that* when the Outside Nations offer food to spirit-images, they are not offering it to the Great Spirit but to evil spirits. And I do not want you to participate in following those evil spirits.

[21]You cannot eat both from the cup of our Honored Chief and from the cup of evil spirits. *In the same manner,* you cannot eat bread from the ceremonial table of our Honored Chief and from the table of evil spirits. [22]Are we trying to anger our Honored Chief by making him jealous? Do we think we are stronger than he is?

[23]We may be free to do anything we desire, but not all things we can do will lead to harmony *with one another or with the Great Spirit.* Not all things bring help and strength to each other. [24]*So then,* no one should seek only what is good for oneself, but also what brings good to others.

[25]*Go ahead and* eat the food offered at the trading posts without asking any questions. Then you will not have to trouble yourself about it. [26]"For the earth and all that is in it belongs to the Great Spirit."[a]

[27]In the same manner, if you are invited to the home of someone who is not a member of the sacred family, eat whatever is set before you without asking any questions. Then no one's sense of wrong or right will be questioned. [28-29]But if they say to you, "This food has been offered to spirit-images," do not eat it. Not because you think it is wrong to eat, but for the sake of the one who told you.

But someone might say, "Why is my freedom to eat being decided by what someone else thinks is right or wrong?

[30]If I give thanks for it, then why should anyone be able to accuse me of wrongdoing?"

[31]*Here is my answer:* whatever you do, whether it is eating or drinking or anything else, do it all to bring honor to the Great Spirit. [32]Walk softly in a manner that will not offend Tribal Members or Wisdom Seekers (Greeks) or anyone who belongs to the sacred family of the Great Spirit.

[33]This is the manner in which I also walk. For I am not looking out only for my own good, but also for the good of others. I do this so they too may be set free and made whole.

11 ◄►◄►◄►◄►◄►◄►◄►◄►◄►

FOLLOWING TRADITIONS

[1]Walk *this road of life* following in my footsteps, as I also walk this road following in the footsteps of the Chosen One. [2]I have great respect for you. You have never forgotten to hold on to the things I have taught you. You have followed the traditions that I entrusted to you in the same manner that I gave them to you.

[3]Here is another tradition I want you to understand: the Chosen One is headman over each and every man, *giving each one loving guidance. In the same way* the husband is headman over his wife *and his family, giving them loving guidance.* In a similar manner the Great Spirit is headman over the Chosen One, *giving loving guidance to all.*

[4]So then, any man who prays or speaks for the Great Spirit with his head covered brings shame to his head.

This could be because, in the traditions of the tribes of Wrestles with Creator (Israel), some men would cover their heads and faces when they prayed, being ashamed of their broken ways. So covering their heads and faces would then be a sign of shame. The Chosen One has taken away all shame, so men should not cover their heads in shame when they pray.[a]

[5]But any woman who prays or speaks for the Great Spirit with her head uncovered brings shame to her head. She would then be the same as a woman who has cut all the hair from her head.[b] [6]If a woman is unwilling to cover herself in this way, she should cut off all her hair. But if this would bring shame to her, then she should cover her head.

This was most likely a strong cultural tradition that Small Man (Paul) was respecting. It might be similar to some of our Native cultures in which women are not permitted to sit at the drum with men or to dance in the circle without wearing a shawl. It would bring shame to her and her husband or to the sacred family. Small Man (Paul) only sets this rule for women who pray and speak for the Great Spirit, which would have applied only to those who were leaders in the sacred family. This tradition was most likely not for all times, cultures, and places.

[7]A man should not cover his head, for man was created to reflect the image of the Great Spirit and bring him honor. But the Great Spirit took the woman *from the man's side* to bring honor to the man. [8]In the beginning the man came first, and then the woman came from the man. [9]For the man was not created because the woman needed him, the woman was created because the man needed her.

[10]It is for this reason that a woman *who prays or speaks for the Great Spirit* should wear on her head the sign of her right to speak. In this way, she will show respect to the spirit-messengers[c] *who watch over the sacred family.*[d]

[11]On the other hand, because of our Honored Chief, we should see that women need men and men need women. [12]For even though the first woman was made from the man, men are now born from women, and both come from the Great Spirit, who created all things.

[13]So you must decide for yourselves whether it is right for a woman to pray to the Great Spirit without a covering on her head. [14]Does not our own tradition and culture teach you that it is not natural or honorable for a man to wear his hair long, [15]but that for a woman to wear her hair long brings honor to her? For her hair is given to her as a natural covering.

[16]Anyone who does not agree with me about these things should know that in the Sacred Families of the Great Spirit we follow no other tradition.

SMALL MAN BRINGS STRONG CORRECTION

[17]As I instruct and guide you in these things, I find nothing honorable about your gatherings. For when you come together, you are doing more harm than good. [18]First of all, when you have your sacred family gatherings, I have heard that you divide up into opposing groups, and I can see some truth in this. [19]For these kinds of splinter groups are certain to happen and make it easy to see who among you walks in a good way and who does not.

---

[a]**11:4** Hebrews 4:15-16; 2 Corinthians 3:17-18
[b]**11:5** Deuteronomy 21:12

[c]**11:10** Or possibly human messengers. See glossary of biblical terms.
[d]**11:10** Revelation 2:1

²⁰At your gatherings, you are not eating the ceremonial meal in the manner given to us by our Honored Chief. ²¹For each one of you hurries to fill his own belly first, with no thought for the hungry among you. So then, one has too much to eat, and another too much to drink, *while others remain hungry and thirsty.*

²²This should never be! Do you not have food and drink in your own homes? Are you trying to shame those who are poor? Have you no respect for Creator's sacred family? What can I say to you? Did you think I would speak well of you for this? I will not!

THE CEREMONIAL MEAL OF THE CHOSEN ONE

²³This is the sacred tradition that came from our Honored Chief, a tradition that I have received and passed on to you: On the night that Creator Sets Free (Jesus) our Honored Chief was betrayed, he took some frybread. ²⁴He then gave thanks *to the Great Spirit*, broke the frybread *into pieces*, and said, "This is my body, broken for you. Eat it to remember me."

²⁵In the same manner, when the evening meal was over, he took the cup *of wine*, gave thanks to the Great Spirit, and said, "This cup represents the new peace treaty, brought into being at the cost of my lifeblood. Whenever you drink this cup, drink it to remember me."

²⁶For until our Honored Chief returns, each time you ceremonially eat from this frybread and drink from this cup, you are retelling the story of his death *and its full meaning and purpose.*

THE WRONG WAY TO EAT THE CEREMONIAL MEAL

²⁷For this reason, if you eat from the fry-bread or drink from the cup of our Honored Chief in a way that does not honor him, you will have to give an answer. For you have dishonored his body and blood. ²⁸Before you eat the fry-bread and drink from the cup, you should think deeply about yourself *and the part you have played in this story. Then with good hearts you may eat and drink.*

²⁹All who eat and drink without recognizing that this is the body of our Honored Chief will bring judgment on their own heads. For they have not thought about what it means to take part in the body of the Chosen One. ³⁰It is for this reason that many among you are weak and sick, and a number of you have fallen into *the* sleep *of death.*[a] ³¹But if we would be deeply honest with ourselves, we would not need to be judged.

³²When the Great Spirit judges us, it is for our own good to teach us how to walk in his ways. Then we will not be found guilty along with those who walk in the ways of this world.

³³So then, my sacred family members, when you gather to share in this ceremonial meal, show respect and wait for each other. ³⁴If you are hungry, you should eat something at home *before you come.* In this way, you will not be found guilty *in the way you treat the body of the Chosen One and those who belong to him.*

I will give further instructions about the other things when I come to you again.

12

UNDERSTANDING SPIRITUAL THINGS

¹Now, my sacred family members, you have much to learn about spiritual things,

---

[a] **11:30** John 11:11-13; Acts 7:60

so I will teach you what I know. ²For you know that when you followed the ways of the Outside Nations, their spirit-images tricked you and led you from one false path to another, even though they have no mouths to speak with. ³So now you should know that no one who is guided by Creator's Spirit says that Creator Sets Free (Jesus) is cursed. *You should also know that* no one can say *from their heart* that Creator Sets Free (Jesus) is the Honored Chief unless guided by the Holy Spirit.[a]

DIFFERENT KINDS OF GIFTINGS

⁴There are different kinds of spiritual giftings, but they all come from the same Spirit. ⁵There are also different ways of serving, but *the example to serve comes from* the same Honored Chief. ⁶Creator's power works in different ways through different people, but it is the same Great Spirit who is at work in all of them.

⁷It is in these many ways that the *Holy* Spirit makes himself known in and through each of us, for the good of all.

⁸Creator's Spirit gives to one person words full of wisdom, and the same Spirit gives another person words full of knowledge. ⁹The Spirit gives a different person great faith and still another healing powers by the same Spirit. ¹⁰The Holy Spirit gives to one person miraculous powers, to another the power to speak Creator's words. To another the Spirit gives the ability to tell good spirits from bad ones. To another the Spirit gives the ability to speak in different languages, and to another the ability to interpret those languages.

¹¹The power to do all these things comes from the one Spirit. It is this Spirit who decides which powers are to be given to each person.

THE BODY OF THE CHOSEN ONE

¹²Human beings have one body made up of many parts that all work together. It is the same for the body of the Chosen One. ¹³For through the one Spirit we all participated in the purification ceremony[b] that joined us together into one body. *That body is made up of* Tribal Members, Wisdom Seekers (Greeks), slaves and free. But none of that matters because we all drink *living water* from the same Spirit.

¹⁴Now, the body is not made up of one part but of many. ¹⁵If the foot should say, "Because I am not a hand, I am not part of the body," would that make the foot any less a part of the body? ¹⁶If the ear should say, "Because I am not an eye, I am not a part of the body," would that make the ear any less a part of the body? ¹⁷If the whole body were an eye, how could it hear? If the whole body were an ear, how could it smell?

¹⁸But *in his wisdom* the Great Spirit has given each body part its own place, so it can fulfill the purpose it was created for and make Creator's heart glad.

¹⁹If all the parts were the same, how could there be a body? ²⁰Even though there is only one body, it was made to have many parts. ²¹So the eye cannot say to the hand, "I have no need of you." Neither can the head say to the feet, "I have no need of you."

²²But the parts of the body that are thought to be of little use are needed just as much as the other parts. ²³The parts we see as lowly we honor by wrapping them in beauty. We respectfully cover those parts of the body that should not be

---

[a] **12:3** Romans 10:9-10

[b] **12:13** Baptism

seen. 24But the more publicly respectable parts of the body do not need this kind of treatment. So the Great Spirit has put the body together in a way that gives more honor to the parts that need it the most. 25*This makes it clear that* Creator's purpose is to keep the body *of the Chosen One* from division. It shows each of us how much we need each other.

26If one part of the body hurts, the whole body hurts. If one part of the body is honored, the whole body celebrates. 27So then, *together* you all form the body of the Chosen One, and each one of you has a place in that body.

28The Great Spirit has set in place those members of his body that he has gifted to care for his sacred family.[a] He set in place first message bearers, second prophets, and third wisdomkeepers who teach. After that comes some with miraculous powers, some with healing gifts, some who help and serve, some who bring guidance, and some who have the gift of speaking in other languages.

29Can you see that not all are message bearers, or prophets, or wisdomkeepers? That not all have miraculous powers, 30or healing gifts, or the gift of speaking in other languages, or interpreting those *languages*?

31I want you to set your hearts on the chief gifts, *the ones that will bring the greatest blessing to the sacred family.*

Now I will show you the most beautiful path of all.

13

THE WAY OF LOVE

1I may have the gift of speaking in both the languages of human beings and of spirit-messengers, but if I fail to love, my words become like the screech of a cat or the yelping of a wild dog.[b]

2I may have prophetic powers and the ability to see into sacred mysteries and understand all things. I might even have faith strong enough to make mountains move. But if I fail to love, I am nothing.

3I may give all my possessions to the poor and give my body to be burned as a sacrifice, but if I fail to love, I have gained no honor.

4Love is patient and kind. Love is never jealous. It does not brag or boast. It is not puffed up or big-headed. 5Love does not act in shameful ways, nor does it care only about itself. It is not hot-headed, nor does it keep track of wrongs *done to it.* 6Love is not happy with lies and injustice, but truth makes its heart glad. 7Love keeps walking even when carrying a heavy load. Love keeps trusting, never loses hope, and stands firm in hard times. 8The road of love has no end.

The time will come when prophets are no longer needed, when people will stop speaking in unknown languages, and when the need for knowledge will fade away. 9For we only know some of the story and can only prophesy small parts of it, 10but the time is coming when we will know the whole story from beginning to end.

11When I was a child, I spoke like a child, I thought like a child, and I saw through the eyes of a child. But when I became fully grown, I put my childish ways behind me. 12For now, it is as if we are looking at a poor reflection *in muddy water,* but then we will see face to face. For now, my knowledge is full of holes,

---

[a]**12:28** Ephesians 4:11-13

[b]**13:1** Lit. *like a noisy gong or a clanging cymbal*

but when that time comes, I will know *the Great Spirit* as well as I am known *by him.* ¹³But until then, these three remain—faith, hope, and love—and love is the greatest!

GUIDANCE FOR SPIRITUAL GIFTINGS

¹Above all other things, make love your aim. Keep the desire for spiritual gifts burning in your hearts, but most of all for the gift of prophecy. ²*Prophesying is better than speaking in unknown languages, because* the ones who speak in unknown languages do not speak to human beings, but to the Great Spirit. No one understands them, for they speak mysteries in the Spirit.

³On the other hand, the ones who prophesy speak to human beings *in a language they understand.* They speak words that give strength, courage, and comfort. ⁴The ones who speak in unknown languages give strength only to themselves, but those who prophesy give strength to the whole sacred family gathering.

⁵It is my desire that all of you would speak in unknown languages, and even more that you would prophesy. Now, the ones who prophesy do a greater thing than the ones who speak in unknown languages, unless someone explains the meaning of what is said. Then the sacred family would be strengthened.

⁶So then, my sacred family members, what if I came to you speaking only in unknown languages? What good would it do you? For unless my words reveal something new, or give deeper understanding, or speak a prophecy, or bring forth a teaching, you will learn nothing.

⁷Some things such as drums or flutes, even though they have no *human* life, must make sounds that have the right beats or tones, or no one will know what they are hearing. ⁸If an eagle bone whistle[a] is not sounded in the right way, who will prepare for battle? ⁹In the same manner, if you speak in an unknown language, how will the hearers know what is being said? The sound of your voice will be lost in the wind. ¹⁰A great number of languages are spoken throughout this world, and all tribes understand their own language. ¹¹If I do not speak the language of a tribe, they will not know my language and I will not know theirs. Our languages will sound strange to each other.

¹²Here is what I am saying to you: since you have such a strong desire for spiritual powers, desire those powers that will help the sacred family grow stronger. ¹³So the one who speaks in an unknown language should pray for the power to interpret its meaning for others.

¹⁴Now, if I pray in an unknown language, I am praying with my spirit and not in a language my mind understands. ¹⁵So what is the right thing to do? I will pray with my spirit and also with my mind. In the same manner, I will sing with my spirit *in unknown words* and with words I understand. ¹⁶So then, if you only give thanks *in an unknown language,* speaking with your spirit, then how could someone who does not understand say "Aho! May it be so" at your prayer of giving thanks? ¹⁷For you may be praying in a good way, but it does not help others to grow *spiritually* strong.

---

[a]**14:8** Lit. *trumpet,* or in Hebrew *shofar,* meaning "ram's horn"

¹⁸I give thanks to the Great Spirit that I speak in unknown languages more than any of you. ¹⁹But at our sacred family gatherings it would be better for me to speak five words of instruction that all can understand than to speak ten thousand words in an unknown language.

²⁰My sacred family members, do not think in childish ways. In the ways of evil be as innocent as a baby in a cradleboard, but in your understanding *of spiritual things* be as wise as an elder.

²¹It has been written down in our Sacred Teachings, "I will speak to my people through the mouths of people with strange languages," says our Honored Chief, "but even so my people will not hear me."

²²This means that unknown languages are a sign for how Creator speaks to the ones who do not want to hear him,[a] but prophecy is a sign for those who want to hear what the Great Spirit is saying.[b]

²³So then, if everyone at a gathering of the sacred family began to speak in unknown languages, and if someone came to the gathering who knew nothing about these things or who did not walk in our ways, would they not think you had lost your minds? ²⁴But on the other hand, if everyone prophesied, the secrets hidden in their hearts would be made known, and they would clearly see how their broken ways will bring them to a bad end. ²⁵They would then humble themselves before Creator and tell everyone that the Great Spirit truly walks among you.

GUIDANCE FOR SACRED GATHERINGS

²⁶So, my sacred family members, what is the path forward? When you gather for ceremony, each one has a gift to share. Some may sing sacred songs, and others might bring a teaching or tell a story. Some might share something new that has been revealed to them, while others may speak in an unknown language and then tell the meaning of it. All these things must be done in a good way to help others grow strong.

²⁷Only two or three should speak in unknown languages. Let each of them speak, one at a time. Then someone must interpret the meaning of what has been said. ²⁸If no one can interpret, let the speakers *of unknown languages* remain silent during the sacred gathering and speak quietly in their hearts to the Great Spirit.

²⁹*In the same manner*, only two or three prophets should speak, and the others should weigh what has been said. ³⁰But if anything is revealed *by the Spirit* to another who is seated in the circle, the first should stop speaking and give way to the other. ³¹The prophets should speak one at a time, so that all may learn and find comfort in their words. ³²Prophets have power over their own spirits, ³³for disorder and confusion do not come from Creator, for he is the Great Spirit of peace and harmony. This is the way these things are to be done wherever Creator's holy people come together at our sacred family gatherings.

GUIDANCE FOR WOMEN IN THE SACRED GATHERING

³⁴During our sacred gatherings wives should remain silent, for they are not permitted to speak *out of place*. They should remain under the guidance of their husbands, as our Sacred Teachings tell us. ³⁵So then, if they have any questions, they should ask their husbands at home, for it is a shameful thing for a

---

[a]**14:22** Lit. *the ones who do not believe*
[b]**14:22** Lit. *for those who believe*

married woman to speak *out of place* during our sacred gatherings.

[36]What are you saying to me? Did the message of the Great Spirit come first from you *who gather in Village of Pleasure (Corinth)*? Are you the only ones whom Creator has entrusted with his message? [37]If anyone among you thinks of himself as a prophet, or thinks of himself to be spiritual, he should *be the first* to see that my instructions come from our Honored Chief. [38]Any who set aside what I am saying are only showing how ignorant they are.

[39]I say to you once more, my sacred family members, fan into flame your desire to prophesy and do not forbid speaking in unknown languages. [40]Let everything be done with respect, in a good and orderly manner.

15

SMALL MAN RETELLS THE GOOD STORY

[1]Now, my sacred family members, I want to talk to you about the good story. I was the one who told you the good story, which you took to heart and continue to stand firmly on. [2]This good story will set you free and make you whole as long as you hold on tightly to the truth of it. If not, then your faith would have no meaning.

[3]This is the first and most important truth I passed on to you: The Chosen One died for our bad hearts and broken ways, just as our Sacred Teachings foretold.[a] [4]The Chosen One was buried, and on the third day his dead body was raised to life, which our Sacred Teachings also foretold.[b] [5]Then he showed himself alive to Stands on the Rock (Cephas) and his twelve

message bearers. [6]After that he showed himself to more than five hundred of his followers at the same time. Most of them live to this day, while others have fallen into the sleep of death. [7]He also showed himself to He Leads the Way (James), then to all the message bearers.

[8]Last of all the Chosen One showed himself to me, as if I were a child that was born past its time of birth. Among the message bearers I am the least. [9]I have no right even to be called a message bearer, since I hunted down and brought harm to Creator's sacred family. [10]But because of the gift of his great kindness, I am what he has called me to be. His gift was not wasted on me. I worked harder than any of the message bearers. But it was not me. It was the gift of his great kindness at work in me.

[11]It matters not whether you first heard the good story from me or from the other message bearers. This is the story we tell, and this is the story in which you have put your trust.

UNDERSTANDING THE RISING FROM THE DEAD

[12]So then, if the good story tells us that the Chosen One has risen from the dead, how can any among you say there will be no rising from the dead? [13]If there is no rising from the dead, it would mean the Chosen One has not risen. [14]If the Chosen One has not risen, then the story we tell means nothing, and your faith is a dried-up spring. [15]If it is true that the dead do not rise, this would mean that we falsely represented the Great Spirit when we told everyone that he raised the Chosen One from the dead.

[16]If the dead are not raised, then the Great Spirit did not raise up the Chosen One. [17]If this were true, your faith would

---

[a]**15:3** Isaiah 53:5-12
[b]**15:4** Psalm 16:8-11

have no meaning, and your broken ways would still rule over you. [18]It would also mean that our sacred family members who have fallen asleep in death while trusting in the Chosen One have faded away, never to rise again. [19]If our hope in the Chosen One is only for this life, then we should be pitied more than all other human beings.

[20]But the truth is the Chosen One has risen from the dead! He is the firstfruits of the harvest to come. He is the first to rise from the dead and the sign that all who have fallen asleep in death will also rise.

WHEN WILL THE DEAD BE RAISED?

[21]Since death came through a human being, the victory over death has also come through a human being. [22]Everyone dies in Red Clay (Adam), and everyone comes to life in the Chosen One. [23]But all in their own time. The Chosen One rose first—the firstfruits of the harvest to come. Then, when the Chosen One returns, all who are his *will live again.*

WHAT HAPPENS AFTER THE DEAD ARE RAISED?

[24]Then, after the Chosen One has brought down all rulers, powers, and authorities, the good road will reach its goal. Then the Chosen One will give the well-traveled good road over to his Father, the Great Spirit. [25]But until then, he must continue his chiefly rule until he has defeated and humbled all his enemies.[a]

[26]Then the last enemy—death itself—will come to an end. [27]For *it says in the book of Sacred Songs*[b] that the Great Spirit has put all things under the power of the True Human Being. But when it says that "all things" are put under his power, this

does not include his Father, the Great Spirit. For he is the one who gave the Chosen One this power in the beginning. [28]And once all things surrender to his power, the Son will then honor his Father, turn all this power over to him, and take his proper place under his loving rule. In this way, the Great Spirit will bring all things into harmony with himself.[c]

MORE ANSWERS ABOUT THE RISING FROM THE DEAD

[29]If there is no rising from the dead, then what do the ones who perform the purification ceremony[d] for the dead hope to accomplish? Why perform this ceremony for them if the dead do not rise? [30]If the dead do not rise, why would we *message bearers* keep putting our lives in danger? [31]I stare death in the face every day. I say this not to boast in myself but in what our Honored Chief Creator Sets Free (Jesus), the Chosen One, has done in your lives. [32]If the dead do not rise, why would I risk my life fighting with the wild beasts at Village of Desire (Ephesus)?

If the dead do not rise, *some will say,* "Let us eat and drink, for tomorrow we die!"[e] [33]But do not let people who think like this fool you, for bad company will bring ruin to good character. [34]Return to the right way of thinking and stop walking in broken ways. Some of you have no understanding of the ways of the Great Spirit. It is to your shame that I have to speak in this way. *Have you no respect for yourselves?*

HOW DO THE DEAD RISE?

[35]Now someone may ask, "How do the dead rise? What kind of body will they have when they come back to life?"

---

[a] **15:25** Psalm 110:1
[b] **15:27** Psalm 8:9
[c] **15:28** Lit. *the Great Spirit will be all in all*
[d] **15:29** Baptism
[e] **15:32** Isaiah 22:13; Luke 12:19

[36]How can one be so foolish? When you plant a seed, it does not come to life unless it first dies. [37]The seed that is buried does not look like the full-grown plant that it will become. It is only a seed, perhaps of wheat or something else. [38]But the Great Spirit gives it the body he wants it to have. He gives each seed its own kind of body.

[39]Two-legged human beings and four-legged animals and winged ones and fish all have bodies of flesh, but each one has its own kind of body. [40]There are bodies in the sky above and on the earth below, but each of them has a special kind of beauty. [41]The sun shines with its own blinding brightness, the moon reflects the light of the sun with a beauty all its own. The stars have a bright-shining tapestry that has no rival, and each star is beautiful in its own way.

[42]This is how it will be when Creator raises the dead to life. Our death-doomed bodies, which have been planted like a seed into the ground, will come to life never to die again. [43]When our bodies are planted into the ground, they are plain and weak. When they rise to life, they will be beautiful and strong.

[44]Our bodies are unspiritual, made from the earth and planted into the earth when buried. But when our bodies rise from their earth graves, they will be spiritual bodies—made from the spirit-world above. If there is an earthly body, there must also be a spiritual body.

[45]It is written in our Sacred Teachings, "The first man, Red Clay (Adam), became a living being."[a] But the last Red Clay (Adam),[b] *the Chosen One,* became a life-giving spirit. [46]But it was not the spiritual body that came first. It was first the earthly *body* and then the spiritual.

[47]The first man came from the ground and was made of dirt. The second man, *who is our Honored Chief,* came from the spirit-world above. [48]The ones *born* on earth are like the man who was made from the ground. The ones *born* from the spirit-world above are like the man who came from above.[c] [49]Just as we have worn the image of the man from the earth, we will also wear the image of the man from the spirit-world above.

[50]My sacred family members, here is what I am saying to you: human beings, in their *death-doomed* flesh-and-blood bodies, cannot share in the *full* blessings of Creator's good road. Neither can bodies that die share the same blessings of bodies than cannot die.

[51]Behold! I am about to show you a mystery. We will not all fall into the sleep of death, but all of us will be changed. [52]It will happen faster than the blink of an eye, when the eagle bone whistle[d] sounds for the last time. When it sounds, the dead will come to life never to die again, and we will all be changed. [53]For these old, worn-out, death-doomed bodies must be taken off, and our new bodies that will never die must be put on.

[54]When this happens, the saying that has been written down in our Sacred Teachings will find its full purpose and meaning, "Death has been defeated, let the victory dance begin!"[e] [55]"O Death, where is your victory? O Grave, where is your sting?"[f]

---

[a]**15:45** Genesis 2:7
[b]**15:45** The name *Red Clay* is similar in the Hebrew language to the word *man*.

[c]**15:48** See John 3:3-7.
[d]**15:52** Lit. *trumpet,* or in Hebrew *shofar,* meaning "ram's horn"
[e]**15:54** Isaiah 25:8
[f]**15:55** Hosea 13:14

56For our broken ways give death its sting, and our broken ways give the law its power. *But no more!* **57**We give thanks to the Great Spirit, who has given us the victory *over our broken ways and over death* through our Honored Chief Creator Sets Free (Jesus) the Chosen One!

58So then, my much-loved family members, you must stand strong, with your feet planted firmly on the ground. Never give up working hard for our Honored Chief, for you know that whatever you do for him will never fade away.

16

OFFERINGS TO HELP CREATOR'S HOLY PEOPLE

1Now, in respect to the taking of offerings to help Creator's holy people who live in Village of Peace (Jerusalem): I am giving you the same instructions that I gave to the sacred families who gather in the territory of Land of Pale Skins (Galatia).

2*When you gather* on the first day of the week, take from as much as you have been blessed with and set it aside. Keep it in a safe place until I come. In this way no offerings will need to be taken when I come. **3**Then, when I arrive, I will send your trusted messengers, along with letters of approval, to Village of Peace (Jerusalem). **4**If you think it wise for me to travel with them, we will walk the road together.

5But on my way to you I must first pass through Land of Tall People (Macedonia). After that I will come to you **6**and perhaps stay for a while, or even for the winter. Then when I leave, you can sing a traveling song over me as I continue my journey to wherever I may go.

7I am trusting that it is Creator's plan for me to stay with you for a season, instead of just passing through. **8**But for now I will be staying at Village of Desire (Ephesus) until the Festival of Weeks, **9**for a wide path filled with new possibilities has opened before me, even though there are many trying to block the way.

> The Festival of Weeks Small Man (Paul) is speaking of is a ceremonial harvest festival that the tribes of Wrestles with Creator (Israel) celebrated. It was called the Festival of Weeks[a] or Pentecost, meaning "fifty," because it was celebrated after seven weeks, on the fiftieth day, following another festival called Passover.[b]

10If He Gives Honor (Timothy) comes to you, calm his fears about being with you, for he is working at doing what the Great Spirit wants, just as I am. **11**So make sure no one looks down on him. Then send him on his way in peace, for I am waiting for him to come to me along with other brothers *in the sacred family.*

12Now about our *spiritual* brother He Tears Down (Apollos): more than once I have encouraged him and others to come and stay awhile with you, but for him it was not a good time to come. He will come to you when the time is right.

SMALL MAN'S FINAL WORDS

13Keep your eyes wide open. Stand firm in the faith. Be brave and strong. **14**Let love be the reason behind all that you do.

15Do not forget about Headdress of Many Feathers (Stephanas) and all who live in his house. They were the first to follow the way of the Chosen One in Land of Sorrow (Achaia). They set their hearts to serving Creator's holy people. I

---

[a]**16:9** See "Festival of Weeks" in the glossary of biblical terms.
[b]**16:9** See "Passover Festival" in the glossary of biblical terms.

beg of you, my sacred family, **16**to follow their guidance and to walk in the footsteps of all who serve in this manner.

17It made my heart glad when Headdress of Many Feathers (Stephanas) and Lucky Man (Fortunatus) and Man of Sorrows (Achaicus) came to me. They have been walking in your footsteps by helping me while you have been away. **18**My spirit has been renewed by them in the same way they have renewed yours. You should make sure men like these are given the honor they deserve.

19The sacred families who gather in Land of the Rising Sun (Asia) send their greetings to you. Strong Eagle (Aquila) and Lives Long (Priscilla)[a] and the sacred family that meets for ceremony in their home also send warm greetings to you in our Honored Chief. **20**All the sacred family members send their greetings to you. Welcome each other with a holy kiss.

21I, Small Man (Paul) write this *final* greeting with my own hand.

22Let all who fail to love our Honored Chief be cut off[b] from the Chosen One![c] Come, O Honored Chief, Come! (Maranatha!)[d]

23May the gift of great kindness that comes through Creator Sets Free (Jesus) remain with you. **24**May the deep love I have for all of you in the Chosen One, Creator Sets Free (Jesus), find its way into your hearts.

Aho! May it be so!

---

[a]**16:19** Lit. *Prisca*, which was probably a nickname for Priscilla. See Acts 18:1-3.

[b]**16:22** Lit. *anathema*, a word meaning "cursed"

[c]**16:22** See Romans 9:3.

[d]**16:22** An Aramaic word that was used in the early church as a prayer for the return of the Chosen One

SECOND LETTER FROM SMALL MAN TO THE SACRED FAMILY IN VILLAGE OF PLEASURE

2 CORINTHIANS

1 ⟡▷⟨⟡▷⟨⟡▷⟨⟡▷⟨⟡▷⟨⟡▷

GREETINGS

1From Small Man (Paul), chosen by the Great Spirit to be a message bearer for the Chosen One, Creator Sets Free (Jesus), and from He Gives Honor (Timothy), our *spiritual* brother.

To the members of Creator's sacred family who gather in Village of Pleasure (Corinth), and to all Creator's holy people who live in the territory of Land of Sorrow (Achaia).

2Great kindness and peace to you from our Father the Great Spirit and from our Honored Chief Creator Sets Free (Jesus) the Chosen One. **3**All blessings belong to the Great Spirit, who is the Father of our Honored Chief Creator Sets Free (Jesus) the Chosen One. He is a kind-hearted and merciful Father, the Maker of Life who walks by our side to give us help, and the Great Spirit of all comfort.

COURAGE AND COMFORT

4The Great Spirit walks with us through times of trouble, giving us courage and well-being so that we can give to others the same comfort he has given to us. **5**When our suffering overflows because we represent the Chosen One, he gives us overflowing strength and well-being.

6Our sufferings and the comfort we receive help us to bring you comfort when you suffer in the same way we have. **7**This gives us great hope, for we know that when you share in our troubles, you will also share in our comfort.

8With this in mind, my sacred family members, we want you to know about the road of suffering we walked in Land of the Rising Sun (Asia). Things could not have been worse. We ran out of strength, and our hearts fell to the ground. It was as if we had come face to face with death. **9**It truly felt as if death were stalking us. This caused us to stop trusting in ourselves and to put our trust in the Great Spirit who brings the dead back to life— and he did! **10**The Great Spirit snatched us from the jaws of death. Yes, we have set our hearts on the one who rescues us, that he will rescue us again and again! **11**We need your prayers, for as you send your voice to the Great Spirit, many will see in our lives the answers to your many prayers and give him thanks.

12We may be bragging, but we are bold enough to tell you that our hearts are pure, for we have walked this road of life in a sacred and true manner. We have not followed the ways of this world, but by the gift of Creator's great kindness we have walked in a good way before the people of this world, and even more toward you. In the same way, our words to you are as straight as an arrow. We do not speak with forked tongues in our letters to you. ¹³What you read in our letters should be clear to you, so I hope you understand everything in the way we mean it.

¹⁴Even now you do not fully know us, and my hope is that you will come to know us for who we truly are. Then on the day of our Honored Chief Creator Sets Free (Jesus), we will take pride in knowing each other. ¹⁵⁻¹⁶It was for this reason that I had planned the blessing of two visits with you. I would have come to you first on my way to Land of Tall People (Macedonia), and then I would have come to you again on my way to Land of Promise (Judea). Then you could have *sung a traveling song over me and* sent me on my way.

A MAN OF HIS WORD

¹⁷So when I had to change my plans, did this make you think that I am not a man of my word? Do you think I say "Yes" when I mean "No," like the people who follow the ways of this world? ¹⁸If you trust the Great Spirit, then you can trust that I am a man of my word. When I say "Yes" or "No" I mean what I say.

¹⁹So you can be sure that the message made known to you by Forest Walker (Silvanus), He Gives Honor (Timothy), and me, Small Man (Paul), remains "Yes" in the Chosen One Creator Sets Free (Jesus) the Son of the Great Spirit, for Creator is true to his word. ²⁰The many promises of the Great Spirit find their "Yes" in the Chosen One. He is the reason we say, "Aho! May it be so!" to honor the Great Spirit.

²¹Creator has set us all firmly on *the rock of* the Chosen One. He poured the oil of the Spirit's power on us. ²²He put his Spirit into our hearts to mark us as his own. His Spirit in us is the promise of our place in the world to come.

²³I call on the Great Spirit to be a witness to the truth I tell you now. The reason I did not come to you in Village of Pleasure (Corinth) was to spare you *the pain my sharp words would bring to you.* ²⁴Instead, we want to work together with you to make your hearts glad. It is not our aim to rule over you but to walk together with you as you stand firm in your faith.

2

¹So I made up my mind not to sadden you with another painful visit. ²If I came to you in this way, there would be no one to make my heart glad, for your hearts would be on the ground. ³I have written this letter so that when I come to you it will be a time of rejoicing instead of sadness. I am sure you also want the same thing.

⁴My heart was on the ground as I wrote *the other letter* to you. I wrote each word in pain, sorrow, and many tears. Not to cause you pain, but to let you know how great my love is for *all of* you.

FORGIVE THE ONE WHO HAS DONE WRONG

⁵But there is one among you who has caused trouble and pain, not so much to me but mostly to all of you. ⁶The discipline most of you have already given him is enough. There is no need to punish him further. ⁷Instead, to keep him from losing heart and falling into deep sorrow and self-pity, you should forgive and speak words of healing over

him. [8]That is why I now beg you to show him once again how much you love him.

[9]The reason for my letter was to find out whether you would follow all of my instructions, even the hard ones. [10]Anyone you forgive, I forgive also. Whatever I have already forgiven, if I have forgiven anything, I forgave knowing that the Chosen One is here with us in spirit.[a] [11]I do this to make sure that Accuser (Satan) gains no foothold, for we know his evil trickster ways.

SMALL MAN AT THE VILLAGE OF CUT THROUGH

[12]On my journey I arrived at *the seaport village of* Cut Through (Troas). For it was there that our Honored Chief had opened a way for me to tell the good story about the Chosen One. [13]But my spirit was restless when I did not find Big Man (Titus) there, for he is like a brother to me. So I left there and journeyed on my way to look for Big Man (Titus) in Land of Tall People (Macedonia).

> *Small Man (Paul) tells us later in this letter that he went to Land of Tall People (Macedonia) with some fellow travelers. When he did not find Big Man (Titus) there, he continued to be restless and even argued with his fellow travelers. But Big Man (Titus) finally arrived, making the heart of Small Man (Paul) glad!*[b]

[14]We are giving thanks to the Great Spirit, for the Chosen One is his headman dancer leading us in the victory dance. Everywhere we go Creator uses us to spread the sweet-smelling smoke of what it means to know the Chosen One. [15]To the Great Spirit we smell like the Chosen One. To those who are being set free and made whole we have the smell of life, [16]but to the ones who are walking the road to a bad end, we have the smell of death. Who among us is able to carry the weight of such a task?

[17]We are not like those who are turning Creator's message into a way to gain possessions. For in the Chosen One, with Creator looking down on us, we speak truth from our hearts as we represent the Great Spirit.

3

SERVANTS OF THE NEW PEACE TREATY

[1]Do you think we are trying to prove ourselves to you once again? Do we, like some others, need letters of approval for you or from you? [2]You are our letter of approval, one that has been written on our hearts, a letter everyone can clearly see and read. [3]Your lives show that you are a letter about the Chosen One, written by us not with pen and ink but by Creator's own Spirit, not with words that have been carved into stone tablets but with words that have been carved into human hearts.

[4]We say such bold things about ourselves because we trust in *what* the Great Spirit *can do* through the Chosen One. [5]We do not think we have the power to do these things on our own. Our power comes from the Great Spirit, *who works in and through us.* [6]For it is Creator himself who has chosen and prepared us to tell others the meaning and purpose of his new peace treaty.

This new peace treaty does not depend on written words, but in what the Spirit says. For the peace treaty written as law ended in death, but what the Spirit writes on our hearts brings life.

[a]**2:10** Matthew 18:20
[b]**2:13** 2 Corinthians 7:5-7

⁷The law of the peace treaty that was given by Drawn from the Water (Moses) became a way of death instead of life. Even so, this law came with so much honor and shining-greatness that the people of Wrestles with Creator (Israel) could not look for long on the face of Drawn from the Water (Moses), even though the brightness was already fading. ⁸In the light of this, how much greater will be the honor and shining-greatness that comes from the Spirit?

THE BEAUTY OF THE NEW PEACE TREATY

⁹If the way that condemns people to death came like a shining light, then the way that gives people good standing and life far outshines it. ¹⁰The shining light that came first has lost its brilliance in the greater light of the beauty and splendor that has now come. ¹¹For if what was fading away came as a shining light, how much more beauty and shining-greatness belongs to what will never fade away! ¹²This kind of hope gives us the courage to speak with brave words about these things.

¹³We will not be like Drawn from the Water (Moses), who hid his face behind a cloth so the people of Wrestles with Creator (Israel) would not see that the brightness was fading away. This kept them from seeing and understanding. ¹⁴Even now, when the old peace treaty is being read, it is as if the same cloth also covers their minds and blinds them to the truth. It is only the Chosen One who can remove their blinders and make them see.

¹⁵But to this day, whenever they hear the words of Drawn from the Water (Moses) being read, a cloth remains over their hearts. ¹⁶But our Honored Chief removes the cloth from the hearts of all who turn to him. ¹⁷The Honored Chief I am talking about here is the Spirit, and wherever the Spirit walks, freedom follows!

¹⁸So then, with uncovered faces, we are seeing the bright and shining face of our Honored Chief. This bright and shining-greatness, which shines from his face into ours, keeps changing us to be more and more like him. This is what the Spirit does for us, for he is the Spirit of our Honored Chief.

4

A LIGHT IN THE DARKNESS

¹Since we have received this sacred task through Creator's mercy, we never lose heart *as we walk this road.* ²For this reason we have put an end to shameful ways that are kept hidden in darkness. We do not walk in the ways of a trickster or misrepresent Creator's message. Instead, under Creator's watchful eyes we openly speak the truth. In this way, all who hear can know within themselves what kind of people we are.

³But even if the good story we tell is hidden from their eyes, it is hidden only to the ones who walk the road to a bad end. ⁴For the ones who do not believe have been blinded in their minds by the evil spirit-ruler of this present world. This blindness keeps them from seeing the light that shines when the good story is told about the beauty of the Chosen One, who is the only one who fully represents the Great Spirit.

⁵The story we tell is not about ourselves. It is about our Honored Chief Creator Sets Free (Jesus) the Chosen One. And because of him we see ourselves as your servants. ⁶For the same Great Spirit who told light to shine out of darkness has shined his light into our hearts. His light

helps us to see the beauty of the Great Spirit in the face of Creator Sets Free (Jesus) the Chosen One.

CLAY POTS FILLED WITH CREATOR'S POWER

7Our bodies are like old clay pots that have been filled with the sacred gift *of his light.* This shows that the great power we have does not come from us but from our Creator. **8**Trouble surrounds us and presses in on us, but we know there is always a way out. Even when we do not know which way to go, we never lose hope or give in to fear. **9**We are hunted down and mistreated, but the Great Spirit never abandons us. Even when beaten to the ground, we get up and keep walking.

10Everywhere we go death bears down on us. Our bodies are dying the kind of death Creator Sets Free (Jesus) died. In this way his life will also be seen in our bodies. **11**It is because of Creator Sets Free (Jesus) that we who are alive are always facing death. It is for this reason that the life of Creator Sets Free (Jesus) will also be seen in our death-doomed bodies. **12**So you can see that we struggle with death, but because of this you have the life of the world to come.

COURAGE TO SPEAK

13It has been written in our Sacred Teachings, "My faith gave me the courage to speak."[a] Since the same faith lives in our spirits, we too have the courage to speak. **14**For we know that the one who raised up Creator Sets Free (Jesus) *to sit beside the Great Spirit* will also raise us up to be with him.[b] Then together, we will all stand before him.

15So then, all that *we suffer* is for your good. This means that Creator's gift of great kindness will reach more and more people. Then many people will give thanks to the Great Spirit, bringing him even greater honor. **16**That is why we never lose heart. For even though our outer being is fading away, our inner being grows stronger every day.

17For the troubles we now face are small *compared to what is coming* and do not last for long. Instead, they are getting us ready for the great and shining beauty of the world to come, a beauty beyond comparison that will never fade away. So we set our minds not on the things we can see but on the things we cannot see. **18**For the things we can see will last only for a short time, but the things we cannot see are from the world to come, which will never fade away.

5

ABOUT OUR NEW BODIES

1*Our bodies are like tipis* that we live in here on earth. If our tipi wears out and is taken down in death, we know *for sure* that the Great Spirit has a better lodge for us in the spirit-world above. That lodge is not made with human hands and will never grow old or wear out.

2As long as we remain here in our earthly tipis, we groan, for we are aching to put on our tipis from the world above. **3**After we have taken off these old bodies, we will be given new bodies to wear.[c] In this way we will not remain spirits without bodies.[d]

4As long as we remain in these tipis *of our earthly bodies,* we keep groaning with

---

[a] **4:13** Possibly Psalm 116:10
[b] **4:14** Ephesians 2:6
[c] **5:3** 1 Corinthians 15:52
[d] **5:3** Lit. *be found naked*

heavy hearts, longing for something more. We do not desire our earthly bodies to be stripped from us, but that we would be fitted with our new bodies. When this happens, these death-doomed bodies of ours will be overtaken with new life.

WALKING BY TRUSTING, NOT BY SEEING

⁵Our Creator is the one who has made us ready for this *new body*. The gift of his Spirit is his proof to us that his promise is trustworthy and true. ⁶This is the reason our hearts remain firm, for we know that as long as we remain in this earthly body, we are not yet at home with our Honored Chief. ⁷As we walk the road of life, we trust in him even though we do not yet see him, for we walk by faith, not by sight.

⁸Our hearts remain so firm in this truth that we can say, "We would rather be at home with our Honored Chief than to remain in these earthly bodies." ⁹So whether we stay here on earth or go to be with him in the spirit-world above, it is our aim to make his heart glad. ¹⁰For we must all stand before the council seat of the Chosen One and give an answer for what we have done in these earthly bodies—whether good or bad. Then the Chosen One will give back to each of us the honor that is due.

¹¹Knowing that all will stand before our Honored Chief in this way fills us with great respect and awe. This is why we work so hard to help all people see and understand this truth. The Great Spirit can see who we are, and we trust that you can also see from your hearts who we truly are.

LIVING OR DYING, WE TRUST IN HIM

¹²We are not trying to make ourselves look big in your eyes, but we do want you to be proud of us *in a good way*. Then you will be able to see through the ones who brag about how things look on the outside rather than what is in the heart. ¹³If we sound as if we have lost our minds, that is between us and the Great Spirit. If we sound as if we are in our right minds, it is for your good.

¹⁴The love shown to us by the Chosen One has taken hold of our hearts, because we know that if one has died for all human beings, then all of us died. ¹⁵He died for all so that those who live should no longer live for themselves, but for the one who died and rose for them.

¹⁶So from now on we will no longer look at others through weak human eyes. Even though we used to see the Chosen One in this way, that is not how we see him now.

NEW CREATION

¹⁷I am saying that anyone who has been joined together with the Chosen One is now part of the new creation. For in the Chosen One the old creation has faded away and the new creation has come into being. ¹⁸It is the Great Spirit himself who has done all of this! Through the Chosen One, Creator has removed the hostility between human beings and himself, bringing all creation into harmony once again. The Great Spirit has chosen us to represent him in the sacred task of helping others find and walk this path of peacemaking and healing—turning enemies into friends.

¹⁹The Great Spirit was not holding people's broken ways against them. Instead, he was working in the Chosen One to bring all people back into harmony with himself. He has now given us the honor of bringing this message to others.

²⁰So we now represent the Chosen One. It is as if Creator is speaking through

us, calling out for all people to walk the path of being restored back to the Great Spirit. ²¹Creator Sets Free (Jesus), the one who knew no broken ways, was chosen by the Great Spirit to bear our broken ways, so that we would become the ones who represent his right ways.

TODAY IS A GOOD DAY

¹As we work side by side with Creator, we are calling out for you to not let the gift of Creator's great kindness fall to the ground. ²For the Great Spirit is speaking to you through the Sacred Teachings, "At the right time I heard your cry, and I set you free on the day you needed my help."ᵃ Behold! Now is the right time, and today is the day to be set free.

WALKING IN A GOOD WAY

³We walk in a way that will make no one else stumble, so that no one has a reason to talk bad about our sacred task. ⁴Instead, we represent ourselves to others in a good way as servants of the Great Spirit. It is with great patience that we walk through times of trouble, suffering, and misery. ⁵We have been beaten, thrown in prison, and faced uprisings. We have worked hard, spent nights with no sleep, and have gone hungry for days. ⁶We walk with clean hearts as we carry sacred knowledge with patience and kindness. We stay in step with the Holy Spirit as we walk the road of love with our hearts open for all to see. ⁷We speak the truth by the power of the Great Spirit. We fight for what is right with spiritual weapons in our right hand and in our left.

WALKING IN THIS WORLD

⁸As we walk the road, we are honored and dishonored. Some speak evil of us, while others speak well of us. Even though we speak the truth, some say we speak with a forked tongue. ⁹We are strangers to some but well known to others. We look as if we are dying, but look again—we live! We have been whipped and mistreated, but death has not found us. ¹⁰Our hearts are glad even in times of sorrow. We may be poor, but we have made many rich. *It looks as if* we have nothing, but the truth is, all things are ours.ᵇ

OPEN MOUTHS AND OPEN HEARTS

¹¹O you who live in Village of Pleasure (Corinth), we have spoken freely to you, and our hearts have been wide open. ¹²Our hearts have not been closed to you. Why have yours been closed to us? ¹³I will speak to you as I would to my own children: let us make a good trade. Since our hearts are wide open to you, you should open wide your hearts *to us.*

CREATOR'S LODGE MUST BE KEPT SACRED

¹⁴Do not try to walk in step with those who do not trust in the Chosen One. How can doing right be in harmony with doing wrong? How can light and darkness walk the same path together? ¹⁵How can there be any agreement between the Chosen One and the Worthless One (Belial)?ᶜ What common ground does one who trusts in the Chosen One share with one who does not? ¹⁶Do spirit-images have any place in Creator's sacred lodge? For we are his sacred lodge, and Creator lives in us.

The Great Spirit himself has said, "I will make my home in them and walk

---

ᵃ**6:2** Isaiah 49:8

ᵇ**6:10** 1 Corinthians 3:21-23
ᶜ**6:15** *Belial* is another name for Satan.

among them. I will be their Great Spirit, and they will be my people."[a]

[17]*That is why our Sacred Teachings also say*, "'Walk away from them and separate yourselves from their ways,' says the Great Spirit. 'Do not join yourself to what is ceremonially impure, and I will welcome you.'"[b] And, [18]"'I will be a father to you, and you will be my sons and daughters,' says the All-Powerful One."

[1]My much-loved friends, since Creator has given us promises such as these, let us cleanse both body and spirit from all impurities. We will continue to walk this path of becoming holy because we have such deep respect for the Great Spirit.

COMFORT AND TROUBLES

[2]Open your hearts and let us in. We have wronged no one. We have harmed no one. We have cheated no one. [3]I do not say this to accuse you. For as I told you before, whether we live together or die together, you remain in our hearts.

[4]I boldly tell others how much I respect you. My heart has been made strong and overflows with joy, even as we walk a troubled path. [5]As soon as we came to Land of Tall People (Macedonia) we found no rest for our bodies. Trouble came at us from all directions, arguments from the outside, and fears on the inside.

[6]But the Great Spirit, who lifts up the downcast, lifted our hearts by sending Big Man (Titus) to us. [7]We were also encouraged when he gave us a good report about your concern for us. He told us of your longing to see me, of your tears,

and your burning desire to defend me. This made my heart glad!

SORROW TURNED TO JOY

[8]I know that letter I wrote caused you sorrow. At first, this made me wish I had not written it, but since your sorrow was only for a short time, I no longer feel that way. [9]Now my heart is glad, not that you were made sad, but that your sadness led you to change your ways. This is what Creator wanted, so that you would not be harmed by our letter. [10]With the help of the Great Spirit, sorrow can create a change of heart that will not turn back, which sets us free and makes us whole. But there is a sorrow in this world that leads only to death.

[11]Look at what Creator has done in you. He has turned your sorrow into something good. You took my warnings to heart, restored your reputation, and put your anger to good use. You treated my counsel with great respect, and your burning desire was to make the wrongs right again. In every way you have represented yourselves in a good and sacred manner.

[12]I wrote that letter not because of the one who did wrong, or because of the one who was harmed. I wrote so that in the eyes of the Great Spirit you would see for yourselves how much we care *for the well-being of all the sacred family.*

TRUST RESTORED BECAUSE OF BIG MAN

[13]You have lifted up our hearts. For when Big Man (Titus) told us of the joy he felt when you refreshed his spirit, our hearts were also filled with joy. [14]I am not ashamed that I bragged about you to Big Man (Titus). For in the same way that we have always spoken truth to you, what we told him about you has also proven

---

[a] **6:16** Ezekiel 37:27; Leviticus 26:12; Jeremiah 31:33
[b] **6:17** Isaiah 52:11

to be true. [15]His care for you has grown even deeper as he remembers the great respect you showed him when he came to you, and how willing you were to follow all of his instructions. [16]All these things make my heart glad and give me the courage to fully trust you.

8

GIVING SACRIFICIALLY

[1]My sacred family members, we want to tell you what the Great Spirit has done among the sacred families who gather in Land of Tall People (Macedonia). The gift of Creator's great kindness has taken hold of their hearts. [2]Even though they were walking a rough and troubled road *with only a few possessions*, they found great joy in giving away as much as they could. [3]I speak truth from my heart. They not only gave as much as they could. They willingly sacrificed even more. Of their own free will [4]they begged us to let them participate in bringing help to Creator's holy people *who live in Village of Peace (Jerusalem)*.

[5]They did much more than we had hoped for. For they first offered their lives to our Honored Chief, and then, under Creator's guidance, they offered their lives to us as well. [6]This is why we asked Big Man (Titus) to once again stir up this gift of great kindness in your hearts. For he is the one who first asked you to join in *with this offering to help Creator's holy people*.

THE RIGHT WAY TO GIVE

[7]You are strong in faith, noble in speech, wise in understanding, and whole-hearted in all that you do. The love we planted in you has grown strong. Since you have done so well in all these things, see to it that you also do well in this gift of giving. [8]I am not demanding that you give, but, by choosing you as an example for others, I am proving how deep your love truly is.

[9]For you know the loving kindness of our Honored Chief Creator Sets Free (Jesus) the Chosen One. Even though had great treasures, he became poor for your sake, that through his poverty you might share in his great treasures.

FINISH WHAT YOU STARTED

[10]The reason I give you this counsel is to help you finish what you started to do last year. You were the first to be willing to help, [11]so now is the time for you to finish the journey you began. Be as eager to finish this journey as you were when you started, and give as much as you are able. I would not ask you to give more than you are able. [12]If you have a willing heart, it is accepted that you give from what you have and not from what you do not have.

[13]It is not that I am trying to lift the burden of others only to burden you. But to restore balance, [14]you who have more than enough should give to the ones in need. Then when they have more than enough and you are in need, they can help you. This is what I mean by restoring balance. [15]Just as it has been written *in our Sacred Teachings*, "The ones who gathered much had nothing left over. The ones who gathered little had all they needed."[a]

HELPERS IN THE GOOD STORY

[16]I give thanks to the Great Spirit, for he put into the heart of Big Man (Titus) the

[a]**8:15** Exodus 16:18

same care that I have for you. [17]When we asked Big Man (Titus) for his help, he welcomed the idea, because going to you was already in his heart. [18]Along with Big Man (Titus) we have sent a *spiritual* brother whose reputation for living the good story is well known and highly respected among all the sacred families.

[19]It is for this reason the sacred families have chosen him to help us in this sacred task. He will journey with us as we take this gift of kindness *to Creator's holy people in Village of Peace (Jerusalem)*. We welcome him to join with us in this sacred task that Creator has called us to. [20]Taking him with us shows our goodwill and helps us prove beyond a doubt that we are doing things in a good way. [21]Our aim is to do what is honorable, not only in the eyes of the Great Spirit but also in the eyes of human beings.

[22]We are also sending another *spiritual* brother to journey with them. He has proven himself to be always willing to help. He has dedicated himself to this sacred task because of the good things he has heard about you.

[23]As for Big Man (Titus), he is my trusted partner as he works by my side to serve you. As for the other *spiritual* brothers, they serve as message bearers for the sacred families and bring honor to the Chosen One. [24]So show these brothers your love in a way that the sacred families can clearly see. This will prove that we had good reason to brag about you.

9 ❖◄❖►◄❖►◄❖►◄❖►◄❖►◄❖►◄❖►

READY AND WILLING TO GIVE

[1]There is no need for me to speak anything more to you about helping Creator's holy people in this matter *of giving*. [2]I know how ready and willing you are. I brag about you *to the sacred families* in Land of Tall People (Macedonia). I tell them that the sacred families in Land of Sorrow (Achaia) have been ready to give since last year. It was your eagerness *to give* that made them want to do the same.

[3]To make sure that my bragging about you will not fall to the ground, I am sending some *spiritual* brothers to you so you will make yourselves ready *to give this gift* just as I said you would be. [4]For if any from Land of Tall People (Macedonia) were to come with me and find you not ready, this would bring shame to us all. [5]It is for this reason I felt that I needed to urge these brothers to come to you ahead of time. They will help make sure your promised gift will be ready. In this way, when we arrive, it will show you gave from your hearts and not because you felt forced to give.

GIVING BRINGS HONOR

[6]Remember this saying: The one who plants only a few seeds will harvest a small crop. The one who plants many seeds will harvest a large crop. [7]Each of you should give what you have decided in your heart to give. You should not feel forced to give out of guilt because someone is shaming you for not giving. For the Great Spirit loves it when people give with glad hearts.

[8]Creator has the power to use the gift of all of his great kindness to provide more than enough for all that you need at all times. In this way you will have plenty to help others, [9]just as it says *in our Sacred Teachings*, "He filled many giveaway blankets with gifts to the poor. His right ways will bring honor to him beyond the end of all days."

¹⁰The one who gives seed for planting and good food for eating will make your seeds grow into a great harvest for doing what is right. ¹¹His blessing will rest on you in every way so that you can always be a blessing to others. In this way, the gift you give to us *for others* will bring *honor and* thanks to the Great Spirit. ¹²This sacred task *of giving* not only helps the poor among Creator's holy people *in Village of Peace (Jerusalem)*, but it also inspires many people to give praise to the Great Spirit.

¹³Your willingness to follow through with this sacred task of giving shows that your faithfulness to the good story of the Chosen One goes beyond words. Your freely given gift to them and to all will bring honor to Creator. ¹⁴With deep feelings for you they will send their voice to the Great Spirit, for they have seen the gift of Creator's great kindness at work in you.

¹⁵Give thanks to the Great Spirit for the gift that goes beyond our weak ways of speaking!

10

SMALL MAN SPEAKS FOR HIMSELF

¹Now I, Small Man (Paul), will speak for myself. With all the humility and kindness of the Chosen One I beg you to listen to what I have to say. Some have said that I am weak when with you and bold when away from you. ²These people think that we walk in weak and broken human ways, but they will soon find out what kind of courage and boldness we can walk in! I beg you not to make me treat you in the same manner *as I must treat those who stand against me.*

³Even though we are walking in weak human bodies, we are not fighting with human strength. We do not make war in the ways of this world. ⁴Our weapons have Creator's power to break through and tear down strongholds. These strongholds are high-minded and wrong ideas about the Great Spirit and his ways. ⁵We help others see clearly about Creator and capture those wrong ideas, so that the truth about the Chosen One becomes a clear path to follow. ⁶Then, when you are fully walking in the ways of the Chosen One, we will be ready to bring Creator's justice to those who fail to walk in his ways.

⁷You are only looking at how things appear on the outside. If you are sure that you belong to the Chosen One, you should remind yourself that we, as much as you, also belong to the Chosen One.

SMALL MAN DEFENDS HIS AUTHORITY

⁸You might think I brag too much about my authority in the Chosen One, but I am not ashamed to boast, for he gave me the right to build you up, not to tear you down. ⁹I say this so you will not think I am trying to make you afraid with my letters.

¹⁰It has been said by some, "In his letters his words carry much weight and power, but face to face his words are weak and empty." ¹¹Those who say this should think again, for what we have said in our letters when away we will do when we are among you.

¹²We dare not measure ourselves or lump ourselves together with those who beat their own drum. For when they measure themselves against each other and compare themselves one with another, they show that they have no wisdom.

¹³So then, unlike the others, we will not boast beyond the territory Creator has assigned to us. It is a far-reaching

territory that includes you *who live in Village of Pleasure (Corinth)*. **14**We did not overstep our boundaries when we came to you, for we were *the very first* to reach all the way to you with the good story about the Chosen One.

15We do not overstep boundaries or take for ourselves honor for what others have done. Instead, our hope is that, as your trust in us grows, our sacred task among you will reach out and touch many more. **16**When that time comes, we will be able to tell the good story to villages beyond you. In this way we will never take for ourselves honor for what others have done.

17For *it says in our Sacred Teachings*, "Let the one who brags boast in what the Great Spirit has done."[a]

18For it is not the ones who honor themselves that are proven worthy, but only those who are honored by the Great Spirit.

11

TRUE AND FALSE MESSAGE BEARERS

1Since you have already been patient with me, I hope you will put up with my boasting a little longer. **2**I am jealous for you with a jealousy that comes from the Great Spirit. For I have promised you in marriage to one husband, the Chosen One, to give you to him as pure as a maiden who has never been with a man.

3*Long ago* the evil snake used his trickster ways to take Life Bearer (Eve) down the wrong path.[b] I fear that, in the same manner she was tricked, false message bearers may take you down the wrong path in your thinking and lead you away from your single-hearted loyalty to the Chosen One.

4I say this because you seem so willing to put up with someone who tells you about another Creator Sets Free (Jesus) who is not the same Creator Sets Free (Jesus) we told you about. You are also willing to welcome a different spirit from the one you welcomed from us. You even welcome a different good story from the good story we told you.

5I do not think I am any less of a message bearer than any of these puffed-up ones you have been listening to. **6**I may not speak with a smooth tongue, but I know what I am talking about. For we have made ourselves clearly understood to you all.

7Was it wrong for me to humble myself by giving you Creator's good story without charge in order to bless you? **8**I felt as if I were stealing from other sacred families when I took gifts from them to serve you. **9**While I was with you, *I did not ask any of you for help, even though* I was in need. Some sacred family members who came from Land of Tall People (Macedonia) gifted me with everything I needed. In this way, I was able to keep myself from becoming a burden to you, and I mean to keep it that way.

10I speak truth from my heart with the Chosen One as my witness. No one throughout the territory of Land of Sorrow (Achaia) will be able to keep me from walking true to my boast *in what the Chosen One has helped me to do*. **11**You may ask why I will not let myself become a burden to you. Do you think it is because I do not love you? The Great Spirit knows I love you!

12I will keep walking this same path, so that these *puffed-up* message bearers will have no solid ground to walk on

---

[a]**10:17** Jeremiah 9:24; 1 Corinthians 1:31
[b]**11:3** Genesis 3:4, 13

when they brag that they walk in the same manner that we do. **13**The ones who make this boast are false message bearers and lying tricksters. They represent themselves as message bearers of the Chosen One, but the regalia they wear does not represent who they truly are. **14**This should not surprise us, for Accuser (Satan) falsely represents himself as a spirit-messenger wearing bright and shining regalia. **15**So it is no surprise that the followers of Accuser (Satan) would falsely represent themselves as servants of *Creator's* right ways. The path they walk will take them to a bad end.

SMALL MAN SPEAKS LIKE A FOOL

16I will say it again: I want no one to think of me as a fool. But if you think of me in that manner, then let me speak as if I were a fool so that I can brag some more. **17**To be clear, I am not speaking as our Honored Chief would have me speak. Instead, I will speak as a fool who brags too much. **18**Since there are so many who brag about who they are and what they have done, I will now do the same!

19If I speak as a fool, this should help you understand me better, for you are so wise that you are glad to put up with many foolish things. **20**You even let others rule over you as if you were their slaves. You put up with them when they devour your goods, trick you, look down on you, and insult you. **21**Shame on me! I was not strong enough to treat you so badly! But if others can boldly brag—I speak like a fool—I dare to brag just as much.

THE MARKS OF A TRUE MESSAGE BEARER

22Are they Tribal Members (Hebrews)? So am I! Are they of the tribes of Wrestles with Creator (Israelites)? So am I! Are they descendants of Father of Many Nations (Abraham)? So am I!

23Are they servants of the Chosen One? Some may think I have lost my mind, but I want to brag even more! I have worked harder. I have been in prison more. I have been beaten more times than I can count. I have faced death many times. **24**Five times I have been beaten with thirty-nine strikes of the whip by the people of my own tribe. **25**I was beaten with clubs three times. Once I was almost killed when they threw stones at me. I was shipwrecked three times, and I drifted on the deep waters of the sea for a night and a day.

26Many times I have traveled far and wide. On these journeys I faced dangers from raging rivers and desperate outlaws. I have faced threats from my own people and from the people of the Outside Nations. I have faced dangers in villages, dangers in the desert, dangers at sea, and dangers from false sacred family members. **27**My hands have been worn to the bone with hard work. On many nights I have gone without sleep. On my journeys I have been hungry and thirsty, often without food, with no blanket to keep me warm.

28Alongside all these challenges, each day I am weighed down with my deep concern for all the sacred families *under my care.* **29**I feel the weakness of any who are weak. I burn with fire in my inner being every time someone is turned away from the good road.

30If I must boast, I choose to brag about the things that show how weak I am. **31**The Great Spirit who is the Father of our Honored Chief Creator Sets Free (Jesus), who is blessed beyond the end of all days, knows that I speak the truth.

32When I was in the village of Silent Weaver (Damascus), the governor representing the ruler named Brave One (Aretas) was on the lookout to capture me. [33]I had to sneak away from there by being lowered in a basket through an opening in the village wall.

12

SACRED VISIONS AND SPIRITUAL EXPERIENCES

[1]It does not seem like a good thing for me to keep "bragging like this," but I now want to tell you about the sacred visions shown to me by the Great Spirit.

[2-3]Let me tell you the story of a man I know, a follower of the Chosen One. Fourteen winters ago this man was taken up into the highest place in the spirit-world above.[a] If this happened to him in the body or outside the body, I do not know. Only the Great Spirit knows. [4]This man was taken up into Creator's Beautiful Garden,[b] where he heard mysterious words that human beings are not permitted to speak.

[5]I will brag about that man, but as for myself I will boast only in how small and weak I am. [6]It would not be a foolish thing for me to brag about this, because I would be speaking the truth about myself. But I will hold back from saying too much, so that none of you will think too highly of me beyond what you hear me say and see me do.

[7]The things that were shown to me were so mysterious and powerful that I was given a thorn to stab me where I was weak, a messenger from Accuser (Satan) to prick my pride and keep me humble. [8]Three times I begged our

---

[a]12:2-3 Often translated in other English translations as "the third heaven"
[b]12:4 Lit. *paradise*

Honored Chief to remove this thorn from me.

[9]"The gift of my great kindness will give you the strength you need," our Honored Chief said to me. "For the greatness of my power comes to the ones who understand how weak they are."

So then, I am glad to brag even more about how weak I am, so it can be clearly seen that the power resting on me comes from the Chosen One. [10]That is why I can take joy in those things that show how weak I am. Others can insult me, mistreat me, hunt me down, and make things hard for me, all because of my trust in the Chosen One. For when I am weak, Creator's strength becomes my own.

[11]I may be acting like a fool, but you are to be blamed for it. You should have shown honor to me, for I am no less a message bearer than these puffed-up ones, even though I am nothing. [12]The powerful signs and wonders that mark one as a true message bearer were performed among you with great patience. [13]What have I done for the other sacred families that I have not done for you? Only that I did not become a burden to you. You must release me from this wrong!

[14]I am now ready to come to you for a third time. Once again I will not be a burden to you. I want you, not what you can give to me. For it is the parents who should provide for their children, and not children for their parents. [15]It would make my heart glad to give all that I have and all that I am to you. If my love for you is so great, then why is your love for me so small?

[16-17]Since it is clear that I did not ask anything for myself, do you think I acted like a trickster to fool and cheat you by sending others to collect the offering? [18]When I sent Big Man (Titus) and the

other *spiritual* brother to you, did they take more than they should? You know that they did not. For Big Man (Titus) and I walk together in the same spirit on the same path.

¹⁹Have you been thinking all this time that we have been trying to prove ourselves to you? *We have nothing to prove to you*, for we speak with the words of the Chosen One and under the eyes of the Great Spirit. You are our much-loved ones, and everything we do is to lift you up and make you strong *in him*.

²⁰But I fear that when I come to you we will not be walking in step with each other. I might find among you that there will be arguing, jealousy, uncontrolled anger, selfish desires, forked tongues, boastful talk, and hostile ways. ²¹This makes me afraid that when I come to you again the Great Spirit will humble me in front of you. For I will weep many tears for the ones who have been following their bad hearts and have not turned away from walking in impurity and uncontrolled sexual desires.

13

FINAL WORDS OF WARNING AND ENCOURAGEMENT

¹This will be the third time I will be coming to you. It says *in the Sacred Teachings* that it takes two or three witnesses to prove a wrongdoing.[a] ²When I came the second time, I warned *the ones who were doing wrong*, and now I warn the rest of you. When I come this time, I will not take pity on anyone. ³You who seek proof that the Chosen One is speaking through me will get all the

proof you need. Do not think that the Chosen One is weak in this matter. His power is at work among you. ⁴Yes, he was nailed to a tree-pole—the cross—and died as a weak human being, but he now lives by the power of the Great Spirit. In the same way we, like him, are also weak human beings, but you will see that, like him, we also live by the power of the Great Spirit as we walk together with you.

⁵Take a good look inside yourselves to see whether you walk true to what you believe. Put yourselves to the test. Do you know who you truly are? Do you not understand that Creator Sets Free (Jesus) the Chosen One lives in and among you? Or have you failed the test *of walking true to this in your own lives*? ⁶It is my hope that you will come to know that I and my fellow workers have not failed this test.

⁷We are sending our voices to the Great Spirit, praying for you to do nothing wrong. This is not to make it look as if we have passed the test, but so that you will do what is good and right even if it looks as if we have failed. ⁸For we must stand firm on the truth and not walk away from it. ⁹So if our being weak means that you are strong, it makes our hearts glad. It is our prayer that you will become strong and mature *followers of the Chosen One*.

¹⁰I am writing this letter to you while I am away, so that I will not have to speak sharp words like this when I come to you. Instead, I want to use the power our Honored Chief has given me to build you up, not to tear you down.

LAST WORDS

¹¹Last of all, my sacred family members, let your hearts be glad. Mend your ways,

---

[a] **13:1** Deuteronomy 19:15

walk side by side with each other, sharing the same purpose and living in harmony with one another. In this way, the Great Spirit who gives love and peace will walk with you *on the road of life.*

¹²Welcome each other with a holy kiss. All of Creator's holy ones *who are with me* send their greetings to you.

¹³May the gift of great kindness that comes from our Honored Chief Creator Sets Free (Jesus), the Chosen One, along with the love of our Creator remain with you as you walk hand in hand together with the Holy Spirit.

Aho! May it be so!

SMALL MAN TO THE SACRED FAMILIES IN LAND OF PALE SKINS

GALATIANS

1

GREETINGS AND FIRST WORDS

1-2 From Small Man (Paul), and from the *spiritual* brothers who are with me. To the sacred families who gather in Land of Pale Skins (Galatia). I was chosen to be a message bearer not from human beings or through human beings, but through Creator Sets Free (Jesus) the Chosen One and through *our* Father the Creator, who brought the Chosen One back to life from the world of the dead.

3I greet you with the great kindness and peace that comes from our Father above and from *our* Honored Chief, Creator Sets Free (Jesus) the Chosen One. **4**He is the one who laid down his life for us to set us free from our bad hearts and broken ways. He did this to rescue us from the evil and worthless ways of the world we now live in. This is what our Father the Great Spirit wanted him to do. **5**All honor belongs to our Father the Great Spirit to the time beyond the end of all days. Aho! May it be so!

A FALSE TELLING OF THE GOOD STORY

6The Chosen One called you by the gift of his great kindness to walk the road with him. I stand amazed that you would so quickly walk away from him to follow a different good story. **7**Not that there is another good story, but there are some who are causing trouble for you by trying to change the meaning and purpose of the Chosen One's good story.

8Should anyone, whether it be one of us or even a spirit-messenger from the spirit-world above, tell you a different good story from the one we already told you, let that person be cut off[a] *from the Chosen One.* **9**I will say it again: if anyone should tell you a different good story from the one you have already welcomed, let that person be cut off *from the Chosen One.*

10Do these words sound as if I am seeking honor from human beings or from the Great Spirit? Do you think I am trying to please human beings? If that were true, then I would not be a willing servant of the Chosen One.

SMALL MAN TELLS HIS STORY

11My sacred family members, I want you to know that the good story I have been telling you did not come from the mind of human beings. **12**It did not come to me from human beings, nor was it taught to me. This good story was revealed to me by Creator Sets Free (Jesus) the Chosen One.

13-14 You have heard the story of how I used to walk as a traditional Tribal

---

[a]**1:8** Lit. *anathema*, a word meaning "cursed" or "cut off." See Romans 9:3.

Member. I was becoming a leader in my tribal nation and was following our tribal traditions far ahead of anyone else my age. You also heard how with great fury I hunted down and brought harm to Creator's sacred family.

[15]But *when I was on the way to the village of Silent Weaver (Damascus),*[a] the Great Spirit *stopped me in my tracks.* He is the one who chose me while I was still in my mother's womb and called me because of the gift of his great kindness. [16]It made his heart glad to show me the truth about his Son, so I would tell his good story to all the Outside Nations.

After this happened, I did not look for guidance from flesh-and-blood human beings. [17]Neither did I go to Village of Peace (Jerusalem) to learn from the ones who were message bearers before me. Instead, I went away into Land of Wanderers (Arabia), and after that I went back to Silent Weaver (Damascus).

[18]Then after three winters I traveled to Village of Peace (Jerusalem) to learn from Stands on the Rock (Cephas-Peter) and remained with him for fifteen days. [19]While I was there, the only other message bearer I saw was He Leads the Way (James), the brother of *Creator Sets Free (Jesus)* our Honored Chief.

[20]I promise you, with the Great Spirit as my witness, that I am telling you the truth about these things. I am not lying!

[21]After that I went into the territories of Bright Sun (Syria) and Turns Over (Cilicia). [22]The sacred families of the Chosen One in Land of Promise (Judea) had not seen me face to face, [23]but they did hear about me. They heard, "The one who was attacking us is now telling the good story he once made war against."

[a]1:15 Acts 22:6

[24]And they gave the Great Spirit the honor for what happened to me.

2

THE COUNCIL AT VILLAGE OF PEACE

[1]Then after fourteen winters had passed, I went once again to Village of Peace (Jerusalem) along with Son of Comfort (Barnabas) and Big Man (Titus). [2]It was the Great Spirit who revealed to me that I should go. I met in a private council with those who seemed to be the spiritual leaders and explained to them the manner in which I tell the good story to people from the Outside Nations. I wanted them to understand so that they would not try to undo all that I had done or wanted to do. I wanted to make sure I was not running a race I could not finish.

[3]*The good news is that* Big Man (Titus), who was with me, was not required to participate in the cutting of the flesh ceremony, even though he was a Wisdom Seeker (Greek), *that is, from an Outside Nation.* [4]*The ceremony was talked about* because some who were not true sacred family members had been sneaked in. They crept in to spy on the freedom we have in Creator Sets Free (Jesus) the Chosen One and to make us slaves *to their understanding of our tribal law.* [5]But we stood firm and gave them no ground, even for a moment, so that the truth of Creator's good story would be preserved for you.

[6]As for those *leaders* who are supposed to hold such a high reputation, their reputation means nothing to me, for the Great Spirit does not judge by outward appearance. Those leaders did not add one thing to *the good story* that I tell.

[7]Instead, it became clear to them that I had been given the sacred task of telling the good story to the Outside Nations,[a] just as Stands on the Rock (Cephas-Peter) was to our Tribal Members.[b] [8]For the Great Spirit who gave Stands on the Rock (Cephas-Peter) the calling and power to be a message bearer to our Tribal Members also gave me the calling and power to serve the Outside Nations.

[9]So when He Leads the Way (James), Stands on the Rock (Cephas-Peter), and He Shows Goodwill (John), who seemed to be the spiritual leaders,[c] came to understand that I had been given this sacred task, they joined hands in agreement with me and Son of Comfort (Barnabas). They agreed that we would go to the Outside Nations and they to our tribal nation. [10]They asked only that we would not forget to help the poor, a desire that was already burning in my heart.

SMALL MAN'S CONFLICT WITH STANDS ON THE ROCK

[11]*After that, something else happened that I need to make clear*: when Stands on the Rock (Cephas-Peter) came to stay for a time at *the village of* Stands Against (Antioch), I had to take a stand against him face-to-face, to clearly show that what he was doing was wrong.

[12]*From Village of Peace (Jerusalem)* He Leads the Way (James) sent some men to Stands Against (Antioch). Before they came, Stands on the Rock (Cephas-Peter) would sit and eat with *the sacred family members from* the Outside Nations. But after those men came, he separated himself from *the sacred family members*

from the Outside Nations, for he was afraid of what these Tribal Members might think of him.

> *Stands on the Rock (Cephas-Peter) was not remaining true to what the Great Spirit had shown him in a sacred vision.*[d]

[13]Then all the other Tribal Members joined with him in his cowardly ways, so that even Son of Comfort (Barnabas) was drawn into their false-faced ways.

GOOD STANDING DOES NOT COME FROM KEEPING THE LAW

[14]When I saw that they were not walking true to the meaning of the good story, I said to Stands on the Rock (Cephas-Peter) in front of everyone there, "You, who are a Tribal Member, have been living in the same manner as the people from the Outside Nations. So how is it that you would force them to follow the traditions of our Tribal Members?

[15]"We who are Tribal Members by birth are not like those 'outcasts' from the Outside Nations *who do not keep our law.* [16]But we *who follow the Chosen One* know that working hard to keep our tribal law does not put us in good standing with Creator. For good standing comes through trusting in what Creator Sets Free (Jesus) the Chosen One has done. *As Tribal Members* we have put our trust in him, so that our good standing comes from trusting in the Chosen One and not by working hard to keep our tribal law. For no human being will be put in good standing *with Creator* by working hard to keep the law.

[17]"If we Tribal Members, while seeking to be in good standing by trusting in the Chosen One, are also found to be outcasts

---

[a]**2:7** Lit. *uncircumcised*, a way to speak of one who is a Gentile outsider
[b]**2:7** Lit. *circumcised*, a way to speak of one who is Jewish
[c]**2:9** Lit. *pillars*

[d]**2:12** See Acts 10:28.

and guilty of wrongdoing, can it be said that the Chosen One is leading us into broken ways? May it never be! ¹⁸For if I were to rebuild the things I have torn down, that would prove that I was *wrong from the first and make me* a lawbreaker. ¹⁹It was through our tribal law that I died to our tribal law, so that I could be set free to live for the Great Spirit. When the Chosen One died on the cross, I died with him.

²⁰"My life is no longer my own, for my life belongs to the Chosen One, who lives in me. The life I now live in my weak human body, I live by trusting in the faithfulness of the Son of the Great Spirit, who loved me and gave up his life for me. ²¹I cannot do away with the gift of Creator's great kindness, for if good standing with Creator could be gained through the law, that would mean the Chosen One died for nothing."

WORKING TO KEEP THE LAW OR TRUSTING IN THE CHOSEN ONE

¹O you foolish ones who live in Land of Pale Skinned People (Galatia)! Did someone put a spell on you? Was it not clearly shown to you that Creator Sets Free (Jesus) the Chosen One was put to death on a tree-pole—the cross? ²I have one chief question to ask you: Did the Holy Spirit come to you because you worked hard to keep our tribal law, or because you heard and trusted in the good story we told you?

³Have you become foolish enough to believe that a journey begun in the power of the Spirit could be finished by weak human strength? ⁴I cannot believe that you have traveled so far just to end up at a dead end.

⁵Does Creator give you his Spirit and work his power among you because you are working hard to keep our tribal law, or because you hear and trust in the good story we told you?

LESSONS FROM THE SACRED TEACHINGS

⁶It was the same for Father of Many Nations (Abraham), *for it says in our Sacred Teachings*, "Father of Many Nations (Abraham) put his trust in Creator. This is what gave him good standing in the eyes of the Great Spirit."ᵃ ⁷It should now be clear to you that the true sons and daughters of Father of Many Nations (Abraham) are the ones who trust *in Creator*.

⁸It was foretold long ago in our Sacred Teachings that it would be through trusting in him that Creator would give good standing to *all* the Outside Nations. The good story was told to Father of Many Nations (Abraham) when Creator said to him, "It is through you that I will bless all nations."ᵇ ⁹So then, all who walk the same path that Father of Many Nations (Abraham), the man of trusting, walked are also blessed with good standing.

¹⁰All who seek good standing with Creator through working hard to keep our tribal law are under the law's curse. For it is written in our Sacred Teachings, "Cursed is anyone who does not perform all that is written down in the book of the law."ᶜ

¹¹It should be clear for all to see that no one is given good standing in the eyes of the Great Spirit by keeping our tribal law, for "The ones in good standing will find life by trusting."ᵈ ¹²Our tribal law is not about trusting. It is about doing. As

---

ᵃ**3:6** Genesis 15:6; Romans 4:3
ᵇ**3:8** Genesis 12:3
ᶜ**3:10** Deuteronomy 27:26; 31:26
ᵈ**3:11** Habakkuk 2:4

our Sacred Teachings tell us, "It is the ones who keep doing what is written in the law who will find life."[a]

SET FREE BY THE CHOSEN ONE

[13]The Chosen One paid a great price to set us free *from the law's demand about doing* by taking on himself the law's curse. As it is written in our Sacred Teachings, "Anyone who has been hanged upon a tree-pole is under a curse."[b] [14]This was done so that the promise made to Father of Many Nations (Abraham) to bless the Outside Nations would come to them through Creator Sets Free (Jesus) the Chosen One. In this way we can all receive the promised Spirit by trusting *in him and what he has done.*

[15]My sacred family members, I will now speak to you from a human point of view. Once a peace treaty has been made between human beings, no one can change or put an end to the agreement. [16]It is the same for the promises made to Father of Many Nations (Abraham) and his descendants.[c] The promises were not made to many descendants—but only to one. And that one descendant is the Chosen One.

[17]Here is what I am saying: our tribal law, which was given four hundred and thirty years after Father of Many Nations (Abraham), does not undo the peace treaty Creator made with him or do away with the promise. [18]For if sharing in these blessings depends on walking the path of the law, then the promise falls to the ground. But the Giver of Life promised it to Father of Many Nations (Abraham) as a gift of his great kindness.

THE PURPOSE OF THE LAW

[19]So then, what was the purpose of our tribal law? The law was added because of bad hearts and broken ways, *but only* until the coming of *the Chosen One*, the descendant to whom the promise was made. The law was put in place by spirit-messengers through a go-between. [20]A go-between is only needed when there is more than one. But the Great Spirit is one.

> *There was no go-between when the Great Spirit gave the promise to Father of Many Nations (Abraham) long before the law was given.*

[21]Does this mean that our tribal law is against Creator's promises? It does not! For if laws had the power to give life, then good standing with Creator would have come through our tribal law. [22]But our Sacred Teachings make it clear that because of broken ways Creator has rounded everyone up into one corral, so that the promise he made to Father of Many Nations (Abraham) would be sure to find its way to all who trust in what Creator Sets Free (Jesus) the Chosen One has done.[d]

THE WAY OF TRUSTING

[23]Before this way of trusting came, we were rounded up and held firmly under the guidance of our tribal law until the time came when the way of trusting would be made clear. [24]Our tribal law was like an elder who watched over the children and told them how to do every little thing, but only until the coming of the Chosen One, who would give us good standing by the way of trusting. [25]But now that the way of trusting has come, we are no longer children needing

---

[a]**3:12** Leviticus 18:5
[b]**3:13** Deuteronomy 21:23
[c]**3:16** Genesis 12:7

[d]**3:22** Romans 11:32

someone to watch over us and tell us what to do. **26**For we are all sons and daughters of the Great Spirit through our trust in Creator Sets Free (Jesus) the Chosen One. **27**All of you who participated in the purification ceremony[a] of the Chosen One have put on the regalia of the Chosen One himself.

28It no longer matters whether you are Tribal Members or Wisdom Seekers (Greeks), slaves or free, male or female. For in Creator Sets Free (Jesus) the Chosen One you are all one people. **29**And since you belong to the Chosen One, you are a descendant of Father of Many Nations (Abraham) and the ones who share in the blessings of the promise Creator made to him.

1What I am saying is that a father might die and leave everything to an only son. As long as that son remains a child, he has no say in the family,[b] even though one day all will be his. **2**He must wait until he reaches the age that was decided by his father. Until then, he is under the care of his aunts and uncles and other relatives.

SET FREE TO BE MATURE
SONS AND DAUGHTERS
3In the same way, we were also children held in bondage under the spiritual powers that rule this world. **4**But when the time was right, Creator sent his Son, who was born of a woman and born under our tribal law. **5**He came to set free[c] the ones who were under the law,

so that all of us could take our place in Creator's family as mature sons and daughters. **6**Because this is true of you, Creator has sent the Spirit of his Son into our hearts, crying out from within us, "Abba! My Father!"

7So then, you are no longer slaves *to the spiritual powers of this world that use the law to accuse you and bring you under bondage.* You are now taking your place as mature sons and daughters ready to share in the family blessing promised by the Great Spirit.

DO NOT TURN BACK TO THE OLD WAYS
8Before you fully knew about the Great Spirit, you served spirits that do not share the nature of the Great Spirit.[d] **9**But now that you know the Great Spirit, and even more, that the Great Spirit knows you, how is it that you desire to turn back to serve those weak and pitiful spirits that *use the law to* make you their slaves? **10**This is what you are doing when you *require people to* take part in *things like* special days, moon cycles, ceremonial seasons, and yearly festivals, *in a useless attempt to gain the blessing of Creator's good road.* **11**I am worried that my work among you has come to nothing.

12My sacred family members, I beg you to become like me, for I was once like you *when I served those weak and pitiful spirits—but now I am free.* You did not treat me in a bad way when I first came to you. **13**As you know, I was sick and weak in my body when I first told you the good story. **14**But even though the weakness in my body was hard for you to bear, you did not look down on me with scorn or turn away from me in disgust. Instead, you welcomed me as if

---

[a]**3:27** Baptism
[b]**4:1** Lit. *no different from a household slave*
[c]**4:5** Lit. *purchase the freedom of*

[d]**4:8** Lit. *those who by nature are not gods*

I were a spirit-messenger from Creator, or even as if I were the Chosen One, Creator Sets Free (Jesus) himself.

15Have you lost your desire to be such a blessing to me? I am telling you the truth that in those days, if it had been in your power, you would have sacrificed anything to help me, even your own eyes. **16**Do you now see me as an enemy because I speak truth to you?

17These false teachers *I am warning you about* are working hard to snatch you away from us and win you over *to their way of thinking. They do not truly care about you.* They only want more followers to help them spread their lies. **18**Yes, to win people over is a good thing, but only when it is done for the right reasons, and not just when I am there with you.

19My little children! Once again I am like a mother struggling to give birth to a child. My struggle will continue until the Chosen One has been fully formed within you. **20**O how I wish I were there with you so we could speak face to face! Then *we could sit in counsel together, where* you could hear my heart and not just my words. I do not know what to do about you.

WHAT IT MEANS TO BE UNDER THE LAW

21So then, you who wish to remain under our tribal law, are you ready to hear what it means to be under the law?

22Let me tell you a story from our Sacred Teachings. Father of Many Nations (Abraham) had two sons. A slave named Wandering Woman (Hagar) gave birth to one son, and Noble Woman (Sarah) gave birth to the other. **23**The son born to the slave woman was born because of broken desires, *by trying to force Creator's promise to come true.* The son born to the

free woman was born because Creator himself made the promise come true.

24-25 This story reveals a deeper truth. These women represent two peace treaties *between the Great Spirit and his people.* One peace treaty was made from Mountain of Small Trees (Mount Sinai), *where our tribal law was given.* This mountain is in Land of Wanderers (Arabia) and is represented by Wandering Woman (Hagar), whose children are all born into slavery. Wandering Woman (Hagar) also represents the present-day Village of Peace (Jerusalem), for this village and its people remain in slavery.

26But the Village of Peace (Jerusalem) from the spirit-world above is *represented by Noble Woman (Sarah), the free woman.* This Village of Peace (Jerusalem) is our mother, *and we are her children, born in freedom.*

27For it is written in our Sacred Teachings, "O childless woman who has never given birth or felt the pains of childbirth, dance for joy and shout as loud as you can! For the woman who was barren has more children than a woman with a husband."[a]

28Now you also, my sacred family members, are children born of promise. For it was by Creator's promise that He Made Us Laugh (Isaac) became the child of Father of Many Nations (Abraham).

29At that time the one who was born from broken desires hunted down and brought trouble to the son born of the Spirit's promise. The same kind of thing is happening today *from our own Tribal People.*

30But what do our Sacred Teachings tell us? "Send the slave woman and her son far away. For the son of the slave

---

[a] **4:27** Isaiah 54:1

woman cannot share the family blessings with the son of the free woman."[a]

31So then, my sacred family members, we *who trust in the Chosen One* are not children of the slave woman but of the free woman.

5 ⬥⬥⬥⬥⬥⬥⬥⬥⬥⬥⬥⬥⬥⬥

1The Chosen One set us free so that we can remain free, so stand firm and do not let anyone rope you into being slaves again. **2**Listen closely to what I, Small Man (Paul), am telling you: if you decide to participate in the cutting of the flesh ceremony *for good standing with Creator,* then what the Chosen One has done will not help you. **3**Again, I speak truth from my heart: any man who participates in the cutting of the flesh ceremony *for good standing* must follow all of the law *given by Drawn from the Water (Moses).* **4**You who trust in the law for good standing have cut yourself off from the Chosen One and walked away from the gift of Creator's great kindness.

THE THING THAT MATTERS MOST
5But through the Spirit we keep trusting *in the Chosen One* for good standing and aim our hearts toward Creator's right ways. **6**So then, in Creator Sets Free (Jesus) the Chosen One, whether or not you participate in the cutting of the flesh ceremony does not matter. What matters is walking out our faith on the road of love.

7You were walking in a good way. Who talked you out of following the path of truth? **8**That counsel did not come from the one who called you *to follow him.* **9***It has been said,* "A little yeast will spread through the whole lump of bread dough."

10But I am sure that our Honored Chief will bring you back into agreement *with the truth.* As for the one who is troubling you, whoever he is, his ways will come back on his own head.

11My sacred family members, if I still teach that the cutting of the flesh ceremony is needed, then why am I under attack? If that is what I truly teach, then the *story of the* cross of the Chosen One would make no one stumble. **12**If only those false teachers who are trying to force their way on you would go the whole way and cut it all off!

FREEDOM TO LOVE AND SERVE
13But you, my sacred family members, have been called to walk in freedom. Do not use this freedom to walk in weak and broken human ways. Instead, walk in love and serve each other. **14**For all of our tribal law finds its full meaning and purpose in this one instruction, "Love your fellow human beings in the same way you love yourself."[b] **15**If you keep on *acting like wild animals*, biting and snapping at each other, watch out! You may end up wiping each other out!

WALKING WITH THE SPIRIT
16So I say to you, if you keep walking by the Spirit's guidance, your weak and broken desires will no longer lead you down the wrong path. **17**For our broken human desires go against the Spirit, and the desires of the Spirit go against our broken human desires. They are at war with each other, and this struggle keeps you from doing the things you want to do. **18**But if you follow the guidance of the Spirit, you are not under tribal law. *You have been set free to follow the Spirit!*

---

[a]**4:30** Genesis 21:10
[b]**5:14** Leviticus 19:18

THE WRONG PATH TO FOLLOW

19We all know the things our weak and broken human ways lead us to do, things such as walking in impure ways, giving in to dark desires, 20following after spirit-images, and participating in witchcraft. Also hostile ways such as fighting, jealousy, lashing out in anger, arguing and making trouble, and dividing into opposing groups. 21Our broken ways also lead us to want what belongs to others, to become drunks, and to participate in wild parties. It is things like this that I am warning you about. For I have already warned you that the ones who walk in these ways will not share in the blessings of Creator's good road.

THE FRUIT OF WALKING WITH THE SPIRIT

22On the other hand, *if we follow the guidance of the Spirit, our lives will bear good spiritual fruit.* The Spirit will grow in us the fruit of love and joy, peace and patience, kindness and goodness, faithful hearts, 23gentle ways, and self-control.

Our tribal law has nothing to say against those who walk in these ways. 24For the ones who belong to Creator Sets Free (Jesus) the Chosen One have nailed their weak and broken humanity to his cross. This puts to death all their wrong desires and broken ways.

25Since our life comes from the Spirit, let us dance in step with the Spirit and follow the Spirit's guidance. 26In this way we will not become big-headed troublemakers who are jealous of each other.

6 ✖◆◇◆▷◁◆◇◆▷◁◆◇◆▷◁◆▷

CALLED TO BE BURDEN BEARERS

1My sacred family members, if someone among you has given in to broken ways, you who are guided by the Spirit should lead this person back to the right path in a spirit of gentleness. But keep a close eye on yourselves, for you may be tempted *to do the same kind of thing.* 2Bear each other's *heavy* burdens, this way you are walking a path that brings full meaning and purpose to the law of the Chosen One. 3The people who see themselves as something when they are nothing have become their own trickster.

4Each one of you should take a good look at your own deeds. Then you can feel honor in the good you have done without comparing yourself with others. 5For all of us have our own burden basket to carry.[a]

GOOD AND BAD SEED PLANTING

6The ones who are instructed in the message of the Chosen One should share all good things with their teacher.

7Let no one mislead you. You cannot make a fool of the Great Spirit. Whatever you plant is what you will harvest. 8If you plant the seeds of your own broken humanity, you will harvest only death and decay. But if you plant the seeds of the Spirit, then from the Spirit you will harvest the life of the world to come that never fades away, full of beauty and harmony. 9Never grow tired of doing what is good. For when the time is right, we will reap a harvest of good things as long as we do not let our hearts fall to the ground. 10So then, whenever we are able, we should do good to everyone, and most of all to the members of our sacred family.

FINAL WORDS TO REMEMBER

11Take a good look at the large letters I use to write to you with my own hand!

---

[a]**6:5** The Apache and some of the other southwestern tribes have burden baskets. They are often used in a coming-of-age ceremony in which the new generation accepts the responsibility to carry the burden for its generation.

¹²These men who try to force you into participating in the cutting of the flesh ceremony do so for the wrong reasons. They do not teach *the full meaning of* the cross of the Chosen One out of fear of being hunted down and harmed *by their own Tribal Members*. ¹³For even those who have participated in the cutting of the flesh ceremony do not themselves keep our tribal law. They only want you to participate in the ceremony so they can brag to others about what they did to your body.

¹⁴May I never brag except in what our Honored Chief, Creator Sets Free (Jesus) the Chosen One, has done by dying on the cross. For I was nailed to the cross with the Chosen One. That is how I died to the ways of this world and how the ways of this world died to me. ¹⁵So it no longer matters whether one participates in the cutting of the flesh ceremony or not. What matters is *that you are* a new creation *in the Chosen One.*

LAST WORDS

¹⁶May peace and mercy rest on all who walk true to this way of seeing and thinking, and on the people of the Great Spirit who together form the tribes of Wrestles with Creator (Israel).

¹⁷Last of all, let no one trouble me any longer, for on my body I bear the scars that mark me as a follower of Creator Sets Free (Jesus).

¹⁸My sacred family members, may the gift of the great kindness of our Honored Chief, Creator Sets Free (Jesus) the Chosen One, guide your spirit on the road of life.

Aho! May it be so!

SMALL MAN TO THE SACRED FAMILY IN VILLAGE OF DESIRE

EPHESIANS

GREETINGS

¹From Small Man (Paul), chosen by the Great Spirit to be a message bearer for Creator Sets Free (Jesus).

To the Great Spirit's holy people who live in Village of Desire (Ephesus), who walk the good path following the Chosen One. ²Great kindness and peace to you from the Father above and from our Honored Chief Creator Sets Free (Jesus), who is the Chosen One.

CHOSEN FOR GREAT KINDNESS

³All blessings belong to the Great Spirit, who is the Father of Creator Sets Free (Jesus). From the spirit-world above he has gifted us with all spiritual blessings found in the Chosen One.

⁴In the same way, before he made all things and because of his great love, the Maker of Life chose to make us pure and holy in his eyes. ⁵He also decided ahead of time, through Creator Sets Free (Jesus), to take us into his family, fulfilling his purpose and making his heart glad. ⁶This great kindness he has shown us brings honor to him and gives us a highly honored place, together with his much-loved Son.

⁷⁻⁸By paying the highest price, offering his own lifeblood, the Chosen One released us from a great captivity caused by our bad hearts and broken ways. He poured out all of this overflowing kindness on us, showing how wise and understanding he is.

HIDDEN WISDOM MADE CLEAR

⁹It makes Creator's heart glad to show us the hidden wisdom of his plan *for all of creation*, now made clear through the Chosen One. ¹⁰This is how Creator brings all things to completion. He makes all things in the spirit-world above and on the earth below come together and find their full meaning and original purpose in the Chosen One.

¹¹⁻¹²The Chosen One has shared with us all that he has been given. This was Creator's plan that he decided long ago to accomplish. A wise and powerful vision he saw within himself. Creator is working out all the details, fitting everything into his purpose, so that we, *who are from the tribes of Wrestles with Creator (Israel)*, who have first put our hope in the Chosen One, will bring praise and honor to him.

¹³And now, not only we but all other Nations who have heard the truth of this message can participate in his plan. This is the good story that sets all people free.

When we trusted in the Chosen One, he marked us as his own by giving us his promised Holy Spirit. [14]He did this to make sure that we, the people he paid a great price for, will receive all that he has planned for us. This brings great praise and honor to him.

SENDING UP PRAYERS

[15]Ever since I heard of the trust you have in Creator Sets Free (Jesus) and your deep love for all of his holy people, [16]I have never stopped giving thanks for you, remembering you when I send my voice to the Great Spirit.

[17]I pray that the Father of honor and beauty, who is the Great Spirit of our Honored Chief Creator Sets Free (Jesus), will gift you with a spirit of wisdom to know him deeply and understand his mysterious ways.

[18]I am asking him to shine his light into your hearts so you can clearly see the hope he has chosen us for and the beautiful treasure he has in us, his holy people.

[19]I pray he will show how much greater his power is for all who put their trust in him. [20]This is the same power he used when he brought the Chosen One back to life from the dead and gave him the seat of honor at his right hand. [21]This is a high spiritual place greater than all rulers, authorities, and powers. It is a place higher and stronger than all names that can be named, not only in this world but also in the one that is coming.

[22]This is how he brought all things, seen and unseen, under his loving power and made him the elder[a] of his sacred family. [23]This sacred family is his body on earth, made whole by the one who gives everything and everyone their full meaning and purpose.

---

[a]1:22 Lit. *head*

2

A DARK PATH

[1]We all once walked a dark and crooked path that led us to death. [2]Our broken ways caused us to miss the mark and wander from the good path, following the worthless ways of this world.

We all once walked the dark path of the evil one who rules the spiritual atmosphere of this world, that evil spirit who is at work in human beings who have lost their way. [3]This is how all of us once lived when we followed our uncontrolled emotions fed by bodily desires and dark thoughts. These broken ways became our natural condition, and, like the rest of humankind, we were children *deserving* of *Creator's* anger.

FROM DEATH TO LIFE

[4]But the Great Spirit, who is kind and forgiving, because of his deep love, [5]raised us up from *spiritual* death. Even though we were walking the road of death, he made us alive again with the Chosen One. This is what it means to be rescued by the gift of his great kindness.

[6]He lifted us up with him to the highest place in the spirit-world above and put us on a seat of honor alongside the Chosen One. [7]He did this to show us the overflowing greatness of his kindness and mercy, not only in this age but in the many ages to come—all because of what the Chosen One has done.

A GREAT GIFT

[8]It is by trusting in the gift of his great kindness that we have been made whole. It is not because of any good thing we have done, but only by accepting a gift that we could never earn. [9]In this way,

no one can brag or boast about themselves, but only humbly give thanks. ¹⁰We are like clay in his hands, molded from the Chosen One, made to be like him, and walking the ancient pathways he originally created us for.

OUTSIDERS AND INSIDERS

¹¹You Nations must not forget that before you knew the Chosen One you were not natural-bornᵃ members of the tribes of Wrestles with Creator (Israel). You were called "the outsiders"ᵇ by the ones who call themselves "the insiders."ᶜ But remember, the sign that marks them as insiders is cut into their flesh with human hands.

¹²You Outside Nations did not share in the promises or the peace treaty that the Great Spirit made with those tribes. You were out from under their special care and protection—unaware of and apart from the Chosen One. You shared no common hope and were outside the help Creator gave to them in this world.

HE IS OUR GREAT PEACE

¹³But no more! Even though you Outside Nations were far away, you have now been made close by the lifeblood offered by Creator Sets Free (Jesus), the Chosen One. ¹⁴He is our great peace, who has brought the people of all Nations together with the tribes of Wrestles with Creator (Israel), making them into one new people by removing the barrier that separated us.

¹⁵In his own human body he removed the hostility between us when he did away with the rules and requirements of our tribal law that separated us. This is

the way he recreates people—making one new humanity out of the two. This brings us all together on the path of peace.

A CLEAR PATH

¹⁶Even though we behaved like enemies, we are now friends with the Great Spirit and with one another. When Creator Sets Free (Jesus) died on the cross, those things that made us enemies died with him. We are now joined together as one people in one body. ¹⁷He brought this good story of peace and harmony to people who were far away from him and to people who were close to him. ¹⁸Because of him we both have a clear path, through one Spirit, to the Father from above.

A NEW SACRED LODGE

¹⁹Now we are all his holy people and members of one new nation. No one is on the outside of this great family that our Father is creating. We are all related to one another and initiated into Creator's lodge that is built together with wooden poles— ²⁰the message bearers and prophets of old. Creator Sets Free (Jesus) is the main pole binding us together, ²¹like branches being weaved into his sacred lodge. ²²Joined together in this way, we become a dwelling place for his Spirit.

3 ◁▷◀▷◀▷◀▷◀▷◀▷◀▷◀▷◀▷◀▷

A GREAT MYSTERY REVEALED

¹Because I, Small Man (Paul), follow the Chosen One and represent you Nations in this way, I have been arrested and put in chains. ²I am sure you have heard how the Great Spirit chose me, because of his great kindness, to be a wisdom-keeper to all Nations. ³Creator chose me, by a sacred vision, to make known this

---

ᵃ2:11 Lit. *Gentiles in the flesh*
ᵇ2:11 Lit. *the uncircumcision*, a way to say non-Jews
ᶜ2:11 Lit. *the circumcision*, a way to say Jews

hidden wisdom that I have already spoken about.

⁴When you hear this message, you will understand how I see the mystery of the Chosen One. ⁵This mystery was not made known to the generations of humankind that walked before us in the same way his Spirit has now told it to his holy message bearers and prophets.

⁶This mystery is that the people of all Nations have equal share in the blessings promised to the tribes of Wrestles with Creator (Israel). They have full membership in the same body and are included in the promise through the Chosen One as told in the good story.

CHOSEN TO TELL THE GOOD STORY

⁷The gift of Creator's great kindness came to me in a powerful way and created in me a desire to serve this good story. ⁸Even though I am small and weak among his holy people, he still chose me to tell all Nations about the mysterious treasures he has hidden in the Chosen One ⁹and about the unfolding of this ancient plan—a great mystery that was hidden away for many ages in Creator's heart. ¹⁰So that now, through his sacred family, his great wisdom, which is like a rainbow with many colors, will be made known to the powers and rulers in the spirit-world above.

¹¹This good story gives full meaning to the ancient purpose he planned before he created all things. This purpose has now been made clear through the Chosen One, Creator Sets Free (Jesus). ¹²Our trust in him opens the way and gives us strong hearts to move close to the Great Spirit. ¹³So do not become weak of heart when you hear about how much I am suffering for you, which is proof of your great worth.

A HUMBLE PRAYER

¹⁴This is the reason I bow down on my knees and humble myself before the Father above, ¹⁵from whom all families, clans, and tribes, in this world and in the spirit-world above, are named.

¹⁶My prayer for you is that from the great treasures of his beauty, Creator will gift you with the Spirit's mighty power and strengthen you in your inner being. ¹⁷In this way, the Chosen One will make his home in your heart.

I pray that as you trust in him, your roots will go deep into the soil of his great love, ¹⁸and that from these roots you will draw the strength and courage needed to walk this sacred path together with all his holy people. This path of love is higher than the stars, deeper than the great waters, wider than the sky. Yes, this love comes from and reaches to all directions.

I pray that you would feel how deep the Chosen One's great love is. ¹⁹It is a love that goes beyond our small and weak ways of thinking. This love fills us with the Great Spirit, the one who fills all things. ²⁰I am praying to the Maker of Life, who, by his great power working in us, can do far more than what we ask for, more than our small minds can imagine.

²¹May his sacred family and the Chosen One bring honor to him across all generations, to the time beyond the end of all days. Aho! May it be so!

A HUMBLE PATH

¹Because I walk the road with our Honored Chief, I have been made a prisoner. I now call on you to join me in representing him in a good way as you

follow the path he has chosen for you. [2]Walk with a humble and gentle spirit, patiently showing love and respect to each other. [3]Let his Spirit weave you together in peace as you dance in step with one another in the great circle of life.

[4]*In this circle* we are joined together in one body, by one Spirit, chosen to follow one purpose. [5]There is only one Honored Chief, one common faith, and one purification ceremony.[a] [6]There is one Great Spirit and Father of us all, who is above all, and who works in and through all.

THE HEADDRESS OF THE CHOSEN ONE

[7]His great kindness has gifted each of us from the headdress[b] of the Chosen One. [8]That is why it is said, "When he was lifted up on high, he captured many warriors, took their spoils of war, and gave them back to the people."[c]

[9]What does "he was lifted up" mean? It could only mean that he had to first come down, into the lowest parts of the earth, [10]so he could be lifted up, to the highest place, and be the one who would restore all things.

WALKING IN HARMONY

[11]He gifted us with message bearers, prophets, tellers of the good story, and wisdomkeepers, who watch over us like a shepherd watches over his sheep. [12]These gifts were given to prepare Creator's holy people for the work of helping others and to make the body of the Chosen One strong [13]until we all follow the good road[d] in harmony with each

other because we know and understand who Creator's Son is.

We will then be like the Chosen One— mature human beings, living and walking in his ways, and fully reflecting who he is. [14]No longer will we be like children who are tossed about by the waves and follow every voice they hear in the wind. We will no longer listen to the ones who behave like tricksters with their forked tongues.

[15]Instead, as true human beings, we will walk out this truth on the path of love. When we become fully grown, we will be like the Chosen One, joined together with him in the same way a body is connected to its head. [16]Every joint in this body is needed to hold it together and help it grow. When all the parts work together the way they should, then the body grows strong in the love of the Great Spirit.

REPRESENTING OUR HONORED CHIEF

[17]I say this to you as one who represents our Honored Chief. You must no longer walk the dark path of the Nations *who have chosen their own ways.* [18]Their minds have no good thoughts, because the darkness has taken away their ability to see and think clearly. Their hearts have become as hard as stone and can no longer beat with the life that comes from the Great Spirit. [19]This takes them down the path of greed and selfish pleasure, leading to an impure life. [20]This is not the path you learned from the Chosen One, [21]for the true path to walk is only found in Creator Sets Free (Jesus).

[22]Take off that worn-out and stained outfit of your past life with its selfish desires and worthless ways of thinking. It no longer represents who you are. [23]You are now true human beings, with a new

---

[a]**4:5** Baptism
[b]**4:7** The headdress was worn among many tribes to represent victory in battle and good deeds accomplished. Here it is used as a metaphor of the Chosen One's victory.
[c]**4:8** Psalm 68:18
[d]**4:13** The faith

way of seeing and thinking. [24]Put on the regalia of your new life. For you have been made new, created again to look like the one who made you, standing in a good way and walking a true and sacred path.

LIVING IN HARMONY

[25]We are all members of one body—*one tribe*—so we must speak truth and be honest with each other, leaving the path of falsehood far behind.

[26]There are times when anger is the right thing, but do not let your anger turn into rage, for it will burn like a wildfire. Work things out before the sun sets that day, [27]or the evil one may use it to burn up all the good things in your life.[a]

There is no room for thieves on this sacred path. [28]The ones among you who have stolen and taken what is not theirs must learn to do good, working hard with their hands. In this way they will not only have enough for themselves but also something to help others.

DO NOT GRIEVE THE HOLY SPIRIT

[29]Keep a close watch over the words you speak, for our mouths can be full of worthless and empty talk that will bring death to others. Let your words be full of wisdom and goodwill that will give strength and bring healing to the ones who hear you. [30]In this way, Creator's Holy Spirit will not be grieved. For it is he who marks you as his own and keeps you safe for the day when all things will be complete.[b]

[31]Let Creator pull the bitter roots from your heart, for they feed the rage and anger that takes you down a path of fighting, hurting, and speaking evil of

---

[a]**4:27** Psalm 4:4
[b]**4:30** The day of redemption or restoration

your fellow human beings. [32]Instead, show goodwill and kindness to others, by releasing them from the things they have done wrong. For this is what the Great Spirit, through the Chosen One, has done for you.

5

WALKING HIS ROAD

[1]We must follow in the steps of the Great Spirit, for we are his much-loved children. [2]Walk the road of love, following the path of the Chosen One, who loved us and offered up his life to the Great Spirit like the smoke of burning sage.

[3]Sexual relations are sacred. They must be kept pure, and free from uncontrolled desire. As his holy people, we must follow Creator's purpose and plan for human beings who represent him. [4]Sexual relations should be spoken of with respect—no foolish talk or dirty jokes. Instead, give thanks *for this sacred gift of creating new life.*

[5]Listen closely, no one who walks an impure path of uncontrolled desires participates in the good road of the Chosen One and the Great Spirit. The ones who walk in this way follow lying spirits that take them down a dark path, far from the sacred ways of the Great Spirit. [6]Do not listen to their empty words and forked tongues, for the Great Spirit's anger will be shown to the ones who follow these ways. [7]Do not walk with them on a path that leads to a bad end.

DARKNESS AND LIGHT

[8]As weak human beings, you were once empty and full of darkness, but now that Creator's Spirit lives in you, you are beings full of light. [9]Walk in the light,

and all things good and right and true will shine out from you. **10**This will prove you are his children—the ones who seek for ways to make his heart glad.

11Turn away from the path of darkness with its worthless ways. Instead, let your light shine into the darkness to show the way out. **12**The shameful things done under the blanket of night should not even be spoken of, **13**for the light shines into the darkness and takes the mask off its empty ways. It is like the sunrise that pushes back the night and brings the light of a new day. **14**This is why it is said, "Wake up, O sleeper, come back from the dead, and the Chosen One will shine on you!"

THE WAY OF WISDOM

15Walk with your eyes wide open and make wise use of your time, **16**for the evil days we live in are full of worthless and troubled ways. **17**Keep foolishness far from you *and welcome the ways of wisdom,* for then you will clearly see the path Creator has chosen for you.

18It is not wise to become a drunk, for it will lead you to a life of emptiness and sorrow. Instead, drink deeply of Creator's Spirit, *and he will lead you into a life of beauty and harmony.*

19*At your gatherings,* tell the ancient stories and sing the traditional songs. Sing spiritual songs from your heart *as you dance before the Great Spirit,* **20**giving thanks to our Father the Creator, as you represent our Honored Chief, Creator Sets Free (Jesus), the Chosen One.

WISDOM FOR HUSBANDS AND WIVES

21If you have respect for the Chosen One, then have respect for each other. **22**Wives, honor your husbands in the same way you honor the Great Spirit. **23**Just as the Chosen One guides and protects his sacred family as his own body when they put their trust in him, **24**so a wife should, in the same way, follow the loving guidance of her husband in all these things.

25Husbands, love your wives just as the Chosen One loved and gave his life for his sacred family. **26**He did this to give them a place of honor and dignity above all others. He washes all with the purifying water of the word he speaks over them. **27**He will clothe his sacred family with the regalia of beauty and harmony with no wrinkles or stains, *like a bride dressed for her wedding day.* **28**This is the manner in which husbands should love their wives, as their own bodies. For the one who loves his wife loves himself. **29-30**No one hates his own body but instead takes good care of it, just as the Chosen One does for his sacred family. We are members of his body, of his flesh, and of his bones.

31"For this purpose a man must leave his father and mother, so he can join with his wife, and the two will become one body."[a] **32**This is a great mystery, but I am telling you that it is about the Chosen One and his sacred family. **33**So each man should love his wife as himself, *treat her as he wants her to treat him,* and each wife is to give respect to her husband.

FURTHER INSTRUCTIONS ON RESPECT

1Children, it is the right thing to follow the guidance of your parents, for this is what Creator wants. **2**"Honor your father and mother." This is the first instruction in our tribal law that carries a promise

---

[a]**5:31** Genesis 2:24

with it— [3]"that it will go well with you, and you will live long on the land."[a]

[4]Fathers, if you push your children too hard, it will only make them angry. Instead, help them to grow strong in the ways of the Great Spirit.

[5]Slaves, do everything your earthly masters tell you to do. Show great respect to them in the same way you serve the Chosen One. Do this from a strong and pure heart, [6]not just to look good to your earthly master, [7]but as if you were serving our Honored Chief, [8]knowing that Creator will see and honor all who serve others, no matter whether they are slaves or free.

[9]Masters, do not use threats, but treat your slaves with the same respect you would give to the Great Spirit. For he is your master from the spirit-world above as well as theirs, and he will not favor one over another.

PREPARING FOR SPIRITUAL WARFARE

[10]Last of all, *I must remind you that we are all fighting in a spiritual battle. We are weak human beings, so* let your strength come from our Great Warrior Chief. [11]The only way to stand strong against the war plans of the evil trickster[b] is to put on Creator's war garments. [12]*But remember*, we are not fighting against human beings. Our battle is against the evil rulers, the dark powers, and the spiritual forces of the spirit-world above and around us.

[13]Once you are fully dressed for this war, you will be able to stand your ground in this day of the enemy's evil rule. You are now ready to make your stand—so stand strong. [14]Wrap the sash of truth around your waist. Cover your heart with the breastplate of making wrongs right again. [15]Put on your feet the moccasins of Creator's peace *treaty*, so you will always be ready to tell the good story *as you walk the road of life.* [16]Then you must raise high the shield of trusting in Creator. This shield will put out the flaming arrows of the evil one. *Do not forget to* [17]put on the headdress of Creator's power to rescue and set free, and use the long knife of the Spirit— which is the word of Creator *coming from your mouth.*

[18]All of this is done by prayer, sending your voice to the Great Spirit, asking him for all that is needed. As you pray with the help of the Spirit, stay alert and keep all of Creator's holy people in your thoughts, praying for their needs. [19]Also ask Creator to give me the right words to speak and the courage to make known the mystery of Creator's good story. [20]This is the reason I now represent the Great Spirit as a captive in chains. Pray that I will speak with boldness and not hold back.

FINAL WORDS

[21-22]So you will know how I am doing, I am sending He Is at Ease (Tychicus), a much-loved *spiritual* brother and one who serves others as a gift from Creator. He will let you know how we are doing so your hearts can be lifted up and strengthened.

[23]Peace be to all the sacred family members, along with love and trust from the Great Spirit, who is our Father, and from our Wisdomkeeper, Creator Sets Free (Jesus), the Chosen One.

[24]May Creator's great kindness rest on all who love the Chosen One, with a love that will never grow old or fade away.

Aho! May it be so!

---

[a]**6:3** Deuteronomy 5:16
[b]**6:11** The devil

SMALL MAN TO THE SACRED FAMILY IN VILLAGE OF HORSES

PHILIPPIANS

1

GREETINGS

¹From Small Man (Paul) and He Gives Honor (Timothy), sacred servants of the Chosen One, Creator Sets Free (Jesus).

To all of Creator's holy people who gather in Village of Horses (Philippi) and to the spiritual leaders and those who have the sacred task of helping others, who together watch over the sacred family.

²May our Father the Great Spirit and our Honored Chief, Creator Sets Free (Jesus) the Chosen One, bless you with the gift of his great kindness and peace.

THOUGHTS AND PRAYERS

³Whenever you come into my thoughts I give thanks to my Creator. ⁴I always pray with a glad heart when I send up prayers for you, ⁵because from the first day until now we have walked side by side in the telling of the good story. ⁶I have no doubts that the one who set your feet on this good path will keep walking it with you until the day that Creator Sets Free (Jesus) the Chosen One appears.

⁷It is right for me to think of you in this way, for you hold a warm place in my heart. You have shared with me in the gift of Creator's great kindness, both in my chains and when I stand on the truth of the good story. ⁸The Great Spirit knows that the longing I have to see you comes from the warm and tender heart of the Chosen One, Creator Sets Free (Jesus).

⁹When I send my voice to the Great Spirit, I pray that the love you have for each other will grow strong and remain steady in wisdom and understanding. ¹⁰In this way, you will be able to make good choices that will lead to a pure heart and keep you from stumbling until the day of the Chosen One. ¹¹*I pray that* your lives will be filled with the good fruit of doing what is right, which comes from remaining true to Creator Sets Free (Jesus) the Chosen One. All of this will bring honor and praise to the Great Spirit.

THE STORY OF THE CHOSEN ONE IS BEING TOLD

¹²My sacred family members, I want you to know that the hard times I find myself facing have not held me back. Instead, new ground has been gained for the telling of the good story. ¹³So now the soldiers who guard the lodge of the People of Iron (Romans) and all the other people here know that I am in chains because I follow the Chosen One.

¹⁴Knowing that I am in chains has given a great number of the sacred family members new courage in our Honored Chief to win the victory over

their fear and boldly tell the good story. **15**It is true that some tell about the Chosen One only because they are full of jealousy and bitterness, while others do so out of a good heart.

16The ones with good hearts do so because of their love, for they know that Creator has given me the sacred task of guarding the truth of the good story. **17**The others, *who are filled with jealousy and bitterness,* tell about the Chosen One with crooked hearts and out of a selfish desire to cause trouble for me while I am *a captive* in chains.

18So here is how I see it. Whether they do these things for the wrong reasons or the right reasons, the story about the Chosen One is being told. This is what makes my heart dance. And my heart will keep dancing, **19**for I know that when I am set free it will be through your prayers and the help given from the Spirit of Creator Sets Free (Jesus) the Chosen One.

HONORING THE CHOSEN ONE

20From deep in my spirit comes the hope that I will never face the shame of defeat but that I will have the courage, now and always, to bring honor to the Chosen One by the way I live or by the way I die. **21**How can I lose? The Chosen One is my life, and death only brings me something better.

22Even if death would be a better choice, living in this world means my work will bear good fruit. So I do not know which way to go. **23**I am being pulled from both directions. On the one hand, I desire to go and be with the Chosen One, which would be far better than staying here in this world.

24But on the other hand, staying here to help you is needed even more. **25**Since I am needed here, I am sure that I will stay, so I can continue to walk you down a road of joy and strengthen your faith. **26**Then when I come face to face with you once again, you can be full of joy *and stand tall* in what the Chosen One, Creator Sets Free (Jesus), has done through me.

WALKING WORTHY OF THE CHOSEN ONE

27Whatever happens, you should walk in a manner that brings honor to the good story about the Chosen One. In this way, whether or not I come to see you, I will hear that you are standing firm in one spirit, having one purpose, and struggling together to hold true to the good story in which we have put our trust.

28Show courage in the face of those who oppose you. This will be a sign to them that they are coming to a bad end, but for you it will be a sign that Creator is setting you free. **29**For you have been given the honor not only to trust in the Chosen One but also to suffer for him. **30**For you are now struggling in the same *spiritual* battle you saw me fight in the past, one I am still fighting.

2

WALKING THE ROAD TOGETHER

1As you walk the road with the Chosen One, have you gained from him courage for the journey? Have you found comfort in his love? Do you share together in his Spirit? Has his tenderness and mercy captured your heart? **2**If so, then have the same kind of thoughts. Love with one heart. Join together in one Spirit. And walk side by side on one path. This will make my heart leap for joy.

3*But when you do these things, make sure you do them for the right reasons.* Do not let selfish ways take you down a path of bragging or trying to look better than others. Instead, let humility be your guide as you honor others above yourself. **4**Each of you should look to the needs of others, not just to your own.

THE HUMILITY OF THE CHOSEN ONE

5Think about yourselves in the same way Creator Sets Free (Jesus) the Chosen One thought about himself.

6Even though Creator Sets Free (Jesus) has always been the same as the Great Spirit and shared everything equally with him, he did not even think of holding on to this in a selfish way.

7Instead, he emptied himself, became nothing, and gave up all he had. Then, having been born as a human being, he took on himself the lowly form of a servant.

8As a True Human Being, he lowered himself even more by following the guidance *of the Great Spirit*, even when death was waiting for him *at the end of the trail*, death on a tree-pole—the cross!

9Because Creator Sets Free (Jesus) did this, the Great Spirit gave him an honored place above all others and bestowed on him a name greater than all other names, **10**so that all who live in the spirit-world above, on the earth below, and underneath the earth will bow their knee to Creator Sets Free (Jesus) in honor of his name. **11**Then everyone, in their native language, will shout out loud that Creator Sets Free (Jesus) the Chosen One is Grand Chief *over all the earth*. This will bring honor and praise to our Father the Great Spirit.

WISE COUNSEL FROM SMALL MAN

12My much-loved family, you have always followed my guidance, not only when I was with you but much more now that I am away. So then, with great respect, you must walk the path Creator has given you for being set free and made whole. **13**For the Great Spirit is creating in you the desire and strength to do what pleases him.

14Do everything without grumbling or arguing. **15**In this way, you will show yourselves to be pure and innocent children of the Great Spirit. Even though you walk among a generation of people who live in bent and twisted ways, your reputation will shine as bright as the stars in the night sky **16**as you hold out to them the words of life. In this way, on the day of the Chosen One, I can stand tall *at the end of the trail* knowing that my hard work was not wasted on you. **17**Even if my lifeblood is to be poured out like a ceremonial drink offering in loving service to your faith, my heart is glad and I share my joy with you. **18**Your hearts should also be glad and share the same joy that I have.

TWO FAITHFUL SPIRITUAL BROTHERS

19I want to hear how you are doing, so I am trusting in our Honored Chief Creator Sets Free (Jesus) to send He Gives Honor (Timothy) to you soon, so that he can encourage me with good news about you. **20**I know of no one else like him who truly cares for your well-being. **21**For all the others care only for their own things, not the things relating to Creator Sets Free (Jesus) the Chosen One.

22But you know the good reputation of He Gives Honor (Timothy). He works side by side with me, like a son with his father, as we tell the good story. **23**That is why I hope to send him to you as soon as I see how things turn out for me. **24**Our Honored Chief gives me hope that I will be coming to you soon.

25*Until then*, I feel the need to send Walks with Beauty (Epaphroditus) back to you. He is a member of our sacred family and warrior who has fought side by side with me *in serving the Chosen One*. He was your message bearer to help me in my need, *and now I am sending him back to you*. **26**He has a deep longing to see all of you again. His heart has been on the ground ever since you heard he was sick. **27**It is true that he was so sick he nearly died. But Creator had pity on him, and on myself as well, to keep my heart from falling to the ground, heavy with sorrow.

28This is the reason I so desire to send Walks with Beauty (Epaphroditus) to you, so that, when you see him, your heart will be glad and my own heart will be free from worry. **29***So when he arrives*, welcome him in our Honored Chief with glad hearts. Show great respect and honor toward people like him. **30**For he came close to death working for the Chosen One. He risked his life to give me the help you were not able to give *because you lived so far away*.

3

BEWARE OF THE FLESH CUTTERS

1So then, my sacred family members, dance with glad hearts in harmony with our Honored Chief. I never grow tired of writing these things to you again, for they give you a safe path to follow. **2**Be on the lookout for those wild-dog men—the flesh cutters and troublemakers *who require others to participate in the cutting of the flesh ceremony*.

3We are the people of the true cutting of the flesh ceremony. For we stand tall in Creator Sets Free (Jesus) the Chosen One and put no trust in a ceremony done with human hands. We honor and serve Creator in the way of his Spirit, *as he cuts from our hearts the worthless and broken ways that dishonor him*.

4I used to trust in outward ceremonies and had a better reason than others to do so. **5**When I was eight days old, the cutting of the flesh ceremony was done for me. I was born a member of the tribes of Wrestles with Creator (Israel). I am of the tribe of Son of My Right Hand (Benjamin). I am a full-blood Tribal Member (Hebrew). As for our tribal law, I was of the Separated Ones (Pharisees). **6**I was so on fire for our law that I hunted down and brought harm to the sacred family. When it came to doing what is right according to our tribal law, I was faultless.

THE GREAT BEAUTY OF KNOWING THE CHOSEN ONE

7But now, because of the Chosen One, I have let go of those things in which I took so much pride. They now mean nothing to me. **8**Even more than this, I now count all things to be worthless compared to the great beauty of knowing the Chosen One, Creator Sets Free (Jesus), as my Honored Chief. Because I follow him, I have lost everything, but compared to knowing the Chosen One, I now count them as dog droppings.

9To be in full harmony with the Chosen One is my desire. I do not want to gain my own good standing with Creator by keeping tribal law but by trusting in the Chosen One. This good standing comes from the Great Spirit by trusting in what he has done, *not what I* *can do.* **10**I want to fully know the Chosen One and the power that raised him from the dead. I want to know what it means to participate in his sufferings and to become like him in his death, **11**living in the hope that, *like the Chosen One*, I will also rise from death to life.

FOLLOWING THE CHOSEN ONE TO VICTORY

12I do not mean to say that I have won the victory or have already arrived at the end of the good road. But I keep dancing the victory dance, staying in step with the Chosen One, who is the headman dancer leading the way. In this way, I can fully become what the Chosen One, Creator Sets Free (Jesus), has made me to be.

13My sacred family members, I do not represent myself as one who has finished the victory dance. My one aim is to forget what is behind me and to keep moving forward, dancing the victory dance with firm steps *to the drumbeat of Creator's heart.* **14**I keep my eyes straight ahead while I dance toward the high honor the Great Spirit has called me to through the Chosen One, Creator Sets Free (Jesus).

KEEP WALKING THE GOOD PATH

15Those among us who have grown spiritually strong should see these things in the same way. If any of you sees differently, Creator will make it clear to you. **16**Until then, let us keep holding true to the path we have already been walking. **17**My sacred family members, I call on you to join with the others who follow me as I walk this road. Keep your eyes on those who walk in the same manner and follow them also.

18I have warned you many times that there are a great number of people who walk as enemies of the cross of the Chosen One. And now with tears I warn you again. **19**A bad end awaits these people. They have made their weak human appetites the spirit they follow. They take pride in doing things they should be ashamed of. They have set their minds on the ways of this world.

THE WAY OF LIFE FROM ABOVE

20But the way of life of the tribe we belong to is found in the spirit-world above, and it is from there that we eagerly wait for the one who has set us free and made us whole, our Honored Chief, Creator Sets Free (Jesus) the Chosen One. **21***When he appears*, he will take our weak, death-doomed bodies and change them into a body like his, a body that shines with beauty and honor. For he is the one who has the power to bring all things into harmony with himself.

1My sacred family members, how I long to be with you. You are like feathers in my headdress, making my heart dance. I have shown you how to stand firm on the solid ground of the Chosen One. So now, my much-loved ones, stand firm!

URGENT COUNSEL FOR TWO WOMEN

2My strong counsel to Good Journey Woman (Euodia) and Blessing Way Woman (Syntyche) is for them to walk hand in hand in their life together with our Honored Chief. **3**I also ask you, Burden Bearer (Syzygus), to be true *to your name* and help these women who have shared my struggle in the telling of the good story. These women have also worked side by side with Walks with Kindness (Clement) and all the others whose names are written down in *Creator's* book of life.

DANCING FOR JOY AND
WALKING IN PEACE

⁴Always dance with joy before our Honored Chief! I will say it again: dance with joy! ⁵Let everyone see how kind and thoughtful you are. Our Honored Chief is close at hand. ⁶Do not let your hearts be weighed down with anything. Instead, with every step you take, send your voice to the Great Spirit, asking him for the things you need. And in all your prayers *remember to* give him thanks. ⁷Then the peace and harmony of the Great Spirit, which goes far beyond our small and weak ways of thinking, will watch over your hearts and minds through the Chosen One, Creator Sets Free (Jesus).

⁸Last of all, my sacred family members, if anything can be seen as good and honorable, think *deeply* about these things. Things that are true and noble, upright and pure, full of beauty and worthy of respect. ⁹Follow the way of life you have seen in me, the things you have learned from me, heard from me, and received from me. Keep walking in the traditions I have passed on to you. Then the Great Spirit of Peace will continue to walk with you on this road.

CREATOR WILL TAKE CARE
OF ALL OUR NEEDS

¹⁰My heart is dancing for joy before our Honored Chief! For even though in the past you did not have the chance to show how deeply you care for me, you have shown once again how much you truly care.

¹¹You should not think that I am looking for you to take care of my needs, for I have learned how to be at peace with whatever the Great Spirit has provided. ¹²I have lived with less than I need, and I have lived with more than I need. I have learned the secret of walking the road of life. Whether I am well-fed or hungry, whether I have more than I need or not enough, ¹³I can do all things through the Chosen One who gives me strength! ¹⁴All the same, you have done well to help me during my time of trouble.

¹⁵My friends who live in Village of Horses (Philippi), you remember those early days when I first told you about the good story. How that after I left Land of Tall People (Macedonia), you were the only sacred family that walked together with me in giving and receiving. ¹⁶Even when I was in the village of False Victory (Thessalonica), you sent gifts to me more than once. ¹⁷It is not your gifts that I am seeking after but all the good things that giving will add to your lives.

¹⁸But now I have received more than I need. My blanket has been filled with good things. The gifts that Walks with Beauty (Epaphroditus) brought from you are like a sweet-smelling smoke offering —a sacrificial gift, pleasing to the Great Spirit. ¹⁹And I know that my Creator will take care of all your needs from the great treasures of his beauty through the Chosen One, Creator Sets Free (Jesus).

LAST WORDS

²⁰All honor and beauty belong to our Father the Great Spirit to the time beyond the end of all days. Aho! May it be so!

²¹Greet all of Creator's holy ones among you, each one who belongs to the Chosen One, Creator Sets Free (Jesus). The sacred family members who are with me send their greetings. ²²All *of Creator's* holy ones send their greetings to you, most of

all the ones who serve in the royal lodge of the Ruler of the People of Iron (Caesar).

²³May the great kindness of our Honored Chief, Creator Sets Free (Jesus) the Chosen One, guide your spirit *on the road of life.*

▌ *Aho! May it be so!*

SMALL MAN TO THE SACRED FAMILY IN VILLAGE OF GIANTS

COLOSSIANS

1 ⋈⊰⋈⊰⋈⊰⋈⊰⋈⊰⋈⊰⋈⊰⋈

GREETINGS

¹From Small Man (Paul), chosen by the Great Spirit to be a message bearer for Creator Sets Free (Jesus) the Chosen One, and from He Gives Honor (Timothy).

²To the Great Spirit's holy people and sacred family members[a] who live in Village of Giants (Colossae) and have been faithful to walk the path of the Chosen One. We greet you with the great kindness and peace that comes from our Father, the Great Spirit.

GIVING THANKS TO THE FATHER

³When we send up prayers for you, we always give thanks to the Father of our Honored Chief, Creator Sets Free (Jesus) the Chosen One. ⁴We thank him for the good words we have heard about your trust in Creator Sets Free (Jesus) the Chosen One and your deep love for all his holy family members. ⁵This love and trust come from the hope you have in Creator's promises kept safe for you in the spirit-world above. It is the same hope you heard about when you were told the words of truth found in Creator's good story.

GOOD FRUIT COMES FROM THE GOOD STORY

⁶The seeds of this good story have been planted throughout the whole world, and now the message is growing and bearing good fruit. In the same way, it took root and began to grow in you, when you first heard and understood the truth about the gift of Creator's great kindness.

⁷Walks in Beauty (Epaphras) was the seed planter who first taught you these things. He is a faithful servant of the Chosen One, for your sakes, and also a much-loved helper who walks beside us on the road of life. ⁸He is the one who told us about the love of the Spirit that is in you.

SENDING UP PRAYERS

⁹Ever since we heard about you, we have never stopped praying for you. When we send our voices to the Great Spirit, we ask that he will fill your heart and mind with the knowledge you need to walk in his ways with all spiritual wisdom and understanding. ¹⁰That you will walk in a manner that is worthy of our Honored Chief, making his heart glad and bearing good fruit as you walk the path he has chosen for you. In this way, you will grow wise in your understanding of our Great Creator.

---

[a]1:2 Lit. *brothers*

11-12We pray that you will grow strong with the strength that comes from the honor and shining-greatness of his power. Then you will be able to stand firm in a calm and unhurried manner, as you give thanks with glad hearts to the Great Spirit who is our Father from above. For he is the one who has made you ready to take your place on this road of life, a place he prepared for you among all the holy ones who walk in his light.

SET FREE BY THE SON

13The Giver of Life has set us free from the dark ruler of this world. He has brought us safely onto his good road to walk it together with Creator's much-loved Son. 14He is the one who paid a great price to release us from our bad hearts and broken ways.

15He is the visible representation of our invisible Creator. All that the Father has belongs to this Son. He existed before creation and is above all created things. 16For it was in him that all things in the spirit-world above and on the earth below were created, all things seen and unseen. Yes, even governments, rulers, powers, and authorities were all created by him and for him.

HE GIVES ALL THINGS THEIR FULL MEANING

17He is the one who is in first place and the head of all things. It is in him that all things come together and find their full meaning and purpose. 18He is also the head of his body *on earth*, the sacred family. He is in first place before all other things, the first[a] to rise to life from among those who have died. In this way, he remains chief in all things.

19It made our Great Father's heart glad to have all that he is living in his Son. 20Through his Son he brought together everything in the spirit-world above and on the earth below into harmony with himself, making peace through his life-blood poured out on the cross.

OUTSIDERS BECOME INSIDERS

21At one time you were outsiders, separated from Creator by your hostile thoughts that led to evil ways. 22But now in the physical body of the Chosen One, through his death, he has turned you from an enemy into a friend. He did this so that you can stand without shame before the Great Spirit as a people who have been made holy, washed clean from guilt and free from all accusation.

23Yes, all this is yours as you make your path straight on the road that leads to this hope, trusting in the good story that you have heard. This is the same story that is being told to all in creation who live under the spirit-world above. And I, Small Man (Paul), have dedicated my life to serve this good story.

SUFFERING WITH THE CHOSEN ONE

24Even though I have been suffering for you, it makes my heart glad. There are still many things that the Chosen One must suffer through his sacred family in his body on earth.

My suffering, in my human body,[b] is my part in bringing full meaning and purpose to these remaining afflictions. This I gladly do for the sake of the sacred family, the body of the Chosen One.

A GREAT MYSTERY REVEALED

25The Great Spirit has given me the solemn task of serving his sacred family, the

---

[a]1:18 Lit. *firstborn*

[b]1:24 Lit. *flesh*

family you are now part of, by teaching you the full meaning and purpose of Creator's message. 26This message is a mystery that was hidden for many ages and generations but now has been made clear to his holy ones.

27Creator also did this to show the Outside Nations the mystery of the beauty and honor he has bestowed on them. This mystery is that Chosen One also lives in you, the Outside Nations. For the Chosen One in you is the hope of this beauty and honor.

28Yes, he is the one we tell others about, teaching and instructing them with wise counsel, so that they may stand tall as mature human beings, like the Chosen One. 29I give all I am to this task, drawing my strength from the Great Spirit who works so powerfully in me.

SPIRITUAL WARFARE

1I want you to know about the fierce spiritual battle that I fight for you who live in Village of Giants (Colossae). I also fight for you who live in the village of The People Will Decide (Laodicea) and for all who have never seen me face to face. 2I pray that all of you would have strong hearts that beat together with the love of the Great Spirit. Then your understanding will grow strong and you will see clearly into the mystery of our Father the Great Spirit, and this mystery is the Chosen One.

TREASURES OF WISDOM
AND KNOWLEDGE

3For the Great Spirit has hidden all the treasures of wisdom and knowledge in the Chosen One. 4I am making this known to you so that no humans behaving like

tricksters will fool you with their smooth words and sly arguments. 5For even though my body may be far away, in my spirit I am close to you. I can see you standing strong and walking a straight path with firm steps as you trust in the Chosen One.

WALKING THE GOOD ROAD

6So, in the same way you welcomed the Chosen One, Creator Sets Free (Jesus), to be your Honored Chief, continue to walk with him on this road of life. 7Let your roots grow deep into him, and then your faith will grow strong and your steps will become firm on this path that you have learned to follow, always giving thanks to the Great Spirit.

WATCH OUT FOR LYING SPIRITS

8Make sure no one steals your faith from you with fine-sounding words spoken with hollow tongues. These people make up their own traditions as they follow the lying spirits of the ways of this world,[a] instead of simply trusting in the Chosen One. 9For all that the Great Spirit is fills the physical body of the Chosen One. 10He is the one above all other powers and forces, and you have been made complete in him.

CUTTING OFF WEAK HUMAN WAYS

11In the Chosen One, you received a spiritual cutting of the flesh ceremony done without human hands. The Chosen One did this for you, by the cutting off of your weak human ways.[b]

12This is what happened when you were buried with him during your purification ceremony.[c] You were also raised

---

[a] 2:8 Lit. *elemental spirits* or *principles of this world*
[b] 2:11 Lit. *the flesh*
[c] 2:12 Baptism

up with him through your trust in Creator's great power that raised the Chosen One from the dead.

SILENCING ALL ACCUSATIONS

¹³You were *spiritually* dead because your weak human ways had not yet been cut away and because you were still following your bad hearts, walking in your broken ways. Even so the Great Spirit has made you *spiritually* alive along with the Chosen One by releasing you from all wrongdoings.

¹⁴When Creator did this, he wiped away and silenced every accusation that could be made against us for not following tribal law. When the Chosen One was nailed to the cross, the accusations the law made against us were nailed there with him, releasing us from those charges.

VICTORY DANCE

¹⁵This is how the Great Spirit, through what the Chosen One did on the cross, defeated the *spiritual* powers that ruled over us by using our tribal law to accuse us and hold us captive. He now dances the victory dance with us, for the whole world to see, to celebrate the defeat of those powers!

NO MORE SHADOWS

¹⁶From now on do not accept anyone's accusation against you for not following laws about what you should eat or drink, or whether you participate in celebrating festivals, or New Moon ceremonies, or a Day of Resting. ¹⁷These laws and ceremonies were only dim shadows of what was coming, but the reality is found in the Chosen One.

HOLD ON FIRMLY TO THE CHOSEN ONE

¹⁸Do not permit anyone to talk you out of what the Chosen One has done for you. That kind of humility is only a mask to fool you into humbling yourselves before wayward spirit-messengers. The visions they claim to have seen are only puffed-up images that come from their own prideful imaginations and weak ways of thinking.

¹⁹These people have lost their way because they did not hold on firmly to the Chosen One, who is the head of his body, *the sacred family*. When the members of this body depend on the Chosen One, they are nourished and held together by the body's joints and tendons. This is how Creator helps them grow into maturity.

FOLLOWING THE CHOSEN ONE INSTEAD OF RULES

²⁰If you have died with the Chosen One to the powers and ideas that rule the ways of this world, why would you follow the kind of rules these people require? ²¹Rules like, "Do not handle this! Do not taste that! Do not go near this!" ²²The problem is, these things they make rules about eventually get used up and ultimately fade away, because they are only rules and instructions made up by weak human beings. ²³They may put on a show of wisdom and humble, self-imposed spirituality, along with harsh treatment of their bodies, but these rules are without honor and have no power to keep us from following our broken human ways.

3

KEEP LOOKING UP

¹Since you have been raised up to a new life with the Chosen One, then keep looking upward toward him into the spirit-world above, where he sits in the place of greatest honor at Creator's right

hand. ²Keep your thoughts and desires centered on the spirit-world above, not on the things from the earth below.

HIDDEN IN THE CHOSEN ONE

³You died with the Chosen One, and now your life is hidden with the Chosen One in the Great Spirit. ⁴When the Chosen One is revealed, then you will be revealed with him and share in his beauty and honor.

THINGS THAT MUST DIE

⁵So let the death of the Chosen One kill in you all that is of the ways of this world. These are things such as improper sexual desires, spiritual impurity, uncontrolled emotions that lead to wrong desires, evil ways, and always wanting more than you need. These desires come from listening to lying spirits.ᵃ ⁶It is things such as these that will bring down the great anger of Creator on the ones who refuse to follow his ways.

⁷All of you once followed this dark path when you walked in these ways, ⁸but it is now time to walk away from these things, things such as uncontrolled anger that turns into rage, dark selfish desires, speaking lies against others, and insulting them with foul words from mouths that have no respect. ⁹So stop lying to each other and speaking with forked tongues!

WALKING THE NEW PATH

These bad-hearted ways must come to an end, for they no longer represent who you are. The person you were has died, so quit walking the path like that worn-out person you used to be. ¹⁰Instead, begin to walk in the ways of the new person you have been created to be. This new person is being created to look like the Great Spirit and to think his thoughts.

THE CHOSEN ONE IS ALL IN ALL

¹¹In the Chosen One there are no longer Insiders or Outsiders,ᵇ or those who ceremonially cut the flesh and those who do not. We no longer see ourselves or others as uncivilized, ruffians,ᶜ slaves or free. For there is only the Chosen One. All are in him, and he is in all!

NEW REGALIA FOR A NEW LIFE

¹²The Great Spirit has chosen you to be his holy and deeply loved children, so put on the new regalia he has provided for you. Put on deep feeling for the pain of others, kindness, humbleness of heart, gentleness of spirit, and be patient with one another. ¹³If there are any complaints against each other, then carry that burden basket and learn to forgive. For we must forgive others in the same manner that our Honored Chief has freely forgiven us.

¹⁴When all this new regalia is in place, let the love of the Great Spirit gather all the loose threads and braid them together in unity with one another. ¹⁵Let the Chosen One guide you on the path of peace and harmony, and then as his one body this peace will be the guiding light in your hearts as you give thanks to the Great Spirit.

DANCING OUR PRAYERS

¹⁶Let the message of the Chosen One become a deep watering hole inside you. It will then become a refreshing spring as you teach and guide one another with wisdom and understanding. You will sing traditional prayers, sacred chants,

---

ᵃ**3:5** Lit. *which is idolatry*

ᵇ**3:11** Lit. *Jews or Greeks*

ᶜ**3:11** Lit. *Scythian,* a people group known to be barbaric and uncivilized

and spiritual songs, *as you dance your prayers before the Great Spirit* with glad and thankful hearts.

[17]Every step taken and each word spoken should be done to represent our Honored Chief Creator Sets Free (Jesus), as you dance your prayers and give thanks through him to our Father the Creator.

GUIDANCE FOR FAMILY MEMBERS

[18]Wives, listen to and follow the loving guidance of your husbands, for this is a good thing in Creator's sight. [19]Husbands, love your wives *in the same manner that Creator loves you*, and never let bitter roots grow in your heart toward them.

[20]Children, follow the *wise* guidance of your parents in all you do, for this will make Creator's heart glad. [21]Fathers, do not push your children too hard, for this may make their hearts fall to the ground.

GUIDANCE FOR SLAVES AND MASTERS

[22]If you are a slave, then do everything your earthly master tells you to do, not just when he has his eye on you but from a good heart and out of deep respect for the Great Spirit. [23]Do everything from a strong heart, knowing you are serving our Creator and not weak human beings. [24]For you know it is our Honored Chief, the Chosen One, whom you serve, who will honor you with all that he has promised. [25]*It does not matter whether one is master or slave:* if wrong is done, then wrong will come back—full circle. Creator will not favor one over another.

4

[1]If you are a master, then treat your slaves in Creator's right ways, with respect and honor, for you know that you also have a Master in the spirit-world above.

NEVER GIVE UP PRAYING

[2]When you send your voice to the Great Spirit, stay alert and never give up praying and giving thanks. [3-4]Keep us in your thoughts and prayers also. Ask Creator to open the way for our message to be heard, and that I would clearly make known the mystery of the Chosen One. It is for this reason that I have been captured and put in chains.

[5]Use great wisdom as you walk among those who are not yet part of the sacred family, and make full use of every opportunity *as you represent our Honored Chief.* [6]Think before you speak and let your words be clear. Then, like salt that brings out the good flavor, you will know how to give each person the right answer.

FINAL WORDS AND FAREWELLS

[7-8]I am sending He Is at Ease (Tychicus) to you, a much-loved *spiritual* brother, one who faithfully serves our Honored Chief by also serving others. I am sending him to bring you news about me, so you will know how we are doing and that your hearts may be lifted up and made strong. [9]Along with him is He Is Helpful (Onesimus), a much-loved and faithful *spiritual* brother, who is also from the sacred family that meets in your village. They will give you a full report about everything here.

[10]I send you greetings from Good Chief (Aristarchus), who is in prison with me. War Club (Mark), the cousin of Son of Comfort (Barnabas), also sends his greetings. He is the one I already instructed you about. If he comes to you, welcome him. [11]Creator Rescues (Jesus), who is also named Stands Upright (Justus), also sends his greetings. These are the only Tribal Members who walk with me on Creator's good road, working with me

side by side. They have been a great comfort to me.

¹²Walks in Beauty (Epaphras), who is a member of the sacred family of your village,ᵃ sends his greetings also. He is a true servant of the Chosen One, Creator Sets Free (Jesus). He wrestles for you in his prayers, that you will stand strong and walk Creator's path with firm steps as you grow into mature human beings. ¹³I speak from my heart, he has worked with all his strength for you and for those who live in the village of The People Will Decide (Laodicea) and in Medicine Village (Hierapolis).

¹⁴Our much-loved friend Shining Light (Luke), the medicine man, sends you his greetings, along with Leader of the People (Demas).

ᵃ4:12 Lit. *one of you*

¹⁵Send my greetings to the sacred family members in the village of The People Will Decide (Laodicea), to Bride Woman (Nympha), and to the sacred family members that gather in her home.

¹⁶After you who live in Village of Giants (Colossae) have read this message from me, make sure it is also read by the sacred family at The People Will Decide (Laodicea), and then you can also read the message I sent to them.

¹⁷Give this message to Horse Chief (Archippus), "See to it that you finish the work our Honored Chief entrusted to you."

¹⁸I, Small Man (Paul), write this greeting with my own hand. Remember me in my chains! May the gift of Creator's great kindness rest on you.

Aho! May it be so!

FIRST LETTER FROM SMALL MAN TO THE SACRED FAMILY IN VILLAGE OF FALSE VICTORY

1 THESSALONIANS

1

GREETINGS

1From Small Man (Paul), Forest Walker (Silvanus), and He Gives Honor (Timothy).

To the sacred family that gathers in the village of False Victory (Thessalonica), who belong to our Father the Great Spirit and to our Honored Chief, Creator Sets Free (Jesus) the Chosen One. We greet you with the gift of *Creator's* great kindness and peace.

2We never stop giving thanks for you, speaking your names as we send our voice to the Great Spirit. **3**We remember how your trust became a labor of love and how hope kept you hand in hand with our Honored Chief, Creator Sets Free (Jesus) the Chosen One, as you walked under the shadow of the Great Spirit, who is our Father *from above.*

WELCOMING THE GOOD STORY

4My sacred family members who are loved by Creator, we know he has chosen you to be his own. **5**For when we told you the good story, it was not with words only but with the power and assurance that comes from the Holy Spirit. For you know that we lived and walked among you in a good way. **6**So you followed in our footsteps and those of our Honored Chief, welcoming the good story in a time of much hardship and trouble with the joy of the Holy Spirit. **7**In this way, you became an example for all the members of the sacred family in Land of Tall People (Macedonia) and in Land of Sorrow (Achaia).

8The message from our Honored Chief has sounded out from you, not only in Land of Tall People (Macedonia) and Land of Sorrow (Achaia), but everywhere we go the word has gone out about your trust in Creator, and we have nothing to add to what has been said. **9**They keep talking about the kind of welcome you gave us. They tell how you walked away from spirit-images to serve the living and true Great Spirit **10**and how you now wait for his Son Creator Sets Free (Jesus), the one he raised up from the dead, to return from the spirit-world above. He is the one who rescues us from the coming storm of *Creator's* anger.

2

SEEKING TO PLEASE THE GREAT SPIRIT

1So then, my sacred family members, you can see that our time with you did not fail in its purpose. **2**For you already know about the mistreatment and insults we faced at Village of Horses (Philippi). But in the midst of such hostility Creator gave us the boldness to tell you his good story.

³Our message to you had no false purpose. We were not trying to trick or fool anyone. ⁴For it is the Great Spirit himself who has approved and entrusted us with the good story. We do not speak to please human beings but to please the Great Spirit, the one who puts our hearts to the test.

⁵As you know, we did not try to sweet-talk you into giving us your possessions. Creator is our witness. ⁶We were not looking for you or anyone else to give us honor, ⁷even though as message bearers of the Chosen One we could have required it. *Instead*, we were as gentle among you as a nursing mother caring for her own children. ⁸We cared so much for you that we were willing to share with you not only Creator's good story but our own lives as well. That is how deep our love for you has become.

WORKING HARD, NIGHT AND DAY

⁹My sacred family members, I am sure you remember how hard we worked night and day so we would not be a burden to anyone as we told Creator's good story to you. ¹⁰Along with the Great Spirit, you who trust our message are witnesses to the honest, good, and blameless ways we walked among you. ¹¹For you know that we treated you as parents would treat their own children. We begged and comforted and urged you ¹²to walk in ways that bring honor to Creator, the one who chose you to walk his good road that shines like the sun.

¹³This is why we never stop giving thanks to the Great Spirit for the manner in which you welcomed his message. You received it for what it truly is, the word of Creator and not the word of human beings. His word is now at work in you who trust in its message.

HOSTILE TO THE GOOD STORY

¹⁴You, my spiritual relatives, have followed in the footsteps of Creator's sacred families who gather in Land of Promise (Judea), who are also joined together in Creator Sets Free (Jesus) the Chosen One. For you have suffered mistreatment at the hands of your people, just as they did from their own Tribal Members. ¹⁵They are the ones who killed our Honored Chief Creator Sets Free (Jesus) and the prophets and have driven us away. They fail to please the Great Spirit and are hostile to all humankind. ¹⁶They try to keep us from telling the Outside Nations the good story so they can be set free and made whole. Their broken ways have always taken them down the wrong path, but now the storm of *Creator's* great anger is catching up with them, leading to a bad end.

HINDERED FROM COMING TO YOU

¹⁷My sacred family members, we may have been physically separated from you, but you were still in our hearts. This made us long for you even more and to try to see you face to face. ¹⁸Our desire was to come to you. I, Small Man (Paul), tried more than once, but Accuser (Satan) held us back. ¹⁹For who else but you will be our headdress of honor making our hearts glad before our Honored Chief Creator Sets Free (Jesus) when he appears? ²⁰Yes, you are our honor and our joy!

FACING HARD TIMES

¹When we could not wait any longer to see you, we felt it was best to stay alone

in Wondering Place (Athens) and send He Gives Honor (Timothy) to you. ²He is our spiritual brother who works hand in hand with Creator telling the good story of the Chosen One. We sent him to lift you up and strengthen you in your spiritual ways,ᵃ ³so that no one would be shaken by the hard times we are facing. For you know that this is the path *Creator has* chosen for us. ⁴When we were with you, we made it clear that a trail of sorrow and trouble lay ahead of us. As you know, we had to walk that path.

A GOOD REPORT FROM HE GIVES HONOR

⁵So because I could not bear waiting any longer, I sent He Gives Honor (Timothy) to see whether you were still walking in our spiritual ways.ᵇ For I feared that the evil trickster may have drawn you away, and our work among you would come to nothing. ⁶But He Gives Honor (Timothy) has now come back from you and brought the good news that you still walk in love and in our spiritual ways.ᵇ He told us that you have good thoughts about us and long to see us as much as we long to see you.

⁷So, my sacred family members, this good news about your spiritual walk has comforted us during all the trouble and suffering we have faced. ⁸We came to life when we heard that you are standing firm trusting in our Honored Chief. ⁹When we stand *in prayer* before Creator, we cannot thank him enough for all the joy you have brought to us. ¹⁰With all our heart we send up prayers night and day, asking to see you face to face, so we can give you all you need to further strengthen your spiritual ways.ᵃ

¹¹Now may our Father the Great Spirit himself and Creator Sets Free (Jesus) our

Honored Chief guide our steps to you. ¹²May our Honored Chief make your love for each other and for all people grow deep and wide, just as our love does for you. ¹³This love will give you strong hearts, so you will be able to stand holy and pure before our Father the Great Spirit when our Honored Chief Creator Sets Free (Jesus) appears with all his holy ones.

KEEP WALKING IN A SACRED WAY

¹My sacred family members, I have more I want to say to you. You are walking in a way that makes Creator's heart glad, the way we taught you to walk. Now our firm counsel to you from our Honored Chief Creator Sets Free (Jesus) is that you must keep walking more and more in this way. ²For the instructions we gave you came from Creator Sets Free (Jesus) our Honored Chief himself.

³Our Creator wants you to walk in a sacred way, keeping yourself free from sexual impurity. ⁴He wants each of you to control your own body in a sacred manner with honor and respect, ⁵not with uncontrolled desire, like the people from the Outside Nations who do not know the Great Spirit. ⁶No one should abuse a sacred family member in this manner, for our Honored Chief will punish those who do, just as we have already *solemnly* warned you. ⁷For our Creator has not called us to walk in impurity but in a sacred manner. ⁸So the one who turns away from this instruction is not turning away from a human being, but from Creator himself, who has given his Holy Spirit to you.

ᵃ3:2, 10 Lit. *your faith*
ᵇ3:5, 6 Lit. *our faith*

LOVING EACH OTHER

⁹There is no need for us to instruct you about the love we share as sacred family members. Creator himself has taught you how to love each other. ¹⁰It is clear that you show love to all the sacred family throughout Land of Tall People (Macedonia). So then, my sacred family members, keep loving like this more and more. ¹¹Make it your aim to live a quiet and peaceful life, to mind your own business, and to work with your own hands, just as we have instructed. ¹²By walking in this good way, you will win the respect of outsiders and not have to look to others for your needs.

ABOUT THOSE WHO HAVE DIED

¹³Now, my sacred family members, we want you to understand what will happen to those who have walked on so that you will not be filled with sorrow like the others who have no hope. ¹⁴We believe that Creator Sets Free (Jesus) died and rose again. We can be just as sure that the Great Spirit will, along with him, bring back *to life* those who when they died were *trusting* in him.

¹⁵What we are telling you comes from the words of our Honored Chief. We who remain alive until his coming will not come face to face with him ahead of the ones who have walked on. ¹⁶For our Honored Chief himself will come down from the spirit-world above with a war cry. The voice of the chief spirit-messenger will join with him, and the eagle bone whistle will sound.ᵃ First, the ones who died trusting in the Chosen One will rise. ¹⁷Then, together with them, we who have remained alive will be taken up into the clouds to meet our

Honored Chief in the air. Then we will always be with him. ¹⁸Use these words to lift up each other's hearts.

THE DAY OF OUR HONORED CHIEF

¹Now, my sacred family members, we have no need to write to you about the times and seasons *that have been set in place by our Creator.* ²For you know very well that the day of our Honored Chief will come *without warning* like a thief in the night. ³At a time when people are saying, "Peace and safety," sudden destruction will come down on their heads, like the pains of birth that come upon a woman with child, and there will be no way to escape.

⁴⁻⁵But that day should not catch you off guard like a thief in the night. For you, my sacred family members, are children of the light. You belong to the day. We are not of the night, nor of darkness. ⁶So let us not fall asleep as others do. Instead, we should stay sober and alert. ⁷For it is during the night that people sleep or get drunk. ⁸But since we are children of the day, let us walk in sobriety and put on faith and love as a breastplate, and for a headdress let us put on the hope of being set free and made whole.

⁹For the Great Spirit has not chosen us as targets for his great anger, but *as targets for his great love.* He will set us free and make us whole through our Honored Chief Creator Sets Free (Jesus) the Chosen One. ¹⁰He died for us so that we might live together with him, whether we remain alive *until he comes* or have died and walked on. ¹¹So encourage each other and help each other grow strong, just as you are already doing.

ᵃ**4:16** Lit. *trumpet,* or in Hebrew *shofar,* meaning "ram's horn"

WISE COUNSEL AND LAST WORDS

[12]So, my sacred family members, we have something to ask of you. Honor the spiritual leaders who work hard among you. For they watch over you and give you wise and firm counsel as they serve our Honored Chief. [13]Treat them with great respect and love for the work they do, and be at peace with each other.

[14]Now, my sacred family members, we call on you to give firm and wise counsel to those whose hands do nothing. Comfort those whose hearts are on the ground. Help the ones who are weak, and be patient with everyone. [15]Make sure no one gives back to anyone evil for evil. Instead, seek to walk in a good way with each other and with all people.

[16]Dance for joy at all times! [17]Never stop sending up prayers. [18]Give thanks to the Great Spirit in all things, for this is what he wants from you as you dance in step with Creator Sets Free (Jesus) the Chosen One. [19]Do not put out the fire of the *Holy* Spirit. [20]Do not look down on or turn away from words spoken as prophecies, [21]but think deeply about what is said and hold firmly to what is good. [22]Make sure to turn away from all kinds of evil.

PRAYERS AND BLESSINGS

[23]Now may the Giver of Peace, Creator himself, make you holy in every way. May your whole spirit, soul, and body be kept pure and without blame at the coming of our Honored Chief, Creator Sets Free (Jesus) the Chosen One. [24]The one who called you is faithful, and he will do it.

[25]My sacred family members, keep sending up prayers for us, [26]and greet all the members of the sacred family with a holy kiss. [27]Give me your solemn promise that you will read this letter to all of them. [28]May the gift of great kindness from Creator Sets Free (Jesus) the Chosen One be with you all.

Aho! May it be so!

SECOND LETTER FROM SMALL MAN TO THE SACRED FAMILY IN VILLAGE OF FALSE VICTORY

2 THESSALONIANS

GREETINGS

¹From Small Man (Paul), Forest Walker (Silvanus), and He Gives Honor (Timothy).

To the sacred family that gathers in village of False Victory (Thessalonica) who belong to our Father the Great Spirit and to Creator Sets Free (Jesus) the Chosen One. ²*We greet you with* the gift of great kindness and peace that comes from our Father the Great Spirit and from our Honored Chief, Creator Sets Free (Jesus) the Chosen One.

GIVING THANKS FOR YOU

³My sacred family members, it is only right and good that we are always giving thanks to Creator for you. *We give thanks for the way your trust in him and your love for each other keeps growing stronger day by day.* ⁴We tell the other Sacred Families of Creator about you, bragging about the way you keep trusting even when the path you walk is full of pain and trouble from others.

CREATOR WILL HONOR YOU

⁵⁻⁶Creator will honor you as you walk his good road even when it means suffering. This shows that it is right for Creator to punish those who have made you suffer.

⁷It is also right that he will bring comfort to all of us who share in these troubles. This will happen when our Honored Chief Creator Sets Free (Jesus) is revealed from the spirit-world above along with all his powerful spirit-messengers.

In flaming fire ⁸he will punish the ones who refuse to see who Creator truly is, and those who do not respect and follow the good story of our Honored Chief Creator Sets Free (Jesus). ⁹They will come to a bad end and to a punishment that will last beyond the end of all days. They will be removed far away from the beauty and power that shines from the face of our Honored Chief. ¹⁰*This will happen* on the day he comes to be honored by all his holy people and to be looked on in amazement by all who have trusted in him. *This includes you*, because you trusted the truth we told you.

SENDING UP PRAYERS

¹¹This is the reason we never stop sending our voice to the Great Spirit for you. We pray that our Creator will give you what you need to walk with honor on the path he has chosen for you. We pray that, as you trust in his power, he will fulfill every desire you have to walk in a good way. ¹²We also pray that you will show the beauty that is in the name

of our Honored Chief Creator Sets Free (Jesus) and that his beauty will be seen in you. *He will do this* by the gift of Creator's great kindness that comes through our Honored Chief, Creator Sets Free (Jesus) the Chosen One.

2

THE DAY OF OUR HONORED CHIEF

¹My sacred family members, we have something to say to you about the time when our Honored Chief, Creator Sets Free (Jesus) the Chosen One, will appear and we will all be gathered around him. ²Do not be suddenly shaken in your mind or troubled if you hear that the day of our Honored Chief has already arrived. *It does not matter whether you hear it* by a prophecy or a spoken word or by a written message that someone says came from us.

BEFORE THAT DAY COMES

³Do not be fooled by anyone. Before that day comes, there must first be an uprising —a turning away *from Creator*. Then the man who respects no law will be revealed, the son whose father is destruction. ⁴He will speak out against and consider himself to be greater than all the so-called powerful spirit-beings and all that is seen as sacred or holy. He will even set himself up in Creator's sacred lodge and represent himself as the Great Spirit. ⁵Have you forgotten that when I was still with you I told you about these things?

MORE ABOUT THE LAWLESS ONE

⁶You know what it is that now holds him back until it is time for him to be revealed. ⁷For the mysterious power of the lawless one is already at work in secret. The lawless one is ready and waiting to be revealed, but not until the one who holds him back steps out of the way. ⁸Then *the mask will come off and* the lawless one will be revealed. And when Creator Sets Free (Jesus) our Honored Chief comes, he will destroy him with the breath of his mouth and put an end to him with the light that shines from his face.

⁹This lawless one will come performing all kinds of misleading signs and wonders, but the one who gives him this power is Accuser (Satan) *the evil trickster*. ¹⁰He will use his trickster ways to lead people down a path to a bad end. They will follow him because they did not love the truth that would rescue them and set them free. ¹¹Because *they did not love the truth*, the Great Spirit will give them over to the full power of this lie, so they will believe it. ¹²In this way, all who did not trust the truth but instead found joy in wrongdoing will come to the bad end they deserve.

STAND STRONG AND HOLD ON FIRMLY

¹³My sacred family members loved by our Honored Chief, we owe thanks to the Great Spirit for you. He has chosen you to be first among those he will set free and make whole, as you trust in the truth through his Spirit who makes you holy. ¹⁴Creator used our telling of the good story to call you to himself so that you would share in the honor that shines from the face of our Honored Chief, Creator Sets Free (Jesus) the Chosen One.

¹⁵So then, my sacred family members, stand strong and hold firmly to the traditions we taught you, either by voice or by letter. ¹⁶We are loved by our Honored Chief, Creator Sets Free (Jesus) the Chosen One, and by our Father the Great Spirit. It is through the gift of his great kindness that he has given us good hope and

comfort that will never fade away. ¹⁷*We pray that* he will now lift up your hearts and strengthen you in all the good things you do or say.

3

MORE PRAYER IS NEEDED

¹Now, my sacred family members, I have some final things to write to you. Would you send up prayers for us asking that the message of our Honored Chief will run like the wind and be given honor in the same way it has among you? ²Pray that we will be rescued from bad-hearted and evil men—for not all follow our spiritual ways.^a ³But our Honored Chief is trustworthy. He will set your feet on solid ground and protect you from the evil one.

⁴The trust we have in our Honored Chief makes us feel sure that you will keep following all the instructions we gave you. ⁵So we pray that he will guide your hearts into the path of Creator's love and help you walk in the steady steps of the Chosen One.

FOLLOW THE TRADITIONS WE GAVE YOU

⁶So, my sacred family members, as we represent our Honored Chief, Creator Sets Free (Jesus) the Chosen One, we instruct you to keep away from any sacred family member who walks in a bad way and fails to follow the traditions we gave you. ⁷For you all know that you should walk in our footsteps. We walked in a good way when we were with you. ⁸We did not expect people to feed us for free. Instead, we wore ourselves out working hard night and day so we would not be a burden to anyone.

⁹We had the right not to work, but we wanted to set a good example for you to follow. ¹⁰*Do you remember* when we were still with you, we gave you the instruction, "The ones who will not work should not be fed"? ¹¹We say this because we hear that there are some among you who are walking in a bad way. They do nothing but put their noses into the business of others.

¹²So, representing our Honored Chief, Creator Sets Free (Jesus) the Chosen One, we speak firmly to those who walk in this way, "Settle down, *go to work*, and *quietly* earn your own food."

WORDS OF ENCOURAGEMENT

¹³But to the rest of you, my sacred family members, do not let your hearts fall to the ground as you keep walking in a good way. ¹⁴Take note of any among you who do not follow these instructions. Have nothing to do with them, so they will feel the shame of their ways. ¹⁵Do not see them as enemies, but give them this firm and wise counsel as members of the sacred family.

FINAL WORDS

¹⁶Now may our Honored Chief of peace give his peace to you at all times and in every way. May our Honored Chief be with you all.

¹⁷I, Small Man (Paul), write this *final* greeting with my own hand. Take note of how I sign my letters. This way you will know the letter is from me.

¹⁸May the gift of great kindness that comes from our Honored Chief, Creator Sets Free (Jesus) the Chosen One, be with you all.

Aho! May it be so!

---

^a**3:2** Lit. *the faith*

FIRST LETTER FROM SMALL MAN TO HE GIVES HONOR

1 TIMOTHY

1

GREETINGS

¹From Small Man (Paul), a message bearer of Creator Sets Free (Jesus) the Chosen One. I was instructed to be a message bearer by the Great Spirit himself, our Sacred Deliverer, and by Creator Sets Free (Jesus) the Chosen One, our hope.

²To He Gives Honor (Timothy), my true spiritual son. I greet you with the gift of great kindness, mercy, and peace that comes from our Father the Great Spirit and from Creator Sets Free (Jesus) the Chosen One, our Honored Chief.

SMALL MAN'S WISE COUNSEL BEGINS

³When I left to travel to Land of Tall People (Macedonia), I urged you to remain at Village of Desire (Ephesus) to instruct certain people not to teach things that are not true ⁴and to turn away from stories with no meaning and from long ancestral histories. These things only cause arguments *and confuse people* instead of helping them to trust in the good road of the Great Spirit.

⁵My aim in telling you these things is that you would walk the path of love with a pure heart, being true to what you trust in and honest to who you are deep inside. ⁶For there are some who have wandered from this good path and turned aside to nothing but worthless talk. ⁷They want to be seen as teachers of our tribal law,ᵃ but they do not understand the words they speak or the things they so boldly teach.

USING THE LAW IN THE RIGHT WAY

⁸We know that the law is good if it is used in the right way. ⁹For we understand that the law was not made for those who walk in a good way. The law was made for outlaws, rebels, and those who follow their bad hearts and have no respect for what is spiritual. It was made for the unholy ones who walk in worthless ways, and for the ones who kill their own fathers or mothers and take the lives of others. ¹⁰The law was made for men who sell their bodies for sex or abuse the sacred gift of sex with each other, for slave traders, forked-tongue talkers, those who tell lies about their fellow human beings, and for anything else that goes against the kind of teaching ¹¹found in the good story that shows the beauty of the Blessed One, our Creator. *This is the teaching* that was entrusted to me.

SMALL MAN TELLS ABOUT HIMSELF

¹²I give thanks to the Chosen One, Creator Sets Free (Jesus) our Honored Chief, for

---

ᵃ**1:7** Luke 5:17; Acts 5:34

the strength he gives me to walk out this sacred task. [13]He chose me even though I used to speak evil against him. I even hunted down and attacked his followers. But he took pity on me because I did not know what I was doing and did not yet believe who he was.

[14]The gift of Creator's great kindness overflowed to me along with the trust and love found in Creator Sets Free (Jesus) the Chosen One. [15]Here is a saying that you can be sure of: Creator Sets Free (Jesus) the Chosen One came into this world to set bad-hearted people free from their broken ways—and I am the worst one of all. [16]But I was shown mercy so that in me Creator Sets Free (Jesus) the Chosen One could show that he does not give up on even the worst bad-hearted person. In this way, I became an example of his patience that never runs dry for the ones who would put their trust in him for the life of the world to come that never fades away, full of beauty and harmony.

HONORING OUR GREAT CHIEF

[17]So let us honor the Great Chief of all the ages, the one whom death has no power over, who cannot be seen with human eyes. He is the only true and Great Spirit. All honor and shining-greatness belong to him to the time beyond the end of all days. Aho! May it be so!

MORE WISE COUNSEL

[18]Now, He Gives Honor (Timothy) my *spiritual* son, the instructions I give you are the same ones that were spoken over you as prophecies. Use these as weapons to keep fighting this *spiritual* battle in a good way. [19]Keep your trust *in the Chosen One* strong and follow what you know deep inside to be true. Some have not listened to this inner voice, and their trust *in the Chosen One* has fallen to the ground. [20]This happened to Sings with a Glad Heart (Hymenaeus) and Man Fighter (Alexander). I had to hand them over to Accuser (Satan) that they might learn not to speak against the Great Spirit.

GUIDANCE FOR SENDING UP PRAYERS

[1]First of all, I call on you to send your voice to the Great Spirit with many kinds of prayer. Give thanks as you ask him to bless all people everywhere with the things they need. [2]Send up prayers for rulers and all governing authorities, so we may live our lives in a peaceful and sacred way, walking together with harmony and respect. [3]This will make Creator's heart glad and will be seen as a good thing by the one who sets us free and makes us whole.

CREATOR LONGS FOR ALL PEOPLE TO BE FREE

[4]Our Creator longs to set all people free and guide them into the full understanding of the truth. [5]For there is only one Great Spirit, and only one who can bring the Great Spirit and human beings together in peace. That one is Creator Sets Free (Jesus) the Chosen One, who is himself human. [6]He gave up his own life to set all people free, so that, when the time was right, this truth would be made clear to all humankind.

[7]The reason I was given the sacred task of a truth teller and a message bearer is to tell others this good story. I am not speaking with a forked tongue! Creator has sent me to be a faithful and true wisdomkeeper to the Outside Nations.

GUIDANCE FOR MEN AND WOMEN

[8]So in every place *you gather as a sacred family*, I want the men who pray to lift up their hands in a sacred manner, putting away all anger and disagreement.

[9]In the same way, I want the women *who pray in the sacred family gathering* to wear clothes that represent them well. They should dress in a modest and respectful manner. There is no need *to try to look better than others* with fancy hair, or with gold, pearls, or clothes that cost too much. [10]It is only right that a woman who represents herself as walking in a sacred manner should show her beauty in the good things she does for others.

[11]*At our sacred family gatherings*, a woman should remain quiet while learning from those who teach and humbly follow their instructions. [12]I do not permit a woman to teach or take over for a man, but to listen quietly. [13]For Red Clay (Adam) was formed first and then Life Bearer (Eve). [14]Also, Red Clay (Adam) was not fooled *by the evil trickster*. It was the woman who was fooled and walked where she should not. [15]But women will be kept safe through *the pain and labor of* childbirth if they keep walking a sacred path of trust, love, and self-control.

3 ✕)‹‹✕)‹‹✕)‹‹✕)‹‹✕)‹‹✕)‹‹✕)‹‹✕)‹

GUIDELINES FOR SPIRITUAL LEADERS

[1]It is a true saying that anyone who desires the solemn task of watching over the sacred family desires a good thing. [2]Elders like this must be free from accusation, faithful in marriage,[a] clear-minded, self-controlled, honorable, welcoming to strangers, and able to teach others. [3]They must not be heavy drinkers, nor given to violence, but gentle peacemakers who are free from the love of possessions.

[4]These *elders* must guide their own families in a good way, having children who are respectful and well-behaved. [5]For if they cannot guide their own families, how will they take care of Creator's sacred family? [6]They also should not be new followers *of Creator Sets Free (Jesus)*, or they might get a big head and give the evil trickster the right to accuse them.

[7]*And last of all*, they must have a good reputation with those who are outside the sacred family, so they will not be shamed and fall into the trap set by the evil trickster.

GUIDELINES FOR SACRED SERVANTS

[8]In the same way, those who have the sacred task of helping others must walk in an honorable way, not be double-tongued, nor heavy drinkers, and not greedy for possessions. [9]From deep within they must hold firm to the mystery of our spiritual ways.[b] [10]They must first prove themselves. Then if they are found to be free from blame, let them walk true to the sacred task of serving others. [11]Their wives[c] must walk with dignity, never speak evil of others, and be clear-minded and faithful in every way.

[12]These sacred servants must also be faithful in marriage[d] and guide their own families in a good way. [13]The ones who have served well as helpers gain the respect of others, and their trust in Creator Sets Free (Jesus) the Chosen One will grow strong.

[14]I hope to come to you soon. But I am writing this letter to you [15]so that, if I am

---

[a]**3:2** Lit. *the husband of one wife*

[b]**3:9** Lit. *mystery of the faith*
[c]**3:11** Or *the women helpers*
[d]**3:12** Lit. *husbands of one wife*

held back, you will know how to live together in Creator's household. This household is the sacred family of the Living Great Spirit, the family that holds high the truth.

A GREAT MYSTERY MADE KNOWN

16The mystery of this great and sacred truth has now been made known. He who appeared as a human being was shown to be in the right by the Spirit. He was seen by spirit-messengers, made known among the nations, trusted in by people in the world, and taken up to be honored *in the spirit-world above.*

WARNINGS ABOUT THE LAST TIMES

1The Spirit clearly says that in the last times some will turn away from their trust in Creator Sets Free (Jesus) and listen to lying spirits and their evil teachings. **2**It is through people with forked tongues and false faces that these lies will be spoken. The truth inside them has been burned away until they no longer know right from wrong. **3**They stop people from getting married and tell people to stay away from eating certain kinds of foods. These foods were created by the Great Spirit to be received with grateful hearts by those who trust in and know the truth. **4**For all of his creation is good, and nothing is to be refused if it is received with a grateful heart. **5**For it is made holy and good to eat by Creator's word and prayer.

SERVING THE SACRED FAMILY

6If you make these things clear to the members of the sacred family, you will be a good servant of Creator Sets Free (Jesus) the Chosen One. *This shows that* the trust you have in the message of our spiritual ways and the good teaching you have been following has helped you to grow *spiritually strong.*

7Have nothing to do with made-up stories and worn-out tales that have been passed on from long ago. Instead, learn to walk in a sacred manner. **8**Physical discipline is good for the life we now live, but spiritual discipline is good in every way, since it holds promise not only for this life but also for the life *of the world* to come. **9**This saying is honorable and should be fully welcomed by all.

THE ONE WHO SETS ALL PEOPLE FREE

10This is the reason we struggle and work so hard, for we have put our hope in the Living Great Spirit. He is the one who sets free and makes whole all of humankind, but first and foremost those who put their trust in him.

11Teach and instruct others in all these things. **12**Let no one look down on you because you are young. Lead the way for others in all that you say and do, and also by trusting, loving, and walking with a pure heart. **13**Until I come to see you, make sure you read the Sacred Teachings out loud at our sacred family gatherings, and teach with words that lift people's spirits high.

DO NOT NEGLECT YOUR SPIRITUAL GIFT

14Do not neglect the spiritual gift that is in you. This gift came to you through a word of prophecy that was given when the council of elders laid their hands on you *to set you in place as a spiritual leader.* **15**Meditate on these things. Give all your time and energy to doing them. In this way, everyone will see how far down the good road you have traveled. **16**Keep a close watch on yourself and on what you are teaching. Keep doing *all that I have told you*. In this way, you will set free and make whole not only yourself but all who listen to you.

5

HONORING THE ELDERS

[1] Never speak sharp words to a man who is your elder. Instead, speak respectfully to him as to a father. Speak to the younger men as brothers, [2] to the women elders as mothers, and to the young women as sisters, keeping your thoughts pure.

THE CARE OF WIDOWS

[3] Honor and take care of the women whose husbands have walked on, if they truly need help. [4] But if any among them have children or grandchildren, they should take care of her with respect as she once did for them, for this is what Creator wants them to do. [5] *The sacred family* should take care of women who have no one to care for them as long as they are looking to Creator for their help and continue to send up prayers night and day. [6] But the ones who live only to please themselves are *spiritually* dead even while they live.

[7] Instruct *the sacred family members* *about* these things, so no one will have a reason to accuse or look down on them. [8] For all who fail to care for the members of their own family have denied the truth of our spiritual ways[a] and are worse than an outsider who does not trust as we do.

WIDOWS WHO ARE ELDERLY

[9] To be counted as a widow *to be taken care of by the sacred family*, a woman must be an elder of sixty winters or older

who was faithful to her husband.[b] [10] She must also have a reputation for doing good. Has she raised her children in a good way? Has she welcomed travelers into her home? Has she washed the feet of Creator's holy ones?[c] Has she offered help to people during hard times? Has she always been willing to do good for others?

WIDOWS WHO ARE YOUNG

[11] Do not include the younger widows for *this kind of care*. For when their natural human desires draw them away from their devotion to the Chosen One, they will want to get married. [12] Then they will be found guilty of breaking the sacred promise they made *to remain unmarried*. [13] They make a habit of going around from home to home doing nothing and helping no one. Not only that, they talk about people behind their backs, stick their noses into places they do not belong, and say things that should not be said.

[14] That is why I want the younger widows to get married, have children, and take good care of their own families. Then the enemy will have nothing to say against them. [15] For some *of the younger widows* have already wandered away to follow Accuser (Satan) *the evil trickster snake*.

[16] If sacred family members have a widow in the family, let them take her in and care for her. This will lift the burden from the sacred family so the widows who have no family will be cared for.

HONORING THE SPIRITUAL LEADERS

[17] The elders who are spiritual leaders are to be given double honor—most of all, the ones who work hard at instructing and teaching others. [18] For our Sacred Teachings tell us, "When an ox is used to

---

[a] **5:8** Lit. *our faith*

[b] **5:9** Lit. *a wife of one man*

[c] **5:10** John 13:14

harvest corn, do not cover its mouth and keep it from eating,"[a] and "Those who work hard should be given the honor and goods they have worked hard for."[b]

[19]If someone accuses an elder who is a spiritual leader with wrongdoing, do not listen unless two or three others say the same thing. [20]Even so, a spiritual leader who continues in wrongdoing must be brought before all *of the council of elders* for correction as a warning to others.

MORE WORDS OF WISDOM AND COUNSEL

[21]With the Great Spirit as my witness, along with Creator Sets Free (Jesus) the Chosen One and his chief[c] spirit-messengers, I call on you, *He Gives Honor (Timothy)*, to follow my instructions by treating everyone the same and not taking the side of one over another. [22]Do not be in a hurry to lay your hands on others *to choose them as spiritual leaders.* Do not take part in the broken ways of others. Keep yourself pure.

[23]No longer drink only water, and from now on use a little wine *to purify the water.* This will be good medicine for the times you have a bad stomach.

[24]Some people's broken ways are plain to see even before their guilt is decided. The guilt of others becomes clear later on. [25]In the same way, the good deeds of some are clearly seen, and even if they are not clear for all to see, they will not be hidden for long.

INSTRUCTIONS FOR SLAVES

[1]Any *sacred family members* who are slaves should treat their earthly masters with respect. In this way Creator will not be given a bad reputation, and no one will speak against him or what we teach. [2]Those who are slaves to masters who are sacred family members should not for that reason look down on them. Instead, they should serve them all the more, for the ones who benefit from their service are also much-loved sacred family members. Teach and urge others to walk in these ways.

A WARNING ABOUT TROUBLEMAKERS

[3]There are some who teach things that are not in agreement with the good words spoken by our Honored Chief, Creator Sets Free (Jesus) the Chosen One, and with the teaching that keeps us walking in a sacred way. [4]Teachers like this think they know it all, but they really understand nothing. There is a sickness in the way they think. They argue over the meaning of words, which takes people down a path of envy, fighting, name-calling, and evil mistrust of each other.

[5]They keep stirring up trouble between people whose minds have wandered away from the truth. They even think that walking in the ways of the Great Spirit is a path to getting more and more possessions. [6]It is true that following the ways of the Great Spirit will lead to great possessions, but only when people are at peace with what they have. [7]For we came into this world with nothing and can take nothing with us when we leave it. [8]So, as long as we have food to eat and a roof over our heads, we should be at peace with what we have.

A WARNING TO THOSE WHO LONG TO BE RICH

[9]Those who long for more and more possessions stumble into temptation and are

---

[a]**5:18** Deuteronomy 25:4; 1 Corinthians 9:9
[b]**5:18** Leviticus 19:13
[c]**5:21** Lit. *chosen*

trapped by many foolish desires that drag them down and take them to a bad end. [10]For the love of possessions is the root of many evil, thorny branches. Some, who have made possessions their aim in life, have walked away from the good road and have been pierced by thorns that bring them much pain and sorrow.

FIGHT THE GOOD FIGHT OF TRUSTING

[11]But you, O man who follows the Great Spirit, run away from these things and pursue doing what is right, living in a sacred way, trusting, loving, never giving up, and walking softly and in a humble manner. [12]Fight the good fight of trusting *Creator*. Get a firm hold on the life of the world to come that never fades away, full of beauty and harmony. *The Great Spirit* called you to this life when you said yes to him and made it known before many people that you had chosen to walk the good road *with Creator Sets Free (Jesus) the Chosen One.*

[13]As you stand before the Great Spirit who gives life to all things, and before Creator Sets Free (Jesus) the Chosen One, who told the truth in a good way when he stood before Spear of the Great Waters (Pilate), I call on you [14]to follow through with this way of life to which he has called you. Keep walking a path that no one can find fault with until the day comes when our Honored Chief, Creator Sets Free (Jesus) the Chosen One, will appear.

THE GRAND CHIEF ABOVE ALL CHIEFS

[15]That day will be revealed when the time is right by the Blessed One who alone rules above all others, the Grand Chief Above All Chiefs. [16]He is the only one over whom death has no power. His life shines so bright no one can even come near him, and no human eye has ever been able to *fully* see him. To him belongs all honor and power to the time beyond the end of all days. Aho! May it be so!

FOR THOSE WHO HAVE MANY POSSESSIONS

[17]Instruct the ones who have many possessions in this present world not to see themselves as better than others. They must not put their hope in their many possessions, which cannot be depended on, but in the Great Spirit, who, from his great possessions, provides all we need to enjoy life. [18]Instruct them to walk in a good way, to possess many good deeds, and to be willing and ready to share *with those in need.* [19]In this way, they will be storing up and preparing themselves for the life of the world to come, the true life *of beauty and harmony that never grows old or fades away.*[a]

CLOSING WORDS

[20]O He Gives Honor (Timothy), keep a close watch over the things that you have been entrusted with. Turn away from foolish and empty talk and arguments about what is falsely called knowledge. [21]For there are some who, having held this "knowledge" to be true, have strayed away from the good road in which we trust.

May the gift of Creator's great kindness walk with you on the road of life.

Aho! May it be so!

---

[a]**6:19** Matthew 6:19-21

SECOND LETTER FROM SMALL MAN TO HE GIVES HONOR

2 TIMOTHY

GREETINGS

1From Small Man (Paul), a message bearer for Creator Sets Free (Jesus) the Chosen One. The Great Spirit chose me to be a message bearer in harmony with the life he has promised through Creator Sets Free (Jesus) our Honored Chief.

2To He Gives Honor (Timothy), my much-loved *spiritual* son. I greet you with the gift of Creator's great kindness, mercy, and peace that comes from our Father the Great Spirit and from Creator Sets Free (Jesus) the Chosen One, our Honored Chief.

NIGHT-AND-DAY PRAYER

3When I send my voice to the Great Spirit, I speak your name before him as I give thanks to him night and day. I serve Creator with a pure heart, doing what I know deep inside to be good and right, just as my ancestors did. **4**Oh how I long to see you! I look back on your tears, which makes me want to see you again so that my heart will dance for joy.

FAN INTO FLAME CREATOR'S GIFT

5I remember how deep your faith truly is. That faith was alive first in your grandmother Woman Who Walks with Kindness (Lois), then in your mother Woman Who Wins (Eunice). I know that this same faith lives in you as well. **6**This is why I now remind you to fan into flame the gift Creator gave you when I laid my hands on you *as you were set in place as a spiritual leader.* **7**Creator has not given us a timid spirit but one of power, love, and clear thinking.

DEATH DEFEATED

8So do not be timid[a] in telling others about our Honored Chief or that I am in prison because of him. But walk with me on this road of suffering for the sake of the good story as Creator gives us strength. **9**For he is the one who has made us whole and called us to walk a sacred path. He did not choose us because of any good thing we have done. He chose us in harmony with his own purpose and by the gift of his great kindness. This gift was given to us through Creator Sets Free (Jesus) the Chosen One before time began. **10**But now that the Chosen One has appeared, his purpose has been made clear. For he has defeated death and has, through the good story, brought into the light the kind of life that will never again taste death.

NOT ASHAMED

11He chose me to be a message bearer and a wisdomkeeper so I could make

---

[a]**1:8** Lit. *be ashamed*

this good story known to all. ¹²This is the reason I walk a path of hardship and suffering. But I am not ashamed, for I know the one in whom I have put my trust. I am sure that he will watch over me as I walk this sacred path toward that day.

¹³Hold true to the words of good medicine you have heard from me, for they came from the trust and love found in Creator Sets Free (Jesus) the Chosen One. ¹⁴Watch over these sacred truths by the Holy Spirit who lives in us.

BETRAYAL AND COURAGE

¹⁵As you know, *almost* everyone in Land of the Rising Sun (Asia) turned away from me, along with Man Who Runs Away (Phygelus) and Born with Good Luck (Hermogenes). ¹⁶May our Honored Chief show kindness to the family of Bringer of Good Things (Onesiphorus), for he was like a drink of cool water to me and was never ashamed to visit me in prison. ¹⁷When he was in Village of Iron (Rome), he searched hard until he found me. ¹⁸I pray that our Honored Chief will show kindness to him when that day comes. For you know very well the many ways he helped me at Village of Desire (Ephesus).

2 ◁▷◁▷◁▷◁▷◁▷◁▷ ◁▷◁▷

¹So then, my *spiritual* son, let the gift of great kindness from Creator Sets Free (Jesus) the Chosen One be your strength. ²You have heard the things I have spoken of *as we sat together* with many others who heard the same things. Pass these teachings on to those who can be trusted to teach the same to others.

STAND STRONG

³Walk with me on this path of suffering as a good *spiritual* warrior of Creator Sets Free (Jesus) the Chosen One. ⁴During times of war, no warrior gets involved in everyday life, for he must please the war-chief who chose him. ⁵Those who run in a race must follow the rules in order to win. ⁶The one who works hard to plant a field should be the first to share in the harvest. ⁷Think about what I am saying, and our Honored Chief will help you to understand these things.

⁸Keep your thoughts centered on Creator Sets Free (Jesus) the Chosen One, who was raised from the dead and is a descendant of *Chief* Much Loved One (David). This is the good story that I tell. ⁹It has taken me down a troubled path, one that includes being put in chains as an outlaw. But Creator's message can never be locked up. ¹⁰So I keep walking through these troubled times for the sake of the ones whom the Great Spirit has chosen as his own. I want them to be set free and made whole through Creator Sets Free (Jesus) the Chosen One and be honored with him to the time beyond the end of all days.

A VERY WISE SAYING

¹¹Here is a wise saying you can fully trust: If we died with him, we will live with him. ¹²If we never give up, we will share in his chiefly rule. If we deny him, he will deny us. ¹³If we fail to trust him, he will remain faithful, for he cannot deny himself.

¹⁴Keep reminding others about these things. Warn them in the sight of the Great Spirit not to fight over the meaning of words, for these are empty arguments that only bring a bad end to those who listen. ¹⁵Make it your aim to present yourself to Creator as one who is tried and true, a hard worker, without shame, who guides Creator's message of truth down a straight path.

WORTHLESS AND EMPTY TALK

[16]Turn away from worthless and empty talk, for it will take people down a path far away from what is sacred and pure. [17]Talk like this will spread like a disease that eats away at the body. Sings with a Glad Heart (Hymenaeus) and Friendly Man (Philetus) are two men who have been talking like this. [18]They have turned away from the truth, saying that the rising of the dead has already taken place, harming the faith of some.

[19]But the solid rock of Creator's truth stands firm. Carved into it are these words: "Our Honored Chief knows the ones who belong to him," and "All those who say they honor his name must turn away from all wrongdoing."

VESSELS OF HONOR AND DISHONOR

[20]In a great lodge there are not only vessels made of gold and silver but also pots made of wood and clay. Some are for special use and others for ordinary use. *This is true in the lodge that is Creator's sacred family.* [21]Those who wash themselves clean from these worthless ways will be vessels of honor, made holy for the Headman's use and ready to do many good deeds.

[22]So flee from youthful desires and pursue right living, trusting, love, and peace, along with all who call out to our Honored Chief from a pure heart. [23]Have nothing to do with foolish and ignorant disputes, knowing that they stir up further arguments. [24]For Creator's sacred servant must not be eager to argue but kind to all. He must also be a good and patient teacher, [25]humbly instructing those who stand against him. For it could be that Creator will return them to the right way of thinking and lead them back to the path of truth. [26]Then they will come to their senses and escape the trap of the evil trickster, who held them captive to serve his purposes.

WARNINGS ABOUT THE LAST DAYS

[1]I want you to remember that the last days will be violent and dangerous times. [2]People will love only themselves and possessions. They will be puffed up, bigheaded, troublemakers, disobedient to parents, unthankful, and unspiritual. [3]People will be cold-hearted, merciless, full of accusations, without self-control, savage, and haters of what is good. [4]They will be traitors, reckless and arrogant people who love pleasure more than they love the Great Spirit. [5]Stay clear of people like this, for they make a big show of being spiritual but deny its *true* power.

[6]Some of these are men who trick their way into people's families to manipulate vulnerable women who have given themselves over to broken ways to be burdened down with all kinds of evil desires. [7]They are always looking to learn new things but never able to find and understand the truth. [8]In the same way that Greedy Man (Jannes) and Hostile Man (Jambres) stood against Drawn from the Water (Moses),[a] these men also stand against the truth. They are men of bent and twisted minds, whose understanding of our spiritual ways[b] is worthless. [9]But they will not fool many, for their trickery will be easy to see, just as it was for Greedy Man (Jannes) and Hostile Man (Jambres).

SMALL MAN'S WALK OF SUFFERING

[10]But you, He Gives Honor (Timothy), have followed my teachings, my way of life, my

---

[a]3:8 Exodus 7:11
[b]3:8 Lit. *the faith*

purpose, and what I believe. *You know* how patient I am, how much I love others, and how I have never given up. [11]You also know how much I suffered when I was at Stands Against (Antioch), Spirit Village (Iconium), and Set Free (Lystra), how they hunted me down to bring harm to me. But our Honored Chief rescued me in each of those places. [12]It is a true saying that all who want to live their lives in harmony with Creator Sets Free (Jesus) the Chosen One will suffer harm at the hands of those who stand against him.

SACRED TEACHINGS WILL MAKE YOU WISE

[13]Bad-hearted people will go from bad to worse. These are humans behaving like tricksters who lead people down the same kind of path they have been tricked into walking. [14]But you should keep following the ways you have been taught, the teachings you are sure of, for you know who it was who taught you. [15]From the time you were a young boy you have known the Sacred Teachings that are able to make you wise as you trust in the one who has set you free and made you whole, Creator Sets Free (Jesus) the Chosen One.

[16]All the Sacred Teachings come from the breath of the Great Spirit and help us to teach others about Creator's ways. They help us correct wrong thinking and bring lives into balance. They show the good and right way to walk the road of life. [17]In this way, those who walk with the Great Spirit will have everything that is needed to do good things for others.

4

MAKE HIS MESSAGE KNOWN

[1]When the Chosen One appears, he will decide the fate of the living and the dead

and bring his good road to us in all its fullness. In light of these things and in the sight of the Great Spirit and Creator Sets Free (Jesus) the Chosen One, I call on you to complete the sacred task [2]of making his message known! Be ready whether the time seems right or not. Patiently instruct others. Give strong counsel, warnings, and firm words to strengthen their hearts. [3]For a day will come when people will not listen to good teaching. They will gather around themselves teachers who will tell them what their itching ears want to hear. [4]They will turn their ears away from the truth and believe made-up stories.

BE A GOOD STORYTELLER

[5]But you must remain clear-minded in every way, stand strong in hard times, and do the work of a good storyteller. Keep doing what Creator has called on you to do. [6]For my life is already being poured out like a *ceremonial* drink offering, and the time for me to walk on has come. [7]I have fought the good fight. I have walked the good road to its end and stayed true to our spiritual ways.[a] [8]There is a chief's headdress for doing what is right waiting for me in the spirit-world above. Our Honored Chief, whose decisions are always right, will honor me with a headdress on that day, and not only me but also all who have loved his appearing.

CLOSING WORDS AND WARNINGS

[9]Try to come and see me soon. [10]For Leader of the People (Demas), because he loved this present world, has run away to village of False Victory (Thessalonica) and left me alone. He Grows More (Crescens) has gone to Land of Pale Skins (Galatia),

---

[a] **4:7** Lit. *the faith*

and Big Man (Titus) to Land of Holy Robes (Dalmatia). **11**Only Shining Light (Luke) is with me. When you come, bring War Club (Mark) with you, for he is a good help to me as I serve our Creator. **12**I sent He Is at Ease (Tychicus) to Village of Desire (Ephesus). **13**And I left my coat at Cut Through (Troas) with He Grows Good Fruit (Carpus). So when you come, bring it to me along with the books, and above all bring the animal-skin scrolls.

14Man Fighter (Alexander), who works with copper, did much harm to me. Our Honored Chief will do to him what he has done to hurt others. **15**Be on the lookout for him, for he stands strongly against all we teach.

16At my first council hearing, no one spoke up for me and everyone left me alone. May this not be counted against them. **17**But Our Honored Chief stood with me and gave me strength, so that through me the Outside Nations would hear the whole good story. I was set free from the mouth of the lion.[a] **18**Our

Honored Chief will rescue me from every evil scheme and carry me safely onto his good road from above. All honor belongs to him to all the ages. Aho! May it be so!

FINAL WORDS

19I send greetings to Lives Long (Priscilla)[b] and Strong Eagle (Aquila) and to the family of Bringer of Good Things (Onesiphorus). **20**Much Desired (Erastus) remained behind at Village of Pleasure (Corinth), and He Eats Well (Trophimus) was sick so I left him at White Sheep Wool (Miletus). **21**Try to come to me before winter. Wise Counselor (Eubulus) sends greetings to you, along with Hides His Face (Pudens), Sweet Grass (Linus), Limping Woman (Claudia), and all the members of the sacred family.

22May our Honored Chief be with your spirit, and may the gift of his great kindness rest on you.

Aho! May it be so!

---

[a]**4:17** "Mouth of the lion" is a possible reference to death at the hands of the Roman Empire.

[b]**4:19** Lit. *Prisca*, which was probably a nickname for Priscilla. See Acts 18:1-3.

SMALL MAN TO BIG MAN

TITUS

1

GREETINGS

¹From Small Man (Paul), a *sacred* servant of the Great Spirit and a message bearer for Creator Sets Free (Jesus) the Chosen One. *I have been sent to strengthen the* spiritual ways of Creator's chosen ones and their understanding of the truth that guides them on this sacred path. ²This way of trusting and understanding rest on the hope of the life of the world to come that never fades away, full of beauty and harmony. It was long ago, before the beginning of time, that the Great Spirit, who always speaks the truth, promised this life to us. ³So when the time was right, the Great Spirit, who is our Sacred Deliverer, trusted me with this message and told me to make it known *to all who will hear.*

⁴To Big Man (Titus), my true son in our spiritual ways.ᵃ I greet you with the gift of great kindness that comes from our Father the Great Spirit and from Creator Sets Free (Jesus) the Chosen One, our Sacred Deliverer.

CHOOSING SPIRITUAL LEADERS

⁵I left you behind at Flesh Eater Island (Crete) so you would finish setting things in order for the sacred family who gathers there and put in place the elders *who will be the spiritual leaders* in all the villages, just as I have instructed you.

⁶These spiritual leaders must be free from accusation, faithful in marriage,ᵇ and have children who are not wild and rebellious, but respectful followers of our spiritual ways. ⁷Because they represent the Great Spirit, the elders who watch over the sacred family must have a good reputation *with outsiders.* They must not be stubborn, hot-headed, heavy drinkers, violent, or greedy for possessions.

⁸Instead, they must be willing to open their homes to others, love what is good, and think clearly. With self-discipline, they must walk with a good heart in our sacred ways ⁹and stay true to the faithful message they have been taught. Then these elders will be able to encourage others by teaching the truth about our spiritual ways. Then they will be able to *stand up to and* prove wrong those who oppose them.

A WARNING ABOUT TROUBLEMAKERS

¹⁰There are many troublemakers with forked tongues and empty words. Most of them are from our own Tribal Members, flesh cutters *who require others to participate in the cutting of the flesh ceremony.* ¹¹These men must be silenced, for they are troubling whole families by teaching wrong things. They are behaving like tricksters using people for their own gain.

¹²One of their own prophets said, "People from Flesh Eater Island (Crete) always speak with forked tongues. They

---

ᵃ**1:4** Lit. *the faith*

ᵇ**1:6** Lit. *the husband of one wife*

are evil beasts who are lazy and eat too much." [13]I have found this to be true *of some of them*. So speak sharply to them, that they may learn to find health in our spiritual ways.[a] [14]Tell them not to listen to made-up stories from our Tribal Members or to instructions from those who are turning away from the truth.

[15]To the pure, all things are pure. But to those who are unclean because they do not believe the truth, nothing is pure, for both in their minds and deep within their hearts they have been made unclean. [16]They represent themselves as those who know the Great Spirit, but the path they walk proves they do not. They show themselves to be disgusting, rebellious, and worthless for any kind of good deed.

2

GUIDANCE FOR THE SACRED FAMILY

[1]But as for you, teach those things that lead to a healthy spiritual walk. [2]Expect the older men to be sober-minded, worthy of respect, and self-disciplined as they walk with firm steps on a path of trust and love. [3]In the same way, expect the elder women to walk a sacred path. They should not talk in a bad way about others or be heavy drinkers. They should be wisdomkeepers, [4]teaching young women to love their husbands and their children. [5]They should show the *young women* how to be self-disciplined, pure-minded, working at home, kind, and following the loving guidance of their husbands. In this way, they will not bring dishonor to the message of the Great Spirit.

[6]In the same manner, urge the young men to be self-disciplined in every way.

[7]*As for yourself,* be an example to them by the good deeds you do, and in the heartfelt and respectful ways you teach. [8]Speak with firm words and with an honesty that cannot be spoken against, so that those who oppose will be put to shame, with nothing bad to say about you.

[9]As for *those sacred family members who are* slaves, teach them to do all that their masters require in a good way, and not to argue [10]or steal from them. Instead, they should show that they can be fully trusted. In this way, they will properly show the beauty of the teaching of the Great Spirit, our Sacred Deliverer.

WALKING WITH WISDOM

[11]For the gift of Creator's great kindness that sets people free has shined its light on all human beings. [12]It instructs us to turn away from all that does not honor our Creator and from the desire to walk in the ways of this world. It instructs us to walk with straight and firm steps on a good and sacred path in this present world. [13]For we are looking and waiting for the blessing of the bright-shining appearance of the one who set us free and made us whole—our Great Spirit, Creator Sets Free (Jesus) the Chosen One. [14]He paid the highest price to set us free from all our wrongdoings and purify for himself a people whose hearts burn with fire to do good deeds.

[15]So speak out boldly about these things. Strengthen the hearts of the ones who are doing good and set straight the ones who are doing wrong. Let no one ignore you.

.

3

MORE GUIDANCE AND WISDOM

[1]Remind *the sacred family members* to give way to the powers and authorities

---

[a]**1:13** Lit. *the faith*

that rule the land. They must follow their laws and be ready to do any good deed. ²Make sure they do not speak evil of anyone. Instead, they should be peacemakers who are gentle and humble toward all people. ³For it was not that long ago that we were also foolish and misled rebels who let our evil desires rule over us. Some of us were even badhearted, jealous troublemakers, hated by others and hating each other.

⁴But then the kindness of the Great Spirit who sets us free and makes us whole appeared, along with his love *for all human beings.* ⁵He set us free *from our bad hearts and broken ways,* not because of any good thing we did to deserve this, but because in his love he took pity on us. He set us free by the washing that birthed us into a new life through the power of the Holy Spirit. ⁶*Creator* freely rained down his Spirit on us through Creator Sets Free (Jesus) the Chosen One, our Sacred Deliverer. ⁷We have been given good standing by his great kindness, so that we now can have our share in the hope of the life of the world to come that never fades away, full of beauty and harmony.

STAY AWAY FROM FOOLISH ARGUMENTS

⁸You can be sure that the things I have told you are true and good and helpful for everyone. I want you to speak boldly about these things, so that those who trust in Creator will give themselves to doing good things for others. ⁹But stay away from foolish arguments about ancestors, from things that cause division, and from conflicts about our tribal law. Arguments like these are worthless and will not help anyone. ¹⁰If anyone among you keeps stirring up division, warn him once, then a second time. After that have nothing more to do with him. ¹¹For you know that people like this are walking in broken and twisted ways that show how guilty they are.

FINAL WORDS

¹²After I send Free from Harm (Artemas) or He Is at Ease (Tychicus) to you, make it your aim to come to me at Village of Victory (Nicopolis). I have decided to stay there for the winter. ¹³Do all you can to give traveling help to Counsel Giver (Zenas), who is an expert in tribal law, and He Tears Down (Apollos), so they will have all they need. ¹⁴Our *sacred* family members must learn to give themselves to doing good for others when they are in need. In this way, they will not fail to bear good fruit in their lives.

¹⁵All who are with me send greetings to you. Pass on our greetings to all who share our deep friendship in our spiritual ways.^a

May the gift of Creator's great kindness rest on all of you.

Aho! May it be so!

---

^a**3:15** Lit. *the faith*

SMALL MAN TO HE SHOWS KINDNESS

PHILEMON

GREETINGS

¹From Small Man (Paul), a prisoner of Creator Sets Free (Jesus) the Chosen One, and from He Gives Honor (Timothy) our spiritual brother.

To He Shows Kindness (Philemon), our much-loved friend who works side by side with us *as we walk the good road.* ²And also to our *spiritual* sister Protected One (Apphia), to Horse Chief (Archippus) our fellow warrior, and to all the sacred family members who gather *for ceremony* at your house.

³I greet you with peace and the gift of great kindness that comes from our Father the Great Spirit and from our Honored Chief, Creator Sets Free (Jesus) the Chosen One.

SENDING UP PRAYERS

⁴When I send my voice to the Great Spirit, I always remember to thank him for you. ⁵For I keep hearing about the trust you have toward our Honored Chief Creator Sets Free (Jesus) and the love you have for all his holy ones. ⁶I pray that as you share with others the trust you have *in the Chosen One,* your understanding of all the good things we have in him will keep growing deeper and stronger. ⁷The love you have shown *toward others,* my *much-loved spiritual* brother, has encouraged me and made my heart glad and has refreshed the hearts of Creator's holy ones.

A PERSONAL REQUEST

⁸I have the freedom in the Chosen One to boldly order you to do the right thing, ⁹but instead, I am asking for your help out of love. I ask as Small Man (Paul), your elder, who is a prisoner because of Creator Sets Free (Jesus) the Chosen One.

¹⁰I call on you for the sake of He Is Helpful (Onesimus) my *spiritual* child, to whom I have become a *spiritual* father while in prison. ¹¹In the past he was not helpful to you, but he has now become helpful to both you and me. ¹²I am now sending him back to you, and with him I send my own heart. ¹³I would have liked to keep him here with me, so that while I am in prison for telling the good story he would take your place in serving me.

¹⁴But I do not want to do anything unless you agree to it. In this way, you will help me willingly and not because you think you must. ¹⁵It may be that he was away from you for a little while so he can remain with you from now on. ¹⁶*Treat him* not as a slave, but as more than your slave—*treat him* as a much-loved *spiritual* brother. If he is loved by me in this way, he should be loved all the more by you, both as a human being and as one who belongs to our Honored Chief.

¹⁷So if you think of me as a fellow traveler on the good road, then welcome him the same way you would welcome me. ¹⁸If he has done you any wrong or owes you anything, tell me how much is owed and I will make it right. ¹⁹I, Small

Man (Paul), write this with my own hand—I will pay what is owed. But must I remind you that you owe me your whole life as well? **20**Yes, I am asking you to do this for me as a brother in the family of our Honored Chief. Then you will make this old heart glad in the Chosen One.

FINAL WORDS

21I write this letter to you knowing you will do all I have asked and much more. **22**I also ask you to get a guest room ready for me, for my hope is that through your prayers I will be given back to you.

23Walks in Beauty (Epaphras), my fellow prisoner in Creator Sets Free (Jesus) the Chosen One, sends his greetings to you, **24**along with War Club (Mark), Good Chief (Aristarchus), Leader of the People (Demas), and Shining Light (Luke), who work side by side with me.

25May the gift of great kindness that comes from our Honored Chief, Creator Sets Free (Jesus) the Chosen One, be with your spirit.

Aho! May it be so!

TO THE PEOPLE OF THE TRIBES OF WRESTLES WITH CREATOR

HEBREWS

THE GREAT SPIRIT SPEAKS THROUGH HIS SON

1 Long ago, in many ways and at many times, the Great Spirit spoke to our tribal ancestors through the prophets. ²But now, in these last days, he has spoken to us through his Son—the one he has chosen to give all things to. It is through his Son that the Great Spirit made the world that is, the world that was, and the one that is coming.

³This Son is the light coming from the face of the Great Spirit in all its bright-shining beauty. What is true about the Great Spirit is true about the Son, for he represents Creator in every way. It is his powerful word that holds *the stars above, the earth below, and* all things *seen and unseen* in their place. He came into this world to purify the bad hearts and broken ways of all people. When he was finished, he *returned to the One Above Us All* to sit in the place of greatest honor at the right hand of the Great Mystery.

GREATER THAN SPIRIT-MESSENGERS

⁴The Son was lifted up to a higher place than all the spirit-messengers, for the name that he was given has much more beauty and honor than theirs.

⁵For did the Great Spirit ever say to a spirit-messenger, "You are my Son. Today I make it known that I am your Father"?ᵃ

Or again, "I will be a Father to him, and he will be a Son to me"?ᵇ

⁶And again, when the Great Spirit was about to bring his honored Sonᶜ into the world *above*, he said, "Let all of Creator's spirit-messengers honor and serve him."

⁷When speaking of his spirit-messengers the Sacred Teachings tell us, "He makes the winds his spirit-messengers, and flames of fire to be his servants."ᵈ

⁸But when speaking of the Son the Sacred Teachings tell us, "O Great Spirit, your seat of honor will last beyond the end of all days. Your chief's staff is your walking stick on the good road where you make wrongs right again. ⁹You love right ways and hate wrong ways. So the Great Spirit, your Creator, has chosen you to be a Chief, by pouring the oil of joy on you, honoring you more than all who walk the road with you."ᵉ

¹⁰Our Sacred Teachings have also said *of the Son*, "O Honored Chief, in the beginning

---

ᵃ**1:5** Psalm 2:7
ᵇ**1:5** 2 Samuel 7:14
ᶜ**1:6** Lit. *firstborn Son*. In the Jewish culture of that day, the firstborn son was honored as the head of the family.
ᵈ**1:7** Psalm 104:4
ᵉ**1:9** Psalm 45:6-7

it was you who formed the earth and sky. **11-12**They will fade away, but you will live on. They will become old, and you will roll them up like a worn-out blanket. You will take them off like old, ragged clothes. But you remain the same, and your years will never come to an end."[a]

13Has the Great Spirit said this to any spirit-messenger, "Sit down beside me at my right hand, my place of greatest honor, until I defeat your enemies and humble them before you"?[b]

14Are not all spirit-messengers spirits who have been sent out with the sacred task of serving those who will share in the blessings of being set free and made whole?

2 ⟨⟩⟨⟩⟨⟩⟨⟩⟨⟩⟨⟩⟨⟩⟨⟩⟨⟩

WALKING WITH FIRM STEPS
1This is the reason we, who are followers of the Chosen One, must walk with firm steps, holding true to what we have heard, so we will not wander away *from the good road.* **2**For if the message *of our tribal law,* spoken to us by spirit-messengers, has always stood firm, and every failure to walk in that law was given the punishment deserved, **3**how will we escape if we do not honor such a great and powerful way to be set free and made whole?

It was our Honored Chief Creator Sets Free (Jesus) himself who first spoke about this. Then those who heard him clearly passed on to us what they heard. **4**The Great Spirit also confirmed the truth of what they were saying with many signs, wonders, and works of power. He also gave them gifts of the Holy Spirit in harmony with his desire.

WHY CARE ABOUT HUMAN BEINGS?
5The Great Spirit did not put the world that is coming, which we will now speak about, under the guidance of spirit-messengers. **6**Instead, somewhere *in our Sacred Teachings* it has been said, "O Great Spirit, why do you think so much of humanity? Why do you watch over human beings so carefully? **7**For a short time you made them a little lower than the spirit-messengers. You placed a headdress of honor on their heads **8**and made them the caretakers over all things."[c]

When Creator gave human beings the sacred calling of being the caretakers over all things, he left nothing that was not under their care. But we still do not see all things under the care of humankind.

THE TRUE HUMAN BEING
9But we can see *that there is one human being who has taken on himself this sacred calling*—Creator Sets Free (Jesus). For a short time he was made a little lower than the spirit-messengers so that by the gift of Creator's great kindness, he might taste death for everyone. Because he did this, he has been highly honored with the headdress of a chief.

10The Great Spirit is the maker and upholder of all things. So it was only right that he would be the one to lift his children back up to the honored place for which he created them. The one who would blaze the trail before them had to suffer, so he would be fully prepared to set them free and make them whole. **11**Creator Sets Free (Jesus) is the one who makes people holy, and those he makes holy are all from one *Father.* For this reason he is not ashamed to call them his family.

---

[a]**1:11-12** Psalm 102:25-27
[b]**1:13** Psalm 110:1

[c]**2:8** Psalm 8:4-6

¹²For *Creator Sets Free (Jesus)* speaks to us *through our Sacred Teachings*, saying, "O Great Spirit, I will honor your name before my brothers *and sisters*. I will sing sacred songs to you when we gather as a sacred family."[a]

¹³He also says, "I will trust in the Great Spirit." And again he says, "Behold! Here I am standing side-by-side with the brothers and sisters *of the sacred family* Creator has given to me."[b]

¹⁴So then, since these brothers and sisters all share in what it means to be weak human beings, he also became a weak human being just like them. He did this so that by dying he would bring an end to the one who holds the power of death—the evil trickster. ¹⁵He *died to* set all people free who have lived their lives as slaves *to the evil trickster* because of their fear of death.

¹⁶It is clear that he did not come for spirit-messengers, but he came to set free the descendants of Father of Many Nations (Abraham). ¹⁷I am saying that Creator Sets Free (Jesus) needed to become fully and truly human. In this way, he could serve as Creator's honorable and merciful chief holy man and perform the ancient mercy-seat ceremony *one last time*[c] to heal the bad hearts and broken ways of the people. ¹⁸Since Creator Sets Free (Jesus) suffered temptation, he is able to help all who are being tempted.

The tribes of Wrestles with Creator (Israel) were given this mercy-seat ceremony to show that the Great Spirit had washed them clean from their bad hearts and broken ways. Once a year the chief holy man would take the blood of a ceremonial ani-

mal into the Most Holy Place in Creator's sacred lodge and sprinkle the blood onto the lid of a wooden box covered with gold. The lid of this wooden box was called the mercy seat.

3 ⟨◆⟩◀◆▶◀◆▶◀◆▶◀◆▶◀◆▶◀◆▶

A NEW AND GREATER CHIEF HOLY MAN

¹So then, my sacred family members, you who share in Creator's high calling, take a good look at Creator Sets Free (Jesus). He is the *great* message bearer and chief holy man of our spiritual ways. ²He stayed true to the purpose for which he was chosen, just as Drawn from the Water (Moses) stayed true to serving the people of Creator's lodge.

³But Creator Sets Free (Jesus) has been given greater honor than Drawn from the Water (Moses), just as the maker of a lodge is given more honor than the lodge itself. ⁴Now every lodge has a builder, but the builder and maker of all things is the Great Spirit.

⁵Drawn from the Water (Moses), as Creator's family servant, stayed true to Creator's family. He was a truth teller who prophesied about what would be said in the last days.[d] ⁶But the Chosen One is Creator's own Son, the headman who stayed true to *the people of* Creator's lodge, and we are his people if we keep holding firmly and honorably to our hope in him.

CREATOR'S PLACE OF REST

⁷So then, we should do what the Holy Spirit, through our Sacred Teachings, tells us.

He says, "Today, when you hear his voice ⁸⁻⁹do not harden your hearts as your ancestors did when they turned away

[a]**2:12** Psalm 22:22
[b]**2:13** Isaiah 8:17-18
[c]**2:17** Exodus 25:17-20
[d]**3:5** Hebrews 1:1-2

from me and put me to the test in the desert wilderness. It was there that they tested my patience and saw the powerful things I did for forty winters. [10]I became angry with them and said, 'You are a people with wandering hearts who have not learned my ways.' [11]Then in my great anger, I made a solemn promise that they would not enter my *place of rest.*"[a]

[12]So then, my sacred family members, make sure none of you have wandering hearts that fail to trust, hearts that turn you away from our living Creator. [13]Speak courage to each other every day, as long as it is still called "today," so that no one's heart will grow hard and be led astray by broken ways. [14]As long as we keep walking this road with firm steps from beginning to end, we will share in all the blessings of the Chosen One.

[15]The Sacred Teachings tell us, "Today, when you hear his voice, do not harden your hearts as your ancestors did when they turned away from me and put me to the test."

[16]Who were these people who heard Creator's voice and turned away from him? Was it not all of those who followed Drawn from the Water (Moses) out from Black Land (Egypt)? [17]And who was it who angered the Great Spirit for forty winters? Was it not the ones who followed their bad hearts and broken ways, whose dead bodies lay scattered across the desert? [18]And to whom did Creator make the solemn promise that they would not enter into his rest? It was to the ones who did not trust him and do what he said.

[19]So we can see that our tribal ancestors did not enter *into Creator's place of rest* because they failed to trust him.

4

THE PROMISE OF REST REMAINS OPEN

[1]So then, *my sacred family members,* since the promise of entering into Creator's place of rest still remains open, we must take care that none of you would fail to enter into this promised rest. [2]For this good message has been told to us, just as it was told to our tribal ancestors. But the message they heard did them no good, because they failed to put their trust in the one who gave them the promise.

[3]So then, we are the ones who will enter into this promised rest, but only if we keep trusting in the Great Spirit. For he said, "In my great anger, I made a solemn promise that they would not enter my *place of rest.*"[b] He said this, even though his work was finished from the time the world was formed. [4]As for the seventh day, it has been said in the Sacred Teachings, "The Great Spirit rested on the seventh day from all his work." [5]And again as he already said, "They will never enter into my rest."

[6]This shows us that there are still some who will enter his rest. Since those who first heard this good message did not enter because they failed to trust, [7]*many winters later* Creator chooses another day and calls it "today," as he speaks through the mouth of Much Loved One (David) and says again, "Today, when you hear his voice, do not harden your hearts." [8]If Creator Gives Freedom (Joshua) had led our ancestors into their place of rest, then Creator would not have spoken through *Chief* Much Loved One (David) of another day of rest for his people.

[9]There now remains a *sacred* rest, a *true and spiritual* Day of Resting, for the

---

[a]3:11 Psalm 95:7-11

[b]4:3 Psalm 95:11, also in verse 5

people of the Great Spirit. ¹⁰For just as Creator rested from his work *after creating the world,* the ones who enter into Creator's promised rest have also rested from their work. ¹¹So then, let us pour all of our strength into entering Creator's rest. In this way, no one will stumble away from the path of trusting, like our ancestors did.

CREATOR'S LIVING WORD

¹²For the Word of the Great Spirit is alive, powerful, and sharper than any two-edged long knife. His Word cuts deep into the inner being, separating soul from spirit and joints from marrow. His Word uncovers the true nature of the human heart, its thoughts and intentions. ¹³Not one thing in all creation is hidden from his sight. All things are stripped bare before the eyes of the one to whom we must give an answer *for how we have walked on this earth.*

A NEW CHIEF HOLY MAN

¹⁴Seeing that we are served by such a great chief holy man who has walked the road of the spirit-world above, Creator Sets Free (Jesus), the Son of the Great Spirit, let us walk true to this way of life in which we have put our trust. ¹⁵For we do not have a chief holy man who is unable to feel the same kind of pain and sorrow we feel. Even though he faced the same temptations we face, he never gave in to them or did anything wrong. ¹⁶So with brave hearts let us come before Creator's seat of honor to receive mercy and the gift of his great kindness to help us in our time of need.

HOW A CHIEF HOLY MAN IS CHOSEN

¹*Among the tribes of Wrestles with Creator* (Israel) every chief holy man is chosen from among the men of his tribe. He is given the sacred task of representing the people to the Great Spirit by offering ceremonial gifts and sacrifices for the people's bad hearts and broken ways. ²Since the chief holy man is also a weak human being, he can take pity on those whose understanding is weak and have lost their way. ³And because he is a weak human being, he must *first* offer sacrifices for his own broken ways and then for the broken ways of the people. ⁴No one chooses this honor for himself. It is the Great Spirit who chooses a chief holy man, just as he chose *the first chief holy man* Light Bearer (Aaron).

CHOSEN TO BE A HOLY MAN

⁵In the same way, the Chosen One did not take for himself the honor of being the chief holy man. It was the Great Spirit who chose him by saying to him, "You are my Son. Today I make it known that I am your Father."ᵃ ⁶And in another place Creator says *to him,* "You are a holy man whose days will never end. The same kind of holy man as Chief Who Stands for What Is Right (Melchizedek)."ᵇ

⁷In the days when Creator Sets Free (Jesus) walked among us as a human being, he sent his voice to the Great Spirit with tears and loud cries to the only one who could rescue him from death. His prayers were heard because of the honor and respect he showed *to the One Above Us All.* ⁸Even though he was *Creator's* Son, he still had to learn, through suffering, what it means to stay true to the ways of the Great Spirit. ⁹When he was fully prepared, he became the one through whom all people who listen and do what he says will be set

---

ᵃ**5:5** Psalm 2:7
ᵇ**5:6** Psalm 110:4

free and made whole, to the time beyond the end of all days. [10]This is because the Great Spirit chose him to be a chief holy man just like Chief Who Stands for What Is Right (Melchizedek).

SPIRITUAL MILK OR SOLID FOOD

[11]I have much more I would like to say about this, but it is hard to make the meaning clear because your ears have become slow to hear. [12]By now you should be able to teach others, but instead you need someone to teach you the simple spiritual truths of Creator's message all over again. You are like children who need milk and are not ready for solid food. [13]For all those who drink only milk are still like nursing babies who have not yet learned how to walk in right ways. [14]But solid food is for those who are mature. For the ones who have walked the road many times have learned the difference between what is right and what is wrong.

6 ◀▶◀▶◀▶◀▶◀▶◀▶◀▶◀▶◀▶

WALKING TOWARD MATURITY

[1]It is time for us to move beyond the beginning spiritual truths of the teachings *that prepared the way* of the Chosen One and start to see things through more mature eyes. There is no need to go back to the beginning of the trail to learn things all over again. *You have already been taught* to turn away from meaningless efforts to please the Great Spirit and to *simply* trust him. [2]*You have been given* instructions about different kinds of ceremonies for purification and for laying on of hands. *You have also been taught* about the rising of the dead and the final judgment. [3]So then, as the Great

Spirit permits, we will now walk forward toward more mature teachings.

WALKING AWAY FROM THE GOOD PATH

[4]For there are some who once walked in the light. They tasted the gift that comes from the spirit-world above. They shared together with us in the Holy Spirit. [5]They tasted Creator's good word and the powers of the world to come. [6]If people like this walk away from the path, it is not possible to bring them back. For to their own harm they are nailing the Son of the Great Spirit to the cross again and shaming him before others.

[7]The ground that drinks the rain that often falls on it and grows many plants that are useful for those who work the ground shares in the blessings of the Great Spirit. [8]But if the ground grows only thorns and thistles, it has failed in its purpose, and will soon be seen as cursed and its crops burned.

BETTER THINGS FOR YOU

[9]My much-loved relatives, even though we are speaking in this way, we are sure of much better things about you, the things that come from being set free and made whole. [10]The Great Spirit will not fail to do what is right. He will not forget how hard you have worked and how much love you have shown in representing him. He sees how you have served his holy ones, in the past and even now.

[11]It is our desire that you walk with firm steps, keeping your eyes straight, as you travel this sure path of hope to its end. [12]Do not limp along, dragging your feet, but follow firmly in the footsteps of those who through trust and patience share in the promises.

[13]When the Great Spirit made his promise to Father of Many Nations

(Abraham), it was a solemn promise. And since there was no one greater to hold him to his promise, he held himself to it. **14**He said, "I give you my word of honor that I will greatly bless you and give you many descendants."[a] **15**So by staying true to the path and never giving up, Father of Many Nations (Abraham) received what had been promised.

A SOLEMN PROMISE FROM THE GREAT SPIRIT

16When people give their word of honor and make a solemn promise, they make it before someone who is greater than themselves. This kind of promise brings an end to all disagreements. **17**The Great Spirit wanted to prove to his people that his promise would remain true and never change, so he made this kind of solemn promise. **18**The Great Spirit cannot speak with a forked tongue! So his word of honor and his solemn promise are two things that can never be changed. This gives us, the ones who have taken shelter under his wings, brave hearts to take a firm hold on the hope he has set before us.

19This hope is like a tent-stake, holding our lives firmly and safely in place. This hope goes behind the blanket that hangs in the sacred lodge and reaches into the Most Holy Place in the spirit-world above.

Creator's sacred lodge on earth had a blanket that separated the Holy Place from the Most Holy Place. This earthly lodge was a symbol of the true sacred lodge in the spirit-world above spoken of here.

20Creator Sets Free (Jesus) is the one who was first to enter into this Most Holy Place in the spirit-world above to open the way for us to follow. For he has been made chief holy man whose days will never end, the same kind of holy man as Chief Who Stands for What Is Right (Melchizedek).

7

A DIFFERENT KIND OF HOLY MAN

1Chief Who Stands for What Is Right (Melchizedek) was both the chief of a village named Peace (Salem) and a holy man of Creator Most High. When Father of Many Nations (Abraham) was returning from the battle where he defeated many warring chiefs, Chief Who Stands for What Is Right (Melchizedek) met with him and blessed him.[b] **2**Then Father of Many Nations (Abraham) gave him a tenth of all the spoils of war. The meaning of the name of Chief Who Stands for What Is Right (Melchizedek) comes first from his being a chief who stands for what is right, and then also from being chief of Salem, which means chief of peace. **3**There is no record of his father or mother or a family ancestry of any kind. No one knows when his life began or when it ended. In this way, he is like the Son of the Great Spirit, whose place as a holy man continues without end.

4Can you see how great this man was? Our ancestor, Father of Many Nations (Abraham), gave him a tenth of the best of the spoils of war! **5**Our tribal law instructs the descendants of He Brings Together (Levi), who are the holy men of our tribes, to receive a tenth from their own tribal family—even though our tribal family is also descended from Father of Many Nations (Abraham).

6But this man, Chief Who Stands for What Is Right (Melchizedek), received a

---

a6:14 Genesis 22:17

b7:1 Genesis 14:17-20

tenth from Father of Many Nations (Abraham), even though he is not descended from He Brings Together (Levi), and he blessed the one to whom the Great Spirit gave the promises. [7]Everyone knows that the one with the power to bless is greater than the one to whom the blessing is given.

[8]*There is another way to see what I am saying.* Our tribes pay a tenth to holy men who die, but here a tenth is paid to a holy man who, we are told, continues to live. [9]It could be said that He Brings Together (Levi), the ancestor of the tribe of holy men who receive a tenth, also paid a tenth through Father of Many Nations (Abraham), [10]because he was still in the body of his ancestor when Chief Who Stands for What Is Right (Melchizedek) met Father of Many Nations (Abraham).

A NEW KIND OF HOLY MAN
AND A NEW LAW

[11]So then, if Creator's full purpose was to come through the holy men who are descended from He Brings Together (Levi), for our tribal law was given in harmony with these holy men, why would there be a need for another holy man to appear, one like Chief Who Stands for What Is Right (Melchizedek), instead of one who is descended from Light Bearer (Aaron)? [12]For if the way to become a holy man has changed, then it means our tribal law must also change.

[13]Now *Creator Sets Free (Jesus)*, the one spoken of here, is not from the tribe that holy men come from. He is from another tribe, and no one from that tribe has ever served at the *ceremonial* altar. [14]We all know that our Honored Chief *Creator Sets Free (Jesus)* is descended from Give Him Praise (Judah), and Drawn from the Water (Moses) never said anything about holy men coming from that tribe.

[15]So if another holy man appears, one who is like Chief Who Stands for What Is Right (Melchizedek), it becomes even more clear [16]that it is the power of a life that can never end that makes him a holy man, not a law about physical ancestry. [17]For it says in our Sacred Teachings, "You are a holy man whose days will never end, the same kind of holy man as Chief Who Stands for What Is Right (Melchizedek)."

[18]Because it was weak and useless, the former instruction had to be done away with. [19]For our tribal law could not bring anyone or anything to full meaning and purpose. But the Chosen One has brought to us an even greater hope, and it is this hope that moves us to draw near to the Great Spirit.

[20-21]Under our tribal law no one was ever made a holy man by a solemn promise. But it was by a solemn promise that the Chosen One was made a holy man, when it was said to him, "The Great Spirit has made a solemn promise and will never change his mind, 'You are a holy man whose days will never end.'"[a] [22]In this way, Creator Sets Free (Jesus) has become the promise keeper of a better peace treaty.

A CHIEF HOLY MAN WHO WILL NEVER DIE

[23]The holy men who came before were many in number, because death kept them from continuing. [24]But since Creator Sets Free (Jesus) will never die, his place as a holy man will never come to an end. [25]This means he is able to fully set free and make whole all who draw near to the Great Spirit through him, since he always lives to pray and represent them in a good way.

---

[a]7:17, 20-21 Psalm 110:4

26This kind of chief holy man is just what we weak human beings need. One who remains holy, blameless and pure. One who differs from weak human beings because he has a good heart with no broken ways. One who has been lifted up to the highest place in the spirit-world above. 27He has no need to make offerings every day like other chief holy men. They make offerings first for their own broken ways, and then for the broken ways of the people. But when Creator Sets Free (Jesus) offered himself *on the cross*, he performed a ceremony—once for all time—to set people free from their bad hearts and broken ways.

28So *you can see that* our tribal law chooses weak human beings *with broken ways* to be chief holy men. But it was a solemn promise, given many winters after our tribal law, that chose the Son *of the Great Spirit*. His suffering has fully prepared him to be a chief holy man whose days will never end.

8 ◆▷◁◆▷◁◆▷◁◆▷◁◆▷◁

THE NEW CHIEF HOLY MAN

1The heart of what I am saying is that we now have this kind of chief holy man, one who has taken his place in the spirit-world above at the right hand of the seat of honor held by the Great Honored One. 2He serves as a holy man in the true sacred tent, the one pitched by our Honored Chief and not by human beings.

3Every chief holy man is chosen to offer ceremonial gifts and sacrifices, so our chief holy man must also have something to offer. 4*Remember*, if he were on earth, he would not be a holy man, seeing that there are holy men *on earth* who offer gifts required by our tribal law. 5But

these holy men serve in a sacred tent that is only a dim shadow of the one in the spirit-world above. For Drawn from the Water (Moses) was given this counsel by the Great Spirit just before he completed making the sacred tent, "Make sure that everything you make follows the pattern that was shown to you on the mountain."a

A NEW AND BETTER PEACE TREATY

6So you can see that the Chosen One has been given a more honorable place as chief holy man than all the others. In the same way, the peace treaty he made for us with the Great Spirit is better than the first one, for it depends on better promises. 7For if there had been nothing wrong with the first peace treaty, then there would have been no need to look for a second one.

8But finding something wrong, the Great Spirit said to his people, "Behold! The time is coming when I will make a new peace treaty with the *northern* tribes of Wrestles with Creator (Israel) and the *southern* tribes of Give Him Praise (Judah). 9This peace treaty will not be like the one I made with their ancestors when I took them by the hand to walk them out of Black Land (Egypt). They did not honor that peace treaty, so I let them go their own way.

10"But here is the *new* peace treaty I will make with the tribes of Wrestles with Creator (Israel) after that time. I will plant my laws in their minds and carve them into their hearts. I will be their Great Spirit, and they will be my people, *my sacred family*. 11There will be no need to teach others to know their Honored Chief, for all, whether small or great, will know me. 12I will take pity on

---

a**8:5** Exodus 25:40

wrongdoers, and their broken ways I will remember no more."[a]

13When Creator tells of a new peace treaty, this means he has done away with the first one—for it is old, worn out, and ready to fade away.

CEREMONIES AND THE FIRST PEACE TREATY

1Under the first peace treaty, there were instructions for ceremonies and a sacred lodge tent that is of this world. 2The first room in the sacred lodge tent was called the Holy Place. In that room, there was a lampstand and a table for the sacred bread *and other ceremonial items.*

3A blanket was hung between the Holy Place and the next room, which was called the Most Holy Place. 4In this room, there was a sacred altar for the burning of sweet-smelling herbs and spices, and a cedar box[b] of the peace treaty that was covered with gold on all sides.

Inside the cedar box was a golden pot filled with the mysterious bread,[c] the walking stick of Light Bearer (Aaron) that blossomed, and the stone tablets of the peace treaty. 5Above the cedar box were the bright-shining winged ones whose wings overshadowed the mercy seat. But we cannot speak at length about these things at this time.

6When all these things had been made ready in a good way, the holy men would go into the outer room of the sacred lodge tent over and over again to perform the sacred ceremonies. 7But only the chief holy man could enter into the second room, the Most Holy Place, and then only once a year. He must also take blood from a sacrificed animal in with him to offer first for himself and then for the wrongs the people did not mean to do.

A NEW WAY IS REVEALED

8By all these things the Holy Spirit is showing us that the way into the Most Holy Place *in the spirit-world above* was not yet open as long as the first sacred lodge tent *in this world* was still standing. 9This has spiritual meaning for the time we live in. It shows us that the gifts and offerings *made in the sacred lodge tent that now stands* cannot truly set free the heart and mind of the one who brings the offerings. 10These things are only concerned with food and drink and different kinds of ceremonial washings— rules about outward things. *They were needed* until it was time for a new way *to be revealed.*

11But now the Chosen One has appeared as the chief holy man of the good things that have now come. He entered into the true and greater sacred tent lodge, the one not made with human hands, meaning not of this creation. He entered into the Most Holy Place once for all time and for all people. 12He did not go in with the blood of goats and calves but with his own lifeblood. In doing so, he paid the highest price to set us free and make us whole for all time.

A ONCE-FOR-ALL-TIME CEREMONY

13If the blood of goats and young bulls and the ashes of a young cow sprinkled on those who are ceremonially unclean can purify our bodies, 14then how much

---

[a]8:12 Jeremiah 31:34
[b]9:4 The ark or box was made of acacia wood. We use *cedar* here because many Native Americans use a cedar box to hold ceremonial items.
[c]9:4 Lit. *manna,* meaning "what is it?" A mysterious food. See Exodus 16:33; John 6:32-33, 48-51.

more will the lifeblood of the Chosen One accomplish? Through the eternal Spirit he offered his life to the Great Spirit to purify our hearts and minds from the meaningless things we have done to try to please the Great Spirit. Now we can serve the living Creator *with the life that comes from him!*

15This is why it must be the Chosen One who makes a new peace treaty *between human beings and the Great Spirit.* His death was the price he paid to release people from their failure to walk true to the first peace treaty. This new peace treaty was needed so that those who answer his call will share in all the promised blessings that will never fade away.

DEATH AND THE NEW PEACE TREATY

16-17This kind of peace treaty[a] does not begin while the one who made it remains alive. It begins after the death of the one who made it. 18This is why even the first peace treaty required blood to be shed. 19Drawn from the Water (Moses) told the people all that our tribal law required them to do. Then he used red wool and a hyssop[b] branch to sprinkle the book of the law and the people with water and the blood of bulls and goats.

20He said to our people, "This is the blood of the peace treaty the Great Spirit has made with you. You must do all that it says."[c]

21In the same way, he sprinkled the sacred lodge tent and all the ceremonial objects with blood. 22So then, according to our tribal law, almost all things need to be washed clean with blood, and

---

[a]**9:16-17** Similar to a last will and testament
[b]**9:19** An herbal plant with long stems. Used ceremonially to sprinkle the blood of a sacrifice. See Psalm 51:7.
[c]**9:20** Exodus 24:8

unless lifeblood has been poured out in death there is no being set free *from broken ways.* 23If the earthly copies of what is in the spirit-world above needed purification in this way, then better offerings are needed to purify the things in the spirit-world above.

HE REPRESENTS US

24For the Chosen One did not go into a Holy Place made with human hands—an *earthly* copy of the true Holy Place. He went into the spirit-world above, where he now represents us before the Great Spirit. 25He did not go in to offer himself again and again like the chief holy man who every year goes into the *earthly* Holy Place with lifeblood that is not his own. 26For then, from the time when the world was formed, he would have had to suffer over and over again. But now, at the fullness of the ages, he appeared to bring an end to broken ways by performing the once-for-all-time ceremony when he offered himself.

27Human beings die once, and then they must stand before the one who decides what they have done right and what they have done wrong. 28So the Chosen One also died once when he took on himself the bad hearts and broken ways of many people. He will appear a second time, not to die for broken ways but to set free and make whole all who keep their eyes wide open as they wait for him.

10

A DIM SHADOW

1Our tribal law is only a dim shadow of the good things to come, not the things themselves. The ceremonial sacrifices and offerings required by our law are repeated over and over again year after year. These ceremonies cannot fully set free and make whole those who draw near to the Great Spirit. ²If they could, would they not have stopped offering them? For once the ceremonies had been performed, the people would be purified in their hearts and minds, and no longer feel the guilt of their broken ways.

³But these yearly ceremonies keep reminding the people that their bad hearts and broken ways have not been fully purified. ⁴For it is not possible for the blood of bulls and goats to take away bad hearts and broken ways.

NO MORE SACRIFICES

⁵So then, when the Chosen One came into this world, he said, "*O Great Spirit, sacrifice and offering is not what you want, but you have given me a human body to bring an end to these sacrifices once and for all.* ⁶Burnt animal sacrifices and other offerings for broken ways do not make your heart glad." ⁷Then *the Chosen One* said, "In the Sacred Book, it has been written about me. 'Behold! I have come to do what you want done, O Great Spirit.'"

⁸First, the Chosen One said that "the Great Spirit does not want sacrifices and offerings, nor is he pleased with them," even though they are required by our tribal law. ⁹Then he said, "Behold, I have come to do what you, the Great Spirit, wants done." *This means that* he has taken away the first peace treaty *with its law of sacrifices and offerings* to put in its place the second. ¹⁰The Chosen One did what Creator wanted when he made us holy by offering his body once for all time.

¹¹*Under our tribal law* holy men keep performing the same ceremonies day after day and making the same sacrifices over and over again. Those sacrifices can never take away bad hearts and broken ways.

¹²But the Chosen One, after performing the once-for-all-time ceremony to heal our broken ways, sat down at Creator's right hand—the place of greatest honor. ¹³He now *rules from there and waits until all his enemies have been defeated and humbled.*[a] ¹⁴For by this one offering he has for all time completely set free the ones he is making holy.

¹⁵The Holy Spirit tells us the same truth. First, he says, ¹⁶"'This is the peace treaty I will make with them in the coming days,' says the Great Spirit Chief. 'I will carve my laws on their hearts and plant them into their minds.'"[b]

¹⁷Then he says, "And their broken ways and wrongdoings I will remember no more."[c]

¹⁸Now when broken ways and wrongdoings have been forgiven like this, there is no longer any need for further offerings.

A NEW AND LIVING WAY

¹⁹So then, my sacred family members, since Creator Sets Free (Jesus) has offered his own lifeblood in this way, this gives us the courage to walk boldly into the Most Holy Place. ²⁰He has made a new and living way for us to pass through the blanket—that is, his human body—*to go into the Most Holy Place.*

²¹Since we have such a great chief holy man, who is headman of Creator's family lodge, ²²let us draw near with honest hearts, trusting fully *in what the Chosen One has done.* For our hearts

---

[a] **10:13** Psalm 110:1
[b] **10:16** Jeremiah 31:33
[c] **10:17** Jeremiah 31:34

have been washed clean from guilt and shame and our bodies washed with pure water. 23Let us get a firm and steady hold on this hope we say is ours, for the one who made the promise to us can be fully trusted.

24We should think about how to stir each other up toward love and doing good. 25To do this, we must never give up on gathering together, as some have. Instead, we should encourage each other, and all the more as you see the day of his appearing coming near.

26For if we keep stubbornly walking in broken ways after the truth has been made clear to us, then no further sacrifice can be made for our broken ways. 27All that remains is to wait for the fiery judgment that will burn up all who are hostile to Creator's right ways.

28Under the law given by Drawn from the Water (Moses), anyone who set aside that law was put to death without pity on the word of two or three witnesses. 29How much worse punishment do you think is deserved by the one who has trampled underfoot the Son of the Great Spirit, who treats the lifeblood of the peace treaty that makes us holy as having no value, and treats with disrespect the Spirit who gives us the gift of his great kindness?

30For we know Creator has said, "Punishment for wrongs belongs to me. I will make sure that wrongs are made right again."a And the Sacred Teachings have also said, "The Great Spirit Chief will decide for all his people who has done right and who has done wrong."b 31It is a fearful thing to come before the living Creator to give an answer for the wrongs we have done.

KEEP WALKING FORWARD

32Remember those early days when you first started walking in the light *of the good story.* You kept walking the road even when the way forward was a struggle filled with *pain and* suffering. 33At times the path was hard to walk, as you faced open shame and insults. At other times you walked side by side with those who were being mistreated. 34You shared in the pain of those who were in prison. When your own possessions were stolen, you accepted it with glad hearts, knowing that you have been given better possessions that will never fade away.

35So keep your hearts from falling to the ground. Hold your heads high. For a great honor awaits you at the end of the trail. 36All you need is to keep walking with firm steps, doing what Creator wants. He will make sure you receive all that he has promised.

37For *the Sacred Teachings tell us,* "It will not be long until the Coming One arrives. He will be here soon! 38Until then the ones who are in good standing with Creator will walk the road of life by trusting in him. But he will not be pleased with any who turn back."c

39We are not the ones who turn back and lose their way, but we are the ones whose whole beings are kept safe and made whole by trusting in him.

11

BRAVE ONES WHO TRUSTED CREATOR

1Trusting Creator is the solid ground our hope rests on. It means we can be sure of the things we do not yet see. 2For it was this kind of trusting that brought honor

---

a**10:30** Deuteronomy 32:35
b**10:30** Deuteronomy 32:36

c**10:38** Habakkuk 2:3-4

to our tribal ancestors. ³By trusting, we understand that the Great Spirit, by his voice, created all that we can see. By trusting we understand that the things we see were brought into being by that which we cannot see.

⁴Because he trusted Creator, His Breath Goes Up (Abel) offered a ceremonial gift that was more acceptable to the Great Spirit than the offering of Spear Maker (Cain).ᵃ Because he trusted, Creator was pleased with his gift, which gave him the reputation of being in good standing. So because he trusted, his voice still speaks to us today, even though he died long ago.

⁵Because he trusted *the Great Spirit*, Walks with Creator (Enoch) did not die. No one could find him because Creator took him.ᵇ Before he was taken, he had the reputation of one who makes Creator's heart glad. ⁶For no one can make Creator's heart glad without trusting him. So then, those who draw near to the Great Spirit must believe that he is and that he honors all who truly seek him.

⁷Because he trusted *the One Above Us All*, One Who Rests (Noah) took to heart the warning given to him by the Great Spirit and made a great wooden canoe for the safety of his family. By trusting he showed the world how terrible their ways had become. By trusting he took his place among those who, by trusting, share in the blessing of good standing with Creator.

⁸Because he trusted *the Great Mystery*, Father of Many Nations (Abraham) left his homeland to go to another land that was promised to him and his descendants. He followed the voice of the Great Spirit even though he was going to a land he had never been before. ⁹By trusting *in*

this way, he lived in the Land of Promise as a stranger in a strange land. Father of Many Nations (Abraham) settled his family in tents, along with his sons, He Made Us Laugh (Isaac) and Heel Grabber (Jacob), who would share with him in the same promise. ¹⁰*There he waited*, for he was looking for a village that would remain—one built on solid ground. A village whose maker and builder is the Great Spirit.

¹¹Because he trusted *the Maker of Life*, Father of Many Nations (Abraham) was able to father a child, even though his wife Noble Woman (Sarah) was barren and they were both too old. For they were sure the Great Spirit could be trusted to keep the promise he made to them. ¹²So from this one man, his body as good as dead, many descendants were born, as many as the stars in the sky and as countless as the sand on the seashore.

LONGING FOR A BETTER LAND

¹³Every one of these people died still trusting *in Creator*. Even though they did not receive all that had been promised, they took the promises to heart and welcomed them from afar. They said of themselves, "We are strangers and wanderers on the land." ¹⁴People who say things like this make it clear that they are looking for a land of their own. ¹⁵If they had been longing for the land from which they had come, they could have returned. ¹⁶But they are longing for a better land—one from the spirit-world above. That is why Creator is not ashamed to be called their Great Spirit and has prepared for them a village to live in.

MORE EXAMPLES OF TRUSTING

¹⁷⁻¹⁸Because he trusted *the Giver of Breath*, Father of Many Nations (Abraham), when he was tested by the Great Spirit, offered

ᵃ**11:4** Genesis 4:4-5
ᵇ**11:5** Genesis 5:21-24

up He Made Us Laugh (Isaac) as a ceremonial sacrifice. For Creator had promised him, "It is through He Made Us Laugh (Isaac) that your descendants will be born." But there he was, ready to offer up his only son! **19**For he was sure that Creator had the power to raise him up, even from the dead. So in a spiritual way of thinking, he did receive He Made Us Laugh (Isaac) back from the dead.

20Because he trusted *the Most Holy One*, He Made Us Laugh (Isaac), when he spoke the family blessing over Heel Grabber (Jacob) and his brother Hairy Man (Esau), told them about things to come.

21Because he trusted *the Great Spirit*, Heel Grabber (Jacob), at the end of his days, blessed each of the sons of Creator Gives More (Joseph) as he leaned on his walking stick and humbled himself before Creator.

22Because he trusted *the One Above Us All*, Creator Gives More (Joseph), at the end of his days, spoke of the time when the children of the tribes of Wrestles with Creator (Israel) would go out from Black Land (Egypt), and he gave instructions about *where to bury* his bones.

23Because his parents trusted *the Great Mystery*, they hid Drawn from the Water (Moses) for three moons. They saw Creator's beauty in the child and did not fear the instructions of the ruler of Black Land (Egypt).

24Because he trusted *the Maker of Life*, Drawn from the Water (Moses), as a full-grown man, refused to be called the son of the daughter of Great House (Pharaoh), *the ruler of Black Land (Egypt)*. **25**He chose to suffer with Creator's people, rather than finding joy in the *passing* pleasures of the broken ways of Black Land (Egypt). **26**He knew that the honor he would receive by suffering with the Chosen One was greater than all the treasures of Black Land (Egypt), because he kept his eyes on the honor that was to be his. **27**By trusting he left Black Land (Egypt) without fear of its ruler. He kept walking forward, keeping his eyes on the one who cannot be seen.

28Because he trusted *the Giver of Breath*, Drawn from the Water (Moses) participated in the *first* Passover while he was still in Black Land (Egypt) when the blood of a lamb was sprinkled on the doorposts. This is how the firstborn sons of the tribes of Wrestles with Creator (Israel) were not killed by the spirit-messenger of death.[a] **29**By trusting *Creator*, the people walked through the Red Sea as if they were on dry land. But when the soldiers of Black Land (Egypt) tried to cross, they were swallowed up by the sea.[b]

30Because the people trusted *the Great Spirit*, they walked around Moon Village (Jericho) for seven days, and the walls fell to the ground. **31**Boastful Woman (Rahab), *who lived in Moon Village (Jericho)*, made her living by trading her body for possessions. But because she trusted and welcomed the spies with peace, she did not die with the ones who refused to obey Creator.

SO MANY BRAVE ONES TO HONOR

32If I had more time, I would tell you about He Tears Down (Gideon), Lightning Flashing Across the Sky (Barak), Strength of the Sun (Samson), and He Breaks Out (Jephthah). I would also tell the stories of Chief Much Loved One (David), of Creator Hears Him (Samuel), and the prophets. **33**Because men such as these trusted *the Great Spirit*, they won the victory over nations, made wrongs right again, took hold of promises, and closed the mouths of

[a] **11:28** Exodus 12:21-30
[b] **11:29** Exodus 14:21-31

mountain lions. **34**They defeated the power of fire and escaped the long knives of *their enemies*. The weak were made strong and became great warriors who drove their enemies away. **35**Women received their loved ones back from the dead.

Others were tortured, refusing to be set free, knowing they would be honored when the dead are raised. **36**Some were insulted and mocked, whipped with leather straps, or chained and thrown into prison. **37**Some were killed with rocks. Others were cut in two. Others faced temptation. And some were cut down by long knives. They wandered about in sheepskins and goatskins, hunted down, mistreated, and in need of many things. **38**They roamed aimlessly through deserts and mountains, living in caves and holes in the ground. The world is not worthy of people like this.

CREATOR PROVIDED SOMETHING BETTER

39Even though these *faithful ones* have been honored for showing what it means to trust Creator, they did not receive all that was promised. **40**But the Great Spirit has provided something better for us *who live in these last days*. So now those who came before us can finally see Creator's promise come to its full meaning and purpose. For without us they would not be complete *in the Chosen One*.

12

A GREAT CLOUD OF TRUTH TELLERS

1We are surrounded by a great cloud of truth tellers *who have shown us what it means to trust the Great Spirit*. So let us lay to the side everything that weighs us down and the broken ways that so easily wrap around *our legs to trip us*. And let us run as if we are in a long-distance race, setting a steady pace and heading toward the goal.

2This means we must keep our eyes on Creator Sets Free (Jesus), the trailblazer of our spiritual ways,[a] the one who was first to reach the end of the trail. The joy that lay before him gave him the strength to suffer on the cross and willingly bear its shame. He now sits at Creator's right hand in the place of greatest honor.

3If you will keep your thoughts on how much hostility Creator Sets Free (Jesus) endured from those with bad hearts and broken ways, it will keep you from growing weary and your hearts from falling to the ground. **4**For in your struggle against bad hearts and broken ways you have not yet had to face your own blood being shed.

THE DISCIPLINE OF THE GREAT SPIRIT

5Have you forgotten the wise counsel *in our Sacred Teachings* that speaks to you as mature sons *and daughters*? "Do not treat lightly the wise counsel of the Great Spirit Chief or let your heart fall to the ground when he shows you where you have gone wrong. **6**For he brings correction to the ones he loves and disciplines every child he takes into his family."[b] **7**So accept difficult times as the loving discipline of a parent, for Creator is treating you as one of his children. Are not all children disciplined by their fathers? **8**But if you never receive the discipline that all take part in, it means you are not truly his children and not part of the family.

9When our earthly fathers disciplined us, we respected them for it. So how much more should we accept and respect Creator's discipline, for he is our spiritual

---

[a]**12:2** Lit. *our faith*
[b]**12:6** Proverbs 3:11-12

Father and the one who gives us the life of beauty and harmony! [10]For a short time, our earthly fathers disciplined us as they saw best, but the Great Spirit disciplines us for our own good, so we can be holy like him.

[11]Now, all discipline at the time seems to create more sorrow than joy. But for those who have learned its worth, it grows into a life of peace and doing what is right. [12]So lift up your arms that hang down and begin using your weak knees. [13]Make the path you walk straight, so that those with weak knees may not stumble from the path but instead be healed.

WALK IN PEACE WITH EVERYONE

[14]Live in a sacred way by walking the road of peace with all people, for those who fail to walk in this way will not see our Honored Chief. [15]See to it that no one among you misses out on the gift of Creator's great kindness and that no bitter root springs up among you, making trouble and poisoning many hearts. [16]See that no one becomes an impure or unspiritual person like Hairy Man (Esau), who for a single meal traded away his family birthright. [17]For you know that later on, he wanted it back. But even though he begged his father with many tears, it was too late to undo what he had done.

LEARN FROM THE ANCESTORS

[18]For you have not come, *as your ancestors did*, to something that can be touched—a mountain blazing with fire and smoke, with clouds of darkness and gloom, and a windstorm.

> *This happened long ago when Drawn from the Water (Moses) was given the tribal law on Mountain of Small Trees (Sinai).*[a]

[19]There the eagle bone whistle[b] was sounded. A voice spoke *out from the mountain*, but the people begged the voice to stop and not speak to them again. [20]For the instruction, "Even if an animal touches the mountain, it must be put to death with stones,"[c] was too much for them to bear. [21]The vision set before their eyes was so fearful that Drawn from the Water (Moses) cried out, "I am trembling with fear!"

A NEW PEACE TREATY

[22]*But you, my much-loved relatives, have not come to a mountain like this.* Instead, you have come to Strong Mountain (Zion) and to the Village of Peace (Jerusalem) from the spirit-world above, the village of our Creator who is the Maker of Life. This is where many thousands of the spirit-messengers have gathered to celebrate a great festival!

[23]This is also a gathering of the great sacred family, who are the firstborn whose names have been written down *in the book of life kept* in the spirit-world above. You have come to the Great Spirit, the one who decides for everyone who has done right and who has done wrong, and to the ones in good standing whose spirits have been made whole. [24]Yes, you have come to Creator Sets Free (Jesus), the peacemaker of the new peace treaty between the Great Spirit and human beings. You have come to the blood that has been sprinkled, which says better things than the blood of His Breath Goes Up (Abel).

A SHAKING OF ALL THINGS

[25]Make sure you do not turn away from the voice of the one who now speaks! For

---

[b]**12:19** Lit. *trumpet*, or in Hebrew *shofar*, meaning "ram's horn"
[c]**12:20** Exodus 19:12-13

[a]**12:18** See Exodus 19.

if the ones who turned away from him who warned them on earth did not escape, how will we escape if we turn away the one who speaks from the spirit-world above? 26At that time his voice shook the earth, but he has now promised once more to shake both the earth and the spirit-world above.a 27When he says "once more," this means he is removing those things that can be shaken, things that are of this creation, so that which cannot be shaken will remain.

28So then, since we are welcoming a good road that cannot be shaken, let us give thanks to the Great Spirit and serve him in a good way, with much honor and respect. 29For our Creator is an all-consuming fire.

13

LOVE AS BROTHERS AND SISTERS

1Keep loving each other as brothers and sisters *of the sacred family.* 2Do not forget to be kind and welcoming to strangers, for in this way some have welcomed spirit-messengers without knowing it. 3Keep the ones who are in prison in your thoughts as if you were there with them, and those who are mistreated as if you in your own body shared their suffering.

4Marriage is honorable, and the marriage bed is pure, but Creator will decide the guilt of all who are sexually impure and unfaithful in marriage. 5Keep yourselves free from the love of possessions and be at peace with what you have. For the Great Spirit himself has said, "I will never leave you or give up on you."b 6Because of this we can boldly say, "The Great Spirit Chief is the one who stands

with me. Why would I fear what human beings can do?"c

WISE WORDS OF COUNSEL AND COURAGE

7Never forget the ones who blazed the trail before you, the ones who were first to tell you the message of Creator's *good story.* Think deeply about the manner in which they lived and died, and follow in their way of trusting.

8Creator Sets Free (Jesus) the Chosen One remains the same yesterday, today, and to the time beyond the end of all days.

9Do not let all kinds of strange teachings take you down a wrong path. For our hearts are made strong by the gift of *Creator's* great kindness, not from following rules about what foods to eat. These kinds of rules have not helped those who have followed after them.

10The ones who still serve in the tent lodge *on earth* have no right to share ind our ceremonial altar. 11For *each year* the chief holy man takes the blood of animals into the Most Holy Place as an offering for the people's broken ways. The bodies of those animals are then burned outside the camp. 12Creator Sets Free (Jesus) offered his own lifeblood to make the people holy and suffered outside the village gate. 13So then, let us join him outside the camp, sharing in the same kind of disrespect and shame that he suffered. 14For we are not seeking an earthly village that will fade away. We are seeking the village that is coming *down from the spirit-world above, one that will remain.*e

MORE WISE COUNSEL

15So then, through Creator Sets Free (Jesus), let us keep giving thanks as a

---

a**12:26** Haggai 2:6
b**13:5** Deuteronomy 31:6
c**13:6** Psalm 118:6
d**13:10** Lit. *eat from*
e**13:14** Revelation 21:2

sacrificial offering to the Great Spirit. This is the fruit of our lips, giving honor to him and all that his name represents. 16And do not forget to do good and share with those who are in need, for these are also sacrificial gifts that make Creator's heart glad.

17Follow the guidance of your spiritual leaders and give way to their instructions. For they must give an answer for the guidance they provide. So let them do so with glad hearts and not with sorrow, for that would not be a good thing for you.

KEEP SENDING UP PRAYERS

18Keep sending up prayers for us, for deep inside we are sure that we are walking in a good and honorable way. 19I ask you this with all my heart, so that I may soon return to you.

20The Great Spirit of Peace is the one who raised up from the dead our Honored Chief Creator Sets Free (Jesus), the Great Shepherd of the sheep. It is through his lifeblood that we now have a peace treaty that will last beyond the end of all days. 21*May the Great Provider* give you everything you need to do what he wants done. He is working, through Creator Sets Free (Jesus) the Chosen One, to do in us the things that make his heart glad. He is to be given all honor to the time beyond the end of all days. Aho! May it be so!

FINAL WORDS

22So now, my relatives, I counsel you to take to heart this short message. I have written it to lift you up and give you strength. 23I want you to know that our *spiritual* brother He Gives Honor (Timothy) has been set free *from prison*. If he comes soon, we will travel together to see you. 24Greet all your spiritual leaders and all of Creator's holy ones. I send you greetings from those in Land of Young Bulls (Italy).

25May the gift of *Creator's* great kindness be with you all.

Aho! May it be so!

HE LEADS THE WAY TO THE SCATTERED TRIBES

JAMES

GREETINGS

¹From He Leads the Way (James), a *sacred* servant of the Great Spirit and of our Honored Chief, Creator Sets Free (Jesus) the Chosen One.

To the twelve tribes scattered *like seeds* among the nations. I send *joyful* greetings!

WISDOM FOR TIMES OF TESTING

²My *sacred* family members, whenever your trust *in the Great Spirit* is tested, count it as a reason to dance for joy. ³For you know that when your trust is put to the test, your ability to stand firm grows stronger. ⁴So keep standing firm until you have passed the test. Then you will have gained all the maturity and strength of character needed to finish *walking the good road.*

⁵If wisdom is needed, ask the Great Spirit, for he freely gives wisdom to all who ask and never holds back. ⁶But when you ask, you must put all your trust in him without doubting. For the one who doubts is like a wave in the sea tossed about by the wind. ⁷People *who doubt* should not hope to receive anything from our Honored Chief, ⁸for they have two minds, not knowing which one to follow.

WISDOM FOR THE POOR AND THE RICH

⁹Those sacred family members who have little should take joy in the honor Creator bestows on them. ¹⁰And the ones who have much should take joy in knowing that they will be humbled because they will fade away like a wildflower *in the grass.* ¹¹For the sun rises with its fiery heat and dries up the grass, causing the wildflower to fall *to the ground* and its beauty to fade away. This is how it will be for those who go about working so hard to get many possessions.

¹²Creator's blessing rests on the ones who stand firm under testing, for once they have passed the test, they will receive the headdress of life that has been promised to those who love the Great Spirit.

WISDOM FOR TIMES OF TEMPTATION

¹³When tempted, no one should say, "Creator is tempting me." For the Great Spirit cannot be tempted by evil, nor does he tempt anyone. ¹⁴We are the ones who tempt ourselves when we are lured away and trapped by our own desires. ¹⁵When an evil desire takes root in our hearts, it gives birth to broken ways. When these broken ways have taken over, they drag us down a path that leads to death.

GOOD GIFTS COME FROM
THE FATHER ABOVE

16Do not be misled, my sacred family members. **17**Every good and perfect gift comes down from the Father above, who gave us the sun, moon, and stars. But unlike them, *the light that comes from the Great Spirit* never dims, flickers, or casts a shadow. **18**Creator is the one who chose to birth us into being by his word of truth so that we would be the first of all creation to truly be who he made us to be.

TURN AWAY FROM HUMAN ANGER

19Knowing this, my much-loved family members, we must all be quick to listen, slow to speak, and slow to become angry. **20**For human anger will not take us down the path of Creator's right ways. **21**So scrape off all the mud of your evil ways and humbly receive the message that the Great Spirit has planted deep within you. This will set your heart free and make your mind whole.

DO NOT ONLY HEAR THE MESSAGE

22But make sure you do not fool yourselves. You must not only hear this message. You must also walk in its truth. **23**For if you only hear but fail to walk true to the message, you are like a man who sees his own face reflected in a pool of water. **24**Then, right after looking at himself, he walks away and forgets what he looks like. **25**But take a good long look into the perfect way of life, the law of love that sets people free. Stay true to its message, not forgetting what you have heard but walking in all its ways, and Creator's blessing will rest on all you do.

26All who represent themselves as spiritual but do not keep their tongue under control are only fooling themselves—their spirituality is worthless.

27But the one whose spirituality is pure and spotless before our Father the Great Spirit takes care of widows and orphans, and keeps himself free from the evil ways of this world.

TREAT ALL PEOPLE IN THE SAME WAY

1My *sacred* family members, as you trust in our bright and shining Honored Chief, Creator Sets Free (Jesus) the Chosen One, do not treat one person better than another. **2**Let us say someone comes into your sacred gathering wearing fine clothes and costly jewelry, and some poor person comes in dressed in rags. **3**Then you give more honor to the one wearing fine clothes, saying, "Come, sit here in this honored place," but you say to the one dressed in rags, "Go, stand over there," or, "Sit here on the floor where people lay their feet." **4**If you treat people in this way, have you not decided that some among you are better than others and acted like crooked council members with bad hearts?

5Hear me, my much-loved *sacred* family members! Did not the Great Spirit choose the ones the world looks down on as poor to be rich in trusting and sharers together in the good road that Creator has promised to those who love him? **6**Why would you show no respect for the poor? Is it not the rich who drag you down and bring you before their own *corrupt* councils? **7**Are they not the ones who speak evil against the Honorable Name spoken over you?

THE TRUE MEANING AND
PURPOSE OF THE LAW

8If you "love your fellow human beings in the same way you love yourselves," as it says in our Sacred Teachings,[a] you are doing well, for you are walking in the true meaning and purpose of the law of our Honored Chief. [9]But if you treat one person better than another, you are walking in broken ways and guilty of not following our Sacred Teachings. [10]For whoever does everything our tribal law requires yet fails in one thing is guilty of breaking all of it. [11]The one who told us to be faithful in marriage[b] also told us not to take the life of another.[c] If you are faithful in marriage but take away the life of another, you have become one who fails to keep the law.

[12]In all that you say or do, remember that it is the *Chosen One's* law of freedom that Creator will use to decide for or against you. [13]When the Great Spirit decides, no mercy will be shown to those who have not shown mercy. *On the other hand, the ones who have shown mercy will have mercy shown to them. So then,* mercy wins the victory over judgment.

HARMONY BETWEEN FAITH AND DEEDS

[14]What good is it, my *sacred* family members, if a man says "I have faith," but has no deeds to show for it? Can that kind of "faith" set him free and make him whole? [15]If a family member *or any human being* has no clothes to wear or no food to eat, [16]and you say, "Go in peace, stay warm, and eat well," but fail to give what is needed, what good have you done?

[17]In the same way, without deeds, faith by itself is dead. [18]But someone will say, "Faith is what is needed," while another says, "Good deeds are what is needed."[d] *I say that both are needed. You show me your faith without good deeds, and I will show you my faith by the good deeds I have done.*

EXAMPLES OF FAITH AND GOOD DEEDS

[19]You believe there is only one Great Spirit. Good! But evil spirits also believe and tremble with fear! [20]Are you the kind of shallow person who needs to be shown over and over again that faith without good deeds has no worth? [21]*So I ask you,* was not Father of Many Nations (Abraham) shown to be in good standing when he put his son He Made Us Laugh (Isaac) on the sacred altar as a sacrifice?

Long ago the Great Spirit promised Father of Many Nations (Abraham) a son even though he was too old to father a child. For many winters he kept trusting that the promise would come true. Finally, his promised son was born, the son whom the Great Spirit said his descendants would come from and through whom all nations would be blessed. But Creator told Father of Many Nations (Abraham) to take his son and offer him as a sacrifice. His trust in the Great Spirit was so strong that he believed even if he sacrificed his only son Creator would bring him back from death. So he began to do what he was told, but the Great Spirit sent a spirit-messenger to stop him just as he was about to sacrifice his son.[e]

[22]It is clear to see that his faith was in harmony with what he did. His faith was completed by his deeds. [23]This gives full meaning to the Sacred Teaching that says, "Father of Many Nations (Abraham) trusted the Great Spirit, and this gave him good standing in Creator's eyes." It

---

[a]**2:8** Leviticus 19:18; Romans 13:10
[b]**2:11** Exodus 20:13
[c]**2:11** Deuteronomy 5:17

[d]**2:18** Lit. *You have faith and I have good deeds*
[e]**2:21** See Genesis 22:1-15.

was for this reason that he was called the friend of the Great Spirit.

²⁴So you can see that human beings do not have good standing only by trusting but also by what they do.

²⁵It was the same for Boastful Woman (Rahab), one who traded her body for possessions. Did she not do what was right in Creator's eyes when she took in the spies that were sent from our tribes and *helped them escape* by sending them out another way?

²⁶In the same way that a body has no life without the spirit, so faith has no life without deeds.

THE POWER OF WORDS

¹My *sacred* family members, not many of you should become teachers *of our spiritual ways.* For you know that we who teach will face a stricter judgment. ²We all stumble *on the path* in many ways. But if we could keep our words from hurting others, we would be mature human beings, able to aim our whole lives in the right direction.

³Those who put bits into the mouths of horses are able to move them in the direction they want them to go. ⁴It is the same with a canoe. Even when a large canoe is being pushed by strong winds, it takes only a small paddle to steer it where someone wants it to go.

⁵In the same way, the tongue is a small part of the body, but it boasts about great things. A large forest can be set on fire by a tiny flame, ⁶and the tongue is itself a flame of fire. The tongue is a world full of evil and spreads its poison throughout the body. The words spoken by the tongue have the power to set on fire the very circle of life itself, and its flames come from the Valley of Smoldering Fire.ᵃ

NO ONE CAN TAME THE TONGUE

⁷Every kind of four-legged beast or winged one of the air and every reptile or sea creature can be tamed and have been tamed by human beings. ⁸But no one can tame the tongue. It is an evil that never rests, full of deadly poison. ⁹With it we bless the Great Spirit, our Honored Father, and with it we curse human beings who are made in his image. ¹⁰Blessing and cursing come out of the same mouth. My *sacred* family members, this should not be. ¹¹Does both sweet and bitter water come from the same spring? ¹²Can olives and figs come from the same tree? Can a grapevine bear figs, my *sacred* family members? *Not at all!* And neither can saltwater be used to make water fresh again.

TRUE AND FALSE WISDOM

¹³Are any among you wise and understanding? Then show it in the way you live, doing good from a humble and wise heart. ¹⁴But if your hearts are full of bitter envy and selfish desires, then stop boasting and speaking lies to cover up the truth *about yourselves.* ¹⁵This is not the kind of wisdom that comes down from the One Above Us All. Instead, it is from this world. It is unspiritual and of the evil one. ¹⁶For where there is jealousy and selfish ways, you will also find confusion and all kinds of evil at work.

¹⁷But the wisdom that comes from the One Above Us All is first of all pure, then peace-loving, gentle, full of mercy, and open to another's way of seeing and thinking. People with this kind of wisdom are like trees filled with good fruit. They

---

ᵃ**3:6** See glossary of biblical terms.

have open hearts with nothing to hide. [18]This wisdom will bring about a harvest of doing what is right, because they are peacemakers planting seeds of peace.

4

WARS, FIGHTS, AND ARGUMENTS

[1]Where do the wars, fights, and arguments among you come from? Do they not come from the selfish desires that wage war in your own bodies? [2]You want what you do not have, so you kill for it. You want what belongs to others, but you cannot get it from them, so you fight and wage war. You do not have because you do not ask the Great Spirit. [3]When you ask for things, you do not receive them because you ask for the wrong reasons, wanting to satisfy your own selfish desires. [4]You are unfaithful people! You must know that if you become friends with *the ways of* this world, you make yourself an enemy of the Great Spirit.

HUMBLE YOURSELVES

[5]Do you think our Sacred Teachings have no meaning when they tell us that Creator's Spirit in us longs for us to be faithful and true to him? [6]But his gift of great kindness is more than enough, just as our Sacred Teachings also say, "The Great Spirit stands against the proud and arrogant, but he shows great kindness to the humble of heart."[a] [7]So humbly follow all of Creator's ways. Make your stand against the evil trickster,[b] and he will turn and run from you. [8]Draw near to the Great Spirit, and he will draw near to you. Wash your hands clean of your broken ways, and purify your hearts and minds

from trying to walk two different roads. [9]Cry out in your misery. Be sad and weep. Turn your laughter into sadness, and your joy into tears. [10]Humble yourselves in the sight of the Great Spirit, and he will lift you up *to a place of honor.*

DO NOT ACCUSE EACH OTHER

[11]My *sacred* family members, do not speak accusations against each other. If you do, you are putting yourselves above the law, deciding who is guilty or not. When you do this, you are acting against the law itself instead of doing what it says. [12]There is only one *true* Lawgiver and Judge who has the power to decide who has done right or wrong. He is the one with the right to set people free or bring them to a bad end. So who are you to judge a fellow human being?

LOOK OUT FOR EVIL BOASTING

[13]Listen to me, you who say, "Today or tomorrow we will go to a trading post in some village. There we will stay for a year trading our goods and gaining more than we started with." [14]You do not even know what tomorrow will bring. Your life is like the *morning* mist *over a lake* that is there for a short time and then gone. [15]Instead, here is what you should say, "If it is what Creator wants, then we will live and do these things." [16]But as it stands, you are making prideful boasts. All such boasting is evil. [17]So then, the one who knows to do good but fails to do it is walking in broken ways.

5

A WARNING TO THOSE WITH GREAT POSSESSIONS

[1]Listen to me, you who have great possessions, weep and howl over the times

[a]4:6 Proverbs 3:34
[b]4:7 The devil

of trouble and sorrow that are coming your way. ²Even now your treasured possessions are rotting away and moths are eating your fine garments. ³Your gold and silver will waste away. It will be a witness against you and eat your flesh like fire. For you have piled up many possessions in the last days.

⁴Behold! You have held back the goods you owed to the workers who harvest your crops. Their cries *for justice* have reached the ears of the Chief of Spirit Warriors. ⁵Your life on this earth has been one of getting for yourselves whatever you want to satisfy your selfish desires. You have fattened yourselves[a] *like an animal prepared* for a day of slaughter. ⁶You have falsely accused and put to death the innocent, who did not even try to stand against you.

WAITING FOR HIS APPEARING

⁷So be patient, my *sacred* family members, until our Honored Chief appears. Look at the worker in the field who patiently waits for the seasonal rains to fall so the land can bring forth its fruits. ⁸In the same way, you must also be patient and stand firm, for the appearing of our Honored Chief is close at hand. ⁹*So then, my sacred* family members, do not grumble against each other or you may be found guilty. Look! The Judge who decides is right outside, ready to come in.

¹⁰*My sacred* family members, follow in the footsteps of the prophets who spoke for the Great Spirit. Even in times of suffering, they remained patient *and strong.* ¹¹Look at how we honor those who have stood firm *in troubled times.* You have heard the story of Turns to Creator (Job), how he stood firm to the

end and found the Great Spirit to be kind and merciful. *The Great Spirit will do the same for you.*

¹²The chief thing I want to say to you, my *sacred* family members, is that you are not to make solemn promises. Do not promise by the spirit-world above, or by the earth below, or make a solemn promise in any other way. Your simple "yes" or "no" is enough. You may be found guilty if you say more.[b]

THE POWER OF PRAYER

¹³Are you suffering? Send up prayers. Are your hearts glad? Sing traditional songs of honor and praise. ¹⁴Are any among you sick? Call on the elders of the sacred family to pray over them and smudge them with sweet-smelling smoke[c] in the name of our Honored Chief. ¹⁵When you send your voice to our Honored Chief, trusting in him, he will heal the sick ones and restore them to health. He will forgive and set free any who have been following their bad hearts and broken ways.

¹⁶So admit your broken ways one to another and pray for each other that you may be healed. The prayer of one in good standing *with Creator* is powerful and good medicine.

¹⁷Great Spirit Is Creator (Elijah) was a weak human being, the same as we are. He prayed with much prayer that it would not rain, and for three winters and six moons no rain fell on the land. ¹⁸Then, when he prayed for the rain to fall, down it came, and once again *mother* earth gave a harvest *of good food.*

FINAL WORDS

¹⁹*My sacred* family members, has any of you wandered from the truth? Has

anyone helped you find the way back? 20If so, then let them know, the one who helps someone return from broken ways has rescued their soul from death and hidden the many paths that lead to broken ways.

Aho! May it be so!

FIRST LETTER FROM
STANDS ON THE ROCK

1 PETER

1

GREETINGS

1From Stands on the Rock (Peter), a message bearer from Creator Sets Free (Jesus) the Chosen One.

To Creator's chosen ones who have been scattered *like seeds* throughout Land of Black Waters (Pontus), Land of Pale Skins (Galatia), Land of Handsome Horses (Cappadocia), Land of the Rising Sun (Asia), and the territory of Rushing Storm (Bithynia), who live like strangers among them.

2Our Father the Great Spirit knew long ago that he would take you into his family. By his Spirit he is making you holy so you will obey Creator Sets Free (Jesus) the Chosen One and be sprinkled with his lifeblood. May the gift of his great kindness and peace overflow to you.

SHARED BLESSINGS

3All blessings belong to the Great Spirit, the Father of our Honored Chief, Creator Sets Free (Jesus) the Chosen One! In his great mercy, when he raised Creator Sets Free (Jesus) the Chosen One from the dead, we were given new birth, and our hope came to life. We now share with the Chosen One all the blessings he has received. **4**These shared blessings are kept safe in the spirit-world above, where they will never grow old, become impure, or fade away.

THE TESTING OF YOUR TRUST

5Creator's plan to set you free and make you whole is ready to be fully revealed when the time for the end has come. Until then you are kept safe by trusting in Creator's power. **6**You dance for joy now because you know that day is coming, even though for a short time you may have to walk a trail of tears because of the many kinds of troubles *you are facing.*

7These *troubles* will test the purity of your trust in him, just like fire tests the purity of gold. Your trust in him is worth more than gold that can fade away. After you have passed through the fire and come out pure, it will bring praise, honor, and shining-greatness to Creator Sets Free (Jesus) the Chosen One when he is revealed. **8**You have never seen him, yet you love him. You cannot see him now, yet you trust him. This makes your heart so glad that you cannot find words beautiful enough, so you have to dance for joy. **9**For your trust in him is bringing you to the end of the trail, where your whole being will be set free and made whole.

FORETOLD BY THE PROPHETS

10This time of being set free and made whole was foretold by the prophets, who prophesied about Creator's gift of great kindness that would come to you. The prophets wondered about these things, so they searched deeply into the meaning of it all. [11]The Spirit of the Chosen One in them told them ahead of time about the sufferings of the Chosen One and the honor that would follow. They wondered whom the Spirit was speaking about and when these things would take place. [12]The Spirit made it known to them that the things they searched out were for you and not for themselves. You have now learned these things from those who told you the good story by the Holy Spirit, who was sent down from the spirit-world above. Even the spirit-messengers long to see and understand more about these things.

STAND READY IN YOUR MIND

[13]In light of all of this, stand ready in your mind to face what is ahead. Think clearly and set all your hope on the gift of great kindness that will be yours when Creator Sets Free (Jesus) the Chosen One is revealed. [14]Because you are the children of the Great Spirit, follow all his instructions. Do not walk with a bad heart, as you did in the past when you did not know the things you know now. [15]Walk in a sacred manner in everything you do. For you were called away from your old life by the Holy One, who walks ahead of you on a sacred path. [16]For it is written *in our Sacred Teachings*, "Be holy, for I am holy."[a]

THE PRICE HE PAID TO SET US FREE

[17]If you call on the Great Spirit as your Father, walk with great respect and awe for him on your journey through this life. Creator decides who has done right or wrong without favoring one person over another. [18-19]For you know that the price

to set you free was not paid with silver or gold or anything that can fade away. It was the lifeblood of the Chosen One, a spotless lamb with no defect, that set you free from empty ways handed down to you from your ancestors. [20]He was chosen *to walk this path* before the world was made, but he has been revealed in these last days for your good. [21]Through him you trust in the Great Spirit, who raised him to life from death and honored him with shining-greatness. *Creator did this* so you would put all your hope and trust in him.

THE LIVING WORD GIVES US NEW BIRTH

[22]You have purified your souls by fully following the truth. Now your love for each other can come from a true heart. So keep loving each other in this way. [23]You have been given new birth through the living word of the Great Spirit. This living Word is like a seed planted within you that will never decay and will remain to the time beyond the end of all days.

[24]*Just as our Sacred Teachings tell us*, "Human beings are like grass. Their beauty is like a wildflower growing in the grass. The grass dries up and the wildflower falls *to the ground*, [25]but Creator's Word never fades away."

And that word is the good story that was told to you.

2

GROWING UP SPIRITUALLY

[1]So turn away from hatred, lying, cheating, and any false face you have been wearing. Stop bad-mouthing others and being jealous. [2]Like newborn babies who long for their mother's milk, *you should* long for milk that is spiritually pure. This milk will help you grow strong

---

[a]1:16 Leviticus 19:2

in the one who sets you free and makes you whole. ³For you have already tasted the goodness of our Honored Chief.

THE CHIEF LODGEPOLE

⁴You are drawing near to the living Lodgepole,ᵃ *the Chosen One* who was rejected by human beings but highly honored in the eyes of the Great Spirit. ⁵You are also like living wooden polesᵇ whose branches are being woven together into a spiritual and sacred lodge. In this spiritual lodge, as holy men and women, you will send up spiritual offerings that will be like sweet-smelling smoke to the Great Spirit through Creator Sets Free (Jesus) the Chosen One.

⁶For it stands true in our Sacred Teachings, "Behold, in Strong Mountain (Zion) I am setting in place the Chief Lodgepole that I have chosen, one that is highly honored. The hearts of all who trust in him will never fall to the ground."ᶜ

⁷He is highly honored by all who trust in him. But for those who fail to put their trust in him, "The tree the lodge builders threw away has become the Chief Lodgepole.ᵈ ⁸He is a tree pole that many will trip over, a wooden poleᵉ that will make them stumble."ᶠ They stumble because they do not do what Creator's message requires them to do. This is what was decided ahead of time for all who do not trust his message.

CREATOR'S CHOSEN PEOPLE

⁹But you *who trust in Creator Sets Free (Jesus)* are a chosen people. You are a family of chiefs who serve as holy men and women. You are a sacred nation, a people who belong to the Great Spirit *alone*. You are the ones who will show forth the beautiful ways of the one who called you out of darkness and brought you into his wondrous light. ¹⁰You are now the people of the Great Spirit, even though at one time you were not known in this way.ᵍ In the past you had not known mercy, but now you have found it.

WALK IN A GOOD WAY

¹¹So then, my much-loved ones, *you who are* strangers and outsiders to the ways of this world, I speak to you now with strong words. Stay far away from the weak and broken desires within you that make war against who you are. ¹²Walk in a good way among those who are outsiders to our spiritual ways. In this way, even though they falsely accuse you of wrongdoing, when they see the good you have done they will give honor to the Great Spirit on the day he comes to visit us.

COMING UNDER HUMAN AUTHORITIES

¹³On behalf of our Honored Chief, I call on you to come under all human governments. This includes the Ruler of the People of Iron (Caesar), as the highest authority, ¹⁴and all who represent him. They have been sent to punish wrongdoers and honor those who do what is right. ¹⁵Creator wants you to walk in his right ways so that the ignorant and foolish will have nothing to say against you. ¹⁶Do this as a people who have been set free, but do not use your freedom as a cover-up for evil ways. Instead, walk out your freedom as willing servants of the Great Spirit. ¹⁷Show respect to all people. Love the members of our sacred

---

ᵃ**2:4** Lit. *the living Stone*
ᵇ**2:5** Lit. *living stones*
ᶜ**2:6** Isaiah 28:16
ᵈ**2:7** Psalm 118:22
ᵉ**2:8** Lit. *rock*
ᶠ**2:8** Isaiah 8:14

ᵍ**2:10** Hosea 1:10

family. Treat Creator with great respect, and show honor to the Ruler of the People of Iron (Caesar).

INSTRUCTIONS FOR HOUSEHOLD SERVANTS

[18]Household servants, I call on you to respectfully come under the master of the house. *Serve with respect* not only masters who are good and kind, but also the ones who treat you in a bad way. [19]For the gift of great kindness rests on the ones who, out of respect for the Great Spirit, patiently suffer even when they have done nothing wrong. [20]There is no honor in suffering for wrongs you have done. But if you suffer with patience for doing what is right, then Creator will look on you with great kindness.

THE PATH OF SUFFERING

[21]Suffering in this way is part of what you have been called to do. It was for you that the Chosen One walked a path of suffering, showing you the way to follow in his footsteps. [22]*Our Sacred Teachings tell us,* "He did nothing wrong and never spoke with a forked tongue."[a] [23]He did not return insult for insult. When he suffered, he made no threats. Instead, he kept looking to the one who is always right when he decides who has done right or who has done wrong.

[24]He took on himself our broken ways when he hung on a tree-pole—the cross. He did this so we could die to our broken ways and come alive to his right ways. By his wounds we have been made whole. [25]At one time you were like sheep wandering away, but you have now returned to the one who watches over you like a shepherd *who watches over the sheep.*

[a]2:22 Isaiah 53:9

3

INSTRUCTIONS FOR WIVES AND HUSBANDS

[1]In the same way, you wives are to come under the guidance of your husbands. In this way, even husbands who do not follow Creator's message might be won over without a word by the way their wives treat them. [2]For they will see the honest and respectful way you live your life. [3]Your beauty should not be only on the outside, with fancy braided hair, costly beaded jewelry, or dressing up in fine clothes. [4]But let your beauty shine out from who you are deep within your heart—a gentle spirit filled with peace and harmony. That kind of beauty never fades and has great value in the eyes of the Great Spirit.

[5]For this was how the holy women in times past who put their hope in Creator made themselves beautiful. They followed the guidance of their husbands [6]like Noble Woman (Sarah) did. She followed the guidance of *her husband,* Father of Many Nations (Abraham), and respectfully called him her honored chief. You are her daughters if you do not let fear keep you from doing what is right.

[7]In the same way, you husbands, live in an understanding way with your wife. She may be physically weaker, but she deserves honor as one who shares equally with you in the gift of great kindness as you walk together on the road of life. Then nothing will stand in the way of your prayers.

LOVE EACH OTHER AS FAMILY

[8]I have some last things to say to all of you. Walk side by side in harmony with each other. Try to feel what others feel.

Love each other as family. Be tenderhearted and walk with a humble spirit. [9]Never return evil for evil or insult for insult. Instead, speak words of blessing over each other, for you were chosen to share together in Creator's blessings.

[10]*Our Sacred Teachings tell us,* "Let the ones who love life and long to see good days keep their tongue from evil and their lips from speaking lies. Let them turn away from doing evil and do what is good. [11]Let them seek peace and choose to walk in its good ways. [12]For the eyes of our Honored Chief watch over the ones who do what is right. His ears are open to their prayers. But his face is against all who do what is evil."[a]

SUFFERING FOR DOING GOOD

[13]If you give yourselves fully to doing good, who would want to harm you? [14]But even if you should suffer for doing what is right, remember that Creator's blessing rests on you. So do not fear what they can do to you or be troubled by their threats. [15]Instead, set your hearts on the Chosen One as your Honored Chief. Always be ready to give an answer to the ones who ask about the hope you carry inside you. [16]Give your answer to them in a kind and respectful way. Do what you know deep inside to be right, so when outsiders accuse you, they will be put to shame as you walk in a good way following the Chosen One. [17]For if it is what the Great Spirit wants, it is better to suffer for doing good than for doing wrong.

[18]The Chosen One died once for the broken ways of all people. The one who always does right suffered for those who do wrong to make a way for us to come to the Great Spirit. In his weak human body he was put to death, but he was made alive in the Spirit.

LESSONS FROM THE TIME OF THE GREAT FLOOD

[19]In the Spirit the Chosen One went and told his story to the spirits that had been held captive from long ago. [20]These were the spirits of human beings who refused to walk in the ways of the Great Spirit. This was before the great flood in the time of One Who Rests (Noah), when Creator waited patiently for the great wooden canoe to be built. A small number, only eight people, were brought safely through the waters of the flood.

This happened long ago in ancient times when the world was filled with violence and almost every human heart was taken over with violence and evil. Creator had to cleanse the earth with a great flood that drowned all living things. The only ones who survived were the family of One Who Rests (Noah), along with the animals he chose, who entered into the great wooden canoe Creator told him to build.[b]

[21]The story of what happened then is a way to understand our purification ceremony with water,[c] a ceremony that is performed to set us free and make us whole. This ceremony does not just wash the dirt from our bodies. It shows that from deep inside we are crying out for Creator to set us free by what he did when he raised Creator Sets Free (Jesus) the Chosen One from the dead.

[22]The Chosen One now sits in his honored place at Creator's right hand in the spirit-world above. From there the Chosen One rules over all spirit-messengers, authorities, and powers.

---

[a]**3:12** Psalm 34:12-16

[b]**3:20** Genesis 6–9; Hebrews 11:7
[c]**3:21** Baptism

4 ▸◂▸◂▸◂▸◂▸◂▸◂▸◂▸

SUFFERING WITH THE CHOSEN ONE

¹Since the Chosen One suffered for us while in his earthly body, we must also be ready to suffer and to think about it in the same way he did. The ones who are willing to suffer while still in their weak human bodies have chosen to stop walking in broken ways. ²They also have chosen to live out their remaining days in these weak human bodies doing what the Great Spirit wants and not following broken human desires. ³For in the past you walked long enough following the evil desires of the nations who have lost their way. *Like them*, you walked a path of selfish and uncontrolled desires. You became drunks who went to wild drinking parties. You even prayed to forbidden spirit-images.

⁴The ones *who walk in this way* think it strange that you no longer join them in their wild and reckless way of life, so they speak evil of you. ⁵But they will have to give an answer to the Great Spirit for what they have done. He stands ready, for both the living and the dead, to decide who has done right and who has done wrong. ⁶This is the reason the good story has been told to the dead. In this way, even though they were found guilty in their weak human bodies, they might still live spiritually before the Great Spirit.

NEVER STOP LOVING AND SERVING

⁷The end of all things is near, so think good thoughts and be single-minded in your prayers. ⁸Above all, never stop loving each other, for *like a warm blanket* love covers a great number of broken ways. ⁹Open your homes to each other and share your food without grumbling.

¹⁰Each one of you has been given a gift, so use it to serve one another, as a good manager of the many kinds of gifts Creator gives. ¹¹If your gift is speaking, then your words should come from the Great Spirit. If your gift is serving, then serve with the strength Creator gives you. In this way, the Great Spirit will be honored by everything you do through Creator Sets Free (Jesus) the Chosen One. To him belongs all power and shining-greatness to the time beyond the end of all days. Aho! May it be so!

MORE ABOUT SUFFERING

¹²My much-loved ones, do not be caught off guard by the fiery trial that you now face, as if something strange were happening to you. ¹³Instead, be glad that you share in the sufferings of the Chosen One. The more you share in his sufferings, the more you will dance for joy when his shining-greatness is revealed. ¹⁴If you are treated with scorn and contempt because you follow the Chosen One, you are blessed. For this is a sign that the beauty of his Spirit and of Creator is resting on you. ¹⁵Make sure no one among you suffers as a murderer, a thief, an evildoer, or a troublemaker. ¹⁶But if you suffer as a follower of the Chosen One, do not be ashamed. Represent his name well, and you will bring honor to the Great Spirit.

¹⁷The time has come for judgment to begin with Creator's own family. If it begins with us, what will become of the ones who do not respect and follow Creator's good story? ¹⁸If the ones in good standing come through with much difficulty, then what will be the end of the bad-hearted ones and those who walk in broken ways? ¹⁹So the ones who suffer for doing what is right, as the

Great Spirit wants them to, should fully trust our faithful Creator with their lives and continue to do good.

5 ⟨X⟩⟨X⟩⟨X⟩⟨X⟩⟨X⟩⟨X⟩

WISDOM FOR THE ELDERS

1*Knowing the times we live in,* I speak with strong words to the elders among you who serve as spiritual leaders. I am a fellow elder who saw the sufferings of the Chosen One with my own eyes and who will share in the beauty of his shining-greatness that will be revealed. **2***I counsel you to* watch over Creator's family like a shepherd watching over a flock of sheep. Do this willingly, as Creator wants you to, not to gain more possessions but from an honest desire to serve. **3**Do not use your authority to boss people around. Instead, show them the way by doing first what you are asking of them. **4**Then, when the Chief Shepherd appears, he will honor you with a headdress of many feathers that will never lose its beauty.

WISDOM FOR THE YOUNG

5In the same way, those who are young should listen to their elders. All of you must wear the regalia of humility as you walk together. "The Great Spirit stands against the proud and arrogant, but he shows great kindness to the humble of heart."[a] **6**So humble yourselves under Creator's powerful hand, and when the time is right he will highly honor you. **7**The Great Spirit cares deeply about you, so gather all your worries into a blanket and throw them on his shoulders. He will carry them for you.

STAND FIRM AGAINST THE EVIL ONE

8Stay alert and remain calm, for your opponent, the evil trickster,[b] prowls about, roaring like a *mountain* lion, looking for someone to devour. **9**Take your stand against him, firm in your trust, knowing that all over the world other sacred family members are suffering in the same way. **10**But you will not have to suffer for long, for the Great Spirit who gives us his gift of great kindness will restore you, set your feet on solid ground, and strengthen you. For he has called you into the bright-shining greatness of the Chosen One that will never fade away. **11**All power belongs to him to the time beyond all days. Aho! May it be so!

12I have written this short letter to you by the hand of Forest Walker (Silvanus). He is a *spiritual* brother whom I count as trustworthy. With a few strong words, I have told you the truth about the gift of Creator's great kindness. So stand firm in this truth!

13The sacred family[c] who gathers in Village of Confusion (Babylon) and who were chosen in the same way you were sends greetings to you. Also War Club (Mark), who is a son to me, sends his greetings.

14Greet each other in a loving way with a *holy* kiss. Peace be upon all of you who belong to the Chosen One.

Aho! May it be so!

---

[b]**5:8** The devil
[c]**5:13** Lit. *She*

[a]**5:5** Proverbs 3:34

SECOND LETTER FROM STANDS ON THE ROCK

2 PETER

GREETINGS

1From Stands on the Rock (Peter), a *sacred* servant and message bearer of Creator Sets Free (Jesus) the Chosen One.

To all who have taken hold of and share together with us in the way of trusting that comes from the right ways of the Great Spirit and from our Sacred Deliverer, Creator Sets Free (Jesus) the Chosen One.

SHARING HIS SACRED NATURE

2May the gift of Creator's great kindness and peace rest on you in greater measure as you grow in your knowledge *and understanding* of the Great Spirit and Creator Sets Free (Jesus), our Honored Chief. **3**Creator's own power has given us all we need to walk the road of life in a sacred manner. This power comes from knowing the Chosen One, who has called us to share in his honor and goodness. **4**He has given us promises full of honor and beauty so that through them we may share the sacred nature that belongs to him and, *through these promises*, be set free from the evil desires that corrupt this world.

5This is why you must put your whole heart into uniting trust with goodness, goodness with knowledge, **6**and knowledge with self-discipline. Unite self-discipline with never giving up, and never giving up with walking in a sacred way. **7**Unite walking in a sacred way with family kindness, and family kindness with love. **8**For if you are growing in these things, they will keep you spiritually strong and fruitful in the true knowledge of our Honored Chief, Creator Sets Free (Jesus) the Chosen One.

MAKE SURE YOU HAVE HEARD HIS CALL

9The ones who do not walk in these ways are nearsighted and blind *to spiritual things*, and have forgotten that they were washed clean from their old broken ways. **10**So then, my *sacred* family members, do all you can to make sure you are among the ones Creator has called and chosen to be his own. If you walk in these ways, you will never stumble. **11**And you will be given a warm welcome onto Creator's good road that never fades away, the same road walked by our Honored Chief and Sacred Deliverer, Creator Sets Free (Jesus) the Chosen One.

12-13 Even though you know these things and stand firm in the truth you now have, as long as I live in this body I will never stop reminding you about these things. I think it is the right thing to do, **14**for our Honored Chief, Creator Sets Free (Jesus) the Chosen One, has made it clear to me that I will soon walk on. [15]I am making it my aim to share these things with you, so that after I have walked on you will always be able to remember what you have been taught.

A TRUE WORD OF PROPHECY

[16]We were not following slyly crafted, manmade stories when we made known to you the power and coming of our Honored Chief, Creator Sets Free (Jesus) the Chosen One. With our own eyes we saw his chiefly greatness. [17]For he received honor and shining-greatness from his Father, the Great Spirit, who spoke to him with his voice of honor, saying, "This is my much-loved Son, the one who makes my heart glad."

[18]With our own ears we message bearers who were with him on the sacred mountain heard this voice from the spirit-world above.[a] [19]We have an even more sure word of prophecy—one that will guide you well if you follow it as you would a torch that shines in the dark. So stay alert until the day dawns and the morning star rises in your hearts.

[20]Above all else, you must understand that no prophecy found in our Sacred Teachings is a matter of one's own interpretation. [21]For prophecy did not come from the mind[b] of human beings but from those who through the Holy Spirit spoke Creator's words.

2

A WARNING ABOUT FALSE TEACHERS

[1]But just as there were false prophets among the people *of tribes of Wrestles with Creator (Israel)*, there will also be false teachers among you. They will sneak into your gatherings and teach things that are harmful to our spiritual ways. They will even deny the Honored One who paid a great price to set them free. In doing so, they will quickly bring ruin down on their own heads. [2]Many will follow their shameful ways, and because of them the way of truth will be spoken against. [3]Because of their greed, they will use made-up stories to prey on you for their own gain. Their punishment *for this* that was spoken of long ago is not sleeping. It is still coming and will not fail to bring them to a bad end.

EXAMPLES FROM THE PAST

[4]The Great Spirit did not take pity on spirit-messengers who were guilty of wrongdoing. He banished them into the dark caves of the underworld, to be held there until the time comes for their fate to be decided. [5]Neither did he spare the ancient world when he sent a great flood to cleanse the world from evil. But along with seven others he spared One Who Rests (Noah), who told others about Creator's right ways.

[6]Creator decided that the people of Village of Bad Spirits (Sodom) and the people of Village of Deep Fear (Gomorrah) needed to be punished for their evil ways. So he covered them with burning ashes. He left those ruined villages as a warning for all who would walk in evil ways. [7]But he rescued Covers His Head (Lot), a good-hearted man living among them, who was deeply troubled by the people who had given themselves over to their bad hearts and evil ways. [8]The soul of this good man was tormented day after day by the evil things he saw and heard.

---

[a]**1:18** Matthew 17:5; Mark 9:7; Luke 9:35
[b]**1:21** Lit. *will*

WARNINGS ABOUT BAD-HEARTED ONES

⁹So then, all of these stories show us that the Honored One knows how to rescue his holy ones from trouble and hold the bad-hearted ones captive until the day comes when he will decide their punishment. ¹⁰This is true most of all for those who give themselves over to their bad-hearted, corrupt desires and who have no respect for authority. These *bad-hearted ones* are reckless, stubborn, and puffed up with pride. They do not even tremble with respect when they speak evil against spirit-beings of shining-greatness. ¹¹Even so the spirit-messengers, who are greater in strength and power, do not accuse *these bad-hearted ones* or speak evil of them before our Honored Chief.

¹²But these people act without thinking. They are like wild animals born to be captured and killed. They speak against things they know nothing about, but they will be captured in their own cages and come to a bad end. ¹³In this way, they will suffer for the wrongs they have done. It makes their hearts glad to run wild in the light of day. They are dark spots and stains *on your garments*, gladly feasting with you while deep inside they laugh *about how they have tricked you.* ¹⁴They are always looking for someone willing to be unfaithful in marriage. They lure weak souls into their evil ways. Their hearts are well trained to want more and more. They are children living a cursed life, ¹⁵who have left the good road *to walk a path of lies.* They have followed in the footsteps of People Destroyer (Balaam), the son of Burning Man (Beor), who loved the things he could gain from wrongdoing. ¹⁶But a donkey, which cannot talk, spoke with a human voice and gave him a good tongue-lashing, turning the prophet away from his madness.

¹⁷These *bad-hearted ones* are like dried-up watering holes and clouds that scatter and melt in the wind. A place of deep darkness is kept ready for them. ¹⁸With empty boasts and puffed-up words, they prey on people's weak human desires and lure them back into the wrong ways of those they have just escaped from. ¹⁹They promise them freedom, but they are themselves slaves to evil desires, for people are slaves to whatever controls them.

BAD HEARTS LEAD TO A BAD END

²⁰What would happen to those who, after being set free from the shameful ways of the world through knowing our Honored Chief and Sacred Deliverer, Creator Sets Free (Jesus) the Chosen One, were to be overcome by these ways and to choose to walk once again on that bad path? If that happened, they would be in a worse place than they were at first. ²¹It would have been better if they had never known about the good road than, after learning about it, to walk away from the sacred teaching that was handed down to them. ²²They have proved the truth of these wise sayings: "A dog returns to its own vomit,"ᵃ and, "A pig after being washed goes back to wallowing in the mud."

3 ⟡⟡⟡⟡⟡⟡⟡⟡⟡⟡⟡⟡

WISDOM FOR THE LAST DAYS

¹My much-loved ones, this is now my second letter to you. I have written both letters to stir up your memories and awaken good thoughts. ²I want you to

---

ᵃ**2:22** Proverbs 26:11

remember the things foretold by the holy prophets of old and the instructions given by the message bearers of our Honored Chief and Sacred Deliverer.

³I want to remind you, first of all, that in the last days there will come scoffers who will laugh with scorn. Following their own bad hearts, ⁴they will say *things like*, "Where is he? Did he not promise to appear again? Our fathers have walked on since then, but all things remain the same as they were at the creation of the world."

⁵But they choose to ignore the truth that long ago, when Creator spoke his word, the universe came into existence, and the land was brought forth from water and by water. ⁶It was also through water that the ancient world was brought to an end by a great flood. ⁷By the same word, the skies above and the earth below that now exist will be brought to an end by fire. They will remain until the *great* day of deciding arrives, which will bring an end to those who walk in evil ways.

⁸But do not forget this one thing, my much-loved friends: with the Great Spirit there is no difference between one day or one thousand winters. ⁹*So then,* our Honored Chief is not slow in keeping his promise, even if some see it that way. *Instead,* he is being patient with you. He does not want anyone to come to a bad end. He wants all people to return to the right way of thinking.

THE DAY OF OUR HONORED CHIEF

¹⁰But *you can be sure that* the day of our Honored Chief will come. *It will come without warning*, like a thief. Then with a loud sound like rushing wind, the skies above will come to an end. The elemental things will melt away in the fierce heat.

And the earth and the things done on it will be laid bare.ᵃ

¹¹Seeing that all these things will come to an end in this manner, you should be a people who walk a sacred path that brings honor to the Great Spirit. ¹²*Keep walking in this way* as you wait for the coming day of Creator, doing what you can to help it come more quickly. When that day comes, the skies above will burn away, and the elemental things will melt in the fierce heat. ¹³But we are looking to what the Great Spirit has promised—a new spirit-world above and a new earth below where all people will walk in his right ways.

WISDOM FROM SMALL MAN

¹⁴So then, my much-loved friends, since you are looking for these things, make it your aim to be found by him walking in peace, having no spot or stain *on your souls*. ¹⁵Remember, the reason our Honored Chief is being patient is to give more time for people to trust him to rescue them from what is coming. This is what our much-loved *spiritual* brother Small Man (Paul) wrote to you about, through the wisdom he was given. ¹⁶He writes about these things in all his letters. Some of the things he writes about are hard to understand. In their ignorance, people who have lost their *spiritual* balance misrepresent these teachings, as they do other sacred teachings, to their own bad end.

CLOSING WORDS

¹⁷So then, my much-loved friends, since I have warned you ahead of time, stay alert! Then none of these bent and twisted people will lead you down the

---

ᵃ**3:10** Some manuscripts read *burned up.*

wrong path and cause you to lose your own spiritual balance. [18]Instead, keep growing in the gift of great kindness and knowledge that is yours through our Honored Chief and Sacred Deliverer, Creator Sets Free (Jesus) the Chosen One.

To him be all honor and bright-shining greatness, both now and to the time beyond the end of all days.

Aho! May it be so!

FIRST LETTER FROM HE SHOWS GOODWILL

1 JOHN

THE STORY OF THE WORD OF LIFE

¹There is one who has existed from the beginning. We heard his story. We saw him with our own eyes. We stared *in wonder* at him and touched him with our own hands. He is the one we call the Word of Life.

²This Life was made known to us. We have seen it, we give witness to it, and we are now telling you the story of the life of the world to come that never fades away, full of beauty and harmony. This Life was with our Father *the Great Spirit* and has now been revealed to us.

³We are telling you about the things we have seen and heard so that you may share with us the same life we share in harmony with our Father *the Great Spirit* and his Son, Creator Sets Free (Jesus) the Chosen One. ⁴We write these things to you so that our hearts can dance together *in the circle of life.*

THE GREAT SPIRIT IS LIGHT

⁵The Great Spirit is light, and in him there is no darkness. This is the message we heard from the Chosen One and are now telling you. ⁶If we say we are in harmony with him yet walk a path of darkness, we are living a lie and not following the truth. ⁷But if we walk in the light, as he is in the light, we will be in harmony with each other as the lifeblood shed by Creator Sets Free (Jesus), the Son of the Great Spirit, cleanses us from all our broken ways.

⁸If we say that we have no broken ways, we are lying to ourselves, and the truth is not alive in us. ⁹If we name our broken ways, our Creator can be trusted to release us from them and purify us from all wrongdoing. ¹⁰If we say we have never walked in broken ways, we are calling him a liar, and his words are not at home in us.

THE ONE WHO REPRESENTS US

¹My much-loved children, I am writing these things to you so you will not walk a path of broken ways. But if anyone does, we have one who represents us before our Father the Great Spirit. He is Creator Sets Free (Jesus) the Chosen One, who has always done what is right. ²He paid a great price to set us free from our bad hearts and broken ways, not only for us but for all people.

³We can be sure that we truly know him if we follow the teachings of the Chosen One. ⁴The ones who say, "I know the Great Spirit," yet do not follow his teachings, are lying, and the truth does not live in them. ⁵⁻⁶But for those who

walk in his message, Creator's love has found its true meaning and purpose. The ones who say they are in harmony with the Great Spirit must walk in the footsteps of Creator Sets Free (Jesus). This is how we know we are living in harmony with him.

AN OLD AND NEW TEACHING

[7]My much-loved friends, I am not giving you a new teaching[a] but an old one, the same one you were given at first. The old teaching is the message you have heard. [8]On the other hand, I am giving you a new teaching. Its truth is found in Creator Sets Free (Jesus) and also in you. For the darkness is fading, and the true light is already shining. [9]Anyone who says, "I walk in the light," but hates another[b] is still walking in darkness. [10]Anyone who loves others is walking in the light and has no reason to trip or fall. [11]But anyone who hates others is in darkness and walks in darkness. Such ones have lost their way because the darkness has blinded their eyes.

WISDOM FOR ALL AGES

[12]I write to you children because you have been released from your broken ways through the name of Creator Sets Free (Jesus). [13]I write to you elders because you have known the one who was there from the beginning. I write to you young ones because you have won the victory over the evil trickster.

[14]I have written to you children because you have known the Father, *who is the Great Spirit*. I have written to you elders because you have known Creator Sets Free (Jesus), the one who was there from the beginning. I have written to

you young ones because you are strong, with Creator's message firmly planted in your hearts, and you have won the victory over the evil trickster.

DO NOT LOVE THE WAYS OF THE WORLD

[15]Do not love the *ways of this* world, nor the things *you can get* from the world. When you love the world, it shows that the love of our Father *the Great Spirit* is not alive in you. [16]For all the things found in the world—desiring to walk in broken ways, longing to have everything you see, thinking you are better and more deserving than others—these things are not from our Father *the Great Spirit* but from the world. [17]This world is coming to an end along with all its broken desires, but the ones who walk in the ways of the Great Spirit will remain to the time beyond the end of all days.

THE FALSE CHOSEN ONE

[18]My *much-loved* children, the time of the end[c] has come! You have heard that a false chosen one is coming. *I tell you* even now that many false chosen ones have appeared. This is how we know that the time of the end[d] has come. [19]These false chosen ones were among us, but they did not belong, so they left. If they had truly belonged, they would have remained—but they left, showing that they did not belong.

[20]But as for you, the Holy One has poured out *his Spirit* as a sweet-smelling ointment on you, *choosing you as his own*, and all of you know the truth. [21]I write this to you not because you do not know the truth, but because you know it, and because no lie comes from the truth. [22]Who is the liar? It is the one who denies

---

[a]**2:7** Instruction or commandment
[b]**2:9** Lit. *brother*. Also in verses 10-11.

[c]**2:18** Lit. *the last hour*
[d]**2:18** Lit. *the last hour*

that Creator Sets Free (Jesus) is the Chosen One. This is the false chosen one, the one who denies both Father and Son. **23**The ones who deny the Son do not have the Father. The ones who speak well of the Son have the Father also.

HARMONY WITH CREATOR

24So then, let the message you first heard remain in you. If you do, then you will also remain in harmony with the Son and with the Father. **25**His promise to us is the life of the world to come that never fades away, full of beauty and harmony.

26I write to you to warn you about the ones who are trying to lead you down the wrong path. **27**But the sweet-smelling ointment *of his Spirit* remains within you, and there is no need for anyone to teach you. The sweet-smelling ointment *of his Spirit* is your teacher in all things. Through it, he speaks only the truth and never anything false. So remain in harmony with him just as he has taught you.

28So I say again, my much-loved children, remain in *harmony with* him, so that when he appears we may stand boldly before him and not have to hang our heads in shame. **29**Since you know that *the Chosen One* always does what is right, you can be sure that the Great Spirit is the father of all who walk in his right ways.

CHILDREN OF THE GREAT SPIRIT

1Behold the greatness of the love shown to us by our Father the Great Spirit that he would call us his children! And so we are! The ones who belong to *the ways of* this world do not know the Giver of Life, so they do not see us in this way.

2Much-loved friends, we are now Creator's children. It is not yet clear what we will be. But we know that when the Chosen One appears, we will be like him, for we will see him as he truly is. **3**All who through him have this hope will keep themselves pure, in the same way that he is pure.

A WARNING ABOUT BROKEN WAYS

4All who walk in broken ways are trampling over the law *of the Chosen One*, for all broken ways go against his law. **5**You know that he came to do away with bad hearts and broken ways and that in him there are no broken ways. **6**The ones who remain in harmony with him do not walk in broken ways. Those who walk in broken ways have not truly seen or known him.

7My much-loved children, do not let anyone take you down the wrong path. The Chosen One always did what was right. So the ones who keep walking his right ways show that they are in good standing with him. **8**The ones who stay with walking in broken ways are following the evil trickster, for he has been walking in broken ways from the beginning. The reason Creator's Son appeared was to bring an end to the ways of the evil trickster. **9**Those who have been born from the Great Spirit do not keep walking in broken ways. They are not able to, for Creator is their Father and he has planted his message[a] deep within them to stay.

LOVING EACH OTHER

10There is a clear difference between Creator's children and the children of the evil trickster. The ones who do not

---

[a]**3:9** Lit. *seed*. See Matthew 13:18-23.

walk in a good way do not belong to Creator, nor do those who do not love the sacred family. **11**The message you heard from the beginning was that we should love each other. **12**Do not be like Spear Maker (Cain), who gave himself to the ways of the evil trickster and killed his *own* brother. Why did he kill him? Because what he was doing was wrong, and what his brother was doing was right. **13**So then, my much-loved family members, do not be surprised if the world hates you.

14We know that we have crossed over from death to life, because we love each other. The ones who do not love remain under the power of death. **15**All who hate others have murder in their hearts, and you know that murderers do not have the life of the world to come that never fades away, remaining in them.

16The Chosen One laid down his life for us. This is how we know what love is. In the same way, we should lay our lives down for each other. **17**If someone who has many possessions sees another in need and shows no pity, how can Creator's love remain in that person? **18***My* much-loved children, our love must not be empty words on our tongues but deeds done in truth. **19-20**This is how we can be sure we belong to the way of truth. Whenever our hearts make us feel guilty, we can still have peace when we stand before him. For Creator is greater than our hearts and knows all things.

21*My* much-loved friends, if our hearts are free from guilt, this gives us the courage to stand boldly before Creator. **22**He will give us whatever we ask of him because we keep his instructions and do the things that make his heart glad.

23This is his instruction to us, that we trust in the name of his Son, Creator Sets Free (Jesus) the Chosen One, and love each other as he taught us to do. **24**The ones who follow these instructions remain in him, and he remains in them. We know that he remains in us by the Spirit he has gifted to us.

4

TESTING THE SPIRITS OF THE PROPHETS

1*My* much-loved friends, do not trust every spirit, but test the spirits *of the prophets* to see whether Creator sent them, for there are many false prophets who have gone out into the world. **2**This is how to know whether a spirit comes from Creator: Every spirit that says Creator Sets Free (Jesus) the Chosen One came to us as a human being is from the Great Spirit. **3**Every spirit that does not speak of Creator Sets Free (Jesus) in this manner is not from the Great Spirit. This is the spirit of the false chosen one, the one you have heard was coming and who is now already in the world.

4Much-loved children, you have been born of Creator and have won the victory over these *false prophets*. For the Spirit[a] in you is much greater than the spirit[a] in the world. **5**These *false prophets* are of this world, so they speak the way the world speaks, and the world listens. **6**We are of the Great Spirit, and those who know the Great Spirit listen to us. The ones who are not of the Great Spirit do not listen to us. This is how we can tell the Spirit that is true from the spirit that is false.

MORE ABOUT LOVE

7*My* much-loved friends, love each other, for love comes from the Great Spirit. All

---

[a] **4:4** Lit. *one*

who love have been born of him and know him. **8**Those who do not love do not know him, for the Great Spirit is love. **9**Creator showed his love for us by sending the only Son who fully represents him into this world, so that we could live through him. **10**This is love, not that we loved Creator, but that he loved us and proved his love by sending his Son to take on himself the burden of our broken ways.

11*My* much-loved friends, if Creator loved us like that, then we should also love each other. **12**No one has ever seen the Great Spirit, but as long as we love each other, he remains in us, and his love is made complete in us. **13**We know that we live in him and he lives in us because Creator has shared his Spirit with us. **14**We have seen and now tell you the truth about what our Father the Great Spirit has done. He sent his Son to be the Sacred Deliverer of the world. **15**Those who tell others that Creator Sets Free (Jesus) is the Son of the Great Spirit are the ones Creator lives in, and they live in him.

THE GREAT SPIRIT IS LOVE

16We have come to know and trust the love Creator has for us. The Great Spirit is love. He remains in those who love and keep on loving, and they remain in him. **17**Love is made complete in us so that we will stand without fear on the day Creator decides who has done right or wrong. For in this world, *when we love as he loves*, we are just like him.

18Where love is there can be no fear, for mature love drives all fear away. Fear comes from the thought of punishment. So love has not yet matured in those who continue to be afraid. **19**We love because he first loved us. **20**If we say that we love the Great Spirit but hate others, then we are speaking with a forked tongue. If we

do not love someone we can see, then how can we love a Creator we cannot see? **21**And from him we have been given this instruction: the ones who love the Great Spirit must also love the members of his family.

5 ◆◇◆◇◆◇◆◇◆◇◆◇◆◇◆◇◆◇

LOVE WINS THE VICTORY

1All who believe that Creator Sets Free (Jesus) is the Chosen One have the Great Spirit as their Father. All who love the Father will also love his children. **2**We can be sure that we are loving Creator's children when we love Creator and follow all of his instructions. **3**For when we follow his instructions, it shows our love for the Great Spirit. And his instructions are not hard to follow. **4**Whoever has the Great Spirit as their Father wins the victory over *the ways of* the world. For it is our trust *in him and his way of love* that wins the victory.

THE WATER, THE BLOOD, AND THE SPIRIT

5Who is able to win the victory over *ways of* the world? Those who trust that Creator Sets Free (Jesus) is the Son of the Great Spirit. **6**He is the one who came through water and blood—Creator Sets Free (Jesus) the Chosen One. He did not come by water only, but by both water and blood. It is the *Holy* Spirit who tells us that this is true, for the Spirit himself is the truth. **7**So then, we have three who witness to this truth— **8**the Spirit, the water, and the blood—and these three are in harmony.

TRUE LIFE IS FOUND IN CREATOR'S SON

9If we accept truth from human beings, then how much more should we accept the truth of what the Great Spirit has told us about his Son! [10]The ones who trust in the Son of the Great Spirit have accepted this truth in their inner beings. But those who do not trust in him are making Creator out to be a liar, because they do not believe he has told the truth about his Son. [11]And the truth we have heard from Creator is that he has gifted us with the life of the world to come that never fades away, full of beauty and harmony—and this life is *found* in his Son. [12]The ones who have the Son have life. The ones who do not have Creator's Son do not have life.

BOLDNESS IN PRAYER

[13]I have written these things to you who trust in the name of Creator's Son, so that you may know you have the life of the world to come that never fades away, full of beauty and harmony. [14]We can be sure that if we ask anything of the Great Spirit that is in harmony with his will, he will hear us. [15]If we know that he hears us, then we know we have whatever we have asked of him.

SPECIAL INSTRUCTIONS FOR PRAYER

[16]You might see a sacred family member walking in a broken way that does not end in death. You should pray and that person will be given life, as long as the broken way does not end in death. There is a broken way that ends with death. If that is so, prayer will not help. [17]All who do wrong walk in broken ways, but not all broken ways end in death.

LAST WORDS

[18]We know that all who have the Great Spirit as their Father do not continue to walk in broken ways. They are kept safe by the Son, who fully represents his Father, and the evil one cannot harm them. [19]We know that we are children of the Great Spirit. We know that the evil one rules over *the ways of* this world. [20]We also know that the Son of the Great Spirit has come. He has given us a way to know the True One. It is through his Son, Creator Sets Free (Jesus) the Chosen One, that we are in *harmony with* the True One. This is the one true Great Spirit and the life of the world to come that never fades away, full of beauty and harmony.

[21]*My* much-loved children, keep away from spirit-images *or anything that would take the place of the Great Spirit in your hearts.*

Aho! May it be so!

SECOND LETTER FROM
HE SHOWS GOODWILL

2 JOHN

GREETINGS AND FIRST WORDS

¹From *He Shows Goodwill (John)*, the elder.

To the honored woman and her children who have been chosen *by the Great Spirit*. You are all truly loved, not only by myself but by all who know the truth. ²This love comes from the truth that lives in us and will remain with us to the time beyond the end of all days.

³It is this truth and love, coming from our Father the Great Spirit and from his Son, Creator Sets Free (Jesus) the Chosen One, that blesses us with the gift of his great kindness, mercy, and peace.

WALKING IN LOVE

⁴It made my heart dance for joy when I found some of your children following the way of truth, just as our Father *from above* has instructed us. ⁵I now call on you, honored woman, to make sure that we love each other. This is not a new instruction I am writing to you, but the same one we were given from the first. ⁶Love means we are following his instructions. This is the same instruction you heard from the beginning—that we should walk in love.

WARNINGS ABOUT FALSE TEACHERS

⁷For in this world there are many false teachers, *leading people down the wrong path*. They say that Creator Sets Free (Jesus) did not come into this world as a human being. Those who say this are deceivers and *of* the false chosen one. ⁸Guard your hearts. You do not want to lose what we all have worked so hard for and fail to receive the full honor that should be yours.

⁹All who go too far in their thinking and do not remain true to the teaching about the Chosen One have walked away from the Great Spirit. But the ones who remain true to this teaching walk together both with the Father and with his Son. ¹⁰If any of these people come to you who do not agree with this teaching, do not welcome them to stay in your home or greet them *as members of the sacred family*. ¹¹For greeting them *in this way* means you are joining with them in their evil deeds.

FINAL WORDS

¹²I have much more to tell you, but I do not want to use paper and ink. I am hoping to come and speak with you face to face. In this way, our hearts will dance for joy.

¹³The children of your honored sister who have been chosen *by the Great Spirit* send their greetings *to you*.

Aho! May it be so!

THIRD LETTER FROM
HE SHOWS GOODWILL

3 JOHN

GREETINGS AND FIRST WORDS

1From *He Shows Goodwill (John)*, the elder.

To my much-loved *spiritual* brother Glad Heart (Gaius), whom I truly love. **2**My close friend, I pray that good things will come your way and that you will remain in good health, even as your soul does well.

WALKING THE PATH OF TRUTH

3It made my heart dance for joy when some of the members of the sacred family came and told me of your great respect for the truth—a path you now walk. **4**Nothing gives me more joy than to hear that my *spiritual* children are walking the path of truth.

TREATING TRAVELERS WELL

5My much-loved brother, it is good that you keep treating the *traveling* members of our sacred family so well, even though they are strangers to you. **6**At a gathering of our sacred family they told us about the love *you showed to them*. You are doing a good thing when you send these family members on their way in a manner that honors the Great Spirit. **7**For they went out to make his name known without taking any help from those outside the sacred family.[a] **8**So it is up to us to help them on their way. In this way, we share together with them in making known the truth.

A WARNING TO THE HEADMAN

9I wrote to the sacred family *that gathers with you*, but Raised by the Sky Spirit (Diotrephes), who loves to be the headman, will not listen to us. **10**So if I come, I will give him a stern talking-to, for he has spoken foolishly, accusing us with evil words. As if this were not enough, he also refuses to welcome *traveling* members of the sacred family. He puts a stop to those who want to welcome them and forces them out of the sacred family gathering.

A GOOD REPORT

11My much-loved brother, do not follow these evil ways, but walk in step with those who do good. The ones who walk in a good way are of the Great Spirit. The ones who walk in evil ways have not truly seen the Great Spirit.

12Everyone has something good to say about Corn Spirit (Demetrius), and what they say agrees with the truth. We also say good things about him, and as you know, we always speak the truth.

CLOSING WORDS

13I have much *more* to say to you, but I do not want to use pen and ink. **14**I hope to see you soon, so we can speak face to face.

15Peace be with you. Our friends *from the sacred family who gather here* send their greetings to you. Please greet our friends *from the sacred family who gather with you*. Greet each of them by name.

Aho! May it be so!

STRONG OF HEART

JUDE

GREETINGS

¹From Strong of Heart (Jude), a brother of He Leads the Way (James) and a *sacred* servant of Creator Sets Free (Jesus) the Chosen One.

To all whom our Father the Great Spirit has called, who are loved by him, and kept safe by Creator Sets Free (Jesus) the Chosen One. ²May Creator's mercy, peace, and love flood into your lives *like a rushing river.*

FIRST WORDS

³*My* much-loved friends, I was eagerly preparing to write to you about how we have all been set free and made whole. As I thought about this, I felt that I needed to urge you to wage a *spiritual* battleª for the faith that was once and for all handed down to his holy ones. ⁴For there are some bad-hearted people who have snuck in among you. They twist the gift of Creator's great kindness into an excuse to give in to uncontrolled selfish pleasures. In doing so, they deny our only Headman and Honored Chief, Creator Sets Free (Jesus) the Chosen One. It was written long ago that people like this would come to a bad end.

A SOLEMN REMINDER

⁵I want to remind you of some things you already know. *First*, that our Honored Chief who rescued his people from Black Land (Egypt) later stuck down the ones who turned away from trusting him.

⁶You also know about the spirit-messengers who did not remain in their place of authority and deserted their rightful dwelling. They are bound continually in a place of deep darkness waiting to face their fate on the great day of deciding.

⁷In the same way, Village of Bad Spirits (Sodom) and Village of Deep Fear (Gomorrah) and the small villages nearby gave themselves over to sexual impurity and to twisted and shameful ways. These villages, which were punished with a fire that burned on and on, are now set before us as a warning against such things.

DECEITFUL DREAMERS

⁸But the bad-hearted people I have been telling you about ignore these warnings. They are deceitful dreamersᵇ who through their corrupt desires reject all authority and speak against spirit-beings of shining-greatness. ⁹Not even Who Is Like Creator (Michael), who is himself a very powerful spirit-messenger, dared to speak in this way against the evil trickster when they both argued over the body of Drawn from the Water (Moses). *Instead* he said, "May the Great Spirit Chief rebuke you!" ¹⁰But these bad-hearted ones speak against things they do not understand. They are like wild

---

ª**1:3** Ephesians 6:10-17

ᵇ**1:8** Jeremiah 23:25-27

beasts who do not think but act only on instinct. These things are taking them to a bad end.

LESSONS FROM THE PAST

[11]Sorrow and trouble are coming their way! They are following in the footsteps of Spear Maker (Cain), *who out of anger and jealousy killed his own brother.*[a] In their longing for more possessions they have given themselves over to the greedy ways of People Destroyer (Balaam), *a prophet who would have brought a curse on Creator's people for pay.*[b] And like Bald-headed Man (Korah), who led an uprising[c] *against Drawn from the Water (Moses),* they will come to the same bad end.

LOST AND WANDERING STARS

[12]These *bad-hearted ones* have no respect for the love you share when they feast with you *at your sacred family gatherings.* They are dark spots and stains on your gatherings, caring only for themselves. They are clouds with no rain, blown about by the winds. They are trees that have no fruit at the harvest moon. They are twice dead, with their roots plucked from the ground. [13]Their shameful ways are like the foam churned up by the storm-tossed waves of the sea. They are lost and wandering stars that have strayed from their proper path in the night sky. A place of deep darkness that goes on and on is kept ready for them.

THE COMING OF OUR HONORED CHIEF

[14]It was people like this that Walks with Creator (Enoch), the seventh generation from Red Clay (Adam), prophesied about when he said, "Behold! Our Honored Chief is coming with many thousands of his holy ones. [15]*When he comes*, he will carry out the decision he has made against the ones who have followed their bad hearts and broken ways. Their shameful ways will be exposed along with all the insulting things they have spoken against the Great Spirit." [16]These people keep grumbling and complaining, even as they try to satisfy all of their own broken desires. They speak big, boastful words and use flattery to get what they want from others.

END-TIME SCOFFERS

[17]But I call on you, *my* much-loved friends, to remember the words spoken by the message bearers of our Honored Chief, Creator Sets Free (Jesus) the Chosen One, as they warned us of what was coming. [18]They told you that in the time of the end there would be scoffers who would follow their own selfish desires. [19]They were talking about these troublemakers who turn people against each other—beast-like people—who do not have the Spirit.

STAY ROOTED IN LOVE

[20]But you, *my* much-loved friends, use your trust in our sacred and spiritual ways[d] to grow even stronger as you pray with the words the Holy Spirit gives you. [21]Keep yourselves *deeply rooted* in the love of the Great Spirit, as you keep looking and waiting for the mercy of our Honored Chief, Creator Sets Free (Jesus) the Chosen One, who gives us the life of the world to come that never fades away, full of beauty and harmony.

[22]Show this same mercy to some among you who are doubting, [23]and rescue some as if you were snatching

---

[a]**1:11** Genesis 4:1-8
[b]**1:11** Numbers 22–24
[c]**1:11** Numbers 16:1-2

[d]**1:20** Lit. *your most holy faith*

them from flames of fire. To others show mercy as you tremble in fear, hating the broken ways that have stained their regalia and ruined their lives.

CLOSING WORDS

24Now to the one who is able to keep you from stumbling, who can make you pure and blameless, so that with great joy you can stand before his bright-shining greatness. 25To the one Great Spirit, who has set us free and made us whole through our Honored Chief Creator Sets Free (Jesus) the Chosen One. Bright-shining greatness, beauty, power, and chiefly rule belong to him from the time before all days, today, and to the time beyond the end of all days.

Aho! May it be so!

BOOK OF THE GREAT REVEALING

REVELATION

OPENING WORDS

¹Written down in this sacred scroll are the things the Great Spirit revealed to Creator Sets Free (Jesus) the Chosen One. This *great* revealing was given to the ones who serve him, to show them what will soon happen. He sent his spirit-messenger to He Shows Goodwill (John), his sacred servant, to make this message known to him *through signs, omens, and sacred visions.*

²He Shows Goodwill (John) as a truth teller wrote down everything he saw and heard as a witness to this message from the Great Spirit and the things told to him by Creator Sets Free (Jesus) the Chosen One.

³Creator's blessing rests on the one who reads aloud the words of this prophecy, and on those who hear and take to heart what is written in it, for the time it speaks about is almost here.

THE MESSAGE BEGINS

⁴From He Shows Goodwill (John) to the seven sacred families in Land of the Rising Sun (Asia):

I greet you with great kindness and peace from One Who Is and Was and Is to Come, and from the seven spirits who stand face to face with him as he sits in his seat of honor. ⁵I also greet you from Creator Sets Free (Jesus) the Chosen One.

He is the honorable witness, the first to rise from among the dead, and the Grand Chief over all who rule on earth. All honor belongs to the one who loves us, the one who, by giving up his own life-blood, set us free from our bad hearts and broken ways.

⁶He has made us to be chiefs of a sacred nation of holy men and women who represent the good road of his Father the Great Spirit. All honor and power belong to him from the ages past to the time beyond the end of all days. Aho! May it be so!

CLOUD RIDER IS COMING

⁷Behold! He comes riding on the clouds! Every eye will see him, even the ones who pierced him. When all the tribes of the land see him, their hearts will be pierced through with sorrow and fall to the ground.ᵃ Aho! May it be so.

⁸"I am Alpha and Omega,ᵇ the one who is before all things and beyond all things," says the Great Spirit Chief. "I am One Who Is and Was and Is to Come, the All-Powerful One."

ON THE ISLAND OF WALKING PLACE

⁹I, He Shows Goodwill (John), am your brother in the sacred family and one who walks a path of suffering with you

---

ᵃ1:7 Zechariah 12:10
ᵇ1:8 Alpha and omega are the first and last letter of the Greek alphabet, the language of the New Testament.

as we walk the good road with firm steps following Creator Sets Free (Jesus) the Chosen One. I had been banished to the island called Walking Place (Patmos) because I had spoken the truth about Creator Sets Free (Jesus) and his message from the Great Spirit.

A LOUD VOICE SPEAKS

10I was taken up into the spirit *world* on the day *we gather in honor* of our Great Chief. I heard a loud voice from behind me that sounded like an eagle bone whistle.[a]

11The voice said, "Write down in a scroll the things that you see. Send this scroll to the seven sacred family gatherings in Land of the Rising Sun (Asia).

"Send it to the sacred family gatherings in Village of Desire (Ephesus), Village of Bitter Herbs (Smyrna), First in Courage (Pergamum), High Rock House (Thyatira), Safe Place (Sardis), Family of Friends (Philadelphia), and The People Will Decide (Laodicea)."

THE TRUE HUMAN BEING IS REVEALED

12I turned around to see the voice that was speaking to me. When I turned, I saw seven golden lampstands. **13**The lampstands encircled one who looked like a True Human Being.[b] His regalia was a robe that reached all the way to his feet. He wore a golden sash that was wrapped across his chest. **14**The hair on his head was as white as the tip of an eagle's tail feathers,[c] as white as freshly fallen snow, and his eyes blazed like flames of fire. **15**His feet glowed like molten bronze purified in a furnace of fire, and his voice roared like the sound of great rushing waters. **16**In his right hand he was holding seven stars. Out from his mouth came a sharp, two-edged long knife, and his face shone with the full strength of the sun.

17When I saw him, I dropped to the ground and lay at his feet as a dead man.

I AM FIRST AND LAST

He put his right hand on me and said, "Do not fear! **18**I am first and last, the Living One, who was dead, and now, behold! I am alive, never to die again. And in my hands I hold the power[d] to free people from the Dark Underworld of Death (Hades).

19"So then," he said to me, "Write down the things you have just seen and the things that will be shown to you. **20**I will tell you the mystery of the seven stars you saw in my right hand and the mystery of the seven golden lampstands. The seven stars are the messengers of the seven sacred family gatherings, and the seven lampstands are the seven sacred families.

2

TO VILLAGE OF DESIRE

1"Write this to the messenger of the sacred family that gathers in Village of Desire (Ephesus):

These are the words of the one who holds the seven stars in his right hand, the one who walks among the seven golden lampstands: **2**I know what you have been doing, how hard you have worked, and the rough path you

---

[a]**1:10** Lit. *trumpet*, or in Hebrew *shofar*, meaning "ram's horn"
[b]**1:13** Daniel 7:13
[c]**1:14** Lit. *white like wool*

[d]**1:18** Lit. *keys*

have walked with firm steps. I also know that you do not put up with evil and worthless ways. You have put to the test the ones who *falsely* call themselves message bearers and have proven them to be liars who speak with forked tongues.

³I know you have never grown tired of representing me, even when thorns grew across the path. ⁴But I have against you this one thing—you have walked away from the love you had at first. ⁵So remember what made you stumble, go back and find that first love, and do what needs to be done. Unless you change your thinking about this, I will have to come and remove your lampstand. ⁶But you have this in your favor: like me, you hate what the Rulers of the People (Nicolaitans) do.

⁷Let the one who has ears hear and do what the Spirit is saying to the sacred families. To the ones who win the victory, I will give them fruit to eat from the tree of life that grows in Creator's Beautiful Garden.

TO VILLAGE OF BITTER HERBS
⁸"Write this to the messenger of the sacred family that gathers in Village of Bitter Herbs (Smyrna):

These are the words of the one who is the first and last, who died and came back to life. ⁹I know that you have walked a troubled path and that you are poor, but *spiritually* you are rich. I also know the lies spoken against you by those who claim to be Tribal Members, but they are not. They are a tribal gathering house for Accuser (Satan), and not true-hearted Tribal Members.

¹⁰Do not fear the suffering you must soon face. The evil trickster snake will put you to the test. I tell you, he will have some of you thrown into a prison house, and you will walk a troubled path for ten days. Even if you must face death, stay true to the path, and I will honor you with a headdress of life that has many feathers.

¹¹Let the one who has ears hear and do what the Spirit is saying to the sacred families. The ones who win the victory will not be hurt at all by the second death.

TO VILLAGE OF FIRST IN COURAGE
¹²"Write this to the messenger of the sacred family that gathers in the village of First in Courage (Pergamum):

These are the words of the one who has the sharp, two-edged long knife: ¹³I know you live where Accuser (Satan) rules. You have stood strong and true, representing my name in the days when Looks Like His Father (Antipas), my truth teller, was killed in your village where Accuser (Satan) makes his home. Even then you refused to turn your back on me and stayed true to my good road.

¹⁴But even so, I have a few things against you: Some among you walk in the teachings of People Destroyer (Balaam), who instructed People Swallower (Balak) to put stumbling stones before the children of Wrestles with Creator (Israel). He tempted them to ceremonially eat food that had been offered to spirit-

images and to give themselves to sexual impurity. [15]Like them, you also have among you some who follow the teachings of the Rulers of the People (Nicolaitans).

[16]Unless you change your thinking about these things, I will come suddenly to you and make war against them with the words of my mouth that will cut like a two-edged long knife.

[17]Let the one who has ears hear and do what the Spirit is saying to the sacred families. I will give the mysterious bread[a] to the ones who win the victory. I will also give them a new name carved into a white stone. A name known only to the one who receives it.

TO VILLAGE OF HIGH ROCK HOUSE

[18]"Write this to the messenger of the sacred family that gathers in the village of High Rock House (Thyatira):

These are the words of the Son of the Great Spirit, who has eyes that blaze like flames of fire and feet that glow like molten bronze: [19]I know how hard you work, how truly you love, how faithfully you serve others, and how you never give up walking the good road. I also know that you are doing even more now than you did at first.

[20]But even so, I have something against you. You permit Bad Spirit Woman (Jezebel), the one who calls herself a prophetess, to teach my sacred servants. She takes them down a path of sexual impurity and teaches them to ceremonially eat food that has been offered to spirit-images. [21]I have given her time to return to the right way of thinking, but she would not change her mind about her impure ways. [22]Behold, I am putting her into a bed of sorrow and suffering. And all who participate with her will also suffer greatly, unless they turn from her impure ways. [23]I will turn her *spiritual* children over to death. Then all the sacred families will know that I am the one who looks into the thoughts and sees the hearts of all people. I will make sure each person is given what is deserved for all that he has done.

[24]But to the rest of you who live in the village of High Rock House (Thyatira), the ones who do not walk in her ways and know nothing about the so-called deep things of Accuser (Satan), I require nothing more of you, [25]except to say, Hold tightly to what you already have until I come to you.

[26-27]To the ones who win the victory and keep walking in my ways to the end of the trail, I will give them the right to rule over all nations with an unbreakable iron *chief's* staff, one that can break pots made of clay into pieces.[b] [28]This is the same right my Father has given to me. I will also gift them with the morning star. [29]Let the one who has ears hear and do what the Spirit is saying to the sacred families.

---

[a]**2:17** Lit. *manna*, meaning "what is it?" A mysterious food. See Exodus 16:33; John 6:32-33, 48-51.

[b]**2:26-27** Psalm 2:9

3

TO VILLAGE OF SAFE PLACE

¹"Write this to the messenger of the sacred family that gathers in the village of Safe Place (Sardis):

These are the words of the one who has the seven spirits of the Great Mystery and the seven stars: I know what you have been doing. I know you have a reputation of being alive. But while others may see you as alive, I see you as dead. ²Wake up! Do not let death defeat you! Strengthen those things that remain alive before it is too late. For I can see that you have not finished what the Great Spirit has called you to do. ³So remember what you have been given and what you have heard. Return to the right way of thinking. Walk with firm steps and do what needs to be done. But if you fail to wake up, you will not be prepared for my coming. Then for you I will be like a thief who comes when you do not expect it.

⁴But there are a few among you in the village of Safe Place (Sardis) with a good reputation, who have not stained their regalia. Dressed in pure white regalia, they will dance by my side in the circle of life, for they are worthy of this honor. ⁵All others who win this victory will also wear pure white regalia. I will not remove their names from the book of life, and I will represent them by speaking their names before my Father and his spirit-messengers. ⁶Let the one who has ears hear and do what the Spirit is saying to the sacred families.

TO VILLAGE OF FAMILY OF FRIENDS

⁷"Write this to the messenger of the sacred family that gathers in the village of Family of Friends (Philadelphia):

These are the words of the holy and true One, the one who has the rightful power[a] of Much Loved One (David). When he opens the way, no one can close it, and when he closes the way, no one else can open it.

This is what the holy and true One has to say: ⁸I know what you have been doing. Behold! I have opened a way before you that no one can block. Even though your strength is small, you have stayed true to my message and have not turned away from representing me. ⁹Look at what I will do to the members of the gathering house of Accuser (Satan) who falsely represent themselves as true-hearted Tribal Members. I will cause them to humble themselves before you to honor you. I will make sure they clearly see that I have loved you.

¹⁰Because you have walked with firm steps and stayed true to my message, I will watch over you and keep you safe from the time of great trouble that is coming upon the world, to test the ones who walk the land. ¹¹*It will not be long, for* I am coming soon. Hold on to what you already have with a strong hand. Then no one will be able to take your headdress of honor away from you.

¹²To the ones who win the victory I will make them a strong pole in the sacred lodge of my

---

[a] 3:7 Lit. *key*

Father the Great Spirit—and there they will remain. I will carve into them the name of my *Father the* Great Spirit and the name of his sacred village that comes down from the world above—the new Village of Peace (Jerusalem). I will also carve into them my own new name. **13**Let the one who has ears hear and do what the Spirit is saying to the sacred families.

TO THE VILLAGE OF THE PEOPLE WILL DECIDE

14"Write this to the messenger of the sacred family that meets in the village of The People Will Decide (Laodicea):

These are the words of Heart Speaker, the one who is the trustworthy and honest truth teller. He is the wellspring and chief of all the Great Spirit has created:

15I know what you have been doing, and that *spiritually* you are neither cold nor hot. How I wish you were either cold or hot! **16**But because you are only warm, neither hot nor cold, I am about to vomit you out of my mouth. **17**The reason for this is that you say, 'I have acquired great possessions, more than I could ever need.' But you cannot see that you are to be pitied, for *spiritually* you are full of misery—poor and blind and naked. **18**I counsel you to acquire from me gold that has been purified by fire, and then you will truly have great possessions. You must also acquire from me pure white regalia, to hide the shame of your nakedness, and healing ointment to put on your eyes, so you can see.

19It is from my love that I speak sharply to you, so that you will learn to follow my ways. And then from your heart you will return to my right ways of thinking and doing.

20I stand before the entrance of your tipi, asking you to welcome me in. If any of you welcome me in, I will sit down with you, and we will share a good meal together.

21I will give the ones who win the victory the right to sit with me on my seat of honor in the same way that I also won the victory and sat down with my Father on his seat of honor.

22Let the one who has ears hear and do what the Spirit is saying to the sacred families."

THE SACRED VISION BEGINS

1After this I looked up and *in my sacred vision* I saw an opening into the spirit-world above. I heard the voice of the one who had spoken to me at first. The voice that sounded like an eagle bone whistle.[a]

"Come up here," the voice said, "and I will show you the things that will take place following *what you have seen and heard.*"

A VISION OF THE SEAT OF HONOR

2Right then, *in my sacred vision*, I was taken up *through the opening* into the spirit-world above. I looked and saw a seat of honor in the world above—and someone was seated on it!

3The one who sat on it had the appearance of a fiery red but clear crystal

---

[a]**4:1** Lit. *trumpet*, or in Hebrew *shofar*, meaning "ram's horn"

stone.ᵃ A rainbow that looked crystal greenᵇ encircled the seat of honor.

⁴Encircling the seat of honor were twenty-four elders sitting on twenty-four seats of honor. They wore pure white regalia and golden headdresses.

THE SEVEN SPIRITS OF THE GREAT MYSTERY

⁵From the seat of honor came flashes of lightning and rolling thunder. There were seven torches of fire burning before the seat of honor, which are the seven spirits of the Great Mystery. ⁶Before the seat of honor there was what looked like a great sea, smooth and crystal clear.

Four living *spirit* animals, with eyes in the front and back, closely encircled the seat of honor.

THE SPIRIT ANIMALS ARE REVEALED

⁷The first *spirit* animal was like a lion. The second *spirit* animal was like a young bison. The third *spirit* animal had the face of a human being. And the fourth *spirit* animal was like a soaring eagle.

⁸These four *spirit* animals each had six wings and were covered with eyes all around and even under their wings. Day and night they never stop saying, "Holy, holy, holy is the all-powerful Great Spirit, One Who Is and Was and Is to Come!"

⁹⁻¹⁰The *spirit* animals give shining-greatness and honor and thanks to the one who sits in the seat of honor, all to the one who lived before all days and lives beyond the end of all days. Then the twenty-four elders humble themselves, remove their headdresses, and offer them to the one who sits on the seat of honor.

¹¹"All honor belongs to you, O Great Spirit Chief," the twenty-four elders say

with one voice. "For you are the one who made everything there is. It is from your sacred vision that all things came into being and were created!"

5 ❖◀✖▶◀✖▶◀✖▶◀✖▶◀✖▶◀✖▶◀✖▶

A SCROLL WITH SEVEN SEALS

¹*In my sacred vision,* I then saw a scroll resting on the right hand of the one sitting on the seat of honor. The scroll was sealed with seven seals, and full of words inside and out.

²Then I saw a powerful spirit-messenger with a thundering voice saying for all to hear, "Who has gained the honor to take the scroll and break open its *seven* seals?"

³But no one in the spirit-world above or on the earth below or under the earth was able to open the scroll or see what was inside. ⁴*Many tears ran down my face as* I wept and cried because there was no one who had gained the honor to open the scroll and look inside.

THE LION WHO IS THE LAMB

⁵But one of the elders *came to me.* "Do not weep!" he said. "Look, there is the Lion from the tribe of Give Him Praise (Judah), *the one who has sprouted from* the Root of Much Loved One (David). He has won the victory and gained the honor to take the scroll and break open its seven seals."

⁶Then I looked and saw a Lamb that looked as if he had been violently killed standing in the center near the seat of honor. He stood encircled by the four living *spirit* animals and the elders. The Lamb had seven horns and seven eyes. These are the seven spirits of Creator that he has sent out into all the earth.

ᵃ**4:3** Lit. *jasper and carnelian,* which are crystalline jewels. Carnelian is clear and sometimes has a red cast. Jasper is red.
ᵇ**4:3** Lit. *like an emerald,* a clear, green-colored jewel

⁷Then the Lamb stepped forward and took the scroll from the right hand of the one who sat in the seat of honor. ⁸When he took the scroll, the four living *spirit* animals and the twenty-four elders all humbled themselves before the Lamb to honor him. They each held a stringed musical instrument and a golden smudge bowl full of sweet-smelling smoke, which are the prayers of Creator's holy people.

A NEW SONG FOR THE LAMB

⁹Then they sang a new song with these words:

"To you belongs the honor to take hold of the *sacred* scroll and break open its seven seals, for you died as a lamb led to the slaughter. You paid the highest price by offering your lifeblood to bring people back to the Great Spirit from every tribe and language and people and nation. ¹⁰You have made them chiefs of a sacred nation of holy men and women who will give guidance to all the earth as they represent the good road of the Great Spirit."

SPIRIT-MESSENGERS HONOR THE LAMB

¹¹Then I heard the sound of countless numbers of spirit-messengers, thousands upon thousands of them, and ten thousand times ten thousand. They made a grand circle around the seat of honor, the *spirit* animals, and the elders.

¹²With one thunderous voice, they sang, "The Lamb that was violently killed has been honored with power, riches, wisdom, chiefly rule, respect, blessing, greatness, and praise!"

¹³Then I heard all of creation, those in the spirit-world above, on the earth below, under the earth, and in the sea of great waters.

They were singing, "All blessing, respect, honor, and chiefly rule belong to the one who sits on the seat of honor and to the Lamb, to the time beyond the end of all days!"

¹⁴Then the four *spirit* animals said, "Aho! May it be so!" And the elders humbled themselves before the Great Spirit and before the Lamb to give them the honor they deserved.

A WHITE HORSE AND ITS RIDER

¹I watched as the Lamb broke open the first of the seven seals. Then I heard the first of the four *spirit* animals speak.

"Come forth!" it said with a voice of thunder.

²And when I looked, I saw a white horse with its rider holding a bow. He was given a headdress, and he rode out as a conqueror to conquer again.

A RED HORSE AND ITS RIDER

³When the Lamb broke open the second seal, I heard the voice of the second *spirit* animal.

"Come forth!" it said.

⁴Another horse came forth—fiery red. Its rider was permitted to take away peace from the land, so that war and violence would break out among the people. And he was given a great and powerful long knife.

A BLACK HORSE AND ITS RIDER

⁵When the Lamb broke open the third seal, I heard the voice of the third *spirit* animal.

"Come forth!" it said.

I looked, and there before me was a black horse. Its rider had balancing scales in his hand.

⁶From the center of the four *spirit* animals, I heard a sound like a voice.

"A small basket of wild rice[a] or three small baskets of corn[b] to trade for a day's work," the voice said. "But do no harm to the *olive* oil and the wine."

A PALE HORSE AND ITS RIDER

[7]When the Lamb broke open the fourth seal, I heard the voice of the fourth spirit animal.

"Come forth!" it said.

[8]I looked, and there before me was a *sickly* pale-*green* horse. The name of its rider was Death. Following close behind him was the Dark Underworld of Death (Hades). They were given power over a fourth of the land, to kill with the long knife, hunger, deadly disease, and by the wild beasts of the land.

THE VOICE OF THE HONORED DEAD

[9]When the Lamb broke open the fifth seal, I looked under the sacred altar and saw the souls of the ones who had been killed for remaining true to the message Creator had given them.

[10]They cried out with a loud voice, "O Honored One, who is holy and true! How long will it be before you right the wrong done against us by the people in the land who have shed our blood?"

[11]Then each of them was gifted with white regalia and told to rest for a little while longer. For there were still a number of their brothers and sisters—who also serve the Great Spirit—who must be killed in the same manner they were.

THE DAY OF FIERCE ANGER HAS COME

[12]When the Lamb broke open the sixth seal, I looked, and there was a great earthquake. The sun became as dark as a black cloth, the full moon became blood red, [13]and, like wild figs flung from a tree shaken by a fierce wind, the stars in the sky fell down on the land. [14]The sky went away like a scroll being rolled up and set to the side. And every mountain and island was moved from its place.

[15]The chiefs who ruled the land, the headmen and the war chiefs, the rich and powerful, and everyone, slave or free, hid themselves in caves and behind the rocks in the mountains.

[16]"Fall on us!" they said to the mountains and rocks. "Hide us from the face of the one who sits on the seat of honor and from the anger of the Lamb. [17]For the great day of their fierce anger has come, and who is able to stand *against them*?"

7

THE FOUR WINDS ARE HELD BACK

[1]After this I saw four spirit-messengers standing at the four corners of the land.[c] They were holding back the four winds of the earth to keep them from blowing on the land, on the sea, or against any tree.

[2]Then I saw another spirit-messenger rising from the place where the sun rises, holding the branding iron[d] of the living Creator. With a loud voice the messenger called out to the four spirit-messengers who were permitted to harm the land and the sea.

THE SEALING OF THE SERVANTS OF CREATOR

[3]"Bring no harm to the land, sea, or trees," the messenger instructed them, "until we have sealed the mark *of the Great Spirit* on the foreheads of the ones who serve him."[e]

---

[a]**6:6** Lit. *a liter of wheat*
[b]**6:6** Lit. *barley*
[c]**7:1** Ezekiel 7:2
[d]**7:2** Lit. *seal*
[e]**7:3** Ezekiel 9:4

[4]I then heard the number that would be sealed—one hundred forty-four thousand—from all of the tribes of children of Wrestles with Creator (Israel).

[5-8]Twelve thousand were sealed from each of the tribes named and represented here:

Give Him Praise (Judah), Son of My Vision (Reuben), Counting Many Coups (Gad), Walks with a Glad Heart (Asher), He Will Wrestle (Naphtali), He Made Them Forget (Manasseh), Creator Hears (Simeon), He Brings Together (Levi), He Is My Reward (Issachar), Honored Dwelling (Zebulun), Creator Gives More (Joseph), Son of My Right Hand (Benjamin).

EVERY TRIBE AND LANGUAGE

[9]After this I saw a great crowd of people, too many to count, from every nation, tribe, clan, and language. They were standing before the seat of honor and before the Lamb, dressed in pure white regalia, holding palm tree branches in their hands.

[10]They lifted their voices and shouted, "The power to set us free and make us whole belongs to the Great Spirit who sits upon the seat of honor, and to the Lamb!"

[11]All the spirit-messengers who encircled the seat of honor, along with the elders and the four living *spirit* animals, humbled themselves and fell face down on the ground before the Great Spirit to give him the honor that he deserves.

[12]"Aho! It is so!" they said *with one voice*. "Praise and honor and wisdom and respect and power and strength belong to the Great Spirit to the time beyond the end of all days! Aho! It is so!"

WHO ARE THESE PEOPLE?

[13]Then one of the elders spoke to me, "Who are these people who are dressed in white regalia? And from where did they come?"

[14]"Honored one," I said to him, "you must know."

Then he said *to me*, "These are the ones who have come through the time of great trouble and suffering. They have washed their regalia in the lifeblood shed by the Lamb, making their regalia pure white.

[15]"Because of this they stand before the seat of honor, and they serve the Great Spirit day and night in the inner court of his sacred lodge. The one who sits on the seat of honor will spread his sacred tent over them and cover them in the shadow of his wings. [16]Never again will they hunger or thirst or suffer under the heat of the *desert* sun.

[17]"The Lamb at the center of the seat of honor will watch over them like a shepherd watches over his sheep. He will guide them to springs of life-giving water, and there the Great Spirit will perform the wiping of tears ceremony for each of them."

8

SILENCE IN THE WORLD ABOVE

[1]When the Lamb broke open the seventh seal, a *powerful* silence fell on the spirit-world above that remained for about half an hour. [2]Then I saw the seven spirit-messengers that stand before the Great Spirit. They were given seven eagle bone whistles.[a]

SMOKE AND PRAYERS GO UP

[3]Another spirit-messenger, holding a golden smudge bowl in his hands, came

---

[a]**8:2** Lit. *trumpet,* or in Hebrew *shofar,* meaning "ram's horn"

and stood before the *sacred* altar. He was given much incense to burn as a sweet-smelling smoke offering above the *sacred* golden altar and offer it up along with the prayers of all the holy ones. ⁴From the golden smudge bowl in the hand of the spirit-messenger the sweet-smelling smoke, mixed with the prayers of Creator's holy ones, began to rise to the Great Spirit.

PURIFYING FIRE

⁵Then the spirit-messenger filled the smudge bowl with fiery coals from the sacred altar and threw it down on the land. I heard the crashing and rolling thunder and saw flashes of lightning, and the earth began to shake.

⁶Then the seven spirit-messengers who were holding the seven eagle bone whistlesᵃ got ready to sound them.

**THE SOUNDING OF THE
EAGLE BONE WHISTLES**

⁷The first spirit-messenger sounded his eagle bone whistle, and hail and fire mixed with blood came *out from the altar* and were thrown down on the land. A third part of the land was burned with fire, and a third of the trees, and all the green grass.

⁸The second spirit-messenger sounded his eagle bone whistle, and what looked like a great mountain burning like a wildfire was thrown into the sea. A third of the waters turned into blood, ⁹a third of all the living sea creatures died, and a third of the sea-canoes sank.

¹⁰The third spirit-messenger sounded his eagle bone whistle, and from the sky came a great star flaming like a torch. The flaming star fell down on a third of the rivers and on the springs of water.

¹¹The name of the star was Bitterness, and a third of the waters became bitter, and many people died because the water had been made bitter.

¹²The fourth spirit-messenger sounded his eagle bone whistle, and a third of the sun, moon, and the stars were struck with darkness. So for a third of the day the sun gave no light, and for a third of the night the moon and stars did not shine.

¹³Then I heard the screech of an eagle above me, so I looked up and saw an eagle soaring in the sky.

"Warning, warning, warning!" the eagle screeched, "to those who live on the land, because of the remaining eagle bone whistlesᵇ to be sounded by the last three spirit-messengers!"

THE BOTTOMLESS PIT IS OPENED

¹The fifth spirit-messenger sounded his eagle bone whistle,ᶜ and I saw a star falling to earth from the spirit-world above. The star was given the powerᵈ to open the way to the deep, dark underworld.

²The star opened the way, and smoke began to rise from the pit, like smoke from a great fiery furnace. The air was filled with the smoke, and the sun was darkened.

FIERCE GRASSHOPPERS EMERGE

³Out of the smoke came *fierce* giant grasshoppers on the land. They were given power to sting like earthly scorpions. ⁴They were told not to harm any of the earth's grass or any green plant or tree,

---

ᵃ**8:6** Lit. *trumpet*, or in Hebrew *shofar*, meaning "ram's horn"

ᵇ**8:13** Lit. *trumpet*, or in Hebrew *shofar*, meaning "ram's horn"

ᶜ**9:1** Lit. *trumpet*, or in Hebrew *shofar*, meaning "ram's horn"

ᵈ**9:1** Lit. *key*

but only the human beings who had not been marked on their foreheads with the seal of the Great Spirit. ⁵They were not permitted to kill anyone, but only to bring them pain and suffering for five moons—pain like the sting of a scorpion.

⁶In those days people will seek death but will not find it. They will long to die, but death will run *and hide* from them.

⁷The grasshoppers looked like war-horses prepared for battle. They wore golden headdresses, and their faces looked human. ⁸They had hair like a woman and teeth like a *mountain* lion. ⁹They wore breastplates of iron, and their wings sounded like many horses galloping into battle. ¹⁰Their tails were like a scorpion's, and their sting had the power to greatly wound people for five moons. ¹¹Their war-chief is the spirit-messenger of the deep dark underworld. The name of the war-chief in our tribal language[a] is Abaddon, meaning Destroyer, and in the language of the Outside Nations[b] his name is Apollyon, also meaning Destroyer.

¹²The first time of terrible pain and suffering has passed, but two more times of terrible pain and suffering will soon follow.

A GREAT ARMY OF MANY HORSEMEN

¹³When the sixth spirit-messenger sounded an eagle bone whistle,[c] I heard a voice coming from the four horns of the golden altar that is before the Great Spirit. ¹⁴The voice spoke to the spirit-messenger, saying, "Unleash the four spirit-messengers who are bound at the great river called Much Fruit (Euphrates)."

---

¹⁵Then the four spirit-messengers who had been held ready for that very hour and day and moon and year were unleashed to kill a third of humankind. ¹⁶I heard the number of this great herd of horse riders. It was twice ten thousand multiplied by ten thousand.

THE APPEARANCE OF THE HORSES AND RIDERS

¹⁷In my sacred vision I could see the appearance of the riders and their horses. The riders wore breastplates that were fiery red, smoky blue, and yellow like sulfur that burns. The horses had heads like *mountain* lions, and out from their mouths came fire, smoke, and burning sulfur. ¹⁸It was these three things that killed a third of humankind—the fire, smoke, and burning sulfur that came from the horses' mouths. ¹⁹The power of the horses was in their mouths and tails, for on the end of their tails were snake-like heads that could *bite and* injure people.

THE PEOPLE WHO WERE NOT KILLED

²⁰The rest of the people who were not killed in this way did not turn away from the spirit-images they made with their own hands. They continued to follow evil spirits and pray to these spirit-images made of gold, silver, bronze, stone, and wood—things that cannot see, hear, or walk. ²¹They also did not turn away from their murders, witchcraft, and sexual impurity, or from taking what is not theirs.

A SPIRIT-MESSENGER AND THE VOICE OF SEVEN THUNDERS

¹Then I saw another powerful spirit-messenger coming down from the

spirit-world above. He was clothed with a cloud, and a rainbow was over his head. His face was like the sun, his legs were like towers of fire, ²and a small scroll lay open in his hand. He put his right foot on the sea and his left foot on the land. ³He cried out with a loud voice that roared like a lion. And when he cried out, the seven thunders spoke with rumbling voices.

⁴I was about to write down the message spoken by the seven thunders when I heard a voice from the spirit-world above.

"Do not reveal what the seven thunders have spoken," the voice instructed me. "Seal up the words and do not write them down."

THE ANCIENT MYSTERY IS FINISHED

⁵Then the spirit-messenger whom I saw standing on the sea and on the land raised his right hand to the spirit-world above. ⁶He made a solemn promise representing the one who lives to the time beyond all days, the one who created all things in the spirit-world above, on the earth below, the great waters of the sea, and all that is in them.

"There shall be no more delay," *he cried out,* ⁷"for the time has come for the seventh spirit-messenger to sound his eagle bone whistle!ᵃ When he sounds, the ancient mystery spoken by the Great Spirit will be complete, bringing the full meaning and purpose of the good story that he revealed to his prophets who served him."

THE SMALL SCROLL IS SWEET AND BITTER

⁸Then I again heard the voice that had spoken to me from the spirit-world above.

"Go," the voice said to me, "and take the scroll that is lying open in the hand of the spirit-messenger who is standing on the sea and on the land."

⁹I did as I was told and instructed the spirit-messenger to give me the scroll.

"Take it and eat it," the messenger said to me. "It will be as sweet as honey in your mouth, but it will turn bitter in your stomach."

¹⁰So I took the small scroll from the hand of the spirit-messenger and ate it. It was as sweet as honey in my mouth, but when I swallowed, it became bitter in my stomach.

¹¹Then I was told, "You must once again prophesy to many peoples, nations, languages, and rulers."

11

MEASURING THE SACRED LODGE

¹A measuring reed the size of a walking stick was given to me.

"Rise up," a voice said to me, "and measure Creator's sacred lodge and the altar, and count the ones who make their prayers and serve him there. ²But do not measure the courtyard that is outside of the lodge, for it has been given over to the Outside Nations. And for forty-two moons they will trample the sacred village under their feet.

THE TWO TRUTH-TELLER PROPHETS

³"And I will give power to my two truth tellers, and they will prophesy for one thousand two hundred sixty days, wearing rough animal hidesᵇ to show the sorrow in their hearts."

⁴These are the two olive trees and the two lampstands that stand before the Honored One of all the earth. ⁵Fire will

---

ᵃ**10:7** Lit. *trumpet,* or in Hebrew *shofar,* meaning "ram's horn"

ᵇ**11:3** Lit. *sackcloth*

come out from their mouths to burn up all their enemies. All who try to harm them must die in this manner. **6**They also have the power over the sky to hold back the rain during the days of their prophesying. And they have power over the waters, to turn them into blood, and the power to bring all kinds of disasters on the land as often as they desire.

THE TWO PROPHETS ARE KILLED

7When they have completed their time of truth telling, the wild beast who rises from the deep, dark underworld will make war with them and defeat and kill them. **8**Their bodies will lie dead in the pathway of the great Village of Peace (Jerusalem), where our Honored Chief was killed by being nailed to a tree-pole—the cross. This village is spiritually known as Village of Bad Spirits (Sodom) and as Black Land (Egypt).

9For three and a half days people from many tribes, languages, and nations will stare at their dead bodies and will not permit them to be buried properly. **10**Those who dwell in the land will celebrate with glad hearts and send gifts one to another, because these two prophets had caused them such great suffering.

THE PROPHETS RETURN TO LIFE

11But after three and a half days, the breath of the Great Spirit entered into them. When they rose to their feet, great fear fell on all who were watching. **12**Then the two prophets heard a loud voice from the spirit-world above.

"Come up here!" the voice said to them. As their enemies watched, a cloud took them up into the spirit-world above.

13At that same time there was a great shaking of the earth. A tenth of the village came crashing down, and seven thousand people were killed. Those who remained were filled with fear and gave honor to the Great Spirit of the world above.

14The second time of terrible pain and suffering has passed, but a third time of terrible pain and suffering will soon follow.

THE SEVENTH EAGLE BONE WHISTLE

15*Then when* the seventh spirit-messenger sounded his eagle bone whistle,[a] I heard loud voices in the spirit-world above.

"The power to rule this world now belongs to our Great Spirit Chief and to his Chosen One," the voices thundered, "and the guidance of his good road will last beyond the end of all days!"

16Then the twenty-four elders, who sit in seats of honor before Creator, fell face down on the ground to give honor to the Great Spirit.

17"We offer thanks to you, O Honored One," they said *with one voice*. "You are the All-Powerful One, Who Is and Was, for you have revealed your great power and established your good road. **18**The nations were furious, but now the time of your fierce anger has come. It is time for you to decide the fate of the dead and to honor the ones who serve you—both prophets and holy ones—all who have deep respect for your name, from the smallest to the greatest among us. And *it is time for you* to bring to an end the ones who have brought destruction to the land."

19Then I looked and saw that the *way into* Creator's sacred lodge in the spirit-world above was open. Inside the lodge the cedar box of the peace treaty came into view. Lightning flashed with the sound of crashing thunder, and the earth

---

a11:15 Lit. *trumpet,* or in Hebrew *shofar,* meaning "ram's horn" shook while large hailstones fell from the sky.

12 ⟨X⟩◂⟨X⟩◂⟨X⟩◂⟨X⟩◂⟨X⟩◂⟨X

OMENS IN THE WORLD ABOVE

¹A great and mysterious omen was seen in the spirit-world above: a woman wearing the sun for her regalia, with the moon under her feet, and on her head a headdress of twelve stars. ²She was with child and cried out in agony as she was giving birth.

³Then another omen was seen in the spirit-world above: a great fiery-red sea serpent with seven heads and ten horns. On each of its seven heads it wore the headdress of a chief. ⁴With its tail the sea serpent reached up into the spirit-world above and pulled down a third of all the stars and threw them down on the land. Then the fiery-red sea serpent, wanting to swallow up her child as soon as it was born, placed itself in front of the woman, waiting for her to give birth.

A SON IS BORN TO RULE THE NATIONS

⁵The woman gave birth to a son, a male child, the one who holds an iron chief's staff to rule over all nations. And her child was taken up to the Great Spirit and to his seat of honor.

⁶The woman found safe passage into the desert wilderness, to the place Creator had prepared for her. There she would be fed and kept safe for one thousand two hundred sixty days.

WARFARE IN THE WORLD ABOVE

⁷I looked up and saw that there was an uprising in the spirit-world above. Who Is Like Creator (Michael) and his spirit-messengers were waging war with the fiery-red sea serpent and its spirit-messengers. They fought back, ⁸but they were not powerful enough, and the sea serpent and its spirit-messengers lost their foothold in the spirit-world above.

⁹The great fiery-red sea serpent was thrown down from the spirit-world above. He is the ancient trickster snake, who is also called the evil one and Accuser (Satan). He is the one who takes the whole world down a false path. He was thrown down to the ground, along with all his spirit-messengers.

CREATOR'S GOOD ROAD HAS ARRIVED

¹⁰Then I heard a voice thundering in the spirit-world above, saying, "The good road of the Great Spirit has finally arrived! This good road has the power to set us free and make us whole! The Chosen One has walked this good road to the end and has the right to bring it to us. And now, the one who by day and by night accuses the sacred family members before the Great Spirit has been thrown down to the ground. ¹¹Creator's holy ones won the victory over him by the lifeblood shed by the Lamb and by boldly telling his story, and, when faced with death, they loved him more than they loved their own lives.

¹²"So let your hearts be glad, you who live in the spirit-world above. But to those who live on land and sea there will be great sorrow and trouble, for the evil trickster snake has come down upon you with great anger, because he knows that his time will soon come to an end."

EAGLE HELPS THE WOMAN

¹³So when the fiery-red sea serpent saw that he had been thrown down to the ground, he hunted down and mistreated the woman who had given birth to the

male child. **14**But the woman was given two wings of a great eagle, so she could fly deep into the desert wilderness to a place where she would be cared for. There she was hidden from the face of the evil trickster snake—for a season, and seasons, and half a season.[a]

THE LAND HELPS THE WOMAN

15The sea serpent spewed a raging river of water out from its mouth at the woman, to carry her away in its flood. **16**But the land helped the woman by opening its mouth to swallow the river the sea serpent had spewed from its mouth.

17The serpent's anger toward the woman grew fierce, so it left her and attacked the rest of her descendants—the ones who walk in the ways of the Great Spirit and stand true to the message of Creator Sets Free (Jesus).

13

THE WILD BEAST FROM
THE GREAT WATERS

1The fiery-red sea serpent took its stand on the shore of the great waters. Then I saw a wild beast with ten horns and seven heads emerging from the waters. On each horn was a headdress like a chief would wear. Its heads had names carved into them that spoke evil against the Great Spirit. **2**I saw that the wild beast looked like a leopard with feet like a bear and a mouth like a *mountain* lion. The fiery-red sea serpent gave the wild beast its power, its seat of ruling, and its far-reaching dominion.

3I saw that one of the heads of the wild beast was fatally wounded, but the wound had healed, and all the people of the land were filled with wonder as they followed after the wild beast. **4**They were all bowing down and honoring the fiery-red sea serpent, because it had given power to the wild beast. So they gave honored service to the wild beast, saying, "Who can be compared to the wild beast? Who can make war with it?"

5The fiery-red sea serpent filled the mouth of the wild beast with arrogant words and insults spoken against the Great Spirit. And for forty-two moons the wild beast was permitted to do whatever it wanted. **6**So it spoke with boldness against the Great Spirit, his name, his sacred lodge in the spirit-world above, and against all who live there. **7**The wild beast was given the ability to make war against Creator's holy people and defeat them. It was also given authority over every tribe and people and language and nation. **8**All who dwell in the land will honor and serve the wild beast—all whose names have not been written down in the book of life belonging to the Lamb who was *chosen to be* violently killed from the formation of the world.[b]

9Let the one who has ears, hear this: **10**"All who lead others into captivity will themselves become captive. All who take up the long knife to kill will by the long knife be killed."[c]

This will test the faithfulness of Creator's holy ones to stay true to the path of trusting in the ways of the Great Spirit.

THE WILD BEAST FROM THE LAND

11Then I saw another wild beast emerging from the land. This beast had two horns like a lamb, but it spoke like a fiery-red

---

[a]**12:14** Meaning three and a half years, which is the same as 1,260 days or forty-two moons

[b]**13:8** 1 Peter 1:19-20
[c]**13:10** Matthew 26:52

sea serpent. ¹²Representing the first wild beast, it used its power to make all who dwell in the land honor and serve the first wild beast whose deadly wound had been healed. ¹³It performed great signs and wonders in the sight of everyone, even making fire come down on the land from the sky.

¹⁴Because of the signs that were done as it represented the first wild beast, it was able to trick the people who live in the land. It instructed them to carve an image to honor the *first* wild beast who was fatally wounded by the long knife yet lived. ¹⁵It was given the power to give breath to the *carved* image and make it speak. It could then have anyone killed who would not bow down to honor the *carved* image of the *first* wild beast.

¹⁶The second wild beast then required everyone, small or great, rich or poor, slave or free, to be tattooed on their right hand or on their forehead, ¹⁷so that no one could buy or sell without this mark, which represents the name of the wild beast or the number of its name.

¹⁸Wisdom is needed here. The one who understands will count the number representing the name of the wild beast. It is the number of a human being, and this one's number is six hundred sixty-six.

14

THE ONE HUNDRED AND FORTY-FOUR THOUSAND

¹Then I looked, and there on Strong Mountain (Mount Zion) stood the Lamb. Standing with him were one hundred forty-four thousand who had his name and the name of his father tattooed on their foreheads. ²And coming from the spirit-world above I heard a voice that sounded like the roar of rushing water

or the sound of loud thunder. And the voice I heard was like the sound of music being played on stringed instruments.

³The singers were standing before the seat of honor and the four living *spirit* animals and the elders. They sang a new song that no one was able to learn except for the one hundred forty-four thousand, who, at a great cost, had been rescued from the land. ⁴These are the ones who have kept themselves *spiritually* as pure as a virgin. Wherever the Lamb goes, they walk the road with him. They are the first from among humans to be set apart for the Great Spirit and for the Lamb. They are the ceremonial first fruits of the harvest, for a great price has been paid to rescue them and set them free. ⁵They speak only what is true, for they are spiritually pure and have no false ways within them.

A SPIRIT-MESSENGER ANNOUNCES THE GOOD STORY

⁶Then I saw another spirit-messenger flying high above me. The messenger had the words of the good story that tells about the good things of the world to come. This good story is to be told to all who dwell in the land, to every nation, tribe, language, and people!

⁷"Show great respect and honor to the Great Spirit," the messenger said with a loud voice, "for the time has come for him to decide who has done right and who has done wrong. Bow down and humble yourselves before the one who created the sky above, the earth below, the great waters of the sea, and the springs of water *that flow out from the ground*."

⁸A second spirit-messenger followed the first, saying, "It has fallen! The great Village of Confusion (Babylon) has fallen! She is the village that has made the

nations drink of the wine of Creator's anger toward her *spiritual* impurity."

A WARNING TO THE FOLLOWERS OF THE WILD BEAST

⁹The first two spirit-messengers were followed by a third spirit-messenger, who spoke with a thundering voice, saying, "All who bow down to serve the wild beast or its carved image or any who accept its mark on their foreheads or on their hands ¹⁰will also drink the wine of Creator's great anger. The wine in the cup of his deep anger will not be watered down, and those who drink it must face great suffering with fire and burning rocks in the presence of the holy spirit-messengers and the Lamb. ¹¹And the smoke from their suffering will rise to the time beyond the end of all days. And there will be no rest day or night for all who bow down to serve the wild beast or its *carved* image, or for any who accept the mark that represents its name."

¹²This is the time when Creator's holy people, who follow his instructions and trust in the way of Creator Sets Free (Jesus), will be required to walk with firm steps and stay true to the path.

¹³Then I heard a voice from the spirit-world above saying to me, "Write this down: from this time forward Creator's blessing will rest on those who die, the ones who will make the ultimate sacrifice for their Honored Chief."

"It is true!" says the Spirit. "The weary will find rest from their troubled path, and what they have done will follow them *into the world to come*."

THE LAND IS RIPE FOR THE HARVEST

¹⁴Then I looked up and saw a bright cloud, and there seated on the cloud was one that looked like a True Human Being. He wore a golden headdress and held a sharp harvesting stick in his hand. ¹⁵Another spirit-messenger came out from the sacred lodge. With a loud voice he called out to one who was seated on the cloud, "Take your stick and start harvesting, for the time has come and the land is ripe."

¹⁶Then the one seated on the cloud swung his stick over the land and harvested the crop.

¹⁷Another spirit-messenger came out from the sacred lodge that is in the spirit-world above. He also had a sharp harvesting stick. ¹⁸He was followed by another spirit-messenger, one who has the power of fire. The messenger came out from the sacred altar and called out to the spirit-messenger with the sharp harvesting stick, "Take your sharp stick and harvest the grapes from the land, for her grapes are ripe."

¹⁹So the spirit-messenger swung his harvesting stick over the land, gathered the grapes, and threw them into the great winepress of Creator's fierce anger. ²⁰Then, outside the village, the grapes were trampled on, and blood poured out from the winepress to the height of a horse's shoulders for a distance of about two hundred miles.

15

A POWERFUL OMEN FROM ABOVE

¹Then in the spirit-world above I saw another omen. It was powerful enough to take one's breath away! There were seven spirit-messengers with seven last disasters. After these, Creator's fierce anger will come to an end.

²And then I saw what seemed to be a great sea, smooth and crystal clear,

glowing with fire. And standing on this great sea were the ones who had won the victory over the wild beast, its carved image, and its mark. In their hands they held stringed instruments gifted to them from the Great Spirit. ³They were singing the song of Creator's servant Drawn from the Water (Moses) and the song of Creator's Lamb.

"O Great Creator and Honored One!" *they sang with one voice.* "All that you do is powerful and full of wonder! Your ways are right and true, O Chief of All Nations! ⁴Who is there who does not honor you with deep respect for who you are and what your name represents? Only you are holy! Because your right ways have been clearly shown to all nations, they will come to bring honor to you and serve you."ᵃ

THE SEVEN SPIRIT-MESSENGERS

⁵After this I looked up and in the spirit-world above I saw that the sacred tent of Creator's peace treatyᵇ was opened. ⁶The seven spirit-messengers who hold the power of the seven disasters came out from the sacred tent. They wore regalia made from pure, shining white garments with golden sashes wrapped around their chests.

⁷Then one of the four living *spirit* animals gave to the seven spirit-messengers seven golden smudge bowls that were filled with the fiery anger of the Great Spirit, the one who lives beyond the end of all days. ⁸Smoke that came from Creator's shining-greatness filled the sacred tent, and no one was able to enter until the seven disasters from the seven spirit-messengers had come to an end.

ᵃ**15:4** Psalm 86:9-10
ᵇ**15:5** Acts 7:44

16 ▷◁▶◁▶◁▶◁▶◁▶◁▶◁

THE SEVEN SMUDGE BOWLS POURED OUT

¹I then heard a loud voice coming from the sacred lodge *in the spirit-world above.*

"Go!" the voice said to the seven spirit-messengers, "and pour out on the land the seven smudge bowls of Creator's fiery anger."

²So the first spirit-messenger poured his smudge bowl onto the land, and horrible and painful sores broke out on the people who had the mark of the wild beast and bowed down to serve its carved image.

³The second spirit-messenger poured his smudge bowl into the waters of the sea. And the waters turned into blood that was like the blood of a dead body—and all living things in the sea died.

⁴The third spirit-messenger poured his smudge bowl into rivers and springs of water, and their waters also turned into blood.

⁵Then I heard the spirit-messenger of the waters say, "You are upright and true, O Holy One Who Is and Was. Your decisions are right and true! ⁶For the ones who shed the blood of your holy ones and prophets have been given blood to drink, and this is what they deserve."

⁷And I heard a voice from the sacred altar, saying, "All your decisions are upright and true, O Honored and all-powerful Great Spirit!"

⁸Then the fourth spirit-messenger poured out his smudge bowl on the sun, which was permitted to scorch people with fire. ⁹When scorched by the fierce heat, they cursed the Great Spirit, the one who had the power over these disasters. But they did not return to Creator's right ways and give him the honor he deserves.

¹⁰The fifth spirit-messenger poured out his smudge bowl on the wild beast's seat of power. And all that the wild beast ruled over was covered in darkness. The people *the wild beast ruled over* gnawed their tongues in pain ¹¹and cursed the Great Spirit from the spirit-world above. But they would not turn back from their evil ways to Creator's right ways.

¹²The sixth spirit-messenger then poured out his smudge bowl on the great river named Much Fruit (Euphrates). The waters of the river dried up to prepare the way for the rulers that would come from the east.

¹³Then I saw three impure frog-spirits coming out from the mouth of the fiery-red sea serpent, the wild beast, and the false prophet. ¹⁴These spirits are evil demons, performing *misleading* signs and omens. These spirits go out into all the lands, to gather their rulers to make war against the Great Spirit on the day of the great battle when he shows his mighty power.

HE COMES LIKE A THIEF

¹⁵"Behold, I am coming like a thief!" says *Creator Sets Free (Jesus).*[a] "Creator's blessing will rest on the one who remains awake, wearing regalia, and not naked and ashamed for all to see."

¹⁶And the evil frog-spirits gathered the rulers together to the place called in our tribal language[b] Mountain of Invasion (Armageddon).

¹⁷Then the seventh spirit-messenger poured out his smudge bowl in the air. Out of the sacred lodge came a loud voice from the seat of honor. "It is done!" the voice roared.

¹⁸The lightning flashed, the thunder rumbled, and the earth shook violently! The earthquake was greater than humankind has ever seen or felt before! ¹⁹The great village was split into three parts, and the villages of the Outside Nations fell to the ground. Creator remembered all that the great Village of Confusion (Babylon) had done and gave her the cup that was filled with his fierce anger.

²⁰Every island sank into the great waters, and the mountains could not be found. ²¹Monstrous one-hundred-pound hailstones fell from the sky onto the people. The people cursed the Great Spirit for the hailstones that brought on them such a great disaster.

17

THE FATE OF THE GREAT VILLAGE OF CONFUSION

¹One of the seven spirit-messengers who had the seven smudge bowls came to talk with me.

"Come," the spirit-messenger said to me, "and I will show you the fate of the infamous woman who sits on many waters and trades her body for possessions. ²The rulers of the land have participated in her broken and impure ways. And the people of the land have become drunk on the wine of her impurities."[c]

THE WOMAN WHO SITS ON THE WILD BEAST

³The spirit-messenger carried me away in the spirit to a desert wilderness. I saw a woman sitting on a wild beast that was red in color. The wild beast had seven

---

[a]**16:15** Matthew 24:42-44; 1 Thessalonians 5:2
[b]**16:16** Hebrew

[c]**17:2** Isaiah 1:21

heads with ten horns and was filled with names that spoke evil against the Great Spirit.

⁴The woman wore purple and red garments sparkling with gold, costly stones, and pearls. She held in her hand a golden cup filled with all of her horrible, shameful, and impure ways. ⁵Carved into her forehead was a mysterious name:

VILLAGE OF CONFUSION,
MOTHER OF ALL WHO DWELL
IN THE LAND AND FOLLOW
SHAMEFUL AND IMPURE WAYS

⁶I could see that this woman was drunk with the blood of Creator's holy ones and with the blood of the truth tellers for Creator Sets Free (Jesus). I could only stare at this woman with wonder and amazement.

**THE MYSTERY OF THE
WOMAN IS REVEALED**

⁷"Why are you amazed?" the spirit-messenger asked me. "I will tell you the mystery of this woman and the wild beast with seven heads and ten horns that she rides on.

⁸"The wild beast, which you saw, once was and now is not, but will soon emerge from the dark and bottomless pit and meet with disaster. All who live on the land, whose names have not been written in the book of life from the creation of the world, will be amazed when they see the wild beast that once was and now is not, but will soon emerge from the dark and bottomless pit.

WISDOM IS NEEDED

⁹"Much wisdom is what is needed to understand this mystery. The seven heads *of the wild beast* represent the seven

mountains that the woman sits on. The seven heads also represent seven rulers— ¹⁰five who have fallen, one who now rules, and the seventh, who has not yet come into power. But when he does, he will remain for only a short time. ¹¹The wild beast that once was and now is not is an eighth ruler, who is of the seven and will come to a bad end.

¹²"The ten horns you saw are ten rulers. They have not yet risen in power. But when they do, they will rule for *only* one hour with the wild beast. ¹³Their one purpose is to give their power and authority to the wild beast.

MAKING WAR AGAINST THE LAMB

¹⁴"They will make war against the Lamb, but the Lamb will win the victory, because he is Grand Chief over All Chiefs! And those who stand with him are the called-out ones, who have been chosen and are loyal *to the Great Spirit.*"

THE WOMAN AND THE WILD BEAST

¹⁵Then the spirit-messenger said to me, "The *many* waters you saw the woman sitting on, the one who trades her body for possessions, are many peoples, tribal groups, and languages. ¹⁶The ten horns and the wild beast that you saw will hate the impure woman. They will ruin her, strip her naked, and eat her flesh, and with fire they will burn her until nothing is left.

¹⁷"With one heart and mind the ten horns gave their ruling power over to the wild beast. This is what Creator wanted them to do, so that the words he had spoken would finally happen.

¹⁸"The woman whom you saw," *the spirit-messenger reminded me,* "is that great village that rules over all rulers of the land."

18

THE GREAT VILLAGE HAS FALLEN

¹After this I saw another spirit-messenger, one with great power and authority, coming down from the spirit-world above. The whole land was filled with the light that shined out from him. ²With a powerful and thundering voice he cried out: "She has fallen! The great Village of Confusion (Babylon) has fallen! She has become a lair for demons and impure spirits, and a corral for every impure despised bird and wild beast. ³For all the nations have drunk the wine of her furious impurities. The rulers of the land have joined themselves to her, and those in the land who trade in goods have grown rich from the corrupting power of her dark and evil ways."

COME OUT FROM HER, MY PEOPLE

⁴Then from the spirit-world above I heard another voice.

"My people," *the voice warned*, "remove yourselves from her so you will not participate in her wrong ways and suffer under the disasters that will come upon her. ⁵For her wrongdoings have piled up to the spirit-world above, and the Great Spirit has not forgotten the evil she has done. ⁶Do to her twice as much as she has done to others. Make her drink wine from a wineskin *of sorrows* that is twice as strong as the wine she gave to others. ⁷As much as she boasted in her rich living, give to her the same in sorrow and suffering.

"For this is what she thinks about herself, 'I rule as a woman chief. I am not like a woman who has lost her husband. I will never know sorrow or grief.'

⁸"This is the reason the disasters of death, misery, and great hunger will fall on her in one day. A raging fire will make her a wasteland. For the one who has decided her fate is our Great and Honored Creator."

THE RULERS WEEP OVER HER

⁹*Again, a voice came from the spirit-world above.*

"The rulers of the land," *the voice said*, "who participated in her evil desires, will weep many tears when they see the smoke rise from the raging fire that burns her *to the ground.* ¹⁰And these rulers, because they are afraid to look on her agony, will stand watching from afar.

"'How terrible! How terrible!' they will cry out, 'O great and strong village! O Village of Confusion (Babylon), your fate has come upon you suddenly—in one hour!'"

THE TRADERS IN GOODS WEEP OVER HER

The voice from the spirit-world above continued. ¹¹"And the traders of the land will weep and wail over her. For there will be no one left to trade for all their goods. ¹²No one to trade for their goods of gold, silver, jewels, or pearls. No one to trade for their fancy purple, red, and silk cloths. No one to trade for their sweet-smelling wood and carvings made from wood and animal horns. No one to trade for things made from bronze, iron, or polished rock. ¹³Nor for their cinnamon, spices, sweet-smelling herbs, myrrh, frankincense, wine, olive oil, ground flour, wheat, cattle, sheep, horses, and chariots. And none to participate in the slave-trading of human beings.

¹⁴"The traders of the land will say, 'All the fruits you were longing to taste are gone! All the rich and fancy things you hoped for have melted away, never to be found again.'

¹⁵"The ones who gained great possessions from trading with her will stand weeping and wailing, and because they are afraid to look on her agony they will watch from afar ¹⁶and cry out, 'How terrible! How terrible, O great village! She who was clothed in beautiful red and purple regalia sparkling with gold, costly stones, and pearls has come to a bad end. ¹⁷For in such a short time all her great wealth and many possessions have been burned up.'

"All who travel the waters by canoe, both great and small, and those who make their living on the sea stood far away watching her smoke rise ¹⁸as they cried out, 'Is there another village as great as this one?'

¹⁹"They threw dirt on their heads as they cried out with many tears and much sorrow, 'How terrible! How terrible! The great village that made the sea travelers rich with her many possessions has come to a bad end in such a short time!'ᵃ

²⁰"Dance with joy, you who live in the spirit-world above! Let your hearts beat with gladness you holy ones, message bearers, and prophets! For the Great Spirit has decided the fate of the great Village of Confusion (Babylon) for what she did to you."

A GREAT STONE THROWN INTO THE SEA

²¹Then I saw a powerful spirit-messenger take a great stone the size of a huge boulderᵇ and throw it into the waters of the sea.ᶜ

"In this manner the great Village of Confusion (Babylon) will be violently thrown down, never to be found again," the voice said. ²²"The sound of the music makers, with their drums and flutes, and the shrill of eagle bone whistlesᵈ will not be heard in you any longer. No tentmaker, drum maker, or carver will be found in you, not even the sound of bark being stripped from trees.ᵉ ²³The light from torches will not shine in you. The voice of the bridegroom and the bride will be heard in you no longer. For your traders in goods were the noble people of the land, and all the Outside Nations were led down a false path by your witchcraft. ²⁴The blood of Creator's prophets and holy people has stained her village pathways. Yes, the blood of all who have been violently killed has been spilled by her throughout the land."ᶠ

19

PRAISING THE GREAT SPIRIT

¹After this I heard what sounded like the roar of many voices coming from a great gathering in the spirit-world above.

"Give Praise to the Great Spirit (Hallelujah)!" they shouted *with one voice*. "For his great and shining power has set us free! ²His decisions are upright and true! He has made right the wrongs done by the woman who traded her body for possessions and brought ruin to the land filled with her impure ways. He has carried out his decision against the Village of Confusion (Babylon), which shed the blood of those who faithfully serve him."

³Then they shouted once again, "Give Praise to the Great Spirit (Halle-

---

ᵃ**18:17, 19** Lit. *one hour*
ᵇ**18:21** Lit. *a millstone*
ᶜ**18:21** Matthew 18:6; Mark 9:42; Luke 17:2

ᵈ**18:22** Lit. *the sound of trumpeters*
ᵉ**18:22** Lit. *the sound of a millstone*
ᶠ**18:24** Luke 11:49-50

lujah)! The smoke from her burning will keep rising to the time beyond the end of all days."

⁴Then the twenty-four elders and the four living spirit animals humbled themselves before the Great Spirit, who sits on his seat of honor, and gave him the praise and honor only he deserves.

With one voice they said, "Aho! It is so! Give Praise to the Great Spirit (Hallelujah)!"

⁵Then a voice came from the seat of honor, saying, "Give praise to our Creator, all you who respect and serve him, both small and great."

⁶Then like the roar of many waters came what sounded like rolling thunder. The sound was like the voices of a great crowd!

"Give Praise to the Great Spirit (Hallelujah)!" they cried out. "For our Creator, the All-Powerful and Honored One, rules over us!"

THE BRIDE IS READY FOR THE WEDDING

The voices continued to shout, ⁷"Dance for joy with glad hearts and give honor to the Great Spirit, for the time for the wedding ceremony of the Lamb has come, and his bride has made herself ready."

⁸The wedding regalia she was given to wear was made from soft buckskin,ᵃ bright and shining, pure and white. For pure white buckskin represents the good things done by Creator's holy people.

⁹Then the spirit-messengerᵇ said to me, "Write this down, 'Creator's blessing rests on the ones who are invited to the marriage feast of the Lamb.' These words are true," he said *with firm words,* "for they come from the mouth of the Great Spirit."

THE TRUE SPIRIT OF PROPHECY

¹⁰I then humbled myself before the spirit-messenger to give him praise and honor.

"Do not humble yourself to me in this way," he said. "I am one who stands by your side to serve the Great Spirit. I stand with you and all the sacred family members who have stood firm as truth tellers for Creator Sets Free (Jesus). Give praise and honor only to the Great Spirit. For the spirit of prophecy is at work when the truth is told about Creator Sets Free (Jesus)."

RIDER ON A WHITE HORSE

¹¹I looked up and saw the sky open, and out rode a white warhorse whose rider is called Honorable and True! He rides to make wrongs right again, and his judgments are as straight as an arrow. ¹²His eyes blaze like flames of fire. His headdress has many feathers. He has a name written down that only he knows. ¹³His regalia is dipped in blood. And his name is known as Word of Creator.ᶜ

¹⁴Following behind him were all the warriors from the spirit-world above, clothed in pure white buckskin and also riding white warhorses. ¹⁵Out from his mouth comes a sharp long knife to strike down the opposing nations. He will rule over them with an unbreakable iron chief's staff. He tramples the grapes in the winepress of the fierce anger of the all-powerful Great Spirit. ¹⁶He has this name carved into his regalia and tattooed on his thigh:

GRAND CHIEF OF ALL CHIEFS

¹⁷Then I saw a spirit-messenger standing in *the blazing light of* the sun.

ᵃ**19:8** Lit. *fine linen*
ᵇ**19:9** Revelation 17:1

ᶜ**19:13** John 1:1

With a loud voice he spoke to the winged ones who were flying high in the sky.

"Come," *he cried out to them,* "gather together for the great feast offered by Creator. [18]Come and feast on the flesh of rulers, war chiefs, strong warriors, and horses with their riders. Feast on the flesh of all, whether slave or free, small or great."

THE WILD BEAST AND HIS ARMY

[19]Then I saw the wild beast along with the rulers of the land and their armies. They had gathered to make war against the rider on the *white* horse and against his band of warriors.

[20]The wild beast was taken captive along with the false prophet who had stood before the wild beast and performed signs and wonders. These signs and wonders were used to trick those who had accepted the mark of the wild beast and those who had bowed down to honor its *carved* image. The wild beast and the false prophet were thrown alive into a fiery lake that blazed with burning rocks. [21]The others were killed by the long knife coming out from the mouth of the rider on the white horse. And all the winged ones ate from their *dead* flesh until they were full.

20 ▶◀▶◀▶◀▶◀▶◀▶◀▶

THE BINDING OF ACCUSER

[1]Then I saw a spirit-messenger coming down from the spirit-world above. *In his hand* he held the power[a] to open or close the way in or out of the dark and bottomless pit. In his hand he also held a large iron chain. [2]The spirit-messenger

---

[a] 20:1 Lit. *key*

took hold of the fiery-red sea serpent, that ancient trickster snake who is also called the evil one and Accuser (Satan). He wrapped the chain around him and bound him for a thousand winters. [3]He then threw him into the dark and bottomless pit, closed the way in or out, and sealed it tight. He did this so Accuser (Satan) could no longer blind the nations and lead them down a false path until a thousand winters have passed. But after that he will be released for a short time.

ONE THOUSAND WINTERS

[4]Then I saw many seats of honor, and sitting on them were those who had been given the right to decide who has done right and who has done wrong. I saw the souls of those who had their heads cut off because they told the truth about Creator Sets Free (Jesus) and stayed true to Creator's message. I also saw the souls of the ones who had not bowed down to honor the wild beast or its carved image and did not accept its tattoo on their foreheads or hands. All these came to life and ruled with the Chosen One for a thousand winters. [5]The rest of those who were dead did not come to life until after the thousand winters were complete. This is the first rising from the dead.

[6]The ones who participate in this first rising from the dead are blessed and holy *in Creator's sight.* The second death has no power over them. They will be holy men and women representing the Great Spirit and his Chosen One. They will rule by his side for a thousand winters.

ACCUSER IS RELEASED

[7]After a thousand winters Accuser (Satan) will be released from the dark and bot-

tomless pit. **8**He will go out into the four corners of all the land to gather the Gog and Magog[a] nations and trick them into going to war.

Their number is as great as the number of sands on the seashore. **9**They spread out over the whole width of the land. And when they had surrounded the encampment of Creator's holy people and his much-loved village, fire came down from the spirit-world above and devoured them. **10**The evil one who had deceived them was thrown into the fiery lake that blazes with burning rocks— where the wild beast and false prophet were thrown. There they will suffer greatly day and night to the time beyond the end of all days.

THE FINAL JUDGMENT

11Then I saw a great seat of honor shining bright and clear, and the one seated there. The land and sky fled from his face, and no place was found for them *to hide.* **12**And I saw the dead, both small and great, standing before his seat of honor. Books were opened, and then another book was opened, the book of life. The fate of the dead was decided by what was written down in the books, according to what they had done.

13All the great waters of the sea gave up the dead in them. Death and the Dark Underworld of Death (Hades) gave up the dead that were in them, and their fate was decided by what they had done. **14**Then death itself and the Dark Underworld of Death (Hades) were thrown into the fiery lake. The fiery lake is the second death. **15**Anyone whose name was not found written down in the book of life was thrown into the fiery lake.

21

A NEW SPIRIT-WORLD AND A NEW EARTH

1Then I saw a new spirit-world above and a new earth below, for the first spirit-world and the first earth had gone away, and the great waters of the sea were no longer there. **2**I saw a new Sacred Village of Peace (Jerusalem), coming down from the Great Spirit in the world above and dressed in wedding regalia, like a bride made ready for her husband.

WIPING OF TEARS CEREMONY

3I heard a voice coming from the seat of honor. "Behold," the voice said, "the Great Spirit has pitched his sacred tent among human beings. They will be his people, and Creator himself will make his home among them and will be their Great Spirit. **4**He will perform a wiping of tears ceremony, for death will be no more. There will be no sorrow, or weeping, or pain, because these former things have faded away."

5Then the one on the seat of honor spoke again. "Behold," he said, "I am making all things fresh and new." Then he added, "Write these words down, for they are true and trustworthy."

6"It is done!" he said to me. "I am Alpha and Omega,[b] the beginning and the end. I will give the free gift of the wellspring of life-giving water to all who are thirsty. **7**All these blessings will belong to the ones who win the victory. I will be their Great Spirit, and they will be my sons *and daughters.*

8"But the fearful, the untrustworthy, the doers of shameful things, those who

---

[a] **20:8** Gog and Magog are enemy nations of Creator and his people. See Ezekiel 38–39.

[b] **21:6** Alpha and omega are the first and last letter of the Greek alphabet, the language of the New Testament.

murder, the sexually impure, the bad medicine people, the ones who pray to spirit-images, and all who speak lies, their place will be in the fiery lake of burning rocks. This is the second death."

THE BRIDE, THE LAMB'S WIFE

[9]*Then* one of the seven spirit-messengers who had the seven smudge bowls that were filled with the seven last disasters came and spoke to me.

"Come," he said, "and I will show you the bride, the Lamb's wife."

[10]The spirit-messenger took me on a spiritual journey to a great and high mountain. There he showed me the Sacred Village of Peace (Jerusalem) coming down from the Great Spirit in the spirit-world above. [11]It was filled with Creator's beauty and honor. The sacred village was bright and shone like a costly stone, like a jasper stone as clear as crystal.

[12]The sacred village had a great and high wall with twelve gates and twelve spirit-messengers, one at each gate. Carved into the gates were the names of the twelve tribes of the families of Wrestles with Creator (Israel). [13]There were three gates on the east wall, three gates on the south, three gates on the west, and three gates on the north. [14]The wall encircling the sacred village was built on twelve stones. Carved into the stones were the names of the twelve message bearers of the Lamb.

[15]The spirit-messenger who spoke to me had a golden measuring stick to measure the sacred village, both its gates and walls. [16]The sacred village was laid out in a square. It measured twelve thousand stadia.[a] Its width, length, and height were the same. [17]The spirit-messenger was using human measurements. He measured the wall to be one hundred and forty-four cubits.[b] [18]The wall was made of jasper, and the sacred village was made of pure gold, as clear as crystal.

[19]The stones the village wall was built on were made of all kinds of costly gemstones. The first stone was jasper, the second sapphire, the third agate, the fourth emerald, [20]the fifth sardonyx, the sixth sardius, the seventh chrysolite, the eighth beryl, the ninth topaz, the tenth turquoise, the eleventh jacinth, and the twelfth amethyst.[c]

[21]The twelve gates of the sacred village were made of pearl, and each gate was made from a single pearl. The village had a wide pathway made of gold that was crystal clear.

[22]I could see no sacred lodge within the village, because the all-powerful and honored Spirit Chief and the Lamb are its sacred lodge. [23]In this village there is no need for the sun or the moon to shine its light, for the light comes from the beauty of the Great Spirit shining through the Lamb.

[24]All the nations will walk by its light, and the chiefs of the earth will bring their honor and beauty into the sacred village. [25]Its gates will not be closed during the day, night will never come, [26]and the beauty and honor of all nations will be brought into it. [27]Nothing impure or anyone who participates in shameful ways will go through the gates. Only the ones whose names are written down in the Lamb's book of life will be able to enter.

---

[a]**21:16** A stadia is equal to about six hundred feet. Twelve thousand stadia would be about fourteen hundred miles.

[b]**21:17** A cubit is the distance from elbow to fingertip, or about eighteen inches. The wall would be about two hundred feet thick.

[c]**21:20** The identity of some of these stones is uncertain.

22

THE RIVER OF LIFE-GIVING WATER

¹The spirit-messenger then showed me the river of life-giving water shining as bright as crystal. It flowed out from the seat of honor of the Great Spirit and the Lamb. ²The river flowed down the center of the village's wide pathway. On each side of the river was the life-giving tree. Every moon this tree was bearing *fresh* fruit—twelve *different* crops a year! Its leaves were good medicine for the healing of all nations.

³No curse will be found there, for the seat of honor of the Great Spirit and the Lamb will be in that village, and in that place his people will honor him with their service. ⁴They will see his face, and his name will be tattooed on their foreheads.

⁵Night will be no more. There will no longer be any need of a torch to light the way, or for the light of the sun, because Creator himself, who is their Honored Chief, will be their light. And they will rule with him to the time beyond the end of all days.

⁶"These words are true and trustworthy," the spirit-messenger said to me, "for our Honored Chief, the Great Spirit of the spirits of the prophets, has sent his spirit-messenger to show the ones who serve him what must soon take place."

⁷"Behold! I am coming very soon," *said Creator Sets Free (Jesus).* "Creator's blessing rests on the ones who follow the instructions of the words of the prophecy of this sacred book."

FINAL WORDS

⁸I, He Shows Goodwill (John), am the one who heard and saw these things. And when I did, I humbled myself before the spirit-messenger who was showing these things to me.

⁹"Do not humble yourself before me," the spirit-messenger told me. "I stand beside you and your family members who are prophets and *beside* all who follow the words of this book, as one who serves the Great Spirit. Honor the Great Spirit and serve him *alone*!

¹⁰"Do not seal up the words of the prophecy of this sacred book," the spirit-messenger continued, "for the time is almost upon us. There is little time left for those who do wrong to change their ways, or for the impure to cleanse themselves. ¹¹So leave the evil and the impure to continue in their wrong ways. Let the ones who do what is right stay on a good path, and the holy ones, let them continue to walk that good road."

¹²"Behold! I am coming very soon," *said Creator Sets Free (Jesus).* "I am ready to reward everyone for what they have done, *whether good or bad.* ¹³I am Alpha and Omega,[a] first and last. beginning and end.

¹⁴"Creator's blessing rests on the ones who have washed their regalia. This gives them the right to *eat from* the life-giving tree and to enter through the gates into the sacred village. ¹⁵Outside the gates are wild-dog people, bad-medicine people, the sexually impure, those who murder, the ones who pray to spirit-images, and all who love to speak lies.

¹⁶"I, Creator Sets Free (Jesus), have sent my spirit-messenger to you to tell you these things for the sacred families. I am the descendant of Much Loved One (David), who has sprouted from his roots. I am the bright Morning Star."

---

[a]**22:13** Alpha and omega are the first and last letter of the Greek alphabet, the language of the New Testament.

17The Spirit and the Bride say, "Come." Let the ones who hear say, "Come." Let all who hear say, "Come." Let all who are thirsty come and freely drink from the wellspring of life-giving water.

18To all who hear the words of this prophecy, I speak from my heart, "If anyone adds anything to them, Creator will add to that person the disasters found in this book. 19If anyone takes away from the words of this book of prophecy, then Creator will take away that person's place in the life-giving tree and in the sacred village this book tells about."

20The one who tells the truth about these things, *Creator Sets Free (Jesus)*, says, "Yes, I am coming soon!"

Aho! May it be so! Come, our Honored Chief Creator Sets Free (Jesus)!

21May the gift of great kindness from Creator Sets Free (Jesus) remain with everyone.

Aho! It is so!

GLOSSARY OF BIBLICAL TERMS

TO HELP THE READER with the historical and cultural context, we have included some background information here. While this is not comprehensive, it should provide guidance to help set the story in its proper context and explain some cultural crossovers. The Bible is a book, the writing of which spans several millennia, and by the time of Creator Sets Free (Jesus), many thousands of years of history had already passed.

Also, there are many important key terms in Bible translation. The author has worked with both biblical and Native cultural consultants to determine the most appropriate ways to translate these key terms for general relevance to our First Nations people. Below are a few of the more important biblical terms with some explanation of why these terms were chosen.

APOSTLE (MESSAGE BEARER)

The Greek word translated as *apostle* literally means "sent one." It is used as the carrier of an official message. These sent ones not only carried a message but also carried with it the authority of the person sending them. In this translation, we have translated *apostle* as "message bearer."

BAD HEARTS AND BROKEN WAYS (SIN)

For many of our Native people, the English word *sin* evokes the memories of boarding school, where "sin" was often the length of our hair, or speaking in our native language, or anything related to our cultures. The biblical concept of sin is expressed in the Greek word *hamartia*, which means "to miss the mark" or "to fail to do what is right"—in other words, not living in the ways Creator wants us to live. All human beings are broken and fail to live in Creator's ways. Some try but fail, some don't even try, and others give themselves over to evil ways. We have translated *sin* as either "bad hearts," "wrongdoings," or "broken ways," depending on which one best fits the context.

CEREMONIAL FESTIVALS

The tribes of Wrestles with Creator (Israel) were given three primary annual festivals to remind them of Creator's goodness when he set them free from slavery in Black Land (Egypt) and made them into a holy nation. We will list them here, with a short explanation.

Passover Festival (Passover). This festival is celebrated in conjunction with the Feast of Unleavened Bread. It commemorates the time when Creator delivered the tribes of Wrestles with Creator (Israel) from slavery in Black Land (Egypt) through Drawn from the Water (Moses). The highlight of this story is when the blood of a slain lamb was put on the doorposts of each home for protection from a destroying spirit-messenger, who would "pass over" the house with blood on the doorposts. According to 1 Corinthians 5:7, Creator Sets Free (Jesus) is the fulfillment of the Passover Lamb we now celebrate in the bread and wine of the ceremonial meal of the Chosen One in 1 Corinthians 11:23-26 (see Deuteronomy 16:1-8; Leviticus 23:4-8).

Festival of Weeks (Pentecost). The word *Pentecost* means "fifty," and is called that because it was celebrated seven weeks from the Passover Festival, on the fiftieth day. The Festival of Weeks was a harvest festival when the people would bring the firstfruits of the harvest to Creator's sacred lodge in the Village of Peace (Jerusalem) to give thanks for his provision and remember how he provided for them in the desert wilderness. This festival found its fulfillment in Acts 2 with the outpouring of the Holy Spirit (see Deuteronomy 16:9-12; Leviticus 23:15-22).

Festival of Shelters (Feast of Tabernacles). This festival was celebrated at the end of the harvest. The tribes were instructed to make temporary shelters made from tree branches. They were to live in these shelters for seven days. In this way, they remembered the time after they had been set free from slavery in Black Land (Egypt) when their ancestors migrated in the desert wilderness under the care of Drawn from the Water (Moses) and lived in temporary shelters. It was during this time in the wilderness that Creator gave them water to drink from a rock (Exodus 17:5-7). Creator Sets Free (Jesus) announced himself as the fulfillment of this during this festival when he said, "The ones who thirst must come to me and drink" (John 7:37). Small Man (Paul) confirms this in 1 Corinthians 10:4 (see Leviticus 23:33).

CHOSEN ONE (CHRIST)

Creator spoke to the tribes of Wrestles with Creator (Israel) through many prophets. These prophets spoke of a coming deliverer called Messiah, which means "Anointed One." In the Greek language of the New Testament, Messiah is translated as *Christos* and then in English as "Christ," which means "Anointed

One." This Messiah, or Christ, was to be Creator's Chosen One to set his people free. In this retelling of the story of Creator Sets Free (Jesus), we use the term *Chosen One* in place of *Christ*, since few English-speaking people understand the meaning of the word *Christ*. Scripture uses the term *Chosen One* to refer to Jesus in many English translations (see Luke 9:35).

CREATOR SETS FREE (JESUS)

The name Jesus was a common name in first-century Palestine. The name Jesus finds its roots in the Hebrew language. His name in Hebrew is Yeshua (pronounced *yeh-shoo-wah*). The name comes from two words. The first is *Yah*, the shortened form of Yahweh, the Hebrew name for Creator. The second comes from a word that means "to rescue, deliver, save, or simply set free"—Yah Sets Free. From the Hebrew to the Greek of the New Testament, Yeshua became *Iesous* (pronounced *yeh-soos*). From the Greek to the English, *Iesous* became Jesus.

The Jewish people in biblical times gave names that had meaning. For example, Abraham means "Father of Many Nations." This is similar to the traditions of our First Nations people, so we decided to follow this practice in the First Nations Version. We have chosen to call Jesus by the translated meaning of his name, which is Creator Sets Free. This is one possible rendering of his name in English as it would have been heard and understood in the language of his own people. We have also done this with all other names found in the New Testament.

DAY OF RESTING (SABBATH)

The instructions from the law given by Drawn from the Water (Moses) included a day of resting called the Sabbath, which means "rest." This was to honor the Great Spirit, who created all things in six days and then rested on the seventh. It was also given as a reminder to the tribes of Wrestles with Creator (Israel) of their time of forced labor in Black Land (Egypt), where they had no day of resting (see Deuteronomy 5:15). From sunset Friday evening until sunset Saturday evening, no work was to be done (see Exodus 20:8-11). Also, how far a person could walk on that day was limited by this law. Its proper interpretation and practice became a point of controversy between the spiritual leaders and Creator Sets Free (Jesus) (Matthew 12:1-8) and later by his first followers.

GATHERING HOUSES (SYNAGOGUES)

In the time of the gospel story, the Jewish people in most villages had a meeting place called the synagogue, which simply means "gathering place." The synagogue was used primarily for religious purposes, such as the study of the Scriptures and prayer, but also for local village council meetings. We have chosen to call synagogues simply "gathering houses."

GOOD ROAD (KINGDOM OF GOD)

Today, many First Nations people speak of the "good way" or "red road" as a way to understand a way of life that seeks to live in harmony with the Great Spirit's plan for all of creation. To live in harmony with fellow human beings and all of creation could be called "walking the good road."

With the advice of some of our Native American friends and insights from prominent American Indian theologian George E. Tinker, we have chosen to translate *kingdom of God* as "Creator's good road."[a] Creator Sets Free (Jesus) came to call us to walk in a new way, a way of beauty and harmony, that reflects the government of God/heaven. To walk the road with Creator Sets Free (Jesus) is to be on this path.

HOLY MEN (PRIESTS)

According to the law of Moses, only men were permitted to be priests. By this same law, priests could only be chosen from the tribe of He Brings Together (Levi). We have translated *priest* in the following ways: for the *high priest* we chose "chief holy man," for the *chief priests* we chose "head priests," and for *priest* we chose "holy man."

OUTCASTS (SINNERS)

The Separated Ones (Pharisees) identified certain people as "sinners." This word carries a more disturbing meaning than just someone who sins. These "sinners" were the outcasts of Jewish society and designated as such by the Pharisees' oppressive interpretation of the law of Moses. These outcasts were not permitted to enter the gathering houses and were despised by the Separated Ones (Pharisees). Outcasts included tribal tax collectors, prostitutes, people who ate and drank too much, those with diseases that made them ceremonially unclean, and all Gentiles (non-Jews).

OUTSIDE NATIONS (GENTILES)

The members of the tribes of Wrestles with Creator (Israel) called all people from other nations Gentiles. No Gentile was permitted to enter the sacred lodge under the penalty of death. There was a Court of the Gentiles in the temple where they could learn about the Great Spirit. In this translation, for the word *Gentiles* we have used "Nations," "other nations," "Outside Nations," "Outsider," and in certain contexts "People of the Village of Iron" when referring to the Romans, who were also Gentiles.

PURIFICATION CEREMONY (BAPTISM)

In the time of Creator Sets Free (Jesus), baptism in water was a cultural and

---

[a]George E. Tinker, *Spirit and Resistance* (Minneapolis: Fortress, 2004), 91-99.

spiritual practice among the Jewish people. Baptism was a sacred ceremony symbolizing purification or cleansing. It also was used as an initiation rite into the spiritual and social community. To be baptized in the name of someone was to accept their teachings and become identified with them. Baptism was most often practiced by immersing a person in flowing water, which is why rivers were often used. In this translation, we have chosen to call baptism "the purification ceremony."

SACRED FAMILY (CHURCH)

Most English translations translate the Greek word *ekklesia* as "church." This word literally means "called-out ones" and was used for community gatherings, whether religious, social, or governmental. We have chosen "sacred family" for this translation, highlighting the relational aspect of this sacred gathering of the followers of Creator Sets Free (Jesus). This meaning is reflected in several Scriptures where the *ekklesia* is called a "household," Greek *oikos*, meaning a family member or one living in the same house. First Timothy 3:15; Ephesians 2:19; and 1 Peter 4:17 are examples of this. We have also used sacred family members in many places where "brothers" is used. This was a familial term referring to both men and women as believers in Creator Sets Free (Jesus), making them members of the *ekklesia* or "sacred family members."

SACRED OR CEREMONIAL LODGE (TEMPLE)

Under Chief Much Loved One (King David), Creator instructed the tribes of Wrestles with Creator (Israel) to build a sacred lodge in Jerusalem. This sacred lodge was a permanent structure to replace the tent also called the tabernacle, which was used when Israel was wandering in the wilderness. Creator did not allow Much Loved One (David) to build the sacred lodge because he was a man of violence and warfare.

The first sacred lodge was built by Chief Stands in Peace (King Solomon) and was later destroyed by the People of the Village of Confusion (Babylonians) who defeated the tribes and took most of the people into exile in a foreign land. When they returned from their exile, they built a second sacred lodge, but it was smaller and much less impressive. Leading up to the time of Creator Sets Free (Jesus), Chief Looks Brave (King Herod the Great) had used his fantastic wealth to further rebuild the sacred lodge in an attempt to restore much of its ancient glory. The sacred lodge built by Looks Brave (Herod) contained four courtyards— the Court of the Holy Men, the Court of the tribes of Wrestles with Creator (Israel), the Court of the Women, and the Court of the Gentiles. Many biblical scholars agree that it was in the Court of the Gentiles that Creator Sets Free (Jesus) drove out the moneychangers. In the FNV we have translated *temple* as "lodge," "sacred lodge," and "ceremonial lodge."

The Holy Place was another inner chamber within the sacred lodge. The Holy Place was entered often by holy men who performed daily ceremonies and offered morning and evening prayers.

The Most Holy Place, also called the Holy of Holies, was the innermost chamber of the temple, a small room separated from the Holy Place by a thick double curtain. It contained sacred objects from Israel's tribal history. No one was allowed to see behind this curtain except the chief holy man, and then only once a year, when he entered for a special ceremony. It was this curtain that was torn in two, from top to bottom, when Creator Sets Free (Jesus) gave up his Spirit.

SPIRIT-MESSENGERS (ANGELS)

In the Greek of the New Testament, the word most often translated as "angel" is *angelos*. The primary meaning of this word is "messenger." It can refer to human messengers or spirit-messengers, which are spirits sent from Creator to help humans in distress or simply to convey a message. In the FNV we have translated this word as "spirit-messenger" or "messenger" depending on the context.

SPIRITUAL LEADERS

In the time of Creator Sets Free (Jesus), the tribes of Wrestles with Creator (Israel), were divided into many different religious groups with differing beliefs. The members of these religious groups had set themselves up as the spiritual leaders of Israel.

Separated Ones (Pharisees). Pharisees are mentioned most often. The title *Pharisees* means "separated ones." The Pharisees were the most vocal and influential of the spiritual leaders and held a very strict and oppressive interpretation of the law of Moses. As their name indicates, they separated themselves from those they deemed to be sinners and pressured others to do the same. They also banned people from participating in their local synagogues or gathering houses. We have translated *Pharisees* as "Separated Ones."

Upright Ones (Sadducees). Sadducees, which means "righteous or upright ones," were a sect of the high priests who were often rich and held positions of power within Israel's religious and political establishments. They differ from the Pharisees in several ways. Most significantly, they did not believe in spirits or in a resurrection from the dead. We have translated *Sadducees* as "Upright Ones."

Scroll keepers (scribes and lawyers). Scroll keepers are mentioned quite often in the Gospels, and both titles describe the same group. The scribes were the keepers of the sacred scrolls, the Scriptures. Since they knew how to write, they became scroll copiers, making copies of the Scriptures. Since they spent so much time reading and writing the Scriptures, they became experts in the interpretation of the law of Moses. We have translated *scribes* as "scroll keepers."

Friends of Herod (Herodians). These are believed to have been a small group of Jews who supported the family dynasty and political interests of King Herod. We have translated *Herodians* as "Friends of Herod."

Firebrands (Zealots). This group is indirectly referred to in the Gospels. *Zealot* means "one who is on fire or full of zeal." In practice, however, the Zealots were insurrectionists using violent terrorist methods. Many of the Zealots were openly rebellious and wanted to lead a violent uprising against the People of Iron (Romans). Son of His Father (Barabbas) was most likely a Zealot, and one of Creator Sets Free's (Jesus') own followers appears to have been a former Zealot (Simon the Zealot). Some historians speculate that Speaks Well Of (Judas), who betrayed Creator Sets Free (Jesus), may have also been a Zealot. We have not offered a translation other than for Simon the Zealot, referring to him as One Who Listens (Simon)—the Firebrand.

SPIRITUAL WARFARE

In Ephesians 6 there is a section on the "war garments of Creator," also called the "armor of Creator." It is important to understand that this warfare is not a physical battle or a contest of brute power between the Great Spirit and the Accuser (Satan), even though it affects things in this natural world. Rather, it is a war of methods and ideals (2 Corinthians 10:3-6). The powerful weapon Creator gives us is the word of truth that Creator Sets Free (Jesus) reveals about who the Great Spirit is and about his great love for all humankind.

TRIBAL MEMBERS (JEWS)

The people of the tribes of Wrestles with Creator (Israel) were also called "Jews" in the Bible. The name *Jew* comes from the time when Israel was divided into two nations. The northern nation was called Israel and consisted of ten tribes. The southern nation was called Judah and consisted of two tribes. The name *Jew* is simply a reference to Judah and became a way of referring to all the people of the tribes of Wrestles with Creator (Israel). We have simply used "Tribal Members" and "Tribal People," or, when the context seemed appropriate, "Spiritual Leaders" or "Tribal Leaders" to translate *Jews*.

TRIBAL TAX COLLECTORS (TAX COLLECTORS)

Tax collectors were often Jewish Tribal Members who contracted with the Roman government for the procurement of taxes. They could force the people, under the threat of violence, to pay them. They often became extremely rich off the suffering of poor people and were hated by everyone. We have chosen to call them "tribal tax collectors" of the colonial Roman government.

TRUE HUMAN BEING (SON OF MAN)

Creator Sets Free (Jesus) most often referred to himself as the Son of Man. This title is full of meaning from the Old Testament Scriptures. In the book of Ezekiel it is used over ninety times and simply means a human being. There it is not meant to be a title of prestige but of humility. In using this title, Creator Sets Free (Jesus) is presenting himself as a common human being, as one of us.

In the book of Daniel, the title "Son of Man" takes on an expanded meaning. Daniel sees a vision of one like a Son of Man coming before the Ancient of Days (Creator) on the clouds of heaven. This person is given authority, glory, and sovereign power from the Great Spirit. His rule is over all peoples and languages and his chiefly rule will never come to an end. Even though he is a human being, he will be worshiped (see Daniel 7:13-14).

So Creator Sets Free (Jesus) as the True Human Being shows us that the good road or the kingdom of God is a kingdom of humility, love, and service to others. He is a common man and at the same time the almighty Creator who alone is worthy of worship. As Son of the Great Spirit, he is divine. As Son of Man, he is a True Human Being.

We have used the title "True Human Being" for "Son of Man." For he is one of us and what a human being should truly be like. As we walk the road with him, we are on the path to becoming true human beings.

WISDOMKEEPER (RABBI)

In the time of Creator Sets Free (Jesus), there were spiritual leaders who traveled about gaining followers. These leaders were often called *rabbi*, meaning "teacher." They functioned as a sage or wisdomkeeper as they taught their interpretation of the written and oral Torah (Jewish laws). Creator Sets Free (Jesus) is called "rabbi" in the Gospels. It is a title of respect and honor. Rabbis were held in high esteem, even though they held no official status. In our translation, we have used "wisdomkeeper" for "rabbi." When appropriate we also used this title for "Lord" when people addressed Creator Sets Free (Jesus) in this honorable way.

THE WORD (*LOGOS*)

Just as many English translations have done, we have translated the Greek word *Logos* found in John 1 and 1 John 1 as "Word." The word *logos* has great cultural and theological depth and meaning. In the time of the New Testament, it was used by both Jews and Greeks. It was understood as the means by which Creator revealed himself to the world. It was also understood as the unseen power that held the universe together. The Jewish people understood that there was a wisdom persona that came from the Great Spirit and created all things (Proverbs 8:22-23). In the time of the New Testament, the term *Logos* took on a similar meaning. Even though *logos* can be translated as "word," that does not mean it indicates a single word in a sentence. It is better understood as "message" or "communication" or as "reason." Creator Sets Free (Jesus) reveals the entirety of who Creator is, what he has done, and what he will do. He is truly the Word or Story of the Great Spirit and embodies the message Creator is revealing through him.

FOR MORE INFORMATION, VISIT

WWW.FIRSTNATIONSVERSION.COM

WWW.FACEBOOK.COM/FIRSTNATIONSVERSION